J.K. LASSER'S™

SMALL BUSINESS TAXES

Look for these and other titles from J.K. Lasser™—Practical Guides for All Your Financial Needs

J.K. LASSER'S™

SMALL BUSINESS TAXES

Your Complete Guide to a Better Bottom Line

2006 Edition

Barbara Weltman

WILEY

John Wiley & Sons, Inc.

This book is dedicated with love to my understanding husband, Malcolm Katt.

For general information on our other products and services or for technical support, please contact our Customer Care Department within the United States at (800) 762-2974, outside the United States at (317) 572-3993 or fax (317) 572-4002.

Wiley also publishes its books in a variety of electronic formats. Some content that appears in print may not be available in electronic books. For more information about Wiley products, visit our web site at www.wiley.com.

ISBN-13 978-0-471-73311-9
ISBN-10 0-471-73311-3

Printed in the United States of America.

10   9   8   7   6   5   4   3   2   1

Contents

Preface

According to the Internal Revenue Service (IRS), about 80 percent of small businesses use paid professionals to handle their tax returns. So why do you need to read up on taxes? The answer is simple: You, and not your accountant or other financial adviser, run the business, so you can't rely on someone else to make decisions critical to your activities. You need to be informed about tax-saving opportunities that continually arise so you can strategically plan to take advantage of them. Being knowledgeable about tax matters also saves you money; the more you know, the better able you are to ask your accountant key tax and financial questions that can advance your business, as well as to meet your tax responsibilities.

This is a great time to be a small business. Not only is small business the major force in our economy but it also is the benefactor of new tax rules that make it easier to write off expenses and minimize the taxes you owe. This is the eighth edition of this book, and it has been revised to include all of the new rules taking effect for 2005 returns. It also provides information about future changes scheduled to take effect in order to give you an overall view of business tax planning. Most importantly, it addresses the many tax questions I have received from readers as well as visitors to my web site, <www.barbaraweltman.com>.

This book focuses primarily on federal income taxes. But businesses may be required to pay and report many other taxes, including state income taxes, employment taxes, sales and use taxes, and excise taxes. Some information about these taxes is included in this book to alert you to your possible obligations so that you can then obtain further assistance if necessary.

It is important to stay alert to future changes. Pending or possible changes are noted in this book. Be sure to check on any final action before you complete your tax return or take any steps that could be affected by these changes. Changes can be found at my web site.

For a free update on tax developments affecting small businesses and a free download of the Supplement to this book (available February 1, 2006), go to <www.jklasser.com>.

How to Use This Book

The purpose of this book is to make you acutely aware of how your actions in business can affect your bottom line from a tax perspective. The way you organize your business, the accounting method you select, and the types of payments you make all have an impact on when you report income and the extent to which you can take deductions. This book is not designed to make you a tax expert. It is strongly suggested that you consult with a tax adviser before making certain important decisions that will affect your ability to claim tax deductions. I hope that the insight you gain from this book will allow you to ask your adviser key questions to benefit your business.

In Part 1, you will find topics of interest to all businesses. First, there is an overview of the various forms of business organization and an explanation of how these forms of organization affect reporting of income and claiming tax deductions. The most common forms of business organization include independent contractors, sole proprietors, and sole practitioners—individuals who work for themselves and do not have any partners. If self-employed individuals join with others to form a business, they become partners in a partnership. Sometimes businesses incorporate. A business can be incorporated with only one owner or with many owners. A corporation can be a regular corporation (*C corporation*), or it can be a small business corporation (*S corporation*). The difference between the C and S corporations is the way in which income of the business is taxed to the owner (which is explained in detail in Part 1). There is also a relatively new form of business organization called a *limited liability company* (LLC). Limited liability companies with two or more owners generally are taxed like partnerships even though their owners enjoy protection from personal liability. The important thing to note is that each form of business organization will affect what deductions can be claimed and where to claim them. Part 1 also explains tax years and accounting methods that businesses can select.

Part 1 contains another topic of general interest to all businesses. It covers important recordkeeping requirements and suggestions to help you audit-proof your return and protect your deductions and tax credits. In the course of business you may incur certain expenses, but unless you have specific proof of those expenses, you may not be able to claim a deduction or credit. Learn how to keep the necessary records to back up your write-offs in the event your return is questioned by the IRS.

Part 2 details how to report various types of income your business may receive. In addition to fees and sales receipts—the bread-and-butter of your business—you may receive other types of ordinary income such as interest income, dividends, and rents. You may have capital gain transactions as well as sales of business assets. But you may also have losses—from operations or the sale of assets. Special rules govern the tax treatment of these losses. The first part of each chapter discusses the types of income to report and special rules that affect them. Then scan the second part of each chapter, which explains where on the tax return to report the income or claim the loss.

Part 3 focuses on specific deductions. It will provide you with guidance on the various types of deductions you can use to reduce your business income. Each type of deduction is explained in detail. Related tax credits are also explained in each deduction chapter. In the first part of each chapter, you will learn what the deduction is all about and any dollar limits or other special requirements that may apply. As with the income chapters, the second part of each deduction chapter explains where on the tax return you can claim the write-off. The answer depends on your form of business organization. You simply look for your form of business organization to learn where on the return to claim the deduction. The portion of the appropriate tax form or schedule is highlighted in certain instances. For your convenience, key tax forms for claiming these deductions have been included. While the forms and schedules are designed for the 2005 returns, they serve as an example for future years. Also, in Chapter 22, Miscellaneous Business Deductions, you will find checklists that serve as handy reference guides on all business deductions. The checklists are organized according to your status: self-employed, employee, or small corporation. You will also find a checklist of deductions that have not been allowed.

Part 4 contains planning ideas for your business. You will learn about strategies for deferring income, boosting deductions, starting up or winding down a business, and avoiding audits. It also highlights the most common mistakes that business owners make in their returns when claiming deductions. This information will help you avoid making the same mistakes and losing out on tax-saving opportunities. You will also find helpful information about electronic filing of business tax forms and how to use the Internet for tax assistance and planning purposes. And you will find information about other taxes on your business, including state income taxes, employment taxes, sales and use taxes, and excise taxes.

In the Appendix, you will see a listing of information returns you may be required to file with the IRS or other government agencies in conjunction with your tax obligations. These returns enable the federal government to cross-check tax reporting and other financial information.

Several forms and excerpts from forms have been included throughout the book to illustrate reporting rules. These forms are not to be used to file your return. (In many cases, the appropriate forms were not available when this book was published, and older or draft versions of the forms were included.) You can obtain the forms you need from the IRS's web site at <www.irs.gov> or where otherwise indicated.

Another way to stay abreast of tax and other small business developments that can affect your business throughout the year is by subscribing to *Barbara Weltman's Big Ideas for Small Business*®, a newsletter geared for small business owners and their professional advisers at <www.barbaraweltman.com>.

I would like to thank Sidney Kess, Esq. and CPA, for his valuable suggestions in the preparation of the original tax deduction book; Donna LeValley, Esq., for reviewing the new materials; and Elliott Eiss, Esq., for his expertise and constant assistance with this and other projects.

Barbara Weltman
September 2005

Introduction

Small businesses are big news today. They employ 51 percent of the country's private sector workforce, produce 51 percent of private sector output, and now contribute more than half of the nation's gross national product. Small businesses create 75 percent of all new jobs.

Small businesses fall under the purview of the Internal Revenue Service's (IRS) Small Business and Self-Employed Division (SB/SE). This division handles businesses with assets under $10 million and services approximately 45 million tax filers, more than 33 million of whom are full-time or partially self-employed. The SB/SE division accounts for about 40 percent of the total federal tax revenues collected. Headquartered in New Carrolton, MD, the SB/SE has service centers in Brookhaven, New York; Cincinnati, Ohio; Memphis, Tennessee; Ogden, Utah; and Philadelphia, Pennsylvania. The goal of this IRS division is customer assistance to help small businesses comply with the tax laws.

Toward this end, the Small Business Administration (SBA) has teamed up with the IRS to provide small business owners with help on tax issues. A special CD-ROM called *Small Business Resource Guide 2005: What You Need to Know About Taxes and Other Products,* is available free of charge through the IRS web site <www.irs.gov> and IRS tax experts now participate in SBA Business Information Centers where tax forms and publications are also available.

There is also an IRS web site devoted exclusively to small business and self-employed persons <www.irs.gov/business/small/index.htm>. Here you will find special information for your industry—agriculture, automotive, child care, construction, entertainment, gaming, gas retailers, manufacturing, real estate, restaurants, and even tax professionals are already covered, and additional industries are set to follow. You can see the hot tax issues for your industry, find special audit guides that explain what the IRS looks for in your industry when examining returns, and links to other tax information.

As a small business owner, you work, try to grow your business, and hope to make a profit. What you can keep from that profit depends in part on the income tax you pay. The income tax applies to your net income rather than to your gross income or gross receipts. You are not taxed on all the income you bring in by way of sales, fees, commissions, or other payments. Instead, you are essentially taxed on what you keep after paying off the expenses of providing the services or making the sales that are the crux of your business. Deductions for these expenses operate to fix the amount of income that will be subject to tax. So deductions, in effect, help to determine the tax you pay and the profits you keep. And tax credits, the number of which has been expanded in recent years, can offset your tax to reduce the amount you ultimately pay.

Special Rules for Small Businesses

Sometimes it pays to be small. The tax laws contain a number of special rules exclusively for small businesses. But what is a small business? The Small Business Administration (SBA) usually defines small business by the number of employees—size standards range from 50 employees to 1,500 employees, depending on the industry or the SBA program (these new size standards are currently under review). For tax purposes, however, the answer varies from rule to rule, as explained throughout the book. Sometimes it depends on your revenues and sometimes on the number of employees. In Table I.1 are various definitions from the Internal Revenue Code on what constitutes a small business.

Reporting Income

While taxes are figured on your bottom line—your income less certain expenses—you still must report your income on your tax return. Generally all of the income your business receives is taxable unless there is a specific tax rule that allows you to exclude the income permanently or defer it to a future time.

When you report income depends on your method of accounting. *How* and *where* you report income depends on the nature of the income and your type of business organization. Over the next several years, the declining tax rates for owners of pass-through entities—sole proprietorships, partnerships, limited liability companies (LLCs), and S corporations—requires greater sensitivity to the timing of business income as these rates decline.

TABLE I.1 Examples of Tax Definitions of Small Business

Tax Rule	Definition
Accrual method exception for small inventory-based businesses (Chapter 2)	Average annual gross receipts of no more than $10 million in the three prior years (or number of years in business if less)
Bad debts deducted on the nonaccrual-experience method (Chapter 11)	Average annual gross receipts for the three prior years of no more than $5 million
Corporate alternative minimum tax (AMT) exemption for small C corporations (Chapter 22)	Average annual gross receipts of no more than $1 million for a three-year period
Disabled access credit (Chapter 10)	Gross receipts of no more than $1 million in the preceding year or no more than 30 full-time employees
Electronic deposits of federal employment taxes (Chapter 7)	Aggregate tax liability exceeding $200,000 in the year before the prior year
First-year expensing election (Chapter 14)	Equipment purchases for 2005 of no more than $525,000
Independent contractor versus employee determination—shifting burden of proof to IRS (Chapter 7)	Net worth of business does not exceed $7 million
Late filing penalty cap (Appendix)	Average annual gross receipts of no more than $5 million for a three-year period
Reasonable compensation—shifting the burden of proof to the IRS (Chapter 7)	Net worth of business not in excess of $7 million
Retirement plan start-up credit (Chapter 16)	No more than 100 employees with compensation over $5,000 in the preceding year
Savings Incentive Match Plans for Employees (SIMPLE) plans (Chapter 16)	Self-employed or businesses with 100 or fewer employees who received at least $5,000 in compensation in the preceding year
Small business stock—deferral or exclusion of gain on sale (Chapter 5)	Gross assets of no more than $50 million when the stock is issued and immediately after
UNICAP small reseller exception (Chapter 2)	Average annual gross receipts of no more than $10 million for a three-year period
UNICAP simplified dollar value last-in, first-out (LIFO) method (Chapter 2)	Average annual gross receipts of no more than $5 million for a three-year period

Claiming Deductions

You pay tax only on your profits, not on what you take in (gross receipts). In order to arrive at your profits, you are allowed to subtract certain expenses from your income. These expenses are called "deductions."

The law says what you can and cannot deduct (see below). Within this framework, the nature and amount of the deductions you have often vary with the size of your business, the industry you are in, where you are based in the country, and other factors. The most common deductions for businesses include car and truck expenses, utilities, supplies, legal and professional services, insurance, depreciation, taxes, meals and entertainment, advertising, repairs, travel, rent for business property and equipment, and in some cases, a home office.

Are your deductions typical? The General Accounting Office has compiled statistics on deductions claimed by sole proprietors for 2001. These numbers show the dollars spent on various types of deductions, the percentage of sole proprietors who claimed the deductions, and what percentage of total deductions each expense represented. For example, 25 percent of sole proprietors with business gross receipts under $25,000 claimed a deduction for advertising costs. This percentage rose to 65 percent when gross receipts exceeded $100,000. You can view these statistics at <www.gao.gov/new.items/d04304.pdf>.

What Is the Legal Authority for Claiming Deductions?

Deductions are a legal way to reduce the amount of your business income subject to tax. But there is no constitutional right to tax deductions. Instead, deductions are a matter of legislative grace; if Congress chooses to allow a particular deduction, so be it. Therefore, deductions are carefully spelled out in the Internal Revenue Code (the Code).

The language of the Code in many instances is rather general. It may describe a category of deductions without getting into specifics. For example, the Code contains a general deduction for all *ordinary and necessary* business expenses, without explaining what constitutes these expenses. Over the years, the IRS and the courts have worked to flesh out what business expenses are ordinary and necessary. Often the IRS and the courts reach different conclusions, leaving the taxpayer in a somewhat difficult position. If the taxpayer uses a more favorable court position to claim a deduction, the IRS may very well attack the deduction in the event that the return is examined. This puts the taxpayer in the position of having to incur legal expenses to bring the matter to court. On the other hand, if the taxpayer simply follows the IRS approach, a good opportunity to reduce business income by means of a deduction will have been missed. Throughout this book, whenever unresolved questions remain about a particular deduction, both sides have been explained. The choice is up to you and your tax adviser.

Sometimes the Code is very specific about a deduction, such as an employer's right to deduct employment taxes. Still, even where the Code is specific and there is less need for clarification, disputes about applicability or terminology may still arise. Again, the IRS and the courts may differ on the proper conclusion. It will remain for you and your tax adviser to review the different authorities for the positions stated and to reach your own conclusions based on the strength of the different positions and the amount of tax savings at stake.

A word about authorities for the deductions discussed in this book: There are a number of sources for these write-offs in addition to the Internal Revenue Code. These sources include court decisions from the U.S. Tax Court, the U.S. district courts and courts of appeal, the U.S. Court of Federal Claims, and the U.S. Supreme Court. There are also regulations issued by the Treasury Department to explain sections of the Internal Revenue Code. The IRS issues a number of pronouncements, including Revenue Rulings, Revenue Procedures, Notices, Announcements, and News Releases. The department also issues private letter rulings, determination letters, field service advice, and technical advice memoranda. While these private types of pronouncements cannot be cited as authority by a taxpayer other than the one for whom the pronouncement was made, they are important nonetheless. They serve as an indication of IRS thinking on a particular topic, and it is often the case that private letter rulings on topics of general interest later get restated in revenue rulings.

What Is a Tax Deduction Worth to You?

The answer depends on your tax bracket. The tax bracket is dependent on the way you organize your business. If you are self-employed and in the top tax bracket of 35 percent in 2005, then each dollar of deduction will save you 35 cents. Had you not claimed this deduction, you would have had to pay 35 cents of tax on that dollar of income that was offset by the deduction. If you have a personal service corporation, a special type of corporation for most professionals, the corporation pays tax at a flat rate of 35 percent. This means that the corporation is in the 35-percent tax bracket. Thus, each deduction claimed saves 35 cents of tax on the corporation's income. Deductions are even more valuable if your business is in a state that imposes income tax. The impact of state income tax and special rules for state income taxes are not discussed in this book. However, you should explore the tax rules in your state and ascertain their impact on your business income.

When Do You Claim Deductions?

Like the timing of income, the timing of deductions—when to claim them—is determined by your tax year and method of accounting. Your form of business organization affects your choice of tax year and your accounting method.

Even when expenses are deductible, there may be limits on the timing of those deductions. Most common expenses are currently deductible in full. However, some expenses must be capitalized or amortized, or you must choose between current deductibility and capitalization. Capitalization generally means that expenses can be written off ratably as amortized expenses or depreciated over a period of time. Amortized expenses include, for example, fees to incorporate a business and expenses to organize a new business. Certain capitalized costs may not be deductible at all, but are treated as an additional cost of an asset (*basis*).

Credits versus Deductions

Not all write-offs of business expenses are treated as deductions. Some can be claimed as tax credits. A tax credit is worth more than a deduction since it reduces your taxes dollar for dollar. Like deductions, tax credits are available only to the extent that Congress allows. In a couple of instances, you have a choice between treating certain expenses as a deduction or a credit. In most cases, however, tax credits can be claimed for certain expenses for which no tax deduction is provided. Business-related tax credits, as well as personal credits related to working or running a business, are included in this book.

Tax Responsibilities

As a small business owner, your obligations taxwise are broad. Not only do you have to pay income taxes and file income tax returns, but you also must manage payroll taxes if you have any employees. You may also have to collect and report on state and local sales taxes. Finally, you may have to notify the IRS of certain activities on information returns.

It is very helpful to keep an eye on the tax calendar so you will not miss out on any payment or filing deadlines, which can result in interest and penalties. You might want to view and print out or order at no cost from the IRS its Publication 1518, *Small Business Tax Calendar* (go to <www.irs.gov/businesses/small/article/0,,id=101169,00.html>).

You can obtain most federal tax forms online at <www.irs.gov>.

Organization

CHAPTER 1

Business Organization

If you have a great idea for a product or a business and are eager to get started, do not let your enthusiasm be the reason you get off on the wrong foot. Take a while to consider how you will organize your business. The form of organization your business takes controls how income and deductions are reported to the government on a tax return. Sometimes you have a choice of the type of business organization; other times circumstances limit your choice. If you have not yet set up your business and do have a choice, this discussion will influence your decision on business organization. If you have already set up your business, you may want to consider changing to another form of organization. In this chapter you will learn about:

- Sole proprietorships (including independent contractors)
- Partnerships and limited liability companies
- S corporations and their shareholder-employees
- C corporations and their shareholder-employees
- Employees
- Factors in choosing your form of business organization
- Forms of business organization compared
- Changing your form of business

For a further discussion on worker classification, see IRS Publication 15-A, *Employer's Supplemental Tax Guide.*

Sole Proprietorships

If you go into business for yourself and do not have any partners, you are considered a *sole proprietor* and your business is called a *sole proprietorship.* You may think that the term *proprietor* connotes a storekeeper. For purposes of tax treatment, proprietor means any unincorporated business owned entirely by one person. Thus, the category includes individuals in professional practice, such as doctors, lawyers, accountants, and architects. Those who are experts in an area, such as engineering, public relations, or computers, may set up their own consulting businesses and fall under the category of sole proprietor. The designation also applies to independent contractors.

There are no formalities required to become a sole proprietor; you simply conduct business. You may have to register your business with your city, town, or county government by filing a simple form stating that you are doing business as the "Quality Dry Cleaners" or some other business name. This is sometimes referred to as a DBA.

From a legal standpoint, as a sole proprietor, you are personally liable for any debts your business incurs. For example, if you borrow money and default on a loan, the lender can look not only to your business equipment and other business property but also to your personal stocks, bonds, and other property. Some states may give your house homestead protection; state or federal law may protect your pensions and even Individual Retirement Accounts (IRAs). Your only protection for your personal assets is adequate insurance against accidents for your business and other liabilities and paying your debts in full.

Simplicity is the advantage to this form of business. It is the reason why 72.7 percent of all U.S. firms operate as sole proprietorships. This form of business is commonly used for sideline ventures, as evidenced by the fact that half of all sole proprietors earn salaries and wages along with their business income.

Independent Contractors

One type of sole proprietor is the *independent contractor*. To illustrate, suppose you used to work for Corporation X. You have retired, but X gives you a consulting contract under which you provide occasional services to X. In your retirement, you decide to provide consulting services not only to X, but to other customers as well. You are now a consultant. You are an independent contractor to each of the companies for which you provide services.

More precisely, an independent contractor is an individual who provides services to others outside an employment context. The providing of services becomes a business, an independent calling. In terms of claiming business deductions, classification as an independent contractor is generally more favorable than classification as an employee. (See "Tax Treatment of Income and Deductions in General," later in this chapter.) Therefore, many individuals whose employment status is not clear may wish to claim independent contractor status. Also, from the employer's perspective, hiring independent contractors is more favorable because the employer is not liable for employment taxes and need not provide employee benefits. Federal employment taxes include Social Security and Medicare taxes under the Federal Insurance Contribution Act (FICA) as well as unemployment taxes under the Federal Unemployment Tax Act (FUTA).

You should be aware that the Internal Revenue Service (IRS) aggressively tries to reclassify workers as employees in order to collect employment taxes from employers. The IRS agents are provided with a special audit manual designed to help the agents reclassify a worker as an employee if appropriate (view this manual at <www.irs.gov/pub/irs-utl/emporind.pdf>). The key to worker classification is control. In order to prove independent contractor status, you, as the worker, must show that you have the right to control the details and means by which your work is to be accomplished. You may also want to show that you have an economic stake in your work (that you stand to make a profit or loss depending on how your work turns out). It is helpful in this regard to supply your own tools and place of work, although working from your home, using your own computer, and even setting your own hours (flex time) are not conclusive factors that preclude an employee classification. Various behavioral, financial, and other factors can be brought to bear on the issue of whether you are under someone else's control. You can learn more about worker classification in IRS Publication 15-A, *Employer's Supplemental Tax Guide*.

There is a distinction that needs to be made between the classification of a worker for income tax purposes and the classification of a worker for employment tax purposes. By statute, certain employees are treated as independent contractors for employment taxes even though they continue to be treated as employees for income taxes. Other employees are treated as employees for employment taxes even though they are independent contractors for income taxes.

There are two categories of employees that are, by statute, treated as non-employees for purposes of federal employment taxes. These two categories are real estate salespersons and direct sellers of consumer goods. These employees are considered independent contractors (the ramifications of which are discussed later in this chapter). Such workers are deemed independent contractors if at least 90 percent of the employees' compensation is determined by their output. In other words, they are independent contractors if they are paid by commission and not a fixed salary. They must also perform their services under a written contract that specifies they will not be treated as employees for federal employment tax purposes.

Statutory Employees

Some individuals who consider themselves to be in business for them-selves—reporting their income and expenses as sole proprietors—may still be treated as employees for purposes of employment taxes. As such, Social Security and Medicare taxes are withheld from their compensation. These individuals include:

- Corporate officers
- Agent-drivers or commission-drivers engaged in the distribution of meat products, bakery products, produce, beverages other than milk, laundry, or dry-cleaning services
- Full-time life insurance salespersons
- Homeworkers who personally perform services according to specifications provided by the service recipient
- Traveling or city salespersons engaged on a full-time basis in the solicitation of orders from wholesalers, retailers, contractors, or operators of hotels, restaurants, or other similar businesses

Full-time life insurance salespersons, homeworkers, and traveling or city salespersons are exempt from FICA if they have made a substantial investment in the facilities used in connection with the performance of services.

One-Member Limited Liability Companies

Every state allows a single owner to form a limited liability company (LLC) under state law. From a legal standpoint, an LLC gives the owner protection from personal liability (only business assets are at risk from the claims of creditors) as explained later in this chapter. But from a tax standpoint, a one-member LLC is treated as a "disregarded entity" (the owner can elect to have the LLC taxed as a corporation, but there is probably no compelling reason to do so). If the owner is an individual (and not a corporation), all of the income and expenses of the LLC are reported on Schedule C of the owner's Form 1040. In other words, for federal income tax purposes, the LLC is treated just like a sole proprietorship.

Tax Treatment of Income and Deductions in General

Sole proprietors, including independent contractors and statutory employees, report their income and deductions on Schedule C, see *Profit or Loss From Business* (Figure 1.1). The net amount (profit or loss after offsetting income with deductions) is then reported as part of the income section on page one of your Form 1040. Such individuals may be able to use a simplified form for reporting business income and deductions: Schedule C-EZ, *Net Profit From Business* (see Figure 1.2). Individuals engaged in farming activities report business income and deductions on Schedule F, the net amount of which is then reported in the

SCHEDULE C
(Form 1040)

Department of the Treasury
Internal Revenue Service

Profit or Loss From Business
(Sole Proprietorship)

▶ Partnerships, joint ventures, etc., must file Form 1065 or 1065-B.

▶ Attach to Form 1040 or 1041.   ▶ See Instructions for Schedule C (Form 1040).

OMB No. 1545-0074

2005

Attachment
Sequence No. **09**

Name of proprietor

Social security number (SSN)

A   Principal business or profession, including product or service (see page C-2 of the instructions)

B   Enter code from pages C-7, 8, & 9 ▶

C   Business name. If no separate business name, leave blank.

D   Employer ID number (EIN), if any

E   Business address (including suite or room no.) ▶
City, town or post office, state, and ZIP code

F   Accounting method: (1) ☐ Cash   (2) ☐ Accrual   (3) ☐ Other (specify) ▶

G   Did you "materially participate" in the operation of this business during 2005? If "No," see page C-3 for limit on losses   ☐ Yes   ☐ No

H   If you started or acquired this business during 2005, check here   ▶ ☐

Part I   Income

1   Gross receipts or sales. **Caution.** If this income was reported to you on Form W-2 and the "Statutory employee" box on that form was checked, see page C-3 and check here   ▶ ☐ | 1 |
2   Returns and allowances | 2 |
3   Subtract line 2 from line 1 | 3 |
4   Cost of goods sold (from line 42 on page 2) | 4 |
5   **Gross profit.** Subtract line 4 from line 3 | 5 |
6   Other income, including Federal and state gasoline or fuel tax credit or refund (see page C-3) | 6 |
7   **Gross income.** Add lines 5 and 6   ▶ | 7 |

Part II   Expenses. Enter expenses for business use of your home **only** on line 30.

8	Advertising	8	18	Office expense	18
9	Car and truck expenses (see page C-3)	9	19	Pension and profit-sharing plans	19
10	Commissions and fees	10	20	Rent or lease (see page C-5):	
11	Contract labor (see page C-4)	11	a	Vehicles, machinery, and equipment	20a
12	Depletion	12	b	Other business property	20b
13	Depreciation and section 179 expense deduction (not included in Part III) (see page C-4)	13	21	Repairs and maintenance	21
			22	Supplies (not included in Part III)	22
			23	Taxes and licenses	23
			24	Travel, meals, and entertainment:	
14	Employee benefit programs (other than on line 19)	14	a	Travel	24a
15	Insurance (other than health)	15	b	Deductible meals and entertainment (see page C-5)	24b
16	Interest:		25	Utilities	25
a	Mortgage (paid to banks, etc.)	16a	26	Wages (less employment credits)	26
b	Other	16b	27	Other expenses (from line 48 on page 2)	27
17	Legal and professional services	17			

28   **Total expenses** before expenses for business use of home. Add lines 8 through 27 in columns   ▶ | 28 |
29   Tentative profit (loss). Subtract line 28 from line 7 | 29 |
30   Expenses for business use of your home. Attach **Form 8829** | 30 |
31   **Net profit or (loss).** Subtract line 30 from line 29.
• If a profit, enter on **Form 1040, line 12,** and also on **Schedule SE, line 2** (statutory employees, see page C-6). Estates and trusts, enter on Form 1041, line 3.
• If a loss, you **must** go to line 32. | 31 |
32   If you have a loss, check the box that describes your investment in this activity (see page C-6).
• If you checked 32a, enter the loss on **Form 1040, line 12,** and also on **Schedule SE, line 2** (statutory employees, see page C-6). Estates and trusts, enter on Form 1041, line 3.
• If you checked 32b, you **must** attach **Form 6198.** Your loss may be limited.   32a ☐ All investment is at risk.   32b ☐ Some investment is not at risk.

For Paperwork Reduction Act Notice, see Form 1040 instructions.   Cat. No. 11334P   Schedule C (Form 1040) 2005

FIGURE 1.1   Schedule C, Profit or Loss From Business

Part III **Cost of Goods Sold** (see page C-6)

33 Method(s) used to
value closing inventory: **a** ☐ Cost **b** ☐ Lower of cost or market **c** ☐ Other (attach explanation)

34 Was there any change in determining quantities, costs, or valuations between opening and closing inventory? If
"Yes," attach explanation . . . . ☐ **Yes** ☐ **No**

35	Inventory at beginning of year. If different from last year's closing inventory, attach explanation . .	35
36	Purchases less cost of items withdrawn for personal use	36
37	Cost of labor. Do not include any amounts paid to yourself	37
38	Materials and supplies	38
39	Other costs	39
40	Add lines 35 through 39	40
41	Inventory at end of year	41
42	**Cost of goods sold.** Subtract line 41 from line 40. Enter the result here and on page 1, line 4 . .	42

Part IV **Information on Your Vehicle.** Complete this part **only** if you are claiming car or truck expenses on
line 9 and are not required to file Form 4562 for this business. See the instructions for line 13 on page
C-4 to find out if you must file Form 4562.

43 When did you place your vehicle in service for business purposes? (month, day, year) ▶ ....../....../......

44 Of the total number of miles you drove your vehicle during 2005, enter the number of miles you used your vehicle for:

a Business .... **b** Commuting (see instructions) .... **c** Other ....

45 Do you (or your spouse) have another vehicle available for personal use?. . . . . ☐ **Yes** ☐ **No**

46 Was your vehicle available for personal use during off-duty hours? . . . . ☐ **Yes** ☐ **No**

47a Do you have evidence to support your deduction? . . . . ☐ **Yes** ☐ **No**

 b If "Yes," is the evidence written? . . . . ☐ **Yes** ☐ **No**

Part V **Other Expenses.** List below business expenses not included on lines 8–26 or line 30.

....	
....	
....	
....	
....	
....	
....	
....	

48	**Total other expenses.** Enter here and on page 1, line 27	48

✪ *Printed on recycled paper*

FIGURE 1.1 *(Continued)*

SCHEDULE C-EZ (Form 1040) Department of the Treasury Internal Revenue Service	**Net Profit From Business** (Sole Proprietorship) ▶ Partnerships, joint ventures, etc., must file Form 1065 or 1065-B. ▶ Attach to Form 1040 or 1041. ▶ See instructions on back.	OMB No. 1545-0074 20**05** Attachment Sequence No. **09A**
Name of proprietor		Social security number (SSN)

Part I   General Information

You May Use Schedule C-EZ Instead of Schedule C Only If You:	• Had business expenses of $5,000 or less. • Use the cash method of accounting. • Did not have an inventory at any time during the year. • Did not have a net loss from your business. • Had only one business as either a sole proprietor or statutory employee.	**And You:** • Had no employees during the year. • Are not required to file **Form 4562**, Depreciation and Amortization, for this business. See the instructions for Schedule C, line 13, on page C-4 to find out if you must file. • Do not deduct expenses for business use of your home. • Do not have prior year unallowed passive activity losses from this business.

A   Principal business or profession, including product or service

B   Enter code from pages C-7, 8, & 9
▶

C   Business name. If no separate business name, leave blank.

D   Employer ID number (EIN), if any

E   Business address (including suite or room no.). Address not required if same as on Form 1040, page 1.

City, town or post office, state, and ZIP code

Part II   Figure Your Net Profit

1	**Gross receipts. Caution.** If this income was reported to you on Form W-2 and the "Statutory employee" box on that form was checked, see **Statutory Employees** in the instructions for Schedule C, line 1, on page C-3 and check here . . . . ▶ ☐	**1**
2	**Total expenses** (see instructions). If more than $5,000, you **must** use Schedule C.	**2**
3	**Net profit.** Subtract line 2 from line 1. If less than zero, you **must** use Schedule C. Enter on **Form 1040, line 12,** and **also** on **Schedule SE, line 2.** (Statutory employees **do not** report this amount on Schedule SE, line 2. Estates and trusts, enter on Form 1041, line 3.)	**3**

Part III   Information on Your Vehicle. Complete this part **only** if you are claiming car or truck expenses on line 2.

4   When did you place your vehicle in service for business purposes? (month, day, year) ▶ ...... / ...... / ....

5   Of the total number of miles you drove your vehicle during 2005, enter the number of miles you used your vehicle for:

a Business .... **b** Commuting (see instructions) .... **c** Other ....

6   Do you (or your spouse) have another vehicle available for personal use? . . . . ☐ **Yes** ☐ **No**

7   Was your vehicle available for personal use during off-duty hours? . . . . ☐ **Yes** ☐ **No**

8a Do you have evidence to support your deduction?   . . . . ☐ **Yes** ☐ **No**

  b If "Yes," is the evidence written?   . . . . ☐ **Yes** ☐ **No**

For Paperwork Reduction Act Notice, see Form 1040 instructions.   Cat. No. 14374D   Schedule C-EZ (Form 1040) 2005

FIGURE 1.2   Schedule C-EZ, Net Profit From Business

income section on page one of your Form 1040. Individuals who are considered employees cannot use Schedule C to report their income and claim deductions. See page 21 for the tax treatment of income and deductions by employees.

Partnerships and Limited Liability Companies

If you go into business with others, then you cannot be a sole proprietor. You are automatically in a *partnership* if you join together with one or more people to share the profits of the business and take no formal action. Owners of a partnership are called *partners*.

There are two types of partnerships: *general partnerships* and *limited partnerships*. In general partnerships, all of the partners are personally liable for the debts of the business. Creditors can go after the personal assets of any and all of the partners to satisfy partnership debts. In limited partnerships, only the general partners are personally liable for the debts of the business. Limited partners are liable only to the extent of their investments in the business plus their share of recourse debts and obligations to make future investments.

Example

If a partnership incurs debts of $10,000 (none of which are recourse), a general partner is liable for the full $10,000. A limited partner who initially contributed $1,000 to the limited partnership is liable only to that extent. He or she can lose the $1,000 investment, but creditors cannot go after personal assets.

General partners are jointly and severally liable for the business's debts. A creditor can go after any one partner for the full amount of the debt. That partner can seek to recoup a proportional share of the debt from other partner(s).

Partnerships can be informal agreements to share profits and losses of a business venture. More typically, however, they are organized with formal partnership agreements. These agreements detail how income, deductions, gains, losses, and credits are to be split (if there are any special allocations to be made) and what happens on the retirement, disability, bankruptcy, or death of a partner. A limited partnership must have a partnership agreement that complies with state law requirements.

Another form of organization that can be used by those joining together for business is a limited liability company (LLC). This type of business organization is formed under state law in which all owners are given limited liability. Owners of LLCs are called *members*. These companies are relatively new but have attracted great interest across the country. Every state now has LLC statutes to permit the formation of an LLC within its boundaries. Most states also permit limited liability partnerships (LLPs)—LLCs for accountants, attorneys, doctors, and other professionals—which are easily formed by existing partnerships filing an LLP election with the state. And Delaware now permits multiple LLCs to operate under a single LLC umbrella called a series LLC. The debts and liabilities of each LLC remain separate from those of the other LLCs, something that is ideal for those owning several pieces of real estate—each can be owned by a separate LLC under the master LLC. At present, state law is evolving to determine the treatment of LLCs formed in one state but doing business in another.

As the name suggests, the creditors of LLCs can look only to the assets of the company to satisfy debts; creditors cannot go after members and hope to recover their personal assets. For federal income tax purposes, LLCs are treated like partnerships unless the members elect to have the LLCs taxed as corporations. Tax experts have yet to come up with any compelling reason for LLCs to choose corporate tax treatment, but if it is desired, the businesses just check the box on a special form (IRS Form 8832, Entity Classification Election. See Figure 1.3). For purposes of our discussion throughout the book, it will be assumed that LLCs have not chosen corporate tax treatment and so are taxed the same way as partnerships. A one-member LLC is treated for tax purposes like a sole proprietor if it is owned by an individual who reports the company's income and expenses on his or her Schedule C.

Tax Treatment of Income and Deductions in General

Partnerships and LLCs are *pass-through* entities. They are not separate taxpaying entities; instead, they pass income, deductions, gains, losses, and tax credits through to their owners. The owners report these amounts on their individual returns. While the entity does not pay taxes, it must file an information return with IRS Form 1065, U.S. Return of Partnership Income, to report the total pass-through amounts. Even though the return is called a *partnership return*, it is the same return filed by LLCs with two or more owners. The entity also completes Schedule K-1 of Form 1065 (Figure 1.4), a copy of which is given to each owner. The K-1 tells the owner his or her allocable share of partnership/LLC amounts. Like W-2 forms used by the IRS to match employees' reporting of their compensation, the IRS now employs computer matching of Schedules K-1 to ensure that owners are properly reporting their share of their business's income.

There are two types of items that pass through to an owner: trade or business income or loss and separately stated items. A partner's or member's share is called the *distributive share*. Trade or business income or loss takes into account most ordinary deductions of the business—compensation, rent, taxes, interest, and so forth. Guaranteed payments to an owner are also taken into account when determining ordinary income or loss. From an owner's perspective, deductions net out against income from the business, and the owner's allocable share of the net amount is then reported on the owner's Schedule E of Form 1040. Figure 1.5 shows a sample portion of Schedule E on which a partner's or member's distributive share is reported.

Form **8832** (Rev. September 2002) Department of the Treasury Internal Revenue Service	**Entity Classification Election**	OMB No. 1545-1516

	Name of entity	EIN ▶
Type or Print	Number, street, and room or suite no. If a P.O. box, see instructions.	
	City or town, state, and ZIP code. If a foreign address, enter city, province or state, postal code and country.	

1   Type of election (see instructions):

a ☐ Initial classification by a newly-formed entity.

b ☐ Change in current classification.

2   Form of entity (see instructions):

a ☐ A domestic eligible entity electing to be classified as an association taxable as a corporation.

b ☐ A domestic eligible entity electing to be classified as a partnership.

c ☐ A domestic eligible entity with a single owner electing to be disregarded as a separate entity.

d ☐ A foreign eligible entity electing to be classified as an association taxable as a corporation.

e ☐ A foreign eligible entity electing to be classified as a partnership.

f ☐ A foreign eligible entity with a single owner electing to be disregarded as a separate entity.

3   Disregarded entity information (see instructions):
a Name of owner ▶ ....
b Identifying number of owner ▶ ....
c Country of organization of entity electing to be disregarded (if foreign) ▶ ....

4   Election is to be effective beginning (month, day, year) (see instructions) . . . . ▶ ___ / ___ / ___

5   Name and title of person whom the IRS may call for more information | **6   That person's telephone number**
(   )

Consent Statement and Signature(s) (see instructions)

Under penalties of perjury, I (we) declare that I (we) consent to the election of the above-named entity to be classified as indicated above, and that I (we) have examined this consent statement, and to the best of my (our) knowledge and belief, it is true, correct, and complete. If I am an officer, manager, or member signing for all members of the entity, I further declare that I am authorized to execute this consent statement on their behalf.

Signature(s)	Date	, Title

For Paperwork Reduction Act Notice, see page 4.   Cat. No. 22598R   Form **8832** (Rev. 9-2002)

FIGURE 1.3   Form 8832, Entity Classification Election

Schedule K-1
(Form 1065)

2005

Department of the Treasury
Internal Revenue Service

For calendar year 2005, or tax
year beginning _____ , 2005
ending _____ , 20___

Partner's Share of Income, Deductions,
Credits, etc. ▶ See back of form and separate instructions.

Part I	Information About the Partnership

A Partnership's employer identification number

B Partnership's name, address, city, state, and ZIP code

C IRS Center where partnership filed return

D ☐ Check if this is a publicly traded partnership (PTP)
E ☐ Tax shelter registration number, if any _____
F ☐ Check if Form 8271 is attached

Part II	Information About the Partner

G Partner's identifying number

H Partner's name, address, city, state, and ZIP code

I ☐ General partner or LLC member-manager   ☐ Limited partner or other LLC member

J ☐ Domestic partner   ☐ Foreign partner

K What type of entity is this partner? _____

L Partner's share of profit, loss, and capital:

	Beginning		Ending	
Profit		%		%
Loss		%		%
Capital		%		%

M Partner's share of liabilities at year end:
Nonrecourse . . . . $_____
Qualified nonrecourse financing . . $_____
Recourse . . . . $_____

N Partner's capital account analysis:
Beginning capital account . . . . $_____
Capital contributed during the year . $_____
Current year increase (decrease) . . $_____
Withdrawals & distributions . . . $(_____)
Ending capital account . . . . $_____

☐ Tax basis ☐ GAAP ☐ Section 704(b) book
☐ Other (explain)

☐ Final K-1   ☐ Amended K-1   OMB No. 1545-0099

Part III	Partner's Share of Current Year Income, Deductions, Credits, and Other Items

1	Ordinary business income (loss)	15	Credits & credit recapture
2	Net rental real estate income (loss)		
3	Other net rental income (loss)	16	Foreign transactions
4	Guaranteed payments		
5	Interest income		
6a	Ordinary dividends		
6b	Qualified dividends		
7	Royalties		
8	Net short-term capital gain (loss)		
9a	Net long-term capital gain (loss)	17	Alternative minimum tax (AMT) items
9b	Collectibles (28%) gain (loss)		
9c	Unrecaptured section 1250 gain		
10	Net section 1231 gain (loss)	18	Tax-exempt income and nondeductible expenses
11	Other income (loss)		
		19	Distributions
12	Section 179 deduction		
13	Other deductions		
		20	Other information
14	Self-employment earnings (loss)		

*See attached statement for additional information.

For IRS Use Only

For Privacy Act and Paperwork Reduction Act Notice, see Instructions for Form 1065.   Cat. No. 11394R   Schedule K-1 (Form 1065) 2005

FIGURE 1.4 Schedule K-1, Partner's Share of Income, Credits, Deductions, etc.

14 ORGANIZATION

Schedule K-1 (Form 1065) 2005

Page 2

This list identifies the codes used on Schedule K-1 for all partners and provides summarized reporting information for partners who file Form 1040. For detailed reporting and filing information, see the separate Partner's Instructions for Schedule K-1 and the instructions for your income tax return.

1. Ordinary business income (loss). You must first determine whether the income (loss) is passive or nonpassive. Then enter on your return as follows:

	Enter on
Passive loss	See the Partner's Instructions
Passive income	Schedule E, line 28, column (g)
Nonpassive loss	Schedule E, line 28, column (h)
Nonpassive income	Schedule E, line 28, column (j)

2. Net rental real estate income (loss) — See the Partner's Instructions

3. Other net rental income (loss)

Net income	Schedule E, line 28, column (g)
Net loss	See the Partner's Instructions

4. Guaranteed payments — Schedule E, line 28, column (j)

5. Interest income — Form 1040, line 8a

6a. Ordinary dividends — Form 1040, line 9a

6b. Qualified dividends — Form 1040, line 9b

7. Royalties — Schedule E, line 4

8. Net short-term capital gain (loss) — Schedule D, line 5, column (f)

9a. Net long-term capital gain (loss) — Schedule D, line 12, column (f)

9b. Collectibles (28%) gain (loss) — 28% Rate Gain Worksheet, line 4 (Schedule D Instructions)

9c. Unrecaptured section 1250 gain — See the Partner's Instructions

10. Net section 1231 gain (loss) — See the Partner's Instructions

11. Other income (loss)

Code		
A	Other portfolio income (loss)	See the Partner's Instructions
B	Involuntary conversions	See the Partner's Instructions
C	Sec. 1256 contracts & straddles	Form 6781, line 1
D	Mining exploration costs recapture	See Pub. 535
E	Cancellation of debt	Form 1040, line 21 or Form 982
F	Other income (loss)	See the Partner's Instructions

12. Section 179 deduction — See the Partner's Instructions

13. Other deductions

A	Cash contributions (50%)	Schedule A, line 15
B	Cash contributions (30%)	Schedule A, line 15
C	Noncash contributions (50%)	Schedule A, line 16
D	Noncash contributions (30%)	Schedule A, line 16
E	Capital gain property to a 50% organization (30%)	Schedule A, line 16
F	Capital gain property (20%)	Schedule A, line 16
G	Investment interest expense	Form 4952, line 1
H	Deductions—royalty income	Schedule E, line 18
I	Section 59(e)(2) expenditures	See Partner's Instructions
J	Deductions—portfolio (2% floor)	Schedule A, line 22
K	Deductions—portfolio (other)	Schedule A, line 27
L	Amounts paid for medical insurance	Schedule A, line 1 or Form 1040, line 29
M	Educational assistance benefits	See the Partner's Instructions
N	Dependent care benefits	Form 2441, line 12
O	Preproductive period expenses	See the Partner's Instructions
P	Commercial revitalization deduction from rental real estate activities	See Form 8582 Instructions
Q	Pensions and IRAs	See the Partner's Instructions
R	Reforestation expense deduction	See the Partner's Instructions
S	Domestic production activities information	See Form 8903 Instructions
T	Qualified production activities income	Form 8903, line 7
U	Employer's W-2 wages	Form 8903, line 13
V	Other deductions	See the Partner's Instructions

14. Self-employment earnings (loss)

Note. *If you have a section 179 deduction or any partner-level deductions, see the Partner's Instructions before completing Schedule SE.*

A	Net earnings (loss) from self-employment	Schedule SE, Section A or B
B	Gross farming or fishing income	See the Partner's Instructions
C	Gross non-farm income	See the Partner's Instructions

15. Credits & credit recapture

A	Low-income housing credit (section 42(j)(5))	Form 8586, line 4
B	Low-income housing credit (other)	Form 8586, line 4
C	Qualified rehabilitation expenditures (rental real estate)	Form 3468, line 1
D	Qualified rehabilitation expenditures (other than rental real estate)	Form 3468, line 1
E	Basis of energy property	Form 3468, line 2
F	Other rental real estate credits	See the Partner's Instructions
G	Other rental credits	See the Partner's Instructions
H	Undistributed capital gains credit	Form 1040, line 70; check box a
I	Credit for alcohol used as fuel	Form 6478, line 4

Code		Enter on
J	Work opportunity credit	Form 5884, line 3
K	Welfare-to-work credit	Form 8861, line 3
L	Disabled access credit	Form 8826, line 7
M	Empowerment zone and renewal community employment credit	Form 8844, line 3
N	Credit for increasing research activities	Form 6765, line 40
O	New markets credit	Form 8874, line 2
P	Credit for employer social security and Medicare taxes	Form 8846, line 5
Q	Backup withholding	Form 1040, line 64
R	Recapture of low-income housing credit (section 42(j)(5))	Form 8611, line 8
S	Recapture of low-income housing credit (other)	Form 8611, line 8
T	Recapture of investment credit	See Form 4255
U	Other credits	See the Partner's Instructions
V	Recapture of other credits	See the Partner's Instructions

16. Foreign transactions

A	Name of country or U.S. possession	Form 1116, Part I
B	Gross income from all sources	Form 1116, Part I
C	Gross income sourced at partner level	Form 1116, Part I

Foreign gross income sourced at partnership level

D	Passive	Form 1116, Part I
E	Listed categories	Form 1116, Part I
F	General limitation	Form 1116, Part I

Deductions allocated and apportioned at partner level

G	Interest expense	Form 1116, Part I
H	Other	Form 1116, Part I

Deductions allocated and apportioned at partnership level to foreign source income

I	Passive	Form 1116, Part I
J	Listed categories	Form 1116, Part I
K	General limitation	Form 1116, Part I

Other information

L	Total foreign taxes paid	Form 1116, Part II
M	Total foreign taxes accrued	Form 1116, Part II
N	Reduction in taxes available for credit	Form 1116, line 12
O	Foreign trading gross receipts	Form 8873
P	Extraterritorial income exclusion	Form 8873
Q	Other foreign transactions	See the Partner's Instructions

17. Alternative minimum tax (AMT) items

A	Post-1986 depreciation adjustment	
B	Adjusted gain or loss	See the Partner's
C	Depletion (other than oil & gas)	Instructions and
D	Oil, gas, & geothermal—gross income	the Instructions for
E	Oil, gas, & geothermal—deductions	Form 6251
F	Other AMT items	

18. Tax-exempt income and nondeductible expenses

A	Tax-exempt interest income	Form 1040, line 8b
B	Other tax-exempt income	See the Partner's Instructions
C	Nondeductible expenses	See the Partner's Instructions

19. Distributions

A	Cash and marketable securities	See the Partner's Instructions
B	Other property	See the Partner's Instructions

20. Other information

A	Investment income	Form 4952, line 4a
B	Investment expenses	Form 4952, line 5
C	Fuel tax credit information	Form 4136
D	Look-back interest—completed long-term contracts	Form 8697
E	Look-back interest—income forecast method	Form 8866
F	Dispositions of property with section 179 deductions	
G	Recapture of section 179 deduction	
H	Special basis adjustments	
I	Section 453(l)(3) information	
J	Section 453A(c) information	
K	Section 1260(b) information	See the Partner's
L	Interest allocable to production expenditures	Instructions
M	CCF nonqualified withdrawals	
N	Information needed to figure depletion—oil and gas	
O	Amortization of reforestation costs	
P	Unrelated business taxable income	
Q	Other information	

Printed on recycled paper

FIGURE 1.4 *(Continued)*

Schedule E (Form 1040) 2005   Attachment Sequence No. **13**   Page **2**

Name(s) shown on return. Do not enter name and social security number if shown on other side.	Your social security number

Caution. The IRS compares amounts reported on your tax return with amounts shown on Schedule(s) K-1.

Part II   Income or Loss From Partnerships and S Corporations   **Note.** If you report a loss from an at-risk activity for which **any** amount is **not** at risk, you **must** check the box in column **(e)** on line 28 and attach **Form 6198.** See page E-1.

27 Are you reporting any loss not allowed in a prior year due to the at-risk or basis limitations, a prior year unallowed loss from a passive activity (if that loss was not reported on Form 8582), or unreimbursed partnership expenses? ☐ **Yes** ☐ **No**
   If you answered "Yes," see page E-6 before completing this section.

28	(a) Name	(b) Enter **P** for partnership; **S** for S corporation	(c) Check if foreign partnership	(d) Employer identification number	(e) Check if any amount is not at risk
A			☐		☐
B			☐		☐
C			☐		☐
D			☐		☐

	Passive Income and Loss		Nonpassive Income and Loss		
	(f) Passive loss allowed (attach **Form 8582** if required)	(g) Passive income from **Schedule K-1**	(h) Nonpassive loss from **Schedule K-1**	(i) Section 179 expense deduction from **Form 4562**	(j) Nonpassive income from **Schedule K-1**
A					
B					
C					
D					
29a Totals					
b Totals					

30	Add columns (g) and (j) of line 29a	30	
31	Add columns (f), (h), and (i) of line 29b	31	( )
32	**Total partnership and S corporation income or (loss).** Combine lines 30 and 31. Enter the result here and include in the total on line 41 below	32	

FIGURE 1.5   Schedule E, Part II, Income or Loss From Partnerships and S Corporations

Separately stated items are stand-alone items that pass through to owners apart from the net amount of trade or business income. These are items that are subject to limitations on an individual's tax return and must be segregated from the net amount of trade or business income. They are reported along with similar items on the owner's own tax return.

Example

A charitable contribution deduction made by a partnership passes through separately as a charitable contribution. The partner adds the amount of the pass-through charitable contribution to his or her other charitable contributions. Since an individual's cash contributions are deductible only to the extent of 50 percent of adjusted gross income, the partner's allocable share of the partnership's charitable contribution is subject to his or her individual adjusted gross income limit.

Other items that pass through separately to owners include capital gains and losses, Section 179 expense deductions, investment interest deductions, and tax credits.

When a partnership or LLC has substantial expenses that exceed its operating income, a loss is passed through to the owner. A number of different rules operate to limit a loss deduction. The owner may not be able to claim the entire loss. The loss is limited by the owner's *basis*, or the amount of cash and property contributed to the partnership, in the interest in the partnership.

Example

You contributed $2,000 to the AB Partnership. In 2005 the partnership had sizable expenses and only a small amount of revenue. Your allocable share of partnership loss is $3,000. You may deduct only $2,000 in 2005, which is the amount of your basis in your partnership interest. You may deduct that additional $1,000 of loss when you have additional basis to offset it.

There may be additional limits on your write-offs from partnerships and LLCs. If you are a passive investor—a silent partner—in these businesses, your loss deduction is further limited by the passive activity loss rules. In general, these rules limit a current deduction for losses from passive activities to the extent of income from passive activities. Additionally, losses are limited by the individual's economic risk in the business. This limit is called the *at-risk rule*. The passive activity loss and at-risk rules are discussed in Chapter 4. For a further discussion of the passive activity loss rules, see IRS Publication 925, *Passive Activity and At-Risk Rules*.

S Corporations and Their Shareholder-Employees

S corporations are like regular corporations (called *C corporations*) for business law purposes. They are separate entities in the eyes of the law and exist independently from their owners. For example, if an owner dies, the S corporation's existence continues. S corporations are formed under state law in the same way as other corporations. The only difference between S corporations and other corporations is their tax treatment for federal income tax purposes.

For the most part, S corporations are treated as pass-through entities for federal income tax purposes. This means that, as with partnerships and LLCs, the income and loss pass through to owners, and their allocable share is reported by S corporation shareholders on their individual income tax returns. The tax treatment of S corporations is discussed more fully later in this chapter.

Note

State laws vary on the tax treatment of S corporations for state income tax purposes. Be sure to check the laws of any state in which you do business.

S corporation status is not automatic. A corporation must elect S status in a timely manner. This election is made on Form 2553, Election by Small Business Corporations to Tax Corporate Income Directly to Shareholders. It must be filed with the IRS no later than the fifteenth day of the third month of the corporation's tax year.

Example

A corporation (on a calendar year) that has been in existence for a number of years wants to elect S status. It has to file an election no later than March 15, 2006 to be effective for its 2005 tax year. If a corporation is formed on August 1, 2005, and wants an S election to be effective for its first tax year, the S election must be filed no later than November 15, 2005.

If an S election is filed after the deadline, it is automatically effective for the following year. A corporation can simply decide to make a prospective election by filing at any time during the year prior to that for which the election is to be effective.

Example

A corporation (on a calendar year) that has been in existence for a number of years wants to elect S status for its 2006 tax year. It can file an election at any time during 2005.

To be eligible for an S election, the corporation must meet certain shareholder requirements. Starting in 2005, there can be no more than 100 shareholders. For this purpose, all family members (up to six generations) can be treated as a single shareholder. Only certain types of trusts are permitted to be shareholders. There can be no nonresident alien shareholders.

An election cannot be made before the corporation is formed. The board of directors of the corporation must agree to the election and should indicate this assent in the minutes of a board of directors meeting.

Remember, if state law also allows S status, a separate election may have to be filed with the state. Check with all state law requirements.

Tax Treatment of Income and Deductions in General

For the most part, S corporations, like partnerships and LLCs, are pass-through entities. They are generally not separate taxpaying entities. Instead, they pass through to their shareholders' income, deductions, gains, losses, and tax credits. The shareholders report these amounts on their individual returns. The S corporation files a return with the IRS—Form 1120S, U.S. Income Tax Return for an S Corporation—to report the total pass-through amounts. The S corporation also completes Schedule K-1 of Form 1120S, a copy of which is given to each shareholder. The K-1 tells the shareholder his or her allocable share of S corporation amounts. The K-1 for S corporation shareholders is similar to the K-1 for partners and LLC members.

Unlike partnerships and LLCs, however, S corporations may become taxpayers if they have certain types of income. There are only three types of income that result in a tax on the S corporation. These three items cannot be reduced by any deductions:

- **Built-in gains.** These are gains related to appreciation of assets held by a C corporation that converts to S status. Thus, if a corporation is formed and immediately elects S status, there will never be any built-in gains to worry about.

- **Passive investment income.** This is income of a corporation that has earnings and profits from a time when it was a C corporation. A tax on the S corporation results only when this passive investment income exceeds 25 percent of gross receipts. Again, if a corporation is formed and immediately elects S status, or if a corporation that converted to S status did not have any earnings and profits at the time of conversion, then there will never be any tax from this source.

- **LIFO recapture.** When a C corporation uses last-in, first-out or LIFO to report inventory converts to S status, there may be recapture income that is taken into account partly on the C corporation's final return, but also on the S corporation's return. Again, if a corporation is formed and immediately elects S status, there will not be any recapture income on which the S corporation must pay tax.

To sum up, if a corporation is formed and immediately elects S status, the corporation will always be solely a pass-through entity and there will never be any tax at the corporate level. If the S corporation was, at one time, a C corporation, there may be some tax at the corporate level.

C Corporations and Their Shareholder-Employees

A *C corporation* is an entity separate and apart from its owners; it has its own legal existence. Though formed under state law, it need not be formed in the state in which the business operates. Many corporations, for example, are formed in Delaware or Nevada because the laws in these states favor the corporation, as opposed to the investors (shareholders). However, state law for the state in which the business operates may still require the corporation to make some formal notification of doing business in the state. The corporation may also be subject to tax on income generated in that state.

For federal tax purposes, a C corporation is a separate taxpaying entity. It files its own return (Form 1120, U.S. Corporation Income Tax Return) to report its income or losses (or Form 1120-A, U.S. Corporation Short-Form Income Tax Return, for corporations with gross receipts under $500,000). Shareholders do not report their share of the corporation's income. The tax treatment of C corporations is explained more fully later in this chapter.

Personal Service Corporations

Professionals who incorporate their practices are a special type of C corporation called **personal service corporations (PSCs)**.

Personal service corporation (PSC) A C corporation that performs personal services in the fields of health, law, accounting, engineering, architecture, actuarial science, performing arts, or consulting and meets certain ownership and service tests.

Personal service corporations are subject to special rules in the tax law. Some of these rules are beneficial; others are not. Personal service corporations:

- Cannot use graduated corporate tax rates; they are subject to a flat tax rate of 35 percent.
- Are generally required to use the same tax year as that of their owners. Typically, individuals report their income on a calendar year basis (explained more fully in Chapter 2), so their PSCs must also use a calendar year. However, there is a special election that can be made to use a fiscal year.
- Can use the cash method of accounting. Other C corporations cannot use the cash method and instead must use the accrual method (explained more fully in Chapter 2).
- Are subject to the passive loss limitation rules (explained in Chapter 4).
- Can have their income and deductions reallocated by the IRS between the corporation and the shareholders if it more correctly reflects the economics of the situation.
- Have a smaller exemption from the accumulated earnings penalty than other C corporations. This penalty imposes an additional tax on corporations that accumulate their income above and beyond the reasonable needs of the business instead of distributing income to shareholders.

Tax Treatment of Income and Deductions in General

The C corporation reports its own income and claims its own deductions on Form 1120, U.S. Corporation Income Tax Return. Shareholders in C corporations do not have to report any income of the corporation (and cannot claim any deductions of the corporation). Figure 1.6 shows a sample copy of page one of Form 1120.

Form 1120

U.S. Corporation Income Tax Return

Department of the Treasury
Internal Revenue Service

For calendar year 2005 or tax year beginning .... , 2005, ending .... , 20 ....
▶ See separate instructions.

OMB No. 1545-0123

2005

A Check if:
1 Consolidated return (attach Form 851) ☐
2 Personal holding co. (attach Sch. PH) ☐
3 Personal service corp. (see instructions) ☐
4 Schedule M-3 required (attach Sch. M-3) ☐

Use IRS label. Otherwise, print or type.

Name

Number, street, and room or suite no. If a P.O. box, see instructions.

City or town, state, and ZIP code

B Employer identification number

C Date incorporated

D Total assets (see instructions)
$

E Check if: (1) ☐ Initial return (2) ☐ Final return (3) ☐ Name change (4) ☐ Address change

Income

1a	Gross receipts or sales ⌊___⌋ b Less returns and allowances ⌊___⌋ c Bal ▶	1c
2	Cost of goods sold (Schedule A, line 8)	2
3	Gross profit. Subtract line 2 from line 1c	3
4	Dividends (Schedule C, line 19)	4
5	Interest	5
6	Gross rents	6
7	Gross royalties	7
8	Capital gain net income (attach Schedule D (Form 1120))	8
9	Net gain or (loss) from Form 4797, Part II, line 17 (attach Form 4797)	9
10	Other income (see instructions—attach schedule)	10
11	**Total income.** Add lines 3 through 10 ▶	11

Deductions (See instructions for limitations on deductions.)

12	Compensation of officers (Schedule E, line 4)	12
13	Salaries and wages (less employment credits)	13
14	Repairs and maintenance	14
15	Bad debts	15
16	Rents	16
17	Taxes and licenses	17
18	Interest	18
19	Charitable contributions (see instructions for 10% limitation)	19
20a	Depreciation (attach Form 4562) 20a	
b	Less depreciation claimed on Schedule A and elsewhere on return ... 20b	20c
21	Depletion	21
22	Advertising	22
23	Pension, profit-sharing, etc., plans	23
24	Employee benefit programs	24
25	Domestic production activities deduction (attach Form 8903)	25
26	Other deductions (attach schedule)	26
27	**Total deductions.** Add lines 12 through 26. ▶	27
28	Taxable income before net operating loss deduction and special deductions. Subtract line 27 from line 11	28
29	**Less:** a Net operating loss deduction (see instructions) 29a	
	b Special deductions (Schedule C, line 20) 29b	29c

Tax and Payments

30	**Taxable income.** Subtract line 29c from line 28 (see instructions if Schedule C, line 12, was completed)	30
31	**Total tax** (Schedule J, line 11)	31
32	Payments: a 2004 overpayment credited to 2005 . 32a	
b	2005 estimated tax payments . . . 32b	
c	Less 2005 refund applied for on Form 4466 32c ( ) d Bal ▶ 32d	
e	Tax deposited with Form 7004 32e	
f	Credit from (1) Form 2439 _____ (2) Form 4136 _____ 32f	32g
33	Estimated tax penalty (see instructions). Check if Form 2220 is attached ... ▶ ☐	33
34	**Tax due.** If line 32g is smaller than the total of lines 31 and 33, enter amount owed	34
35	**Overpayment.** If line 32g is larger than the total of lines 31 and 33, enter amount overpaid ...	35
36	Enter amount of line 35 you want: **Credited to 2006 estimated tax** ▶ Refunded ▶	36

Sign Here ▶

Under penalties of perjury, I declare that I have examined this return, including accompanying schedules and statements, and to the best of my knowledge and belief, it is true, correct, and complete. Declaration of preparer (other than taxpayer) is based on all information of which preparer has any knowledge.

|___| Signature of officer   Date   ▶ Title

May the IRS discuss this return with the preparer shown below (see instructions)? ☐ Yes ☐ No

Paid Preparer's Use Only

Preparer's signature ▶		Date	Check if self-employed ☐	Preparer's SSN or PTIN
Firm's name (or yours if self-employed), address, and ZIP code ▶			EIN	
			Phone no. ( )	

For Privacy Act and Paperwork Reduction Act Notice, see separate instructions.   Cat. No. 11450Q   Form **1120** (2005)

FIGURE 1.6 Form 1120, U.S. Corporation Income Tax Return

Distributions from the C corporation to its shareholders are personal items for the shareholders. For example, if a shareholder works for his or her C corporation and receives a salary, the corporation deducts that salary against corporate income. The shareholder reports the salary as income on his or her individual income tax return. If the corporation distributes a dividend to the shareholder, again, the shareholder reports the dividend as income on his or her individual income tax return. In the case of dividends, however, the corporation cannot claim a deduction. This, then, creates a two-tier tax system, commonly referred to as *double taxation*. First, earnings are taxed at the corporate level. Then, when they are distributed to shareholders as dividends, they are taxed again, this time at the shareholder level. There has been sentiment in Congress over the years to eliminate the double taxation, but as of yet no legislation to accomplish this end other than the relief provided by capping the rate on dividends at 15 percent.

Other Tax Issues for C Corporations

In view of the favorable corporate rate tax structure (compared with the individual tax rates), certain tax penalties prevent businesses from using this form of business organization to optimum advantage.

- **Personal holding company penalty.** Corporations that function as a shareholder investment portfolio rather than as an operating company may fall subject to the personal holding corporation (PHC) penalty tax of 15 percent in 2005 on certain undistributed corporate income. The tax rules strictly define a PHC according to stock ownership and adjusted gross income. The penalty may be avoided by *not* triggering the definition of PHC or by paying out certain dividends.

- **Accumulated earnings tax.** Corporations may seek to keep money in corporate accounts rather than distribute it as dividends to shareholders with the view that an eventual sale of the business will enable shareholders to extract those funds at capital gain rates. Unfortunately, the tax law imposes a penalty on excess accumulations at 15 percent in 2005. Excess accumulations are those above an exemption amount ($250,000 for most businesses, but only $150,000 for PSCs) *plus* amounts for the reasonable needs of the business. Thus, for example, amounts retained to finance planned construction costs, to pay for a possible legal liability, or to buy out a retiring owner are reasonable needs not subject to penalty regardless of amount.

Employees

If you do not own any interest in a business but are employed by one, you may still have to account for business expenses. Your salary or other compensation is reported as wages in the income section as seen on page one of your Form 1040. Your deductions (with a few exceptions), however, can be claimed only as miscellaneous itemized deductions on Schedule A. These deductions are subject to two limitations. First, the total is deductible only if it exceeds 2 percent of adjusted gross income. Second, high-income taxpayers have an overall reduction of itemized deductions when adjusted gross income exceeds a threshold amount.

Under the 2-percent rule, only the portion of total miscellaneous deductions in excess of 2 percent of adjusted gross income is deductible on Schedule A. *Adjusted gross income* is the tax term for your total income subject to tax (gross income) minus business expenses (other than employee business expenses), capital losses, and certain other expenses that are deductible even if you do not claim itemized deductions, such as qualifying IRA contributions or alimony. You arrive at your adjusted gross income by completing the Income and Adjusted Gross Income sections on page one of Form 1040.

Example

You have business travel expenses that your employer does not pay for and other miscellaneous expenses (such as tax preparation fees) totaling $2,000. Your adjusted gross income is $80,000. The amount up to the 2-percent floor, or $1,600 (2 percent of $80,000), is disallowed. Only $400 of the $2,000 expenses is deductible on Schedule A.

The second deduction limitation applies to higher-income taxpayers whose adjusted gross income exceeds a threshold amount that is adjusted annually for inflation. For example, for 2005 the limitation applies to taxpayers with adjusted gross income over $145,950, or over $72,975 if married and filing separately. If the limitation applies, itemized deductions other than medical expenses, investment interest, casualty or theft losses, and gambling losses are generally reduced by 3 percent of the excess of adjusted gross income over the annual threshold ($145,950 or $72,975). A worksheet included in the IRS instruction booklet is used to calculate the reduction.

For the Future

The overall limit on itemized deductions for high-income taxpayers that can affect the actual business write-offs for employees is set to be phased out starting in 2006. It will be fully phased out by 2010.

If you fall into a special category of employees called *statutory employees*, you can deduct your business expenses on Schedule C instead of Schedule A. Statutory employees were discussed earlier in this chapter.

Factors in Choosing Your Form of Business Organization

Throughout this chapter, the differences of how income and deductions are reported have been explained, but these differences are not the only reasons for choosing a form of business organization. When you are deciding on which form of business organization to choose, many factors come into play.

Personal Liability

If your business owes money to another party, are your personal assets—home, car, investment—at risk? The answer depends on your form of business organization. You have personal liability—your personal assets are at risk—if you are a sole proprietor or a general partner in a partnership. In all other cases, you do not have personal liability. Thus, for example, if you are a shareholder in an S corporation, you do not have personal liability for the debts of your corporation.

Of course, you can protect yourself against personal liability for some types of occurrences by having adequate insurance coverage. For example, if you are a sole proprietor who runs a store, be sure that you have adequate liability coverage in the event someone is injured on your premises and sues you.

Even if your form of business organization provides personal liability protection, you can become personally liable if you agree to it in a contract. For example, some banks may not be willing to lend money to a small corporation unless you, as a principal shareholder, agree to guarantee the corporation's debt. In this case, you are personally liable to the extent of the loan to the corporation. If the corporation does not or cannot repay the loan, then the bank can look to you, and your personal assets, for repayment.

There is another instance in which corporate or LLC status will not provide you with personal protection. Even if you have a corporation or LLC, you can be personally liable for failing to withhold and deposit payroll taxes, which are called trust fund taxes (employees' income tax withholding and their share of FICA taxes, which are held in trust for them) to the IRS. This liability is explained in Chapter 27.

Profitability

All businesses hope to make money. But many sustain losses, especially in the start-up years. The way in which a business is organized affects how losses are treated.

Pass-through entities allow owners to deduct their share of the company's losses on their personal returns (subject to limits discussed in Chapter 4). If a business is set up as a C corporation, only the corporation can deduct losses.

Thus, when losses are anticipated, for example in the start-up phase, a pass-through entity generally is a preferable form of business organization. However, once the business becomes profitable, the tables turn. In that situation, C corporations can offer more tax opportunities, such as fringe benefits.

Fringe Benefits

The tax law gives employees of corporations the opportunity to enjoy special fringe benefits on a tax-free basis. They can receive employer-provided group term life insurance up to $50,000, health insurance coverage, dependent care assistance up to $5,000, education assistance up to $5,250, adoption assistance, and more. They can also be covered by medical reimbursement plans. This same opportunity is not extended to sole proprietors. Remember that sole proprietors are not employees, so they cannot get the benefits given only to employees. Similarly, partners, LLC members, and even S corporation shareholders who own more than 2 percent of the stock in their corporations are not considered employees and thus not eligible for fringe benefits.

If the business can afford to provide these benefits, the form of business becomes important. All forms of business can offer tax-favored retirement plans.

Nature and Number of Owners

With whom you go into business affects your choice of business organization. For example, if you have any foreign investors, you cannot use an S corporation, because foreign individuals are not permitted to own S corporation stock directly. An S corporation also cannot be used if investors are partnerships or corporations. In other words, in order to use an S corporation, all shareholders must be individuals who are not nonresident aliens (there are exceptions for estates, certain trusts, and certain exempt organizations).

The number of owners also presents limits on your choice of business organization. If you are the only owner, then your choices are limited to a sole proprietorship or a corporation (either C or S). All states allow one-member LLCs. If you have more than one owner, you can set up the business in just about any way you choose. S corporations cannot have more than 100 shareholders, but this number provides great leeway for small businesses.

If you have a business already formed as a C corporation and want to start another corporation, you must take into consideration the impact of special tax rules for multiple corporations. These rules apply regardless of the size of the business, the number of employees you have, and the profit the businesses make. Multiple corporations are corporations under common control, meaning they are essentially owned by the same parties. The tax law limits the number of tax breaks in the case of multiple corporations. Instead of each corporation enjoying a full tax benefit, the benefit must be shared among all of the corporations in the group. For example, the tax brackets for corporations are graduated. In the case of certain multiple corporations, however, the benefit of the graduated rates must be shared. In effect, each corporation pays a slightly higher tax because it is part of a group of multiple corporations. If you want to avoid restrictions on multiple corporations, you may want to look to LLCs or some other form of business organization.

Tax Rates

Both individuals and C corporations (other than PSCs) can enjoy graduated income tax rates. The top tax rate paid by sole proprietors and owners of other pass-through businesses is 35 percent for 2005. The top corporate tax rate imposed on C corporations is also 35 percent. Personal service corporations are subject to a flat tax rate of 35 percent. (The domestic production activities deduction in Chapter 21 effectively lowers the top rate in 2005 to 34 percent.) But remember, even though the C corporation has a lower top tax rate, there is a two-tier tax structure with which to contend if earnings are paid out to you—tax at the corporate level and again at the shareholder level.

While the so-called double taxation for C corporations has been eased by lowering the tax rate on dividends, there is still some double tax because dividends remain nondeductible at the corporate level. The rate on dividends is 15 percent (5 percent for shareholders in the 10 percent and 15 percent tax brackets; zero for these taxpayers in 2008).

The tax rates on capital gains also differ between C corporations and other taxpayers. This is because capital gains of C corporations are not subject to special tax rates (they are taxed the same as ordinary business income), while owners of other types of businesses may pay tax on the business's capital gains at no more than 15 percent (or 5 percent if they are in the 10 percent or 15 percent tax brackets). Of course, tax rates alone should not be the determining factor in selecting your form of business organization.

Social Security and Medicare Taxes

Owners of businesses organized any way other than as a corporation (C or S) are not employees of their businesses. As such, they are personally responsible for paying Social Security and Medicare taxes (called *self-employment taxes* for owners of unincorporated businesses). This tax is made up of the employer and employee shares of Social Security and Medicare taxes. The deduction for one-half of self-employment taxes is explained in Chapter 13.

However, owners of corporations have these taxes applied only against salary actually paid to them. Owners of unincorporated businesses pay self-employment tax on net earnings from self-employment. This essentially means profits, whether they are distributed to the owners or reinvested in the business. The result: Owners of unincorporated businesses can wind up paying higher Social Security and Medicare taxes than comparable owners who work for their corporations. On the other hand, in unprofitable businesses, owners of unincorporated businesses may not be able to earn any Social Security credits, while corporate owners can have salary paid to them on which Social Security credits can be generated.

Restrictions on Accounting Periods and Accounting Methods

As you will see in Chapter 2, the tax law limits the use of fiscal years and the cash method of accounting for certain types of business organizations. For example, partnerships and S corporations in general are required to use a calendar year to report income.

Also, C corporations generally are required to use the accrual method of accounting to report income. There are exceptions to both of these rules. However, as you can see, accounting periods and accounting methods are important considerations in choosing your form of business organization.

Multistate Operations

Each state has its own way of taxing businesses subject to its jurisdiction. The way in which a business is organized for federal income tax purposes may not necessarily control for state income tax purposes. For example, some states do not recognize S corporation elections and tax such entities as regular corporations.

A company must file a return in each state in which it does business and pay income tax on the portion of its profits earned in that state. Income tax liability is based on having a *nexus*, or connection, to a state. This is not always an easy matter to settle. Where there is a physical presence—for example, a company maintains an office—then there is a clear nexus. But when a company merely makes sales to customers within a state or offers goods for sale from a web site, there is generally no nexus.

Assuming that a company does conduct multistate business, then its form of organization becomes important. Most such businesses are C corporations because only one corporate income tax return needs be filed in each state that they do business. Doing business as a pass-through entity means that each owner would have to file a tax return in each state the company does business.

Audit Chances

Each year the IRS publishes statistics on the number and type of audits it conducts. The rates for fiscal year 2004, the most recent year for which statistics are available, show a slight increase in audit activity for most types of business returns.

The chances of being audited vary with the type of business organization, the amount of income generated by the business, and the geographic location of the business. While the chance of an audit is not a significant reason for choosing one form of business organization over another, it is helpful to keep these statistics in mind.

Table 1.1 sheds some light on your chances of being audited, based on the most recently available statistics.

TABLE 1.1 Percentage of Returns Audited

	FY 2004*	FY 2003*
Sole proprietors (Schedule C) (based on gross receipts)		
Under $25,000	3.15%	3.00%
$25,000 to under $100,000	1.47	1.33
$100,000 and over	1.86	1.47
Farming (Schedule F) (based on gross receipts)		
Under $100,000	.91	0.57
$100,000 and over	1.61	0.78
Partnerships	.26	0.35
S corporations	.19	0.30
C corporations (based on assets)		
Under $10 million	.31	0.49

*Fiscal year from October 1 through September 30.

Filing Deadlines and Extensions

How your business is organized dictates when its tax return must be filed, the form to use, and the additional time that can be obtained for filing the return. Table 1.2 lists the filing deadlines for calendar-year businesses, the available automatic extensions, and the forms to use in filing the return or requesting a filing extension. Note that these dates are extended to the next business day when a deadline falls on a Saturday, Sunday, or legal holiday.

Tax Treatment on Termination

The tax treatment on the termination of a business is another factor to consider. While the choice of entity is made when the business starts out, you

TABLE 1.2 Filing Deadlines, Extensions, and Forms

Type of Entity	Return Due Date	Income Tax Return	Automatic Filing Extension	Form to Request Filing Extension
Sole proprietorship	April 15	Schedule C of Form 1040	August 15	Form 4868
Partnership/LLC	April 15	Form 1065	July 15	Form 8736
S corporation	March 15	Form 1120S	September 15	Form 7004
C corporation	March 15	Form 1120	September 15	Form 7004

cannot ignore the tax consequences that this choice will have when the business terminates. The liquidation of a C corporation produces a double tax—at the entity and owner levels. The liquidation of an S corporation produces a double tax *only* if there is a built-in gains tax issue—created by having appreciated assets in the business when an S election is made. However, the built-in gains tax problem disappears 10 years after the S election so termination after that time does not result in a double tax.

If the termination of the business results in a loss, different tax rules come into play. Losses from partnerships and LLCs are treated as capital losses (explained in Chapter 5). A shareholder's losses from the termination of a C or S corporation may qualify as a Section 1244 loss—treated as an ordinary loss within limits (explained in Chapter 5).

Forms of Business Organization Compared

So far, you have learned about the various forms of business organization. Which form is right for your business? The answer is really a judgment call based on all the factors previously discussed. You can, of course, use different forms of business organization for your different business activities. For example, you may have a C corporation and personally own the building in which it operates—directly or through an LLC. Or you may be in partnership for your professional activities, while running a sideline business as an S corporation.

Table 1.3 summarizes two important considerations: how the type of business organization is formed and what effect the form of business organization has on where income and deductions are reported.

Changing Your Form of Business

Suppose you have a business that you have been running as a sole proprietorship. Now you want to make a change. Your new choice of business organization is dictated by the reason for the change. If you are taking in a partner, you would consider these alternatives: partnership, LLC, S corporation, or C corporation. If you are not taking in a partner, but want to obtain limited personal liability, you would consider an LLC (if your state permits a one-person LLC), an S corporation, or a C corporation. If you are looking to take advantage of certain fringe benefits, such as medical reimbursement plans, you would consider only a C corporation.

Whatever your reason, changing from a sole proprietorship to another type of business organization generally does not entail tax costs on making the changeover. You can set up a partnership or corporation, transfer your business assets to it, obtain an ownership interest in the new entity, and do all this

TABLE 1.3 Comparison of Forms of Business Organization

Type of Business	How It Is Formed	Where Income and Deductions Are Reported
Sole proprietorship	No special requirements	On owner's Schedule C or C-EZ (Schedule F for farming)
Partnership	No special requirements	Some items taken into account in figuring (but generally have trade or business income directly on partnership agreement) Form 1065 (allocable amount claimed on partner's Schedule E); separately stated items passed through to partners and claimed in various places on partner's tax return
Limited special partnership	Some items taken into account in figuring partnership under state law	Trade or business income directly on Form 1065 (allocable amount claimed on partner's Schedule E); separately stated items passed through to partners and claimed in various places on partner's tax return
Limited liability company	Organized as such under state law	Some items taken into account in figuring trade or business income directly on Form 1065 (allocable amount claimed on member's Schedule E); separately stated items passed through to members and claimed in various places on member's tax return
Limited liability partnership	Organized as such under state law	Some items taken into account in figuring trade or business income directly on Form 1065 (allocable amount claimed on member's Schedule E); separately stated items passed through to members and claimed in various places on member's tax return
S corporation	Formed as corporation under state law; tax status elected by filing with IRS	Some items taken into account in figuring trade or business income directly on Form 1120S (allocable amount claimed on shareholder's Schedule E); separately stated items passed through to shareholders and claimed in various places on shareholder's tax return
C corporation	Formed under state law	Claimed by corporation in figuring its trade or business income on Form 1120 or 1120-A
Employee	No ownership interest	Income reported as wages; deductions as itemized deductions on Schedule A (certain expenses first figured on Form 2106)
Independent contractor	No ownership interest in a business	Claimed on individual's Schedule C

on a tax-free basis. You may, however, have some tax consequences if you transfer your business liabilities to the new entity.

But what if you now have a corporation or partnership and want to change your form of business organization? This change may not be so simple. Suppose you have an S corporation or a C corporation. If you liquidate the corporation to change to another form of business organization, you may have to report gain on the liquidation. In fact, gains may have to be reported both by the business and by you as owner.

Before changing your form of business organization it is important to review your particular situation with a tax professional. In making any change in business, consider the legal and accounting costs involved.

CHAPTER 2

Tax Year and Accounting Methods

Once you select your form of business organization, you must decide how you will report your income. There are two key decisions you must make: What is the time frame for calculating your income and deductions (called the tax year or accounting period), and what are the rules that you will follow to calculate your income and deductions (called the accounting method). In some cases, as you will see, your form of business organization restricts you to an accounting period or accounting method. In other cases, however, you can choose which method is best for your business.

In this chapter you will learn about:

- Accounting periods
- Accounting methods
- Uniform capitalization rules

For a further discussion on tax years and accounting methods, see IRS Publication 538, *Accounting Periods and Methods*. Inventory rules are discussed in Chapter 4.

Accounting Periods

You account for your income and expenses on an annual basis. This period is called your *tax year*. There are two methods for fixing your tax year: *calendar* and *fiscal*. Under the calendar year, you use a 12-month period ending on December 31. Under the fiscal year, you use a 12-month period ending at the end of any month other than December.

You select your tax year when you first begin your business. You do not need IRS approval for your tax year; you simply use it to govern when you must file your first return. You use the same tax year thereafter. If you commence your business in the middle of the tax year you have selected, your first tax year will be short.

Example

You start your S corporation in May 2005. It uses a calendar year to report expenses. The corporation will have a short tax year ending December 31, 2005, for its first tax year. Then, for 2006, it will have a full 12-month tax year.

A short tax year may occur in the first or final year of business. For example, if you closed the doors to your business on May 1, 2005, even though you operated on a calendar year. Your final tax year is a short year because it is only seven months. You do not have to apportion or prorate deductions for this short year because the business was not in existence for the entire year. Different rules apply if a short year results from a change in accounting period.

Seasonal Businesses

Seasonal businesses should use special care when selecting their tax year. It is often advisable to select a tax year that will include both the period in which most of the expenses as well as most of the income is realized. For example, if a business expects to sell its products primarily in the spring and incurs most of its expenses for these sales in the preceding fall, it may be best to select a fiscal year ending just after the selling season, such as July or August. In this way, the expenses and the income that are related to each other will be reported on the same return.

Limits on Use of the Fiscal Year

C corporations, other than personal service corporations (PSCs), can choose a calendar year or a fiscal year, whichever is more advantageous. Other entities, however, cannot simply choose a fiscal year even though it offers tax advantages to its owners. In general, partnerships, limited liability companies

(LLCs), S corporations, and PSCs must use a **required year.** Since individuals typically use a calendar year, their partnership or LLC must also use a calendar year.

Required year   For S corporations, this is a calendar year; for partnerships and LLCs, it is the same year as the tax year of the entity's owners. When owners have different tax years, special rules determine which owner's tax year governs.

Business Purpose for Fiscal Year

The entity can use a fiscal year even though its owners use a calendar year if it can be established to the satisfaction of the IRS that there is a business purpose for the fiscal year. The fact that the use of a fiscal year defers income for its owners is not considered to be a valid **business purpose** warranting a tax year other than a required tax year.

Business purpose   This is shown if the fiscal year is the natural business year of the entity. For a PSC, for example, a fiscal year is treated as a natural business year if, 25 percent or more of its gross receipts for the 12-month period ending on the last month of requested tax year are received within the last two months of that year.

Section 444 Election for Fiscal Year

If an entity wants to use a fiscal year that is not its natural business year, it can do so by making a Section 444 election. The only acceptable tax years under this election are those ending September 30, October 31, and November 30. Use of these fiscal years means that at most there can be a three-month deferral for the owners. The election is made by filing Form 8716, Election to Have a Tax Year Other Than a Required Tax Year, by the earlier of the due date of the return for the new tax year (without regard to extensions) or the fifteenth day of the sixth month of the tax year for which the election will be effective.

If the election is made, then partnerships, LLCs, and S corporations must make certain *required payments*. These essentially are designed to give to the federal government the tax that has been deferred by reason of the special tax year. This payment can be thought of as simply a deposit, since it does not serve to increase the tax that is otherwise due. The payment is calculated using the highest individual income tax rate plus 1 percentage point. Therefore, the rate for 2005 is 36 percent. The required payment is made by filing Form 8752, Required Payment or Refund Under Section 7519 for Partnerships and S Corporations, by May 15 of the calendar year following the calendar year in which the election begins. For example, if the election begins on October 1, 2005, the required payment must be made no later than May 15, 2006. In view of the high required payment and the complications involved in making and maintaining a Section 444 election, most of these entities use a calendar year.

Personal service corporations that make a Section 444 election need not make a required payment. Instead, these corporations must make *required distributions*. They must distribute certain amounts of compensation to employee-owners by December 31 of each year for which an election is in effect. The reason for the required elections is to ensure that amounts will be taxed to owner-employees as soon as possible and will not be deferred simply because the corporation uses a fiscal year. Required distributions are figured on Part I of Schedule H of Form 1120, Section 280H Limitations for a Personal Service Corporation.

Pass-Through Business on a Fiscal Year

Owners in pass-through entities who are on a calendar year report their share of the business's income, deductions, gains, losses, and credits from the entity's tax year that ends in the owners' tax year.

Example

You are in a partnership that uses a fiscal year ending October 31. The partnership's items for its 2005 fiscal year ending October 31, 2005, are reported on your 2005 return. The portion of the partnership's income and deductions from the period November 1, 2005, through December 31, 2005, are part of its 2006 fiscal year, which will be reported on your 2006 return.

Short Tax Years

You may have a year that is less than a full tax year. This results most commonly in the year you start or end a business.

Example

You start an LLC on August 1, 2005, and use a calendar year to report your income and expenses. The LLC's first tax year is a short tax year, running from August 1, 2005, through December 31, 2005.

A short tax year can also result when a C corporation that had been reporting on a fiscal year elects S status and adopts a calendar year. The tax year of the C corporation ends on the date the S election becomes effective.

Alternatively, if an S election is terminated within the year, then the corporation can have two short tax years in this case.

Example

A C corporation with a fiscal year ending on June 30 elects to become an S corporation and adopts a calendar year. The election is effective on January 1, 2005. The C corporation has a short tax year starting on July 1, 2004, and ending on December 31, 2005.

Example

An S corporation reporting on a calendar year has its election involuntarily terminated on July 31, 2005, when another corporation becomes a shareholder. The corporation has two short tax years: The S tax year running from January 1, 2005, through July 31, 2005, and the C tax year running from August 1, 2005, through December 31, 2005.

Change in Tax Year

If your business has been using a particular tax year and you want to change to a different one, you must obtain IRS approval to do so. Depending on the reason for the change, approval may be automatic or discretionary. You can request a change in your tax year by filing Form 1128, Application to Adopt, Change, or Retain a Tax Year. You must also include a user fee (an amount set by the IRS) for this request.

Accounting Methods

There are two principal methods of accounting: *cash basis* and *accrual basis*. Use of a particular method determines when a deduction can be claimed. However, restrictions apply for both methods of accounting. Also, the form of business organization may preclude the use of the cash method of accounting even though it may be the method of choice.

Cash Method

Cash method is the simpler accounting method. Income is reported when it is actually or constructively received and a deduction can be claimed when and to the extent the expense is paid.

Example

You are a consultant. You perform services and send a bill. You report the income when you receive payment. Similarly, you buy business cards and stationery. You can deduct this expense when you pay for the supplies.

Actual receipt is the time when income is in your hands. Constructive receipt occurs when you have control over the income and can reduce it to an actual receipt.

Example

You earn a fee for services rendered but ask your customer not to pay you immediately. Since the customer was ready and able to pay immediately, you are in constructive receipt of the fee at that time.

Payments received by check are income when the check is received even though you may deposit it some time later. However, if the check bounces, then no income results at the time the check was received. You only report income when the check is later honored.

You may not be able to deduct all expenses when they are paid because there are some limitations that come into play. Generally, you cannot deduct advance payments (so-called prepaid expenses) that relate to periods beyond the current tax year.

Example

You take out a three-year subscription to a business journal and pay the three-year subscription price this year. You can deduct only one-third of the payment—the amount that relates to the current year. You can deduct another one-third next year, and the final third the following year.

Prepayments may occur for a number of expenses. You may prepay rent, insurance premiums, or subscriptions. Generally, prepayments that do not extend beyond 12 months are currently deductible.

In the case of interest, no deduction is allowed for prepayments by businesses. For example, if you are required to pay points to obtain a mortgage on your office building, these points are considered to be prepaid interest. You must deduct the points ratably over the term of the loan.

Example

If the mortgage on the office building runs for 30 years (or 360 months) and you pay the points on July 1, you can deduct 6/360 of the points in the first year. In each succeeding year you would deduct 12/360 of the points. In the final year, you would again deduct 6/360.

If you pay off the mortgage before the end of the term (you sell the property or refinance the loan), you can then write off any points you still have not deducted.

RESTRICTIONS ON THE USE OF THE CASH METHOD. You cannot use the cash method of accounting if you maintain inventory unless you qualify for a small business exception. If you are barred from using the cash method, you must use the accrual method or another method of accounting.

SMALL INVENTORY-BASED BUSINESS EXCEPTION. Even though you maintain inventory, you are permitted to use the cash method if your average annual gross receipts for the three prior years do not exceed $10 million. More specifically, you can use the cash method if your average annual gross receipts for the three tax years (or the years in which you are in business if less than three years) ending with each prior taxable year ending on or after December 31, 2000, do not exceed $10 million. In effect, in order to qualify for the cash method under this exception in 2005, your average annual gross receipts must not exceed $10 million in each of these three-year periods: 1998–2000, 1999–2001, 2000–2002, 2001–2003, and 2002–2004.

You can use the cash method of accounting even though you use the accrual method for financial accounting purposes (for example, on profit and loss statements). However, you do not qualify for this exception if your principal business activity is retailing, wholesaling, manufacturing (other than custom manufacturing), mining, publishing, or sound recording. (Principal business activity is based on the largest percentage of your gross receipts using the North American Industry Classification System [NAICS], published by the U.S. Department of Commerce.)

In addition to the inventory limitation, certain types of business organizations generally cannot use the cash method of accounting. These include:

- Corporations other than S corporations
- Partnerships that have a corporation (other than an S corporation) as a partner
- Tax shelters

However, there are exceptions under which some of these businesses can still use the cash method of accounting.

If you are a small inventory-based business that has been using the accrual method but is qualified to change to the cash method, you can make the change under an automatic change of accounting rule. For more information about qualifying for the cash method and changing to it, see Revenue Procedure 2002-28.

FARMING EXCEPTION.   A farming business with gross receipts of $25 million or less can use the cash method. A farming business includes any business that operates a nursery or sod farm or that raises or harvests trees bearing fruit, nuts, or other crops and ornamental trees.

PSC EXCEPTION.   A **qualified personal service corporation** (PSC) can use the cash method of accounting.

Qualified personal service corporation   A corporation (other than an S corporation) with a substantial amount of activities involving the performance of personal services in the fields of medicine, law, accounting, architecture, actuarial sciences, performing arts, or consulting by someone who owns stock in the corporation (or who is retired or the executor of the estate of a deceased former employee).

SMALL BUSINESS EXCEPTION.   Corporations other than S corporations and partnerships that have a corporation (other than an S corporation) as a partner can use the cash method of accounting if they are considered to be a *small business* even if they do not qualify for the inventory-based exception above. A small business for this purpose is one that has average annual gross receipts of $5 million or less in at least one of three prior taxable years. In view of the gross receipt rule, you can see that a business may be able to use the cash method for one year but be precluded from using it in the following year. As a practical matter, if a business gets big enough to approach $5 million in gross receipts, it may have outgrown the cash method and may prefer to change permanently to the accrual method to avoid changes dependent upon **gross receipts.**

Gross receipts   All the income is taken in by the business without offsets for expenses. For example, if a consultant receives fees of $25,000 for the year and has expenses of $10,000, gross receipts are $25,000.

Accrual Method of Accounting

Under the accrual method, you report income when it is earned rather than when it is received, and you deduct expenses when they are incurred rather than when they are paid. There are two tests to determine whether there is a fixed right to receive income so that it must be accrued and whether an expense is treated as having been incurred for tax purposes.

ALL EVENTS TEST. All events that fix the income and set the liability must have occurred. Also, you must be able to determine the amount of the income or expense with reasonable accuracy.

ECONOMIC PERFORMANCE TEST. In order to report income or deduct an expense, economic performance must occur. In most cases, this is rather obvious. If you provide goods and services, economic performance occurs when you provide the goods or services. By the same token if goods or services are provided to you, economic performance occurs when the goods or services are provided to you. Thus, for example, if you buy office supplies, economic performance occurs when the purchase is made and the bill is tendered. You can accrue the expense at that date even though you do not pay the bill until a later date.

There is an exception to the economic performance test for certain recurring items (items that are repeated on a regular basis). A deduction for these items can be accrued even though economic performance has not occurred.

There is a special rule for real estate taxes. An election can be made to ratably accrue real property taxes that are related to a definite period of time over that period of time.

Example

You own a building in which you conduct your business. Real property taxes for the property tax year ending June 30 are $12,000. You are an accrual method taxpayer on a calendar year of reporting. You can elect to ratably accrue the taxes. If the election is made, you deduct $6,000 in the current year, the amount of taxes that relates to the period for your tax year. The balance of the taxes is deductible next year.

Any real property taxes that would normally be deductible for the tax year that apply to periods prior to your election are deductible in the year of the election.

The election must be made for the first tax year in which real property taxes are incurred. It is made simply by attaching a statement to the return for that tax year. The return must be filed on time (including any extensions) in order for the election to be valid. Include on the statement the businesses to which the election applies and their methods of accounting, the period of time to which the taxes relate, and the computation of the real property tax deduction for the first year of the election.

Once you make this election, it continues indefinitely unless you revoke it. To revoke your election you must obtain the consent of the IRS. However, there is an automatic procedure rule that allows you to elect or revoke an election by attaching a statement to your return. Under this method you may assume you have IRS consent; you do not have to request it and wait for a reply.

If you have been accruing real property taxes under the general rule for accrual, you must file for a change in accounting method which is explained later in this chapter.

You can make an election to ratably accrue real property taxes over the period to which they relate for each separate business you own.

TWO-AND-A-HALF-MONTH RULE. If you pay salary, interest, or other expenses to an unrelated party, you can accrue the expense only if it is paid within two and a half months after the close of the tax year.

Example

You declare a year-end bonus for your manager (who is not related to you under the rules discussed). You are on the calendar year. You can accrue the bonus in the year in which you declare it if you actually pay it no later than March 15.

RELATED PARTIES. If expenses are paid to related parties, a special rule applies. This rule, in effect, puts an accrual taxpayer on the cash basis so that payments are not deductible until actually paid. Related parties include:

- Members of an immediate family (spouses, children, brothers and sisters of whole or half blood, grandchildren, and grandparents).
- An individual and a C corporation (other than a PSC) in which he or she owns more than 50 percent of the corporation's outstanding stock (based on the stock's value). Stock ownership may be *direct* or *indirect*. Direct means that the individual holds the stock in his or her name. Indirect ownership means the stock is owned by a member of the individual's immediate family (listed above) or by a corporation, partnership, estate, or trust owned in full or in part by the individual. If the individual has only a partial ownership interest, that same proportion of stock owned by the entity is treated as owned by the individual. For example, if an individual owns 75 percent of stock in Corporation X and X owns 100 percent of the stock in Corporation Y, the individual is treated as owning 75 percent of the stock in Y for purposes of this accrual method limitation.
- An individual and an S corporation in which he or she owns any of the corporation's outstanding stock.

- A PSC and any owner-employee (regardless of the amount of stock ownership). Thus, if an individual owns 10 percent of the stock in Corporation X (a PSC), and X owns 100 percent of the stock in Y, the individual is treated as owning 100 percent of the stock in Y.
- Other categories of related parties (e.g., two corporations that are members of a controlled group—they have certain owners in common).

If you fall under this related party rule, you cannot deduct the expense until payment is actually made and the related party includes the payment in his or her income.

Example

You have an accrual business in which your child is an employee. Your business is on the calendar year. On December 31, 2005, you declare a year-end bonus of $5,000 for your child. You may not accrue the bonus until you pay the $5,000 to your child and your child includes the payment as income. Therefore, if you write a check on January 15, 2006, for the bonus and your child cashes it that day, you can accrue the expense in 2006.

Accounting Methods for Long-Term Contracts

For businesses involved in building, constructing, installing, or manufacturing property where the work cannot be completed within one year, special accounting rules exist. These rules do not affect the amount of income or expenses to be reported—they merely dictate the timing of the income or expenses.

Generally, you must use the percentage-of-completion method to report income and expenses from these long-term contracts. Under this method, you must estimate your income and expenses while the contract is in progress and report a percentage of these items relative to the portion of the contract that has been completed. However, income and expenses are not fully accounted for until the earlier of completion of the job and acceptance of the work or the buyer starts to use the item and 5 percent or less of the total contract costs remain to be completed.

You may also have to use a *look-back method* (discussed later) to compensate for any inaccuracies in your estimates for income or expenses.

EXCEPTIONS FROM THE PERCENTAGE-OF-COMPLETION METHOD. Under this method you account for your income and expenses when, as the name implies, the contract has been completed. You can account for income and expenses using the completed-contract method if:

1. The contracts are small construction contracts that will be completed within two years and average annual gross receipts for the three preceding years from the start of the contract do not exceed $10 million.

2. The contracts are for the construction of homes containing four or fewer dwelling units. Eighty percent or more of the estimated total costs of the contract must be for these homes plus any related land improvements.

3. The contracts are for the construction of residential apartments (80 percent or more of the total contract costs are attributable to these buildings).

You can account for your income and expenses using the completed-contract method if you meet either of the first two exceptions. If you meet the third exception, you account for your income and expenses under a special method called the percentage-of-completion/capitalized-cost method. Under this hybrid method, 70 percent of income and expenses are reported under the percentage-of-completion method while 30 percent of income and expenses are reported under the completed-contract method.

Manufacturing contracts are treated as long-term contracts only if they involve the manufacture of unique items that cannot be completed within a 12-month period. Thus, income and expenses relating to most manufacturing contracts are reported under the company's usual method of accounting.

LOOK-BACK METHOD.   At the end of the contract period you must look back to each year that the contract was in progress and recalculate the income using the correct contract price and costs. These revised numbers determine whether the business owes additional interest on the taxes it should have paid or it is entitled to receive interest on the taxes already paid. Interest for this purpose is hypothetical interest on the overpayment and underpayment for each of the years in issue. This interest is calculated on Form 8697, Interest Computation Under the Look-Back Method for Completed Long-Term Contracts.

Small business owners, however, may escape the application of the look-back method. This method is *not* required if the contract is completed within a two-year period and the contract's gross sale price does not exceed the lesser of $1 million or 1 percent of the business' average annual gross receipts for the three years preceding the tax year in which the contract is completed.

Even if the exception for small businesses cannot be met, it is still possible to avoid the look-back method and its complications. You can elect not to use the look-back method if the estimated income and expenses are within 10 percent of the actual income and expenses. Once this election is made it applies to all future contracts. In order to make the election, you must make the recalculations of the actual income and expenses for the prior years to see if the 10 percent threshold has been satisfied.

Other Accounting Methods

The cash and accrual methods of accounting are the most commonly used methods. There are, however, other accounting methods. For example, if you sell property and receive payments over time, you generally can account for your gain on the *installment method*. More specifically, the installment method applies if one or more payments are received after the year of the sale. *Gain* is reported when payments are received. This method can be used by taxpayers who report other income and expenses on the cash or accrual method.

Example

You sell business property and figure your gain to be $10,000. Under the terms of sale you receive $5,000 in 2005, the year of sale, and $5,000 in 2006. You report one-half of your gain, or $5,000, in 2005 and the other half of your gain, $5,000, in 2006.

However, if the sale involves depreciable property, the recapture rules trigger the immediate reporting of this portion of the gain—without regard to payments received. Recapture rules are discussed in Chapter 6.

The installment method applies only to gains on certain sales; it generally cannot be used for inventory sales even though payment is received over time. The installment method does not apply to losses. It cannot be used by dealers in personal property or for real estate held for resale to customers.

You can elect *not* to report on the installment basis and instead report all of the gain in the year of sale. The election is made simply by reporting all of the gain on the appropriate tax form or schedule. Once made, however, this election generally is irrevocable.

Other accounting methods include, for example: Special Accounting for Multi-Year Service Warranty Contracts and Special Rules for Farmers.

ACCOUNTING FOR DISCOUNTS YOU RECEIVE. When vendors or other sellers give you cash discounts for prompt payment, there are two ways to account for this discount, regardless of your method of accounting. They are:

- Deduct the discount as a purchase in figuring the cost of goods sold.
- Credit the discount to a special discount income account you set up in your records. Any balance in this account at the end of the year is reported as other income on your return.

Trade discounts are not reflected on your books or tax returns. These discounts are reductions from list price or catalog prices for merchandise you purchase. Once you make the choice, you must continue to use it in future years to account for all cash discounts.

Uniform Capitalization Rules

Regardless of your method of accounting, special tax rules limit your ability to claim a current deduction for certain expenses. These are called the *uniform capitalization rules*, sometimes referred to as the UNICAP rules for short. The uniform capitalization rules are a form of accounting method that operates in coordination with the accrual method, but overrides it. In essence, these rules require you to add to the cost of property certain expenses—instead of currently deducting them. The cost of these expenses, in effect, are recovered through depreciation or amortization, or as part of the costs of goods sold when you use, sell, or otherwise dispose of the property. The uniform capitalization rules are complex. Important things to recognize are whether you may be subject to them and that expenses discussed throughout this book may not be currently deductible because of the application of the uniform capitalization rules.

Capitalization Required

Unless one of the exceptions is applicable, you must use the uniform capitalization rules and add certain expenses to the basis of property if you:

- Produce real property or tangible personal property for use in your business or for sale to customers (producers), or
- Acquire property for resale (resellers).

EXCEPTIONS TO THE UNICAP RULES.   There are many exceptions to the uniform capitalization rules. Small businesses may be able to escape application of the uniform capitalization rules by relying on one of these exceptions.

- You do not have to capitalize costs if the property you produce is for your personal or nonbusiness use.
- You do not have to capitalize costs if you acquire property for resale and your average annual gross receipts do not exceed $10 million (small reseller exception). If a reseller has been in business for less than three years, application of the exception is determined by annual gross receipts for the shorter period.
- Creative expenses incurred by freelance authors, photographers, and artists are not subject to the uniform capitalization rules. According to the IRS, this exception does not apply to a musician's demo tape or other sound recording.

- There is a *de minimis* exception for certain producers who use a simplified method and whose total indirect costs are $200,000 or less.

- There are other exceptions not detailed here, for certain farming businesses and other types of businesses.

CAPITALIZED COSTS.   If you are subject to the uniform capitalization rules, you capitalize all direct costs of your production or resale activities. Direct costs for producers include direct material costs and direct labor costs. Direct costs for resellers mean acquisition costs.

You also capitalize a portion of indirect costs. Indirect costs for producers and resellers include costs of purchasing, handling, and storage, as well as taxes, interest, rent, insurance, utilities, repairs, engineering and design costs, quality control, tools and equipment, licensing, and more.

Change in Accounting Method

If you want to change your method of accounting (for example, from the accrual method to the cash method), you must file Form 3115, Application for Change in Accounting Method, during the year for which the change is to be effective. (Instructions on how and where to file this form are included in instructions to the form.) Some changes are automatic—just by filing you are ensured that your change is recognized; other changes require the consent of the IRS.

Periodically the IRS modifies its list of automatic changes (for example, see Revenue Procedures 99-49 and 2002-9). These include changing to a required accounting method from an incorrect one, switching to the cash method by an eligible small inventory-based business, and deducting the cost of "smallwares" (such as dishes and glassware) in the year they are first put to use by restaurants.

CHAPTER 3

Recordkeeping for Business Income and Deductions

Recordkeeping is a tiresome and time-consuming task. Still, you have little choice but to do it. You need records to determine your gain or loss when you sell property. And as a general rule, you must be able to back up your deductions with certain clear proof, such as receipts, canceled checks, and other documentation. If you do not have this proof, your deductions may be disallowed. Certain deductions require specific evidence. Other deductions are based on more general means of proof. In this chapter you will learn about:

- General recordkeeping
- Specific substantiation requirements for certain expenses
- Records for depreciation, basis, carryovers, and prepaid expenses
- How long you should maintain records

This chapter is concerned with recordkeeping for income tax purposes. However, it is equally important to maintain good records to help you to manage your business efficiently and to apply for business loans. For further information on recordkeeping, see IRS Publication 334, *Tax Guide for Small Business (for Individuals Who File Schedule C or C-EZ)*; IRS Publication 552, *Recordkeeping for Individuals*; and IRS Publication 583, *Starting a Business and Keeping Records*.

General Recordkeeping

The tax law does not require you to maintain books and records in any particular way. It does, however, require you to keep an accurate and complete set of books for each business you operate. Statistics show that this can be an awesome task averaging 10 hours each week (that amounts to about 520 hours each year) for small business owners.

Set up your books when you begin your business. Your books are based on your choice of tax year and accounting method, as explained in Chapter 2. You also need to choose a bookkeeping method—single-entry or double-entry. If you are a service business, single-entry bookkeeping may be sufficient. However, if your business involves inventory or is complicated, double-entry should be used.

Your books should be set up with various accounts in order to group your income and expenses. The broad categories of accounts include income, expenses, assets, liabilities, and equity (or net worth). Within these accounts you can keep various subaccounts. For example, in an account called Expenses you can have subaccounts for advertising, bad debts, interest expense, taxes, rents, repairs, and more. In fact, your subaccounts should reflect the various income and deduction topics discussed throughout this book.

Keeping Records by Computer

With more than 70 percent of small business owners owning computers, more and more businesses are using computers to maintain books and records rather than having bookkeepers make handwritten entries. Computer-generated records save time—an important commodity for the small business owner—and generally are more accurate than handwritten entries.

The IRS accepts computer-generated records if they are legible and provide all the necessary information. You are required to keep a description of the computerized portion of your accounting system. You must keep this documentation as long as you keep the records themselves. Your document should show:

- Applications being performed
- Procedures used in each application
- Controls used to ensure accurate and reliable processing
- Controls used to prevent the unauthorized addition, alteration, or deletion of retained records

Use recordkeeping software that facilitates recordkeeping both for tax purposes as well as for financial matters. Using programs such as Intuit's Simple Start or Quickbooks enables you to forward data to your tax professional as well as transfer information into tax return preparation programs at tax time, saving you both time and money.

Your books alone do not entitle you to deductions; you need supporting evidence. This evidence includes sales slips, invoices, canceled checks, paid bills, time sheets for part-time help, duplicate deposit slips, brokerage statements on stock purchases and sales, and other documents that help to explain a particular entry in your books. Certain deductions—travel and entertainment expenses and charitable contributions—require specific types of supporting evidence, as explained later in this chapter. The IRS considers your own memoranda or sketchy records to be inadequate when claiming deductions. Keep these records and documentation in an orderly fashion. Use files or other storage facilities to retain receipts and other evidence.

Keep your files in a safe place. For example, keep a copy of computer files off premises, and store paper files in a fireproof safe. If you lose files with receipts because they were not stored safely, you may lose deductions and face penalties as well. If you "lose" records before or during an audit, you may be charged with a hefty fraud penalty. If, despite your best efforts, files and records are lost or destroyed by a casualty (such as a fire, storm, earthquake, or flood), you may be permitted to reconstruct records if you can prove those records existed before the casualty. Of course, reconstruction takes considerable time, and it is probably impossible to reconstruct all of your expenses. Therefore, take special care to safeguard your records.

Electronic Imaging Systems

Storage of receipts and other records in paper form makes retrieval of wanted items difficult. This is especially so for large companies, but it can be problematic for smaller businesses as well. Recognizing the problem, the IRS now allows books and records to be maintained by **electronic imaging systems**.

Electronic imaging system A system that prepares, records, transfers, indexes, stores, preserves, retrieves, and reproduces books and records by electronically imaging hard copy to an electronic storage media or transferring computerized books and records to an electronic storage media using a technique such as COLD (computer output to laser disk). This technique allows books and records to be viewed or reproduced without the use of the original program.

If an electronic imaging system is used, it must ensure accurate and complete transfer of the hard copy or the computerized books and records. It must include:

- Reasonable controls to ensure the integrity, accuracy, and reliability of the system
- Reasonable controls to prevent and detect the unauthorized creation of, addition to, alteration of, deletion of, or deterioration of records
- An inspection and quality assurance program evidenced by regular evaluations of the electronic storage system
- A retrieval system that includes an indexing system
- The ability to reproduce legible hard copies of electronically stored books and records

In the past, most small businesses could not undertake the expense of using an electronic imaging system for their books and records with the technology that was available. However, today's technology allows you to use an alternative imaging method that is acceptable to the IRS. You can transfer data to a CD-ROM—you burn the information onto the disk and cannot alter it thereafter. You can scan the information to be transferred into your computer and then transfer it to the disk.

Specific Substantiation Requirements for Certain Expenses

Travel and Entertainment Expenses

The tax law imposes special substantiation requirements for claiming travel and entertainment expenses. If you fail to satisfy these requirements, your deduction for these business expenses may be disallowed. There are two types of records you need in order to claim deductions for your travel and entertainment expenses: *written* substantiation in a diary, log book, or other notation system containing certain specific information, and *documentary evidence* (receipts, canceled checks, or bills) to prove the amount of the expense. The IRS now accepts certain electronic or faxed information to be treated as documentary evidence (e.g., a faxed statement attesting to a "ticketless" airline ticket is considered documentary evidence). Personal digital assistants (PDAs) and BlackBerries may also be used for written substantiation in lieu of a logbook. You may even be able to use software for your PDA, such as Pocket Quicken, to easily track travel and entertainment costs and transfer data to your PC.

There are a number of elements to substantiate for each business expense. In general, to substantiate each item you must show the amount, time, place, and business purpose for the travel or entertainment expense or the business relationship with the person or persons you entertain or provide gifts to and, in some cases, a description of the item. The exact substantiation requirements depend on the type of business expense.

In all cases, you are strongly advised to use a daily log or diary to record expenses. As you will see, you need written proof of your expenses, and this proof must be recorded "contemporaneously" with the expenses—generally meaning at the time you incur the expense or as soon as is practical thereafter to record it. It may be helpful to use a separate credit card for business expenses. The monthly statement from the credit card company is also useful in substantiating these expenses.

TRAVEL. You must show the amount of each separate expense for travel, lodging, meals, and incidental expenses. You can total these items in any reasonable category. For example, you can simply keep track of meals in a category called Daily Meals. You must also note the dates you left for the trip and returned, as well as the days spent on the trip for business purposes. You must list the name of the city or other designation of the place of the travel, along with the reason for the trip or the business benefit gained or expected to be gained from it.

While this may sound like a great deal of recordkeeping, as a practical matter, hotel receipts may provide you with much of the information necessary. For example, a hotel receipt typically shows the dates you arrived and departed, the name and location of the hotel, and separate charges for lodging, meals, telephone calls, and other items. A sample log for travel expenses can be found in Chapter 8.

ENTERTAINMENT.   Again, you must list each separate expense. Incidental expenses, such as taxis and telephone calls, may be totaled on a daily basis. You must list the date of the entertainment. For meals or entertainment directly before or after a business discussion, list the date and duration of the business discussion. Include the name and address or location of the place of entertainment, as well as the type of entertainment if it is not apparent from the name of the place. Also list the place where a business discussion was held if entertainment took place directly before or after the discussion. Again, state the business reason or the business benefit gained or anticipated and the nature of the business discussion. Include the names of the persons entertained, including their occupations or other identifying information, and the names of those who took part in the business discussion. If the deduction is for a business meal, you must note that you or your employer were present at the meal.

Again, a restaurant receipt typically supplies much of the information required. It shows the name and location of the restaurant, the number of people served, and the date and amount of the expense. As a practical matter, the back of American Express credit card slips provides the space necessary to enter all the elements for substantiating an entertainment deduction. It may be helpful to use this credit card when entertaining for business and to complete the back of the slip. Be sure to retain these slips as your proof. A sample log for entertainment expenses can be found in Chapter 8.

GIFTS.   Show the cost of the gift, the date it was given, and a description of the gift. Also show the business reason for the gift or the business benefit gained or expected to be gained from providing it. Include the name of the person receiving the gift, his or her occupation or other identifying information, and his or her business relationship to you.

A canceled check, along with a bill, generally establishes the cost of a business item. However, the check alone does not prove a business expense without other evidence of its business purpose.

If you do not have adequate records and your return is questioned, you may still be able to deduct an item if you can prove by your own statement or other supporting evidence an element of substantiation. Where receipts are destroyed, you may be able to reconstruct your expenses. You must, of course, show that you actually maintained records and how the records were destroyed (for example, in a fire, storm, or flood). The IRS may require additional information to prove the accuracy or reliability of the information contained in your records.

CAR EXPENSES.   Show the number of miles driven for business purposes (starting and ending odometer readings), the destination, the purpose of the trip, and the name of the party visited (if relevant). Simply jot down the odometer reading on January 1 to start a good recordkeeping habit. Include notations of expenses for gas, oil, parking, tolls, and other expenses. A sample log for keeping track of car expenses can be found in Chapter 9.

RECORDKEEPING RELIEF.   You do not need receipts, canceled checks, bills, or other proof of the cost of a travel or entertainment expense in the following situations:

- You use a standard rate (such as a standard mileage rate for car use or a per diem rate for meals and lodging). Per diem rates are explained in Chapter 8; the standard mileage rate is explained in Chapter 9.
- The expense is less than $75. However, you cannot use this exception for lodging (you must have documentary evidence for lodging regardless of amount).
- You have a transportation expense (such as a taxi fare) for which a receipt is not readily available.

THE COHAN RULE.   While the IRS says that deductions will be disallowed if you do not have adequate substantiation, you may be able to rely on a special rule developed by the courts. The *Cohan rule*, named after noted songwriter/showman George M. Cohan, is based on approximation. A court may agree to approximate your travel and entertainment expenses if your records are inadequate to establish actual expenses and you have some way to show your approximate expenses. A court cannot be compelled to use the Cohan rule; it must be persuaded to do so because of special circumstances. The Cohan rule is only a last resort for claiming unsubstantiated travel and entertainment expenses.

Charitable Contributions

In the past, canceled checks were sufficient evidence to support charitable contributions by individuals and corporations alike. Now special substantiation rules apply.

If you make contributions up to $75, your canceled check is considered to be adequate substantiation of your contributions. A receipt from the charity is also considered adequate substantiation. If you make contributions over $75 but not more than $250, your canceled check or a receipt from the charity also remains sufficient. What is more, the charity will notify you in writing on a disclosure statement if you received any goods or services by virtue of your contribution (e.g., your contribution entitles you to attend a charity dinner). The disclosure statement will state the amount of the benefit you are entitled to receive. You then subtract this benefit from your contribution and deduct only the net amount.

If you make donations of $250 or more, your canceled check is not considered to be adequate substantiation. You must get a written receipt or acknowledgment from the charity by the due date of your return (or the extended due date if you receive a filing extension) describing your contribution (the amount of cash contributed or a description of property contributed). Each payment to the same charity is treated as a separate payment unless you designed the payment plan to avoid this substantiation requirement.

Example

If you gave a charity $100 in February, $100 in June, and $100 in November, your canceled check is considered adequate substantiation of the donation unless you arranged these contributions to avoid having to obtain a written receipt or acknowledgment.

If a property donation is valued at over $5,000, you may also be required to obtain an appraisal and keep a record of this appraisal.

Records for Depreciation, Basis, Carryovers, and Prepaid Expenses

For some tax items you must keep a running account, because deductions will be claimed not only in the current year but also in years to come.

Depreciation

Depreciation allows you to recover the cost of property over the life of that property by deducting a portion of the cost each year. In order to claim your annual deductions, you must keep certain records:

- Costs and other information necessary to calculate your depreciation
- Capital improvements to depreciable assets
- Depreciation deductions already claimed
- Adjustments to basis as a result of depreciation deductions

This information not only is necessary for depreciation purposes but will also be needed to calculate gain or loss and any depreciation recapture on the sale or other disposition of a depreciable asset. For full details on claiming depreciation, see Chapter 14.

The same recordkeeping rules apply not only to depreciation but also to amortization and depletion deductions.

Basis

Basis is the cost of property or some other value assigned to property. Basis is used for several purposes: It is the amount on which depreciation deductions are based, as well as the amount used to determine gain or loss on the sale or other disposition of property.

The basis of property can vary from its basis upon acquisition. Some items increase basis; others decrease it. Keep track of changes in basis. These can result from:

- Depreciation deductions or first-year expensing
- Casualty deductions relating to the property
- Certain tax credits
- Capitalized costs

Carryovers

A number of deductions may be limited in a current year, but you may be able to carry over any unused portion to other years. In order to take advantage of carryover opportunities, you must keep records of deductions you have already taken and the years in which they were taken. What is more, you must maintain relevant records for the carryover periods. The following list details the types of carryovers for which records should be maintained and limits on the carryover period, if any:

- *At-risk losses.* Losses disallowed because of the application of the at-risk rules (see Chapter 4) can be carried over indefinitely.
- *Capital losses.* There is no limit on the carryover period for individuals. There is a five-year limit on carryover losses for corporations.
- *Charitable contributions.* Individuals who cannot fully use current charitable contributions because of adjusted gross income limits can carry over the unused deductions for a period of five years. C corporations that cannot fully use current charitable contributions because of the 10-percent-of-taxable-income limit can carry over the unused deductions for a period of five years. If the deductions cannot be used within that five-year period (there is insufficient taxable income to offset the deduction in the carryover years), the deductions are lost forever.
- *Home office deductions.* Individuals who maintain an office in their home and whose home office deductions are limited in the current

year by gross income earned in the home office can carry forward unused deductions indefinitely. The unused deductions can be used in a future year if there is gross income from the home office activity to offset it.

- *Investment interest.* Individuals (including partners, LLC members, and S corporation shareholders) may be limited in their current deduction for investment interest by the amount of their net investment income. Excess investment interest can be carried forward indefinitely. There is no limitation on corporations, so there is no carryover.

- *Net operating losses.* When operating losses cannot be used in full in the current year, they may be applied against income in certain other years. The carryover period depends on the year in which the net operating loss arises. There is a three-year carryback period and a 15-year carryforward period for losses arising in tax years beginning before August 5, 1997. There is a two-year carryback (or three years for certain disaster losses affecting small businesses, five years for losses in 2001 and 2002 and for farmers and ranchers in any year, and 10 years for product liability) and a 20-year carryforward for net operating losses arising in tax years beginning after August 5, 1997. Thus, a 2005 net operating loss can be carried back for two years and forward for up to 20 years. Alternatively, each year in which a net operating loss arises, you can elect to forgo the carryback period and just carry forward the net operating losses. The same carryover periods apply to individuals and corporations.

- *Passive activity losses.* Losses disallowed because of the application of the passive activity loss rules (*suspended losses*) can be carried forward indefinitely. The same rules apply to credits from passive activities.

- *Cash basis and prepayment.* Depreciation and carryovers are not the only tax items that may run beyond the current tax year. If you are on the cash basis and prepay certain expenses, you may not be allowed a current deduction for your outlays. You may be required to deduct the expenses ratably over the period of time to which they relate. Some examples of commonly prepaid expenses that may have to be deducted ratably include:

  Insurance premiums. If your insurance premiums cover a period of more than 12 months, you may be required to deduct them over the term covered by the policy.

  Prepaid interest. If you pay points or other amounts treated as prepaid interest to obtain financing to acquire real estate for your business, you deduct the prepaid interest ratably over the term of the loan. If you dispose of the property or refinance the loan before the end of the term, you can then deduct any unused portion of the prepaid interest in that final year.

Rents. If you prepay rents for a period of more than 12 months, you may be required to deduct the rents over the term of the lease.

Subscriptions. If you pay for subscriptions running more than 12 months, you generally have to deduct the cost over the term of the subscriptions. For example, if you pay in full the cost of a three-year subscription to a business journal, you generally must deduct the cost over the same three-year period.

You need to keep a running record of Section 1231 losses—losses on the sale of certain business assets. This is because of a special recapture rule that applies to net ordinary losses from Section 1231 property. A net Section 1231 gain is treated as ordinary income to the extent it does not exceed nonrecaptured net Section 1231 losses taken in prior years. *Nonrecaptured losses* are the total of net Section 1231 losses for the five most recent years that have not yet been applied (recaptured) against any net Section 1231 gains in those same years. In order to determine this recapture, you must retain information on Section 1231 gains and losses. Section 1231 losses are explained in more detail in Chapter 6.

Finally, you need to keep track of tax credits that are not completely used in the current year. Tax credits that are part of the general business credit (such as the research credit, empowerment zone credit, employer Social Security credit, and the disabled access credit) are subject to a carryback and carryforward period depending on the year in which the excess credits result. For credits arising in years beginning before January 1, 1998, the excess credits are carried back three years and forward for up to 15 years. For credits arising in years beginning after December 31, 1997, the excess credits are carried back one year and forward for up to 20 years. No election can be made to forgo this carryback period.

How Long You Should Maintain Records

Your books and records must be available at all times for inspection by the IRS. You should keep these books and records at least until the time when the IRS's ability to question your deductions runs out. This time is called the *statute of limitations.* In general, the statute of limitations is either three years after the due date of your return or two years after the date the tax was paid—whichever is later. Some records must be kept even longer. You need to keep records to support the basis in property owned by the business. You also need to keep records for depreciation and carryovers, as discussed earlier.

Tax Returns

Keep copies of tax returns to help you prepare future returns, as well as to help you if your return is questioned by the IRS. While you can obtain old returns from the IRS, this entails unnecessary time and expense. Although you may only need information on an old return for three additional years, it is a good idea to keep old tax returns indefinitely. If the IRS claims you never filed a return it has an unlimited number of years in which to audit you. But if you have your old return along with proof that you filed it (for example, a certified receipt), the IRS only has three years, in most cases, to start an audit.

Keep a record of the basis of property used in your business for as long as you own the property, plus the statute of limitations on filing the return for the year in which property is sold or otherwise disposed of. For example, if in 2005 you buy equipment that you will sell in 2007, keep records on the basis of the property until 2011 (three years from the due date of the return for the year in which the property was sold).

Employer Records

If you have employees, special recordkeeping rules apply. You are required to keep records on employment taxes for at least four years after the due date of the return or after the tax is paid, whichever is later. Keep copies of all returns you have filed and the dates and amount of tax deposits you have made. Your records should also show your *employer identification number (EIN)*. Every business, sole proprietorship, partnership, and corporation must have one if wages are paid. The EIN is a nine-digit number assigned to each business and used to report the payment of employment taxes and to file certain returns.

If you are just starting your business and do not have an EIN, you can obtain one instantaneously online at <www.irs.gov/businesses/small/article /0,,id=102767,00.html> or by filing Form SS-4, Application for Employer Identification Number, with the IRS service center in the area in which your business is located. Application by mail takes several weeks. An SS-4 can be obtained from the IRS web site at <www.irs.gov> or by calling a special business phone number (1-800-829-4933) or the special Tele-TIN phone number. The number for your service center is listed in the instructions to Form SS-4. If you call for a number, it is assigned immediately, after which you must send or fax a signed SS-4 within 24 hours.

Income Tax Withholding

You must keep records of each employee's name, address, and Social Security number, the amount of each wage payment, the amount of each payment subject to income tax withholding, and the amount of income tax withheld. You must also keep copies of all employees' withholding allowance certificates (Form W-4). Similarly, you must keep any earned income credit advance payment certificates (Form W-5) filed with you by low-income wage earners who want to receive an advance on their earned income credit.

Other Employment Taxes

Similar records must be kept for each employee for Social Security and Medicare taxes, as well as for federal unemployment taxes (FUTA).

Business Income and Losses

CHAPTER 4

Income or Loss from Business Operations

The fees you earn for your services or the receipts you collect from the sale of goods are the bread-and-butter income of your business. Hopefully your pricing policies are realistic and you have a strong customer or client base so that you can make a profit.

Even if sales are healthy, expenses can outrun receipts, resulting in a loss for the business. You will not know whether you have net income or loss until all of the expenses discussed throughout the book have been taken into account. If there is a net loss, then limitations may come into play on when and the extent to which business losses can be deducted.

In this chapter you will learn about:

- Income for service businesses
- Income from the sale of goods
- Income from farming
- Investment-type income
- Miscellaneous business income
- Net operating losses
- Limitations on business losses
- Where to report business income

For further information about business income and losses, see IRS Publication 225, *Farmer's Tax Guide*, IRS Publication 334, *Tax Guide for Small Business*, Publication 541, *Partnerships*, IRS Publication 542, *Corporations*, and IRS Publication 911, *Direct Sellers*. A further discussion of the hobby loss rules may be found in IRS Publication 535, *Business Expenses*. For information on the at-risk rules and passive activity loss limitations, see IRS Publication 925, *Passive Activity and At-Risk Rules*.

Business Income

Whether you work full-time or part-time, income received for your business activity is part of your business income. How you report it depends on your accounting method (explained in Chapter 2).

Where you report it depends on how your business is organized. For example, self-employed individuals report income on Schedule C or Schedule C-EZ or on Schedule F if the business is farming. Partnerships and LLCs report income on Form 1065, S corporations use Form 1120S, and C corporations report income on Form 1120. Where to report income is explained at the end of this chapter.

Payment Methods

Most business transactions are in cash. For tax purposes the term *cash* includes checks or credit card charges. However, in some cases, payments may take a different form.

PAYMENTS IN KIND.   If you exchange your goods or services for property, you must include the fair market value of the property you received in income. Bartering does not avoid the requirement to report income. This is true whether you barter directly—one-on-one—or receive property through a barter exchange that gives you credit for the goods or services you provide.

Bartering through a barter exchange is reported to the IRS on Form 1099-B, Proceeds from Broker and Barter Exchange Transactions.

CAUTION

Bartering does not avoid sales taxes. For example, if you barter your goods to dispose of excess inventory, be sure to follow the same sales tax rules that you would if you had been paid in cash. See Chapter 27.

PAYMENTS IN SERVICES.   If you exchange your goods or services for someone else's services, you are also taxed on the value of the services you receive. If services are exchanged for services, you both can agree to the value of the services you report as income.

CONSIGNMENTS.   If items owned by others are consigned to you for sale, do not include these items in your inventory. Instead, report income from any commissions or profits you are entitled to upon sale.

Example

You are a house painter who paints the offices of an attorney who handles a legal matter for you in exchange for your work. You must include the value of the attorney's services in your income. You may value this according to what the attorney would have charged you if you had paid cash for the work. Or you can both agree to the value of the services, assuming that value is reasonable.

If you consign your goods to others, do not report this arrangement as a sale. You report income from the sale of consigned goods when they are sold by the consignee. Do not remove the items from your inventory until a sale by the consignee.

KICKBACKS. Amounts you receive as kickbacks are included in income. However, do not include them as a separate income item if you properly treat these amounts as a reduction to the cost of goods sold, a capital expenditure, or an expense item.

LOANS. If you obtain business loans, do not include the proceeds in income. They are merely loans that must be repaid according to the terms of the loan agreement.

Income for Service Businesses

If your main business activity is providing services to customers and clients, you are in a service business. As such, reporting business income is generally a simple matter. You report as income all of your revenues from performing services according to your method of accounting. Since most service businesses are on the cash basis, income usually is reported when fees are collected.

1099 Income

If you are an independent contractor, your clients or customers are required to report income paid to you on Form 1099-MISC, Miscellaneous Income. This informs the IRS of income you have received. Income is required to be reported on Form 1099 if annual payments are at least $600, but you are required to report on your tax return *all* income you receive (even if no 1099 has been issued).

Advances and Prepayments

If you receive income for services to be performed in the future, you report the income if you have free and unrestricted use of the money.

Accrual basis businesses receiving advance payments may defer the reporting of income to the following year *if* services are to be performed by the end of that year (the income is accrued at the time the services are performed). However, no deferral is permitted beyond the year after the year of receiving the advance.

Similarly, accrual basis businesses receiving advance payments for service agreements (including agreements that include incidental parts or materials) can defer the income if the services will be performed by the end of the next year.

Income from the Sale of Goods

Reporting income from the sale of goods involves a two-step process. First you must figure your *gross receipts*—amounts received from sales (determined by your method of accounting). Then you must subtract from gross receipts your **cost of goods sold.**

Cost of goods sold   The cost of buying raw materials and producing finished goods. Essentially it is the cost of buying inventory or manufacturing inventory.

Cost of Goods Sold

Cost of goods sold is determined each year by adjusting beginning inventory for changes made during the year. Inventory at the beginning of the year (generally your closing inventory reported on last year's return) is increased by adding any inventory purchases or manufactured items purchased that year. Include not only purchases but also the cost of labor and other costs required to be included under the uniform capitalization (UNICAP) rules explained in Chapter 2. Decrease this figure by sales from inventory.

To know what your opening inventory and closing inventory is, you need to take a physical inventory. A physical inventory must be taken at reasonable intervals and the actual count must be used to adjust the inventory figures you have been maintaining all along. Generally, a physical inventory is taken at year-end. You are permitted to estimate year-end inventory by factoring in a reasonable allowance for shrinkage (for example, loss due to theft that you failed to detect). If you make such an estimate, then you must take a physical count on a consistent basis and adjust—upward or downward—the actual inventory count.

There are four methods for reporting inventory. They are:

1. Cost
2. Lower of cost or market method
3. Write-down of subnormal goods
4. Other inventory methods

Resellers—those who buy items for sale to others—use certain rules and methods to assign the cost of these items to those sold during the year:

* *First-in, First-out (FIFO).* An item sold is deemed to be the first item booked into inventory. For example, if you bought 10 widgets on three oc-

casions at a cost of 10¢ each, 15¢ each, and 20¢ each and you sell 15, under FIFO you have sold 10 at 10¢ each and 5 at 15¢ each.

- *Last-in, First-out (LIFO).* An item sold is deemed to be the last item booked into inventory. In the widge example, you have sold 10 at 20¢ each and 5 at 15¢ each.

- *Specific identification method.* The actual cost of the items is used. This method generally is used when a business owns large or unique items (for example, an antique store would use this method for its objects since items are not identical and cannot be commingled).

Small businesses are allowed to use a simplified value LIFO method that makes it easier to determine the value of inventory. If you elect FIFO, you must use the lower of cost or market method to report inventory. If you elect LIFO, you must use cost to report inventory.

Gross Profits

Gross profits from the sale of goods is the difference between the gross receipts (sales revenues) and the cost of goods sold (as well as other allowances). If you remove items from inventory for your personal use, be sure to adjust your figures accordingly.

You generally cannot use the installment method of accounting to report the sale of inventory items—even if you receive payment on an installment plan. You report the sale according to your usual method of accounting so that on the accrual basis you pick up the income in full in the year of sale even though the full payment will not be received at that time.

Other Income for Direct Sellers

In addition to income from sales of products to customers, direct sellers may receive income in other ways:

- Commissions, bonuses, or percentages you receive for sales and the sales of others who work under you.

- Prizes, awards, and gifts resulting from your sales activities.

Income from Farming

When a business earns its income from sales of livestock and produce, payments from agricultural programs and farm rents and other similar sources, it is considered a farming business. Since most small farms use the cash method of accounting to report income and expenses, the following discussion is limited to this method of accounting. However, if items regularly produced in the farming business or used in the farming business are sold on an installment basis, the sale can be reported on the installment method, deferring income until payment is received.

While many income items of farms are similar to nonfarm businesses, there are a number of income items unique to farming. These include:

- *Sales of livestock (including poultry) and produce.* The sale of livestock classified as Section 1231 property may result in Section 1231 gain or loss (explained in Chapter 6). If crops are sold on a deferred payment contract, you report the income when payment is received.

- *Sales of livestock caused by drought, flood or other weather conditions.* While such sales are generally reported in the current year, you can opt to report them in the following year if you can show that you would not have sold the livestock this year but for the weather conditions *and* you are eligible for federal assistance because of the weather conditions. You must file a separate election with your tax return for the year of the weather conditions for each class of animals (e.g., cattle, sheep). Alternatively, deferral is indefinite if proceeds are reinvested in similar livestock within four years.

- *Sales of timber.* Outright sales of timber qualify for capital gain treatment if the timber was held for more than one year before the date of disposal. Similar treatment applies to sales of timber under a contract with a retained economic interest. However, for purposes of outright sales, the date of disposal is not deemed to be the date timber is cut; you can elect to treat the payment date as the date of disposal.

- *Rents, including crop shares.* Generally, rents are not treated as farm income but rental income and these rents are not part of your net income or loss from farming. However, rents are treated as farm income if you materially participate in the management or operations of the farm (material participation is explained later in this chapter).

- *Agricultural payments* (cash, materials, services or commodity certificates) from government programs generally are included in income. If you later refund or repay a portion of the payments, you can deduct these amounts at that time. For details on how to treat specific government payments, see IRS Publication 225, *Farmer's Tax Guide.*

- *Patronage dividends* from farm cooperatives through which you purchase farm supplies and sell your farm products are included in income.

- *National Tobacco Settlement payments* to landowners, producers, and tobacco quota owners in Alabama, Florida, Georgia, Indiana, Kentucky, Maryland, Missouri, North Carolina, Ohio, Pennsylvania, South Carolina, Tennessee, Virginia, and West Virginia.

Farmers who pledge part or all of their production to secure a Commodity Credit Corporation (CCC) loan can make a special election to treat the loan proceeds as income in the year received and obtain a basis in the commodity for the amount reported as income. Farmers who do not make this election must report market gain as income.

Not all income received by farmers and ranchers is includible in gross income. You may exclude payments received under the following federal programs:

- Agricultural Management Assistance Program
- Soil and Water Conservation Assistance Program

Farm Income Averaging

You can choose to figure the tax on your farming income (*elected farm income*) by averaging it over the past three years. If you make this election, it will lower the tax on this year's income if income was substantially lower in the three prior years. However, it does not always save taxes to average your farming income—it is a good idea to figure your tax in both ways (the usual way and averaging) to determine which method is more favorable to you.

The same averaging option applies to commercial fishermen.

Investment-Type Income

Operating income from a business includes certain investment-type income, such as interest on business bank accounts and rents from leasing property. Except for C corporations, these items are not listed separately on the return but instead reported together as other income. How to report this income can be found later in this chapter. Capital gains are discussed in Chapter 5 and other gains from the sale of business property are discussed in Chapter 6.

Interest Income

Interest received on business bank accounts and on accounts or notes receivable in the ordinary course of business is a common type of ordinary business income. If the business lends money, interest received on business loans is business income. Deductions for business loans that go sour are explained in Chapter 22.

Businesses that make below-market or interest-free loans may be deemed to receive interest, called *imputed interest*. Below-market loan rules from the deduction perspective are discussed in Chapter 13.

Dividends

Dividends payable by corporations in which the business owns shares is reported as ordinary business income.

DIVIDENDS-RECEIVED DEDUCTION.   C corporations that receive dividends from domestic (U.S.) corporations can effectively exclude some or all of these dividends by claiming a special dividends-received deduction. The amount of the dividends-received deduction depends on the percentage of ownership in the corporation paying the dividend. This special write-off for C corporations is discussed in Chapter 22.

Rents

Rents can be generated from leasing personal property items such as equipment, formal wear, or videos. Rents can also be generated from leasing out real property.

REAL ESTATE RENTS. A business that provides services in conjunction with rentals reports rents as business income. For example, if you own a motel, you report your rentals as business income because you provide maid service and other services to your business guests.

If your tenant pays expenses on your behalf in lieu of making rental payments to you, these payments to third parties are part of your business income. For example, if your tenant pays your property taxes, you report the payment of taxes as rental income.

PREPAID RENT. Advances, including security deposits, must be reported as income if you have unrestricted right to them. If you are required by law or contract to segregate these payments, you do not have to report them as income until you are entitled to enjoy them (the restrictions no longer apply).

LEASE BONUS OR CANCELLATION PAYMENTS. Amounts your tenant pays to secure a lease (lease bonus payments) or to get out of a lease early (cancellation payments) are income to you.

Cancellation of Debt

If you owe money and some or all of your debt is forgiven by the lender, you generally must include this debt forgiveness in income. However, you do not have to include debt forgiveness in income if any of the following conditions apply:

- You file for bankruptcy under Title 11 of the U.S. Code.
- You are insolvent at the time of the cancellation. Your exclusion is limited to the extent of your insolvency.
- The canceled debt is a qualified farm debt. This is a debt incurred by a business that receives at least 50 percent of its gross receipts in the prior three years from farming activities. This debt must be owed to one who is regularly engaged in lending money, including the U.S. Department of Agriculture.

- The canceled debt is qualified real property business debt—secured by the property and incurred before January 1, 1993, or after December 31, 1992, if incurred or assumed to acquire, construct, or substantially improve real property used in the business. You must elect this exclusion for the year in which the cancellation occurs. The exclusion cannot exceed certain amounts.

Instead of reporting the cancellation of debt as income, you may elect to reduce certain **tax attributes**. Making this election has the effect of limiting your future write-offs with respect to these tax attributes. Generally the amount excluded from income reduces the tax attributes (in a certain order) on a dollar-for-dollar or 33⅓ cents basis. The election is made on Form 982, Reduction of Tax Attributes Due to Discharge of Indebtedness.

Tax attributes   These are tax aspects that provide a tax benefit in the current year or future years. They include the basis of depreciable real property, the basis of other depreciable property, net operating losses and loss carryovers, general business credit carryovers, minimum tax credit, capital losses and loss carryovers, passive activity loss and credit carryovers, and foreign tax credit carryovers.

Damages and Other Recoveries

If you receive damages for patent, copyright or trademark infringement, breach of contract, or other business-related injuries, you report the damages as business income.

Miscellaneous Business Income

Almost any type of income earned by a business is considered to be business income. In addition to the types of income already discussed, the following are other examples of business income you must report:

- Recovery of bad debts previously deducted under the specific charge-off method
- Taxable income from insurance proceeds (such as key person insurance)
- Income adjustments resulting from a change in accounting method
- Scrap sales
- Finance reserve income
- Prizes and awards for the business
- Credit for alcohol used as fuel (for details see the instructions to Form 6478, Credit for Alcohol Used as Fuel)
- State gasoline or fuel tax refunds received in the current year

- Credit for federal tax paid on gasoline or other fuels claimed on the prior year return
- Recapture of the deduction for clean-fuel vehicles used in the business and clean-fuel refueling property (for details see IRS Publication 535, *Business Expenses*)
- Recapture of first-year expensing deduction (first-year expensing is explained in Chapter 14)
- Recapture of Sec. 280F if listed property's business use drops below 50 percent (figure recapture amount on Form 4797 in Chapter 6)
- State grants to businesses whose property is damaged or destroyed in a disaster (but gain on the resulting income may be postponed under the rules for involuntary conversions discussed in Chapter 6)
- World Trade Center grants made to businesses

For the Future

Starting in 2006, employers can receive subsidies from the federal government if they provide retiree health coverage. The subsidy is figured on a per retiree basis.

Special Income Items for S Corporations

If a corporation operated as a C corporation and then converted to S status, certain unique income items may result. These items are taxed to the S corporation; they are not pass-through items taxed to the shareholders. These items include:

- *Last-in, first-out inventory recapture on the conversion from C status to S status.* It can also result from the transfer of LIFO inventory by a C corporation to the S corporation in a transaction in which no income was recognized. Recapture results in an income adjustment payable in four equal installments, one reported on the final return of the C corporation (or the year of the transfer), and one fourth each in the first, second, and third years of the S corporation's life (or the year of the transfer and the two successive years).
- *Excess net passive income.* If there were accumulated earnings and profits (E&P) from the time when the corporation was a C corporation *and* it has passive income for the year in excess of 25 percent of gross receipts, then tax is due at the rate of 35 percent. The S corporation must have taxable income for the year to be subject to this special tax.

- *Built-in capital gains.* If the corporation has appreciated property when it converts, the appreciation to the date of conversion is reported as built-in gains if the property is sold or otherwise disposed of within 10 years of the conversion. The tax on net recognized built-in capital gains is 35 percent.

If a corporation elects S status for its first year of existence it need not be concerned with any of these income items; they will never arise.

Special Income Items for C Corporations

If a C corporation converts to S status and reports inventory using LIFO, it must recapture one fourth of the resulting income adjustment, reporting it as income on its final return (the year of conversion).

If the corporation receives a tax refund of taxes deducted in a prior year, the refund must be reported as income to the extent it produced a tax benefit for the corporation.

State Income Taxes on Business Income

Federal income taxes on your business income may not be your only concern. You may also be subject to state income taxes. This liability depends on whether you do business within the state. Generally, this means having a nexus (connection) to the state. This is based on having a physical presence there, which may be evidenced by maintaining an office or sending a sales force into the state; merely shipping goods into the state without some additional connection is not enough to prove a business presence within the state. You may have a nexus to more than one state, no matter how small your business is.

If there is a business connection, the business income is apportioned among the states in which you do business. Apportionment is based on a sales factor, a payroll factor, and a property factor (the states have different apportionment rules). The rules are highly complex, but there is considerable wiggle room to shift income into the state with the lowest taxes.

For more information about state income taxes, contact the tax or revenue departments of each state in which you do business.

Net Operating Losses

If deductions and losses from your business exceed your business income, you may be able to use the losses to offset income in other years. Net losses from the conduct of your business are *net operating losses* (*NOLs*). In 2001 (the last year for which statistics are available), NOLs claimed on individual returns exceeded $5.8 billion.

Net operating losses are not an additional loss deduction. Rather, they are the result of your deductions exceeding the income from your business. The excess deductions are not lost; they are simply used in certain other years.

You have an NOL if you have deductions from a trade or business, deductions from your work as an employee, or deductions from casualty and theft losses.

Only individuals and C corporations can claim NOLs. Partnerships, limited liability companies (LLCs), and S corporations cannot have NOLs, since their income and losses pass through to owners. However, partners, LLC members, and S corporation shareholders can have NOLs on their individual returns. These NOLs are created by their share of the business's operating losses.

Calculating NOLs

After you have completed your tax return for the year, you may find that you have an NOL. If you are an individual, you may have an NOL if your adjusted gross income, reduced by itemized deductions or the standard deduction (but before personal exemptions), is a negative figure. C corporations may have an NOL if taxable income is a negative figure. This negative figure merely indicates a possibility of an NOL; then you must determine whether, in fact, there actually is one. This is due to the fact that certain adjustments must be made to that negative figure in arriving at an NOL. Individuals and corporations calculate NOLs in a slightly different manner.

INDIVIDUALS. An NOL does not include personal exemptions, net capital losses, nonbusiness losses, or nonbusiness deductions. The NOL can be computed on Schedule A of Form 1045. This form adds back to taxable income any of these items claimed on the return and makes other adjustments required to compute the NOL. For example, individuals must add back to taxable income any deductions for Individual Retirement Account (IRA) contributions, alimony, the standard deduction, and charitable contributions. More specifically, nonbusiness deductions in excess of nonbusiness income get added back. Do not add back business-related deductions for:

- One-half of self-employment tax
- Moving expenses
- State income tax on business profits
- Interest and litigation expenses on state or federal income taxes related to business
- Payments by a federal employee to buy sick leave
- Loss on rental property
- Loss on the sale or exchange of business real estate or depreciable business property
- Loss on the sale of accounts receivable if you are on the accrual method

- Loss on the sale or exchange of stock in a small business company or small business investment company if the loss is treated as an ordinary loss (such as loss on Section 1244)

CORPORATIONS.   The NOL for corporations generally is calculated by reducing gross income by deductions. Special rules then apply to adjust the NOL. They are:

- A full dividends-received deduction is taken into account in calculating the NOL. For example, the 70-percent or 80-percent limit is ignored.
- NOLs from other years are not taken into account in calculating a current NOL.
- Losses that fall under the passive activity rules cannot be used to calculate an NOL.

If a corporation's ownership changes hands, limits apply on the use of NOL carryforwards. The tax law does not want one corporation to acquire another for the purpose of using NOLs of the target corporation to offset the income of the acquiring corporation. These rules are highly complex.

S corporations do not have net operating losses. Instead, losses are passed through to owners who figure their NOLs on their individual returns. NOL carryovers of a C corporation cannot be claimed after the conversion to S corporation status (they remain in limbo and can be used by the corporation if it terminates its S status and returns to being a C corporation). However, the S corporation can use the C corporation's NOL carryover as a deduction to offset any net recognized built-in gain (built-in gain is explained earlier in this chapter).

Carrybacks and Carryovers

Net operating losses may be carried back and, if not used up, carried forward for a certain number of years. The carryback and carryforward periods depend on the year in which the NOL arose.

For NOLs arising in tax years beginning before August 6, 1997, the carryback period was three years and the carryforward period continues to be 15 years.

For NOLs arising in tax years beginning after August 5, 1997, generally there is a two-year carryback and a 20-year carryforward period. However, for small businesses (those with average annual gross receipts of $5 million or less during a three-year period), a three-year carryback applies to NOLs arising from government-declared disasters and for farmers and ranchers, there is a five-year carryback for all NOLs. For NOLs arising in 2001 and 2002, there is a five-year carryback. There is a 10-year carryback for NOLs arising from product liability.

If you have an NOL in 2005, you first carry the loss back to a year that is two years before the year in which the NOL arose (the NOL year), which is 2003. If it is not used up in that year, carry it to the year before the NOL year, which is 2004. If the NOL is still not used up, you can begin to carry it forward (with modifications explained below). However, if it is not used up after carrying it forward for 20 years, it is lost forever.

Be sure to keep track of each category of NOL. For example, do not lump your pre-August 6, 1997, carryforwards together with your post-August 5, 1997, carryforwards.

Personal service corporations (PSCs) are not allowed to carry back an NOL to any year in which there is a Section 444 election in effect to use a tax year other than a required tax year.

If your marital status in the carryback or carryover years differs from your status in the NOL year, only the spouse who has the NOL can claim it. If you file a joint return, the NOL deduction is limited to the income of the spouse who had the NOL. Special rules apply for carrybacks to a year involving a different marital status than the status in the year the NOL arises.

Example

In 2004 you divorce after many years of marriage. In 2005 you have an NOL. If you do not forgo the two-year carryback, the NOL carryback is applied only against your income on the 2003 return, which was a joint return (in 2004 you were divorced by the end of the year and your filing status was single). After you deduct the NOL calculated with reference to your taxable income, you then apply the tax rates for married filing jointly.

If your NOL is greater than the taxable income for the year to which you carried it, you must make certain modifications to taxable income to see how much of the NOL is used up in that carryback/carryover year and how much is still available as a *carryover*. The carryover is the excess of the NOL deduction over modified taxable income for the carryback/carryforward year. *Modified taxable income* is taxable income without regard to the NOL and with no deduction for net capital losses or personal exemptions. Also, you must recalculate items affected by a change in adjusted gross income. Your modified taxable income cannot be less than zero. You can determine your modified taxable income using Schedule B of Form 1045 for any carryback years and for carryovers from those years. If you have carryovers from more than one year, you use the carryovers in the order in which they were incurred.

ELECTION TO FORGO CARRYBACK.   Instead of carrying a 2005 NOL back two years and then forward, you can elect to forgo the carryback and just carry forward the loss for 20 years. You make this election in the NOL year by attaching a statement to your return if you are an individual, or by checking the appropriate box on the corporate return for C corporations. Once the election is made, it cannot be changed. If you incur another NOL in a subsequent year, you must make a separate election if you also want to forgo the carryback.

Some taxpayers prefer to forgo the carryback because they are afraid of calling attention to prior tax years and risking an audit. While this is certainly a possibility, claiming a carryback will not necessarily result in an audit of a prior year.

The election to forgo the NOL carryback applies not only to regular income tax purposes but also to alternative minimum tax purposes.

QUICK REFUNDS FROM CARRYBACKS. If your business is struggling, you can use an NOL carryback to generate quick cash flow. The carryback will offset income in the carryback years, and you will receive a refund of taxes paid in those years.

Individuals can file Form 1045, Application for Tentative Refund, to obtain a relatively quick refund. The IRS generally will act on the refund within 90 days of the filing of the form. When you carry back an NOL, you may have to recalculate certain deductions, credits, and other items in the carryback years. These are items figured with respect to adjusted gross income. For example, the NOL will lower your adjusted gross income in the carryback years and therefore allow for greater itemized deductions that have an adjusted-gross-income floor. You may also have to recalculate alternative minimum tax.

Corporations can expedite a refund from an NOL carryback by using a special form, Form 1139, Corporation Application for Tentative Refund, to obtain a quick refund. This form cannot be filed before the income tax return for the NOL year is filed and it must be filed no later than one year after the NOL year. What is more, if a corporation expects to have an NOL in the current year, it can delay filing the income tax return for the prior year with the knowledge that the tax on the prior year's return will be fully or partially offset by the NOL.

A corporation that expects an NOL for the current year may extend the time for payment of tax for the immediately preceding tax year by filing Form 1138, Extension of Time for the Payment of Taxes by a Corporation Expecting a Net Operating Loss Carryback. This form is filed *after* the start of the year in which the NOL is expected but *before* the tax for the preceding year is required to be paid. Such corporations can also further extend the time for payment by filing Form 1139, explained earlier. Doing so extends the time for payment of tax for the immediately preceding tax year until the IRS has informed the corporation that it has allowed or disallowed its application in whole or in part.

You can also claim an NOL on an amended return, Form 1040X or Form 1120X. Individuals who carry back NOLs cannot recalculate self-employment tax and get a refund of this tax. The NOL applies for income tax purposes only.

Limitations on Business Losses

Once you figure whether your business has sustained operating losses, you must then determine the extent to which you can deduct these losses. A number of limits apply that restrict full and immediate write-offs of business losses. Not all of the rules that follow apply to all types of businesses, so only review those rules applicable to your company.

Basis

If you own a pass-through entity, business losses claimed on your personal return cannot exceed your tax basis in the company. Losses in excess of basis can be carried forward and used in future years to the extent of basis at that time. There is no time limit on these carryforwards.

PARTNERSHIPS AND LLCS.   Basis is determined, in part, by the way in which a partner or member acquires his interest in the entity.

- If the interest is acquired by contributing directly to the entity (typically in the start-up of the business), then basis is the cash and owner's basis of the property contributed to the entity.
- If the interest is purchased from an owner (for example, a retiring partner), then basis is the cash and value of the property paid.
- If the interest is acquired by performing services for the business, then basis is the amount of compensation reported. However, the receipt of an interest in the profits of the business (and not a capital interest) is not taxable under certain conditions and so does not give rise to any basis.
- If the interest is inherited from a deceased owner, then basis is the value of the interest for estate tax purposes (typically the value of the interest on the date of the owner's death).

If property transferred to the entity is subject to liabilities, owners increase their basis by their share of the liabilities.

After the initial determination of basis, it may be increased or decreased annually. Basis is increased by the following items (determined on a per-share, per-day basis):

- The owner's distributive share of entity income
- The owner's share of tax-exempt income (such as life insurance proceeds)
- Excess of depletion deductions over the basis of depletable property
- Additional capital contributions
- Share of new partnership liabilities (Limited partners in limited partnerships do not increase their basis by a share of liabilities assumed by the general partners.)

Basis is decreased (on a per-share, per-day basis), but not below zero, by:

- The owner's distributive share of entity losses (including capital losses)
- The owner's share of expenses that are not deductible in figuring entity income
- Distributions to the owner by the entity

S CORPORATIONS. Basis for the purpose of deducting pass-through losses means your basis in your S corporation stock—what you contributed to the corporation to acquire your shares—plus the amount of any money you loaned to the corporation. If S corporation stock is acquired by inheritance, the basis, which is generally the value of the stock on the date of the owner's death, is reduced by the portion of the value attributable to income in respect of a decedent. This is income earned by the owner prior to death that is received by and reported by the person who inherits the stock.

Guaranteeing corporate debt, which is a common practice for bank loans to S corporations, does not give rise to basis. However, if you are called on to make good on your guarantee, then you can increase your basis by the amount you pay to the bank on the corporation's behalf.

A shareholder's basis is not affected by the corporation's liabilities. Unlike a partner who can increase his basis by his share of partnership liabilities, an S corporation shareholder may not increase his basis by his share of corporate liabilities.

After the initial determination of basis, it may be increased or decreased annually. Basis is increased by:

- The shareholder's share of the corporation's ordinary income
- The shareholder's share of separately stated items reported on the Schedule K-1 (including tax-exempt income)
- Excess of depletion deductions over the basis of depletable property
- Additional capital contributions

Basis is decreased (but not below zero) by:

- The shareholder's share of the corporation's losses
- The shareholder's share of expenses and losses that are not deductible in figuring ordinary income
- Noncapital and nondeductible corporate expenses reported on the Schedule K-1 (e.g., 50 percent of meal and entertainment costs and nondeductible penalties)
- Distributions not includible in the shareholder's income (e.g., dividends in excess of basis)

Hobby Losses

If your unincorporated business sustains losses year after year, you may not be able to deduct the losses in excess of your business income unless you can show that you have undertaken the business in order to make a profit. This limitation on losses is called the *hobby loss rule*, because it is designed to prevent individuals who collect coins and stamps, breed dogs or cats, or carry on other hobby activities from deducting what the tax law views as personal expenses. Any activity you do mainly for recreation, sport, or personal enjoyment is particularly suspect.

But the hobby loss rule is not limited to these types of activities. It can apply to any activity—even investment activities intended to produce only tax losses for investors. In fact, the IRS even tried to apply the hobby loss rule to a young attorney just starting her practice. The IRS argued that the losses she sustained were not deductible because of the hobby loss rule. The attorney was able to show a profit motive (proof of a profit motive is explained later) and she was allowed to deduct her losses.

The hobby loss rule applies to individuals (including partners and LLC members) and S corporations. It does not apply to C corporations. For partnerships, LLCs, and S corporations whose business losses pass through to owners, the determination of whether there is a profit motive is made at the business level rather than at the owner level. In other words, the business itself must have a reasonable expectation of making a profit. The fact that an individual owner has a profit motive does not transform a hobby loss into a deductible loss if the business does not reasonably have a profit motive.

IMPACT OF HOBBY CLASSIFICATION.   If your business is classified as a hobby, then any year in which you make a profit you must pay taxes on your entire profit. Any year you have losses (expenses exceeding income), you cannot deduct them. What is more, you cannot carry over the unused losses to claim them in another year. You lose the deduction for your losses forever.

PROVING A PROFIT MOTIVE.   There is no hard and fast way for proving that you have a *profit motive*. Rather, a profit motive is something that is inferred on the basis of various factors. The burden of proof is on you, the taxpayer. No single factor is determinative. Some or all of the factors used to determine profit motive include:

- Whether you carry on the activity in a *businesslike manner*. This means that you keep good books and records separate and apart from your personal records, and have a business bank account, telephone, stationery, and other indices of a business.
- Whether the time and effort you put into the activity shows that you intend to make a profit. If you spend only a small amount of time

on it, this may show that there is no realistic way in which you can make a profit.

- Whether you depend on the income from the activity for your livelihood. If you do, then obviously you hope to make a profit to live on.
- Whether you change methods of operation to improve profitability. If you get the advice of experts, this shows you want to make a profit.
- Whether the activity is profitable in some years, and how much profit is realized in those years. Certainly an activity may not always be profitable, but if there has already been a profit in some years and that profit is substantial, this shows an expectation of continued profit.
- Whether you or your advisers have the know-how needed to carry on your business at a profit. If you undertake some activity that you enjoy but know nothing about, this may indicate a lack of profit motive.
- Whether you can expect to see a profit from the appreciation of the assets used in the activity. You may not necessarily realize profit from the operations of the business, but its assets may prove to be profitable. A realistic expectation of this profit from the appreciation of business assets shows profit motive.

PRESUMPTION OF A PROFIT MOTIVE.   Your business may not be profitable, particularly in the early or start-up years. The tax law gives you a special presumption on which you can rely to show a profit motive (and delay an IRS inquiry into your activity). An activity is presumed to be engaged in for profit if you have a profit in at least three out of five years. If the activity is breeding, training, showing, or racing horses, the presumption period is two out of seven years. If you meet this presumption, then the hobby loss rules do not apply and your losses in the off years can be claimed in excess of your income from the activity.

You can rely on this presumption and avoid having the IRS question your losses by filing Form 5213, Election to Postpone Determination as to Whether the Presumption Applies that an Activity Is Engaged in for Profit. In effect, the form asks the IRS to delay a determination of your profit motive until the end of the five-year (or seven-year) period.

Generally, you must file Form 5213 within three years of the due date of the return for the year in which you first carry on the activity. You should know within this time whether you can reasonably expect to be profitable and avoid the hobby loss rules or whether you need to rely on the presumption to gain additional time for the business to make a profit.

The downside to filing this form is that it extends the statute of limitations (the period in which the IRS can question your return and assess additional taxes). In this case, the statute of limitations is extended to two years after the due date of the return for the last year of the presumption period. However, it is extended only for deductions from the activity and any related deductions. Other items on your return, such as your personal itemized deductions, are not affected by this extension of the statute of limitations.

Is it a good idea to file Form 5213 and raise the presumption? Doing so is almost a guarantee that the IRS will look closely at your return. Should you not show a profit in the required number of years during the presumption period, you will be forced to argue that you have a profit motive despite recurrent losses. Thus, you are no better off than if you had not filed the form.

At-Risk Rules

In the past it was not uncommon for someone to invest in a business by contributing a small sum of cash and a large note on which there was no personal liability. The note increased the investor's basis against which tax write-offs could be claimed. If the business prospered, all was well and good. If the business failed, the individual lost only the small amount of cash invested. Congress felt this arrangement was unreasonably beneficial to investors and created *at-risk rules*. At-risk rules operate to limit your losses to the extent of your at-risk amounts in the activity. Your at-risk amounts are, in effect, your economic investment in the activity. This is the cash you put into a business. It also includes the adjusted basis of other property you contribute and any debts secured by your property or for which you are personally liable for repayment.

You are not considered at risk if you have an agreement or arrangement that limits your risk. As a practical matter, if you set up and conduct an active business operation, you probably do not have to be concerned with the at-risk rules. First, you may qualify for an exception to the at-risk rules for closely held C corporations (discussed later). Also, in all probability your investment is what has started and sustained the business. But, if you are an investor, your contribution may be limited, and your losses may be limited as well.

Example

You invest in a partnership to distribute a motion picture. You invest $1,000 cash and sign a promissory note for $9,000. The note is nonrecourse (you are not personally liable for the debt). Your at-risk amount is $1,000, the cash you invested. You cannot deduct losses from this activity in excess of $1,000.

If you are subject to the at-risk rules, you do not lose your deductions to the extent they exceed your at-risk amounts; you simply cannot claim them currently. The losses can be carried forward and used in subsequent years if your at-risk amount increases. There is no limit on the carryover period. If the activity is sold, your gain from the disposition of property is treated as income from the activity and you can then offset the gain by the amount of your carried-over losses.

At-risk rules do not apply to investments in closely held C corporations that meet active business tests and that do not engage in equipment leasing or any business involving master sound recording, films, videotapes, or other artistic, literary, or musical property.

CALCULATING YOUR AT-RISK LIMITATION. Your at-risk amounts—cash, adjusted basis of property contributed to the activity, and recourse loans—form your *at-risk basis*. It is this basis that is used to limit your losses. Your at-risk basis is calculated at the end of the year. Losses allowed reduce your at-risk basis. Thus, once you have offset your entire at-risk basis, you cannot claim further losses from the activity until you increase your at-risk basis.

Partners and LLC members are treated as at risk to the extent that basis in the entity is increased by their share of the entity's income. If the partnership or LLC makes distributions of income, the amount distributed reduces the partner's or LLC member's at-risk amount.

If you are subject to the at-risk rules, you must file Form 6198, At-Risk Limitations, to determine the amount of loss you can claim in the current year. You file a separate form for each activity. If you have an interest in a partnership, LLC, or S corporation that has more than one investment in any of the four categories listed, you can aggregate these activities. The four categories subject to these aggregation rules are:

1. Holding, producing, or distributing motion picture films or videotapes
2. Exploring for or exploiting oil and gas properties
3. Exploring for or exploiting geothermal deposits
4. Farming (but not forestry)

For example, if your S corporation distributes films and videotapes, you can aggregate these activities and treat them as one activity. In addition, all leased depreciable business equipment is treated as one activity for purposes of the at-risk rules.

You may also aggregate activities that you actively manage. This allows you to use losses from one activity as long as there is sufficient at-risk basis from another. If you invest in a partnership, LLC, or S corporation, the activities of the entity can be aggregated if 65 percent or more of the losses for the year are allocable to persons who actively participate in the management of the entity.

SPECIAL RULE FOR REAL ESTATE FINANCING. You can treat nonrecourse financing from commercial lenders or government agencies as being at risk if the financing is secured by the real estate. This special rule does not apply to financing from related parties, seller financing, or financing from promoters. It does apply to real property placed in service after 1986. However, if you acquire an interest in a partnership, LLC, or S corporation after 1986, you can use this special rule regardless of when the entity placed the realty in service.

Passive Activity Loss Rules

If you work for your business full-time, you need not be concerned with the *passive activity loss (PAL) rules*. These rules apply only to a business in which you have an ownership interest but do not work in the day-to-day operations or management (i.e., **materially participate**) as well as rental real estate activities.

Passive activity   Any activity involving the conduct of a business in which you do not materially participate and all rental activities. These rules operate to limit a current deduction for losses from these activities unless certain exceptions, discussed later in this chapter, apply.

Material participation   Participation in a passive activity that satisfies one of seven tests set forth in the tax law. The basic test requires a minimum of 500 hours of participation during the year. Material participation may be allowed for as little as 100 hours of participation during the year if no other owner in the activity participates more.

The seven tests for proving material participation include:

1. You participate in the activity for more than 500 hours during the year. You need only participate for a mere 10 hours a week for 50 weeks in the year to satisfy this test.

2. Your participation is substantially all of the participation in the activity of all individuals for the year, including the participation of individuals who did not own any interest in the activity. This means that if you are a sole proprietor and do not hire someone else to run the business, you meet this participation test, even if you work only five hours each week.

3. You participate in the activity for more than 100 hours during the tax year, and you participate at least as much as any other individual (including individuals who do not own any interest in the activity) for the year.

4. The activity is a *significant participation activity*, and you participate in all significant participation activities for more than 500 hours.

A significant participation activity is any business in which you participate for more than 100 hours during the year and in which you did not materially participate under any of the other material participation tests.

5. You materially participated in the activity for any five (whether or not consecutive) of the 10 preceding tax years. This rule can be useful to someone who retires from the business while continuing to own an interest but who materially participated prior to retirement.

6. The activity is a personal service activity in which you materially participated for any three (whether or not consecutive) preceding tax years.

7. Based on all the facts and circumstances, you participate in the activity on a regular, continuous, and substantial basis. At a minimum you must have participated during more than 100 hours. Managing the activity is not treated as participation if any person other than you received compensation for managing it or any individual spent more hours during the year managing the activity than you (regardless of whether such individual was compensated).

RENTAL REAL ESTATE EXCEPTIONS. There are two special rules for rental real estate activities that may allow you to claim losses in excess of rental income.

Rule 1 allows a limited amount of loss in excess of income to be deducted if participation is considered to be active (**active participation**). This limited loss deduction is called the $25,000 allowance and can be claimed by individuals whose adjusted gross income does not exceed $100,000. The allowance is phased out for those with adjusted gross income over $100,000 and is entirely eliminated when adjusted gross income is $150,000 or more. Married couples must file jointly to claim this allowance unless they lived apart for the entire year. In this case, up to $12,500 in losses can be deducted on a separate return (with a phase-out of the allowance for adjusted gross income over $50,000).

Active participation Participation in a rental real estate activity that is less than the material participation standard. Participation in decision making may be sufficient. For example, if you set the rents, screen tenants, and review expenses, you may satisfy the active participation test. Having a managing agent to collect rents and see to property repairs does not prevent active participation by an owner.

Rule 2 allows real estate professionals to escape the PAL limitations altogether for purposes of deducting losses from their rental real estate activities.

Individuals can be considered real estate professionals if they meet certain tests regarding their participation in real estate activities in general, including real estate construction, conversion, management, or brokerage activities, as well as rental real estate. If a qualifying real estate professional then meets material participation tests with respect to the rental real estate, losses from the rental real estate activity escape PAL restrictions. (Details of these rules are in the instructions to Form 8582.)

The PAL rules are very complicated. Determine whether you may be subject to the rules or whether you can ignore them. If you are subject to the rules, be sure you understand the potential impact that they can have on deducting expenses of the activity.

If you run a business or work full time, you need not be concerned with the PAL rules. You will certainly meet the tests for material participation. If you are a silent partner in a partnership, LLC, or S corporation, you should be concerned that you may be subject to the PAL rules. However, you may fall within an exception to the PAL rules in order to deduct losses in excess of income from the activity (for example, you may be able to eke out enough participation to be considered a material participant). Keep a diary or log book noting the time you put into the business and the types of activities you perform for the business.

HOW THE PASSIVE ACTIVITY LOSS RULES LIMIT DEDUCTIONS FOR EXPENSES. If the rules apply, your losses from passive activities that exceed income from all other passive activities cannot be deducted in the current year. You can carry over your unused deductions to future years. These are called *suspended losses*, for which there is no limit on the carryover period.

You can claim all carryover deductions from an activity in the year in which you dispose of your entire interest in the activity. A disposition includes a sale to an unrelated party, abandonment of the business, or the business becoming completely worthless. Simply giving away your interest does not amount to a disposition that allows you to deduct your suspended losses.

The PAL limitation for noncorporate taxpayers is computed on Form 8582, Passive Activity Loss Limitations. Closely held C corporations subject to the PAL rules must file Form 8810, Corporate Passive Activity Loss and Credit Limitations. Similar rules apply to tax credits from passive activities. The limitation on tax credits from passive activities for noncorporate taxpayers is computed on Form 8582-CR, Passive Activity Credit Limitations.

COORDINATION WITH AT-RISK RULES. At-risk rules are applied first. Any amounts that are deductible after applying your at-risk loss limitation are then subject to the passive activity loss rules. Complete Form 6198 first; then complete Form 8582.

Where to Report Business Income

Self-Employed (Including Independent Contractors)

Business income generally is reported on Schedule C, Profit or Loss from Business. The results from this schedule are part of your personal income tax return, Form 1040. You may be able to use a simplified return to report your business income—Schedule C-EZ, Net Profit from Business. You can use the simplified return if you meet *all* of the following requirements:

- You are on the cash method of accounting.
- You do not maintain inventory.
- You do not have any employees.
- Your business expenses do not exceed $5,000.
- You do not place in service any depreciable property during the year.
- You do not claim a home office deduction.
- You show a profit for the year.
- You do not have any other sole proprietorship.
- You do not have any passive activity loss carryovers for this business.

If you maintain inventory, you must complete Part III of Schedule C to figure your cost of goods sold.

In reporting the business' investment-type income, the specific items are not listed on Schedule C. Instead attach a schedule detailing these items and report only the total amount on Schedule C. Be sure to distinguish between your business and personal investment-type income. For example, if you own stock, dividends received on the stock generally are reported as personal, not business, income, unless you are a dealer in securities.

Net operating losses are computed on Form 1045, Application for Tentative Refund. Use this form or Form 1040X to claim a net operating loss (NOL) carryback. If you are carrying forward an NOL, you claim the loss as a negative amount entered on Form 1040 as other income.

Farmers

If you are a sole proprietor operating a farming business, instead of using Schedule C (or C-EZ) to report your income, you use Schedule F, Profit or Loss from Farming. The section of the schedule used to report your farm income depends on your method of accounting. Cash basis farmers use Part I of Schedule F to report income. Accrual basis farmers use Part III of Schedule F to report farm income.

If you received rental income based on farm production or crop shares and you did not materially participate in the management or operation of the farm, use Form 4835, Farm Rental Income and Expenses, to report this rental income. Since you did not materially participate, this income is not part of your farming income on which self-employment tax is assessed. If you elect to income-average your farm income, you must file Schedule J, Farm Income Averaging.

Net operating losses are computed on Form 1045, Application for Tentative Refund. You use this form or Form 1040X to claim an NOL carryback. If you are carrying forward an NOL, you claim the loss as a negative amount entered on Form 1040 as other income.

Partnerships and LLCs

Operating income of a partnership or LLC, called *total income* (loss), is reported on Form 1065, U.S. Partnership Return of Income. For inventory-based partnerships and LLCs, the cost of goods sold is figured on Schedule A of Form 1065.

Miscellaneous income items discussed in this chapter are reported separately from the gross profit, fees, and sales. Miscellaneous items are detailed on a separate schedule attached to the return. Partners and members in LLCs then report their share of net income or loss from the business on Schedule E, Supplemental Income and Loss, as part of their personal return.

Other income items are separately stated items that pass through to partners and members apart from the business' total income, and are reported on Schedule K-1, Partner's Share of Income, Credits, Deductions, Etc. Owners then report these separate items on the appropriate place on their personal returns. For example, items considered to be portfolio income—income other than that derived in the ordinary course of business—are separately stated items.

If the partnership or LLC passes through losses to the partners and members, they may be able to claim an NOL deduction on their personal returns. Refer to the earlier discussion of "Self-Employed."

S Corporations

Operating income of an S corporation is reported on Form 1120S, U.S. Income Tax Return for an S Corporation. For inventory-based S corporations, the cost of goods sold is figured on Schedule A of Form 1120S.

Miscellaneous income items discussed in this chapter are reported separately from the gross profit from fees and sales. These miscellaneous items are detailed on a separate schedule attached to the return. Shareholders then report their share of net income or loss from the business on Schedule E, Supplemental Income and Loss.

Income taxed to the S corporation for LIFO recapture, excessive passive income, or built-in gains is explained on a separate schedule. The tax on this income is then reported on Form 1120S.

Other income items are separately stated items that pass through to shareholders apart from the corporation's total income is reported on Schedule K-1, Shareholder's Share of Income, Credits, Deductions, Etc. Shareholders then report these separate items on the appropriate place on their personal returns. For example, items considered to be portfolio income—income other than income derived in the ordinary course of business—are separately stated items.

If the S corporation passes through losses to the shareholders, it may be able to claim an NOL deduction. Refer to the earlier discussion of "Self-Employed."

C Corporations

C corporations report their income on Form 1120, U.S. Corporation Income Tax Return. For inventory-based corporations, the cost of goods sold is figured on Schedule A of Form 1120. Dividends are reported on Schedule C of Form 1120 to enable the corporation to figure its dividends-received deduction. Tax-exempt interest received or accrued is reported on Schedule K of Form 1120.

Miscellaneous income items, such as recoveries of bad debts deducted in prior years or recapture of the first-year expense deduction, are detailed on a separate schedule attached to the return.

Net operating losses carried from other years to the current year are deducted on the specific line provided for this item on Form 1120. If a corporation has an NOL for the current year, it can obtain a quick refund by filing Form 1139, Corporation Application for Tentative Refund. If it expects to have an NOL in the current year and it will be able to offset tax in the prior year, it can delay the filing of the prior year's return by filing Form 1138, Extension of Time for Payment of Taxes by a Corporation Expecting a Net Operating Loss Carryback. On this form you explain why a loss is expected. The extension is in effect until the end of the month in which the return for the NOL year is due, including extensions. If a corporation wants to forgo the carryback, it must indicate this election by checking the appropriate box in Schedule K, Other Information, of Form 1120.

All Taxpayers

Taxpayers subject to the PAL rules and the at-risk rules must figure any limitations on business losses on specific tax forms. Figure the at-risk loss limits first. Then compute the PAL limits.

AT-RISK LOSS LIMITS.   Only individuals and pass-through entities must figure the at-risk loss limits (closely held C corporations that are active companies are exempt from these rules). The limits are figured on Form 6198, At-Risk Limitations.

PASSIVE ACTIVITY LOSS RULES.   Noncorporate taxpayers compute their PAL limits on Form 8582, Passive Activity Loss Limitations. Closely held C corporations subject to the PAL rules must file Form 8810, Corporate Passive Activity Loss and Credit Limitations.

CHAPTER 5

Capital Gains and Losses

Companies may sell assets other than inventory items. These sales may result in gains or losses that are classified as *capital gains or losses*. Similarly, companies may exchange assets, also producing capital gains or losses unless tax-free exchange rules apply. Further, owners may sell their interests in the business for gain or loss.

Capital gains generally are treated more favorably than other types of income. However, C corporations do not realize any significant tax benefit from capital gains. What's more, capital losses may be subject to special limitations.

In this chapter you will learn about:

- What are capital gains and losses
- Tax treatment of capital gains and losses for pass-through entities
- Tax treatment of capital gains and losses for C corporations
- Loss limitations
- Sales of business interests
- Special situations
- Where to report capital gains and losses

The treatment of gains and losses from Section 1231 property and income resulting from depreciation recapture are discussed in Chapter 6.

For further information about capital gains and losses, see IRS Publication

537, *Installment Sales*, IRS Publication 544, *Sales and Other Dispositions of Assets*, and IRS Publication 550, *Investment Interest and Expenses*.

What Are Capital Gains and Losses

The tax law generally looks more favorably on income classified as capital gains than on other types of income—at least for pass-through entities. On the flip side, the tax law provides special treatment for capital losses. To understand how capital gains and losses affect your business income you need to know what items are subject to capital gain or loss treatment and how to determine gains and losses.

Capital Assets

If you own property used in or owned by your business (other than Section 1231 property discussed in Chapter 6, or Section 1244 stock discussed later in this chapter), gain or loss on the disposition of the property generally is treated as capital gain or loss. *Capital gains and losses* are gains and losses taken on **capital assets**.

Capital assets   Property held for investment and other property not otherwise excluded from capital asset treatment. For example, your interest in a partnership or stocks and securities is treated as a capital asset.

Most property is treated as capital assets. Excluded from the definition of capital assets are:

- Property held for sale to customers or property that will physically become part of merchandise for sale to customers (inventory)
- Accounts or notes receivable generated by your business (e.g., accounts receivable from the sale of inventory)
- Depreciable property used in your business, even if already fully depreciated (e.g., telephones)
- Real property used in your business (e.g., your factory)
- A copyright; literary, musical, or artistic composition; a letter or memorandum; or other similar property (e.g., photographs, tapes, manuscripts) created by your personal efforts or acquired from the creator by gift or in another transaction entitling you to use the creator's basis
- U.S. government publications

Determining the Amount of Your Gain or Loss

The difference between the **amount received** for your property on a sale, exchange, or other disposition, and your **adjusted basis** in the property is your gain or loss.

Amount received The cash, fair market value of property, and relief of liability you get when you dispose of your property. For example, if you own a computer system for your business and you upgrade with a new system and sell your old system to another business, any cash you receive is considered an amount received. Upon the sale, you receive $5,000 cash, plus the buyer agrees to pay the remaining balance of $2,000 on a bank loan you took to buy the system; your amount received is $7,000 ($5,000 cash, plus $2,000 liability relieved).

Adjusted basis This is your basis in the property, adjusted for certain items. Start with the original cost if you bought the property (the cash and other property you paid to acquire it). Even if the cash did not come out of your pocket—for example, if you took a loan—the cash you turn over to the seller is part of your basis. Adjust the basis by reducing it for any depreciation claimed (or that could have been claimed) and any casualty loss you claimed with respect to the property. For example, if your original computer system cost you $10,000, and you claimed $2,000 depreciation, your adjusted basis is $8,000.

You adjust basis—upward or downward—for certain items occurring in the acquisition of the asset or during the time you hold it. Amounts that *increase* basis include:

- Improvements or additions to property
- Legal fees to acquire property or defend title to it
- Selling expenses (e.g., a real estate broker's fee or advertising costs)
- Unharvested crops sold with the land

Amounts that *decrease* basis include:

- Amortized bond premiums
- Cancellation of income adjustments (e.g., debt forgiveness because of bankruptcy or insolvency or on farm or business real property)
- Casualty losses that have been deducted (e.g., insurance awards and other settlements)
- Depletion allowances with respect to certain natural resources

- Depreciation, amortization, first-year expensing, and obsolescence. (You must reduce the basis of property by the amount of depreciation that you were entitled to take even if you failed to take it.)

- Investment credit claimed with respect to the property. (The full credit decreases basis but one half of the credit claimed after 1982 is added back for a net reduction of one-half of the credit.)

- Return of capital. (Dividends on stock are paid out of capital or out of a depletion reserve instead of earnings and profits or surplus.)

You do not adjust basis for selling expenses and related costs. These amounts are factored into the amount received (they reduce the amount received on the transaction).

DETERMINING BASIS ON ASSETS TRANSFERRED BETWEEN YOU AND YOUR ENTITY. The entity takes over your basis in any assets you contribute in a nontaxable transaction. Thus, if you contribute property to your partnership, the partnership assumes your basis in the property. Similarly, if you contribute property to your corporation as part of a tax-free incorporation, the corporation takes over your basis in the property. The rules for determining the basis in interests in pass-through entities are explained in Chapter 4.

FIGURING GAIN OR LOSS.   When the amount received exceeds the adjusted basis of the property, you have a gain. When the adjusted basis exceeds the amount received, you have a loss.

Sale or Exchange Requirement

In order to obtain capital gain or loss treatment on the disposition of a capital asset, you generally must sell or exchange property. Typically, you sell your property, but other transactions may qualify for sale or exchange treatment. For example, if your corporation redeems some or all of your stock, you may be able to treat the redemption as a sale or exchange. Capital losses are subject to limitation on current deductibility as explained later in this chapter.

If you dispose of property in some way other than a sale or exchange, gain or loss generally is treated as ordinary gain or loss. For example, if you abandon business property, your loss is treated as ordinary loss, even though the property is a capital asset. However, if the property is foreclosed on or repossessed, your loss may be a capital loss. Ordinary losses are deductible without regard to the results from other transactions and can be used to offset various types of income (such as interest income).

Holding Period

Whether gains and losses are short-term or long-term depends on how long the asset disposed of has been held. If the holding period is more than one year, then gain or loss is long-term. If the holding period is one year or less, then the gain or loss is short-term.

If the business buys an asset, the holding period commences at that time (technically on the day after the acquisition date). If you transfer property to your business, the company's holding period includes your holding period if the transfer is viewed as a nonrecognition transaction (for example, a tax-free incorporation).

Example

You form a corporation and transfer ownership of your truck and other items to the corporation in exchange for all of its stock. You acquired your truck on June 1, 2004, and transfer it to the corporation on July 1, 2005. On November 1, 2005, the corporation sells the truck. Its gain or loss on the sale of the truck is long-term because the holding period for the truck is more than one year—measured from the time you acquired it.

If a partnership makes an in kind (property) distribution to you, include the partnership's holding period in your holding period. However, if the distribution is from the partnership's inventory, then you cannot add the partnership's holding period to yours if you sell the property within five years.

TRANSFERS TO A PARTNERSHIP OR LIMITED LIABILITY COMPANY. If you transfer an asset to your company, the company takes on your holding period since this is a nontaxable transaction. If you sell an asset to your company, the company starts its own holding period since the sale generally is a taxable transaction (the company obtains a stepped up basis for the property).

Tax-Free Exchanges

Gain need not be immediately reported as income if the transaction qualifies as a tax-free exchange. The term *tax-free* is not an entirely apt description because the tax rules for these transactions merely *postpone* the reporting of gain rather than make gain permanently tax free. You reduce the basis of the property you acquire in the exchange by the gain you realized on the trade but did not have to report. Then, when you later sell the replacement property in a taxable transaction, you will report the gain on both initial exchange and the later disposition (if any).

To qualify for the tax-free exchange treatment, both the old property (the property you are giving up) and the new property (the property you are acquiring, called *replacement property*) must be business or investment property (certain property cannot be exchanged tax free). And both of the properties must be *like kind*. This means they must be of the same class of

Example

You exchange one office building for another of equal value. Your building is worth $175,000, but has a basis of $100,000. The value of the new building is $175,000. You have a gain of $75,000, which may be postponed because of the tax-free exchange rules. The basis in the new building is $100,000 ($175,000 minus $75,000 gain not recognized). If you sell the new building in the future for $225,000, you will recognize gain of $125,000 ($75,000 deferred from the initial exchange, plus $50,000 from the appreciation of the replacement building).

property. Depreciable tangible personal property can be either like kind or *like class* (the same General Asset Class or Product Class based on the four-digit codes in the Industrial Classification Manual of the U.S. Department of Commerce). Examples of like-kind property include:

- Vacant lot for a factory building
- Factory building for an office complex
- City property for farmland
- Real estate owned outright for real estate subject to a lease of 30 years or more
- Pickup truck for a panel truck used in the business
- Telephone equipment for computer equipment used in the business

If non–like-kind property is also received in the exchange, you must recognize gain to the extent of this other property, called *boot*.

Example

Use the example of the building, except that the replacement building is only valued at $150,000 and you receive $25,000 cash to make the exchange of equal value. You must recognize gain of $25,000, the extent of the boot received. The basis of the replacement building in this case is reduced by only $50,000, and the gain not recognized.

TIMING. Like-kind exchanges must be completed within set time limits. The new property must be identified within 45 days after you transfer the old property. This identification applies to up to three properties (or any number where the value of the properties is not more than double the value of the property given up). To identify the property, a good description of it must be put in writing. *Incidental property*, property valued at not more than 15 percent of the total value of the other property, is disregarded; it need not be identified. Then, the exchange must be completed (you must receive the new property) within 180 days after you transfer the old property or the due date of your return (including extensions) for the year you gave up the old property if this is earlier than 180 days after the transfer.

Since it is not always easy to locate appropriate exchange property, you may work with a qualified intermediary to locate the property, acquire it, and then exchange it with you. A *qualified intermediary* is someone (other than your attorney, accountant, broker, employee, or a related person) who makes a written agreement to acquire the property you are giving up and to transfer replacement property to you. The agreement must limit your rights to receive, pledge, borrow, or otherwise obtain the benefits of money or other property held by the qualified intermediary.

Installment Sales

Gain need not be reported all at once if the sale is structured as an installment sale. This generally allows you to report gain as payments are received. An *installment sale* occurs when at least one payment is received after the year of sale.

Under the installment method, a portion of each payment received represents a return of your investment (part of your adjusted basis) and another part represents your profit (gain). You figure the amount of gain reported each year by a ratio:

$$\text{Gross profit percentage (reportable gain)} = \frac{\text{Gross profit}}{\text{Selling price (contract price)}}$$

ELECTION OUT OF INSTALLMENT REPORTING.   You can opt out of installment reporting and elect to report the entire gain in the year of sale (even though payments will be received at a later time). The election does not require any special forms. You simply report your entire gain in the year of sale. But once you do so, you generally cannot change your mind later on, even if your choice proved to be the wrong one tax-wise.

Example

You sell property worth $100,000 for five annual installments of $20,000, plus 8 percent interest. Your adjusted basis in the property is $60,000 so your gross profit is $40,000 ($100,000 − $60,000). Your gross profit percentage is 40 percent ($40,000 ÷ $100,000). This means that 40 percent of each installment represents your gain while 60 percent is a return of your investment. Thus, in the first year, $8,000 of the $20,000 payment is gain while $12,000 is a return of your investment.

Why would you want to report all of your gain in one year when you can spread it out over a number of years? Reporting the entire gain in the year of sale may be wise, for example, if you have a net operating loss carryforward that can be used to offset the gain.

INTEREST ON DEFERRED PAYMENTS.   Payments must bear a reasonable rate of interest. If you fail to fix a reasonable rate of interest, then a portion of each payment is deemed to represent interest rather than capital gain. *Reasonable rate of interest* usually is the applicable federal rate (AFR) of interest for the term of the installment sale. (Applicable federal rate is explained in Chapter 7.)

If the seller finances the purchase, the required minimum interest rate is the lower of 9 percent ("safe harbor rate") compounded semiannually or the AFR, provided the financed amount does not exceed $4,483,000 in 2005. With interest rates running below the 9 percent safe harbor rate, charging the AFR will produce a lower allowable interest rate. If the deferred amount exceeds $4,483,000, then the required minimum interest rate is 100 percent of the AFR.

DEPRECIABLE PROPERTY.   If you sell depreciable property on the installment basis, any depreciation recapture must be reported in full in the year of sale regardless of when payments are actually received. In other words, gain resulting from depreciation recapture may exceed the cash payments received in the year of the installment sale but must be reported as income anyway. Installment sales are also discussed in Chapter 2.

Tax Treatment of Capital Gains and Losses for Pass-Through Entities

Capital gains and losses are separately stated items that pass through separately to owners. They are not taken into account in figuring the entity's total income (or loss). The reason for this distinction is to allow individual owners to apply the capital gain and loss rules on individual tax returns.

The impact of pass-through treatment of capital gains and losses is that owners may have favorable capital gains rates applied to their share of the business's capital gains. Similarly they may offset pass-through gains and losses from their business against their personal gains and losses.

Example

In 2005, a shareholder in an S corporation has pass-through capital loss from his corporation of $10,000. He also has a $10,000 capital gain distribution from a mutual fund he owns in his personal investment account. He can offset the business gain by his personal loss on his individual income tax return.

Tax Rates on Capital Gains

Owners who are individuals pay tax on their share of capital gains as they would on their gains from personal investments. Thus, long-term capital gains generally are subject to a basic capital gains rate of 15 percent. However, owners in the 10-percent and 15-percent tax brackets pay only 5 percent on their share of capital gains (zero tax in 2008). These rates apply to sales and exchanges in 2005 as well as to payments received on installment sales made in prior years.

SHORT-TERM GAIN.   This type of gain is subject to the same tax rates as ordinary income. Owners in a pass-through entity may pay different tax rates on the same share of short-term capital gain.

Example

An LLC with two equal owners sells at a profit a capital asset held for six months. In 2005, one owner may be in the 35-percent tax bracket while another is in the 25-percent tax bracket. Even though each owner receives an equal share of the gain, one owner pays a greater amount of tax on that gain than the other according to each owner's own tax bracket.

UNRECAPTURED GAIN.   Gain from the sale of real property on which straight line depreciation was taken results in unrecaptured gain (the amount of straight line depreciation). This portion of capital gain is taxed at the rate of 25 percent if the owner is in a tax bracket higher than the 15-percent tax bracket.

If property with unrecaptured gain is sold on the installment basis (discussed later in this chapter), then the first payment is deemed to reflect unrecaptured gain. When this amount has been fully reported, all additional amounts are capital gains subject to the lower rates detailed above.

CAPITAL LOSSES.   Special rules determine how capital losses of individuals may be used. These rules are discussed later in this chapter.

Tax Treatment of Capital Gains and Losses for C Corporations

C corporations must follow the rules discussed throughout this chapter on reporting capital gains and losses separately from their other income. These gains and losses are detailed on the corporation's Schedule D. However, C corporations at present realize no benefit from capital gains. *Net gains*, capital gains in excess of capital losses, are simply added to other business income. In effect, capital gains are taxed at the same rate of the corporation's other income. In the past, C corporations enjoyed a favorable tax rate on their capital gains and it may be possible that this treatment will be restored in the future.

While there are no benefits from capital gains, capital losses of C corporations are subject to special limitations discussed later in this chapter.

Loss Limitations

In some cases, even if you sell or exchange property at a loss, you may not be permitted to deduct your loss. If you sell, exchange, or even abandon a Section 197 intangible (see Chapter 14 for a complete discussion of the amortization of Section 197 intangibles), you cannot deduct your loss if you still hold other Section 197 intangibles that you acquired in the same transaction. Instead, you increase the basis of the Section 197 intangibles that you still own. This means that instead of deducting your loss in the year you dispose of one Section 197 intangible, you will deduct a portion of the loss over the remaining recovery period for the Section 197 intangibles you still hold.

Similarly, you cannot deduct losses on sales or exchanges of property between related parties (defined later). This related party rule prevents you from deducting a loss if you sell a piece of equipment to your spouse. However, the party acquiring the property from you (the original transferee, or in this case, your spouse) can add to the basis the amount of loss you were not allowed to deduct in determining gain or loss on a subsequent disposition of the property.

Example

You sell your partnership interest to your daughter for $7,500. Your basis in the interest is $10,000. You cannot deduct your $2,500 loss. However, if your daughter then sells the partnership interest for $12,000, her gain is minimized to the extent of your nondeductible loss. Her tentative gain is $4,500 ($12,000 amount received less basis of $7,500). The amount of gain she must report is $2,000 ($4,500 tentative gain less $2,500 nondeductible loss).

Related Parties

The tax law defines who is considered a *related party*. This includes not only certain close relatives (spouses, siblings, parents, children, grandparents, and grandchildren), but also certain businesses you control. A *controlled entity* is a corporation in which you own, directly or indirectly, more than 50 percent of the value of all outstanding stock, or a partnership in which you own, directly or indirectly, more than 50 percent of the capital interest or profits interest.

Businesses may be treated as related parties. These relationships include:

- A corporation and partnership if the same persons own more than 50 percent in the value of the outstanding stock of the corporation and more than 50 percent of the capital interest or profits interest in the partnership.
- Two corporations that are members of the same controlled group (one corporation owns a certain percentage of the other, or owners own a certain percentage of each corporation).
- Two S corporations if the same persons own more than 50 percent in value of the outstanding stock in each corporation.
- Two corporations, one of which is an S corporation, if the same person owns more than 50 percent in value of the outstanding stock of each corporation.
- Special rules are used to determine control. These rules not only look at actual ownership but also take into account certain constructive ownership (ownership that is not actual but has the same effect in the eyes of the tax law). For example, for purposes of the related party rule, you are treated as constructively owning any stock owned by your spouse.

Special rules also apply to transactions between partners and their partnerships. It is important to note that what you may view as a related party may not be treated as such for tax purposes. Thus, for example, your in-laws and cousins are not treated as related parties. If you sell property to an in-law or cousin at a loss, you are not prevented from deducting the loss.

Loss Limits on Individuals

You can deduct capital losses against capital gains without limit. Short-term losses from sales of assets held one year or less are first used to offset short-term gains otherwise taxed up to 35 percent in 2005. Similarly, long-term losses from sales of assets held more than one year offset long-term gains otherwise taxed as low as 15 percent (5 percent for those in the 10-percent and 15-percent tax brackets), depending on when the transaction occurred. Losses in excess of their category are then used to offset gains starting with those taxed at the highest rates. For example, short-term losses in excess of short-term capital gains can be used to offset long-term capital gains from the sale of qualified small business stock, 50 percent of such gain of which is otherwise taxed at up to 28 percent (for an effective tax rate of 14 percent). However, if your capital losses exceed your capital gains, you can deduct only $3,000 of losses against your other income (such as salaries, dividends, and interest income).

If married persons file separate returns, the capital loss offset to other income is limited to $1,500. If you do not use up all of your capital losses, you can carry over any unused amount and claim it in future years. There is no limit on the carryover period for individuals.

Loss Limits on Corporations

If your corporation realizes capital losses, they are deductible only against capital gains. Any capital losses in excess of capital gains can be carried back for three years and then, if not used up, carried forward for up to five years. If they are not used within the five-year carryover period, they are lost forever.

The carryback may entitle your corporation to a refund of taxes from the carryback years. The corporation can apply for this refund by filing Form 1120X, Amended U.S. Corporation Income Tax Return. A corporation cannot choose to forgo the carryback in order to simply carry forward the unused capital losses.

Special rules apply in calculating the corporation's carryback and carryforward. You do not use any capital loss carried from another year when determining the corporation's capital loss deduction for the current year. If you have losses from more than one year carried to another year, you use the losses as follows: First, deduct the loss from the earliest year. After that is fully deducted, deduct the loss from the next earliest year. You cannot use a capital loss carried from another year to produce or increase a net operating loss (NOL) in the year to which you carry it.

Sales of Business Interests

The type of interest you own governs the tax treatment accorded to the sale of your interest.

Sole Proprietorship

If you sell your incorporated sole proprietorship, you are viewed as selling the assets of the business. The sale of all the assets of a business are discussed in Chapter 6.

Partnerships and LLCs

PARTNERSHIPS. Gain or loss on the sale of your partnership interest is treated as capital gain *except* to the extent any gain relates to **unrealized receivables** and inventory items. Gain in this case is ordinary income.

Unrealized receivables These are amounts not previously included in income that represent a right to payments for noncapital assets, which include inventory, services rendered, and services to be rendered.

If you receive items that were inventory to the partnership, they may be treated as capital assets to you. However, if you dispose of the items within five years, then any gain with respect to these items is ordinary income, not capital gain.

LLCs. Generally, the rules governing the sale of a partnership interest apply with equal force to the sale of an interest in an LLC. However, there are two special situations to consider:

1. *Sale of multiple-owner LLC to a single buyer.* The entity is treated as making a liquidating distribution of all of its assets to its owners. This means that gain in excess of basis is capital gain *except* to the extent of unrealized receivables and substantially appreciated inventory. Losses on a liquidating distribution can be recognized if only cash is received and it is less than your basis in your interest or cash, unrealized receivables or substantially appreciated inventory are distributed and they are less than your basis in your interest.

2. *Sale of a single-member LLC to multiple buyers.* This entity is treated as selling its assets and then contributing them to the new entity comprised of multiple buyers (treated as a partnership). You recognize gain or loss on the deemed sale of your interest to the buyers. There is no gain or loss recognition upon the contribution of the assets to the new entity.

S and C Corporations

When you sell your stock in a corporation, you recognize capital gain or loss. The amount of your gain or loss is the difference between your adjusted basis in the stock and the amount received in exchange.

If another corporation acquires 80 percent or more of the stock in your corporation within a 12-month period, it can elect to treat the stock purchase as if they had purchased the underlying asset. If so, your corporation must recognize gain or loss as if it had sold its assets for fair market value. From the buyer's perspective, this enables the corporation to step-up the basis of its assets as if it were a new corporation. The purchase price is allocated to the assets as explained in Chapter 6.

Special Situations

Sale of Qualified Business Stock

Tax laws encourage investments in small businesses by offering unique tax incentives. If you own stock in a corporation treated as a **small business**, you may be able to defer your gain or exclude it entirely.

> *Small business*   For purposes of deferring or excluding gain on the sale of stock, a small business is a C corporation with gross assets of no more than $50 million when the stock is issued. The small business must be an active business and not a mere holding company. The stock must have been issued after August 10, 1993.

There are many conditions surrounding this exclusion:

- It applies only to stock issued by a small business after August 10, 1993;
- As of the date the stock was issued, the corporation was a qualified small business (see definition);
- The company must be a C corporation (not an S corporation);
- You must have acquired the stock at its original issue, either in exchange for money or other property, or as pay for services;
- During substantially all of the time you held the stock:
  - The corporation was a C corporation;
  - At least 80 percent of the value of the corporation's assets were used in the active conduct of one or more qualified businesses; and
  - The corporation was not a foreign corporation, domestic international sales corporation (DISC), former DISC, regulated investment company, real estate investment trust, real estate mortgage investment conduit (REMIC), financial asset securitization investment trust (FASIT), cooperative, or a corporation that has made a section 936 election.

DEFERRING GAIN.   If you own stock in a small business for more than six months and sell it, you can defer any tax on the gain—called Section 1202 gain after the section in the Internal Revenue Code—by acquiring other small business stock within 60 days of the sale. If you reinvest only part of your proceeds, you can defer gain to the extent of your reinvestment.

EXCLUDING GAIN.   If you own stock in a small business for more than five years, and sell it you can exclude one-half of your gain. The other half of the gain that is taxable is subject to tax at up to a 28 percent capital gain tax rate (unless you are in the 10-percent or 15-percent tax bracket). Thus, the effective tax rate on the sale of small business stock is 14 percent (50 percent of 28 percent).

The exclusion increases to 60 percent for gain with respect to empowerment zone business stock. To qualify for the higher exclusion, you must meet two additional requirements:

1. You sell or trade stock in a corporation that qualifies as an empowerment zone business during substantially all of the time you held the

stock. Empowerment zone businesses are explained in Chapter 7 with respect to the empowerment zone employment credit.

2. You acquired the stock after December 21, 2000.

The amount of the exclusion related to stock from a particular company is limited to the greater of 10 times your basis in the stock or $10 million ($5 million if married filing separately) minus any gain on stock from the same company excluded in a prior year.

> **CAUTION**
>
> The excluded gain is a tax preference for the alternative minimum tax (AMT). This means that individuals subject to the AMT lose part of the exclusion. See Chapter 26.

> **Note**
>
> Even though the individual tax rates have declined, the 28 percent rate on Section 1202 gains remains at up to 28 percent. Thus, individuals in tax brackets over 28 percent will pay this rate on their 1202 gains.

DEFERRING GAIN FROM PUBLICLY TRADED SECURITIES BY INVESTING IN A SPECIALIZED SMALL BUSINESS INVESTMENT COMPANY. If you own publicly traded securities, gain from their sale can be deferred by rolling over the proceeds into qualified small business stock. In this case qualified small business stock is stock or a partnership interest in a specialized small business investment company (SSBIC). The rollover must be completed within 60 days. The amount of the gain deferred under this option reduces the basis in the stock or partnership interest you acquire.

This deferral option is limited annually to $50,000 ($25,000 if married filing separately). This deferral option has a lifetime limit of $500,000 ($250,000 if married filing separately).

Zero Percent Gain from Community Renewal Property

If you own a community renewal business that invests in business assets within a specialty designated renewal community and hold the assets for more than five years, you do not have to pay *any* tax on your gain (40 authorized community renewal areas have been designated by the Secretaries of Housing and Urban Development and Agriculture). However, any portion of the gain attributable to periods before January 1, 2002, is ineligible for this special treatment and is taxed in the usual way. The zero percent capital gain rate will not apply to property acquired after December 31, 2009.

Section 1244 losses

If you own stock in a company considered to be a small business and you realize a loss on this stock, you may be able to treat the loss as an ordinary loss (within set limits). This loss is referred to as a *Section 1244 loss* because it is the section in the Internal Revenue Code.

Ordinary loss treatment applies to both common stock issued at any time and preferred stock issued after July 18, 1984. You can claim an ordinary loss if you sell or exchange the stock or if it becomes worthless. This special tax rule for small business stock presents another win-win situation for owners. If the company does well and a disposition of the stock produces a gain, it is treated as capital gain. If the company does not do well and the disposition of the stock results in a loss, the loss is treated as ordinary loss, which is fully deductible against your other income (such as salary, dividends, and interest income).

QUALIFYING FOR ORDINARY LOSS TREATMENT.   The corporation issuing the stock must be a small business. This means that it can have equity of no more than $1 million at the time the stock is issued. This equity is the amount of cash or other property invested in the company in exchange for the stock. The stock must be issued for cash and property other than stock and securities. This definition of small business stock applies only to the loss deduction under Section 1244. Other definitions of small business stock apply for other purposes under the tax law.

You must acquire the stock by purchase. The ordinary loss deduction is allowed only to the original purchaser of the stock. If you inherit stock in a small business, receive it as a gift, or buy it from someone who was the original purchaser of the stock, you do not qualify for ordinary loss treatment.

Most important, the corporation must have derived over half its gross receipts during the five years preceding the year of your loss from business operations, and not from passive income. If the corporation is in business for less than five years, then only the years in which it is in business are considered. If the corporation's deductions (other than for dividends received and NOL) exceed gross income, the five-year requirement is waived.

LIMIT ON ORDINARY LOSS DEDUCTION.   You can treat only the first $50,000 of your loss on small business stock as an ordinary loss. The limit is raised to $100,000 on a joint return, even if only one spouse owned the stock. However, losses in excess of these dollar limits can be treated as capital losses, as discussed earlier in this chapter.

The ordinary loss deduction can be claimed only by individuals. If a partnership owns Section 1244 stock and sustains a loss, an ordinary loss deduction can be claimed by individuals who were partners when the stock was issued. If the partnership distributes stock to partners and the partners then realize a loss on the stock, they cannot treat the loss as an ordinary loss.

If an S corporation owns Section 1244 stock and sustains a loss, it cannot pass the loss through to its shareholders in the same way that partnerships can pass the loss through to their partners. Even though S corporation shareholders receive tax treatment similar to that of partners, one court that has considered this question concluded that the language of the tax law results in a difference in this instance. The denial of an ordinary loss deduction for Section 1244 stock is one important way in which the tax treatment differs between partnerships and S corporations.

Worthless Securities

If you buy stock or bonds (collectively called *securities*) in a corporation and they become worthless, special tax rules apply. In general, loss on a security that becomes worthless is treated as a capital loss. If the stock is Section 1244 stock, you can claim an ordinary loss deduction, as explained earlier.

To claim a deduction, you must be able to show that the securities are completely worthless. If they still have some value, you cannot claim the loss. You must show that there is no reasonable possibility of receiving repayment on a bond or any value for your stock. Insolvency of the corporation issuing the security is certainly indicative of worthlessness. However, even if a corporation is insolvent, there may still be some value to your securities. The corporation may be in a bankruptcy restructuring arrangement designed to make the corporation solvent again someday. In this instance, the securities are not considered to be worthless.

You can claim a deduction for worthless securities only in the year in which worthlessness occurs. Since it is difficult to pinpoint when worthlessness occurs, you have some flexibility. The tax law allows you seven years to go back and amend a prior return to claim a deduction for worthless securities.

Example

In 2006 you learn that stock you owned in a business became worthless in 2002. In general, you have seven years from the due date of your 2002 return, or April 15, 2010, to amend your 2002 return to claim the loss deduction.

If you own stock in a publicly held corporation, it is advisable to check with a securities broker to see whether there has been some definite event to fix the time of worthlessness. If you are unsure whether a security actually became worthless in a particular year, consider claiming it anyway. You can renew your claim in a subsequent year if the facts show worthlessness did, in fact, occur in that subsequent year. If you fail to claim the loss in the earlier year and that year proves to be the year of worthlessness, your claim may be lost forever.

If you own stock in an S corporation that becomes worthless, you must first adjust the basis in the stock for your share of corporate items of income, loss, and deductions. If there is any excess basis remaining, you can then claim the excess as a loss on worthless securities.

Where to Report Capital Gains and Losses

Employees

Employees may buy stock in their employer (or acquire it through stock options or as compensation). When this stock is disposed of at a loss (or it becomes worthless), the loss may be a capital loss or an ordinary loss on Section 1244 stock. Capital losses are reported on Schedule D and are carried over to page one of Form 1040. An ordinary loss on Section 1244 stock is reported in Part II of Form 4797. The results of Form 4797 are then reported on page one of Form 1040. If you need to amend a tax return to claim a deduction for worthless securities, file Form 1040X, Amended U.S Individual Income Tax Return.

Self-Employed

Self-employed individuals report any capital gains and losses on their personal Schedule D—there is no special reporting for the business since these assets are viewed as personal assets, not business assets, even if acquired with business profits.

Partnerships and LLCs

Capital gains and losses are separately stated items that are not taken into account in calculating ordinary business income or loss. However, the entity figures the net amount of capital gains or losses on its own Schedule D. The net amount is then entered on Schedule K, and the partners' or members' allocable share of the capital gains or losses is reported to them on Schedule K-1.

Gain on the sale of qualified small business stock is reported as a gain such to the 28 percent tax rate (although 50 percent of the gain is excluded as explained in this chapter) and is passed through as such. Partners and members must have held their interest in the entity on the date that the pass-through entity acquired the qualified small business stock *and* at all times until the stock was sold in order to qualify for the exclusion.

S Corporations

Capital gains and losses are separately stated items that are not taken into account in figuring the S corporation's ordinary income or loss. However, the corporation figures its net amount of capital gain or loss on its own Schedule D. The net amount is entered on Schedule K, and the shareholder's allocable share of the gain or loss is reported to them on Schedule K-1.

Gain on the sale of qualified small business stock is reported as a gain such to the 28 percent tax rate (although 50 percent of the gain is excluded as explained in this chapter) and is passed through as such. Shareholders must have held their interest in the corporation on the date that it acquired the qualified small business stock *and* at all times until the stock was sold in order to qualify for the exclusion.

Built-in capital gains of the S corporation, however, are *not* passed through to shareholders since they are taxed to the corporation. They are reported on a separate part of Schedule D. The computation of built-in gains is made on a separate attachment (of your own making). If there is an excess of recognized built-in gain over recognized built-in losses for the year and this net amount exceeds taxable income (figured without regard to this net gain), the tax is figured on the net amount. It can be reduced by business credit and minimum tax credit carryforwards from years in which the corporation was a C corporation. The tax is then entered on Form 1120S.

C Corporations

Capital gains and losses are reported on the corporation's Schedule D. The net amount of gain or loss is entered on Form 1120 on the line provided for capital gain net income. If there is a net loss, then the corporation must apply its own limitations on capital losses, as explained in this chapter. If the corporation discovers that it suffered a loss from worthless securities in a prior year and wants to file an amended return, use Form 1120X, Amended U.S. Corporation Income Tax Return.

Tax-Free Exchanges

Regardless of your form of business organization, all tax-free exchanges are reported on Form 8824, Tax-Free Exchanges. Any gain resulting from the exchange is then carried to the appropriate tax schedule or form for the entity. For example, if your C corporation makes a tax-free exchange of capital gain property (other than Section 1231) that results in a gain, the gain is then reported on the corporation's Schedule D. Tax-free exchanges involving Section 1231 property are reported on Form 4797, Sales of Business Property, discussed in Chapter 6.

Installment Sales

Regardless of your form of business organization, all installment sales are reported on Form 6252, Installment Sales. The gain reported in the current year is then carried to the appropriate tax schedule or form for the entity. For example, if your C corporation makes an installment sale of capital gain property (other than Section 1231) that results in a gain, the gain is then reported the corporation's Schedule D. Installment sales involving Section 1231 property are reported on Form 4797, Sales of Business Property, discussed further in Chapter 6.

Gains and Losses from Sales of Business Property

Businesses hold a unique category of assets called *Section 1231 property*. This category is named after the section in the Internal Revenue Code that created them. Upon the disposition of these assets, you can realize the best of both possible worlds—capital gain treatment for profitable sales and ordinary loss treatment for sales that result in a loss. Gain may be recognized all at once or deferred through an installment sale.

You may also realize gains or losses from other transactions involving business property, including involuntary conversions, abandonment or repossession of property, or the sale of all of the assets of the business.

Complex rules govern the overall treatment of these transactions. (The treatment of capital gains and losses from other property is also discussed in Chapter 5.) The purpose of this chapter is to alert you to the basic rules governing certain sales of business property. If any transaction applies to your business, you may wish to delve deeper with the assistance of a tax professional.

In this chapter you will learn about:

- Section 1231 gains and losses
- Installment sales
- Recapture
- Involuntary conversions

- Abandonment, foreclosure, and repossession of property
- Sale of all the assets of the business
- Where to report gains and losses on business property

For further information about capital gains and losses, see IRS Publication 537, *Installment Sales*, and IRS Publication 544, *Sales and Other Dispositions of Assets*.

Section 1231 Gains and Losses

Certain assets used in business are granted special tax treatment. This treatment seeks to provide a win-win situation for a business. If a sale or other disposition of these assets (called **Section 1231 property**) results in a net gain, the gain can be treated as capital gain. If a net loss results, the loss is an ordinary loss.

Section 1231 property   **Property held for more than one year and used in a business or held for the production of rents or royalties.**

Examples of **Section 1231 property** include:

- Real property and depreciable personal property (such as equipment)
- Leaseholds
- Timber, coal, and iron ore
- Certain livestock and unharvested crops

Gains or losses due to casualty, theft, or condemnation may also be treated as Section 1231 gains or losses if the property was held for more than one year. Section 1231 property does *not* include:

- Inventory or other property held for sale to customers
- Copyrights; literary, musical, or artistic compositions; letters or memoranda; or similar property created by your efforts
- Government publications

Determining Section 1231 Gains or Losses

You must use a *netting process* to determine your Section 1231 gains or losses. This means combining all gains and losses from the sale or other disposition of Section 1231 property. If your Section 1231 gains exceed your Section 1231 losses, then all of your gains and losses are treated as capital gains and losses. On the other hand, if your Section 1231 losses equal or exceed your Section 1231 gains, all of your gains and losses are treated as ordinary gains and losses.

If you sell appreciated Section 1231 property to a *related party*, gain that would otherwise be capital gain is recharacterized as ordinary income if the property is depreciable property in the hands of the buyer. Related parties for this purpose means a person and all entities that are controlled entities. A *controlled entity* is:

- A corporation with more than 50 percent of the value of the outstanding stock that is owned, directly or indirectly, by you.
- A partnership with more than 50 percent of the capital interest or profits interest that is owned, directly or indirectly, by you.
- Two corporations that are members of a controlled group.
- A corporation and a partnership if the same person owns more than 50 percent of the value of the stock and more than 50 percent of the capital interest or profit interest in the partnership.
- An S corporation and another S corporation where the same person owns more than 50 percent of each.

LOSSES. The fact that your Section 1231 losses for the year equal or exceed Section 1231 gains does not automatically ensure ordinary loss treatment. You must check to see whether a special recapture rule applies. Under the recapture rule, net Section 1231 gain is treated as ordinary income to the extent it does not exceed **nonrecaptured** net Section 1231 **losses** taken in prior years.

Nonrecaptured losses   Total of net Section 1231 losses for the five most recent preceding tax years that have not been applied (recaptured) against any net Section 1231 gains in those years.

The recapture rules for Section 1231 gains and losses are extremely complex. They are designed to prevent you from being able to time gains and losses from year to year so that you take your gains as capital gains and your losses as ordinary losses. (Do not confuse these recapture rules with those that apply to depreciation which are discussed later in this chapter.) The recapture rules, in effect, treat your gains and losses as occurring in the same year so that what would ordinarily have been treated as capital gains is partially or fully treated as ordinary income.

As you can see from the example, losses are recaptured beginning with the earliest year subject to recapture.

Installment Sales

If you sell property and receive at least one payment after the year of sale, you have automatically transacted an installment sale. You report your gain over the period in which you receive payment *unless* you elect to report all of the gain in the year of sale. Installment reporting does not apply to losses. This is called the installment method. You can use it regardless of your other accounting method for reporting income. Installment reporting does not affect the amount of gain you report, nor the characterization of that gain. It merely affects the timing of reporting the gain. Installment reporting is explained in greater detail in Chapter 2.

Recapture

If part of the gain on an installment sale relates to depreciation recapture, this gain must be reported up front, regardless of the payments received.

Recapture

Certain write-offs you may take can come back to haunt you. The benefit you enjoy now may have to be repaid at a later time. For instance, if you claim certain *depreciation* on business assets (explained in Chapter 14)—a write-off of the cost of the assets over a set time—you must *recapture* the benefit when you dispose of the assets. Recapture in some instances is merely a matter of recharacterizing gain—instead of capital gain the recapture amount is treated as ordinary income. However, in other instances, recapture means reporting income that would not otherwise be due.

Recaptured Depreciation

If you claim accelerated depreciation on realty (generally this applies to realty placed in service before 1987), then you must recapture (report as ordinary income) the portion of gain relating to the excess of accelerated depreciation.

- For equipment and other personal property, recapture all of depreciation claimed (to the extent of gain).

- For nonresidential realty depreciated under The Accelerated Cost Recovery System (ACRS) (placed in service after 1981 and before 1987), recapture the excess of ACRS depreciation in excess of straight-line depreciation. Different rules apply to pre-ACRS property.

Unrecaptured Depreciation

If you claim a home office deduction for business use of a portion of your home (these rules are explained in Chapter 18), you do *not* have to apportion your gain; in effect, you can apply the home sale exclusion to your entire gain. However, all depreciation claimed on a home office after May 6, 1997, is unrecaptured depreciation—it must all be reported as gain upon the sale of the home. This gain is taxed at a maximum of 25 percent.

Recapture on Installment Reporting

When to report recapture on an installment sale depends on the type of recapture involved:

- *For recaptured depreciation*—All of the depreciation must be reported in full in the year of sale. This recapture is reported without regard to the proceeds received in the year of sale.

- *For unrecaptured depreciation*—The gain, with respect to each installment payment received, is reported first at the 25 percent rate. Once unrecaptured depreciation has been fully reported, the balance of any gain is reported at the basic capital gains rate (generally 15 percent).

Example

You purchased realty for $100,000 that you depreciated by $20,000 (for a basis of $80,000). In July 2005, you then sell the property for $130,000, payable in five equal annual installments. Of these installments, $10,000 of gain must be reported each year. (*Gain* is the difference between $130,000 received for the property and $80,000 basis.) Thus, gain on the first two installments is taxed at 25 percent. Gain on the three remaining installments will be taxed at 15 percent.

Involuntary Conversions

If business property is destroyed or stolen, condemned or disposed of through threat of condemnation and you receive insurance proceeds or other funds to compensate you for your loss, you have suffered an *involuntary conversion*. *Condemnations* are the taking of your property for public purposes, such as building roads or putting up utility poles—in effect a forced sale. Threat of condemnation occurs when you learn from a government official or other authorized person that the government intends to take your property. If you do not sell it to the government, it will be condemned.

If the funds you receive for the involuntary conversion of your property exceed your **adjusted basis** in the involuntarily converted property, you have a gain that is currently taxable unless you qualify to postpone your gain (explained later). If the funds you receive are less than your adjusted basis in the involuntarily converted property, you have a loss that is currently deductible (subject to usual loss limitation rules discussed in this chapter and in Chapter 5).

Adjusted basis This is your basis in the property, adjusted for certain items. Start with your original cost if you bought the property (the cash and other property you paid to acquire it). Even if the cash did not come out of your pocket, for example, if you took a loan, the cash you turn over to the seller is part of your basis. Then, adjust the basis by reducing it for any depreciation claimed (or that could have been claimed) and any casualty loss you claimed with respect to the property. For example, if your original computer system cost you $10,000 and you claimed $2,000 depreciation, your adjusted basis is $8,000. (Other basis adjustments are explained in Chapter 5.)

In reporting condemnation awards, you can reduce your receipts by any legal fees or other expenses you incurred to obtain the payment as well as any special assessments levied against the part of the property if only a portion of the property was condemned. If amounts are withheld from the award to pay off your mortgage or outstanding taxes, you treat these amounts as payment you receive. Also add to the amount any severance payments you receive for the decrease in the value of the property you retain if only a portion of the property was condemned. The portion of gain relating to severance damages can be postponed in the same way as direct payments for the condemned property.

In figuring your gain or loss from an involuntary conversion, certain payments related to the event are not taken into account (they are treated separately):

- *Relocation payments from the federal government or an assistance program.* If you are displaced from your business (including a home in which you maintain a home office) or farm, you may be eligible for these funds. These amounts are tax-free payments.

- *Interest on a condemnation award.* The municipality may pay you out over time, plus interest. This interest is reported separately as interest income (see Chapter 4).

Election to Postpone Gain

You make the election to postpone gain by acquiring replacement property within set time limits. In deciding whether or not to postpone gain, keep in mind that you do not have to use the insurance proceeds or other funds to acquire the replacement property—you need only invest a similar amount. You can, for example, spend the proceeds and take a loan to buy the replacement property. First, consider the advantage and disadvantage to help you decide whether or not you want to postpone gain.

- *Advantage*—Postponing gain allows you to use the proceeds undiminished by taxes on your gain.

- *Disadvantage*—You must reduce the basis of the replacement property by the amount of gain not immediately recognized. This results in a lower basis for purposes of figuring depreciation on the replacement property as well as for determining gain or loss on the disposition of the property.

REPLACEMENT PROPERTY. *Replacement property* is property that is similar or related in service or use to the involuntarily converted property. *Similar or related* means that the functions of the old and replacement properties are related. For example, if one piece of machinery is destroyed in a storm and you buy a new machine to perform the same work in your business, the new machine is clearly replacement property.

You need not buy the property directly. You are treated as acquiring replacement property if you buy at least an 80 percent interest in a corporation that owns property similar or related in service or use to the involuntarily converted property. However, you cannot buy replacement property from a *related party*—a business you control or a close relative—if the gain is more than $100,000. You can buy replacement property from a related party if the gain is $100,000 or less.

If your business property is destroyed in a disaster within an area qualifying for federal disaster relief, acquiring *any* tangible property for your business is treated as similar or related even if the functions of the old and new property are entirely different.

REPLACEMENT TIME LIMITS. You must decide whether or not to postpone gain by acting with set time limits to place replacement property in service for your business. Generally you have until the end of the two years following the close of the year in which gain from the involuntary conversion was realized to acquire replacement property. For property involuntarily converted in the New York Liberty Zone (generally the southern portion of Manhattan), the two-year replacement period is extended to five years.

If business property has been condemned (or sold under threat of condemnation), the replacement period is three years from the close of the year in which the gain from condemnation (or threat of condemnation) was realized. However, if you buy replacement property by acquiring a controlling interest in a corporation, then the two-year replacement period applies.

Example

In February 2005, a machine is destroyed by a storm and insurance proceeds you receive produce a gain. You can postpone the reporting of this gain by obtaining replacement property no later than December 2007.

If you decide you want to postpone gain but time is running out on buying replacement property, you can request an extension. For example, if you have already found property but have yet to close on the sale, ask for more time to do so. Address your request to the local district director of the IRS. Do not let the replacement period expire without submitting your extension request—it may be almost impossible to obtain an extension at this late date.

Abandonment, Foreclosure, and Repossession of Property

Disposing of business property by abandonment, foreclosure, or repossession generally produces taxable results.

Abandonment

If you abandon business property, you *automatically* have a loss that is treated as an ordinary loss. The amount of your loss is the adjusted basis of the abandoned property. However, if you effectively abandon inventory that has become unsalable because it is obsolete or defective, you do not report it as a loss. Instead, you adjust your inventory valuation to reflect the actual value of the items, which may be merely their scrap value.

If the property you are abandoning is subject to a debt for which you are personally liable and the debt is canceled, you have ordinary income to the extent of this debt cancellation. Report this income separately from the abandonment loss—do not net one against the other. (Income from the cancellation of debt is also discussed in Chapter 4.)

Foreclosure or Repossession

If you cannot pay a loan or the mortgage on your business property, the lender will recoup this amount by *foreclosing* on the property or *repossessing* it. Foreclosure and repossession are treated as a sale or exchange for tax purposes, producing gain or loss on the transaction. This is the case even if you voluntarily transfer the property back. The amount realized usually is the debt you no longer have to pay. The difference between this amount and the adjusted basis in the property is the amount of your gain or loss.

- *If the debt is recourse debt* (you are personally liable for it)—do not include the debt cancellation in the amount realized (you report the debt cancellation separately as income as explained in Chapter 4). *Exception:* If the value of the property is less than the canceled debt, then the amount realized includes the debt cancellation to the extent of the value of the property.
- *If the debt is nonrecourse debt* (you are not personally liable for it)—include the full debt cancellation in the amount realized, regardless of the property's value.

Example

The business bought a car for $30,000, financing $25,000 of the purchase price. The business stops paying the loan when there is still $20,000 outstanding and the adjusted basis of the car is $22,040. The lender repossesses the car and walks away from the remaining debt. If the debt is nonrecourse, report $2,040 as a loss (the difference between the amount realized of $20,000 and the adjusted basis of the car, $22,040).

Example

Continuing with the car example, except that the debt is recourse. The value of the car at the time of the repossession is $19,000. In this instance, report a loss of $3,040 (the difference between the amount realized of $19,000 less $22,040). But you must also report income of $1,000 (the amount of the canceled debt in excess of the value of the car).

Lender's Perspective

If you are the lender and foreclose or repossess property because of nonpayment, you recognize gain or loss on the transaction. This is so whether or not the debtor cooperates and voluntarily transfers the property back to you.

REAL PROPERTY. Generally, your gain is the difference between the total payments you have already received for the property and the gain you already reported as income. However, your reportable gain on a foreclosure or repossession is limited to the gross profit on your original gain minus any gain already reported. Reduce your profit by any costs related to the foreclosure or repossession, such as legal fees, court costs, and costs of recording or clearing title to the property.

Example

You foreclose on an office building for nonpayment of the mortgage you hold on the property you sold. You figure your basis in the building as follows:

Original basis	$200,000
Plus: Gain reported on principal received	+18,000
Plus: Gain on foreclosure	+27,000
Less: Principal received	(−90,000)
New basis	$155,000

Your basis in the reacquired property is your original basis in the property, increased by any gain recognized on the receipt of principal and foreclosure/repossession, and decreased by any principal payments received.

EQUIPMENT AND OTHER PERSONAL PROPERTY.   If you sold property on the installment method and repossess it for nonpayment, report gain or loss on the transaction. In review, gain or loss is the difference between your basis in the installment obligations and the value of the property you repossess. Reduce the basis in the installment obligations by any costs for the repossession. Increase the value of the property by anything you receive from the debtor upon the repossession, such as a partial payment.

What is your basis in the installment obligations? This depends on how you originally opted to report the sale. If you used the installment method, your basis in the installment obligations is the unpaid balance of the installment obligations divided by your gross profit percentage.

Sale of All the Assets of the Business

If you sell your business by selling all of its assets, the rules for reporting gain or loss are really no different from a single asset sale. You allocate the purchase price of the sale to each of the assets, including goodwill or going concern value, in order to determine your gain or loss. You usually arrive at this allocation through negotiations between you and the buyer.

Asset classes include the following:

- *Class I assets*—cash, demand deposits, and similar bank accounts.
- *Class II assets*—certificates of deposit, government securities, readily marketable stock or securities, and foreign currency.
- *Class III assets*—tangible assets (such as equipment, furniture, and fixtures) and intangible assets not in Classes IV or V (such as accounts receivable).
- *Class IV assets*—Section 197 assets (other than goodwill and going concern value) such as patents, copyrights, licenses, permits, franchises, trademarks, and covenants not to compete. (Section 197 assets are discussed in Chapter 14.)
- *Class V assets*—goodwill and going concern value.

The sale price is allocated in descending order—first to Class I assets, then Class II assets, and so on. There is no debate on allocating part of the purchase price to assets in the first two classes since the value of the assets is not in dispute. But as a seller, you generally want to allocate as much of the remaining purchase price to assets that will produce the most favorable tax results to you. For example, if you can allocate an amount to goodwill, you will achieve capital gain treatment.

In contrast, if such amount is allocated to inventory, you have ordinary income. However, the buyer has competing interests and wants to allocate as much as possible to depreciable assets. That would give him or her the opportunity to maximize depreciation deductions and not to allocate to goodwill, the amount of which is only recoverable upon a future sale of the business. Ultimately, the price you receive for the assets will reflect negotiations that include the allocation process. Corporations that acquire stock in another corporation may, under certain circumstances, elect to treat the stock purchase as an asset sale (see Chapter 5).

Where to Report Gains and Losses on Business Property

For All Taxpayers

Section 1231 gains and losses are reported on Form 4797, Sales of Business Property, regardless of the type of entity. The results from Form 4797 are carried over and reported on the business's tax return. For individuals, Form 4797 gains and losses are reported directly on Form 1040.

Installment sales are figured on Form 6252, Installment Sale Income. The results are carried over to Form 4797 (or Schedule D as explained in Chapter 5). Use a separate Form 6252 for each installment sale you transact. Do not complete the form if you elect out of installment reporting—instead simply report your entire gain on Form 4797 (or Schedule D).

A sale of all the assets of the business is reported on Form 8594, Asset Acquisition Statement. This form is used to allocate the purchase price to specific assets.

Self-Employed

Gains and losses on Section 1231 property are reported on Form 4797. The results are carried over to page one of Form 1040. Do not enter the results on Schedule C (or on Schedule F in the case of farming operations).

If you elect to postpone gain on a casualty, theft, or condemnation, make your election on the return for the year in which you realized gain. If you acquired replacement property before filing your return, attach a statement to the return showing the amount realized, how you computed your gain, and any gain reported. If you have not yet acquired replacement property by the time you must file your return, simply attach a statement to your return showing the circumstances of the casualty, theft, or condemnation giving rise to the gain, how you calculated your gain, and that you intend to acquire replacement property within the replacement period. Then, when you do buy replacement property, attach another statement to the return for the year of the replacement purchase explaining the replacement.

If the replacement period expires before you acquire replacement property (and you do not obtain an extension for the replacement period), you must file an amended return for the year in which you realized gain. You report your full gain on this amended return. You must also file an amended return if you buy replacement property and the cost is not sufficient to postpone the reporting of all of your gain. You report the portion of the gain not covered by the replacement property on this amended return.

Once you have designated certain property as your replacement property, you cannot later substitute other property for it. However, if your replacement property is found to be unsuitable, you can then substitute other qualified property, provided the replacement period has not expired.

Partnerships and LLCs

Section 1231 gains and losses, on the other hand, are calculated on Form 4797 and then entered directly on Form 1065. These losses are part of the ordinary income or loss of the business.

If there is a gain as a result of a casualty or theft to business property, the partnership or LLC must elect to defer the recognition of gain and buy the replacement property. The individual partners or LLC members cannot make a separate election. Each partner or LLC member reports his or her distributive share of business income or loss on his or her personal income tax return.

S Corporations

Section 1231 gains and losses, on the other hand, are computed on Form 4797 and then entered directly on Form 1120S. These losses are part of the ordinary income or loss of the corporation. A shareholder's share of ordinary income or loss is reported on Schedule K-1.

If there is a gain as a result of a casualty or theft to business property, the S corporation must elect to defer the recognition of gain and buy the replacement property. The individual shareholders cannot make a separate election. Each shareholder reports his or her distributive share of S corporation income or loss on his or her personal income tax return.

C Corporations

Section 1231 gains and losses are computed on Form 4797 and then entered on Form 1120. Both capital losses and Section 1231 losses are part of the corporation's taxable income.

If the corporation discovers that it suffered a loss from worthless securities in a prior year and wants to file an amended return, use Form 1120X, Amended U.S. Corporation Income Tax Return.

PART 3

Business Deductions and Credits

CHAPTER 7

Employee Compensation

Salary, Wages, and Employee Benefits

If you are an employee, you do not pay compensation to another individual. You can skip most of this chapter and go on to look at deductible expenses. However, you might want to review the areas covered to understand your employer's burdens and responsibilities for the wages and benefits paid to you. You may also be interested in two tax credits to which you may be entitled by virtue of working.

If you hire someone to work for you, the compensation and benefits you pay to that person may be deductible. You may have additional costs associated with paying wages and providing employee benefits. In this chapter you will learn about:

- Deductible compensation
- Other limits on deducting compensation
- Disallowance repayment agreements
- Employee benefits
- Nonstatutory fringe benefits
- Employment tax credits
- Where to deduct compensation costs

Also discussed in this chapter are the *earned income credit* and the *dependent care credit*. These are not business credits; rather, they are personal credits that arise by virtue of employment. The earned income credit is a refundable credit for low-income householders, and the dependent care credit is designed to offset the costs of babysitting and other dependent-related expenses incurred to allow parents to work.

Employment taxes on compensation you pay to your employees, including federal income tax withholding, FICA (Social Security and Medicare taxes), FUTA (federal unemployment tax), and state taxes (income, unemployment, and disability), are discussed in Chapter 27.

Medical coverage is an important facet of employee compensation. It is also a necessary item for self-employed individuals. Medical coverage for you and your employees is explained in Chapter 19.

For further information about employee compensation, see IRS Publication 334, *Tax Guide for Small Business*, IRS Publication 15, *Circular E*, *Employer's Tax Guide*, IRS Publication 15-A, *Employer's Supplemental Tax Guide*, and IRS Publication 15-B, *Employer's Guide to Fringe Benefits*.

Deductible Compensation

Compensation you pay to your employees can take many forms. In general, most types of compensation are fully deductible by you. *Deductible compensation* includes the more common forms, such as salary, wages, bonuses for services performed, vacation pay, sick pay (not otherwise paid by insurance), and fringe benefits, whether or not they are tax-free to your employee. The deduction for these items must be reduced, however, by any employment tax credits claimed. These tax credits are discussed later in this chapter. The timing of when to deduct year-end bonuses paid after the end of the year is discussed in Chapter 2.

Employees versus Independent Contractors

Compensation discussed throughout this chapter means payments to employees. Payments made to independent contractors are not treated as compensation. These payments may be deductible, but not as compensation. The rules for deducting payments to independent contractors are discussed in Chapter 21.

Since payments to independent contractors are not treated as compensation, they are not subject to withholding and employment taxes (discussed later). Whether someone who works for you is an employee or an independent contractor should be resolved at the commencement of work. The rules for making this determination are discussed in Chapter 1.

It is critical to note that the consequences for misclassifying workers can be dire for an employer. If you fail to treat a worker as an employee when you should do so, you are penalized for not withholding income taxes on wages and paying employment taxes. Penalties and interest in this regard can, in some instances, be enough to bankrupt your company. Misclassification can also wreak havoc with employee benefit plans, including retirement plans. If the IRS successfully reclassifies workers as employees, you will be required to provide back benefits (medical, retirement plan contributions, and other benefits you provided to your correctly classified employees).

You may be able to rely on some special rules to avoid employment tax penalties. As a minimum, if you want to treat workers as independent contractors, make sure you do so consistently and that you have a reasonable basis for doing so. The tax law considers these situations to be a reasonable basis:

- You relied on a court case about federal taxes or a ruling issued to you by the IRS.
- You have already gone through an IRS audit in which the issue of worker classification was raised and your workers were not reclassified.
- A significant segment of your industry (at least 25 percent) treats such workers as independent contractors.

Require your independent contractors to complete Form W-9, Request for Taxpayer Identification Number and Certification, a form on which they accept responsibility for paying their required taxes.

Also make sure you file the required information return for independent contractors (Form 1099-MISC) if the worker earned at least $600 (see Appendix for details).

The IRS has a classification settlement program designed to resolve worker classification issues amicably (and with modest penalties and interest charges). If the IRS questions your worker classification and you cannot prove your position on audit or resolve it through the classification settlement program, you can now bring your case to Tax Court for a determination. This means you do not have to pay the taxes up front to have your case reviewed in court.

General Rules for Deductibility of Compensation

To be deductible, compensation must meet certain tests. First, it must be an *ordinary and necessary* **business expense**. The payments must be directly connected to the conduct of your business and they also must be necessary for you to carry on your business.

Ordinary and necessary business expense An *ordinary expense* is one that is common and accepted in your business. A *necessary expense* is one that is helpful and appropriate to your business.

Second, the compensation must be reasonable. For most employees, this issue never comes up; it is assumed that pay to rank-and-file employees is reasonable. The question of reasonableness typically arises in connection with pay to owners and top executives. There are no absolute guidelines for determining what is reasonable—it depends on the individual facts and circumstances. Ask yourself: "Would another business pay the same compensation under your circumstances?" If you are confident that the answer is yes, most likely the compensation is reasonable.

The IRS uses a number of factors to determine whether compensation is reasonable. These factors include:

- *The job description of the employee.* What duties must the employee perform? How much responsibility does the employee shoulder? How much time is required to perform the job? How much business is handled by the employee?

- *The nature of the business.* What are the complexities of your business? What has been your pay policy for all employees? What is the pay to a particular employee as compared with the gross and net profit of the business and distributions to shareholders?

- *The general cost of living in your locality.* Formula-based compensation (such as a percentage of sales or some other fixed arrangement) may be reasonable if it is an industrywide practice to use these formulas.

Courts have also used a hypothetical independent investor standard to test reasonableness. Under this test, courts decide whether a disinterested investor would approve the compensation level in light of the dividends and return on equity. In determining reasonableness, you must look at the total compensation package and not merely the base salary. Also, each employee's pay package must be reasonable by itself. The fact that your total payroll is reasonable is not sufficient.

Remember, if compensation paid to an employee who is also an owner of the corporation is not reasonable, then it may be viewed as a constructive dividend to such owner-employee. As such, it is not deductible by the corporation even though it is fully taxable to the owner. However, the owner-employee and corporation can enter into a disallowance repayment agreement to preserve deductibility. Such agreements are discussed later in this chapter.

Generally, it is up to you to prove the reasonableness of compensation. However, if the issue goes to court, the burden of proof shifts to the IRS once you have presented credible evidence of reasonableness. Only small businesses (corporations and partnerships whose net worth does not exceed $7 million) can shift the burden of proof to the IRS.

A third test requires that the payment be for services actually performed. This issue does not generally arise for ordinary employees. However, in a family situation, the IRS may pay closer attention to see that work has actually been performed for the compensation paid. Thus, for example, if you employ your spouse, children, or parent, be sure to document their work hours and duties should your return be questioned. In one case, a parent was able to deduct salary paid to his seven-year-old son because he showed that the child performed meaningful tasks for his business. In several cases, a deduction for equal pay to both spouses was denied where one spouse was a professional (e.g., an engineer or a doctor) and the other performed only administrative and secretarial duties. The compensation to the professional might have been reasonable, but the same pay to the spouse clearly was not.

Guaranteed annual wages may be deductible as salary even though work is not performed. The deduction is limited to full-time guaranteed wages paid under a collective bargaining agreement.

A fourth test is that you must actually have paid the compensation if you are on the cash basis, or incurred the expense if you are on the accrual basis. Incurring the expense means that economic performance has occurred. For a complete discussion on economic performance, see Chapter 2.

A fifth test applies to year-end bonuses and other payments by accrual basis businesses. Bonuses accrued before year-end cannot be deducted unless they are actually paid within a certain time. The time limit depends upon who is receiving the payment.

- *Rank-and-file employees*—payment must be completed within two-and-a-half months after the close of the year. For example, a bonus declared on December 24, 2005, by an accrual basis corporation for an employee who is not a shareholder must be paid by March 15, 2006, in order to be deductible in 2005.

- *Shareholders in C corporations*—payments to those owning more than 50 percent of the stock cannot be deducted until actual payment is made. Shareholders who own 50 percent or less are considered rank-and-file employees for purposes of this rule.

- *Owners of pass-through entities*—payments cannot be deducted until actual payment is made, regardless of the percentage of ownership. For example, a year-end bonus paid to an S corporation shareholder by an accrual basis corporation is not deductible until the bonus is actually paid.

Other Types of Deductible Compensation

Here are some less common, but equally deductible, compensation items:

- *Outplacement services provided to workers you have laid off.* The types of outplacement services that are deductible include career counseling, resume assistance, skills assessment, and even the cost of renting equipment to facilitate these services.

- *Black Lung benefit trust contributions made by coal mine operators,* provided the contributions are paid no later than the filing of the return (including extensions). The contribution must be made in cash (check) or property; a promissory note is not currently deductible.

- *Interest-free or below-market loans to employees.* The amount of interest not charged that is less than the applicable federal interest rate (a rate that changes monthly and depends on whether the loan is short-term, mid-term, or long-term) is treated as compensation. Include in your income that same amount as taxable interest.

- *Severance pay.* If you are forced to downsize your work force or otherwise let employees go, you may offer them some benefits package. The IRS has acknowledged that severance pay generally is deductible as an ordinary and necessary business expense even though an argument could be made that it provides some future benefit (which would suggest capitalizing the cost). However, if severance pay is part of a plan, method, or arrangement deferring the receipt of income, then it is deductible only when it is included in the worker's income (whether or not the employer is on the cash or accrual method of reporting).

- *Salary continuation.* If you want to continue paying wages to an owner-employee who becomes disabled and claim a deduction for such payments, do so under a salary continuation plan that you set up for this purpose. Without such a plan in place, you risk having the IRS label the payments as dividends or withdrawals of capital, neither of which are deductible by the company.

- *Director's fees.* A corporation's payment of fees to its directors is deductible, but such fees are not treated as compensation even if the director is also an officer or other employee of the corporation. The fees are deductible as other business expenses (see Chapter 22).

- *Employment agency fees.* If you pay a fee to an employment agency or headhunter to hire an employee, you may deduct the cost as an other business expense.

Note

If you allow employees to donate their vacation, sick or personal leave in exchange for your making cash payments to a qualified tax-exempt organization providing relief for victims of Hurricane Katrina, do not include the donated leave in their income. You deduct the payments as charitable contributions, not wages (see Chapter 22).

Other Limits on Deducting Compensation

Besides the reasonable compensation and other tests discussed earlier, there are several limitations on deducting compensation. For example, if your employee agrees to defer compensation to some future date, you cannot claim a deduction until such time as the employee includes the compensation in his or her income. This is true for accrual method businesses as well as cash basis businesses.

Another form of compensation subject to limitation is prizes and awards. Only certain prizes and awards are deductible, and then dollar limits apply. A deduction may be taken for an *employee achievement award*. This is tangible personal property given for an employee's length of service or safety achievement, awarded as part of a meaningful presentation and under conditions and circumstances that do not create a significant likelihood of disguising the award as compensation. An award is not considered a length-of-service award if it is made within the first five years of employment. An award is not considered a safety achievement award if it is given to a manager, administrator, clerical employee, or other professional employee, or if it is given to more than 10 percent of your employees (other than those just listed). Awards can be qualified or nonqualified. The only significant difference between the classifications is the dollar limit on deductibility. There is no dollar limit on qualified achievement awards. A *qualified achievement award* is one given under a written plan that does not discriminate in favor of highly compensated employees as to eligibility or benefits. There is a specific dollar limit on nonqualified achievement awards: The maximum deduction for nonqualified awards to any one employee is $400 per year. Then, too, your total awards, both qualified and nonqualified, made to any one employee during the year cannot exceed $1,600.

Another form of compensation subject to limitation is vacation pay by accrual basis employers. Vacation pay earned by an employee is deductible in the current year only if you actually pay it out by the close of the year or within two and a half months of the close of the year. If you fail to pay it out within this time frame, it becomes deductible in the year it is actually paid out. Of course, for cash basis employers, vacation pay is deductible as wages when it is paid to an employee.

Noncash Payments

In some cases you may pay your employees with property instead of cash. What is the amount you deduct? Your cost for the property (*basis*), or its value at the time it is paid to employees? You can deduct only your basis in the property, even though its value is included in the employee's income as compensation.

Example

You own a car with a basis (after depreciation deductions) of $8,000. The car is worth $12,000. You give the car to your top salesperson as a bonus. You may deduct $8,000, the basis of the car. On the employee's W-2 form you include $12,000 as compensation.

Restricted Property

If you transfer stock or other property that is subject to restrictions to an employee in payment for services, you generally cannot deduct the expense until such time as the stock or other property is no longer subject to restrictions. Restrictions include limits on transferring the stock or property. The term also covers property that is not **substantially vested** in the employee.

Substantially vested   A person can transfer the property and is not subject to a risk of forfeiture (is not likely to be forced to give up rights in the future).

When and how much you can deduct for this type of compensation depends on a number of factors, such as the kind of property transferred and when the property is included in the employee's gross income. In the past, an employer could deduct restricted property only when such property was subject to withholding. Sometimes this was impossible, because a worker was no longer in the employer's employment. The IRS has eased its position and has dropped the withholding requirement. The property must still be included in the worker's income in order for the employer to claim a deduction. According to the IRS, the worker will be deemed to have included the amount in income in the year for which an employer complies with W-2 reporting requirements.

Disallowance Repayment Agreements

If you are an employee of a corporation you own and a portion of your salary is viewed as unreasonable, the corporation loses its deduction for the payment. You are taxed on the payment in any event—either as compensation or as a constructive dividend. However, there is a way you can ensure that the corporation does not lose out if the IRS later characterizes its compensation deduction as partially unreasonable: You can enter into a *disallowance repayment agreement.*

The repayment agreement provides that if certain payments to you by the corporation are disallowed by the IRS, you are required to repay such amounts to your corporation. The agreement must be in writing and enforceable under local law. The agreement should be reflected not only in a separate written agreement between you and your corporation, such as part of your employment contract with the corporation, but also in the corporate minutes as a resolution of the board of directors. The bylaws of the corporation should also reflect the ability of the board to enforce the agreement.

Effect of the Repayment Agreement

The repayment agreement is a way for you to offset dividend income you are required to report if the IRS considers payments to you to be constructive dividends. By virtue of the repayment agreement you are entitled to deduct the amounts you are contractually required to repay to your corporation. However, some tax experts do not think that a repayment agreement is a good idea. Having one could be viewed as an admission that the corporation expects to pay an unreasonable salary.

Employee Benefits

In General

Employers are not required by law to offer any specific types of employee benefits. However, in today's job market, employers may want to offer various *fringe benefits* (also called perks or perquisites) as a way of attracting and retaining a good work force. Businesses may also want to provide these benefits because owners want such benefits for themselves as well.

If you pay certain expenses for an employee, you can claim a deduction. This is so even though the benefits may be excluded from the employee's gross income. If you are a sole proprietor, partner, or LLC member, you are not an employee and cannot receive these benefits on a tax-free basis. For purposes of this rule, employees who are more than 2-percent shareholders in their S corporations are treated the same as partners and cannot get these benefits on a tax-free basis. Limits on benefits for sole proprietors, partners, LLC members, and more-than-2-percent S corporation shareholders are discussed later in this chapter.

The benefits provided to an employee must be ordinary and necessary business expenses. The cost of the benefits must be reasonable in amount. And, in most cases, the benefits must be provided on a nondiscriminatory basis; they cannot be extended only to owner-employees and highly paid workers.

There are two main categories of employee benefits. The first is called *statutory employee benefits*. These benefits, specifically detailed in the Internal Revenue Code, include health and accident plans, group term life insurance, dependent care assistance, adoption assistance, medical savings accounts, and cafeteria plans.

The other broad category of benefits is called *nonstatutory fringe benefits*. These refer to specific sub-categories into which various miscellaneous benefits can fall. For example, if you provide your employees with a turkey at Christmas, this minimal benefit is classified as a *de minimis fringe*. It is not included in the employee's gross income even though you can claim a deduction for your cost of providing the benefit. Nonstatutory fringe benefits are discussed in greater detail later in this chapter.

Statutory Benefits

Certain types of plans or arrangements are treated as statutory benefits. The law details what constitutes a plan, which employees must be covered, the limits, if any, on the excludability of benefits, and other details.

MEDICAL INSURANCE AND BENEFITS.   In general, medical insurance coverage, along with any reimbursements of medical expenses, is excluded from an employee's gross income. You deduct the cost of the medical insurance premiums. If you are *self-insured* (you reimburse employees for medical costs out of your operating expenses under a written medical reimbursement plan), you deduct reimbursements to the employees when and to the extent made. Medical coverage, including health savings accounts (HSAs), long-term care coverage, and medical reimbursement plans, is discussed more fully in Chapter 19.

DEPENDENT CARE ASSISTANCE.   Up to $5,000 may be excluded from an employee's gross income; your outlays are fully deductible. You must set up a program to provide this benefit—a plan that makes clear to your employees what they may be entitled to. You do not have to fund the plan (set money aside); instead you can pay as you go. However, as a practical matter, this benefit may not make sense for a small business since nondiscrimination rules intended to make sure that the plan does not favor owners prevents more than 25 percent of the amounts paid by the plan from benefiting owners (their spouses or dependents) who own more than 5 percent of the business.

You may allow your employees to pay for their own dependent care on a pretax basis by setting up a flexible spending arrangement (FSA) discussed later in this section.

For information about building child care facilities or offering child care referral services, see Chapter 23.

GROUP TERM LIFE INSURANCE.   You deduct the cost of providing this benefit, which is the cost of the premiums. Typical coverage runs two times or more of the annual salary of the employee. The cost for up to $50,000 of coverage is excludable from an employee's gross income. If coverage over $50,000 is provided, an *imputed income* amount for excess coverage is includible in the employee's gross income. The imputed income is calculated according to an age-based IRS table; it is not based on the actual cost of premiums. While you deduct the actual cost of providing this benefit, your employees will be pleased to learn that the income from excess coverage may be modest. Table 7.1 can be used to figure employee income from excess coverage that is reported on the employee's Form W-2. The amount shown is the cost per $1,000 of excess coverage *each month.*

The cost for up to $2,000 of coverage for spouses and dependents is also excludable from an employee's gross income as a de minimis fringe benefit. If a group insurance plan is considered to be discriminatory, key employees (owners and top executives) will have income from the coverage and will not be able to exclude the cost for the first $50,000 of coverage. In this instance, in-

TABLE 7.1 Employee Income From Excess Coverage

Age	Imputed Income ($)
Under age 25	0.05
25–29	0.06
30–34	0.08
35–39	0.09
40–44	0.10
45–49	0.15
50–54	0.23
55–59	0.43
60–64	0.66
65–69	1.27
70 and older	2.06

come to them is the greater of the actual cost of the coverage, or the imputed amount calculated according to the age-based IRS tables. Special insurance coverage arranged on an individual basis (for example, split-dollar life insurance) is discussed later in this chapter.

EDUCATIONAL EXPENSES. If the courses are job related, your payments are deductible as noncompensatory business expenses. If the courses are not job related, your expenses are deductible as wages. If you lay off workers and pay for their retraining, you may also deduct your payments.

There is a special exclusion of up to $5,250 for employer-financed education assistance, including graduate-level courses, under a qualifying plan.

Amounts you pay for an employee under the plan can be excluded from the employee's income even if the courses are not job related. In that case, your payments under the plan would be deductible as noncompensatory business expenses.

As a practical matter, it is generally not advisable for owners of small businesses to set up educational assistance plans for the same reason that dependent care assistance programs may not make sense—no more than 5 percent of benefits can go to owner-employees or their spouses or dependents.

ADOPTION ASSISTANCE. You may deduct the cost of adoption assistance you provide to your employees. If you set up a special assistance program (a separate written plan to provide adoption assistance), your employees can exclude up to $10,630 per child in 2005. However, in 2005 the exclusion is phased out for those with adjusted gross income (AGI) between $159,450 and $199,450 (regardless of your filing status as married or single).

However, as in the case of educational assistance plans, adoption assistance plans do not make sense for small employers, since no more than 5 percent of benefits can go to owner-employees.

RETIREMENT PLANNING ADVICE. If you maintain a qualified retirement plan, you can pay for expert advice for your employees and their spouses with respect to retirement planning and they are not taxed on this benefit. There is no dollar limit to the exclusion. However, it does *not* apply to tax preparation, accounting, legal, or brokerage services. If you pay for these services on behalf of your employees, they are taxed on this amount, although you can deduct your payments.

HEALTH SAVINGS ACCOUNTS. If you maintain a high-deductible health insurance plan and contribute to a Health Savings Account (HSA) for an employee, you can deduct your contributions. Contribution limits and other rules for Health Savings Accounts are discussed in Chapter 19. Contributions are not taxed to employees and are exempt from payroll taxes. You must complete contributions by April 17, 2006, in order to deduct them on your 2005 return (even if you obtain a filing extension).

Note: If you are a small business or a self-employed individual, you can opt instead to set up an Archer Medical Savings Account (MSA).

HSAs and MSAs are discussed more fully in Chapter 19.

HEALTH REIMBURSEMENT ARRANGEMENTS (HRAs). You can contribute a dollar amount to an account for each employee that can be used to pay for unreimbursed medical expenses. HRAs are discussed more fully in Chapter 19.

CAFETERIA PLANS AND FLEXIBLE SPENDING ARRANGEMENTS. If you make contributions to cafeteria plans or flexible spending arrangements (FSAs), you can claim a deduction as an employee benefit expense. Cafeteria plans are designed to offer employees choices among benefits on a nondiscriminatory basis.

Flexible spending accounts are also nondiscriminatory plans but are funded primarily with employee contributions. Flexible spending arrangements are intended to cover medical costs or dependent care costs on a pre-tax basis. Employees agree to salary reductions (within limits set by you) that are then contributed to the FSA to be used for medical costs or dependent care costs. Salary reductions are made on a "use it or lose it" basis—if employees fail to "spend" their contributions within the year for which contributions are made or within a grace period of up to two and a half months (if the plan provides for such grace period), they cannot recoup them as cash or carry them over to the following year. From your perspective, however, you may be on the hook for payments if the plan pays out more than the employee has paid in and the employee then terminates employment. The reason: The plan must pay out benefits equal to the employee's annual commitment for salary reduction contributions, even if they have not been fully paid.

Example

An employee agrees to contribute $100 at the end of each month to an FSA. In January 2005, the employee submits a claim of $1,200 for dependent care payable to an agency to cover the next six months. The employee quits the job in the first week of February 2005. The business is out $1,100.

Note

You may incur costs to administer these employee benefit plans. If you handle them internally (e.g., with your company bookkeeper), there is no additional cost; it is part of wages you already pay. If you use outside companies to administer these plans, you can separately deduct the costs.

Other Employee Benefits

In addition to the various employee benefit plans just discussed, there are other types of benefits you may provide for employees for which you can claim a deduction for your expenses.

SUPPLEMENTAL UNEMPLOYMENT BENEFITS. If you make contributions to a welfare benefit fund to provide supplemental unemployment benefits for your employees, you may deduct your contributions as ordinary and necessary business expenses. The deduction is claimed as an employee benefit expense, not as a compensation cost. Your deduction cannot exceed the fund's qualified cost for the year. *Qualified cost* is the amount you could have claimed had you provided the benefits directly and been on the cash basis, plus the amount estimated to be actually necessary to build the fund to cover claims incurred but not yet paid and administrative costs for such claims.

MEALS AND LODGING. In general, the costs of providing meals and lodging to your employees are deductible as an expense of operating your business. The costs may or may not be taxable to your employees. The tax treatment of this benefit to your employees affects the amount and how you claim a deduction. Generally, you may deduct only 50 percent of the cost of providing meals.

The 50-percent limit on deducting meals does not apply if your employees must include the benefit in income. In this case, you may deduct 100 percent of the cost as compensation.

The 50-percent limit on deducting meals does not apply if you operate a restaurant or catering business and provide meals to your employees at your restaurant or work site. However, in this case, the full cost of the meals is not deductible as compensation; instead, it is treated as part of the cost of goods sold.

Example

You pay your employee's meal costs when your employee is out of town on a sales call. (Assume proper substantiation and reimbursement arrangements, as explained in Chapter 8.) The meal costs are not included in your employee's gross income. You deduct 50 percent of the meal costs.

Example

You give your employee a $200 meal allowance because of seniority. The $200 is included in your employee's gross income. You deduct 100 percent of the $200 meal allowance.

The 50-percent limit on meals does not apply if you provide the meals as part of the expense of providing recreational or social activities. For example, the cost of a company picnic is fully deductible.

You may deduct the full amount of meal costs if your employees are able to exclude this amount from their gross income. They do this if the meals are furnished on your premises and for your convenience, or if the meals qualify as a de minimis fringe benefit.

Note

Under a safe harbor rule, meals provided to all your employees are treated as furnished for your convenience (and fully deductible) if more than half of the employees to whom such meals are provided are treated as having been furnished meals for your convenience.

Special rules apply for valuing the meals provided at an employer-operated eating facility. An *employer-operated eating facility* is a lunchroom or other facility that you own or lease and operate directly or by a contract to provide meals on or near your business premises during or immediately before or after your employees' workday. Meals provided at an eating facility on or near your business premises are treated as a de minimis fringe benefit. As such, they are excluded from your employee's income and you can claim a full deduction (you do not have to apply the 50-percent limit).

If you provide your employees with lodging on your premises (for example, if you run a motel, nursing home, or rental property and the employee must live on the premises in order to manage it), you may deduct your full expenses according to the particular expense involved. For example, you deduct the cost of heating and lighting as part of your utilities, the cost of bedding as part of your linen expenses, and the use of the room as a depreciation item.

However, if you are a self-employed individual, you cannot make your living costs tax deductible. You may not exclude them even if you live at your business (e.g., you own a motel and live in it) since you are *not* an employee of your business.

TRAVEL AND ENTERTAINMENT COSTS.   If you pay for travel and entertainment costs, you may deduct your outlays, subject to certain limits. These expenses are explained in Chapter 6.

EMPLOYEE USE OF A COMPANY CAR.   If you allow an employee to use a company car for personal purposes, you must value this personal use and include it in the employee's gross income. It is a noncash fringe benefit. There are several valuation methods for calculating personal use of a company car. The method to use depends on your particular circumstances.

One method is based on the actual fair market value (FMV) of the personal use. This is determined by looking at the cost of leasing a comparable car at a comparable price for a comparable period of time. The cost of the vehicle can be its FMV if the car was purchased in an arm's-length transaction. Under a safe harbor rule, you can use the manufacturer's invoice price (including the price for all options), plus 4 percent. Under another safe harbor rule, you can use the manufacturer's suggested retail price, minus 8 percent. Then find out what it would cost to lease a car of this value.

Another method is based on the car's annual lease value (ALV). The ALV is set by the IRS and depends on the FMV of the car on the date the car is first used for personal purposes (see Table 7.2).

TABLE 7.2 Annual Lease Value (ALV) Table for Cars

FMV	ALV
$0 to 999	$ 600
1,000 to 1,999	850
2,000 to 2,999	1,100
3,000 to 3,999	1,350
4,000 to 4,999	1,600
5,000 to 5,999	1,850
6,000 to 6,999	2,100
7,000 to 7,999	2,350
8,000 to 8,999	2,600
9,000 to 9,999	2,850
10,000 to 10,999	3,100
11,000 to 11,999	3,350
12,000 to 12,999	3,600
13,000 to 13,999	3,850
14,000 to 14,999	4,100
15,000 to 15,999	4,350
16,000 to 16,999	4,600
17,000 to 17,999	4,850
18,000 to 18,999	5,100
19,000 to 19,999	5,350
20,000 to 20,999	5,600
21,000 to 21,999	5,850
22,000 to 22,999	6,100
23,000 to 23,999	6,350
24,000 to 24,999	6,600
25,000 to 25,999	6,850
26,000 to 27,999	7,250
28,000 to 29,999	7,750
30,000 to 31,999	8,250
32,000 to 33,999	8,750
34,000 to 35,999	9,250
36,000 to 37,999	9,750

TABLE 7.2 *(Continued)*

FMV	ALV
38,000 to 39,999	10,250
40,000 to 41,999	10,750
42,000 to 43,999	11,250
44,000 to 45,999	11,750
46,000 to 47,999	12,250
48,000 to 49,999	12,750
50,000 to 51,999	13,250
52,000 to 53,999	13,750
54,000 to 55,999	14,250
56,000 to 57,999	14,750
58,000 to 59,999	15,250

Example

During all of 2005 your employee uses a company car 50 percent of the time for personal purposes and 50 percent for business purposes. The fair market value of the car as of January 1, 2005, is $15,000. The ALV is $4,350. The amount included in the employee's gross income is $2,175 ($4,350 × .50).

For cars over $59,999, calculate the ALV as follows: Multiply the fair market value of the car by 25 percent and add $500. The ALV figures apply for a four-year period starting with the year of the ALV election. Thereafter, the ALV for each subsequent four-year period is based on the car's then fair market value.

If the car is used continuously for personal purposes for at least 30 days but less than the entire year, you must prorate the value of personal use.

Example

Using the company car example, except that the employee uses the car from May 1 through September 30. The $2,175 is prorated for the 153 days of personal use. The amount included in the employee's gross income is $911.71 ($2,175 × [153 ÷ 365]).

The ALV method already takes into account maintenance and insurance costs. Fuel provided by an employer is not included in the ALV. Fuel provided in kind can be valued at FMV or 5.5 cents per mile for purposes of including it in the employee's gross income. If fuel is paid by a company credit card, the actual charges are used to compute personal use included in the employee's gross income.

An employer may choose to treat all use by an employee of a company-owned car as personal use and include an appropriate amount in the employee's gross income. In this case, it is up to the employee to maintain records substantiating business use and then deduct such business use on his or her individual income tax return. If personal use of a company car is de minimis, then nothing need be included in the employee's gross income. As a practical matter, when the employee is an owner, the decision on how to value personal use of a company car is a mutual decision. Both the employer and employee in this case agree on which method is preferable. Keep in mind that when valuing personal use for an owner, only the fair market value or ALV methods can be used.

Another valuation method for personal use of a company car is the cents-per-mile special rule. This rule can be used only if a car is valued in 2005 at no more than $14,800 and the car is regularly used in the business (at least 50 percent of total annual mileage is for the business, or the car is used each workday to drive at least three employees to and from work in a carpool) or for a car driven by employees at least 10,000 miles during a calendar year. And the employee cannot be a control employee (see below). If the car is owned or leased for less than a full year, the 10,000 miles are prorated accordingly. The value of personal use is based on the standard mileage rate. For 2005 the standard mileage rate is 40.5 cents per mile. For trucks, the value in 2005 is limited to $16,300.

If you want to use the ALV method or the cents-per-mile method, you must elect to do so. This election must be made no later than the first pay period in which the company car is used for personal purposes. You need not inform the IRS of your election.

COMMUTING VEHICLES.   If you allow your employees to use company cars to commute to and from work, a special valuation rule is used to determine the amount includable in the employee's gross income. The car must be owned or leased by the employer for use in the business, and the employer must have genuine noncompensatory business reasons for requiring an employee to commute in the vehicle. Also, the employer must have a written policy preventing use of the vehicle for personal purposes other than commuting (or de minimis personal use). The employee cannot be a *control employee* (an employee who is a board-appointed, shareholder-appointed, confirmed, or elected officer with compensation of at least $50,000, a director, a 1-percent or greater owner, or someone who receives compensation of $100,000 or more). If the special commuting vehicle rule is met, then the value of commuting is $1.50 each way ($3.00 round trip), regardless of the length of the commute. The same flat rate applies to each employee even if more than one employee commutes in the vehicle. While the commuting vehicle rule is optional at the employer's election, it must be used for valuing all commuting if it is used for valuing any commuting.

The deduction for car expenses—depreciation, insurance, gas, oil, and repairs—is explained in Chapter 9. This chapter covers only business use of a company car.

COUNTRY CLUB DUES.   If you pay the cost of membership at a golf or other country club, the dues are not deductible. However, an employee who uses the club for business can exclude the benefit from income (it is viewed as a working condition fringe benefit explained later even though country club dues are otherwise not deductible). However, you can convert this nondeductible cost of the business into a deductible expense by electing to treat the benefit as additional compensation to the employee—deducting the cost as compensation and not as an entertainment cost. This option is discussed more fully in Chapter 8.

Flights on Employer-Provided Aircraft

Special rules are used to determine the value of personal use of flights provided on employer aircraft. A discussion of these rules is beyond the scope of this book.

Life Insurance Provided on an Individual Basis

Businesses may provide owners and other top employees with coverage on an individual basis. This coverage may be term insurance or permanent insurance (e.g., a whole life policy). This coverage is taxable to the individual and does not have to be provided on a nondiscriminatory basis.

SPLIT-DOLLAR LIFE INSURANCE.   Under a split-dollar life insurance plan, the cost of coverage is shared between the business and the insured. Here is how the plan usually works.

A cash value life insurance policy is used for a split-dollar arrangement, with the business paying some or all of the premiums. At the death of the employee, the business recoups its outlay and the balance of the proceeds is payable to the insured's beneficiary (typically his or her spouse or child). Under final regulations, how the employee is taxed on this benefit depends on who owns the policy:

- *If the employee owns the policy,* premiums paid by the business are treated as loans, with imputed interest taxed to the employee.

- *If the business owns the policy,* the employee is taxed on the value of the life insurance protection (which is the one-year term cost of this protection).

In view of income tax being imposed on split-dollar life insurance arrangements, they are no longer favored as wealth builders for business owners.

Nonstatutory Fringe Benefits

There is a special category of fringe benefits that you may provide to your employees on a tax-deductible basis but which your employees need not include in their income. These are referred to as *nonstatutory fringe benefits* because there is no separate section in the Internal Revenue Code for each particular benefit—they are all covered in the same section. Nonstatutory fringe benefits are not only excludable from the employee's gross income; they are also not subject to employment taxes. In general, these benefits must be provided on a nondiscriminatory basis. Benefits cannot be provided solely to owners and highly paid employees and not to rank-and-file employees. Nonstatutory fringe benefits include:

- *No-additional-cost service.* You need not include in your employee's gross income the value of a service you offer to customers in the ordinary course of the business in which your employee works (e.g., if you run a ferry line and allow employees to ride for free on scheduled runs). In the case of no-additional-cost service, you generally do not have any expense to deduct by virtue of providing the benefit to the employee. You have already deducted costs related to providing the service.

- *Qualified employee discount.* You need not include in your employee's gross income a price reduction you give on certain property or services you offer to customers in the ordinary course of your business in which the employee performs services (e.g., if you own a clothing boutique and give your salespersons a 15-percent discount on your merchandise). A qualified employee discount does not include any discount on property that is more than your *gross profit percent* (total sales price of property less cost of property, divided by total sales price of property) times 20 percent of the price charged to customers, or for services.

  A qualified employee discount does not include any discount on real property. A deduction for the goods or services provided as a qualified employee discount is not taken into account as a compensation expense but rather as some other item. Goods provided to employees at a discount are part of the cost of goods sold.

- *Working condition fringe benefit.* You need not include in your employee's gross income a benefit provided to your employee if the employee could have claimed his or her own deduction had he or she paid for the benefit. For example, if you paid for a job-related course that would have been deductible by your employee had the employee paid for it, the course is a working condition fringe benefit. Other examples of working condition fringe benefits include employer-provided vehicles and outplacement services.

- *De minimis (minimal) fringe.* You need not include in your employee's gross income the value of any small or inconsequential benefits, such as the typing of a personal letter by a company secretary or the occasional use of the company copying machine for personal matters. Holiday gifts of nominal value, such as turkeys and hams, are considered de minimis fringes. However, cash of any amount is not a de minimis fringe and must be included in the employee's gross income. Other examples of de minimis fringes include group term life insurance for spouses and dependents up to $2,000, meals furnished at an eating facility on or near your premises, coffee or soft drinks furnished to employees, occasional tickets to sporting or entertainment events, occasional meal money or transportation fare for employees working overtime, and company events (such as parties or picnics) for employees and their guests.

- *Qualified transportation fringe benefit.* If you provide your employee with a transit pass for mass transit, transportation in a commuter highway vehicle, or qualified parking, you need not include the benefit in your employee's gross income. The 2005 limit on this exclusion is $105 per month for a transit pass or commuter highway vehicle. The 2005 limit on the exclusion for qualified parking is $200 per month. The value of parking is based on what a person would have to pay for space in an arm's-length transaction. If you provide parking space to employees that is primarily available to customers, then the parking has no value. If you give employees who carpool preferential parking, the value of the space must be taken into consideration. Employer-paid parking at a temporary job assignment—one expected to last one year or less that does in fact last that period—is fully excludable as paid under an accountable plan (explained in Chapter 8); there is no dollar limit in this situation. If the dollar limits are exceeded, only the excess is includible in gross income. However, in the case of partners and more-than-2-percent S corporation shareholders who are given public transit passes, the exclusion is limited to $21 per month. If the value of this exceeds the $21 per month limit, then the entire cost of the ticket is includable in the owner's gross income. The entire value of parking provided to partners and more-than-2-percent S corporation shareholders is taxable to them, even if it is less than $200 per month. You can shift the cost of monthly transit passes to employees—they pay for the passes by means of salary reductions (i.e., pretax dollars); all you pay for is the administrative cost of handling the benefit. The fact that you offer an employee a choice between a qualified transportation fringe benefit and cash does not make the benefit taxable if the employee chooses the benefit. The employee is, of course, taxed on cash received in lieu of the transportation fringe benefit.

Note

As an employer you can shift the cost of parking or transit passes to employees while still providing them with a tax advantage by permitting them to pay for these benefits on a pretax basis—through a salary reduction agreement. All that is required is for employees to agree to use their salary for payment for the parking or transit pass. The portion of their salary used for this purpose (up to the dollar limits above) is not taxed to them. The arrangement must be made before the end of the month for which the salary reduction is to be effective.

- *Moving expenses.* Payments to an employee (directly to the mover or as an allowance) for nondeductible moving expenses are deductible as wages and subject to employment taxes. Payments or reimbursements that would be deductible by the employee had the employee paid them are not treated as wages and are not subject to employment taxes. They are still deductible by you as noncompensatory business expenses. Moving expenses are explained further in Chapter 22.

- *Certain athletic facilities.* You need not include in your employee's gross income the value of an on-site gym or other athletic facilities for use by employees, their spouses, and children. However, if you pay for a membership to an outside health club or athletic facility open to the general public, you must include the benefit in the employee's gross income. No deduction can be claimed for club dues (see Chapter 8).

Some companies allow employees to use business-generated frequent flyer mileage for personal purposes. This benefit defies classification and, to date, the IRS has not figured out a way to tax it without causing an administrative nightmare.

Limits on fringe benefits paid for the benefit of sole proprietors, partners, LLC members, and more-than-2-percent S corporation shareholders that are otherwise excludable by rank-and-file employees are taxable to sole proprietors, partners, LLC members, and more-than-2-percent S corporation shareholders. For example, if the business pays their health insurance (which may include long-term care insurance), the coverage is taxable to them. The business can deduct the costs as guaranteed payments to partners or as compensation to S corporation shareholders. Owners can then deduct the amount directly from gross income on page 1 of Form 1040.

The balance can be treated as a deductible medical expense, which is taken as an itemized deduction subject to a 7.5-percent floor. Medical coverage for these owners is discussed in Chapter 19.

If, in 2005, the business provides qualified parking, the benefit is taxable to the sole proprietor, partner, LLC member, or 2-percent S shareholder even though its value is less than $200 per month.

Employment Tax Credits

Tax credits are even better than tax deductions. A tax deduction is worth only as much as the tax bracket you are in. For example, if you are in the top federal income tax bracket for individuals, 35 percent in 2005, a $100 deduction saves $35 in taxes. Tax credits reduce your taxes dollar-for-dollar. A $100 tax credit saves $100 in taxes.

Employer's Employment-Related Tax Credits

There are a number of tax credits related to the employment of workers. These tax credits reduce your deduction for compensation dollar-for-dollar. For example, if your deduction for compensation is $40,000 and you are entitled to claim a $2,000 employment tax credit, you may deduct only $38,000.

Employment-related tax credits reduce your deduction for wages paid to your employees. Employment-related tax credits are part of the general business credit and subject to limitation as explained in Chapter 23.

WORK OPPORTUNITY CREDIT. A credit can be claimed for employing individuals from certain economically disadvantaged groups, such as Aid to Families with Dependent Children (AFDC) recipients, food stamp recipients, ex-felons, and high-risk youths. The credit is 25 percent of the first $6,000 of wages ($3,000 of wages for summer youth) for those who work between 120 and 400 hours. The top credit is $2,400 ($1,200 for summer youth). The credit is 40 percent of the first $6,000 of wages ($3,000 of wages for summer youth) for those who work at least 400 hours. The top credit is $2,100 ($1,050 for summer youth). If you employ an eligible worker, be sure to obtain the necessary certification from your state employment security agency. This is done by completing IRS Form 8850, Pre-Screening Notice and Certification Request for the Work Opportunity and Welfare-to-Work Credits. Without this form, you cannot claim the credit unless you submitted the request and all necessary paperwork but the state agency failed to act on your request.

WELFARE-TO-WORK CREDIT. This credit can be claimed for employing individuals who are considered to be long-term family assistance recipients. The credit is 35 percent of qualifying first-year wages up to $10,000, plus 50 percent of qualifying wages up to $10,000. Thus the maximum credit for the first two years of employment is $8,500 ($3,500 in year one and $5,000 in year two). As with the work opportunity credit, you must obtain the required certification. You may find that your worker qualifies you to claim the work opportunity credit and also the welfare-to-work credit. You cannot take both credits, so, you must make a choice. Choose the credit that provides you with the larger benefit.

FICA ON TIPS. Owners of restaurants and beverage establishments can claim a credit for the employer portion of FICA paid on tips related to the furnishing of food and beverages on or off the premises. This is 7.65 percent of tips in excess of those treated as wages for purposes of satisfying the minimum wage provisions of the Fair Labor Standards Act (FLSA).

EMPOWERMENT ZONE EMPLOYMENT CREDIT. The Departments of Housing and Urban Development and Agriculture initially named six cities and three rural economically distressed areas across the country as *empowerment zones* (Round I zones) and in 1998 named 22 more (Round II). In addition, the District of Columbia is an enterprise zone—another type of economically distressed area—and employers in the zone are eligible for the empowerment zone employment credit. Eight new employment zones have been designated (Round III). All of these designations will continue through 2009. If you do business in one of these economically depressed zones and hire part-time or full-time employees who perform substantially all of their employment services within the zone, you may claim a credit based on their wages. The credit is 20 percent of the first $15,000 of qualified wages. The top credit is $3,000 per employee per year. There is no limit on the number of employees for which you may claim the credit. *Wages* for purposes of calculating the credit include not only salary and wages but also training and educational benefits. To determine whether a particular area has received designation, go to <www.hud.gov/crlocator>.

COMMUNITY RENEWAL EMPLOYMENT CREDIT. This is available for businesses operating in designated renewal communities. The credit is 15 percent of the first $10,000 in wages paid to full-time or part-time employees employed at least 90 calendar days. No credit can be claimed for employees owning more than 5 percent of the business as well as for employees who are their spouses and dependents. To determine whether you are in a renewal community, click on <www5.hud.gov/urban/tour/statestour.asp>.

INDIAN EMPLOYMENT CREDIT. You can claim a credit if you employ part-time or full-time workers who receive more than 50 percent of their wages from services performed on an Indian reservation. The employee must be an enrolled member of an Indian tribe or a spouse of an enrolled member. The employee must also live on or near the reservation on which the services are performed.

The credit is 20 percent of the first $20,000 of excess wages and the cost of health insurance. Excess wages and health insurance costs are such costs over amounts paid or incurred during 1993.

Legislative Alert

The work opportunity credit, the welfare-to-work credit, and the Indian employment credit expire at the end of 2005 unless Congress extends them.

GENERAL BUSINESS CREDIT.   Employment tax credits are part of the general business credit. As such, they not only reduce your deduction for wages but are also subject to special limitations. The general business credit is the sum of employment tax credits and certain other business-related credits. The general business credit cannot exceed your net tax liability (tax liability reduced by certain personal and other credits), reduced by the greater of:

- Tentative minimum tax (the alternative minimum tax before the foreign tax credit), or
- Twenty-five percent of regular tax liability (without regard to personal credits) over $25,000.

The amount of the general business credit in excess of this limit can be carried back for one year. Any additional excess amount can then be carried forward for up to 20 years. You cannot elect to forgo the carryback. (For credits arising in tax years before 1998, the carryback period was three years and the carryforward period was 15 years.)

Example

Your 2005 tax liability (without regard to personal credits) is $15,000 and you have no alternative minimum tax liability. Your general business credit is $17,000. In 2005, you can claim a general business credit of $15,000 (your net tax liability reduced by your tentative minimum tax liability of zero). The $2,000 unused credit is carried back to 2004. If it cannot be fully used on an amended 2004 return, it can be carried forward for up to 20 years starting on your 2006 return.

Employee's Employment-Related Tax Credits

An employee may be entitled to claim certain credits by virtue of working. These include the earned income credit and the dependent care credit. They are personal tax credits, not business credits. They are in addition to any child tax credit to which a person may be entitled ($1,000 in 2005 for each child under age 17 if income is below a threshold amount).

EARNED INCOME CREDIT.   If you employ an individual whose income is below threshold amounts, the employee may be eligible to claim an earned income credit. This is a special type of credit because it can exceed tax liability. It is called a refundable credit, since it can be paid to a worker even though it more than offsets tax liability.

From an employer's perspective, it is important to realize that a portion of the credit can be given to the employee along with the salary check. In essence, the credit is advanced to the employee. This credit belongs to the employee, not the employer. If you think you may have an employee who would qualify for the credit, you are required to inform him or her of eligibility and offer the option of receiving an advanced credit. You must notify employees who have no income tax withheld (other than those who claim exemption from withholding). You are encouraged to notify employees who have a qualifying dependent and compensation of less than a set amount (in 2005, less than $37,263 and two or more qualifying children; less than $33,030 and one qualifying child if married filing jointly; $35,263 or $31,030 if single). (A limited credit may be claimed by low earners without any qualifying dependents, but they cannot receive the credit on an advanced basis.) The IRS has provided notification guidance in Notice 797, *Possible Federal Tax Refund Due to the Earned Income Credit*, and Notice 1015, *Employers—Have You Told Your Employees About the Earned Income Credit?*

DEPENDENT CARE CREDIT.   Whether you are an employee or a business owner, if you hire someone to look after your children under age 13 or a disabled spouse or child of any age so that you can go to work, you may claim a tax credit. This is a personal tax credit, not a business tax credit. You claim the credit on your individual tax return.

The credit is a sliding percentage based on your adjusted gross income (AGI). The top percentage is 35 percent; it scales back to 20 percent for AGI over $43,000. This is the AGI on a joint return if you are married and do not live apart from your spouse for the entire year.

The percentage is applied to certain employment-related expenses up to $3,000 per year for one dependent, or $6,000 per year if you have two or more qualifying dependents. Employment-related expenses include household expenses to care for your dependent—housekeeper, babysitter, or nanny—and out-of-the-house expenses for the care of dependents, such as day-care centers, preschool and kindergarten, and day camps. Not treated as qualifying expenses are the costs of food, transportation, education, and clothing. Also, the cost of sleep-away camp does not qualify as an eligible expense.

If you are eligible for a credit, be sure to get the tax identification number of anyone who works for you and the day-care center or other organization to which you pay qualified expenses. The tax identification number of an individual is his or her Social Security number. You must include this information if you want to claim the credit.

If you hire someone to work in your home, be sure to pay the nanny tax. This is the employment taxes (Social Security, Medicare, and FUTA taxes) on compensation you pay to your housekeeper, babysitter, or other in-home worker. You must pay Social Security and Medicare taxes if annual payments to a household worker in 2005 exceed $1,400. If you paid cash wages of $1,000 or more in any calendar quarter to a household employee during the current tax year or the previous year, you also must pay federal unemployment tax (FUTA) on the first $7,000 of wages. You do not pay these taxes separately but instead can report them on Schedule H and include them on your Form 1040. You should increase your withholding or estimated tax to cover your liability for them to avoid estimated tax penalties. You cannot deduct employment taxes on household workers as a business expense. However, the tax itself is treated as a qualifying expense for the dependent care credit.

Where to Deduct Compensation Costs

Self-Employed (Including Independent Contractors and Statutory Employees)

Compensation paid to employees and employee benefits paid or provided to/for them are deductible on the appropriate lines of Schedule C. The deduction for wages must be reduced by any employment credits paid. Self-employed farmers deduct compensation costs on Schedule F. If you maintain a cafeteria plan for employees, you must file an information return, Form 5500, annually. If you personally incur dependent care costs for which a credit can be claimed, you must file Form 2441, Child and Dependent Care Expenses. The credit is then entered on Form 1040.

Partnerships and LLCs

Compensation paid to employees and employee benefits paid or provided to them are a trade or business expense taken into account in determining the profit or loss of the partnership or LLC on Form 1065, U.S. Partnership Return of Income. Report these items on the specific lines provided on Form 1065. Be sure to offset them by employment tax credits. Salaries and wages paid to employees and employee benefits are not separately stated items passed through to partners and members. Partners and members in LLCs report their net income or loss from the business on Schedule E; they do not deduct compensation and employee benefit costs on their individual tax returns.

Guaranteed payments to partners are also taken into account in determining trade or business profit or loss. There is a specific line on Form 1065 for reporting guaranteed payments to partners. They are also reported on Schedule K-1 as a separately stated item passed through to partners and LLC members as net earnings from self-employment. This will allow the partners and LLC members to calculate their self-employment tax on the guaranteed payments. If the partnership or LLC maintains a cafeteria plan for employees, the business must file an information return, Form 5500, annually. Partners and LLC members who personally incur dependent care costs for which a credit can be claimed must file Form 2441 with their Form 1040.

S Corporations

Compensation paid to employees and employee benefits paid or provided to them are trade or business expenses that are taken into account in determining the profit or loss of the S corporation on Form 1120S, U.S. Income Tax Return for an S Corporation. They are not separately stated items passed through to shareholders. This applies as well to compensation paid to owners employed by the corporation. Note that compensation to officers is reported on a separate line on the return from salary and wages paid to nonofficers. Be sure to reduce salary and wages by employment tax credits.

Shareholders report their net income or loss from the business on Schedule E; they do not deduct compensation and employee benefit costs on their individual tax returns. If the corporation maintains a cafeteria plan for employees, it must file an information return, Form 5500, annually. Shareholders who personally incur dependent care costs for which a credit can be claimed must file Form 2441 with their Form 1040.

C Corporations

Compensation and employee benefits paid to employees are trade or business expenses taken into account in determining the profit or loss of the C corporation on Form 1120, U.S. Corporation Income Tax Return. Compensation paid to officers is segregated from salaries and wages paid to employees. Be sure to reduce salary and wages by employment tax credits. Total compensation exceeding $500,000 paid to officers of the corporation is explained in greater detail on Schedule E of Form 1120. Remember that the corporation then pays tax on its net profit or loss. Shareholders do not report any income (or loss) from the corporation. If the corporation maintains a cafeteria plan for employees, it must file an information return, Form 5500, annually.

Employment Tax Credits for All Businesses

Employment taxes are figured on separate forms, with the results in most cases entered on Form 3800, General Business Credit. Form 3800 need not be completed if you are claiming only one business credit, you have no carryback or carryover, and the credit is not from a passive activity.

The separate forms for employment taxes are the following:

- Empowerment zone credit: Form 8844
- Indian employment credit: Form 8845
- Renewal community employment credit: Form 8844
- Social Security tax credit on certain tips: Form 8846
- Welfare-to-work credit: Form 8861
- Work opportunity credit: Form 5884

CHAPTER 8

Travel and Entertainment Expenses

Technology has enabled small business owners to market their goods and services in a manner similar to that of larger companies. For example, local radio advertising may expand the market for a small business beyond the general area in which its office is located. To service these expanding markets, you may have to travel to see clients, customers, vendors, suppliers, and others who are part of your business operations. If you travel on business or entertain clients, customers, or employees, you may be able to deduct a number of expenses. In this chapter you will learn about:

- Local transportation costs
- Travel within the United States
- Foreign travel
- Conventions
- Living away from home on temporary assignments
- Meal and entertainment expenses
- Business gifts
- Reimbursement arrangements
- Recordkeeping requirements
- Where to deduct travel and entertainment expenses

For further information about travel and entertainment costs, see IRS Publication 463, *Travel, Entertainment, Gift, and Car Expenses*. For a listing of per diem rates, see IRS Publication 1542, *Per Diem Rates*. Business use of your car for travel and entertainment purposes is discussed in Chapter 9.

Local Transportation Costs

Do you travel from your office to see clients or customers? Do you have more than one business location? Do you have an office in your home but go into the field to transact business? If the answer to any of these questions is yes, you may be able to deduct local transportation costs. More specifically, local transportation costs include the cost of work-related travel within the area of your **tax home**.

Tax home In general, your tax home is the entire city or general area of your regular place of business. If you have more than one business interest, then it is the location of your main business interest based on the comparative time spent in each location and the income derived from each business interest. If you do not have a regular place of business, you are considered an itinerant without any tax home.

Deductible Costs

Local transportation costs include the cost of driving and maintaining your car (including tolls and parking) or the cost of taxis, bus fare, train fare, or airfare. Computing the cost of driving and maintaining your car is discussed in Chapter 9.

Commuting Costs

As a general rule, the costs of commuting between your home and workplace are not deductible. Thus, your bus or train fare, gas for your car, bridge and highway tolls, and parking fees are nondeductible. This rule does not change merely because the commute is unusually long or you do work on the way (e.g.,

Example

You have a medical practice with an office across the street from the hospital in which you practice. You sometimes stop to see patients in their homes before going to the office or the hospital. You can deduct the cost of travel from your home to the patients' homes, as well as the cost of travel from their homes to your office or the hospital.

reading reports on the train, talking to clients on your car phone, or displaying advertising on your car). Commuting costs are considered nondeductible personal expenses. However, there are a few exceptions that make certain commuting expenses deductible:

1. If you have one or more regular places of business but work at different locations on a temporary basis (as defined under the following exception), you can deduct the daily cost of travel between your home and the other work site.

2. If you travel from your home to a temporary work site outside the metropolitan area where you live and normally work, you can deduct the daily cost of travel between your home and the temporary work site, regardless of the distance. *Temporary* means that work is realistically expected to last for one year or less. If it turns out to last longer, the period up until the realistic expectation change is treated as temporary.

Example

You have an office downtown but work on a two-month project at a client's facilities in the next city. You can deduct the cost of travel from your home (which is in the same metropolitan area as your office) to the client's facilities (and back) each day.

Note

If you do not have a regular place of business but work at temporary work sites in the metropolitan area of your home, you cannot deduct your transportation costs. Thus, according to the IRS, a lumberjack who worked at a number of temporary cutting sites was not allowed to deduct the cost of transportation to those sites. The entire area of the cutting sites was considered his regular place of business. However, the Tax Court has allowed a deduction for transportation costs in this instance, so the issue is not yet settled.

If you travel outside your **metropolitan area**, both the IRS and courts agree that the costs of traveling between your home and a temporary work site outside your area are deductible.

Metropolitan area   The area within a city and its surrounding suburbs.

3. If you have a home office that is the principal place of business for the activity conducted there, the cost of traveling from your home to your clients or customers or to other business locations is deductible.

Example

You run a tax return preparation business from your home and generally meet clients in your home office. Occasionally you go to clients' homes to do your work. You may deduct the cost of traveling between your home and the clients' homes and back again.

4. If you must haul tools or equipment to your job site and you use a trailer or have to make other special arrangements, the additional cost of commuting with the tools is deductible. The basic transportation costs are still treated as nondeductible commuting expenses.

Example

You rent a trailer to haul tools to and from home and business. You may not deduct the expenses of using your car; however, you can deduct the cost of renting the trailer that you haul with your car.

Travel within the United States

If you travel on business away from home, you can deduct not only the cost of transportation but also personal costs, such as your food, lodging, and incidentals. You must be away from your tax home (defined earlier) for more than the day. You must be required, because of the distance or the length of the business day, to get sleep or rest away from home in order to meet the demands of your work. This is called the *sleep or rest* rule. And your travel away from home must be considered **temporary** (discussed later in this chapter).

Temporary   Travel that is expected to last for no more than one year and does in fact last no more than one year. Travel expected to last for more than a year or that actually lasts for more than a year is considered to be indefinite, not temporary.

Example

You fly from New York to San Francisco to meet with a business client. You stay for five days, after which time you return to New York. In this case, your travel expenses are deductible.

Deductible Costs

Travel costs include transportation costs, lodging, meals, and other related expenses.

TRANSPORTATION COSTS.   The cost of a ticket to travel by air, train, or bus between your home and a business destination is deductible. However, if you receive the fare for free because of frequent flyer miles or otherwise, the cost is not deductible. The cost of travel by ship may not be fully deductible (see the section on Conventions later in this chapter).

Transportation costs also include local costs once you arrive at your business destination. Thus, the cost of taxi fare between the airport and your hotel is deductible. Local transportation costs at the business location, such as taxi fare from your hotel to the location of clients or customers, are also deductible. Other deductible local transportation costs include bus fare and limousine fare. Transportation costs for personal travel—sightseeing, visiting relatives, shopping, and other nonbusiness activities—are not deductible.

If you use your car for travel, see Chapter 9. If you rent a car for travel to or at your business destination, the rental charges, as well as gas, parking, and tolls, are deductible. However, if the rental exceeds 30 days and the value of the car exceeds a dollar limit, there may be income to include, called an *inclusion amount*. This concept is also explained in Chapter 9.

LODGING COSTS.   The cost of hotel, motel, or other accommodations is deductible if the nature of the business trip requires an overnight stay in order for you to sleep or properly perform your job. If you are self-employed you must keep track of all costs and deduct these actual costs. You cannot use a per diem rate as explained below.

For other businesses, you have a choice when deducting lodging costs: (1) keep track of all costs and deduct these actual costs, or (2) use a standard allowance set by the IRS that covers lodging, meals, and incidental expenses. There are two standard allowances—the per diem rates for the continental U.S. or two rates under a high-low method (a high rate applies to high-cost areas and the other rate applies to all other areas in the continental United States). The rates for the high-low method as well as high-cost areas are listed later in this chapter. Other per diem rates may be found at <www.policyworks.gov>.

Note

Using the standard allowance does not eliminate the need for other recordkeeping, as explained later in this chapter.

The daily dollar amount of the standard allowance is fixed by the government and is adjusted each year for inflation. The adjustment is now made on the government's fiscal year beginning October 1 of each year. For your calendar year you may use the rates in effect on January 1 (that become effective the previous October 1) throughout the year. Or you may use the actual rates in effect from January 1 through September 30 and the new rates that commence on October 1. The dollar amount you can deduct using a standard allowance depends on where your business takes you.

Example

Your business is on a calendar year. For 2005, you can use the per diem allowance that becomes effective on October 1, 2004, throughout 2005. Or you can use that allowance through September 30, 2005, and use the rates that take effect on October 1, 2005, for the balance of 2005.

MEALS. The cost of your meals on a trip away from home is deductible (subject to a percent limit, explained later). The cost of meals includes food, beverages, taxes, and tips. However, if the meals are considered to be lavish or extravagant, the deductible portion is limited to the amount that is reasonable. What is considered reasonable is based on the facts and circumstances of the situation. Lavish or extravagant is not automatically the conclusion when the cost of meals exceeds the standard meal allowance rate or when meals are eaten in deluxe hotels, restaurants, nightclubs, or resorts.

You have a choice when deducting meal costs: (1) keep track of all costs and deduct these actual costs, or (2) use a standard meal allowance set by the IRS. The Tax Court has said that even self-employed individuals can use a standard meal allowance even though they cannot use the per diem rates for lodging. There are two allowances to choose from: the maximum federal per diem rates or the rates under the high-low substantiation method.

> **Note**
>
> Using the standard meal allowance does not eliminate the need for other recordkeeping, as explained later in this chapter.

The daily dollar amount of the standard meal allowance is fixed by the government and is adjusted each year for inflation. The adjustment is made on the government's fiscal year beginning October 1 of each year. For your calendar year you may use the rates in effect on January 1 (that become effective the previous October 1) throughout the year. Or you may use the actual rates in effect from January 1 through September 30 and the new rates that commence on October 1. For October 1, 2005, through September 30, 2006, the rates remain unchanged, although areas qualifying for a rate other than the standard rate have changed.

The dollar amount you can deduct using a standard meal allowance depends on where your business takes you. In most of the United States, the daily amount is $31 (for October 1, 2004, through September 30, 2005). In certain areas designated by the IRS the daily amount is slightly higher ($35, $39, $43, $47, or $51). Alternatively, for administrative convenience you can use a two-rate system called the *high-low method*. In this case you use a flat rate of $36 per day for all areas other than those designated by the IRS as high-cost areas. For these high-cost areas you use a rate of $46 per day (for October 1, 2004, through September 30, 2005; rules for October 1, 2005, through September 30, 2006 were not available at press time). You take the daily amount based on the rate in effect for the area where you stop to sleep or rest. The standard meal allowances as well as high-cost areas for the high-low method are listed later in this chapter.

There is a percentage limit applied to the deduction for meal costs. Generally, the deduction is limited to 50 percent of meal costs. There is an exception for those who are subject to the hours of service limitations under the Department of Transportation (DOT), as explained later in this chapter. Thus, if you spend $100 on meals while traveling away from home (and you are not subject to DOT hours of service limits), only $50 are deductible. The 50-percent limit also applies to the standard meal allowance. You will see that this limit is taken into account on the forms that you use for deducting meal costs. For example, self-employed individuals filing Schedule C will note that the total cost of meals is entered and *then* the 50-percent limit is applied so that only one-half of meal costs is deductible.

OTHER DEDUCTIBLE TRAVEL COSTS.   While you are away from home on business, you may incur a number of miscellaneous or incidental travel expenses. These expenses are deductible in full. They include, for example, the reasonable cost of cleaning and laundering your clothes and tips you pay for services rendered in connection with any deductible expenses (such as a meal, a taxi ride, or a bellhop). However, if you use a per diem travel rate covering lodging, meals, and incidental expenses, then these items are not separately deductible. You may also incur any number of miscellaneous expenses that are deductible— telephone charges to talk to your office, fees to send or receive a business fax, computer or cell phone rental fees, or public stenographer's fees. These costs are not considered part of incidental expenses for purposes of per diem allowances, explained later in this chapter.

Travel with Another Person

If you take your spouse, child, or another person on a business trip, the costs related to that person generally are not deductible. The only way in which the costs are deductible is if that person works for you, there is a bona fide business reason for the travel, and the costs would have been deductible had they been incurred by someone who was not accompanying you. If the person provides only incidental services (such as typing notes or acting as assistant), his or her travel expenses are not deductible.

How do you distinguish between expenses that are yours (and deductible), from those of your companion (not deductible)? Clearly, the full cost of the other person's travel fare and meals is not deductible. In the case of lodging costs, if you are sharing a room, you must determine what you would have paid for a single, rather than a double, accommodation. For the most part, this is not simply half the cost. You may be able to deduct two-thirds or more of the cost of lodging.

There is a way for a business to turn nondeductible spousal travel costs into deductible costs. If your corporation treats spousal travel costs as additional compensation to you as an employee, then the corporation can claim a deduction for the costs as compensation rather than as travel and entertainment costs. In most cases, this alternative does not make much sense from your perspective, since it only shifts the tax burden from your corporation to you. However, if your personal tax picture is such that additional compensation will not result in additional tax, consider this alternative.

Major and Minor Job Locations

Some individuals work in more than one location. They may, for example, have a major job in one city and conduct some minor business in another. The cost of travel between the two jobs is deductible.

Part Business—Part Pleasure

If you combine business with pleasure, only part of your costs may be deductible. If your trip was primarily for business, then the portion of the travel costs related to business are deductible. This means that the full amount of airfare may be deductible. Meals and lodging for the days spent on business are also deductible.

Example

An airline pilot based in Minneapolis also flew for the National Guard out of Sioux Falls, South Dakota. His family lived in Sioux Falls. The IRS disallowed his travel expenses from Minneapolis to Sioux Falls, but a district court allowed the deduction. The fact that he derived some pleasure from the trip to Sioux Falls was secondary to the business nature of the trip. He deducted travel costs to that city only when he was required to fly there for Guard Duty.

Whether the time spent is primarily for business is determined by the facts and circumstances. There is no hard-and-fast rule.

Example

You travel from New York to San Diego for five days of business. You spend two more days sightseeing at the zoo and other attractions before returning to New York. All of your airfare is deductible. Five-sevenths of your lodging and food costs are also deductible. Any incidental expenses related to business are deductible. The cost of sightseeing and other personal expenses is not deductible.

If you stay over on a Saturday at a business location in order to obtain a re-duced airfare, the stay is treated as business and the cost of lodging for that stay is fully deductible. This is so even though you spend the time on personal matters. If the trip is primarily for personal reasons but you do conduct some business, you can deduct the direct costs of the business activities but no part of the travel costs.

Example

You spend a week at a resort location. One afternoon you make a business appointment and take a client out to lunch. None of your airfare to the resort or your lodging costs is deductible. You may, however, deduct the cost of the business lunch (assuming it meets general deductibility requirements).

FOREIGN TRAVEL

Entirely for Business

If you travel abroad entirely on business, all of your travel costs are deductible. (Meal and entertainment costs are still subject to the 50-percent limit.) If your trip is considered to be entirely business, then even if some time is spent sightseeing or on other personal activities, all of your transportation expenses are still deductible. There are special rules for determining whether your trip is considered to be *entirely* for business. You are treated as having spent your entire trip on business if you meet any of the following four rules.

1. You do not have substantial control over arranging your trip; travel is presumed to be entirely for business. You do not have control if you are an employee who is reimbursed for travel and are not related to your employer nor a managing executive (someone whose actions are not subject to veto by another). As a small business owner, it is virtually impossible to satisfy this rule. However, you can still fall within one of the other rules.
2. You are outside the United States for a week or less (seven or fewer consecutive days). In counting days, do not count the day you leave the United States, but do count the day of your return.

Example

You fly from Washington, D.C., to London on Sunday, arriving at Heathrow Airport on Monday morning. You work until Friday morning, then spend Friday and Saturday sightseeing and shopping. You fly out on Saturday night, arriving back in Washington on Sunday morning. You are considered to have been abroad for seven days (Monday through Sunday). All of your airfare is deductible. The cost of lodging, meals, and incidentals for the business days are also deductible, but meals are subject to the 50-percent limit.

3. You spend less than 25 percent of the time outside the United States on personal activities, regardless of the length of the stay abroad. In counting days for this rule, count both the day you leave and the day you return.

Example

You fly on Sunday from Chicago to Paris, where you spend 14 days on business and five days on personal matters. You spend one day flying in each direction. Your total time abroad is 21 days (14 days for business, five days for personal activities, and two days for travel). Since the time spent on nonbusiness activities is less than 25 percent of the total travel time abroad (five days personal/21 days total), you may treat the trip as entirely business. Thus, the entire cost of the airfare is deductible. You may treat the days of travel as business days so that 16/21 of the lodging and meal costs (subject to the 50-percent limit on meals) are deductible.

4. You can show that a personal vacation or another personal reason was not the major consideration in arranging the trip. You can use this rule even though you do have substantial control over arranging the trip.

Primarily for Business

If your travel abroad is not treated as entirely business (because you do not meet any of the four rules), you may still deduct some business expenses if the trip is *primarily* business. There is no mechanical rule to establish that the trip is primarily business. However, if you can show a valid business reason for the trip, you can deduct the portion of business expenses allocable to the business part of the trip, including the allocable portion of transportation costs.

Example

You fly from Boston to Rome, where you spend 10 days on business and five days on personal matters. You spend one day flying in each direction. Your total time abroad is 17 days (10 days for business, five days for personal activities, and two days in travel time). You had substantial control over arranging your trip, spent more than a week abroad, more than 25 percent of your time on personal activities, and cannot establish that a personal vacation was not a major consideration. Thus, you cannot show the trip was entirely for business. However, you can show the trip was primarily for business. You spent the greater part of the time on business and arranged the trip accordingly. In this instance, 12/17 of the costs of the airfare and other expenses are deductible business costs; the balance is treated as nondeductible personal expenses.

COUNTING BUSINESS DAYS.   In counting days for business when travel is primarily for that purpose, travel days are treated as business days. However, extra days of travel for personal activities, such as side trips, are not counted. You can also treat any day your presence is required at a business meeting or activity as a business day even if you spend the greater part of the day on personal activities. You can also treat as business days any days you wanted to spend on business but were prevented from doing so by circumstances beyond your control (such as weather, strikes, or civil unrest). Saturday, Sunday, and holidays are treated as business days if they fall between two business days. Thus, if you work on Friday and Monday, you count the weekend days as business days. Weekends following the close of your business activities are not treated as business days if you choose to stay on for personal purposes. However, overnight Saturday stays to obtain a reduced airfare are treated as business even when the time is spent on personal activities.

Primarily for Vacation

If you travel abroad primarily for vacation but attend some business or professional seminar, you may not deduct any portion of the trip as a business expense. You may, however, deduct the cost of the seminar (registration fees and other related expenses) as a business expense.

Example

Your professional association sponsors a two-week trip abroad. It holds two three-hour seminars during the trip and awards a Certificate in Continuing Education to those who attend the seminars. The entire cost of the trip is a nondeductible personal expense, as it is viewed as primarily for vacation. However, the registration fees for the seminars are deductible.

Conventions

Travel expenses to conventions held within the United States are deductible if you can show that your attendance benefits your business. The fact that you are appointed or elected to be a delegate to the convention does not, by itself, mean you can deduct expenses; you must show that attendance is connected to your business. You can do this by showing that the convention agenda is related to the active conduct of your business. The same rule applies to both employees and self-employed persons.

Foreign Conventions

The expenses of attending a convention outside the North American area (see Table 8.1) are not deductible unless the meeting is directly related to your business and it is reasonable to hold it outside the North American area.

A number of facts and circumstances are taken into account in showing that it is reasonable to hold the convention outside the North American area. They are:

- The purpose of the meeting and the activities taking place at the meeting
- The purposes and activities of the sponsoring organizations or groups
- The residences of the active members of the sponsoring organization and the places at which the meetings of the sponsoring organizations or groups have been held or will be held
- Other relevant factors

TABLE 8.1 North American Area

American Samoa	Johnston Island
Antigua and Barbuda	Kingman Reef
Baker Island	Marshall Islands
Barbados	Mexico
Bermuda	Micronesia
Canada	Midway Islands
Costa Rica	Northern Mariana Islands
Dominica	Palau
Dominican Republic	Palmyra
Grenada	Puerto Rico
Guam	Saint Lucia
Guyana	Trinidad and Tobago
Honduras	United States
Howland Island	U.S. Virgin Islands
Jamaica	Wake Island
Jarvis Island	

Cruise Ships

The cost of business conventions or meetings held on a cruise ship is limited. The maximum deduction per year is $2,000. In order to get this deduction, a number of requirements must be met:

1. The meeting must be directly related to your business.
2. The cruise ship must be a vessel registered in the United States. (All ships that sail are considered cruise ships.)
3. All of the ship's ports of call must be located in the United States or in U.S. possessions.
4. You must attach a written statement to your return showing the days of the cruise, the number of hours devoted to business, and a program of scheduled business activities.
5. You must also attach a written statement to your return signed by an officer of the organization or group sponsoring the meeting that shows the schedule of the business activities of each day of the meeting and the number of hours you attended.

Living Away from Home on Temporary Assignments

If you work in a location other than your regular place of business and are forced to live away from your home (because the distance is too great to reasonably expect that you would travel back and forth each day), then not only the cost of your transportation to the **temporary assignment** but also living expenses are deductible.

Temporary assignment   An assignment away from the area of your tax home that is realistically expected to last for no more than a year and does, in fact, end at that time.

An assignment that is expected to last for more than a year, or one that does in fact last for more than a year, is considered indefinite. Also, a series of short jobs in the same location that, taken together, last more than a year are considered an indefinite assignment. Probationary work is also treated as indefinite. Thus, for example, if you relocate with the understanding that your job will be permanent if your work is satisfactory, the job is considered indefinite. Transportation to the location of the indefinite assignment from your general area of your tax home is deductible; personal living expenses are not.

Change in Job Assignments

Suppose your assignment gets extended or shortened. How does this affect whether the assignment is treated as temporary or indefinite?

SITUATION ONE.   You are sent out of town on a job assignment expected to last for 10 months but it is extended and, in fact, lasts for 14 months. As long as the initial expectation of 10 months was reasonable, your living expenses are deductible until the time that the expectation changed. Thus, if at the end of 10 months the assignment projection changed, expenses for the first 10 months are deductible. If, however, at the end of six months the assignment projection changed, only expenses for the first six months are deductible.

SITUATION TWO.   You are sent out of town on a job assignment expected to last 14 months but in fact it is shortened and lasts only 10 months. Since the original expectation of the job length exceeded one year, no part of the living expenses is deductible. The entire assignment is treated as indefinite even though it did in fact end within a year.

Remember, you must have a tax home to be away from when deducting living expenses on temporary assignments. If all of your assignments are away and you have no tax home, no living expenses will be allowed.

Example

An engineering consultant in Florida took temporary engineering assignments for a period of three years in five states as well as in his home state. During this time he maintained a home office in his apartment, where he returned after each assignment for periods of four to six months at a time, and he continued to seek permanent employment there. The IRS argued that he was an itinerant, so his expenses were not deductible. The Tax Court disagreed and found his Florida home to be his tax home. He needed to maintain a permanent address and business number to obtain consulting jobs. He always returned there between assignments and never stopped seeking permanent employment there.

What Expenses Are Deductible?

If a job assignment is temporary, then personal living expenses—rent, utilities, food, and other expenses—are deductible. The reason for this rule: Congress recognized that if you are required to be away from home on a temporary basis, you will have to incur duplicative living expenses, since it would be unreasonable to expect you to relocate for that short period of time. However, if the job assignment is indefinite, it would be reasonable to expect you to relocate and there would be no need for duplicative living expenses. If you do move to a new location, the cost of moving expenses may be deductible (see Chapter 22). If you are on a temporary assignment and return home on weekends, holidays, or visits, the time at home is not treated as away from home and the cost of your lodging at home is not deductible. The cost of your lodging at the temporary work site, however, continues to be deductible. Thus, for example, if you are living away from home in a motel and return home on a weekend but must pay for the motel room anyway, that cost is deductible. The cost of meals on a return trip home is deductible only to the extent that the cost of meals away would have been deductible. The cost of travel from the temporary assignment home and the return trip is also deductible.

Meal and Entertainment Expenses

If you entertain your client, customer, or employee, the cost of your expenses is deductible, subject to the 50-percent limit discussed later. (Meal costs for daycare providers are discussed in Chapter 22.) Entertainment may be an important way for you to generate business, create goodwill, and thank employees for a job well done. You may spend a considerable amount of time and expense wining and dining. Be sure to understand the rules to make your costs deductible to the fullest extent possible. Keep in mind that the area of meals and entertainment expenses attracts particular attention from the IRS, but if you meet the requirements for deductibility, your deductions will withstand IRS scrutiny.

General Rules on Deducting Meal and Entertainment Expenses

In order to be deductible as a meal and entertainment expense, an expense must be:

1. An **ordinary and necessary business expense**, and
2. Able to qualify under a directly related test or an associated test.

Ordinary and necessary business expense   An *ordinary expense* is one that is common and accepted in your business. A *necessary expense* is one that is helpful and appropriate to your business. To be necessary, an expense need not be indispensable.

The Directly Related Test

You satisfy the *directly related test* if you can show that the main purpose of the entertainment activity was the active conduct of business and that you did, in fact, engage in business during the entertainment period. Entertainment in a clear business setting is presumed to meet the directly related test. You must have more than a general expectation of deriving income or some other business benefit from the activity at some future time. You need not devote more time to business than entertainment in order to satisfy this test. You simply have to demonstrate that all the facts, including the nature of the business transacted and the reasons for conducting business during an entertainment, support a business purpose. Nor do you need to show that business income or some other business benefit actually resulted from a specific entertainment event.

You will be presumed to have failed the directly related test if you are on a hunting, skiing, or fishing trip or on yachts or other pleasure boats unless you can show otherwise. Other locations that are presumed to have failed the directly related test include nightclubs, golf courses, theaters, and sporting events.

You bear a heavy burden of proof when the entertainment is held in a place where there are substantial distractions that prevent the possibility of actively conducting any business. This kind of entertainment is presumed to fail the directly related test. Substantial distractions are present at nightclubs, theaters, sporting events, and social gatherings (cocktail parties or meetings that include persons other than business associates). You can, however, overcome the presumption by showing that you engaged in a substantial business discussion during the entertainment despite the distractions.

Example

Entertainment in a hospitality room or suite at a convention where your business products are on display is in a clear business setting. Goodwill is presumed to be created through this entertainment in a clear business setting.

Example

A price rebate on the sale of your products can be entertainment provided in a clear business setting. Thus, if you own a restaurant and offer a free meal to a customer or supplier, this entertainment in a clear business setting is directly related to your business and is deductible.

Example

Where the entertainment itself is of a clear business nature but there is no personal or social relationship between you and the person or persons entertained, the costs are treated as directly related to your business. For example, if you entertain business leaders at the opening of a shopping mall in order to gain publicity, the cost is treated as a deductible entertainment expense.

Associated Test

If you cannot meet the higher standard of directly related, you may still be able to show that the entertainment is *associated* with the conduct of your business. This test requires showing that the expense is associated with your business and directly precedes or follows a substantial business discussion. You must have a clear business purpose for having the entertainment expense. This includes entertainment to get new business or encourage continued business with existing clients or customers.

How do you know if a business discussion is *substantial*? There is no quantitative way to show this. There is no prescribed amount of time you must spend meeting or discussing business, and you do not have to devote more time to business than to entertainment. You do not even have to discuss business during the entertainment itself. Whether the entertainment meets the associated test depends on the facts and circumstances of the situation. You must be able to show that you actually held a business discussion to get income or other business benefit. Goodwill entertainment satisfies the associated test.

If the entertainment is held on the same day as a business discussion, it is treated as held preceding or following a substantial business discussion.

Example

During working hours, a customer visits your offices and you discuss business for some time. That evening after your office is closed, you take your customer to the theater. This satisfies the associated test, since you held a substantial business discussion preceding the entertainment.

Where the business discussion is not held on the same day as the entertainment, all the facts are taken into account in determining whether the associated test is met. Factors considered are the place, the date, and the duration of the business discussion. For example, if you or your customers are out of town, the dates of arrival and departure may affect entertainment expenses.

Example

A customer flies in from out of town on Tuesday afternoon. You take her to the theater that evening and meet with her in your office on the following morning, at which time you hold a substantial business discussion. The associated test is met in this instance.

Other Requirements

In addition to meeting the directly related or associated test, you must show that the cost of the entertainment was not *lavish or extravagant*. There are no dollar figures used in making this determination; rather, it is based on the facts and circumstances. However, no deduction is allowed for fees paid to scalpers, ticket agents, or ticket brokers for tickets to theater, sporting, or other events. Only the face value of the ticket is deductible. Also, the cost of skyboxes and other private luxury boxes at a sports arena is limited. These boxes generally are rented for a season or a series of events, such as playoff games or a World Series. Where the cost covers more than one event, you cannot deduct more than the total of the face values of non-luxury box seats times the number of seats in the box. Then the 50-percent limit applies.

Food, beverages, and other separately stated charges related to the skyboxes are separately deductible (subject to the 50-percent limit).

Home Entertainment

If you entertain business associates, customers, or employees at your home, can you deduct your expenses? The answer depends on whether you discuss specific business during the course of the dinner or other entertainment event. Business dinners may be conducive to business discussions. Other types of social gatherings, such as pool parties, may not be as conducive to business discussions and may raise questions with the IRS. It may be helpful to keep the guest list to a minimum (no more than 12) in order to be able to hold discussions with all guests. If you have a larger group, it may be difficult to show that you had business discussions with each guest.

If you do entertain at home, do not combine business with pleasure. The presence of nonbusiness guests may support the conclusion that the gathering was not for business reasons and that business was not discussed. Taxpayers have not fared well in proving that parties for personal events, such as a child's wedding, birthday, or bar mitzvah, were held for business even though business guests attended.

Limit

There is no dollar limit on what you can spend for meal and entertainment expenses. (Remember, though, that there is a lavish or extravagant limit.) However, only a portion of your costs is deductible. Meals and entertainment expenses generally are deductible only to the extent of 50 percent of cost. The 50-percent limit applies to meals eaten while traveling away from home even if they are paid with a per diem reimbursement rate.

The 50-percent limit does not necessarily apply to all business meals or entertainment. There are some important exceptions:

- Promotional activities.
- Meals paid for recreational, social, or similar activities primarily for the benefit of employees. This exception would apply, for example, to your cost of providing food at a company picnic.

Example

A real estate broker selling vacation property gave potential investors a free meal if they agreed to sit through a sales presentation. The IRS allowed the broker to deduct the full cost of the meals in this case, since they were made available to the general public as part of promotional activities.

- Food and beverages provided to employees as a tax-free de minimis fringe benefit. This exception would apply to your expenses of providing an employee cafeteria on your premises.
- Employees (in the transportation industry) who are subject to DOT hours of service limitations are subject to an increased meal deduction for food and beverages consumed while away from home. See Table 8.2 for these deductions.

Impact of the 50-Percent Limit on Employees

The fact that the company cannot deduct 50 percent of its costs for meals and entertainment does not affect employees. Employees are not taxed on the nondeductible portion of meal and entertainment costs even though they receive a full reimbursement or an advance for these expenses.

Club Dues

You cannot deduct the cost of dues, including initiation fees, to clubs organized for pleasure, recreation, or other social purposes. For example, the cost of airline clubs is not deductible. However, dues to certain business, professional, and civic organizations continue to be deductible. These include:

- *Business organizations*—business leagues, trade associations, chambers of commerce, boards of trade and real estate boards, business lunch clubs
- *Professional organizations*—bar associations, medical associations
- *Civic organizations*—Kiwanis, Lions, Rotary, Civitan

TABLE 8.2 Meal Deductions for DOT Employees

Year	Deductible Percentage
2005	70
2006–2007	75
2008 and later	80

If you pay club dues for an employee, you can turn what would otherwise be a nondeductible expense into a deductible one. You can treat the payment of club dues on behalf of an employee as additional compensation. In this way the business can claim a deduction for club dues as compensation, not as travel and entertainment costs.

This option applies only to club dues that would otherwise be deductible but for the ban on deductibility. Thus, it applies only if the club is used for business. For example, suppose a corporation pays the country club dues of an employee. The employee uses the club 100 percent for entertaining clients for business purposes. The corporation can elect to treat these dues as additional compensation to the employee. Of course, the employee cannot claim any offsetting deduction on his or her individual income tax return. If the country club is used solely for personal purposes, then the cost of dues is not subject to this election rule.

The election to treat club dues as additional compensation can be made on an employee-by-employee basis. Thus, if you own a corporation that pays club dues on behalf of yourself and other employees, the corporation can elect to treat the club dues as additional compensation to your other employees but not to yourself. If the corporation pays your club dues and elects to treat this as compensation to you, all you are really doing is shifting the tax burden from the corporation to you, something that may not have any net advantage. The corporation should weigh this election carefully before making it.

Spouse's Expenses

If you take your spouse or a friend with you on business entertainment or take a client's or customer's spouse along, are the spouse's expenses deductible? In general, the answer is no. However, if you can show that the purpose for including the spouse was clearly for business and not some social or personal purpose, the spouse's costs are deductible.

Example

You entertain a business customer. Assume that the costs of entertaining the customer are clearly deductible. The customer's spouse joins you because it would be impractical to entertain the customer without the spouse. In this case, the cost of the spouse's entertainment is an ordinary and necessary business expense. If your spouse were to join the entertainment because the customer's spouse is along, your spouse's costs would also be deductible.

Business Gifts

In the course of your business, you may give gifts to your dealers, distributors, customers, clients, and employees. The cost of business gifts is deductible, within limits. You may deduct only up to $25 per person per year (the dollar limit that was set back in 1954). This rule applies to both *direct* and *indirect* gifts. An indirect gift includes a gift to a company that is intended for the eventual personal use of a particular person or a gift to a spouse or child of a business customer or client.

In using the $25 limit, do not count incidental costs, such as wrapping, insuring, or shipping the gifts. Also, do not count engraving on jewelry.

Example

You give a $30 gift to client A. You may deduct $25. You give a $20 gift to client B. You may deduct $20.

Exceptions

Certain gifts are not subject to the $25 limit. These include gifts of nominal value ($4 or less) with your company name imprinted on them that you distribute to a number of clients or customers. These gifts would include, for example, pens, plastic bags, kitchen magnets, and calendars. Thus, if you give a customer a $25 gift and also send a calendar, the value of the calendar (assuming it is below $4) is not taken into account. Both gifts are deductible. Another exception to the $25 rule includes signs, display racks, or other promotional material used on business premises. Thus, if you give a dealer a display rack to hold your items, the gift is a deductible business expense, regardless of cost.

In one case the Tax Court recognized another exception to the $25 limit for gifts to employees—gifts designated as an *employee relations expense* rather than as a gift or compensation. The court allowed a deduction in this case of almost $1,500 (the cost of a set of golf clubs) given as incentive for continued good performance by a top salesperson.

Note

Expect the IRS to continue to challenge any gifts in excess of the $25 limit so, if you want to make larger gifts, be sure to have a business rationale for doing so.

When Is an Item an Entertainment Expense?

If you give an item that could be treated as either an entertainment expense or a business gift, how do you know how to classify it? The choice is yours. In making it, take into consideration the fact that an entertainment expense is subject to a 50-percent limit, while a business gift is subject to the $25 limit. Thus, if you give tickets to the theater or a ball game and you do not go with the client or customer to the performance or event, you can choose to treat the cost as either an entertainment expense or a business gift.

Example

You give your client two tickets to the ball game. The tickets cost $20 each. If you treat them as a business gift, you can deduct $25 ($40 business gift up to the $25 limit). However, if you treat the tickets as an entertainment expense, only $20 is deductible ($40 expense subject to the 50-percent limit).

If you treat an item as a business gift but want to change the treatment, you may do so within three years of the filing of your return by filing an amended return.

If you go with the client to the theater or sporting event, you must treat the cost of the tickets as an entertainment expense; you cannot treat it as a business gift. However, if the gift is one of food or beverage intended to be consumed by the client or customer at a later time, you must treat it as a business gift. Thus, if you give bottles of wine or liquor, they constitute business gifts.

Reimbursement Arrangements

If an employer reimburses an employee for travel and entertainment expenses, how you arrange the reimbursement affects what the employer and employee can deduct.

No Reimbursement Arrangement

If an employee on salary has no reimbursement arrangement and is expected or required to pay for travel and entertainment costs by himself or herself, the employee can deduct the expenses on his or her individual income tax return. The business expenses are deductible as miscellaneous itemized deductions. This means that after applying all the limits discussed above, such as the 50-percent limit on meals and entertainment, costs are deductible only to the extent they exceed 2 percent of the employee's adjusted gross income. In this instance, the employee is responsible for record-keeping of business expenses.

Accountable Plans

If an employer maintains an *accountable plan*, the employee does not deduct any expenses. Instead, the employer pays for and deducts all costs. No reimbursements are reported as income to the employee, and the reimbursements are not subject to payroll taxes.

A reimbursement arrangement is treated as an accountable plan if:

1. The expenses have a business connection. This means the expenses must have been incurred while performing services as an employee for an employer.

2. The employee must adequately account to the employer for expenses within a reasonable time. Accounting within 60 days after paying or incurring the expenses is considered a reasonable time. The employee must supply the employer with documentary evidence (canceled checks, receipts, or bills) of mileage, travel, and other business expenses unless reimbursement is made at a per diem rate. All employees must provide the employer with a statement of expense, an account book or diary, or a similar record (including computer logs) in which expenses are entered at or near the time at which they were incurred. All amounts received from an employer must be documented. This includes not only cash advances but also amounts charged to an employer by credit card or other method.

3. The employee must return to the employer within a reasonable period of time any excess reimbursements. Thus, for example, if an employer advances an employee $400 for a business trip and expenses totaled only $350, the employee must return the excess $50 within a reasonable period of time. A reasonable period of time depends on the facts and circumstances. However, it is automatically treated as reasonable if an advance is made within 30 days of the expense, adequate accounting of the expense is made to the employer within 60 days after it was paid or incurred, and any excess reimbursement is refunded to the employer within 120 days after the expense was paid or incurred. It is also automatically treated as reasonable if an employer furnishes an employee with a periodic (at least quarterly) statement requesting reimbursement of excess amounts and reimbursement is in fact made within 120 days after receipt of the statement.

If the employer maintains an accountable plan but an employee does not meet all the rules (for example, the employee fails to return excess amounts or is reimbursed for nonbusiness expenses), then those expenses are treated as paid under a nonaccountable plan. The remaining expenses are treated as paid under an accountable plan.

> ### Example
>
> An employer maintains an accountable plan. During the year, an employee is reimbursed for business travel expenses and also receives reimbursement for meals eaten while working late for the employer. The meals are nonbusiness expenses. The employer is treated as having two plans in this instance: an accountable plan for the travel expenses and a nonaccountable plan for the personal meal expenses.

Nonaccountable Plans

If an employer maintains a reimbursement arrangement but it does not qualify as an accountable plan (for example, excess reimbursements need not be returned or reimbursements cover nondeductible personal expenses), the plan is considered a nonaccountable plan. In this case, the employer must report the reimbursements on an employee's Form W-2. The employee then deducts the expenses on his or her individual income tax return, subject to the 2-percent-of-adjusted-gross-income floor.

Reimbursement at Per Diem Rates

Reimbursing employees for travel and related expenses at a per diem rate simplifies things for all concerned; employees need not keep track of every expense and retain receipts for all of them, and employers can make reimbursements at a flat rate, easing accounting procedures. If an employer pays for business expenses using a per diem rate, special rules apply. If the rate used by the employer is the same as or lower than the federal per diem rate for the area of travel, reimbursements are not reported on an employee's Form W-2. If an employee's actual expenses exceeded the reimbursement at or below the federal rate, the employee can deduct the excess expenses on his or her individual income tax return. However, if the rate used by the employer is higher than the federal rate, the amounts are reported on Form W-2. The amount of the federal rate is not included in an employee's gross income, though excess reimbursements are included in the employee's gross income. The employee can, however, claim business deductions for these excess amounts (subject to the 2-percent floor).

There are several acceptable federal rates that an employer can use to make reimbursements, including the federal per diem rate, high-low method, standard meal allowance, and the incidental rate.

FEDERAL PER DIEM RATE. This is the highest per diem rate paid by the federal government to its employees for lodging, meals, and incidental expenses (or meals and incidental expenses only) while traveling away from home in a particular area. Different per diem rates apply in different areas. Some rates are seasonal. The rates can change annually at the government's fiscal year commencing on October 1. Employers can get these rates from IRS Publication 1542, *Per Diem Rates* or from <www.gsa.gov>.

You can opt to use the rates in effect on January 1 for the entire calendar year, or you can use the new rates effective on October 1 for the final quarter of the year.

HIGH-LOW METHOD.   Instead of finding out about different rates for each area of travel, you can use a simplified method where only two different rates apply. So-called high-cost areas (see Table 8.3) are assigned one rate for lodging, meals, and incidental expenses; all other areas within the continental United States are assigned another rate. The high-cost per diem rate for the government's fiscal year October 1, 2004, through September 30, 2005, is $204; for all other areas within the continental United States, it is $129. (The IRS had used the rates of $199 and $127, respectively, starting October 1, 2004, but revised them as stated here effective January 1, 2005.) The rates for the government's fiscal year 2006 are available in IRS Publication 1542, *Per Diem Rates*.

Where an employer does not reimburse for lodging but only for meals and incidental expenses (M&IE), the allowance for high-cost areas is $46; for all other localities it is $36.

The M&IE portion of the reimbursement under the high-low substantiation method is subject to the 50-percent limit on meals and entertainment. Thus, while the allowance for M&IE for a high-cost area is $46 per day, in actuality only $23 is deductible ($46 × .50). Of the $36 per diem rate for non-high-cost areas, only $18 is deductible ($36 × .50).

"Incidental expenses" include only fees and tips for porters, baggage handlers, hotel maids, and room stewards. They no longer include laundry, dry cleaning, lodging taxes, telegrams, and phone calls. This means that such expenses can be claimed in addition to the M&IE rate, provided there are records (such as receipts or itemization on the room bill) to support them.

STANDARD MEAL ALLOWANCE.   The standard meal allowance in effect for October 1, 2004, through September 30, 2005), is $31 a day for most areas within the continental United States. However, a higher rate may or may not apply (a higher rate applies for lodging that makes it a high-cost area even if the meal portion is the standard $31-a-day limit, see Table 8.4). (The $31-per-day rate

---

Note

Both the high-low substantiation rates and the designation of high-cost areas are subject to change each year.

TABLE 8.3 High-Cost Areas for January 1, 2005, through September 30, 2005

State—Key City	County and Other Defined Location
Arizona	
Phoenix/Scottsdale (January 1 to May 31)	Maricopa
California	
Monterey (February 1 to November 30)	Monterey
Napa (May 1 to October 31)	Napa
Palm Springs (January 1 to May 31)	Riverside
San Diego	San Diego
San Francisco	San Francisco
Santa Barbara	Santa Barbara
Santa Monica	City limits
South Tahoe City	El Dorado
(December 1 to August 31)	
Colorado	
Aspen	Pitkin
Crested Butte (December 1 to March 31)	City limits of Crested Butte
Silverthorne/Breckenridge	Summit
(December 1 to March 31)	
Telluride (December 1 to September 30)	San Miguel
Vail	Eagle
District of Columbia	
Washington, D.C.	Washington, D.C.; the cities of Alexandria, Falls Church, and Fairfax and the counties of Arlington, Loudoun, and Fairfax in Virginia; the counties of Montgomery and Prince George in Maryland
Delaware	
Lewes (July 1 to August 31)	Sussex
Florida	
Daytona Beach (February 1 to March 31)	Volusia
Fort Lauderdale (January 1 to May 31)	Broward
Key West	Monroe
Miami (October 1 to May 31)	Miami-Dade
Naples (January 1 to March 31)	Collier
Palm Beach (October 1 to May 31)	Palm Beach (cities of Boca Raton, Delray Beach, Jupiter, Palm Beach Gardens, Palm Beach Shores, Singer Island, and West Palm Beach)
Illinois	
Chicago	Cook and Lake
Louisiana	
New Orleans (February 1 to April 30 and September 1 to November 30)	Orleans and St. Bernard Parishes
Maryland	
Baltimore	Baltimore
Cambridge/St. Michaels (June 1 to August 31)	Dorchester and Talbot
Ocean City (July 1 to August 31)	Worcester

(Continued)

TABLE 8.3 *(Continued)*

State—Key City	County and Other Defined Location
Massachusetts	
Boston	Suffolk
Cambridge	City limits
Hyannis (July 1 to August 31)	Barnstable
Martha's Vineyard (May 1 to August 31)	Dukes
Nantucket	Nantucket
Michigan	
Traverse City (July 1 to August 31)	Grand Traverse
New Jersey	
Atlantic City (May 1 to October 31)	Atlantic
Cape May (June 1 to August 31)	Cape May (except Ocean City)
Ocean City (June 1 to October 31)	City limits of Ocean City
Princeton/Trenton	Mercer County
New Mexico	Sante Fe
Sante Fe (July 1 to August 31)	
New York	Nassau
Carle Place/Garden City/Glen Cove/Great Neck/Plainview/ Rockville Centre/Syosset/ Uniondale/Woodbury	
Lake Placid (July 1 to August 31)	Essex
New York City	Includes Richmond County; boroughs of Manhattan, Brooklyn, the Bronx, and Queens
Riverhead/Ronkonhoma/Melville	Suffolk
Tarrytown	Westchester (except White Plains)
White Plains	City limits
North Carolina	Dare
Kill Devil (April 1 to October 31)	
Pennsylvania	
Hershey (May 1 to August 31)	City limits of Hershey
Philadelphia	Philadelphia
South Carolina	Beaufort
Hilton Head (April 1 to October 31)	
Utah	Summit
Park City (December 31 to March 31)	
Virginia	
See District of Columbia	
Virginia Beach (June 1 to August 31)	Cities of Virginia Beach, Norfolk, Portsmouth, Chesapeake, and Suffolk
Washington	
Seattle (May 1 to October 31)	King

TABLE 8.4 Domestic Per Diem Rates for January 1, 2005, through September 30, 2005

State/City	County	Seasonal Dates (If Applicable)	Lodging Rate	M&IE Rate	Total Per Diem Rate
Standard rate for any area not listed below			$ 60	$ 31	$ 91
Alabama					
Birmingham	Jefferson; Shelby		77	43	120
Gulf Shores	Baldwin	Jan. 1–Feb. 28	60	39	99
Gulf Shores	Baldwin	Mar. 1–May 31	76	39	115
Gulf Shores	Baldwin	Jun. 1–Aug. 31	94	39	133
Gulf Shores	Baldwin	Sept. 1–Dec. 31	60	39	99
Huntsville	Madison; Limestone		65	39	104
Montgomery	Montgomery		65	43	108
Tuscaloosa	Tuscaloosa		64	35	99
Arizona					
Flagstaff/Kayenta	All points in Coconina County not covered under Grand Canyon per diem area	Jan. 1–Mar. 31	60	39	99
Flagstaff/Kayenta	All points in Coconino County not covered under Grand Canyon per diem area	May 1–Aug. 31	73	39	112
Flagstaff/Kayenta	All points in Coconino County not covered under Grand Canyon per diem area	Sept. 1–Dec. 31	60	39	99
Grand Canyon	Grand Canyon Nat'l Park and Kaibab Nat'l Forest	Jan. 1–Mar. 31	60	47	107
Grand Canyon	Grand Canyon Nat'l Park and Kaibab Nat'l Forest	Apr. 1–Oct. 31	85	47	107
Grand Canyon	Grand Canyon Nat'l Park and Kaibab Nat'l Forest	Nov. 1–Dec. 31	85	47	132
Phoenix/Scottsdale	Maricopa	Jan. 1–May 31	121	47	168
Phoenix/Scottsdale	Maricopa	Jun. 1–Sept. 30	75	47	122
Phoenix/Scottsdale	Maricopa	Oct. 1–Dec. 31	103	47	150

(Continued)

TABLE 8.4 *(Continued)*

State/City	County	Seasonal Dates (If Applicable)	Lodging Rate	M&IE Rate	Total Per Diem Rate
Tucson	Pima	Jan. 1–Apr. 30	105	43	148
Tucson	Pima	May 1–Dec. 31	76	43	119
Yuma	Yuma		63	39	102
Arkansas					
Hot Springs	Garland		66	35	101
Little Rock	Puliski		71	39	110
California					
Antioch/Brentwood/ Concord/Lafayette/ Martinez/Pleasant Hill/Richmond/San Ramon/Walnut Creek	Contra Costa		99	47	146
Bakersfield/Delano	Kern; Naval Weapons Center and Ordnance Test Station, China Lake		67	43	110
Benicia/Dixon/ Fairfield/Vacaville/ Vallejo	Solano		104	47	151
Brawley/Calexico/ El Contro/Imperial	Imperial		64	31	95
Clearlake	Lake		69	35	104
Death Valley	Inyo		71	47	118
Fresno	Fresno		70	35	105
Los Angeles	Orange and Ventura Counties; Edwards AFB; Naval Weapons Center and Ordnance Test Station, China Lake		100	51	151
Mammoth Lakes	Mono		71	47	118
Mill Valley/ San Rafael/Novato	Marin		107	47	154
Modesto	Stanislaus		78	39	117
Monterey	Monterey	May 1–Oct. 31	94	47	141
Monterey	Monterey	Nov. 1–Apr. 30	75	47	122
Monterey	Monterey	Dec. 1–Dec. 31	106	47	153
Napa	Napa	Apr. 1–Nov. 15	125	47	172

TABLE 8.4 *(Continued)*

State/City	County	Seasonal Dates (If Applicable)	Lodging Rate	M&IE Rate	Total Per Diem Rate
Napa	Napa	Nov. 16–Mar. 31	110	47	157
Napa	Napa	Nov. 1–Dec. 31	115	47	162
Oakhurst	Madera		76	43	119
Oakland	Alameda		100	43	143
Ontario/Barstow/ Victorville	San Bernadino		82	43	125
Palm Springs	Riverside	Jan. 1–May 31	140	47	187
Palm Springs	Riverside	Jun. 1–Aug. 31	86	47	133
Palm Springs	Riverside	Sept. 1–Dec. 31	104	47	151
Point Arena/Gualala	Mendocino		65	43	108
Redding	Shasta		76	35	111
Sacramento	Sacramento		91	47	138
San Diego	San Diego		129	51	180
San Francisco	San Francisco		126	51	177
San Luis Obispo	San Luis Obispo		103	43	146
San Mateo/Foster City/Belmont	San Mateo		95	47	142
Santa Barbara	Santa Barbara		143	43	186
Santa Cruz	Santa Cruz	Jan. 1–June 30	74	47	121
Santa Cruz	Santa Cruz	Sept. 1–Dec. 31	74	47	121
Santa Monica	City limits		151	43	194
Santa Rosa	Sonoma		104	47	151
South Lake Tahoe	El Dorado	Jan. 1–Aug. 31	136	47	183
South Lake Tahoe	El Dorado	Sept. 1–Nov. 30	113	47	160
South Lake Tahoe	El Dorado	Dec. 1–Dec. 31	136	47	183
Stockton	San Joaquin		77	31	108
Sunnyvale/Palo Alto/San Jose	Santa Clara		111	51	162
Tahoe City	Placer		97	47	144
Truckee	Nevada		87	47	134
Visalia/Lemoore	Tulare; Kings		66	43	109
West Sacramento	Yolo		97	35	132
Yosemite Nat'l Park	Mariposa		81	47	128

(Continued)

TABLE 8.4 *(Continued)*

State/City	County	Seasonal Dates (If Applicable)	Lodging Rate	M&IE Rate	Total Per Diem Rate
Colorado					
Aspen	Pitkin	Jan. 1–Mar. 31	194	47	241
Aspen	Pitkin	Apr. 1–Nov. 30	138	47	185
Aspen	Pitkin	Dec. 1–Dec. 31	194	47	241
Boulder/Bloomfield	Boulder/Bloomfield		87	47	134
Colorado Springs	El Paso	Jan. 1–Apr. 30	73	43	116
Colorado Springs	El Paso	May 1–Oct. 31	104	43	147
Colorado Springs	El Paso	Nov. 1–Dec. 31	73	43	116
Cortez	Montezuma		65	35	100
Crested Butte	City limits	Jan. 1–Mar. 31	146	47	193
Crested Butte	City limits	Apr. 1–Sept. 30	107	47	154
Crested Butte	City limits	Oct. 1–Nov. 30	98	47	145
Crested Butte	City limits	Dec. 1–Dec. 31	146	47	193
Denver	Denver, Adams, Arapahoe; portion of Westminster in Jefferson; Lone Tree in Douglas		112	47	159
Durango	La Plata	Jan. 1–May 31	77	43	120
Durango	La Plata	Jun. 1–Sept. 30	99	43	142
Durango	La Plata	Oct. 1–Dec. 31	77	43	120
Fort Collins	Larimer (except Loveland)		74	39	113
Glenwood Springs	Garfield	Jan. 1–May 31	61	35	96
Glenwood Springs	Garfield	Jun. 1–Aug. 31	78	35	113
Glenwood Springs	Garfield	Sept. 1–Dec. 31	61	35	96
Grand Junction	Mesa		66	35	101
Gunnison	Gunnison (except Crested Butte)	Jan. 1–May 31	67	39	106
Gunnison	Gunnison (except Crested Butte)	Jun. 1–Aug. 31	86	39	125
Gunnison	Gunnison (except Crested Butte)	Sept. 1–Dec. 31	67	39	106
Loveland	City limits	Jan. 1–Jun. 30	61	35	96

TABLE 8.4 *(Continued)*

State/City	County	Seasonal Dates (If Applicable)	Lodging Rate	M&IE Rate	Total Per Diem Rate
Loveland	City limits	Jul. 1–Aug. 31	76	35	111
Loveland	City limits	Sept. 1–Dec. 31	61	35	96
Montrose	Montrose	Jan. 1–Apr. 30	60	39	99
Montrose	Montrose	May 1–Sept. 30	74	39	113
Montrose	Montrose	Oct. 1–Dec. 31	60	39	99
Pueblo	Pueblo	Jan. 1–May 31	60	39	99
Pueblo	Pueblo	Jun. 1–Aug. 31	66	39	105
Pueblo	Pueblo	Sept. 1–Dec. 31	60	39	99
Silverthorne/ Breckenridge	Summit	Jan. 1–Mar. 31	154	43	157
Silverthorne/ Breckenridge	Summit	Apr. 1–Nov. 30	121	43	164
Silverthorne/ Breckenridge	Summit	Dec. 1–Dec. 31	154	43	197
Steamboat Springs	Routt		105	43	148
Telluride	San Miguel	Jan. 1–Mar. 31	196	47	243
Telluride	San Miguel	Apr. 1–Sept. 30	122	47	169
Vail	Eagle	Dec. 1–Dec. 31	249	47	296
Vail	Eagle	Jan. 1–Mar. 31	249	47	296
Vail	Eagle	Apr. 1–Nov. 30	132	47	179
Connecticut					
Bridgeport/Danbury	Fairfield		89	43	132
Cromwell/ Old Saybrook	Middlesex		77	35	112
Hartford	Hartford		94	43	136
Lakeville/Salisbury	Litchfield		95	43	138
New Haven	New Haven		96	39	135
New London/Groton	New London	Jan. 1–Apr. 30	80	39	119
New London/Groton	New London	May 1–Oct. 31	99	39	138
New London/Groton	New London	Nov. 1–Dec. 31	80	39	119
Putnam/Danielson	Windham		68	35	103
Storrs/Mansfield	Tolland		78	35	113

(Continued)

TABLE 8.4 *(Continued)*

State/City	County	Seasonal Dates (If Applicable)	Lodging Rate	M&IE Rate	Total Per Diem Rate
Delaware					
Dover	Kent	Jan. 1–May 31	71	39	110
Dover	Kent	Jun. 1–Oct. 31	81	39	120
Dover	Kent	Nov. 1–Dec. 31	71	39	110
Lewes	Sussex	Jan. 1–Apr. 30	71	43	114
Lewes	Sussex	May 1–Jun. 30	91	43	134
Lewes	Sussex	Jul. 1–Aug. 31	124	43	167
Lewes	Sussex	Sept. 1–Dec. 31	71	43	114
Wilmington	New Castle		108	39	147
District of Columbia (Washington, DC)					
Alexandria, Falls Church, and Fairfax, VA	Fairfax, Arlington, Loudoun; MD: Prince George, Montgomery		153	51	204
Florida					
Altamonte Springs	Seminole		67	43	110
Bradenton	Manatee		64	35	99
Cocoa Beach	Brevard	After 12/26/04	93	39	132
Daytona Beach	Volusia	Jan. 1–Jan. 31	79	43	122
Daytona Beach	Volusia	Feb. 1–Mar. 31	134	43	177
Daytona Beach	Volusia	Apr. 1–Dec. 31	79	43	122
De Funiak Springs	Walton	Jan. 1–Feb. 28	82	31	113
De Funiak Springs	Walton	Mar. 1–Oct. 31	104	31	135
De Funiak Springs	Walton	Nov. 1–Dec. 31	82	31	113
Fort Lauderdale	Broward	Jan. 1–May 31	137	47	184
Fort Lauderdale	Broward	Jun. 1–Sept. 30	86	47	133
Fort Lauderdale	Broward	Oct. 1–Dec. 31	117	47	164
Fort Myers	Lee	Jan. 1–Jan. 31	61	47	108
Fort Myers	Lee	Feb. 1–Mar. 31	93	47	140
Fort Myers	Lee	Apr. 1–Dec. 31	61	47	108
Fort Pierce	Saint Lucie	Jan. 1–Jan. 31	70	43	113
Fort Pierce	Saint Lucie	Feb. 1–Mar. 31	86	43	129
Fort Pierce	St. Lucie	Apr. 1–Dec. 31	70	43	113

TABLE 8.4 *(Continued)*

State/City	County	Seasonal Dates (If Applicable)	Lodging Rate	M&IE Rate	Total Per Diem Rate
Fort Walton Beach	Okaloosa	Jan. 1–Feb. 28	70	43	113
Fort Walton Beach	Okaloosa	Mar. 1–Aug. 31	105	43	148
Fort Walton Beach	Okaloosa	Sept. 1–Dec. 31	70	43	113
Gainesville	Alachua		71	39	110
Gulf Breeze	Santa Rosa	Jan. 1–Feb. 28	71	43	114
Gulf Breeze	Santa Rosa	Mar. 1–Aug. 31	101	43	144
Gulf Breeze	Santa Rosa	Sept. 1–Dec. 31	71	43	114
Jacksonville/ Mayport	Duval; Mayport Naval Station		78	39	117
Key West	Monroe	Jan. 1–Jan. 31	135	47	182
Key West	Monroe	Feb. 1–Mar. 31	184	47	231
Key West	Monroe	Apr. 1–Dec. 31	135	47	182
Kissimmee	Osceola		69	39	108
Lakeland	Polk		66	39	105
Leesburg	Lake		67	35	102
Miami	Dade	Jan. 1–May 31	138	47	185
Miami	Miami-Dade	Jun. 1–Sept. 30	99	47	146
Miami	Miami-Dade	Oct. 1–Dec. 31	138	47	185
Naples	Collier	Jan. 1–Mar. 31	127	43	170
Naples	Collier	Apr. 1–Dec. 31	79	43	122
Ocala	Marion		69	35	104
Orlando	Orange		98	47	145
Palm Beach	Palm Beach	Jan. 1–Mar. 31	132	47	179
Palm Beach	Palm Beach	Apr. 1–May 31	142	47	189
Palm Beach	Palm Beach	Jun. 1–Sept. 30	97	47	144
Palm Beach	Palm Beach	Oct. 1–Dec. 31	128	47	175
Panama City	Bay	Jan. 1–Feb. 28	68	43	111
Panama City	Bay	Mar. 1–Aug. 31	89	43	132
Panama City	Bay	Sept. 1–Dec. 31	68	43	111
Pensacola	Escambia		67	35	102
Punta Gorda	Charlotte	Jan. 1–Apr. 30	95	39	134
Punta Gorda	Charlotte	May 1–Dec. 31	68	39	107

(Continued)

TABLE 8.4 *(Continued)*

State/City	County	Seasonal Dates (If Applicable)	Lodging Rate	M&IE Rate	Total Per Diem Rate
Sarasota	Sarasota	Jan. 1–Jan. 31	86	43	129
Sarasota	Sarasota	Feb. 1–Apr. 30	110	43	153
Sarasota	Sarasota	May 1–Dec. 31	86	43	129
Sebring	Highlands		63	35	98
St. Augustine	St. Johns		79	43	122
Stuart	Martin	Jan. 1–Jan. 31	60	43	103
Stuart	Martin	Feb. 1–Mar. 31	79	43	122
Stuart	Martin	Apr. 1–Dec. 31	60	43	103
Tallahassee	Leon		73	39	112
Tampa/ St. Petersburg	Pinellas and Hillsborough		93	43	136
Vero Beach	Indian River	Jan. 1–Jan. 31	69	35	104
Vero Beach	Indian River	Feb. 1–Mar. 31	91	35	126
Vero Beach	Indian River	Apr. 1–Dec. 31	69	35	104
Georgia					
Athens	Clarke		72	39	111
Atlanta/Stone Mountain/Smyrna	Fulton; DeKalb; Cobb		113	43	156
Columbus	Muscogee		65	39	104
Conyers	Rockdale		68	39	107
Duluth/Norcross/ Lawrenceville	Gwinnett		67	43	110
Jekyll Island	Glynn	Jan. 1–Mar. 31	77	31	108
Jekyll Island	Glynn	Apr. 1–Aug. 31	100	31	131
Jekyll Island	Glynn	Sept. 1–Dec. 31	77	31	108
Savannah	Chatham		103	43	146
Idaho					
Boise	Ada		70	43	113
Coeur d'Alene	Kootenai	Jan. 1–Apr. 30	78	39	117
Coeur d'Alene	Kootenai	May 1–Sept. 30	114	39	153
Coeur d'Alene	Kootenai	Oct. 1–Dec. 31	78	39	117
Ketchum	Blaine (except Sun Valley)		67	43	110

TABLE 8.4 *(Continued)*

State/City	County	Seasonal Dates (If Applicable)	Lodging Rate	M&IE Rate	Total Per Diem Rate
McCall	Valley	Jan. 1–Jun. 30	63	43	106
McCall	Valley	Jul. 1–Aug. 31	76	43	119
McCall	Valley	Sept. 1–Dec. 31	63	43	106
Sun Valley	City limits		100	43	143
Illinois					
Aurora	Kane (except Elgin)		67	35	102
Chicago	Cook and Lake		149	51	200
Elgin	City limits		64	35	99
Oakbrook Terrace	Du Page		83	43	126
Rockford	Winnebago		65	35	100
Springfield	Sangamon		71	31	102
Indiana					
Bloomington	Monroe		73	31	104
Brownsburg/ Plainfield	Hendricks		64	31	95
Fort Wayne	Allen		66	35	101
Indianapolis	Marion; Hamilton; Fort Benjamin Harrison		87	47	134
Lafayette	Tippecanoe		75	35	110
Michigan City	La Porte		76	39	115
Nashville	Brown		67	43	110
South Bend	St. Joseph		77	39	116
Valparaiso/ Burlington Beach	Porter		69	39	108
Iowa					
Cedar Rapids	Linn		66	31	97
Des Moines	Polk		70	35	105
Kansas					
Fort Riley/ Manhattan	Geary; Riley; Pottawatomie		63	31	94
Kansas City/ Overland Park	Wyandotte and Johnson		98	43	141
Wichita	Sedgwick		67	43	110

(Continued)

TABLE 8.4 *(Continued)*

State/City	County	Seasonal Dates (If Applicable)	Lodging Rate	M&IE Rate	Total Per Diem Rate
Kentucky					
Covington/Hebron/ Florence/Newport	Kenton; Boone; Campbell		87	43	130
Lexington	Fayette		75	35	110
Louisville	Jefferson		81	43	124
Lousiana					
Baton Rouge	East Baton Rouge Parish		70	43	113
Lake Charles	Calcasieu Parish		66	39	105
New Orleans/ St. Bernard	Orleans; St. Bernard; Plaquemines; Jefferson Parishes	Jan. 1–Jan. 31	119	47	166
New Orleans/ St. Bernard	Orleans; St. Bernard; Plaquemines; Jefferson Parishes	Feb. 1–Apr. 30	153	47	200
New Orleans/ St. Bernard	Orleans; St. Bernard; Plaquemines; Jefferson Parishes	May 1–Aug. 31	109	47	156
New Orleans/ St. Bernard	Orleans; St. Bernard; Plaquemines; Jefferson Parishes	Sept. 30–Nov. 30	133	47	180
New Orleans/ St. Bernard	Orleans; St. Bernard; Plaquemines; Jefferson Parishes	Dec. 1–Dec. 31	119	47	166
Shreveport	Caddo; Bossier Parishes		64	43	107
St. Francisville	West Feliciana Parish		62	43	105
Maine					
Bar Harbor	Hancock		116	43	159
Kennebunk/Kittery/ Sanford	York	Jan. 1–Jun. 30	82	43	125
Kennebunk/Kittery/ Sanford	York	Jul. 1–Aug. 31	118	43	161
Kennebunk/ Kittery/ Sanford	York	Sept. 1–Dec. 31	72	43	115

TABLE 8.4 *(Continued)*

State/City	County	Seasonal Dates (If Applicable)	Lodging Rate	M&IE Rate	Total Per Diem Rate
Portland	Cumberland; Sagadahoc; Lincoln	Jan. 1–Jun. 30	72	43	115
Portland	Cumberland; Sagadahoc; Lincoln	Jul. 1–Oct. 31	98	43	141
Portland	Cumberland; Sagadahoc; Lincoln	Nov. 1–Dec. 31	72	43	115
Rockport	Knox		83	47	130
Maryland (see DC)					
Counties of Montgomery and Prince George's			153	51	204
Aberdeen, Bel Air/ Belcamp/ Edgewood	Harford		75	43	118
Annapolis	Anne Arundel	Jan. 1–Apr. 30	93	47	140
Annapolis	Anne Arundel	May 1–Oct. 31	114	47	161
Annapolis	Anne Arundel	Nov. 1–Dec. 31	93	47	140
Baltimore	Baltimore		133	47	180
Cambridge/ St. Michaels	Dorchester; Talbot	Jan. 1–May 31	86	35	133
Cambridge/ St. Michaels	Dorchester; Talbot	Jun. 1–Aug. 31	152	47	199
Cambridge/ St. Michaels	Dorchester; Talbot	Sept. 1–Dec. 31	86	47	133
Columbia	Howard		100	47	147
Frederick	Frederick		75	35	110
Lexington Park/ Leonardtown/Lusby	St. Mary's; Calvert		76	39	115
Ocean City	Worcester	Jan. 1–Apr. 30	71	47	118
Ocean City	Worcester	May 1–Jun. 30	108	47	155
Ocean City	Worcester	Jul. 1–Aug. 31	191	47	238
Ocean City	Worcester	Sept. 1–Oct. 31	98	47	145
Ocean City	Worcester	Nov. 1–Dec. 31	71	47	118
Massachusetts					
Andover	Essex		82	43	125
Boston	Suffolk	Jan. 1–Mar. 31	127	51	178
Boston	Suffolk	Apr. 1–Oct. 31	161	51	212

(Continued)

TABLE 8.4 *(Continued)*

State/City	County	Seasonal Dates (If Applicable)	Lodging Rate	M&IE Rate	Total Per Diem Rate
Boston	Suffolk	Nov. 1–Dec. 31	127	51	178
Burlington/Woburn	Middlesex		94	39	133
Cambridge	City limits	Jan. 1–Mar. 31	127	51	178
Cambridge	City limits	Apr. 1–Oct. 31	161	51	212
Cambridge	City limits	Nov. 1–Dec. 31	127	51	178
Falmouth	City limits	Jan. 1–Jun. 30	66	39	105
Falmouth	City limits	Jul. 1–Aug. 31	117	38	156
Hyannis	Barnstable	Jan. 1–Jun. 30	87	43	130
Hyannis	Barnstable	Jul. 1–Aug. 31	127	43	170
Hyannis	Barnstable	Sept. 1–Dec. 31	87	43	130
Martha's Vineyard	Dukes	Jan. 1–Apr. 30	105	47	152
Martha's Vineyard	Dukes	May 1–Jun. 30	134	47	181
Martha's Vineyard	Dukes	Jul. 1–Aug. 31	199	47	246
Martha's Vineyard	Dukes	Sept. 1–Dec. 31	105	47	152
Nantucket	Nantucket	Jan. 1–Jun. 30	121	47	168
Nantucket	Nantucket	Jul. 1–Aug. 31	199	47	246
Nantucket	Nantucket	Sept. 1–Dec. 31	121	47	168
New Bedford	City limits		86	39	125
Northampton	Hampshire	Jan. 1–Apr. 30	78	39	117
Northampton	Hampshire	May 1–Nov. 30	93	39	132
Northampton	Hampshire	Dec. 1–Dec. 31	78	39	117
Pittsfield	Berkshire	Jan. 1–Jun. 30	86	43	129
Pittsfield	Berkshire	Jul. 1–Oct. 31	112	43	155
Pittsfield	Berkshire	Nov. 1–Dec. 31	86	43	129
Plymouth	Plymouth	Jan. 1–May 31	87	39	126
Plymouth	Plymouth	Jun. 1–Oct. 31	107	39	146
Plymouth	Plymouth	Nov. 1–Dec. 31	87	39	126
Quincy	Norfolk		87	43	130
Springfield	Hampden		83	39	122
Taunton	Bristol (except New Bedford)		77	35	112
Worcester	Worcester		87	39	126

TABLE 8.4 *(Continued)*

State/City	County	Seasonal Dates (If Applicable)	Lodging Rate	M&IE Rate	Total Per Diem Rate
Michigan					
Ann Arbor	Washtenaw		80	43	123
Benton Harbor/ St. Joseph/ Stevensville	Berrien		65	35	100
Charlevoix	Charlevoix	Jan. 1–Jun. 30	64	43	107
Charlevoix	Charlevoix	Jul. 1–Aug. 31	82	43	107
Charlevoix	Charlevoix	Sept. 1–Dec. 31	64	43	107
Detroit	Wayne		107	51	158
East Lansing/Lansing	Ingham, Eaton		74	43	117
Flint	Genesee		70	31	101
Frankenmuth	Saginaw		69	35	104
Frankfort	Benzie	Jan. 1–Feb. 28	111	35	146
Frankfort	Benzie	Mar. 1–May 31	81	35	116
Frankfort	Benzie	Jun. 1–Sept. 30	111	35	146
Frankfort	Benzie	Oct. 1–Nov. 30	76	35	111
Frankfort	Benzie	Dec. 1–Dec. 31	111	35	146
Grand Rapids	Kent		70	39	109
Holland	Ottawa		79	39	118
Kalamazoo/ Battle Creek	Kalamazoo; Calhoun		61	31	92
Leland	Leelanau	Jan. 1–Jun. 30	69	39	108
Leland	Leelanau	Jul. 1–Aug. 31	106	39	145
Leland	Leelanau	Sept. 1–Dec. 31	69	39	108
Mackinac Island	Mackinac		116	47	163
Midland	Midland		69	39	108
Mount Pleasant	Isabella	Jan. 1–Jun. 30	74	39	113
Mount Pleasant	Isabella	Jul. 1–Aug. 31	86	39	125
Mount Pleasant	Isabella	Sept. 1–Dec. 31	74	39	113
Muskegon	Muskegon	Jan. 1–May 31	67	35	102
Muskegon	Muskegon	Jun. 1–Aug. 31	90	35	125
Muskegon	Muskegon	Sept. 1–Dec. 31	67	35	102

(Continued)

TABLE 8.4 *(Continued)*

State/City	County	Seasonal Dates (If Applicable)	Lodging Rate	M&IE Rate	Total Per Diem Rate
Ontonagon/Baraga/ Houghton	Ontonagon; Baraga; Houghton		71	35	106
Petoskey	Emmet	Jan. 1–Jun. 30	70	43	113
Petoskey	Emmet	Jul. 1–Aug. 31	94	43	137
Petoskey	Emmet	Sept. 1–Dec. 31	70	43	113
Pontiac/ Auburn Hills	Oakland		82	43	125
Sault Sainte Marie	Chippewa	Jan. 1–Jun. 30	60	39	99
Sault Sainte Marie	Chippewa	Jul. 1–Aug. 31	72	39	111
Sault Saint Marie	Chippewa	Sept. 1–Dec. 31	60	39	99
South Haven	Van Buren	Jan. 1–Jun. 30	63	39	102
South Haven	Van Buren	Jul. 1–Aug. 31	91	39	130
South Haven	Van Buren	Sept. 1–Dec. 31	63	39	102
Traverse City	Grand Traverse	Jan. 1–Jun. 30	78	47	125
Traverse City	Grand Traverse	Jul. 1–Aug. 31	127	47	174
Traverse City	Grand Traverse	Sept. 1–Dec. 31	78	47	125
Warren	Macomb		74	39	113
Minnesota					
Loon Rapids/Ramsey	Anoka		64	39	103
Duluth	St. Louis	Jan. 1–May 31	68	43	111
Duluth	St. Louis	Jun. 1–Oct. 31	92	43	135
Duluth	St. Louis	Nov. 1–Dec. 31	68	43	111
Minneapolis/ St. Paul	Hennepin; Ramsey		205	51	156
Rochester	Olmsted		68	39	107
Mississippi					
Biloxi/Gulfport	Harrison		65	43	108
Robinsonville	Tunica		68	35	103
Starkville	Oktibbeha		65	31	96
Missouri					
Jefferson City	Cole		61	35	96
Kansas City	Jackson; Clay; Cass; Platte		98	47	145
Osage Beach	Camden; Miller	Jan. 1–Apr. 30	74	35	109
Osage Beach	Camden; Miller	May 1–Aug. 31	99	35	134

TABLE 8.4 *(Continued)*

State/City	County	Seasonal Dates (If Applicable)	Lodging Rate	M&IE Rate	Total Per Diem Rate
Osage Beach	Camden; Miller	Sept. 1–Dec. 31	74	35	109
Springfield	Greene		61	35	96
St. Louis	St. Louis; St. Charles		98	51	149
St. Robert/Fort Leonard Wood	Pulaski		67	35	102
Montana					
Big Sky	Gallatin (except West Yellowstone)		78	47	125
Butte	Silver Bow		63	31	94
Polson/Kalispell	Lake; Flathead	Jan. 1–May 31	60	35	95
Polson/Kalispell	Lake; Flathead	Jun. 1–Sept. 30	83	35	118
Polson/ Kalispell	Lake; Flathead	Oct. 1–Dec. 31	60	35	95
West Yellowstone	City limits	Jan. 1–Mar. 31	67	39	106
West Yellowstone	City limits	Apr. 1–May 31	60	39	99
West Yellowstone	City limits	Jun. 1–Sept. 30	89	39	128
West Yellowstone	City limits	Oct. 1–Dec. 31	67	39	106
Nebraska					
Omaha	Douglas		68	43	111
Nevada					
Incline Village/ Crystal Bay	City limits	Jan. 1–May 31	89	43	132
Incline Village/ Crystal Bay	City limits	Jun. 1–Sept. 30	111	43	154
Incline Village/ Crystal Bay	City limits	Oct. 1–Dec. 31	89	43	165
Las Vegas	Clark	Jan. 1–May 31	122	43	165
Las Vegas	Clark	Jun. 1–Aug. 31	106	43	149
Las Vegas	Clark	Sept. 1–Dec. 31	122	43	165
Stateline	Douglas		80	47	127
New Hampshire					
Concord	Merrimack	Jan. 1–May 31	67	39	106
Concord	Merrimack	Jun. 1–Oct. 31	93	39	132
Concord	Merrimack	Nov. 1–Dec. 31	67	39	106
Conway	Carroll		100	43	143

(Continued)

TABLE 8.4 *(Continued)*

State/City	County	Seasonal Dates (If Applicable)	Lodging Rate	M&IE Rate	Total Per Diem Rate
Durham	Strafford	Jan. 1–May 31	81	34	116
Durham	Strafford	Jun. 1–Oct. 31	108	35	143
Durham	Strafford	Nov. 1–Dec. 31	81	35	116
Laconia	Belknap	Jan. 1–May 31	78	39	117
Laconia	Belknap	Jun. 1–Oct. 31	102	39	141
Laconia	Belknap	Nov. 1–Dec. 31	78	39	117
Lebanon/ Lincoln/ Sunapee	Grafton; Sullivan		97	39	136
Manchester	Hillsborough		86	39	125
Portsmouth	City limits	Jan. 1–May 31	81	43	124
Portsmouth	City limits	Jun. 1–Oct. 31	112	43	155
Portsmouth	Rockingham	Nov. 1–Dec. 31	81	43	124
New Jersey					
Atlantic City	Atlantic	Jan. 1–Apr. 30	100	47	147
Atlantic City	Atlantic	May 1–Oct. 31	123	47	170
Atlantic City	Atlantic	Nov. 1–Dec. 31	100	47	147
Cape May	Cape May (except Ocean City)	Jan. 1–May 31	82	47	129
Cape May	Cape May (except Ocean City)	Jun. 1–Aug. 31	131	47	178
Cape May	Cape May (except Ocean City)	Sept. 1-Dec. 31	82	47	129
Cherry Hill/ Moorestown	Camden; Burlington		78	47	125
Eatontown/ Freehold	Monmouth	Jan. 1–Apr. 30	91	43	134
Eatontown/ Freehold	Monmouth	May 1–Oct. 31	115	43	158
Eatontown/ Freehold	Monmouth	Nov. 1–Dec. 31	91	43	134
Edison	Middlesex (except Piscataway)		120	35	155
Flemington	Hunterdon		98	39	137
Freehold	City limits		85	39	124
Millville	Cumberland		61	35	96
Newark	Essex; Bergen; Hudson; Passaic		83	47	130

TABLE 8.4 *(Continued)*

State/City	County	Seasonal Dates (If Applicable)	Lodging Rate	M&IE Rate	Total Per Diem Rate
Ocean City	City limits	Jan. 1–May 31	91	43	134
Ocean City	City limits	Jun. 1–Oct. 31	166	43	209
Ocean City	City limits	Nov. 1–Dec. 31	91	43	134
Parsippany	Morris		112	43	155
Piscataway/Belle Mead	Somerset; city limits of Piscataway		105	43	148
Princeton/Trenton	Mercer		126	47	173
Springfield/ Cranford	Union		105	43	148
Toms River	Ocean	Jan. 1–Jun. 30	84	43	127
Toms River	Ocean	Jul. 1–Aug. 31	123	43	166
Toms River	Ocean	Sept. 1–Dec. 31	84	43	148
New Mexico					
Albuquerque	Bernalillo		68	43	111
Los Alamos/ Espanola	Los Alamos; Rio Arriba		61	39	100
Santa Fe	Santa Fe	Jan. 1–Jun. 30	94	47	141
Santa Fe	Santa Fe	Jul. 1–Aug. 31	134	47	181
Santa Fe	Santa Fe	Sept. 1–Dec. 31	94	47	141
New York					
Albany	Albany		92	47	139
Buffalo	Erie		81	43	124
Carle Place/ Garden City/ Glen Cove/ Plainview/ Rockville Centre/ Syosset/ Uniondale/ Woodbury	Nassau		141	47	188
Glens Falls	Warren	Jan. 1–May 31	69	39	108
Glens Falls	Warren	Jun. 1–Aug. 31	103	39	142
Glens Falls	Warren	Sept. 1–Dec. 31	69	39	108
Ithaca	Tompkins		100	39	139
Kingston	Ulster		73	43	116
Lake Placid	Essex	Jan. 1–Feb. 28	100	43	143
Lake Placid	Essex	Mar. 1–Jun. 30	81	43	124

(Continued)

TABLE 8.4 *(Continued)*

State/City	County	Seasonal Dates (If Applicable)	Lodging Rate	M&IE Rate	Total Per Diem Rate
Lake Placid	Essex	Jul. 1–Aug. 31	135	43	178
Lake Placid	Essex	Sep. 1–Dec. 31	100	43	143
New York City	Richmond County; boroughs of Manhattan, Brooklyn, the Bronx and Queens	Jan. 1–Apr. 30	177	51	228
New York City	Richmond County; boroughs of Manhattan, Brooklyn, the Bronx and Queens	May 1–Jun. 30	200	51	251
New York City	Richmond County; boroughs of Manhattan, Brooklyn, the Bronx and Queens	Jul. 1–Aug. 31	177	51	228
New York City	Richmond County; boroughs of Manhattan, Brooklyn, the Bronx and Queens	Sept. 1–Dec. 31	208	51	259
Niagara Falls	Niagara	Jan. 1–Apr. 30	60	39	99
Niagara Falls	Niagara	May 1–Sept. 30	95	39	124
Niagara Falls	Niagara	Oct. 1–Dec. 31	60	39	99
Nyack/Palisades	Rockland		100	43	143
Owego	Tioga		80	35	115
Poughkeepsie	Dutchess		100	43	143
Riverhead/ Ronkonkoma/ Melville	Suffolk		126	43	169
Rochester	Monroe		77	47	124
Saratoga Springs/ Schenectady	Saratoga; Schenectady	Jan. 1–Jun. 30	81	43	124
Saratoga Springs	Saratoga	Jul. 1–Aug. 31	118	43	161

TABLE 8.4 *(Continued)*

State/City	County	Seasonal Dates (If Applicable)	Lodging Rate	M&IE Rate	Total Per Diem Rate
Saratoga Springs	Saratoga	Sept. 1–Dec. 31	81	43	124
Syracuse	Onondaga		76	39	115
Tarrytown	Westchester (except White Plains)		121	47	168
Waterloo/Romulus	Seneca	Jan. 1–May 31	67	35	102
Waterloo/Romulus	Seneca	Jun. 1–Oct. 31	86	35	121
Waterloo/Romulus	Seneca	Nov. 1–Dec. 31	67	35	102
West Point	Orange		88	39	127
White Plains	City limits		131	47	178
North Carolina					
Asheville	Buncombe		81	31	112
Atlantic Beach	Carteret	Jan. 1–Mar. 31	60	35	95
Atlantic Beach	Carteret	Apr. 1–May 31	82	35	117
Atlantic Beach	Carteret	Jun. 1–Aug. 31	113	35	148
Atlantic Beach	Carteret	Sept. 1–Oct. 31	75	35	110
Atlantic Beach	Carteret	Nov. 1–Dec. 31	60	35	95
Chapel Hill	Orange		105	43	148
Charlotte	Mecklenburg		76	43	119
Cherokee	Swain		64	35	99
Durham	Durham		74	47	121
Fayetteville	Cumberland		63	39	102
Greensboro	Guilford		84	43	127
Greenville	Pitt		62	35	97
Kill Devil	Dare	Jan. 1–Mar. 31	67	43	110
Kill Devil	Dare	Apr. 1–Oct. 31	124	43	167
Kill Devil	Dare	Nov. 1–Dec. 31	67	43	110
New Bern/Havelock	Craven		68	39	107
Raleigh	Wake		74	43	117
Wilmington	New Hanover		72	39	111
Winston-Salem	Forsyth		62	43	105
Ohio					
Akron	Summit		68	43	111
Bellevue	Huron	Jan. 1–Jun. 31	60	35	95
Bellevue	Huron	Jul. 1–Aug. 31	77	35	112

(Continued)

TABLE 8.4 *(Continued)*

State/City	County	Seasonal Dates (If Applicable)	Lodging Rate	M&IE Rate	Total Per Diem Rate
Bellevue	Huron	Sept. 1–Dec. 31	60	35	95
Cincinnati	Hamilton; Clermont		87	51	138
Cleveland	Cuyahoga		99	47	146
Columbus	Franklin		95	43	138
Dayton/Fairborn	Greene; Darke; Montgomery		75	35	110
Geneva	Ashtabula		67	39	106
Hamilton	Butler; Warren		70	39	109
Lancaster	Fairfield		62	35	97
Port Clinton	Ottawa	Jan. 1–May 31	95	39	134
Port Clinton	Ottawa	Jun. 1–Aug. 31	69	39	108
Port Clinton	Ottawa	Sept. 1–Dec. 31	60	39	99
Sandusky	Erie	Jan. 1–May 31	60	43	103
Sandusky	Erie	Jun. 1–Aug. 31	94	43	137
Sandusky	Erie	Sept. 1–Dec. 31	60	43	103
Toledo	Lucas		65	35	100
Oklahoma					
Oklahoma City	Oklahoma		66	43	109
Tulsa	Tulsa; Osage; Rogers; Creek		64	31	95
Oregon					
Ashland	Jackson	Jan. 1–May 31	68	47	115
Ashland	Jackson	Jun. 1–Sept. 30	100	47	147
Ashland	Jackson	Oct. 1–Dec. 31	68	47	115
Beaverton	Washington		73	43	116
Bend	Deschutes	Jan. 1–Jun. 30	66	43	109
Bend	Deschutes	Jul. 1–Aug. 31	80	43	123
Bend	Deschutes	Sept. 1–Dec. 31	66	43	109
Clackamas	Clackamas		67	39	106
Crater Lake	Klamath	Jan. 1–May 31	60	35	95
Crater Lake	Klamath	Jun. 1–Aug. 31	67	35	102
Crater Lake	Klamath	Sept. 1–Dec. 31	60	35	95
Eugene	Lane (except Florence)		71	43	114

TABLE 8.4 *(Continued)*

State/City	County	Seasonal Dates (If Applicable)	Lodging Rate	M&IE Rate	Total Per Diem Rate
Florence	City limits	Jan. 1–Jun. 30	82	39	121
Florence	City limits	Jul. 1–Aug. 31	99	39	138
Florence	City limits	Sept. 1–Dec. 31	82	39	121
Gold Beach	Curry		67	35	102
Lincoln City	Lincoln	Jan. 1–Aug. 31	84	39	123
Lincoln City	Lincoln	Sept. 1–Dec. 31	70	39	109
Portland	Multnomah		93	43	136
Seaside	Clatsop	Jan. 1–Jun. 30	71	39	110
Seaside	Clatsop	Jul. 1–Aug. 31	88	39	127
Seaside	Clatsop	Sept. 1–Dec. 31	71	39	110
Pennsylvania					
Allentown/Gaston/Bethlehem	Lehigh, Northampton		73	35	108
Chester/Radnor/Essington	Delaware		75	39	114
Erie	Erie		75	35	110
Gettysburg	Adams	Jan. 1–Mar. 31	68	39	107
Gettysburg	Adams	Apr. 1–Oct. 31	94	39	133
Gettysburg	Adams	Nov. 1–Dec. 31	68	39	107
Harrisburg	Dauphin (except Hershey)		81	47	128
Hershey	City limits	Jan. 1–Apr. 30	99	43	142
Hershey	City limits	May 1–Aug. 31	150	43	193
Hershey	City limits	Sept. 1–Dec. 31	99	43	142
King of Prussia/Ft. Washington/Warminster	Montgomery; Bucks		106	47	153
Lancaster	Lancaster		82	43	125
Malvern/Frazer/Exton	Chester		103	43	146
Mechanicsburg	Cumberland		78	35	113
Philadelphia	Philadelphia		116	51	167
Pittsburgh	Allegheny		85	47	132
Reading	Berks		85	43	128

(Continued)

TABLE 8.4 *(Continued)*

State/City	County	Seasonal Dates (If Applicable)	Lodging Rate	M&IE Rate	Total Per Diem Rate
Scranton	Lackawanna		70	35	105
State College	Centre		76	31	107
Rhode Island					
East Greenwich	Kent; Naval Construction Battalion Center, Davisville		100	43	143
Jamestown/ Middletown/ Newport	Newport	Jan. 1–Apr. 30	94	47	141
Jamestown/ Middletown/ Newport	Newport	May 1–Oct. 31	154	47	201
Jamestown/ Middletown/ Newport	Newport	Nov. 1–Dec. 31	94	47	141
North Kingstown	Washington		109	31	140
Providence	Providence	Jan. 1–Apr. 30	128	47	175
Providence	Providence	May 1–Oct. 31	138	47	175
Providence	Providence	Nov. 1–Dec. 31	128	47	175
South Carolina					
Charleston	Charleston; Berkeley, Dorchester		98	43	141
Columbia	Richland		67	35	102
Greenville	Greenville		66	43	109
Hilton Head	Beaufort	Jan. 1–Mar. 31	77	47	124
Hilton Head	Beaufort	Apr. 1–Oct. 31	122	47	169
Hilton Head	Beaufort	Nov. 1–Dec. 31	77	47	124
Myrtle Beach	Horry	Jan. 1–Mar. 31	63	47	110
Myrtle Beach	Horry	Apr. 1–May 31	97	47	144
Myrtle Beach	Horry	Jun. 1–Aug. 31	116	47	163
Myrtle Beach	Horry	Sept. 1–Oct. 31	78	47	125
Myrtle Beach	Horry	Nov. 1–Dec. 31	63	47	110
South Dakota					
Custer	Custer	Jan. 1–Mar. 31	60	35	95
Custer	Custer	Apr. 1–Aug. 31	92	35	127

TABLE 8.4 *(Continued)*

State/City	County	Seasonal Dates (If Applicable)	Lodging Rate	M&IE Rate	Total Per Diem Rate
Custer	Custer	Sept. 1–Dec. 31	60	35	95
Hot Springs	Fall River		70	35	105
Rapid City	Pennington	May 15–Sept. 30	60	35	95
Rapid City	Pennington	Oct. 1–May 14	93	35	128
Rapid City	Pennington	Oct. 1–Dec. 31	60	35	85
Sturgis/Spearfish	Meade; Butte; Lawrence	Jan. 1–May 31	60	40	91
Sturgis/Spearfish	Meade Lawrence	Jun. 1–Sept. 30	84	31	115
Sturgis/Spearfish	Meade; Butte; Lawrence	Oct. 1–Dec. 31	60	31	91
Tennessee					
Brentwood/Franklin	Williamson		66	35	101
Chattanooga	Hamilton		88	31	119
Gatlinburg/Townsend	Sevier; Blount		79	43	122
Knoxville	Knox		65	31	96
Memphis	Shelby		80	43	123
Nashville	Davidson		94	47	141
Texas					
Amarillo	Potter		66	35	101
Arlington/Ft. Worth	Tarrant		96	39	139
Austin	Travis		85	43	128
College Station	Brazos		65	39	104
Corpus Christi	Nueces		76	43	119
Dallas	Dallas		96	51	147
El Paso	El Paso		70	35	105
Galveston	Galveston	Jan. 1–Jan. 31	84	47	131
Galveston	Galveston	Feb. 1–Aug. 31	114	47	161
Galveston	Galveston	Sept. 1–Dec. 31	84	47	131
Grapevine	City limits		111	39	150
Houston	Harris; LBJ Space Center; Montgomery; Fort Bend		99	47	146

(Continued)

TABLE 8.4 *(Continued)*

State/City	County	Seasonal Dates (If Applicable)	Lodging Rate	M&IE Rate	Total Per Diem Rate
Killeen	Bell		62	35	97
Laredo	Webb		81	35	116
McAllen	Hidalgo		68	39	107
Plano	Collin		71	39	110
Round Rock	Williamson		71	31	102
San Antonio	Bexar		93	47	140
South Padre Island	Cameron	Jan. 1–May 31	86	39	125
South Padre Island	Cameron	Jun. 1–Aug. 31	106	39	145
South Padre Island	Cameron	Sept. 1–Dec. 31	86	39	125
Waco	McLennan		64	35	99
Utah					
Bullfrog	San Juan		64	35	99
Park City	Summit	Jan. 1–Mar. 31	150	47	57
Park City	Summit	Apr. 1–Nov. 30	73	47	120
Park City	Summit	Dec. 1–Dec. 31	150	47	197
Provo	Utah		65	43	108
Salt Lake City	Salt Lake; Tooele		79	39	118
Vermont					
Burlington/ St. Albans	Chittenden; Franklin		91	39	130
Manchester	Bennington	Jan. 1–Feb. 28	115	47	162
Manchester	Bennington	Mar. 1–Nov. 30	90	47	137
Manchester	Bennington	Dec. 1–Dec. 31	115	47	162
Montpelier	Washington	Jan. 1–Apr. 30	62	35	97
Montpelier	Washington	May 1–Oct. 31	85	35	120
Montpelier	Washington	Nov. 1–Dec. 31	69	35	104
Stowe	Lamoille		104	31	135
White River Junction	Windsor	Jan. 1–Feb. 28	116	35	151
White River Junction	Windsor	Mar. 1–May 31	84	35	119
White River Junction	Windsor	Jun. 1–Nov. 30	104	35	139
White River Junction	Windsor	Dec. 1–Dec. 31	116	35	151

TABLE 8.4 *(Continued)*

State/City	County	Seasonal Dates (If Applicable)	Lodging Rate	M&IE Rate	Total Per Diem Rate
Virginia (* denotes independent cities)					
Charlottesville*			65	47	112
Fredricksburg	Spotsylvania; Stafford		61	31	92
Lynchburg*			65	43	108
Manassas	Prince William		70	39	109
Petersburg*			63	35	98
Richmond*	Chesterfield; Goochland; Henrico		74	43	117
Roanoke*			68	39	107
Shenandoah	Page	Jan. 1–Mar. 31	60	31	91
Shenandoah	Page	Apr. 1–Nov. 30	84	31	115
Shenandoah	Page	Dec. 1–Dec. 31	60	31	91
Virginia Beach*	Virginia Beach, Norfolk; Portsmouth; Chesapeake; Suffolk*	Apr. 1–Oct. 31	109	43	152
Virginia Beach*	Virginia Beach Norfolk; Portsmouth; Chesapeake; Suffolk*	Nov. 1–Mar. 31	55	43	98
Virginia Beach*	Virginia Beach, Norfolk, Portsmouth, Chesapeake, Suffolk	Apr. 1–Aug. 31	133	43	176
Virginia Beach*	Virginia Beach, Norfolk; Portsmouth; Chesapeake; Suffolk	Sept. 1–Dec. 31	67	43	110
Wallops Island	Accomack	Jan. 1–Jun. 30	71	39	110
Wallops Island	Accomack	Jul. 1–Aug. 31	93	39	132
Wallops Island	Accomack	Sept. 1–Dec. 31	71	39	110

(Continued)

TABLE 8.4 *(Continued)*

State/City	County	Seasonal Dates (If Applicable)	Lodging Rate	M&IE Rate	Total Per Diem Rate
Williamsburg*	Williamsburg; Hampton; Poquoson; Newport News; James and York Counties	Jan. 1–Mar. 31	79	43	122
Williamsburg*	Williamsburg; Hampton; Poquoson; Newport News; James and York Counties	Apr. 1–Aug. 31	101	43	144
Williamsburg	Williamsburg; Hampton; Poquoson; Newport News; James and York Counties	Sep. 1–Dec. 31	79	43	122
Wintergreen	Nelson		76	47	123
Woodbridge	Prince William		70	39	109
Washington					
Anacortes Camano Island/ Coupeville	San Juan (except Friday Harbor); Skagit; Island		67	43	110
Bremerton	Kitsap		66	39	105
Everett	Snohomish (except Lynnwood)		64	43	107
Friday Harbor	City limits	Jan. 1–Jun. 30	74	47	121
Friday Harbor	City limits	Jul. 1–Aug. 31	94	47	141
Friday Harbor	City limits	Sept. 1–Dec. 31	74	47	121
Lynnwood	City limits		79	39	118
Ocean Shores	Grays Harbor	Jan. 1–Jun. 30	80	43	123
Ocean Shores	Grays Harbor	Jul. 1–Aug. 31	104	43	147
Ocean Shores	Grays Harbor	Sept. 1–Dec. 31	80	43	123
Olympia/Tumwater	Thurston		71	43	114
Port Angeles	City limits	Jan. 1–May 31	66	43	109
Port Angeles	City limits	Jun. 1–Sept. 30	86	43	129
Port Angeles	City limits	Oct. 1–Dec. 31	66	43	109

TABLE 8.4 *(Continued)*

State/City	County	Seasonal Dates (If Applicable)	Lodging Rate	M&IE Rate	Total Per Diem Rate
Port Townsend	Jefferson		64	39	103
Seattle	King	Jan. 1–Apr. 30	110	51	161
Seattle	King	May 1–Oct. 31	127	51	178
Seattle	King	Nov. 1–Dec. 31	110	51	161
Spokane	Spokane		67	43	110
Tacoma	Pierce		79	35	114
Vancouver	Clark; Cowlitz; Skamania		93	31	124
West Virginia					
Berkeley Springs	Morgan		61	39	100
Charleston	Kanawha		84	43	127
Martinsburg/ Hedgesville	Berkeley		61	35	96
Morgantown	Monongalia	Jan. 1–Mar. 31	65	39	104
Morgantown	Monongalia	Apr. 1–Nov. 30	77	39	116
Morgantown	Monongalia	Dec. 1–Dec. 31	65	39	104
Shepherdstown	Jefferson		75	39	114
Wheeling	Ohio		67	39	106
Wisconsin					
Brookfield	Waukesha		75	43	118
Green Bay	Brown		67	39	106
Lake Geneva	Walworth	Jan. 1–Jun. 30	76	43	119
Lake Geneva	Walworth	Jul. 1–Aug. 31	102	43	145
Lake Geneva	Walworth	Sept. 1–Dec. 31	76	43	119
Madison	Dane		75	43	118
Milwaukee	Milwaukee		99	47	146
Racine	Racine		77	35	112
Sheboygan	Sheboygan		70	35	105
Sturgeon Bay	Door	Jan. 1–May 31	66	39	105
Sturgeon Bay	Door	Jun. 1–Oct. 31	91	39	130
Sturgeon Bay	Door	Nov. 1–Dec. 31	66	39	105
Wisconsin Dells	Columbia		65	43	108

(Continued)

TABLE 8.4 *(Continued)*

State/City	County	Seasonal Dates (If Applicable)	Lodging Rate	M&IE Rate	Total Per Diem Rate
Wyoming					
Cody	Park	Jan. 1–May 31	60	35	95
Cody	Park	Jun. 1–Sept. 30	91	35	126
Cody	Park	Oct. 1–Dec. 31	60	35	95
Jackson	Teton	Jan. 1–May 31	74	47	121
Jackson	Teton	Jun. 1–Sept. 30	113	47	160
Jackson	Teton	Oct. 1–Dec. 31	74	47	121
Pinedale	Sublette	Jan. 1–May 31	60	31	91
Pinedale	Sublette	Jun. 1–Aug. 31	78	31	109
Pinedale	Sublette	Sept. 1–Dec. 31	60	31	91

applies to areas not listed in Table 8.4.) Be sure to note that these rates may be adjusted for future years.

The standard meal allowances are listed in IRS Publication 1542, *Per Diem Rates*, which can be found on the IRS web site at <www.irs.gov>. Per diem travel rates are also listed at <www.gsa.gov>. These standard meal allowances do not apply outside the continental United States (Alaska, Hawaii, Puerto Rico, or any foreign countries). However, there is a standard federal rate for foreign travel that is published monthly in *Maximum Travel Per Diem Allowances for Foreign Travel*, which is available from the Superintendent of Documents (U.S. Government Printing Office, P.O. Box 371954, Pittsburgh, PA 15250-7954). Foreign rates can also be obtained from the U.S. State Department at <www.state.gov/m/a/als/prdm/>.

You cannot use the standard meal allowance if you are related to your employer. You are considered related if your employer is your brother, sister (half or whole), spouse, parent, grandparent, child, or grandchild. You are also considered related if you own, directly or indirectly, more than 10 percent of the value of your employer's stock. Indirect ownership arises when you have an interest in a corporation, partnership, trust, or estate that owns stock in your employer's corporation or if family members own stock in your employer's corporation. However, you can use the standard meal allowance if you are self-employed.

INCIDENTAL RATE. There is a $2 per day rate for incidental expenses ($3 per day on a ship in international waters), such as tips and transportation between the hotel and place of business. This modest rate can be used to cover incidental expenses only if no meal costs are incurred on such a day (for example, it is a day of personal travel).

PARTIAL DAYS OF TRAVEL. If the federal per diem rate or high-low method is used for any day of travel that does not include a full 24-hour period, the per diem amount must be prorated. The full rate is allocated on a quarterly basis for each six-hour period in the day (midnight to 6 a.m.; 6 a.m. to noon; noon to 6 p.m.; 6 p.m. to midnight).

Recordkeeping Requirements

Business expenses can be disallowed unless there is adequate substantiation for the expenses claimed. For travel and entertainment expenses, there are two main ways to prove costs: actual substantiation, or reliance on a per diem rate. First look at actual substantiation; then consider how recordkeeping can be simplified with the use of per diem rates.

There are a number of elements to substantiate for each business expense. In general, to substantiate each item you must show the amount, the time, the place, the business purpose for the travel or the business relationship with the persons you entertain or provide gifts to, and, in some cases, a description of the item. The exact type of substantiation required depends on the item of business expense.

Travel

You must show the amount of each separate expense for travel, lodging, meals, and incidental expenses. You can total these items in any reasonable category. For example, you can simply keep track of meals in a category called daily meals. You must also note the dates you left for the trip and returned, as well as the days spent on the trip for business purposes. You must list the name of the city or other designation of the place of the travel, along with the reason for the travel or the business benefit gained or expected to be gained from it.

While this may sound like a great deal of recordkeeping, as a practical matter hotel receipts may provide you with much of the information necessary. For example, a hotel receipt typically shows the dates you arrived and departed; the name and location of the hotel; and separate charges for lodging, meals, telephone calls, and other items. The IRS says that a charge slip for hotel costs is no substitute for the hotel receipt itself. You must have documentary evidence for the cost of lodging. You do not need documentary evidence if the item (other than lodging) is less than $75 or, in the case of transportation costs, if a receipt is not readily available. Thus, if a cab ride is $9 and the driver does not provide you with a receipt, you are not required to show documentary evidence of this expense.

Meals and Entertainment

List expenses separately. Incidental expenses, such as taxis and telephone, may be totaled on a daily basis. List each date of the meal or entertainment. For meals or entertainment directly before or after a business discussion, list the date and duration of the business discussion. Include the name and address or location of the place for the entertainment and the type of entertainment if not apparent from the name of the place. Also list the place where a business discussion was held if entertainment was directly before or after the discussion. State the business reason or the business benefit gained or expected to be gained and the nature of the business discussion. Include the names of the persons entertained, including their occupations or other identifying information, and indicate who took part in the business discussion.

If the deduction is for a business meal, you must note that you or your employer was present at the meal. Again, a restaurant receipt typically will supply much of the information required. It will show the name and location of the restaurant, the number of people served, and the date and amount of the expense. Be sure to jot down the business aspect of the meal or entertainment, such as asking a client for a referral or trying to sell your services.

Gifts

Show the cost of the gift, the date given, and a description. Also show the business reason for the gift or the business benefit gained or expected to be gained from providing it. Indicate the name of the person receiving the gift, his or her occupation or other identifying information, and his or her business relationship to you.

A canceled check, along with a bill, generally establishes the cost of a business item. A canceled check alone does not prove a business expense without other evidence to show its business purpose.

Using a Diary or Log

Enter your expenses in a diary (see Table 8.5) or log at or near the time of the event giving rise to the expenses. Computer-generated records are acceptable. Be sure to include all the elements required for the expense (especially the business reason for it).

It is a good idea to total expenses on a monthly basis and then use a recap form to put annual figures together.

Other Substantiation Methods

The IRS has recognized we are in the computer age and has endorsed various computer-based substantiation methods. For example, if each employee has a company credit card, electronic reports from the credit card company can be used to substantiate charged expenses (paper receipts of expenses in excess of $75 are still required).

TABLE 8.5 Sample Expense Diary

Date	Description	Fares	Lodging	Meals	Entertainment	Other
1/10	Breakfast with Sue Smith, CEO, X Corp., Discussed sales.			$21.50		
1/11	Sales trip Buyers in NYC	$408.00	$455.00	$105.00		$28.00
1/14	Lunch with Mark Hess after sales call.			$38.75		
1/15	Gift for John Jones (boss).					$22.00

Missing, Lost, or Inadequate Records

If you do not have adequate records, you may still be able to deduct an item if you can prove by your own statement or other supporting evidence an element of substantiation. A court may even allow an estimation of expenses under certain circumstances. Where receipts have been destroyed, you may be able to reconstruct your expenses. You must, of course, show how the records were destroyed (fire, storm, flood). The IRS may require additional information to prove the accuracy or reliability of the information contained in your records. Recordkeeping alternatives are discussed in more detail in Chapter 3.

Per Diem Rates

If you receive reimbursement using one of the per diem rates discussed earlier, you need not retain documentary evidence of the amount of an expense. The per diem rate is deemed to satisfy the proof of the amount of the expense. However, use of the per diem rate does not prove any of the other elements of substantiation. For example, if an employee is reimbursed for business travel using the high-low method, he or she still must show the time, the place, and the business purpose for business travel.

Where to Deduct Travel and Entertainment Expenses

Employees

You calculate your travel and entertainment expenses on Form 2106, Employee Business Expenses, or Form 2106-EZ, Unreimbursed Employee Business Expenses. You can use the EZ form, which is a simplified version of Form 2106, if you do not get reimbursed by your employer for any expenses and, if you are claiming expenses for a car, you own the car and are using the standard mileage rate (as explained in Chapter 9).

You enter your total from Form 2106 or 2106-EZ on Schedule A, Itemized Deductions, as a miscellaneous itemized expense. These deductions are then limited to the amount they exceed 2 percent of adjusted gross income. If adjusted gross income exceeds a certain amount, the deductions may be further limited. (The threshold for the reduction in itemized deductions is adjusted annually for inflation.)

DISABLED EMPLOYEES. If you have a physical or mental disability, your impairment-related work expenses are deductible as an itemized deduction, but the 2-percent floor does not apply. Impairment-related work expenses include expenses for attendant care at your place of work as well as other expenses that are necessary to enable you to work. General medical expenses, however, are not impairment-related work expenses; they are simply personal medical expenses and are deductible as such.

SPECIAL RULE FOR PERFORMING ARTISTS. If you meet certain requirements, you can deduct all of your car expenses as an adjustment to gross income on page one of Form 1040 instead of claiming them as miscellaneous itemized deductions on Schedule A. You are treated as a qualified performing artist (QPA) if you meet all of the following tests:

1. You perform services in the performing arts for at least two employers in the year.
2. You receive at least $200 each from any two of these employers.
3. Your related performing arts business expenses are more than 10 percent of your adjusted gross income from the performance of such services.
4. Your adjusted gross income from *all* sources does not exceed $16,000 (before deducting business expenses from your performing arts).
5. If you are married and you file a joint return (unless you lived apart from your spouse for the entire year).

You figure tests 1, 2, and 3 based on your separate experience. However, the adjusted gross income in test 4 is based on the combined adjusted gross income of you and your spouse.

If you meet these criteria, you deduct your performing arts business expenses as an adjustment to gross income on page one of Form 1040. Enter these expenses on the line used for totaling adjustments to gross income. Write "QPA" next to your expenses.

Self-Employed (Including Independent Contractor and Statutory Employee)

You enter your travel, meals, and entertainment expenses on Schedule C, Profit and Loss from Business, or Schedule C-EZ, Net Profit from Business. On Schedule C there are separate lines for travel, for meals and entertainment, and for determining the 50-percent limit on meals and entertainment. Business gifts are reported as other expenses, which are explained on page two of Schedule C. Schedule C-EZ can be used only if total business expenses are no more than $5,000. You simply add your travel and entertainment expenses to your other deductible business expenses and enter the total on the appropriate line of Schedule C-EZ. You need not attach an itemized statement explaining the deduction. Be sure that when you total your expenses, you apply the 50-percent limit on meals and entertainment.

Self-employed farmers deduct travel, meals, and entertainment expenses on Schedule F.

Partnerships and LLCs

Travel, meals, and entertainment expenses are reported on Form 1065 and are taken into account in arriving at the business's ordinary income (or loss). They are entered in the category of Other Deductions on the form. A schedule is attached to the return explaining the deductions claimed in this category. Be sure to apply the 50-percent limit to meals and entertainment. Travel, meals, and entertainment expenses are not separately stated items. An owner's share of these expenses is reported on Schedule K-1.

S Corporations

Travel, meals, and entertainment expenses are reported on Form 1120S and are taken into account in arriving at the corporation's ordinary income (or loss). They are entered in the category of Other Deductions on the form. A schedule is attached to the return explaining the deductions claimed in this category. Be sure to apply the 50-percent limit to meals and entertainment. Travel, meals, and entertainment expenses are not separately stated items. A shareholder's share of these expenses is reported on Schedule K-1.

C Corporations

Travel, meals, and entertainment expenses are reported on Form 1120 and are taken into account in arriving at the corporation's taxable income (or loss). They are entered in the category of Other Deductions on the form. A schedule is attached to the return explaining the deductions claimed in this category. Be sure to apply the 50-percent limit on meals and entertainment.

CHAPTER 9

Car and Truck Expenses

Americans are highly mobile, and the car is the method of choice for transportation. If you use your car for business, you may write off various costs. There are two methods for deducting costs: the actual expense method and the standard mileage allowance. In this chapter you will learn about:

- Deducting car expenses in general
- Actual expense method
- Standard mileage allowance
- Leasing a car for business
- Arranging car ownership
- Employee use of an employer-provided car
- Vehicle trade-ins
- Trucks and vans
- Write-offs for hybrid and electric cars
- Reimbursement arrangements
- Recordkeeping for car expenses
- Where to deduct car expenses

For further information about deductions with respect to business use of your car, see IRS Publication 463, *Travel, Entertainment, Gift, and Car Expenses.*

Deducting Car Expenses in General

The discussion in this chapter applies to **cars** used partly or entirely for business.

Car Any four-wheel vehicle made primarily for use on public streets, roads, and highways that has an unloaded gross vehicle weight of 6,000 pounds or less (the manufacturer can provide this information). A truck or van is a "light" truck or van if its unloaded gross weight is 6,000 pounds or less and is subject to rules similar to those for passenger cars. Excluded from the definition is an ambulance, hearse, or combination thereof used in business and any vehicle used in business for transporting people or for compensation or hire.

The law allows you to choose between two methods for deducting business-related expenses of a car: the actual expense method or the standard mileage allowance, both of which are detailed in this chapter.

Choosing Between the Actual Expense Method and the Standard Mileage Allowance

Read over the rules on the *actual expense method* and the *standard mileage allowance*. For the most part, the choice of method is yours. In some cases, however, you may not be able to use the standard mileage rate. Where you are not barred from using the standard mileage rate and can choose between the methods, which is better? Obviously, it is the one that produces the greater deduction. However, there is no easy way to determine which method will produce the greater deduction. Many factors will affect your decision, including the number of miles you drive each year and the extent of your actual expenses. See the example's comparison.

Example

You buy or lease a car in January 2005 for $15,000 and use it 100 percent for business. In 2005, the first year the car is in service, you drive 1,500 miles per month. If you use the standard mileage allowance, your car deduction for 2005 is $7,770 (12,000 miles × 40.5¢ plus 6,000 miles × 48.5¢). If your actual costs exceed this amount, it may be advisable to use the actual expense method. If they are less than $7,770, the standard mileage allowance may be better.

In making your decision, bear in mind that the standard mileage allowance simplifies recordkeeping for business use of the car.

You should make the decision in the first year you own the car. This is because a choice of the actual expense method for the first year will forever bar the use of the standard mileage allowance in subsequent years. If you use the standard mileage rate, you can still use the actual expense method in later years. However, if the car has not yet been fully depreciated (using the deemed depreciation rates discussed later), then, for depreciation purposes, you must use the straight-line method over what you estimate to be the car's remaining useful life.

Actual Expense Method

The *actual expense method* allows you to deduct all of your out-of-pocket costs for operating your car for business, plus an allowance for depreciation if you own the car. Actual expenses include:

Depreciation	Lease fees	Repairs
Garage rent	Licenses	Tires
Gas	Oil	Tolls
Insurance	Parking fees	Towing

For individuals, whether interest on a car loan is deductible depends on employment status. If you are an employee who uses a car for business, you cannot deduct interest on a car loan; the interest is treated as nondeductible personal interest. However, if you are self-employed, the interest may be treated as business interest. For corporations, interest on a car loan is fully deductible.

If you pay personal property tax on a car used for business, the tax is deductible by an employee only as an itemized deduction. Personal property tax is not grouped with other car expenses. Instead, it is listed on an individual's Schedule A as a personal property tax.

If your car is damaged, destroyed, or stolen, the part of the loss not covered by insurance may be deductible. If the car was used entirely for business, the loss is treated as a fully deductible casualty or theft loss. If it was used partly for personal purposes, the loss may be treated as a casualty or theft loss, but the portion of the loss allocated to personal purposes is subject to certain limitations. See Chapter 17 for a discussion of casualty and theft losses.

Not all car-related expenses are deductible. Luxury and sales taxes cannot be separately deducted even if a car is used entirely for business; these taxes are treated as part of the cost of the car and are added to the basis of the car for purposes of calculating depreciation, as well as gain or loss on the future sale of the car.

Fines for traffic violations, including parking violations, are not deductible even when they were incurred in the course of business-related travel.

Depreciation

If you own your car and use it for business, you may recoup part of the cost of the car through a deduction called *depreciation*. The amount of depreciation depends on a great many factors. First, it depends on whether you use the depreciation allowance or claim a Section 179 deduction (discussed later in the chapter). It also varies according to the year in which you begin to use your car for business, the cost of the car, and the amount of business mileage for the year as compared with the total mileage for the year. Depreciation is covered in Chapter 14 as well.

Business Use versus Personal or Investment Use

Whether you claim a depreciation allowance or a Section 179 deduction, you can do so only with respect to the portion of the car used for business. For example, if you use your car 75 percent for business and 25 percent for personal purposes, you must allocate the cost of the car for purposes of calculating depreciation. The allocation is based on the number of miles driven for business compared to the total number of miles driven for the year.

Example

In 2005 you buy a car for $16,000 and drive it 20,000 miles. Of this mileage, 15,000 miles were for business; 5,000 miles were personal. For purposes of depreciation, you must allocate $12,000 for business use. It is this amount on which you figure depreciation.

If you use a car for investment purposes, you can add the miles driven for investment purposes when making an allocation for depreciation.

Depreciation Allowance

A depreciation allowance is simply a deduction calculated by applying a percentage to the **basis** of the car. Cars are treated as five-year property under the Modified Accelerated Cost Recovery System (MACRS), the depreciation system currently in effect, as discussed in Chapter 14. As such, you would think that the cost of the car could be recovered through depreciation deductions over a period of five years. However, this is generally not the case because of a number of different rules that exist. These rules all operate to limit the amount of depreciation that can be claimed in any one year and to extend the number of years for claiming depreciation.

Basis   Generally, this is the original cost of the car. If a car is bought in part with the trade-in of an old car, the basis of the new car is the adjusted basis of the old car plus any cash payment you make. Basis is reduced by any first-year expense deduction, any clean fuel vehicle deduction, and any qualified electric vehicle tax credit. It is adjusted downward for any depreciation deductions.

Depreciation can take several forms. There is *accelerated depreciation* under MACRS, which results in greater deductions in the early years of ownership and smaller deductions in the later years. There is *straight-line depreciation*, which spreads depreciation deductions evenly over the years the car is expected to last (the fixed number of years may, in fact, have no relation to the actual number of years the car is in operation). Tables 9.1 and 9.2

TABLE 9.1 Straight-Line Half-Year Convention*

Year	Rate (Percent)
1	10
2	20
3	20
4	20
5	20
6	10

*Depreciation may not exceed a dollar limit (see page 224).

TABLE 9.2 MACRS Half-Year Convention*

Year	Rate (Percent)
1	20.00
2	32.00
3	19.20
4	11.52
5	11.52
6	5.76

*Depreciation may not exceed a dollar limit (see page 224).

provide the percentage for depreciation under both methods. There is the *first-year expense deduction*, discussed later in this chapter, which is in lieu of depreciation. It takes the place of depreciation for the first year. Any part of the car not recovered through the first-year expense deduction can then be recovered through depreciation deductions in subsequent years.

In the past, you could have claimed an additional first-year deduction, called bonus depreciation. This expired at the end of 2004 and has not been extended.

Business Use

In order for you to claim an accelerated depreciation deduction or a first-year expense, the car must be used more than 50 percent for business. Compare the miles driven during the year for business with the total miles driven. If more than 50 percent of the mileage represents business use, accelerated depreciation (or the first-year expense deduction below) can be claimed.

If you satisfy the 50-percent test, you may also add to business mileage any miles driven for investment purposes when calculating the depreciation deduction. You may not add investment mileage in order to determine whether you meet the 50-percent test. If you fail the 50-percent test (you use the car 50 percent or less for business), you can deduct depreciation using only the straight-line method. Your deduction is limited to the rates listed in the section on "Conventions."

What if the percentage of business use changes from year to year? You may use your car 75 percent for business in one year but only 40 percent the next. Where business use in the year the car is placed in service is more than 50 percent but drops below 50 percent in a subsequent year, you must also change depreciation rates. Once business use drops to 50 percent or below, you can use only the straight-line method thereafter. The depreciation rate is taken from the table for the straight-line method (Table 9.1) as if the car had not qualified for accelerated depreciation in a prior year.

Where business use drops to 50 percent or less, you may have to include in income an amount called *excess depreciation*. This is the amount of depreciation (including the first-year expense deduction) claimed when the car was used more than 50 percent for business over the amount of depreciation that would have been allowable had the car not been used more than 50 percent in the year it was placed in service. In addition to including excess depreciation in income, you must increase the basis of your car by the same amount.

Conventions

There are special rules that operate to limit write-offs for depreciation, called *conventions.* Two conventions apply to depreciation for cars: the half-year convention and the mid-quarter convention.

Example

In 2003 you placed in service a car costing $17,000. (Assume the car was used 100 percent for business, you did not elect first-year expensing, and the half-year convention applied.) In 2005 business use drops to 40 percent. The depreciation claimed for 2003 and 2004 totaled $8,160 using MACRS (subject to dollar limits). Had the straight-line method been used, depreciation would have been $5,100. Thus, the excess of $3,060 ($8,160 – $5,100) must be included in income. Your new adjusted basis for the car is $11,900 ($17,000 – $8,160 + $3,060). When calculating the 2004 depreciation deduction, you use the old basis, $17,000, and take the percentage of business use (40 percent). Your basis for depreciation in 2005 is $6,800 ($17,000 × .40). The depreciation percentage for 2005 is 20 percent. The dollar limit must also be reduced to reflect the percentage of business use.

The *half-year convention*, in effect, assumes that the car was placed in service in the second half of the year. Thus, in the first year you are allowed to claim only one-half the normal rate of depreciation, regardless of when in the year the car was placed in service. Thus, even if the car was placed in service on January 1, the half-year convention must still be used.

You can see in Table 9.1 how the half-year convention operates to limit depreciation in the first year. By the same token, the amount of depreciation denied in the first year will ultimately be allowed in the sixth year. Still, the half-year convention means that even though the car is classified as five-year property, its cost will be recovered only over a period of six years. If the half-year convention applies to property used 50 percent or less for business, the depreciation rate is in Table 9.1. If the half-year convention applies to property used more than 50 percent for business, the depreciation rate is in Table 9.2.

The other convention, the *mid-quarter convention,* applies if more than 40 percent of all the depreciable property you place in service during the year is placed in service in the last quarter of the year.

If the mid-quarter convention applies to property used 50 percent or less for business, the rate is in Table 9.3.

Example

In 2005 you place in service a computer costing $5,000 in January and a car costing $15,000 in December. The mid-quarter convention applies because more than 40 percent of the depreciable property you placed in service during the year was placed in service during the last quarter of the year ($15,000 is 75 percent of the total of $20,000 of depreciable property placed in service in 2005).

TABLE 9.3 Straight-Line Mid-Quarter Convention*

Year Placed in Service	1st quarter	2nd quarter	3rd quarter	4th quarter
1	17.5%	12.5%	7.5%	2.5%
2	20.0	20.0	20.0	20.0
3	20.0	20.0	20.0	20.0
4	20.0	20.0	20.0	20.0
5	20.0	20.0	20.0	20.0
6	2.5	7.5	12.5	17.5

*Depreciation may not exceed a dollar limit (see page 224).

Example

The circumstances are the same, except the car was placed in service in January and the computer was placed in service in December. The mid-quarter convention does not apply because only 25 percent of the depreciable property was placed in service in the last quarter of the year ($5,000 is 25 percent of the total of $20,000 of depreciable property placed in service in 2005).

If the mid-quarter convention applies to property used more than 50 percent for business, the rate is in Table 9.4.

Example

In December 2005 you place in service a car costing $14,000. You use the car 40 percent for business and 60 percent for personal purposes. Assume that this is the only depreciable property you place in service in 2005, so the mid-quarter convention applies. Your depreciation deduction for the first year is $140 (2.5 percent of $5,600 [40 percent of $14,000]).

Example

In December 2005 you place in service a car costing $14,000. You use the car 100 percent for business. Assume that this is the only depreciable property you place in service in 2005, so the mid-quarter convention applies. Your depreciation deduction for the first year is $700 (5 percent of $14,000).

TABLE 9.4 MACRS Mid-Quarter Convention*

Year Placed in Service	1st quarter	2nd quarter	3rd quarter	4th quarter
1	35.00%	25.00%	15.00%	5.00%
2	26.00	30.00	34.00	38.00
3	15.60	18.00	20.40	22.80
4	11.01	11.37	12.24	13.68
5	11.01	11.37	11.30	10.94
6	1.38	4.26	7.06	9.58

*Depreciation may not exceed a dollar limit (see page 224).

Section 179 Deduction

The *Section 179 deduction,* also called the first-year expense allowance, is a one-time write-off for the cost of the car. If you use the first-year expense deduction for the year in which you buy the car and place it in service, you cannot then use depreciation in subsequent years. The annual limit on the first-year expense deduction is $105,000 ($25,000 for heavy SUVs) for 2005. However, because of the dollar limits discussed later, the actual limit on the first-year expense deduction is the dollar limit.

So, should you use the first-year expense deduction or depreciation? As a general rule, it is not advisable to use the first-year expense deduction because of the dollar limit. For example, say you buy a car for $15,000 that you use 100 percent for business. Ordinarily, under the rules for the first-year expense deduction, you would deduct the full $15,000. However, because of the dollar limit, you may be able to deduct only a few thousand dollars. What is more, if you buy other depreciable equipment—a computer, machinery, or other equipment—you may well use up your $105,000 expensing limit on the other equipment.

Dollar Limit on Depreciation Deduction

The law sets a *dollar limit* on the amount of depreciation that can be claimed on a car used for business (see Table 9.5). The dollar limit is intended to limit depreciation that could be claimed on a nonluxury car. In essence, the government does not want to underwrite the cost of buying high-priced cars. However, in reality the dollar limits do not really correlate with luxury cars, since the average cost of a new American car purchased topped $28,000 in April 2003. Still, the dollar limits are a factor you must reckon with in calculating your deduction limit.

TABLE 9.5 Dollar Limit on Depreciation of Passenger Cars

Date Car Placed in Service	1st Year	2nd Year	3rd Year	40th and Later Years
2005	$ 2,960	$4,700	$2,850	$1,675
2004	10,610*	4,800	2,850	1,675
2003	10,710**	4,900	2,950	1,775
2002	7,660***	4,900	2,950	1,775
2001	7,660****	4,900	2,950	1,775
2000	3,060	4,900	2,950	1,775

*$2,960 if the car did not qualify for bonus depreciation (i.e., it was a used car)
**$7,660 if the car was acquired before May 6, 2003; $3,060 if the car does not qualify for bonus depreciation.
***$3,060 if the car did not qualify for bonus depreciation
****$3,060 if the car was acquired before September 11, 2003, the car did not qualify for bonus depreciation or an election out of bonus depreciation is made

Example

In March 2005 you place in service a new car costing $20,000 that is used 100 percent for business and weighs 3,500 pounds. The dollar limit on depreciation for 2005 is $2,960. For 2006 it will be $4,700; for 2007 it will be $2,850, and for each year thereafter it will be $1,675 as long as you use the car for business, until the car is fully depreciated.

Example

In 2002 you placed in service a car costing $20,000. For 2005 and all later years, your dollar limit is $1,775.

The dollar limits in Table 9.5 do not apply to light trucks and vans (those weighing less than 6,000 pounds). Special (higher) limits apply as explained later in this chapter.

The dollar limit applies only to cars with a gross vehicle weight (the manufacturer's maximum weight rating when loaded to capacity) of 6,000 pounds or less. Most cars fall into this category. However, some sport utility vehicles (SUVs) are heavier. If you use an SUV as your business car, check the manufacturer's specifications to see if the weight exceeds 6,000 pounds (but not 14,000 pounds). If so, the dollar limits in Table 9.5 do not apply and the vehicle's cost can be expensed up to $25,000. In addition, depreciation can be claimed on the portion of the car that is not expensed.

Example

In 2005, you buy an SUV weighing 6,500 pounds that costs $55,000 and use it entirely for business. You elect to expense the purchase and use MACRS half-year convention (Table 9.2) for the balance of the purchase price. Your expensing and depreciation deductions in 2005 total $31,000 ($25,000 expensing, plus depreciation of 20 percent of [$55,000 − $25,000]). Your depreciation deductions in future years are:

2006	$9,600
2007	5,760
2008	3,456
2009	3,456
2010	1,728

If the dollar limit applies to your business car, the amount depends on the year in which the car was placed in service and how long you have owned it. Over the years the dollar limits have been modified by law changes. For a number of years they have been adjusted for changes in the cost-of-living index. For 2005, the first-year dollar limit is $2,960.

As a practical matter, most individuals will not get to fully depreciate their cars. They will have sold or traded them in long before the cost has been fully written off. This is because of the dollar limit. In the example on page 224, where a $20,000 car was placed in service in 2005, the car will not be fully depreciated until its ninth year (depending upon whether MACRS or the straight-line method was used).

These dollar amounts apply to cars used 100 percent for business. If you use your car for personal purposes as well as for business, you must allocate the dollar limit. The method for allocating this limit is the same method used for allocating the cost of the car for purposes of depreciation, as described earlier.

Example

In July 2005 you place in service a new car costing $30,000 that is used 75 percent for business and 25 percent for personal purposes. The full dollar limit of $2,960 is allocated 75 percent for business. Thus the 2005 dollar limit for this car is $2,220 (75 percent of $2,960).

For cars propelled primarily by electricity, the dollar limits are approximately tripled (rounding off of inflation adjustments can lead to slightly higher-than-triple figures). You may be entitled to a special tax credit for the purchase of an electric car, as explained later in this chapter. If such credit is claimed, then the basis of the car for purposes of depreciation is reduced by the amount of the credit.

Increase Your Dollar Limit

The dollar limit applies on a per-car basis. If you own two cars and use each for business, you may be able to increase your total dollar limit. Be sure to apply the percentage of business use for each car to the applicable dollar limit.

Example

In June 2005 you buy a new car costing $25,000. Assume you drive 24,000 miles during the year, 90 percent of which (21,600 miles) is for business. Your dollar limit on depreciation is $2,664 (90 percent of $2,960).

Now, instead assume you own two cars, each costing $25,000, which you use for business. You drive car A 22,200 miles, of which 20,000 miles is for business, or 90 percent. You drive car B 4,400 miles, of which 2,200 is for business, or 50 percent. Your dollar limit for car A is $2,664 ($2,960 × .90). Your dollar limit for car B is $1,480 ($2,960 × .50). Your total depreciation deduction is $4,144 ($2,664 + 1,480). By using two cars instead of one, your depreciation limit is $1,185 greater than it would be if you used one car exclusively for business and the other for only personal driving.

Dispositions of a Car

When you sell your car, trade it in for a new one, or lose it as the result of a casualty or theft, you have to calculate your tax consequences.

SALE. If you sell your car, your gain or loss is the difference between what you receive for the car and your adjusted basis. Your adjusted basis is your original basis reduced by any first-year expensing or depreciation (up to the dollar limit each year). If the car has been fully depreciated, anything you receive for the car is all gain.

If you used the standard mileage allowance, you are considered to have claimed depreciation even though you did not have to figure a separate depreciation deduction. The standard mileage allowance automatically takes into account a deduction for depreciation. You figure your *deemed depreciation* according to the number of miles you drove the car for business each year and the years in which it was used (see Table 9.6).

Example

You bought a car and placed it in service at the beginning of 2002. You drove the car 20,000 miles each year for business. You sell it at the end of 2005. You must adjust the basis of the car for purposes of determining gain or loss on the sale by deemed depreciation of $12,800 (20,000 miles × 15 cents/mile + 40,000 miles × 16 cents/mile + 20,000 miles × 17 cents/mile). You reduce your original basis by the total of deemed depreciation but do not reduce the basis below zero.

If you use the actual expense method and sell the car before the end of its recovery period, you can claim a reduced depreciation deduction in the year of disposition. Calculate what the depreciation deduction would have been had you held the car for the full year. Then, if you originally placed your car in service in the first three-quarters of the year (January 1 through September 30), you can deduct 50 percent of the amount that would have been allowed. If you originally placed your car in service in the last quarter of the year (October 1 through December 31), you can deduct an amount calculated by applying the percentage in Table 9.7 to what would have been allowed.

TRADE-IN. Generally, no gain or loss is recognized if you trade in your car to buy another car for business. Such a trade is treated as a like-kind exchange if you opt for this treatment. This nonrecognition rule applies even if you pay cash in addition to your trade-in or if you finance the purchase. However, if the dealer gives you money back (because the new car costs less than the trade-in), you may have gain to recognize. The gain recognized will not exceed the amount of cash you receive.

TABLE 9.6 Deemed Depreciation

Year*	Rate per Mile
2005	17 cents
2003–2004	16
2001–2002	15
2000	14
1994–1999	12

*Different rates per mile apply to cars that used the standard mileage rate prior to 1999.

TABLE 9.7 Depreciation in Year of Sale*

Month Car Sold**	Percentage
January, February, March	12.5
April, May, June	37.5
July, August, September	62.5
October, November, December	87.5

*Table is not for fiscal-year taxpayers.
**Car placed in service October 1–December 31.

If you buy a car by trading in another car, your basis for purposes of determining first-year expensing is only the amount of consideration paid; it does not include the basis of the trade-in. But for purposes of depreciation, the basis of the trade-in is included in the basis of the new car.

Example

You buy a new car that costs $15,000 by paying $9,000 cash and receiving $6,000 for the trade-in of your old car that was used 100 percent for business. The adjusted basis of the old car is $5,000. Your basis for purposes of calculating depreciation is $14,000 ($5,000 adjusted basis of the old car, plus $9,000).

A special basis adjustment rule applies when you trade in a car used partially for business (see vehicle trade-in later in this chapter).

CASUALTY OR THEFT. If your car is damaged or stolen and insurance or other reimbursements exceed the adjusted basis of the car, you have a tax gain. However, if you use the reimbursements to buy another car for business or to repair the old car within two years of the end of the year of the casualty or theft, then no gain is recognized. The basis of the new car for purposes of depreciation is its cost less any gain that is not recognized.

Standard Mileage Allowance

Instead of keeping a record of all your expenses and having to calculate depreciation, you can use a *standard mileage allowance* to determine your deduction for business use of your car. You can use the standard mileage allowance in 2005 whether you own or lease the car. The cents-per-mile allowance takes the place of a deduction for gasoline, oil, insurance, maintenance and repairs, vehicle registration fees, and depreciation (if you own the car) or lease payments (if you lease the car). Towing charges for the car are separately deductible in addition to the standard mileage allowance. Parking fees and tolls are also allowed in addition to the standard mileage allowance. Deductible parking fees include those incurred when visiting clients and customers or while traveling away from home on business. Fees to park your car at home or at your place of work are nondeductible personal expenses.

The standard mileage allowance for business use of a car is 40.5 cents per mile for miles driven January 1, 2005 through August 31, 2005, and 48.5 cents per mile for September 1, 2005, through December 31, 2005. (Rural letter carriers who use their cars to deliver mail can deduct the amount paid to them by the U.S. Postal Service as an equipment maintenance allowance.) This rate is adjusted annually for inflation. See Table 9.8 for mileage allowances.

Standard Mileage Rate Barred

You cannot use the standard mileage rate when:

- You use the car for hire (such as a taxi).
- You operate more than four cars at the same time (such as in a fleet operation). This limit does not apply to the use of more than four cars on an alternate basis. For example, if you own cars and vans and alternate the use of these vehicles for business use, then you are not barred from using the standard mileage rate to account for the expenses of the business use for the vehicles.
- You have already claimed MACRS or a first-year expense deduction on the car.

TABLE 9.8 Sample Deductions Under the Standard Mileage Allowance for 2005*

Miles Driven	Deduction	Miles Driven	Deduction
5,000	$ 2,158	30,000	$12,948
10,000	4,316	35,000	15,106
15,000	6,474	40,000	17,264
20,000	8,632	45,000	19,422
25,000	10,790	50,000	21,580

*Assuming mileage is ratable each month.

Standard Mileage Rate or Actual Expense Method?

As discussed earlier in this chapter, which method is preferable for you depends on a number of variables. The most important is the number of business miles you drive each year. As a rule of thumb, those who drive a great number of miles each year frequently find the standard mileage rate offers the greater deduction. However, even with the adjustment to the standard mileage rate for the last four months of 2005, the rate may not adequately reflect your actual driving costs. It is also important to note that the standard mileage rate is not dependent on the price of the car. Less expensive cars can claim the same deduction as more expensive cars, assuming each is driven the same number of business miles. Certainly, those with heavy SUVs can claim a greater deduction with the actual expense method.

Leasing a Car for Business

Leasing a business car is a popular alternative to buying one. If you use the car entirely for business, the cost of leasing is fully deductible. If you make advance payments, you must spread these payments over the entire lease period and deduct them accordingly. You cannot depreciate a car you lease, because depreciation applies only to property that is owned. However, you can choose to deduct the standard mileage rate in lieu of actual expenses (including lease payments).

Lease with an Option to Buy

When you have this arrangement, are you leasing or buying the car? The answer depends on:

- The intent of the parties to the transaction.
- If any equity results from the arrangement.
- If any interest is paid.
- If the fair market value of the car is less than the lease payment or option payment when the option to buy is exercised.

When the factors support a lease arrangement, the payments are deductible. If, however, the factors support a purchase agreement, the payments are not deductible.

Inclusion Amount

If the car price exceeds a certain amount and you deduct your actual costs (you do not use the standard mileage rate), you may have to include in income an *inclusion amount*. This is because the law seeks to equate buying with leasing. Since there is a dollar limit on the amount of depreciation that can be claimed on a luxury car that is owned, the law also requires an amount to be included in income as an offset to high lease payments on a car that is leased. In essence, the inclusion amount seeks to limit your deduction for lease payments to what it would be if you owned the car and claimed depreciation. The inclusion amount, which is simply an amount that you add to your other income, applies if a car is leased for more than 30 days and its value exceeds a certain amount. Amounts are adjusted annually for inflation. The inclusion amount is added to income only so long as you lease the car. It is based on the value of the car as of the first day of the lease term. If the capitalized cost of the car is specified in the lease agreement, that amount is considered to be the fair market value of the car. At the start of the lease, you can see what your inclusion amount will be for that year and for all subsequent years. The inclusion amount is based on a percentage of the **fair market value** of the car at the time the lease begins. Different inclusion amounts apply to gas-driven cars and to electric cars.

Fair market value The price that would be paid for the property when there is a willing buyer and seller (neither being required to buy or sell) and both have reasonable knowledge of all the necessary facts. Evidence of fair market value includes the price paid for similar property on or about the same date.

The inclusion amount applies only if the fair market value of the car when the lease began was more than $15,800 in 1997 to 1998, $15,500 in 1999 to 2002, $18,000 in 2003, $17,500 in 2004, and $15,200 in 2005. Different thresholds for inclusion amounts are applied for cars leased prior to 1997.

Inclusion amounts in Table 9.9 are taken from IRS tables, which can be found in the appendix to IRS Publication 463, *Travel, Entertainment, Gift, and Car Expenses.* Those rates apply to cars first leased in 2005. The full amount in the table applies if the car is leased for the full year and used entirely for business. If the car is leased for less than the full year, or if it is used partly for personal purposes, the inclusion amount must be allocated to business use for the period of the year during which it was used. The allocation for part-year use is made on a day-by-day basis.

Example

The inclusion amount for your car is $500. You used your car only six months of the year (a leap year). You must include $250 in income (183/366 of $500).

TABLE 9.9 Inclusion Amounts for Cars (Other than Light Trucks and Vans, and Electric Cars) First Leased in 2005

Fair Market Value		Tax Year During Lease				
Over	Not Over	1st	2nd	3rd	4th	Later
$15,200	$15,500	3	6	9	11	13
15,500	15,800	4	9	13	17	19
15,800	16,100	5	12	18	22	26
16,100	16,400	7	15	22	27	32
16,400	16,700	8	18	27	32	39
16,700	17,000	9	21	32	38	44
17,000	17,500	11	25	38	45	52
17,500	18,000	14	30	45	54	63
18,000	18,500	16	35	52	63	73
18,500	19,000	18	40	60	72	83
19,000	19,500	20	46	67	80	94
19,500	20,000	23	50	75	90	104
20,000	20,500	25	55	82	99	115
20,500	21,000	27	61	89	108	125
21,000	21,500	30	65	97	117	135
21,500	22,000	32	70	105	125	146
22,000	23,000	35	78	116	139	161
23,000	24,000	40	88	131	156	182
24,000	25,000	44	98	146	175	202
25,000	26,000	49	108	161	192	223
26,000	27,000	54	118	175	211	244
27,000	28,000	58	128	191	228	265
28,000	29,000	63	138	205	247	285
29,000	30,000	67	149	220	264	306
30,000	31,000	72	159	234	283	326
31,000	32,000	77	168	250	300	348
32,000	33,000	81	179	265	318	367
33,000	34,000	86	189	279	336	389

TABLE 9.9 *(Continued)*

Fair Market Value		Tax Year During Lease				
Over	Not Over	1st	2nd	3rd	4th	Later
34,000	35,000	90	199	295	354	409
35,000	36,000	95	209	309	372	430
36,000	37,000	99	219	325	389	451
37,000	38,000	104	229	339	408	471
38,000	39,000	109	239	354	426	491
39,000	40,000	113	249	370	443	512
40,000	41,000	118	259	384	462	533
41,000	42,000	122	269	400	479	554
42,000	43,000	127	279	414	497	575
43,000	44,000	132	289	429	515	595
44,000	45,000	136	299	444	533	616
45,000	46,000	141	309	459	551	636
46,000	47,000	145	320	473	569	657
47,000	48,000	150	329	489	587	678
48,000	49,000	154	340	504	604	699
49,000	50,000	159	350	518	623	719
50,000	51,000	164	360	533	640	740
51,000	52,000	168	370	548	659	760
52,000	53,000	173	380	563	676	781
53,000	54,000	177	390	578	694	802
54,000	55,000	182	400	593	712	823
55,000	56,000	186	410	609	729	844
56,000	57,000	191	420	623	748	864
57,000	58,000	196	430	638	766	884
58,000	59,000	200	440	653	784	905
59,000	60,000	205	450	668	802	925
60,000	62,000	212	465	691	828	957
62,000	64,000	221	485	721	864	998
64,000	66,000	230	506	750	900	1,039

(Continued)

TABLE 9.9 *(Continued)*

Fair Market Value		Tax Year During Lease				
Over	Not Over	1st	2nd	3rd	4th	Later
66,000	68,000	239	526	780	935	1,081
68,000	70,000	248	546	810	971	1,123
70,000	72,000	258	566	839	1,008	1,163
72,000	74,000	267	586	869	1,044	1,204
74,000	76,000	276	606	899	1,079	1,247
76,000	78,000	285	626	930	1,114	1,288
78,000	80,000	294	646	960	1,150	1,329
80,000	85,000	310	682	1,011	1,213	1,402
85,000	90,000	333	732	1,086	1,303	1,504
90,000	95,000	356	782	1,161	1,392	1,608
95,000	100,000	379	832	1,236	1,481	1,712
100,000	110,000	413	908	1,347	1,616	1,867
110,000	120,000	459	1,009	1,496	1,795	2,073
120,000	130,000	505	1,109	1,646	1,974	2,280
130,000	140,000	551	1,210	1,795	2,153	2,486
140,000	150,000	597	1,310	1,945	2,332	2,693
150,000	160,000	642	1,411	2,094	2,511	2,900
160,000	170,000	688	1,512	2,245	2,690	3,106
170,000	180,000	734	1,612	2,392	2,870	3,313
180,000	190,000	780	1,713	2,541	3,048	3,520
190,000	200,000	826	1,813	2,691	3,227	3,727
200,000	210,000	871	1,914	2,840	3,407	3,933
210,000	220,000	917	2,015	2,989	3,585	4,141
220,000	230,000	963	2,115	3,139	3,764	4,347
230,000	240,000	1,009	2,216	3,288	3,943	4,554
240,000	and up	1,055	2,316	3,437	4,123	4,760

Remember that if you use your car for commuting or other nonbusiness purposes, you cannot deduct that allocable part of the lease; there is no inclusion amount for this portion.

There are separate inclusion amount tables for trucks and vans and for electric cars first leased in 2005. This information can be found in IRS Rev. Proc. 2005-13.

Should You Lease or Buy?

The decision to lease or buy a car used for business is not an easy one. There are many financial advantages to leasing. Most important is that you need not put forth more than a small amount of up-front cash to lease, whereas a purchase generally requires a significant down payment. So leasing can enable you to drive a more expensive car than you could afford to buy. However, as a practical matter, if a car is driven extensively (more than 15,000 miles per year), leasing may not make sense because of the annual mileage limit and the charge for excess mileage. In such cases, owning may be preferable. Take into consideration that at the end of the lease term you own nothing, whereas at the end of the same period of time with a purchased car you own an asset that can be sold or traded in for a newer model.

Whether there are any tax advantages is difficult to say. With leasing, you deduct the entire lease charge; with a purchase, you generally deduct depreciation, although you may be able to fully expense up to $25,000 for a car weighing more than 6,000 pounds. Given the current dollar limits on depreciation, this may not be as great as the lease charge. While the inclusion amount is designed to offset this differential, it may not be sufficient to make leasing and depreciation equate.

The only way to know whether leasing or buying is more advantageous taxwise is to run the numbers. Project your deductible costs of leasing versus your costs of purchasing the car.

Arranging Car Ownership

If you have a corporation, should you or your corporation own the car you will use for business? From a tax standpoint, it is generally wise to have the corporation own the car because the corporation can fully deduct the expenses of the car (subject, of course, to the dollar limit on depreciation). If you own the car, your deductions can be claimed only as itemized deductions subject to a floor of 2 percent of your adjusted gross income. If your adjusted gross income is substantial, your deductions may be further limited by an overall reduction in itemized deductions.

For insurance purposes, it may also be more advantageous to have the corporation own the car. If the corporation owns more than one vehicle, it can command better insurance rates than an individual who owns only one or two cars. Also, if the car is involved in an accident, the corporation's insurance rates are not affected. If you own the car and it is in an accident, your personal insurance rates will be increased.

Finally, if there is a lawsuit involving the car, it is generally preferable to have the corporation sued rather than you personally, since a recovery against the corporation is limited by corporate assets.

Employee Use of an Employer-Provided Car

If your employer gives you a car to use for business, you may be able to deduct certain expenses. Your deduction is limited to the actual expenses of operating the car that were not reimbursed by your employer. The amount of the deduction depends on the amount your employer includes in your income and the number of business and personal miles driven. Your personal use is reported annually on your Form W-2 (see Chapter 7). If your employer owns the car you use, you cannot use the standard mileage allowance for car expenses.

What Is Included on Your W-2?

The employer has a choice of what to report. The employer can either report the actual value of your personal use or assume that you used the car entirely for personal purposes and include 100 percent of the benefit in your income. This 100-percent amount is based on the annual lease value for the car (explained in Chapter 7). The full amount reported on your W-2 is income to you. Your W-2 will note whether the 100-percent annual lease value or actual personal use was reported. Even though you must include the full amount reported on your W-2, whatever it might be, you may be able to reduce your income tax. You can offset this income to the extent that what was reported as personal use was actually business use and you deduct your business expenses. Where to claim these business deductions is detailed at the end of this chapter.

If your employer reported 100 percent of personal use even though you used the car in part for business, you can deduct your actual expenses for business use that were not reimbursed by your employer. If your employer included only a portion of the use of the car designed to reflect your personal use, then you can deduct any actual expenses for business use that were not reimbursed by your employer.

Vehicle Trade-In

When you are ready to dispose of your old car and find a replacement, what is the best way to handle the arrangements from a tax perspective? Trade it in? Sell it?

- If you trade in the old car to buy a new one, the arrangement can be considered a tax-free exchange if you elect this treatment. The result: The basis of the new car is the remaining basis of the old car, if any, plus any cash paid toward the new car. And if the car that is traded in was used only partially for business, a special adjustment is required for purposes of figuring depreciation on the newly acquired car. In this case you figure basis of the old car as if it were used entirely for business (i.e., you must reduce basis as if you had depreciated 100 percent of the car's basis). This severely limits your ability to claim write-offs for the new car.

- If you sell the old car to buy a new one, gain or loss results from the difference between the basis of the old car and the amount you receive for it. If the basis is less than what you receive, you have a taxable gain; if the basis is more than what you receive, you have a taxable loss.

Before deciding on which alternative to use, consider the tax results in your situation. If, for example, you are disposing of a large SUV or truck, you may have a taxable gain since you may have already reduced the basis of the car substantially (remember that vehicles that weigh more than 6,000 pounds are not subject to the depreciation dollar limits). In this case, a trade-in postpones gain recognition. However, if you are disposing of another type of vehicle, one with a tax basis that is higher than its fair market value, a sale can produce a taxable loss so a trade-in is ill-advised.

Trucks and Vans

Trucks (including SUVs) and vans that are configured in such a way as to be used for personal purposes only minimally are not subject to the dollar limits on depreciation that apply to passenger cars weighing no more than 6,000 pounds. These trucks and vans are referred to as qualified nonpersonal use vehicles.

Modifications likely to render a truck or van a qualified nonpersonal use vehicle include having a front jump seat, permanent shelving that fills the cargo area, and advertising or a company name printed on the side.

Trucks and vans that are not qualified nonpersonal use vehicles are subject to the following rules:

- For vehicles with a gross vehicle weight rating in excess of 6,000 pounds but not more than 14,000 pounds, the dollar limits on depreciation do not apply (see the treatment of heavy SUVs earlier in this chapter). Their cost can be expensed up to $25,000 in 2005 or depreciated as five-year property without any dollar limit on the annual deduction.

- For lighter vehicles, special dollar limits apply. These dollar limits are slightly higher than for passenger cars. Table 9.10 shows the dollar limits for light trucks and vans first placed in service in 2005.

TABLE 9.10 Dollar Limits for Light Trucks and Vans

Tax Year	Dollar Limit
First Year (2005)	$3,260
Second Year (2006)	$5,200
Third Year (2007)	$3,150
Each Succeeding Year	$1,875

Write-Offs for Hybrid and Electric Cars

The tax law encourages the use of environmentally sensitive cars, including those powered by gas and electricity (hybrid cars) and those powered primarily by electricity.

Hybrid Cars

You may deduct up to $2,000 for the purchase of a clean-fuel car (different limits apply to trucks and vans weighing more than 10,000 pounds). The deduction applies not only to cars used for business, but also to personal cars.

The deduction is claimed in the year of purchase. If the car is not used entirely for business, then the allocable part of the deduction for personal use is claimed as an above-the-line deduction on Form 1040. No deduction is allowed for the portion of the car taken into account for purposes of first-year expensing. The deduction applies only if you are the original owner of the car; it cannot be claimed for the purchase of a used car.

The deduction relates to the incremental cost of clean fuel (electricity). Manufacturers must tell the IRS this amount and receive certification, a copy of which should be available to purchasers of these cars. To date, the IRS has given certification to:

- Ford Escape Hybrid—model year 2005
- Honda Accord Hybrid—model year 2005
- Honda Civic Hybrid—model years 2003 and 2005
- Honda Insight—model years 2000 through 2005
- Lexus RX 400h—model year 2006
- Toyota Highlander Hybrid—model year 2006
- Toyota Prius—model years 2001 through 2005

For the Future

Starting in 2006, you may be entitled to a tax credit for the purchase of a hybrid vehicle, as well as cars and light trucks that run on a fuel cell, alternative fuel, or so-called "lean-burn" vehicles. The amount of the credit varies with the size of the vehicle and fuel economy.

Electric Cars

There are distinct rules for electric cars. The dollar limit for depreciation on electric cars is higher than for cars powered by other means. The inclusion amounts for leased electric cars are also higher than for nonelectric cars. And there is a special tax credit for the purchase of an electric car.

At present electric cars are not widely available. Even where they are available, they have limited traveling range, which makes them generally impractical for business use (remember that commuting is not considered business use). Still, if you bought an electric car and used it for business, you may be entitled to a tax credit. (If you leased instead of purchased an electric car, be sure to take the inclusion amount into account when figuring your car deductions.) This credit reduces your taxes dollar-for-dollar and generally is worth more to you than deductions. The credit, called the credit for **qualified electric vehicles,** is 10 percent of the cost of the car, up to a maximum credit of $4,000 in 2005.

Qualified electric vehicle   Any motor vehicle that is powered primarily by an electric motor drawing current from rechargeable batteries, fuel cells, or other portable sources of electrical current.

You cannot claim a credit for any portion of the car for which a first-year expense deduction is claimed. You must reduce the basis of the car for purposes of depreciation and otherwise by the amount of the credit. The credit cannot exceed the amount of your tax liability, reduced by certain refundable credits.

To claim the credit, you must be the original owner of the car and must not have bought it for resale (you are not a car dealer). The credit is not limited to the portion of the car for business use. You may claim the credit for the portion of the car used for personal purposes. The credit is computed on Form 8834, Qualified Electric Vehicle Credit.

For the Future

The maximum credit of $4,000 is reduced by 75 percent in 2006 for a top credit of $1,000. No credit may be claimed for any electric car placed in service after 2006 unless Congress extends it.

Reimbursement Arrangements

If your employer reimburses you for the business use of your car, you may or may not need to claim deductions. The answer depends on the reimbursement arrangement with your employer.

Accountable Plan

If your employer maintains an arrangement that reimburses you for business-related use of the car, requires you to adequately account to the employer for these expenses, and also requires you to return within a reasonable time any advances or reimbursements in excess of these expenses, then the plan is treated as an *accountable plan*. (For details on adequate accounting under accountable plans and returning excess amounts within a reasonable time, see Chapter 8.) If your employer maintains an accountable plan for reimbursement of business expenses and the amount of reimbursement does not exceed the standard mileage allowance, the reimbursements are not reported on your W-2 and you do not deduct any expenses. If the reimbursements exceed the standard mileage allowance, only the excess over the standard mileage allowance is included on your W-2. You may then deduct your actual expenses that exceed the standard mileage rate.

Nonaccountable Plan

Your employer must include on your W-2 form all reimbursements made under a nonaccountable plan.

Recordkeeping for Car Expenses

Regardless of whether you use the actual expense method or the standard mileage allowance for your car (or a car that your employer provides you with), certain recordkeeping requirements apply. You must keep track of the number of miles you drive each year for business, as well as the total miles driven each year. You must also record the date of the business mileage, the designation of the business travel, and the business reason for the car expense. It is advisable to maintain a daily travel log or diary in which you record the date, the destination, the business purpose of the trip, and the number of miles driven (use the odometer readings at the start and end of the trip, and then total the miles for each trip). Be sure to note the odometer reading on January 1 each year.

If you use the actual expense method, you must also keep a record of the costs of operating the car. These include the cost of gasoline and oil, car insurance, interest on a car loan (if you are self-employed), licenses and taxes, and repairs and maintenance. Record these amounts in your expense log or diary.

If you lease a car, you must keep track of the amount of the lease payments, in addition to the number of miles driven (and the number of business miles), the dates of travel, the destinations, and the purpose for the travel.

Use a diary or log to keep track of your business mileage and other related costs. You can buy a car expense log in stationery and business supply stores. Table 9.11 is a model of an IRS sample daily business mileage and expense log.

It is essential that you keep a written record of the business use of your car. You must note on your tax return whether you have such a record. Remember that your return is signed under penalty of perjury.

TABLE 9.11 Sample Log

| Date | Destination | Business Purpose | Odometer Readings | | Miles this Trip | Expenses | |
			Start	Stop		Type	Amount
5/4/05	Local—St. Louis	Sales calls	8,097	8,188	91	Gas	$18.00
5/5/05	Indianapolis	Sales calls	8,211	8,486	275	Parking	$5.00
5/6/05	Louisville	Bob Smith (potential client)	8,486	8,599	113	Gas	$17.80
						Repair flat tire	$10.00
5/7/05	Return to St. Louis		8,599	8,875	276	Gas	$18.25
5/8/05	Local—St. Louis	Sales calls	8,914	9,005	91		
Weekly total			8,097	9,005	846		$69.05
Year-to-date total					5,883		$1,014.75

Example

An interior designer who runs her business from home visits clients using her personal car for this business driving. She records her mileage for the first three months of the year, which shows that the car is used 75 percent for business and 25 percent for personal driving. Invoices from her business show that business activity was nearly constant throughout the year, indicating that her driving pattern remained the same. Under these facts, she can extrapolate that 75 percent of her car expenses for the year are business-related.

Example

The same interior designer instead records her mileage for the first week of every month, showing 75 percent business use. Invoices show that business continued at the same rate throughout the month so that the first week's record was representative of the full month. Under these facts, she can extrapolate that 75 percent of her car expenses for the balance of the month (and throughout the year) are business-related.

Proving Expenses with a Mileage Allowance

Generally, required recordkeeping includes tracking the odometer at the start and end of each business trip (as well as the date, destination, and purpose of the trip). However, the IRS permits "sampling" in some situations. You are treated as having adequate substantiation if you keep records for a representative portion of the year and can demonstrate that the period for which records are kept is representative of use for the entire year.

Sampling may not be used if you cannot show a consistent pattern of car use. Also, not all substantiation shortcuts are acceptable. For instance, one taxpayer used mileage figured by a computer atlas to substantiate his car expenses. Unfortunately, the Tax Court rejected this method, observing that he failed to keep track of his odometer readings at the time the expenses were incurred.

If your employer pays for car expenses with a mileage allowance, it generally is considered to be proof of the amount of expenses. The amount of expenses that can be proven by use of this allowance is limited to the standard mileage allowance or the amount of a fixed and variable rate (FAVR) allowance that is not included on your W-2. The FAVR allowance includes a combination of fixed and variable costs, such as a cents-per-mile rate to cover variable operating costs (e.g., gas, oil, routine maintenance, and repairs) and a flat amount to cover fixed costs (e.g., depreciation, insurance, registration and license fees, and personal property taxes). The FAVR allowance applies only if the car is used for certain employees. Thus, use of this allowance is the employer's choice, not the employee's.

Where to Deduct Car Expenses

Employees

You compute your car expenses on Form 2106, Employee Business Expenses, or Form 2106-EZ, Unreimbursed Employee Business Expenses. Form 2106-EZ can be used only if:

1. You were not reimbursed by your employer for expenses or, if you were reimbursed, the reimbursements were included in your income on your W-2, and

2. You use the standard mileage rate for deducting your car expenses. If you use the actual expense method to deduct your car expenses, you must use Form 2106.

Enter your total expenses on Schedule A, Itemized Deductions, as a miscellaneous itemized expense. These deductions are then limited to the amount they exceed 2 percent of adjusted gross income. If adjusted gross income exceeds a certain amount, the deductions may be further limited. (The threshold for the reduction in itemized deductions is adjusted annually for inflation.)

Disabled Employees

If you have a physical or mental disability, your impairment-related work expenses are deductible as an itemized deduction, but the 2-percent floor does not apply. Impairment-related work expenses include costs of attendant care at your place of work and those that are necessary to enable you to work (such as the cost of a driver to bring you to business locations). General medical expenses, however, are not impairment-related work expenses; they are simply personal medical expenses and are deductible as such.

Special Rule for Performing Artists

If you meet certain requirements, you can deduct all of your car expenses as an adjustment to gross income on page one of Form 1040 instead of claiming them as miscellaneous itemized deductions on Schedule A. You are treated as a performing artist if you meet *all* of the following tests:

1. You perform services in the performing arts for at least two employers during the year.

2. You receive at least $200 each from any two of these employers.

3. Your related performing arts business expenses are more than 10 percent of your adjusted gross income from the performance of such services.

4. Your adjusted gross income (and not merely performing arts income) does not exceed $16,000 (before deducting business expenses from your performing arts).

5. If you are married, you file a joint return (unless you lived apart from your spouse for the entire year).

You perform tests 1, 2, and 3 based on your individual experience. However, the adjusted gross income in test 4 is the combined adjusted gross income of you and your spouse. If you meet these tests, you deduct your performing arts business expenses as an adjustment to gross income on page one of Form 1040.

Self-Employed

You enter your car expenses on Schedule C, Profit and Loss from Business, or Schedule C-EZ, Net Profit from Business. If you are not required to complete Form 4562, Depreciation and Amortization, because you did not place any depreciable or amortizable property in service in 2005, then use Part IV of Schedule C and Part III of Schedule C-EZ to report information on your car. You need to know and provide when the car was placed in service and the number of miles driven for business, commuting, or other purposes; whether there is another car available for personal use and whether your business car was available during off-duty hours; evidence to support your deductions and whether this evidence is written. If you are otherwise required to complete Form 4562, then report the information about your car on this form and not on Schedule C or Schedule C-EZ.

Farmers who are self-employed deduct their car expenses on Schedule F. Also complete Part IV of Form 4562, Depreciation and Amortization, to provide information about car use.

Partnerships and LLCs

Expenses of business-owned cars are reported on the business's Form 1065 as part of the business's ordinary income (or loss). They are entered in the category of Other Deductions. A schedule is attached to the return explaining the deductions claimed in this category. Car expenses are not separately stated items. The owner's share of ordinary income (or loss) is reported on Schedule K-1.

S Corporations

Car expenses of business-owned cars are reported on the corporation's Form 1120S as part of the S corporation's ordinary income (or loss). They are entered in the category of Other Deductions. A schedule is attached to the return explaining the deductions claimed in this category. Car expenses are not separately stated items. The shareholder's share of ordinary income (or loss) is reported on Schedule K-1.

C Corporations

Car expenses are reported on the corporation's Form 1120 as part of its taxable income (or loss). They are entered in the category of Other Deductions. A schedule is attached to the return explaining the deductions claimed in this category.

All Businesses

If you claim depreciation for a car used in business, you must complete Form 4562, Depreciation and Amortization. This form is filed for the year the car is placed in service. C corporations must continue to file this for each year thereafter. Other taxpayers need not file the form after the first year (unless other depreciable property is placed in service).

The credit for purchasing an electric car is claimed on Form 8834, Qualified Electric Vehicle Credit.

CHAPTER 10

Repairs and Maintenance

Property and equipment generally need constant repairs to keep them in working order. Preventative maintenance—regular servicing of equipment—can cut down on replacement costs by allowing you to keep your current equipment longer. When your computer goes down, a service person is required to make repairs. When the air-conditioning system in your office building stops working, again, servicing is necessary. If you have property or equipment to which you make repairs, you can deduct these expenses. The only hitch is making sure that the expenses are not *capital expenditures.* Capital expenditures cannot be currently deducted but instead are added to the basis of property and recovered through depreciation or upon the disposition of the property.

In this chapter you will learn about:

- Ordinary repairs
- Rehabilitation plans
- Special rules for improvements for the elderly and handicapped
- Deductible repairs and capital improvements
- Where to take deductions for repairs

For further information about deducting repairs, see IRS Publication 535, *Business Expenses.*

Ordinary Repairs

Deducting Incidental Repairs in General

The cost of repairing property and equipment used in your business is a deductible business expense. In contrast, expenditures that materially add to the value of the property or prolong its life must be capitalized (added to the basis of the property and recovered through depreciation). In most cases, the distinction is clear. If you pay a repair person to service your copying machine because paper keeps getting jammed, the cost of the service call is a repair expense and is currently deductible. If you put a new roof on your office building, you usually must capitalize the expenditure and recover the cost through depreciation. Sometimes, however, the classification of an expense as a repair or a capital expenditure is not clear. For example, in one case the cost of a new roof was currently deductible where it was installed merely to repair a leak and did not change the structure of the building or add to its value.

Guidelines on Distinguishing Between a Repair and a Capital Item

Repairs are expenses designed to keep property in good working condition. This includes the replacement of short-lived parts. Typically, the cost of repairs is small compared with the cost of the property itself.

Capital items, on the other hand, are akin to original construction. They replace long-lived parts or enlarge or improve on the original property. Costs are usually substantial.

Table 10.1 includes some common examples of repairs and capital improvements.

Even though repairs add to the length of a property's useful life, this does not automatically make them capital improvements. It can be argued that *all* repairs produce this result. For example, one business owner with a fleet of tug boats made substantial engine repairs each year. The IRS said that the repairs should be capitalized because they added to the life of the boats, but the Tax Court said no. Despite the cost of the repairs—over $100,000 per tug—

TABLE 10.1 Examples of Repairs versus Capital Items

Repairs	Capital Items
Painting the outside of office building	Vinyl siding the outside of office building
Replacing missing shingles on roof	Replacing entire roof unless strictly for repair purposes
Replacing compressor for air conditioner	Adding air-conditioning system
Cleaning canopy over restaurant entrance	Adding canopy over restaurant entrance
Resurfacing office floor	Replacing office floor

and the fact that the repairs kept the tugs afloat longer—they were still ordinary repairs that were currently deductible.

The fact that certain repairs are necessitated by governmental directives does not change the character of the expense. If it is a required repair, it is currently deductible; if it substantially improves the property, it is a capital expenditure. For example, in one case, rewiring ordered by local fire prevention inspectors was a capital expenditure. The same is true for capital expenditures ordered by the U.S. Public Health Service and state sanitary or health laws.

Repairs made to property damaged by a casualty are deductible if they merely restore the property to its pre-casualty condition. This is so even if a deduction is also claimed for a casualty loss to the property.

Example

Severe flooding destroyed a business owner's property. He was not compensated by insurance. The IRS, in a memorandum to a district counsel, allowed him to deduct the cost of repairs to the property where such repairs merely restored it to its precasualty condition. In addition, he claimed a casualty loss for the same property.

Environmental Protection Agency Compliance

If you are forced to take certain actions to comply with Environmental Protection Agency (EPA) requirements, such as encapsulating or removing asbestos, be sure to understand which expenses are currently deductible and which expenses must be capitalized. Environmental remediation costs can be currently deducted. These are costs of cleanups to comply with environmental laws that effectively restore property to its original (precontamination) condition. The cost of capital improvements to comply with environmental laws, however, must be capitalized.

Example

The cost of encapsulating asbestos in a warehouse is currently deductible. The cost of removing asbestos from a boiler room must be capitalized. (The removal makes the property substantially more attractive to potential buyers.)

For certain environmental cleanup expenditures, you can elect to deduct certain costs that would otherwise be capitalized. Since property that has been contaminated by hazardous substances has been referred to as *brownfields*, you may see this expensing election referred to as a brownfields deduction.

Legislative Alert

The election to deduct the cost of certain environmental cleanup costs expires at the end of 2005 unless Congress again extends it.

Small business refiners (those with no more than 1,500 individuals engaged in refinery activities on any day during the year and the average daily domestic refinery run for the one-year period ending on December 31, 2002, did not exceed 205,000 barrels) can elect to deduct 75 percent of costs paid or incurred to comply with the Highway Diesel Fuel Sulfur Control Requirements of the EPA.

Rehabilitation Plans

If you make repairs as part of a general plan to recondition or improve property—typically, office buildings, stores, and factories—then the expenses must be capitalized. This is so even though the expenses would have been deductible if made outside a general plan of repair. This rule is called the *rehabilitation doctrine*. For example, painting generally is treated as a currently deductible repair expense. However, if you add an extension to your office building, the cost of painting the extension upon completion is a capital item under the rehabilitation doctrine.

Protecting the Deduction for Repairs

With proper planning, you can make sure that repair costs are currently deductible even though you also undertake capital expenditures. Schedule repairs separately from capital improvements so they will not be treated as one rehabilitation plan, and get separate bills for the repairs.

Tax Credits for Rehabilitation

While rehabilitation costs generally must be capitalized, in special instances you can claim a tax credit for your expenditures. If you rehabilitate a nonresidential building that was built before 1936, you can claim a credit for 10 percent of your expenditures. If you rehabilitate a certified historic structure (a building that is listed in the National Register or located in a registered historic district), the credit is 20 percent of costs. The credit is claimed in the year the property is placed in service, not the year in which the expenditures are made.

Example

If you undertake a two-year project beginning in 2004 and do not place the building in service until 2005, the credit is taken in 2005

Rehabilitation requires that you make substantial improvements to the building but leave a substantial portion of it intact. A *substantial portion* means that within any two-year period you select, the rehabilitation expenditures exceed the adjusted basis of the building or $5,000, whichever is greater. In the case of a pre-1936 building, at least 75 percent of the external walls must be left intact and at least 50 percent of external walls must remain as external walls. The Secretary of the Interior must certify that the rehabilitation of certified historic structures will be in keeping with the building's historic status.

The credit is claimed on Form 3468, Investment Credit. For individuals and C corporations, it is part of the general business credit computed on Form 3800, General Business Credit. The credit may be limited by the passive loss rules explained in Chapter 4. The general business credit limitations are explained in Chapter 23.

Demolition Expenses

As a general rule, the costs of demolishing a building are not deductible. Instead, they are added to the basis of the new building (that is, the building put up in the place of the demolished building). However, the costs of demolishing only a part of a building may be currently deductible. According to the IRS, if 75 percent or more of the existing external walls and 75 percent or more of the existing internal framework are both retained, the costs of demolition need not be capitalized (added to basis) but instead can be currently deducted.

For the Future

For 2006 and 2007, a special deduction of $1.80 per square foot can be claimed for the cost of energy-efficient improvements to commercial buildings.

Special Rules for Improvements for the Elderly and Handicapped

The Americans with Disabilities Act (ADA) may require you to make certain modifications to your office, store, or factory if you have not done so already. You may have to install ramps, widen doorways and lavatories to accommodate wheelchairs, add elevators, or make other similar changes to your facilities to render them more accessible to the elderly and handicapped.

These modifications may be more in the nature of capital improvements than repairs. Still, the law provides two special tax incentives to which you may be entitled. One is a tax credit; the other is a special deduction. These incentives allow for a current benefit rather than requiring capitalization of expenditures that will be recovered over long periods of time.

Disabled Access Credit

Small business owners can claim a tax credit for expenditures to remove barriers on business property that impede the access of handicapped individuals and to supply special materials or assistance to visually or hearing-impaired persons.

Small business Businesses with gross receipts of no more than $1 million (after returns and allowances) and no more than 30 full-time employees. Full-time employees are those who work more than 30 hours per week for 20 or more calendar weeks in the year.

The credit cannot exceed 50 percent of expenditures over $250 but not over $10,250. The maximum credit is $5,000.

Example

You, as a small business owner, spend $4,000 to install ramps in your mall. You may take a tax credit of $1,875 ($4,000 − $250 = $3,750 × .50).

The dollar limit applies at both the partner and partnership levels. The same rule applies to shareholders and S corporations, as well as to members and LLCs.

Qualifying Expenditures

Qualifying expenditures are designed to meet the requirements of the ADA. For example, the cost of putting in handicapped parking spaces as required by federal law is a qualified expenditure. Many of these requirements are set forth in connection with the expense deduction for the removal of architectural and transportation barriers. However, eligible expenditures do not include those in connection with new construction. Thus, if you are in the process of building an office complex and you install special bathroom facilities to accommodate a wheelchair, you cannot claim the credit because this is new construction. If you claim the credit, you cannot also claim a deduction for the same expenditures.

Businesses already in compliance with the ADA cannot claim the credit for equipment that may add some benefit for handicapped customers. Also, the IRS has ruled that Web-based businesses using software to enable handicapped customers to shop cannot claim the credit; it is limited to bricks-and-mortar businesses. However, a company with a physical place of business that uses a software service to communicate on-site with hearing-impaired customers qualifies for the credit.

Deduction for Removal of Architectural or Transportation Barriers

As you have seen throughout this chapter, expenditures that improve or prolong the life of property generally must be capitalized and the cost recovered through depreciation. You have already seen two special credits that can be claimed for expenditures that would otherwise have to be capitalized. There is one more important exception to this capitalization rule: You can elect to deduct the expenses of removing architectural or transportation barriers to the handicapped and elderly. The election is made simply by claiming the deduction on a timely filed tax return.

The maximum deduction in any one year is $15,000. If your expenditures for a removal project exceed this limit, you can deduct the first $15,000 of costs and capitalize (and then depreciate) the balance.

The dollar limit applies at both the partner and partnership levels. A partner must combine his or her distributive share of these expenditures from one partnership with any distributive share of such expenditures from any other partnerships. The partner may allocate the $15,000 limit among his or her own expenditures and the partner's distributive share of partnership expenditures in any manner. If the allocation results in all or a portion of the partner's distributive share of partnership's expenditures not being an allocable deduction, then the partnership can capitalize the unallowable portion.

While the regulations on applying the dollar limits at both the partner and partnership levels do not specify other pass-through entities, presumably the same rules that apply to partners and partnerships apply as well to shareholders and S corporations.

If the election is made to expense these expenditures, then no disabled access credit can be claimed for the same expenses.

Example

A partner's distributive share of partnership expenditures (after application of the $15,000 limit at the partnership level) is $7,500. The partner also has a sole proprietorship that made $10,000 of expenditures. The partner can choose to allocate the $15,000 limitation as follows: $5,000 to his or her distributive share of the partnership's expenditures and $10,000 to individual expenditures. If the partner provides written proof of this allocation to the partnership, the partnership can then capitalize $2,500, the unused portion of the partner's distributive share of expenditures ($7,500 distributive share less $5,000 allocated as a deduction).

Qualifying Expenditures

These are expenses that conform a facility or public transportation vehicle to certain standards that make them accessible to persons over the age of 65 or those with physical or mental disability or impairment (see Table 10.2). It does not include any expense for the construction or comprehensive renovation of a facility or public transportation vehicle or the normal replacement of depreciable property.

Recordkeeping

If you elect to deduct these expenditures, you must maintain records and documentation, including architectural plans and blueprints, contracts, and building permits to support your claims. How long these records should be kept is discussed in Chapter 3.

TABLE 10.2 Guidance on Acceptable Standards for the Elderly and Handicapped

Type of Expense	Requirements
Grading	The ground should be graded to attain a level with a normal entrance to make the facility accessible to individuals with physical disabilities.
Walks	A public walk should be at least 48 inches wide and have a gradient of no more than five percent.
	A walkway should have a continuing common surface (not interrupted by steps or abrupt changes in level).
	A walkway or driveway should have a nonslip surface.
Parking lots	At least one space that is accessible and proximate to the facility must be set aside and designated for the handicapped.
	The space must be open to one side to allow wheelchair access.
	For head-on parking, the space must be at least 12 feet wide.
Ramps	A ramp should not have a slope greater than a one-inch rise in 12 inches.
	There must be a handrail 32 inches in height.
	A ramp should have a nonslip surface.
	A ramp should have a level surface at the top and bottom (if a door swings into the platform, the platform should be at least five feet by five feet).
	A ramp should have level platforms at least every 30 feet.
	A curb ramp should be provided at every intersection (the ramp should be four feet wide, with transition between two surfaces and a nonslip surface).
Entrances	A building should have at least one primary entrance wheelchair accessible and on a level accessible to an elevator.
Doors and doorways	A door should have an opening of at least 32 inches.
	The floor inside and outside the doorway should be level for at least 51 inches.
	The threshold should be level with the floor.
	The door closer should not impair the use of the door by someone who is handicapped.
Stairs	Stairs should have handrails at least 32 inches from the tread at the face of the riser.
	Steps should not have risers exceeding 7 inches.
Floors	Floors should have a nonslip surface.

TABLE 10.2 *(Continued)*

Type of Expense	Requirements
Toilet rooms	The rooms should provide wheelchair access. At least one stall should be 66 inches wide by 60 feet deep, with 32-inch door space and handrails.
Water fountains	A water fountain or cooler should have up-front spouts and hand and foot controls.
	A water fountain should not be in an alcove unless there is 36 inches of space.
Public telephones	Each phone should be placed so the dial and headset can be reached by someone in a wheelchair.
	Coin slots should be not more than 48 inches from the floor.
	Public phones should be equipped for those with hearing impairments.
Elevators	An elevator should be on entry levels to buildings and in all areas normally used.
	Cab size should allow a wheelchair to turn.
	The door opening should be at least 32 inches.
Controls	Switches and controls for all essential uses (light, heat, ventilation, windows, draperies, and fire alarms) should be within reach of a person in a wheelchair (no higher than 48 inches from the floor).
Identification	Raised letters or numbers should be used to identify rooms (letters or numbers placed on the left or right of the door at a height of 54 to 66 inches).
Warning signals	A visual beaming signal should be accompanied by an audible sound for the benefit of the blind.
Hazards	Hanging signs, ceiling lights, and similar objects and fixtures should be placed at a minimum height of seven feet (measured from the floor).
International	Wheelchair-accessible entrances should be identified with the accessibility symbol.

Lists of Deductible Repairs and Capital Improvements

Over the years various expenditures have come under review by the IRS and the courts. The following lists, one of deductible repairs and the other of improvements that must be capitalized, are based on actual cases and rulings.

DEDUCTIBLE REPAIRS

- Altering building for street-widening program
- Caulking seams
- Replacing compressor for air conditioner

- Replacing copper sheeting for cornice (blown off by wind)
- Relining basement walls and floors with cement
- Cleaning a restaurant canopy
- Cutting and filling cracks in storage tanks
- Tuck pointing and cleaning exterior brick walls
- Adding timbers to support walkway over basement
- Mending plaster walls and ceilings
- Painting walls and ceiling over basement
- Papering walls
- Patching a leaking roof
- Relocating steam pipes and radiators
- Resurfacing floors
- Repairing sidewalks
- Shoring up building foundation
- Replacing retaining walls
- Repairing gutters

CAPITAL IMPROVEMENTS

- Installing new doors
- Installing new windows
- Replacing a coal burner with an oil burner heating system
- Installing skylights
- Installing fire escapes
- Replacing a roof
- Adding new floor supports
- Replacing iron piping with brass piping in hot water system
- Raising, lowering, or building new floors
- Erecting permanent partitions
- Installing fire sprinklers
- Bricking up windows
- Installing an air-conditioning system
- Installing a ventilation system

- Rewiring or upgrading electrical service

- Replacing windows and doors

- Expanding a building (building an addition)

- Installing a burglar alarm system

- Blacktopping a driveway

- Improving a storefront

- Adding new plumbing fixtures

- Constructing a drainage system

Where to Take Deductions for Repairs

Employees

An employee can deduct repair costs as an itemized employee business expense on Schedule A, subject to the two-percent rule and the reduction for higher-income taxpayers discussed in Chapter 1.

Self-Employed

Repair costs are deductible on Schedule C. This schedule contains a line specifically for repairs and maintenance. Repair costs can also be deducted on Schedule C-EZ if total business expenses do not exceed $5,000. Farmers who are self-employed deduct repair costs on Schedule F.

Partnerships and LLCs

Repair costs are trade or business expenses that are taken into account in determining the profit or loss of the partnership or LLC on Form 1065. There is a specific line for deducting repair and maintenance costs. They are not separately stated items passed through to partners and members. Therefore partners and members in LLCs report their net income or loss from the business on Schedule E; they do not deduct repair costs on their individual tax returns.

An exception applies to expenditures for the removal of architectural and transportation barriers to the elderly and handicapped that are elected to be expensed. These items must be separately stated, since dollar limits apply at both the owner and entity levels.

S Corporations

Repair costs are trade or business expenses that are taken into account in determining the profit or loss of the S corporation on Form 1120S. There is a specific line for deducting repair and maintenance costs. They are not separately stated items passed through to shareholders. Therefore shareholders report their net income or loss from the business on Schedule E; they do not deduct repair costs on their individual tax returns.

An exception applies to expenditures for the removal of architectural and transportation barriers to the elderly and handicapped that are elected to be expensed. These items must be separately stated, since dollar limits apply at both the owner and entity levels.

C Corporations

Repair costs are trade or business expenses that are taken into account in determining the profit or loss of the C corporation on Form 1120. This form contains a separate line for deducting repairs and maintenance costs. Shareholders do not report any income (or loss) from the corporation.

Rehabilitation Credit for All Taxpayers

This credit is computed on Form 3468, Investment Tax Credit. It is part of the general business credit and is subject to the limitations on the general business credit (explained in Chapter 23), which is computed on Form 3800, General Business Credit, filed with Form 1040 and Form 1120. (Partners and S corporation shareholders figure the general business credit limitation on their individual returns.)

Disabled Access Tax Credit for All Taxpayers

This credit is computed on Form 8826, Disabled Access Credit. It is part of the general business credit and is subject to the limitations on the general business credit, which is computed on Form 3800, General Business Credit, filed with Forms 1040 and 1120. (Partners and S corporation shareholders figure the general business credit limitation on their individual returns.)

CHAPTER 11

Bad Debts

No one thinks that the loans they make to others will go unpaid; otherwise, such loans would not be made in the first place. If, in the course of your business, you lend money or extend goods and services but fail to receive payment, you can take some comfort in the tax treatment for these transactions gone sour. You may be able to deduct your loss as a bad debt.

In this chapter you will learn about:

- Bad debts in general
- Business versus nonbusiness bad debts
- Loans by shareholder-employees
- Guarantees that result in bad debts
- Special rules for accrual taxpayers
- Reporting bad debts on the tax return
- Where to deduct bad debts

For further information about deducting bad debts, see IRS Publication 535, *Business Expenses.*

Bad Debts in General

If you cannot collect money that is owed to you in your business, your loss may be deductible. You must prove three factors to establish a bad debt:

1. The debtor-creditor relationship
2. Worthlessness
3. Loss

The Debtor-Creditor Relationship

You must prove that there is a *debtor-creditor relationship.* This means that there is a legal obligation on the part of the debtor to pay to the creditor (you) a fixed or determinable sum of money.

If you lend money to a friend or relative, the relationship between you and the borrower is not always clear. You may, for example, lend the money with the expectation of receiving repayment but later forgive some or all of the payments. This forgiveness with a friend or relative transforms what might have been a bad debt into a gift. The law does not bar loans between relatives or friends, but be aware that the IRS gives special scrutiny to loans involving related parties.

The simplest way to prove a debtor-creditor relationship is to have a written note evidencing the loan. The note should state the following terms:

- The amount of the loan
- A stated rate of interest
- A fixed maturity date
- A repayment schedule

If you have a corporation to which you lend money, establishing the debtor-creditor relationship is crucial. Unless you can show that an advance to the corporation is intended to be a loan, it will be treated as a contribution to the capital of the corporation (which is not deductible). Make sure that not only do you have a written note but also that the corporation carries the advance as a loan on its books.

If your corporation lends money to others, it is advisable to include this arrangement in the corporate minutes (e.g., a corporate resolution authorizing the loan and spelling out the loan terms) as well as to carry the loan on the corporation's books.

Worthlessness

You must also show that the debt has become *worthless* and will remain that way. You must be able to show that you took reasonable steps to collect the debt. It is not necessary that you actually go to court to collect the debt if you can show that a judgment would remain uncollectible. If the borrower is in bankruptcy, this is a very good indication that the debt is worthless, at least in part. Generally, the debt is considered to be worthless as of the settlement date of the bankruptcy action, but facts can show that it was worthless before this time. If you use a collection agency to attempt collection of outstanding accounts receivable or other amounts owed to you and you agree to pay the agency a percentage of what is collected, you can immediately deduct that percentage of the outstanding amount as a bad debt; your agreement establishes that that percentage will never be collected by you.

Example

You have an open accounts receivable of $1,000. After 120 days you turn it over to a collection agency that charges 30 percent of what it collects. At the point of your agreement with the agency you are certain you will never recoup at least $300 of the outstanding amount (the fee that would be paid to the agency if it collects 100 percent of the debt) and can now deduct that amount.

You may, in fact, deduct more if the agency collects less than the full amount of the debt. For example, if it collects $500 of the $1,000 outstanding, it is entitled to a $150 fee, so you recoup only $350 of the $1,000. Result: You deduct a total of $650 ($300 of which you deducted when the agreement with the agency was made).

Whether a loan is fully or only partially worthless affects whether you can claim a deduction for the loss. Business bad debts are deductible whether they are fully or partially worthless. If the loss is a nonbusiness bad debt, it is deductible only if the debt is fully worthless. No partial deduction is allowed for nonbusiness bad debts. The distinction between business and nonbusiness bad debts is explained later in this chapter.

Loss

You must show that you sustained a *loss* because of the debt. A loss results when an amount has been included in income but the income is never received. This might happen, for example, where an accrual method taxpayer accrues income but later fails to collect it. If you sell goods on credit and fail to receive payment, you sustain an economic loss whether you are on the accrual method or the cash method of accounting.

If you are on the cash basis and extend services but fail to collect, you cannot claim a bad debt deduction. You are not considered to have an economic loss even though you might argue that you put in your time and effort and were not justly compensated.

Example

A cash basis accountant prepares an individual's tax return. The bill comes to $400. The accountant never receives payment. She cannot deduct the $400. The accountant never reported the $400 as income, so she is not considered to have suffered an economic loss, even though she extended services and invested her time and energy.

If you make payments to a supplier for future shipments and the supplier fails to deliver because of insolvency, you have a business bad debt, regardless of your method of accounting. Again, you have an economic loss (the money you advanced to the supplier) that gives rise to the bad debt deduction.

Collection of Bad Debts

Suppose you fully investigated a debt, made every effort to collect it, and finally concluded it was worthless. You claim a deduction; then, lo and behold, the debtor repays you a year or two later. You need not go back and amend your return to remove the bad debt deduction. Instead, include the recovery of the bad debt in income in the year you receive payment.

Business versus Nonbusiness Bad Debts

Business bad debts, as the term implies, arise in connection with a business. *Nonbusiness bad debts* are all other debts; they can arise in either a personal or investment context.

Business bad debts are deductible as ordinary losses. A C corporation's debts are always business bad debts. Nonbusiness bad debts are deductible by an individual only as short-term capital losses. As such, they are deductible only to offset your capital gains, and then up to $3,000 of ordinary income.

Business bad debts are deductible if partially or wholly worthless. Nonbusiness bad debts must be wholly worthless to be deductible.

Business Bad Debts

Business bad debts are treated as ordinary losses that offset ordinary business income. To be treated as a business bad debt, the debt must be closely related to the activity of the business. There must have been a business reason for entering into the debtor-creditor relationship.

Business bad debts typically arise from credit sales to customers. They can also be the result of loans to suppliers, customers, employees, or distributors. Credit sales are generally reported on the books of the business as accounts receivable. Loans to suppliers, customers, employees, or distributors generally are reported on the books of the business as notes receivable. When accounts receivable or notes receivable become uncollectible, this results in a business bad debt.

Valuing a Bad Debt

Accounts receivable and notes receivable generally are carried on the books at fair market value (FMV). Thus, when they go bad, they are deductible at FMV. This is so even where that value is less than the face value of the obligations.

Impact of Loans with Your Business or Associates

If you lend money to your corporation and the corporation later defaults, you cannot claim a bad debt deduction unless it was a true loan. If, as explained earlier, the advance to the corporation was in fact a contribution to its capital, then you cannot claim a bad debt deduction.

If you have a partnership that breaks up and there is money owing from the partnership, you may be forced to make payments if your partner or partners do not. This payment may be more than your share of the partnership's debts. In this case, you can claim a bad debt deduction if your partner or partners were insolvent and you were required to pay their share.

If you go out of business but still try to collect outstanding amounts owed to you, potential bad debt deductions are not lost. You can still claim them as business bad debts if the debts become worthless after you go out of business.

Example

An attorney lent money to a friend and is later unable to collect despite a number of attempts. Since the loan had nothing to do with the attorney's business, the failure to collect results in a nonbusiness bad debt if it is wholly worthless.

Nonbusiness Bad Debts

Loans made to protect investments or for personal reasons give rise to nonbusiness bad debts when they go bad.

Loans by Shareholder-Employees

When a shareholder who is also an employee of a corporation lends the corporation money but fails to receive repayment, or guarantees corporate debt and is called upon to make good on the guarantee, it is not always clear whether the resulting debt is a business bad debt or a nonbusiness bad debt.

A business bad debt must arise in the context of a business. A shareholder who lends money to the corporation is doing so to protect his or her investment. An employee who lends money to his or her corporation is doing so to protect his or her business of being an employee. In this instance, employment is treated as a business. When an individual is both a shareholder and an employee, which status governs?

According to the U.S. Supreme Court, the dominant motive for making the loan to the corporation is what makes a debt a business or nonbusiness bad debt. Where the dominant motive is to protect one's investment, then the bad debt is treated as a nonbusiness bad debt. Where the dominant motive is to protect one's employment status to ensure continued receipt of salary, then the bad debt is treated as a business bad debt. In making this assessment, several factors are taken into account:

THE SIZE OF YOUR INVESTMENT IN THE CORPORATION.   If your investment is substantial, it indicates that a bad debt might be the result of a desire to protect this investment.

THE SIZE OF YOUR AFTER-TAX SALARY FROM THE CORPORATION.   If your salary is minimal, this indicates that your real interest may be protecting your investment rather than your salary.

OTHER SOURCES OF INCOME AVAILABLE TO YOU.   If the salary is an important source of income to you, then the debt may have been incurred to protect the income. Where the investment is large compared to the salary received and there are other sources of income available, this tends to support the view that the dominant motive was the protection of investment. On the other hand, where the investment is small compared with the salary received and there are no or only insubstantial other sources of income, then the dominant motive may be viewed as protection of salary.

A person's subjective intention in making a loan or guarantee is a factor to be considered, but it is not controlling. Rather, motive is deduced from all the facts and circumstances surrounding the making of the loan or guarantee.

Example

A retired engineer formed a company of which he was the principal shareholder and chief executive officer (CEO). When the company experienced cash flow problems, he lent it money and gave personal guarantees for third-party loans to the company. When the company went under, he lost $450,000 (in addition to his investment in the company). This $450,000 comprised the loans to the company and the guarantees he had to make good on when the company could not. He claimed a business bad debt deduction, which an appellate court allowed. He was a retiree who wanted to continue to work. In view of his age and background, forming his own company was the way to optimal employment. His guarantees in this case far exceeded his initial investment, which was minimal. Therefore his dominant motive in making the loans and guarantees was to protect his employment.

Example

After being terminated from her job as president of a company and spending a year looking for another job, she formed her own company. She did not take salary for the first year; her salary thereafter was between $30,000 and $50,000. Her outside income was substantially more (over $1 million in the year she drew no salary). She guaranteed more than $1 million of loans to the company, which she was called on to repay. But here her bad debt was treated as a nonbusiness bad debt. Her dominant motive was protection of her investment. She could not prove that her dominant motive was protection of salary, since it is not reasonable to believe someone would guarantee over $1 million in loans to protect a salary of $30,000.

WHICH IS BETTER?   Which position should an owner-employee argue in favor of? Naturally, it depends on the person's overall tax position. But generally, nonbusiness bad debt treatment is the better choice. The reason: Losses are treated as short-term capital losses, a deduction for which may be limited in the current year, but unused amounts can be carried forward indefinitely. In contrast, business bad debts of an owner-employee are deductible only as miscellaneous itemized deductions (subject to the 2-percent-of-AGI floor). And such amounts are *not* deductible for alternative minimum tax (AMT) purposes, so that claiming this write-off can trigger or increase AMT liability.

Guarantees that Result in Bad Debts

Banks and other lending institutions are well aware of the limitation on personal liability of owners in corporations. If corporations are in their infancy and do not have significant assets to use as collateral for loans, shareholders usually are asked to extend their personal guarantees to induce the banks or other lending institutions to advance funds to the corporations.

Initially, you do not lend money directly to your business. However, you guarantee, endorse, or indemnify someone else's loan made to your business and are then called on to make good on your guarantee, endorsement, or indemnity. How do you treat this payment?

If the dominant motive for making the guarantee was proximately related to your business (e.g., you guaranteed a loan to the corporation for which you work), then you claim a business bad debt. If the dominant motive for making the guarantee was to protect an investment, you claim a nonbusiness bad debt.

If the guarantee was made for a friend or relative without the receipt of consideration, no bad debt deduction can be claimed. The reason: You did not enter into the arrangement for profit or to protect an investment.

If there is more than one guarantor but only one co-guarantor pays the debt, the co-guarantor who pays the debt can claim only his or her proportional share of the obligation unless it can be proved that the other guarantors were unable to pay.

Example

Three equal shareholders of Corporation X guarantee a bank loan made to the corporation. X defaults and one of the shareholders pays off the entire loan. That shareholder can deduct only one-third of the debt unless he can prove that the other two shareholders were unable to make any payment.

If you, as guarantor, give your own note to substitute or replace the note of the party for whom you became the guarantor, you cannot claim a bad debt deduction at that time. The deduction arises only when and to the extent you make payments on the notes.

When to Claim the Deduction

In general, a bad debt deduction in the case of a guarantee is claimed for the year in which payment is made by the guarantor. Suppose you guarantee a debt but have the right of subrogation or other right against the debtor to recoup your outlays. In this case, you claim your bad debt deduction only when the right against the debtor becomes worthless.

Special Rules for Accrual Taxpayers

All taxpayers (other than certain financial institutions) use the *specific charge-off method* to account for bad debts. Under this method, business bad debts are deducted when and to the extent that they arise.

Nonaccrual-Experience Method

Taxpayers on the accrual basis have an alternative way to account for bad debts. Income that is not expected to be collected need not be accrued. If, based on prior experience, it is determined that certain receivables will not be collected, then they need not be included in gross income for the year. Since income is not taken into account, there is no need to then claim a bad debt deduction.

The *nonaccrual-experience method* applies only to accounts receivable for performing services in the fields of health, law, engineering, architecture, accounting, actuarial science, performing arts, or consulting. In addition, the business's average annual gross receipts for the three prior years cannot be more than $5 million. It cannot be used for amounts owed from activities such as lending money, selling goods, or acquiring receivables or the right to receive payments. Nor can this method be used if interest or penalties are charged on late payments. However, merely offering a discount for early payment is not treated as charging interest or a late penalty if the full amount is accrued as gross income at the time the services are provided and the discount for early payment is treated as an adjustment to gross income in the year of payment.

This method can be used under either a separate receivable system or a periodic system. The separate receivable system applies the nonaccrual-experience method separately to each account receivable; the periodic system applies it to the total of the qualified accounts receivable at the end of the year. This is a highly technical accounting rule that should be discussed with an experienced accountant. The nonaccrual-experience method is explained more fully in IRS Publication 535, *Business Expenses.*

Reporting Bad Debts on the Tax Return

If you want to claim a bad debt deduction on your return, you must do more than simply enter your loss. You also must attach a statement to your return explaining each element of the bad debt. (There is no special IRS form required for making this statement.) These elements include:

- A description of the debt
- The name of the debtor
- Your family or business relationship to the debtor
- The due date of the loan
- Your efforts to collect the debt
- How you decided the debt became worthless

This reporting requirement applies only to individuals who claim bad debts on Schedule A, C, E, or F. Partnerships, LLCs, S corporations, and C corporations need not attach a statement to their returns explaining their bad debt deductions.

The loss is claimed on the return for the year in which the debt becomes worthless (or partially worthless where applicable). Often this is not known by the end of that particular year. Fortunately, there is a seven-year period in which to amend an old return to claim a bad debt.

Example

In 2000, the Corporation (on the accrual basis) provided goods and services to Corporation Y. Partial payment was made in 2000, but the balance due in 2001 was never paid. Due to poor bookkeeping, AB failed to claim a bad debt deduction for this nonpayment. X has until March 15, 2008, seven years from the due date of its 2000 return, to file an amended return and claim the bad debt deduction.

Where to Deduct Bad Debts

Employees

Nonbusiness bad debts are deducted on Schedule D as a short-term capital loss. On this schedule, enter the amount of the bad debt and Statement Attached. Then include on an accompanying statement more information about the bad debt, as explained earlier.

Nonbusiness bad debts are deductible only to the extent of an individual's capital gains, plus up to $3,000 of ordinary income. These capital loss limits are taken into account when completing Schedule D. Remember that unused capital losses can be carried forward indefinitely and used against future capital gains and up to $3,000 of ordinary income each year.

Business bad debts are deducted as ordinary losses on Schedule A as a miscellaneous itemized deduction subject to the 2-percent rule.

Self-Employed

Business bad debts are deducted from business income on Schedule C as "Other Expenses" (or Schedule F in the case of farming operations). Schedule C does not contain a specific line for claiming bad debts from sales or services. Be sure to attach a statement to the return explaining the bad debts.

Nonbusiness bad debts are reported as short-term capital losses on Schedule D. Self-employed persons report nonbusiness bad debts in the same way as employees.

Partnerships and LLCs

Partnerships and LLCs can deduct business bad debts on their return. Form 1065 contains a specific line for claiming bad debts. These bad debts reduce the partnerships' or LLCs' trade or business income. They are not passed through as separate items to partners or LLC members. Partnerships and LLCs need not attach a statement to the return explaining the bad debts.

To date there have been no cases or rulings in which bad debts of partnerships or LLCs have been treated as nonbusiness bad debts. However, should such debts occur, see the treatment of nonbusiness bad debts for S corporations section on the following page.

S Corporations

Bad debts are usually business bad debts. Business bad debts are not separately stated items passed through separately to shareholders. Instead, they serve to reduce the amount of business income or loss that passes through to shareholders. They are entered on Form 1120S on the line specifically for bad debts. S corporations need not attach a statement to the return explaining the bad debts.

It should be noted that where the loss is considered a nonbusiness bad debt, it must be separately stated on Schedule K-1 and passed through to shareholders. In this way the short-term capital loss for the shareholder is subject to that shareholder's capital loss limits.

C Corporations

Bad debts are always business bad debts in the case of C corporations. They are reported on Form 1120 on the specific line provided for bad debts. Corporations need not attach a statement to the return explaining the bad debts.

CHAPTER 12

Rents

From a financial standpoint, it might make more sense to rent than to buy property and equipment. Renting may require a smaller cash outlay than buying. Also, the business may not as yet have established sufficient credit to make large purchases but can still gain the use of the property or equipment through renting. If you pay rent to use office space, a store, or other property for your business, or you pay to lease business equipment, you generally can deduct your outlays.

In this chapter you will learn about:

- Deducting rent payments in general
- The cost of acquiring or canceling a lease
- Improvements you make to leased property
- Rental of a portion of your home for business
- Leasing a car
- Leveraged leases
- Where to deduct rent payments

Deducting Rent Payments in General

If you pay to use property for business that you do not own, the payments are *rent.* They may also be called *lease payments.* Rents paid for property used in a business are deductible business expenses. These include obligations you pay on behalf of your landlord. For example, if you are required by the terms of your lease to pay real estate taxes on the property, you can deduct these taxes as part of your rent payments.

The rents must be reasonable in amount. The issue of reasonableness generally does not arise where you and the landlord are at arm's length. However, the issue does come up when you and the landlord are related parties, such as family members or related companies. Rent paid to a related party is treated as reasonable if it is the same rent that would be paid to an unrelated party. A percentage rental is also considered reasonable if the rental paid is reasonable.

If the rent payments entitle you to receive equity in or title to the property at the end of some term, the payments are not rent. They may, however, be deductible in part as depreciation (see Chapter 14).

Rent to Your Corporation

If you rent property to your corporation, the corporation can claim a rental expense deduction, assuming the rents are reasonable. However, you cannot treat the rents as passive income that you could use to offset your losses from other passive activities. The law specifically prohibits you from arranging this type of rental for tax benefit.

If you rent a portion of your home to your employer, see the discussion on Rental of a Portion of Your Home for Business later in this chapter.

Rent with an Option to Buy

Sometimes it is not clear whether payments are to lease or purchase property. There are a number of factors used to make such a determination.

NATURE OF THE DOCUMENT.   If you have a lease, payments made pursuant to the lease generally are treated as rents. If you have a conditional sales contract, payments made pursuant to the lease are nondeductible purchase payments. A document is treated as a conditional sales contract if it provides that you will acquire title to or equity in the property upon completing a certain number or amount of payments.

INTENT OF THE PARTIES.   How the parties view the transaction affects whether it is a lease or a conditional sales contract. *Intent* can be inferred from certain objective factors. A conditional sales contract exists if any of the following are found:

- The agreement applies part of each payment toward an equity interest.
- The agreement provides for the transfer of title after payment of a stated amount.

- The amount of the payment to use the property for a short time is a large part of the amount paid to get title to the property.
- The payments exceed the current fair rental value of the property (based on comparisons with other similar properties).
- There is an option to buy the property at a nominal price as compared with the property's value at the time the option can be exercised.
- There is an option to buy the property at a nominal price as compared with the total amount required to be paid under the agreement.
- The agreement designates a part of the payments as interest or in some way makes part of the payments easily recognizable as interest.

Example

You lease an office building for a period of two years. The lease agreement provides that at the end of that term you have the option of buying the property and all of the payments made to date will be applied toward the purchase price. In this case, your payments probably would be viewed as payments to purchase rather than payments to lease the property.

Advance Rents

Generally, rents are deductible in the year in which they are paid or accrued. What happens if you pay rent in advance? The answer depends on your method of accounting. If you are on the accrual basis, prepaid rent must be capitalized (it cannot be deducted at the time of payment).

Example

X corporation, an accrual basis taxpayer, leases office space from Y corporation at a monthly rental rate of $2,000. On August 1, 2005, X prepays its office rent expense for the first six months of 2006 in the amount of $12,000. Because economic performance with respect to X prepayment of rent does not occur until 2006, X's prepaid rent is not incurred in 2005 and therefore is not properly taken into account in 2005.

If you are on the cash basis, prepaid rent can be immediately deducted provided that prepayments do not extend beyond 12 months.

Example

X corporation uses the cash method of accounting and pays Y corporation $12,000 on August 1, 2005, to cover rent for the first six months of 2006. With the 12-month rule, the $12,000 payment is deductible in 2005 because the rights or benefits attributable to X's prepayment of its rent do not extend beyond December 31, 2006.

Security deposits generally are not deductible when paid because the landlord is usually obligated to refund them if the terms of the lease are met. However, if the landlord keeps some or all of the deposit (e.g., because you failed to live up to the terms of the lease), you can then deduct such amount as rent.

Gift-Leasebacks

If you own property you have already depreciated, you may want to create a tax deduction for your business by entering into a *gift-leaseback* transaction. Typically, the property is gifted to your spouse or children, to whom you then pay rent. In the past this type of arrangement was more popular, but the passive loss rules put a damper on deducting losses created by these arrangements. If you still want to shift income to your children (who presumably are in a lower tax bracket than you) while getting a tax deduction for your business, be sure that you meet these requirements:

1. You do not retain control over the property after the gift is given.
2. The leaseback is in writing and the rent charged is reasonable.
3. There must be a business purpose for the leaseback. (For example, where a doctor transferred the property in which his practice was located to his children in fear of malpractice suits, this was a valid business reason for leasing rather than owning the property.)

There are other factors to consider before entering into a gift-leaseback. Consider the impact of the kiddie tax if your children are under the age of 14. It is strongly suggested that you consult with a tax adviser before giving business property to your children and then leasing it back for use in your business.

Miscellaneous Rentals

Some payments for the use of property that you may not otherwise think of as rentals but that may be required by your business include safety deposit box rental fees and post office box rental fees.

The Cost of Acquiring, Modifying, or Canceling a Lease

The Cost of Acquiring a Lease

When you pay a premium to obtain immediate possession under a lease that does not extend beyond the tax year, the premium is deductible in full for the current year. Where the premium relates to a long-term lease, the cost of the premium is deductible over the term of the lease. The same amortization rule applies to commissions, bonuses, and other fees paid to obtain a lease on property you use in your business.

What is the term of the lease for purposes of deducting lease acquisition premiums when the lease contains renewal options? The tax law provides a complicated method for making this determination. The term of the lease for amortization purposes includes all renewal option periods if less than 75 percent of the cost is attributable to the term of the lease remaining on the purchase date. Do not include any period for which the lease may be renewed, extended, or continued under an option exercisable by you, the lessee, in determining the term of the lease remaining on the purchase date.

Example

You pay $10,000 to acquire a lease with 20 years remaining on it. The lease has two options to renew, for five years each. Of the $10,000, $7,000 is paid for the original lease and $3,000 for the renewal options. Since $7,000 is less than 75 percent of the total cost, you must amortize $10,000 over 30 years (the lease term plus the two renewal option periods).

Example

The circumstances are the previous example, except that $8,000 is allocable to the original lease. Since this is not less than 75 percent of the total cost, the entire $10,000 can be amortized over the original lease term of 20 years.

The Cost of Modifying a Lease

If you pay an additional rent to change a lease provision, you amortize this additional payment over the remaining term of the lease.

The Cost of Canceling a Lease

If you pay to get out of your lease before the end of its term, the cost generally is deductible in full in the year of payment. However, where a new lease is obtained, the cost of canceling the lease must be capitalized if the cancellation and new lease are viewed as part of the same transaction.

Example

A company leased a computer system for five years. To upgrade its system, the company canceled the original lease and entered into a new one with the same lessor. Because the termination of the old lease was conditioned on obtaining a new lease, the cost of termination had to be capitalized (i.e., added to the cost of the new lease and deducted ratably over the term of the new lease).

Improvements You Make to Leased Property

If you add a building or make other permanent improvements to leased property, you can depreciate the cost of the improvements using Modified Accelerated Cost Recovery System (MACRS) depreciation. (For a further discussion of depreciation, see Chapter 14.) Generally, the improvements are depreciated over their recovery period, a time fixed by law. They are not depreciated over the remaining term of the lease.

Example

You construct a building on land you lease. The recovery period of the building is 39 years. When the building construction is completed, there are 35 years remaining on the lease. You depreciate the building over its recovery period of 39 years, not over the 35 years remaining on the lease.

If you acquire a lease through an assignment and the lessee has made improvements to the property, the amount you pay for the assignment is a capital investment. Where the rental value of the leased land has increased since the beginning of the lease, part of the capital investment is for the increase in that value; the balance is for your investment in the permanent improvements. You amortize the part of the increased rental value of the leased land; you depreciate the part of the investment related to the improvements.

Special Rule for Improvements after October 22, 2004

Leasehold improvements can be amortized over 15 years instead of depreciated over 39 years. To qualify for the 15-year write-off, all of the following requirements must be met:

- The improvement is made pursuant to the terms of a lease to the interior of nonresidential property.

- The lease is *not* between related parties. Related parties are defined in Chapter 5, except that where 50 percent ownership usually is required, in this case, 80 percent ownership applies.

- The building (or portion of the building to which the improvement is made) is occupied exclusively by the lessee or sublessee.

- The improvement is a structural component that would otherwise qualify for 39-year depreciation.

- The improvement is placed in service more than three years after the date the building is first placed in service.

Certain types of improvements specifically do *not* qualify for the 15-year write-off. These include the enlargement of the building, elevators and escalators, structural components that benefit a common area, and internal structural framework.

This special rule also applies restaurant improvements. To qualify as a restaurant, more than 50 percent of the building's square footage must be devoted to the preparation of meals and seating for the serving of meals on the premises. As in the case of general leasehold improvements, qualified restaurant property must be placed in service more than three years after the building is first placed in service.

> **CAUTION**
>
> The 15-year amortization period applies only to leasehold improvements placed in service before January 1, 2006, unless Congress extends the law.

If you enter into a lease after August 5, 1997, for retail space for 15 years or less and you receive a construction allowance from the landlord to make additions or improvements to the space, you are not taxed on these payments provided they are fully used for the purpose intended.

Rental of a Portion of Your Home for Business

If you rent your home and use part of it for business, you may be able to deduct part of your rent as a business expense. This part of the rent is treated as a home office deduction if you meet certain requirements. See Chapter 18 for details on the home office deduction.

Leasing a Car

If you lease a car for business use, the treatment of the rental costs depends upon the term of the lease. If the term is less than 30 days, the entire cost of the rental is deductible. Thus, if you go out of town on business and rent a car for a week, your rental costs are deductible.

If the lease term exceeds 30 days, the lease payments are still deductible if you use the car entirely for business. If you use it for both business and personal purposes, you must allocate the lease payments and deduct only the business portion of the costs. However, depending on the value of the car at the time it is leased, you may be required to include an amount in gross income called an inclusion amount (explained later).

If you make advance payments, you must spread these payments over the entire lease period and deduct them accordingly. You cannot depreciate a car you lease, because depreciation applies only to property that is owned.

Lease with an Option to Buy

When you have this arrangement, are you leasing or buying the car? The answer depends on a number of factors:

1. Intent of the parties to the transaction.
2. Whether any equity results from the arrangement.
3. Whether any interest is paid.
4. Whether the fair market value (FMV) of the car is less than the lease payment or option payment when the option to buy is exercised.

If the factors support a finding that the arrangement is a lease, the payments are deductible. If, however, the factors support a finding that the arrangement is a purchase agreement, the payments are not deductible.

Inclusion Amount

If the car price exceeds a certain amount (which is adjusted periodically for inflation) and you do not use the standard mileage rate to account for expenses, you may have to include in income an amount called an *inclusion amount*. The law seeks to equate buying with leasing. Since there is a dollar limit on the amount of depreciation that can be claimed on a luxury car that is owned, the law also requires an amount to be included in income as an offset to high lease payments on a car that is leased. In essence, the inclusion amount seeks to limit your deduction for lease payments to what it would be if you owned the car and claimed depreciation.

The inclusion amount, which is simply an amount that you add to your other income, applies if a car is leased for more than 30 days and its value exceeds a certain amount. The inclusion amount is added to income only so long as you lease the car. Inclusion amounts are based on the value of the car as of the first day of the lease term. If the capitalized cost of the car is specified in the lease agreement, that amount is considered to be the car's **fair market value**. At the start of the lease, you can see what your inclusion amount would be for that year and for all subsequent years. The inclusion amount is based on a percentage of the FMV of the car at the time the lease begins. Different inclusion amounts apply to gas-driven cars and to electric cars.

Fair market value   The price that would be paid for the property when there is a willing buyer and seller (neither being required to buy or sell) and both have reasonable knowledge of all the necessary facts. Evidence of fair market value includes the price paid for similar property on or about the same date.

The inclusion amount applies only if the FMV of the car when the lease began was more than $15,500 in 1999 to 2002, $18,000 in 2003, $17,500 in 2004, and $15,200 in 2005. Different thresholds applied to cars leased prior to 1999.

Example

The inclusion amount for your car is $500. You used the car only six months of the year (a leap year). You must include in income $250 (183 ÷ 366 of $500).

The inclusion amounts are taken from IRS tables. (See Chapter 9 for inclusion amounts.) The full amount applies if the car is leased for the full year and used entirely for business. If the car is leased for less than the full year, or if it is used only partly for personal purposes, then the inclusion amount must be allocated to business use for the period of the year in which it was used. The allocation for part-year use is made on a day-by-day basis.

Remember that if you use your car for commuting or other nonbusiness purposes, you cannot deduct that allocable part of the lease.

Car leasing, including the advisability of leasing versus buying a business car, is discussed more fully in Chapter 9.

Leveraged Leases

If you are the lessee in a transaction referred to as a **leveraged lease**, you generally can deduct your lease payments.

Leveraged lease   A three-party transaction in which the landlord (lessor) obtains financing from a third party and in which lease payments are sufficient to cover the cost of repaying the financing. Also, the lease term generally covers the useful life of the property.

It is important that the lessor, and not the lessee, be treated as the owner of the property if lease payments are to be deductible. The lessor is treated as the owner if he or she has a minimum amount at risk (at least 20 percent) during the entire term of the lease and the lessee does not have a contractual right to buy the property at its FMV at the end of the lease term. Other factors that are necessary to show that the lessor and not the lessee is the owner of the property are that the lessor has a profit motive (apart from tax benefits), the lessee does not lend money to the lessor, and the lessee does not invest in the property.

If you are about to become the lessee of a leveraged lease and want to be sure that you will not be treated as the owner (which means your rental expenses would not be deductible), you can ask the IRS for an advance ruling on the issue. (However, the IRS will not issue an advance ruling on leveraged leases of so-called **limited use property**.) There is a user fee for this service. It may be advisable to seek the assistance of a tax professional in obtaining the ruling.

Limited use property   **Property not expected to be either useful to or usable by a lessor at the end of the lease term except for continued leasing or transfer to the lessee or a member of a lessee group.**

Special rules apply to leases of tangible personal property over $250,000.

Where to Deduct Rent Payments

Employees

Rent expenses are deductible as itemized expenses on Schedule A. If you lease a car for more than 30 days, you must complete Form 2106, Employee Business Expenses, to report the lease payments. (You cannot use the simplified form, 2106-EZ, if you lease rather than own your car.) The results of Form 2106 are then entered on Schedule A and are subject to the 2-percent-of-adjusted-gross-income floor discussed in Chapter 1.

If you rent your home and use part of it for business for the convenience of your employer, you can claim a home office deduction for that part of the rent. There is no special form that an employee is required to use for calculating his or her home office deduction. However, you may figure the deduction on a special worksheet for this purpose in IRS Publication 587. The deductible portion of your rent (along with other home office expenses) is entered on Schedule A as an itemized expense, which, again, is subject to the 2-percent floor.

Self-Employed

Rents are deductible on Schedule C. This schedule provides two separate lines for reporting rents and leases so that rents and leases for vehicles, machinery, and equipment are reported separately from those of other business property. If you lease a car for more than 30 days, you must complete Part IV of Schedule C if you are not otherwise required to file Form 4562, Depreciation and Amortization, or directly on this form if you placed in service any property in 2005 that is subject to depreciation or amortization. Farmers who are self-employed deduct rents on Schedule F. Information about leased cars must be entered on Form 4562, Depreciation and Amortization.

If you rent your home and use part of it for business and file Schedule C, you can claim a home office deduction for that part of the rent. Home office expenses, including rent, are computed on Form 8829, Expenses for Business Use of Your Home. The deductible portion is entered on Schedule C. If you are a farmer who files Schedule F, figure your home office deduction on the worksheet found in IRS Publication 587. Then enter the deductible portion on Schedule F.

Partnerships and LLCs

Rent and lease payments are deducted by partnerships and LLCs on their returns as part of the entity's ordinary trade or business income, on Form 1065. The return contains a separate line for reporting rents. Rent and lease payments are not passed through to partners or LLC members as separate items.

If you rent your home and use part of it for the business of the partnership, you can claim a home office deduction for that part of the rent. There is no special form that a partner must use for calculating his or her home office deduction. However, you may figure the deduction on a special worksheet for this purpose in IRS Publication 587. The deductible portion of your rent (along with other home office expenses) is entered on Schedule E as part of your share of partnership income and expenses.

S Corporations

Rents and lease payments are deducted by the S corporation as part of its ordinary trade or business income on Form 1120S. The return contains a separate line for reporting rents. Rents and lease payments are not passed through to shareholders as separately stated items.

C Corporations

C corporations deduct rent and lease payments on Form 1120. The return contains a separate line for reporting rents.

CHAPTER 13

Taxes and Interest

Taxes and interest are two types of expenses that are hard to avoid. In the course of your business activities, you may pay various taxes and interest charges.

In this chapter you will learn about:

- Deductible taxes
- Nondeductible taxes
- Deductible interest
- Nondeductible interest and other limitations on deductibility
- Where to deduct taxes and interest

For further information about deducting taxes and interest, see IRS Publication 535, *Business Expenses*.

Deductible Taxes

General Rules

In order to deduct taxes, they must be imposed on you. The tax must be owed by the party who pays it. If your corporation owns an office building, it is the party that owes the real property taxes. If, as part of your lease, you are obligated to pay your landlord's taxes, you can deduct your payment as an additional part of your rent; you do not claim a deduction for taxes, since you are not the owner of the property.

Taxes must be paid during the year if you are on a cash basis. If you pay taxes at year end by means of a check or even a credit card charge, the tax is deductible in the year the check is sent or delivered or the credit charge is made. This is so even though the check is not cashed until the following year or you do not pay the credit card bill until the following year. If you pay any tax by phone or through your computer, the tax is deductible on the date of payment reported on the statement issued by the financial institution through which the payment is made. If you contest a liability and do not pay it until the issue is settled, you cannot deduct the tax until it is actually paid. It may be advisable to settle a disputed liability in order to fix the amount and claim a deduction. If you pay tax after the end of the year for a liability that relates to the prior year, you deduct the tax in the year of payment.

Example

An S corporation on a calendar year, using the cash basis method, pays its state franchise fee for 2005 in March 2006. The payment is deductible on the S corporation's 2006 income tax return, not on its 2005 return.

Real Estate Taxes

In general, real property taxes are deductible. Assessments made to real property for the repair or maintenance of some local benefit (such as streets, sidewalks, or sewers) are treated as deductible taxes.

If you acquire real property for resale to customers, you may be required under uniform capitalization rules to capitalize these taxes. The uniform capitalization rules are discussed in Chapter 2.

Special rules apply when real estate is sold during the year. Real property taxes must be allocated between the buyer and seller according to the number of days in the real property tax year. The seller can deduct the taxes up to, but not including, the date of sale. The buyer can deduct the taxes from the date of sale onward.

Accrual basis taxpayers can deduct only taxes accruing on the date of sale. An accrual basis taxpayer can elect to accrue ratably real property taxes related to a definite period of time over that period of time.

> ## Example
>
> X Corporation, a calendar-year taxpayer on the accrual basis, owns an office building on which annual taxes are $1,200 for the fiscal year beginning July 1, 2005 through June 30, 2006. If X elects to ratably accrue taxes, $600 of the taxes is deductible in 2005, the balance in 2006.

The election to accrue taxes ratably applies for each separate business. If one business owns two properties, an election covers both properties. The election is binding and can be revoked only with the consent of the IRS. You make the election by attaching a statement to your return for the first year that real property taxes are due on property that includes the businesses for which the election is being made, the period of time to which the taxes relate, and a computation of the real property tax deduction for the first year of the election. The election must be filed with your income tax return (including extensions) on time.

If you have already owned property for some time but want to switch to the ratable accrual method, you must obtain the consent of the IRS. To do so, file Form 3115, Change in Accounting Method, within the year for which the change is to be effective.

State and Local Income Taxes

A corporation that pays state and local income taxes can deduct the taxes on its return. Taxes may include state corporate income taxes and any franchise tax (which is a tax for operating as a corporation and has nothing to do with being a franchise business).

A self-employed individual who pays state and local taxes with respect to business income reported on Schedule C can deduct them only as an itemized deduction on Schedule A. Similarly, an employee who pays state and local taxes with respect to compensation from employment can deduct these taxes only on Schedule A.

Self-Employment Tax

Businesses do not pay self-employment tax; individuals do. Sole proprietors, general partners (whether active or inactive), and certain LLC members pay self-employment tax on their net earnings from self-employment (amounts reported on Schedule C or as self-employment income on Schedule K-1). Limited partners do not pay self-employment tax on their share of income from the business. However, limited partners are subject to self-employment tax if they perform any services for the business or receive any guaranteed payments. LLC members who are like general partners pay self-employment tax; those like limited partners do not. The IRS was precluded from issuing regulations defining a limited partner before July 1, 1998. To date, the IRS has still not issued any regulations nor given any indication when it would.

The tax rate for the Social Security portion of self-employment tax is 12.4 percent and, in 2005, applies to net earnings from self-employment up to $90,000. The Medicare tax rate is 2.9 percent; it applies to *all* net earnings from self-employment (there is no limit for the Medicare portion of self-employment tax).

Those who pay self-employment tax are entitled to deduct one-half of the tax as an adjustment to gross income on their personal income tax returns. The deduction on page one of Form 1040 reduces your gross income and serves to lower the threshold for certain itemized deductions.

While S corporations are pass-through entities similar to partnerships and LLCs, owners of S corporations who work for their businesses are not treated the same as partners and LLC members for purposes of self-employment tax. Owners of S corporations who are also employees of their businesses do not pay self-employment tax on their compensation—they are employees of the corporation for purposes of employment tax. Their compensation is subject to FICA, not to self-employment tax. Individuals who both are self-employed and have an interest in an S corporation cannot use losses from the S corporation to reduce net earnings from self-employment.

Personal Property Tax

Personal property tax on any property used in a business is deductible. Personal property tax is an *ad valorem tax*—a tax on the value of personal property. For example, a *floor tax* is a property tax levied on inventory that is sitting on the floor (or shelves) of your business. Registration fees for the right to use property within the state in your trade or business are deductible. If the fees are based on the value of the property they are considered a personal property tax.

Sales and Use Taxes

Sales tax to acquire a depreciable asset used in a trade or business is added to the basis of the asset and is recovered through depreciation. If sales tax is paid to acquire a nondepreciable asset, it is still treated as part of the cost of the asset and is deducted as part of the asset's expense. For example, sales tax on business stationery is part of the cost of the stationery and is deducted as part of that cost (not as a separate sales tax deduction). Sales tax paid on property acquired for resale is also treated as part of the cost of that property.

Sales tax you collect as a merchant or other business owner and turn over to the state is deductible only if you include it in your gross receipts. If the sales tax is not included, it is not deductible.

When sales tax is imposed on the seller or retailer and the seller or retailer can separately state the tax or pass it on to the consumer, then the consumer, rather than the seller or retailer, gets to deduct the tax. When the consumer is in business the tax is treated differently depending on how the asset is acquired. (See the aforementioned details for depreciable property, nondepreciable property, and property held for sale or resale.)

A compensating use tax is treated as a sales tax. This type of tax is imposed on the use, storage, or consumption of an item brought in from another taxing jurisdiction. Typically, it is imposed at the same percentage as a sale tax.

To learn about obtaining a resale number needed for the collection of sales taxes and your sales tax obligations, contact your state tax department (you can find it through your telephone directory or at <www.sba.gov>).

Luxury Tax

Like sales tax, a luxury tax that is paid to acquire a depreciable asset is added to the basis of the asset; it is not separately deductible. For example, if you pay a luxury tax to acquire a high-priced car to use for business, the amount of the tax becomes part of the car's basis for purposes of depreciation.

Employment Taxes

If you have employees and pay the employer portion of FICA for them, you can deduct this amount as a tax. Tax under the Federal Insurance Contribution Act (FICA) is comprised of a Social Security tax and a Medicare tax. The employer portion of the Social Security tax is 6.2 percent. This tax is applied to a current wage base of up to $90,000 in 2005, which is adjusted annually for inflation. The employer portion of the Medicare tax is 1.45 percent. This is applied to all wages paid to an employee; there is no wage base limit. If you, as an employer, pay both the employer and employee portion of the tax, you may claim a deduction for your full payments.

If you are in a dispute over employment taxes with the IRS and you lose, requiring you to pay back taxes and you pay the employee share to avoid adverse employee reaction, you may deduct the employee share as well. The IRS views your payment in this instance as having a valid business reason even though you are not legally obligated to pay the employee share of FICA.

You may also be liable for federal unemployment tax (FUTA) for your employees. The gross federal unemployment tax rate is 6.2 percent. This is applied to employee wages up to $7,000, for a maximum FUTA tax of $434 per employee. However, you may claim a credit of up to 5.4 percent for state unemployment tax that you pay, bringing the maximum FUTA tax to $56 per employee. If your state unemployment tax rate is 5.4 percent or more, then the net FUTA rate is 0.8 percent. Even if your state unemployment rate is less than 5.4 percent, you are permitted to claim a full reduction of 5.4 percent. However, if your state has failed to repay funds borrowed from the federal government to cover state unemployment tax benefits, the federal credit for FUTA is reduced. For example, in 2004, New York employers had their credit reduced to 5.1 percent, so they paid FUTA at the rate of 1.1 percent (instead of 0.8 percent), for a maximum FUTA tax of $77 per employee. However, if you are exempt from state unemployment tax, you must pay the full FUTA rate of 6.2 percent.

These tax payments are deductible by you as an employer. A complete discussion of employment taxes can be found in Chapter 27.

State Benefit Funds

An employer who pays into a state disability or unemployment insurance fund may deduct the payments as taxes. An employee who must contribute to the following state benefit funds can deduct the payments as state income taxes on Schedule A:

- *California*—Nonoccupational Disability Benefit Fund
- *New Jersey*—Nonoccupational Disability Benefit Fund
- *New York*—Nonoccupational Disability Benefit Fund
- *Rhode Island*—Nonoccupational Disability Benefit Fund
- *West Virginia*—Unemployment Compensation Trust Fund

The deduction for these taxes is not subject to a 2-percent-of-adjusted-gross-income floor (see Chapter 1), as is the case with other employee business expenses.

Franchise Taxes

Corporate franchise taxes (which is another term that may be used for state corporate income taxes and has nothing to do with whether the corporation is a franchise) are a deductible business expense. Your state may or may not impose franchise taxes on S corporations, so check with your state corporate tax department.

Excise Taxes

Excise taxes paid or incurred in a trade or business are deductible as operating expenses. A credit for federal excise tax on certain fuels may be claimed as explained in the following section.

Fuel Taxes

Taxes on gas, diesel fuel, and other motor fuels used in your business are deductible. As a practical matter, they are included in the cost of the fuel and are not separately stated. Thus, they are deducted as a fuel cost rather than as a tax.

However, in certain instances, you may be eligible for a credit for the federal excise tax on certain fuels. The credit applies to fuel used in machinery and off-highway vehicles (such as tractors), and kerosene used for heating, lighting, and cooking on a farm.

You have a choice: claim a tax credit for the federal excise tax or claim a refund of this tax. You can claim a quarterly refund for the first three quarters of the year if the refund is $750 or more. If you do not exceed $750 in a quarter, then you can carry over this refund amount to the following quarter and add it to the refund due at that time. But if, after carrying the refund forward to the fourth quarter you do not exceed $750, then you must recoup the excise tax through a tax credit.

Alternatively, if you have pesticides or fertilizers applied aerially, you may waive your right to the credit or refund, allowing the applicator to claim it (something that would reduce your application charges). If you want to waive the credit or refund, you must sign an irrevocable waiver and give a copy of it to the applicator. For further information on this credit, see IRS Publication 378, *Fuel Tax Credits and Refunds.*

Foreign Taxes

Income taxes paid to a foreign country or U.S. possession may be claimed as a deduction or a tax credit. To claim foreign income taxes as a tax credit, you must file Form 1116, Foreign Tax Credit (unless as an individual you have foreign tax of $300 or less, or $600 or less on a joint return). Corporations claim the foreign tax credit on Form 1118. The same rules apply for foreign real property taxes paid with respect to real property owned in a foreign country or U.S. possession.

Other Rules

If a corporation pays a tax imposed on a shareholder and the shareholder does not reimburse the corporation, then the corporation, and not the shareholder, is entitled to claim the deduction for the payment of the tax.

Nondeductible Taxes

You may not deduct federal income taxes, even the amount paid with respect to your business income. These are nondeductible taxes.

Other nondeductible taxes include:

- Assessments on real property for local benefits that tend to add to the value of the property. Such assessments may be made, for example, to build sidewalks, streets, sewers, or parks. These assessments are added to the basis of the property. But assessments for maintenance purposes (such as for repairs to sidewalks, streets, and sewers) are deductible. Water bills, sewage, and other service charges are not treated as taxes. They are, however, deductible as business expenses.
- Employee contributions to private or voluntary disability plans.
- Fines imposed by a governmental authority. These are not deductible as a tax even if incurred in a trade or business. For example, if while traveling away from home on business you receive a fine for a speeding ticket, the fine is not deductible.

- Penalties imposed by the federal government on taxes or for failing to file returns. These are not deductible even though they may be computed with regard to the length of time the taxpayer has failed to comply with a tax law requirement.
- Occupational taxes.

Deductible Interest

General Rules

Interest paid or incurred on debts related to your business generally is fully deductible as business interest. Business interest is deductible without limitation, except when such interest is required to be capitalized. (Remember, for example, that construction period interest and taxes must be capitalized, as explained earlier in this chapter.) There is one main exception to the general deductibility rule for business interest: interest on life insurance policies. (The limits on deducting interest with respect to life insurance policies are discussed in Chapter 22.)

Interest is characterized by how and what the proceeds of the loan that generated the interest are used. *Personal interest* is nondeductible (except to the extent of qualified home mortgage interest and a limited amount of student loan interest). *Investment interest* is deductible only to the extent of net investment income. Interest characterized as incurred in a passive activity is subject to the passive loss rules. The characterization is not dependent on what type of property—business or personal—was used as collateral for the loan. For example, if you borrow against your personal life insurance policy and use the proceeds to buy equipment for your business, you can deduct the interest as business interest. On the other hand, if you take a bank loan using your corporate stock as collateral, and use the proceeds to invest in the stock market, the interest is characterized as investment interest. Interest on a tax deficiency relating to Schedules C, E, or F is nondeductible personal interest. While the Tax Court had allowed a deduction for this interest, several appellate courts have sided with the IRS in denying a deduction for this interest.

If the proceeds are used for more than one purpose, you must make an allocation based on the use of the loan's proceeds. When you repay a part of the loan, the repayments are treated as repaying the loan in this order:

- Amounts allocated to personal use
- Amounts allocated to investments and passive activities
- Amounts allocated to passive activities in connection with rental real estate in which you actively participate
- Amounts allocated to business use

The interest obligation must be yours in order for you to claim an interest deduction. If you pay off someone else's loan, you cannot deduct the interest you pay. If you are contractually obligated to make the payment, you may be able to deduct your payment as some other expense item, but not as interest.

Debt Incurred to Buy an Interest in a Business

If you use loan proceeds to buy an interest in a partnership, LLC, or S corporation or to make a contribution to capital, this is treated as a *debt-financed acquisition.* In this case, you must allocate the interest on the loan based on the assets of the pass-through business. The allocation can be based on book value, market value, or the adjusted bases of the assets.

Example

You borrow $25,000 to buy an interest in an S corporation. The S corporation owns $90,000 of equipment and $10,000 of stocks (based on fair market value (FMV)). In this case, nine-tenths of the interest on the loan is treated as business interest ($90,000 ÷ $100,000); one-tenth of the interest is treated as investment interest ($10,000 ÷ $100,000).

If you, as an S corporation shareholder, LLC member, or partner, receive proceeds from a debt, you must also allocate the debt proceeds. These are called *debt-financed distributions.* Under a general allocation rule, debt proceeds distributed to an owner of a pass-through entity are allocated to the owner's use of the proceeds. Thus, if the owner uses the proceeds for personal purposes, the pass-through entity must treat the interest as nondeductible personal interest. Under an optional allocation rule, the pass-through entity may allocate the proceeds (and related interest) to one or more of the entity's expenditures other than distributions. The expenditures to which the debt is allocated are those made in the same year as the allocation is made (see IRS Notice 89-35 for allocations in pass-through entities).

If you borrow money to buy stock in a closely held C corporation, the Tax Court considers the interest to be investment interest. The reason: C corporation stock, like any publicly traded stock, is held for investment. This is so even if the corporation never pays out investment income (*dividends*) or the purchase of the stock is made to protect one's employment with the corporation.

Loans between Shareholders and Their Corporations

Special care must be taken when shareholders lend money to their corporation, and vice versa, or when shareholders guarantee third-party loans made to their corporation.

CORPORATION'S INDEBTEDNESS TO SHAREHOLDERS. If a corporation borrows from its shareholders, the corporation can deduct the interest it pays on the loan. The issue sometimes raised by the IRS in these types of loans is whether there is any real indebtedness. Sometimes loans are used in place of dividends to transform nondeductible dividend payments into deductible interest. In order for a loan to withstand IRS scrutiny, be prepared to show a written instrument bearing a fixed maturity date for the repayment of the loan. The instrument should also state a fixed rate of interest. There should be a valid business reason for this borrowing arrangement (such as evidence that the corporation could not borrow from a commercial source at a reasonable rate of interest). If the loan is subordinated to the claims of corporate creditors, this tends to show that it is not a true debt, but other factors may prove otherwise. Also, when a corporation is heavily indebted to shareholders, the debt-to-equity ratio may indicate that the loans are not true loans but are merely disguised equity.

When a corporation fails to repay a loan to a shareholder, this may give rise to a bad debt deduction for the shareholder. Bad debts are discussed in Chapter 11.

SHAREHOLDER GUARANTEES OF CORPORATE DEBT. Often for small businesses, banks or other lenders usually require personal guarantees by the corporation's principal shareholders as a condition for making loans to the corporation. This arrangement raises one of the basic rules for deducting interest discussed earlier: The obligation must be yours in order for you to deduct the interest.

Example

A sole shareholder paid interest on a loan made by a third party to his corporation. He agreed that he would pay any outstanding debt if the corporation failed to do so. He was not entitled to claim an interest deduction because it was the corporation, not he, who was primarily liable on the obligation. The shareholder was only a guarantor.

Below-Market and Above-Market Loans

When shareholders and their corporations arrange loans between themselves, they may set interest rates at less than or more than the going market rate of interest. This may be done for a number of reasons, including to ease the financial burden on a party to the loan or to create tax advantage. Whatever the reason, it is important to understand the consequences of the arrangement.

BELOW-MARKET LOANS. If you receive an interest-free or below-market-interest loan, you may still be able to claim an interest deduction. You can claim an interest deduction equal to the sum of the interest you actually pay, plus the amount of interest that the lender is required to report as income under the below-market loan rules. The amount that the lender is required to report as income is fixed according to interest rates set monthly by the IRS. Different rates apply according to the term of the loan.

- *Short-term* loans run three years or less.
- *Mid-term* loans run more than three but less than nine years.
- *Long-term* loans run more than nine years.

Rates required to be charged in order to avoid imputed interest are called the *applicable federal rates* (AFRs). You can find an index of AFRs by entering "applicable federal rules" in the search box at <www.irs.gov>. If a loan is payable on demand, the short-term rate applies. However, if the loan is outstanding for an entire year, you can use a blended annual rate (3.11 percent for 2005) provided by the IRS to simplify the computation of the taxable imputed interest.

Example

On January 1, 2005, you borrowed $40,000 from your corporation for investments. You were not charged any interest by your corporation and the loan was payable on demand. The AFR for determining interest that the lender must report for 2005 is the blended rate of 3.11 percent for demand loans outstanding for the entire year. Thus, your interest deduction is $1,244 (subject to the limitation on deducting investment interest).

Whether you are required to report this amount as income (which would, in effect, offset the interest deduction) depends on the amount of the loan and the context in which it was made. If it was treated as compensation or a dividend, you have to include it in income; if it was considered a gift loan, you do not have additional income. Gift loans are loans up to $10,000 (as long as the loan is not made for tax avoidance purposes). The corporation (lender) must report the interest as income. If the loan is to an employee, an offsetting deduction can be taken for compensation. But if the loan is to a nonemployee, such as a shareholder who does not work for the corporation, no offsetting deduction can be taken.

ABOVE-MARKET LOANS. Instead of borrowing from a bank, your corporation may be able to borrow from a relative of yours, such as your child or parent, to whom you want to make gifts. You can turn the arrangement into a profitable one for both your corporation and your relative (the lender). Set the interest rate at more than what would be charged by the bank. Provided that the interest is still considered "reasonable" and the loan is an arm's-length transaction, your corporation deducts the interest and the lender receives it. If an unreasonably high rate of interest is charged and the arrangement is not at arm's length, however, the IRS will attack the arrangement and may disallow the interest as being a disguised dividend payment to you.

Home Mortgage Interest and Home Offices

If you are self-employed, use a portion of your home for business, and claim a home office deduction, you must allocate the home mortgage interest. The portion of the interest on the mortgage allocated to the business use is deducted on Form 8829, Home Office Expenses. The balance is treated as personal mortgage interest deductible as an itemized expense on Schedule A.

Nondeductible Interest and Other Limitations on Deductibility

If you borrow additional funds from the same lender to pay off a first loan for business, you cannot claim an interest deduction. Once you begin paying off the new loan, you can deduct interest on both the old and new loans. Payments are treated as being applied to the old loan first and then to the new loan. All interest payments are then deductible.

As in the case of taxes, if interest is paid to acquire a capital asset for resale, you must capitalize the interest expense. The interest is recovered when the asset is sold.

Commitment Fees

Fees paid to have business funds available for drawing on a standby basis are not treated as deductible interest payments. They may, however, be deductible as business expenses. Fees paid to obtain a loan may be treated as deductible interest. However, the fees are not immediately deductible; rather, they are deductible only over the term of the loan. If the loan falls through, the fees can be deducted as a loss.

Similarly, points paid to acquire a loan on business property are treated as prepaid interest. They are not currently deductible as such. Instead, they are deductible over the term of the loan.

Example

Your business pays a $200 commitment fee for a $10,000 loan with a 10-year term. Each year the business may deduct $20 ($200 divided by 10 years).

If you pay off the loan before the end of the term (before you have fully deducted the prepaid interest), you can deduct the remaining balance of prepaid interest in the final year of payment.

Interest Paid on Income Tax Deficiencies

If you pay interest on a tax deficiency arising from business income from your sole proprietorship, S corporation, partnership, or LLC, you cannot deduct the interest on your individual return. This interest is treated as nondeductible personal interest even though business income generated the deficiency.

While a C corporation can deduct interest it pays on any tax deficiency, it cannot deduct tax penalties. This rule applies to both civil and criminal penalties. Amounts assessed for the delay of filing a return are considered penalties. Thus, estimated tax penalties, which are imposed because of a delay in payment, are not deductible even though they are calculated by application of an interest rate. Similarly, amounts owing because of the failure to deposit employment taxes are treated as penalties. Additions to tax contained in sections 6651 through 6658 of the Internal Revenue Code are considered penalties.

Interest Related to Tax-Exempt Income

No deduction is allowed for interest paid or incurred to buy or carry tax-exempt securities.

Where to Deduct Taxes and Interest

Employees

Taxes and interest are deductible only as miscellaneous business expenses reported on Schedule A and subject to the 2-percent-of-adjusted-gross-income floor. However, employees can elect to claim a credit on foreign taxes (see Chapter 1).

Self-Employed

Taxes and interest are deducted on Schedule C (or Schedule F in the case of farming operations). This form provides separate space for claiming deductions for mortgage interest and for other interest. It also provides a specific line for claiming a deduction for taxes and licenses.

Instead of deducting foreign taxes on Schedule C (or Schedule F), a sole proprietor may choose to claim a foreign tax credit. If foreign taxes are $300 or less (or $600 or less if the self-employed person files a joint return) and result from passive income, an election can be made to claim the credit directly on Form 1040. Otherwise, the credit must be figured on Form 1116, Foreign Tax Credit.

Partnerships and LLCs

In general, the partnership and LLC deducts taxes and interest on Form 1065. Separate lines are provided for deducting interest, taxes, and licenses. These items are part of the business's operating expenses and figure into its income or loss passed through to partners or LLC members on Schedule K-1 and then reported on the owner's Schedule E. These items are not separately reported to partners or LLC members on Schedule K-1 for special treatment on an owner's individual income tax return.

However, interest that may be classified as investment interest is separately stated in Schedule K-1, since it is subject to an investment interest limitation on the partner's or member's individual income tax return.

Also, foreign taxes are separately stated items on Schedule K-1 to allow the owner to decide whether to take a deduction or credit on his or her individual return. Partners and LLC members treat foreign taxes in the same manner as self-employed individuals.

S Corporations

In general, the S corporation deducts taxes and interest on Form 1120S. Separate lines are provided for deducting interest, taxes, and licenses. These items are part of the business's operating expenses and figure into its income or loss passed through to shareholders on Schedule K-1 and then reported on the owner's Schedule E. These items are not separately reported to shareholders on Schedule K-1 for special treatment on an owner's individual income tax return.

However, interest that may be classified as investment interest is separately stated in Schedule K-1, since it is subject to an investment interest limitation on the shareholder's individual income tax return.

Also, foreign taxes are separately stated items on Schedule K-1 to allow the shareholder to decide whether to take a deduction or credit on his or her individual return. S corporation shareholders treat foreign taxes in the same manner as self-employed individuals.

C Corporations

C corporations deduct taxes and interest on Form 1120. Separate lines are provided for deducting interest, taxes, and licenses.

The foreign tax credit is figured on Form 1118, Foreign Tax Credit—Corporations.

CHAPTER 14

First-Year Expensing, Depreciation, Amortization, and Depletion

*F*irst-year expensing, which is also called the Section 179 deduction after the section in the Tax Code that creates it, is a write-off allowed for the purchase of equipment used in your business. This deduction takes the place of depreciation—the amount expensed is not depreciated. For example, if you buy a computer for your business for $2,500, you can opt to deduct its cost in full in the year you place the computer into service. If you don't make this election, you must write off the cost over a number of years fixed by law.

Depreciation is an allowance for a portion of the cost of equipment or other property owned by you and used in your business. Depreciation is claimed over the life of the property, although it may be accelerated, with a greater amount claimed in the early years of ownership. The thinking behind depreciation is that equipment wears out. In theory, if you were to put into a separate fund the amount you claim each year as a depreciation allowance, when your equipment reaches the end of its usefulness you will have sufficient funds to buy a replacement (of course, the replacement may not cost the same as the old equipment). To claim a depreciation deduction, you do not necessarily have to spend any money. If you have already bought equipment, future depreciation deductions do not require any additional out-of-pocket expenditures.

Amortization is conceptually similar to depreciation. It is an allowance for the cost of certain capital expenditures, such as goodwill and trademarks, acquired in the purchase of a business. Amortization can be claimed only if it is specifically allowed by the tax law. It is always deducted ratably over the life of the property. As you will see, amortization is also allowed as an election for some types of expenditures that would otherwise not be deductible.

Depletion is a deduction allowed for certain natural resources. The tax law carefully controls the limits of this deduction.

In this chapter you will learn about:

- First-year expensing
- Other expensing opportunities
- General rules for depreciation
- Modified Accelerated Cost Recovery System (MACRS) depreciation
- Limitations on listed property
- Putting personal property to business use
- Amortization
- Depletion
- Where to claim depreciation, amortization, and depletion

For a further discussion of depreciation, amortization, and depletion, see IRS Publication 463, *Travel, Entertainment, Gifts, and Car Expenses*; IRS Publication 534, *Depreciating Property Placed in Service Before 1987*; and IRS Publication 946, *How to Depreciate Property*.

First-Year Expensing

Instead of depreciating the cost of tangible personal property over a number of years, you may be able to write off the entire cost in the first year. This is *first-year expensing* or a *Section 179 deduction* (named after the section in the Internal Revenue Code that governs the deduction). A first-year expense deduction may be claimed whether you pay for the item with cash or credit. If you buy the item on credit, the first-year expense deduction can be used to enhance your cash flow position (you claim an immediate tax deduction but pay for the item over time).

You can elect to deduct up to a set dollar amount of the cost of tangible personal property used in your business. In 2005, you can deduct $105,000 (and more in certain economically distressed communities).

The property must be acquired by purchase. If you inherit property, for example, and use it in your business, you cannot claim a first-year expense deduction. If you acquire property in whole or in part by means of a trade, you cannot claim a first-year expense deduction for the portion of the property acquired by trade.

Example

You buy a new car that is used 100 percent for business. You pay cash and trade in your old car. You cannot compute the first-year expense deduction for the portion of the new car's basis that includes the adjusted basis of the car you traded in.

First-year expensing may be claimed for property that has been pre-owned (i.e., used property), as long as the property is new to you (and you acquire it by purchase).

If you buy property on credit, you can still use the first-year expense deduction even though you are not yet out-of-pocket for the purchase price. A purchase on credit that entitles you to a first-year expense deduction is a strategy for aiding your cash flow (i.e., you gain a tax deduction even though you have not expended the cash).

The property must have been acquired for business. If you buy property for personal purposes and later convert it to business use, you cannot claim a first-year expense deduction. If you are an employee, be prepared to show the property you expense was acquired for business (not personal) purposes. In one case, a sales manager was allowed to expense the cost of a home computer where she convinced the Tax Court that its use was entirely for her job. She had a heavy workload, she could access company information via her modem, and she was not allowed entry to her office after business hours.

Off-the-shelf software is eligible for expensing. (In the past its cost had to be amortized over a period of up to 36 months.)

Generally, the first-year expense deduction does not apply to property you buy and then lease to others. (There is no restriction on leased property by corporations.) However, a first-year expense deduction is allowed for leased property you manufactured and leased if the term of the lease is less than half of the property's class life and, for the first 12 months the property is transferred to the lessee, the total business deductions for the property are more than 15 percent of the rental income for the property.

Limits on First-Year Expensing

Three limits apply for first-year expensing: a *dollar limit*, an *investment limit*, and a *taxable income limit*.

DOLLAR LIMIT. You cannot deduct more than the applicable dollar amount in any one year. This dollar limit ($105,000 in 2005) applies on a per-taxpayer basis. For businesses within empowerment zones, renewal communities, the District of Columbia, or the New York City Liberty Zone, the dollar limit is increased by the smaller of $35,000 or the cost of qualified Section 179 property within these areas. If you qualify for a higher dollar limit, simply cross out the preprinted $105,000 limit on Form 4562 and write in your applicable dollar limit in the margin.

If an individual owns more than one business, he or she must aggregate first-year expense deductions from all businesses and deduct no more than a total of $105,000 in 2005. Married persons are treated as one taxpayer. They are allowed only one $105,000 deduction regardless of which spouse placed the property in service. If they file separate returns, each can claim only one-half or $52,500.

Note

A special dollar limit for cars used in business supersedes the first-year expense deduction limit. (See Chapters 7 and 9 for more details on deducting the costs of business cars.) No first-year expense deduction can be claimed for listed property unless it is used more than 50 percent for business.

For the Future

The $105,000 dollar limit on expensing in 2006 will be adjusted for inflation. The higher dollar limit on expensing is set to expire at the end of 2007 unless Congress extends the law. If it expires, then the dollar limit drops to $25,000.

INVESTMENT LIMIT. The first-year expense deduction is really designed for small businesses. This is because every dollar of investments in equipment over $420,000 reduces the dollar limit.

Example

In 2005 you buy equipment costing $436,000. Your first-year expense deduction is limited to $89,000 ($105,000 – [$436,000 – $420,000]).

If a business buys equipment costing $525,000, the deduction limit is fully phased out, so no first-year expense deduction is allowed.

TAXABLE INCOME LIMIT. The total first-year expense deduction cannot exceed taxable income from the active conduct of a business. You are treated as actively conducting a business if you participate in a meaningful way in the management or operations of a business.

Taxable income for purposes of this limit has a special meaning. Start with your net income (or loss) from all businesses that you actively conduct. If you are married and file jointly, add your spouse's net income (or loss). This includes certain gains and losses, called Section 1231 gains and losses (see Chapter 6), and interest from working capital in your business. It also includes salary, wages, and other compensation earned as an employee, so even though a moonlighting business that bought the equipment has little or no income, you may still be eligible for a full first-year expense deduction if your salary from your day job is sufficient. Reduce your net income (or loss) by any first-year expense deduction, the deduction for one-half of self-employment tax, and net operating loss carrybacks or carryforwards. This, then, is your taxable income for purposes of the taxable income limitation. If your taxable income limits your deduction, any unused deduction can be carried forward and used in a future year.

Example

Your taxable income (without regard to a first-year expense deduction) is $12,000. You place in service in 2005 a machine costing $14,000. Your first-year expense deduction is limited to $12,000. You can carry forward the additional $2,000 to next year.

Carryforwards of unused first-year expense deductions can be used if there is sufficient taxable income in the next year. You can choose the properties for which the costs will be carried forward. You can allocate the portion of the costs to these properties as long as the allocation is reflected on your books and records.

Special Rules for Pass-Through Entities

The dollar limit, investment limit, and taxable income limit apply at both the entity and owner levels. This means that partnerships, as well as their partners, and S corporations, as well as their shareholders, must apply all the limits. The same is true for LLCs and members.

Example

You are a 50-percent shareholder in an S corporation that claims a first-year expense deduction in 2005 of $105,000. Your allocable share as reported on your Schedule K-1 is $52,500. You also own a business that you run as a sole proprietor. You place in service a machine costing $75,000. (Assume sufficient taxable income by the S corporation and for your sole proprietorship.) Your first-year expense deduction for this machine is limited to $52,500. The balance of the cost of the machine, $22,500, cannot be expensed in the current year because of the dollar limit.

Should the First-Year Expensing Election Be Made?

You don't automatically claim this deduction; you must elect it on Form 4562. While first-year expensing provides a great opportunity for matching your tax write-off with your cash outlay, it is not always advisable to take advantage of this opportunity. Consider forgoing the election in the following situations:

- You receive the write-off through a pass-through entity but could claim it for purchases made through a sole proprietorship (see the preceding example).
- You are in a low tax bracket this year but expect to be more profitable in the coming years so that depreciation deductions in those years will be more valuable.
- You want to report income to obtain credits for Social Security benefits.

Making or Revoking an Expensing Election

Usually a first-year expensing election must be made on an original tax return for the year to which the election applies. Revocation can be made only with IRS consent, which will be granted only in extraordinary circumstances. However, for 2003 through 2007, you can make or revoke an election to use expensing without obtaining IRS permission. The change is made on an amended return that must specify the item and portion of its cost for which an election is being made or revoked. You have until the time limit for filing an amended return (e.g., April 15, 2009, for a 2005 return filed on April 17, 2006).

Dispositions of First-Year Expense Property

If you sell or otherwise dispose of property for which a first-year expense deduction was claimed, or cease using the property for business, there may

Example

In 2002, you placed in service office furniture (seven-year property) costing $10,000, which you fully expensed. In 2005 you used the property only 40 percent for business (and 60 percent for personal purposes). You calculate your recapture as shown in Table 14.1.

TABLE 14.1 Calculating Recapture

First-Year Expense Deduction:		$10,000
Allowable Depreciation		
$10,000 × 14.29%*	$1,429	
10,000 × 24.49	2,449	
10,000 × 17.49	1,749	
10,000 × 12.49 × 40%	500	$6,127
Recapture amount		3,873

*MACRS percentages from Table 14.2.

be recapture of your deduction. This means that you must include in your income a portion of the deduction you previously claimed. The amount you must recapture depends on when you dispose of the property. The longer you hold it, the less recapture you have. If you sell property at a gain, recapture is not additional income; it is merely a reclassification of income. If you realize gain on the sale of first-year expense property, instead of treating the gain as capital gain, the recapture amount is characterized as ordinary income.

Recapture is calculated by comparing your first-year expense deduction with the deduction you would have claimed had you instead taken ordinary depreciation.

If you transfer first-year expense property in a transaction that does not require recognition of gain or loss (e.g., if you make a tax-free exchange or contribute the property to a corporation in a tax-free incorporation), an adjustment is made in the basis of the property. The adjusted basis of the property is increased before the disposition by the amount of the first-year expense deduction that is disallowed. The new owner cannot claim a first-year expense deduction with respect to this disallowed portion.

Other Expensing Opportunities

In addition to first-year expensing, the tax law is peppered with provisions that let businesses expense certain types of expenditures instead of amortizing them or treating them simply as a capital cost. Some of these provisions have broad application, while many of them are limited to specific industries.

Film or Television Productions

Small production companies can take an immediate write-off of their costs. You can elect to deduct up to $15 million in production costs of a qualified film or television production. A qualified production is one in which total costs do not exceed $15 million. However, under an exception, the dollar limit increases to $20 million for production costs incurred in certain economically depressed areas.

OTHER EXPENSING OPPORTUNITIES

- Acquired intangibles (later in this chapter)
- Business start-up costs (later in this chapter)
- Corporate organizational expenses (later in this chapter)
- Environmental cleanup costs (Chapter 10)
- EPA sulfur regulation costs (Chapter 10)

- Expenditures to remove architectural barriers to the elderly and the handicapped (Chapter 10)
- Fertilizer used by farmers (Chapter 20)
- Partnership organizational expenses (later in this chapter)
- Reforestation expenses (Chapter 20)

General Rules for Depreciation

Depreciable Property

Depreciation is a deduction allowed for certain property used in your business. It is designed to offset the cost of acquiring it, so you cannot depreciate leased property. To be depreciable, the property must be the kind that wears out, decays, gets used up, becomes obsolete, or loses value from natural causes. The property must have a determinable useful life that is longer than one year. Antiques, for example, generally cannot be depreciated because they do not have a determinable useful life; they can be expected to last indefinitely. The same is true for goodwill you build up in your business (though if you buy a business and pay for its goodwill, you may be able to amortize the cost, as explained later in this chapter).

Land is not depreciable because it, too, can be expected to last indefinitely. Land includes not only the cost of the acreage but also the cost of clearing, grading, planting, and landscaping. However, some land preparation costs can be depreciated if they are closely associated with a building on the land rather than the land itself. For example, shrubs around the entry to a building may be depreciated; trees planted on the perimeter of the property are nondepreciable land costs. Also, the cost of the minerals on the land may not be depreciated but may be subject to depletion.

When you own a building, you must allocate the **basis** of the property between the building and the land, since only the building portion is depreciable.

There is no special rule for making an allocation of basis. Obviously you would prefer to allocate as much as possible to the building and as little as possible to the land. However, the allocation must have some logical basis. It should be based on the relative value of each portion. What is the land worth? What is the building worth? You may want to use the services of an appraiser to help you derive a fair yet favorable allocation that will withstand IRS scrutiny.

Basis   Generally, basis is the amount you pay for property. It does not matter whether you finance your purchase or pay cash. You add to basis sales taxes and other related expenses (such as nondeductible closing costs if you get a mortgage, or attorney's fees). But you cannot include the value of trade-ins in your basis.

Example

In 2005, you begin to use a personal computer for a business you have just started up. You paid $2,500 for it in 2003 and it is now worth $1,200. Your basis for depreciation is $1,200. At the same time, you begin to use one room in your home as a home office. You bought your home in 1997 for $200,000 and it is now worth $300,000 (exclusive of land). Assuming that the home office allocation is 12.5 percent of the home, your basis for depreciation is $25,000 (12.5 percent of $200,000, which is lower than 12.5 percent of $300,000, or $37,500).

If you convert personal property to business use, the basis for purposes of depreciation is the lower of its adjusted basis (generally cost) or fair market value at the time of the conversion to business use. If you acquire replacement property in a like-kind exchange or an involuntary conversion, special rules govern basis for purposes of depreciation (see IRS Publication 946, How to Depreciate Property).

Property that can be expected to last for one year or less is simply deducted in full as some other type of deduction. For example, if you buy stationery that will be used up within the year, you simply deduct the cost of the stationery as supplies. In order to claim depreciation, you must be the owner of the property. If you lease property, like an office, you cannot depreciate it; only the owner can, since it is the owner who suffers the wear and tear on his or her investment.

Depreciable property may be tangible or intangible. *Tangible property* is property you can touch—office furniture, a machine, or a telephone. Tangible property may be personal property (a machine) or real property (a factory). *Intangible property* is property you cannot touch, such as copyrights, patents, and franchises. *Personal property* does not mean you use the property for personal purposes; it is a legal term for tangible property that is not real property.

If you use property for both business and personal purposes, you must make an allocation. You can claim depreciation only on the business portion of the property. For example, if you use your car 75 percent for business and 25 percent for personal purposes (including commuting), you can claim depreciation on only 75 percent of the property.

Certain property can never be depreciated. In addition to land, you cannot depreciate your inventory. *Inventory* is property held primarily for sale to customers in the ordinary course of your business. Sometimes you may question whether an asset is really part of your inventory or if it is a separate asset that can be depreciated. For example, containers generally are treated as part of the cost of your inventory and cannot be separately depreciated. However, containers used to ship products can be depreciated if your invoice treats them as separate items, whether your sales contract shows that you retain title to the containers and whether your records properly state your basis in the containers.

When to Claim Depreciation

You claim depreciation beginning with the year in which the property is **placed in service.** You continue to claim depreciation throughout the life of the asset. The life of the asset is also called its *recovery period*. Different types of assets have different recovery periods. The length of the recovery period has nothing to do with how durable a particular item may be. You simply check the classifications of property to find the recovery period for a particular item.

Placed in service   When an item is ready and available for a specific use, whether or not the item is actually used.

You stop claiming depreciation on the item when the property's cost has been fully depreciated or when the property is retired from service. Property is retired from service when it is permanently withdrawn from use, by selling or exchanging it, abandoning it, or destroying it.

Example

A machine with a five-year recovery period is no longer needed after three years for the task for which it was purchased. The machine is sold to another company that still has a use for it. Once the machine is sold, it has been permanently removed from your service. You cannot claim depreciation after this occurs.

The amount of depreciation you can claim in the year in which property is placed in service or retired from service is limited and is discussed later in this chapter.

Even if you do not actually claim depreciation, you are treated as having done so for purposes of figuring the basis of property when you dispose of it.

If you failed to claim depreciation in the past, file an amended return to fix the error if the tax year is still open (the statute of limitation on amending the

> ## Example
>
> You place a piece of machinery in service in 2003 and claim a depreciation deduction on your 2003 return. In 2004, your revenues are low and you forget to report your depreciation deduction on your 2004 return. In 2005, you sell the machine. In calculating gain or loss on the sale, you must adjust basis for the depreciation you actually claimed in 2003 and the depreciation you should have claimed in 2004.

return has not expired). Alternatively, you can correct the underdepreciation (even for a closed tax year) by filing for a change in accounting method on Form 3115. Under a special IRS procedure, you simply adjust your income in the current year. Be sure to write on Form 3115 "Automatic Method Change under Rev. Proc. 98-60."

If you abandon property before it has been fully depreciated, you can deduct the balance of your depreciation deductions in the year of abandonment. For instance, if you have a machine with a seven-year recovery period that you abandon in the fifth year because it is obsolete, you can claim the depreciation that you would have claimed in the sixth, seventh, and eighth years in the fifth year along with depreciation allowable for that year.

Modified Accelerated Cost Recovery System

Modified Accelerated Cost Recovery System (MACRS) is a depreciation system that went into effect for tangible property placed in service after 1986. It is composed of two systems: a basic system, called the *General Depreciation System* (GDS), and an alternate system, called the *Alternative Depreciation System* (ADS). The difference between the two systems is the recovery period over which you claim depreciation and the method for calculating depreciation. You use the basic system unless the alternate system is required or you make a special election to use the alternate system. You cannot use either system for certain property: intangible property (patents, copyrights, etc.), motion picture films or videotapes, sound recordings, and property you elect to exclude from MACRS so that you can use a depreciation method based on some other measuring rod than a term of years (these other methods are not discussed in this book).

Basic System

You can use the basic system (GDS) to depreciate any tangible property unless you are required to use the alternate system, elect to use the alternate system, or are required to use some other depreciation method. To calculate your depreciation deduction, you need to know:

- *The property's basis.* If you purchase property, basis is your cost. If you acquire property in some other way (get it by gift, inheritance, or in a tax-free exchange), basis is figured in another way. For example, if your corporation acquires property from you upon its formation in a tax-free incorporation, then the corporation steps into your shoes for purposes of basis.

Example

You form a corporation (C or S) and contribute cash and a computer. In exchange you receive all of the stock of the corporation. Your basis for the computer was $4,000. The corporation assumes your basis—$4,000.

A similar rule applies to property you contribute to a partnership or LLC upon its formation. If you are a sole proprietor or an employee and convert property from personal use to business use, your basis for depreciation is the lesser of the fair market value (FMV) on the date of conversion to business use or the adjusted basis of the property on that date.

The cost of property includes sales taxes. If you hire an architect to design a building, the fees are added to the basis of the property and recovered through depreciation. The following are more items to consider when calculating your depreciation deduction.

- *The property's recovery period.* Recovery periods are fixed according to the claim in which a property falls. In the past, recovery period was referred to as the useful life of the property and you may periodically see this old phase still in use.

- *The date the property is placed in service.* Remember, this is the date the property is ready and available for its specific use.

- *The applicable convention.* These are special rules that govern the timing of deductions (explained later in this chapter).

- *The depreciation method.* MACRS has five different depreciation methods.

Recovery Periods

The class assigned to a property is designed to match the period over which the basis of property is recovered (e.g., cost is deducted). Five-year property allows the cost of certain equipment to be deducted over five years (subject to adjustment for conventions discussed later).

THREE-YEAR PROPERTY. This property includes taxis, tractor units for use over the road, racehorses over two years old when placed in service, any other horse over 12 years old when placed in service, breeding hogs, certain handling devices for manufacturing food and beverages, and special tools for manufacturing rubber products. Special rules for computer software are discussed under "Amortization" later in this chapter.

FIVE-YEAR PROPERTY. This property includes cars, buses, trucks, airplanes, trailers and trailer containers, computers and peripheral equipment, some office machinery (calculators, copiers, typewriters), assets used in construction, logging equipment, assets used to manufacture organic and inorganic chemicals, and property used in research and experimentation. It also includes breeding and dairy cattle and breeding and dairy goats.

SEVEN-YEAR PROPERTY. This property includes office fixtures and furniture (chairs, desks, files); communications equipment (fax machines); breeding and workhorses; assets used in printing; recreational assets (miniature golf courses, billiard establishments, concert halls); assets used to produce jewelry; musical instruments; toys; sporting goods; and motion picture and television films and tapes. This class is also the catchall for other property. It includes any property not assigned to another class.

10-YEAR PROPERTY. This property includes barges, tugs, vessels, and similar water transportation equipment; single-purpose agricultural or horticultural structures placed in service after 1988; and trees or vines bearing fruits or nuts.

15-YEAR PROPERTY. This property includes certain depreciable improvements made to land (bridges, fences, roads, shrubbery).

20-YEAR PROPERTY. This property includes farm buildings (other than single-purpose agricultural or horticultural structures) and any municipal sewers.

RESIDENTIAL RENTAL REALTY. Rental buildings qualify if 80 percent or more of the gross rental is from dwelling units. The recovery period is 27.5 years.

NONRESIDENTIAL REALTY. This class applies to factories, office buildings, and any other realty other than residential rental realty. The recovery period is 39 years (31.5 years for property placed in service before May 13, 1993). If you begin to use a portion of your home for business (e.g., a home office), use the recovery period applicable on the date of conversion. For example, if you begin to use a home office in 2004, depreciate that portion of your home using a 39-year recovery period, even if you bought your home in 1990.

COMPONENTS OF REALTY. Structural components of a building are part and parcel of the realty and generally must be depreciated as such (e.g., over 39 years). However, certain components, such as electrical systems and wiring, carpeting, floor covering, plumbing connections, exhaust systems, handrails, room partitions, tile ceilings, and steam boilers, can be treated as tangible personal property instead of realty. As such, they can be depreciated over shorter recovery periods rather than being treated as part of realty subject to longer recovery periods. Obtain a cost segregation analysis when buying, building, or improving realty.

Example

You install a fake floor to cover wiring needed for your computers. The IRS originally said that the floor can be depreciated as personal property over five years rather than as part of the realty depreciated over 39 years. However, it later said it would take another look at this conclusion, so beware.

Note

Obtain a cost segregation (or component of cost) analysis when buying, building, or improving realty. This analysis can be the basis for allocating costs to components that will be separately depreciated. The analysis should be performed by an engineer, architect, or realty appraiser and not by you or your accountant.

IMPROVEMENTS OR ADDITIONS.   In general, improvements or additions to property are treated as separate property and are depreciated separately from the property itself. The recovery period for improvements begins on the later of the date the improvements are placed in service or the date the property to which the improvements are made is placed in service. Use the same recovery period for the improvements that you would for the underlying property (unless an improvement is a component of realty that can be depreciated according to its own recovery period).

PROPERTY ACQUIRED IN A LIKE-KIND EXCHANGE.   The property acquired in a like-kind exchange is depreciated over the remaining recovery period of the *old* property. Thus, the new property, which has the basis of the old property, also has the old property's remaining recovery period. This enables you to write off the newly acquired asset more rapidly than if the recovery period of the new asset were used.

Conventions

There are three conventions that affect the timing of depreciation deductions. Two apply to property other than residential or nonresidential real property (essentially personal property such as equipment); the other applies to residential or nonresidential real property (rental units, offices, and factories).

HALF-YEAR CONVENTION.   The *half-year convention* applies to all property (other than residential or nonresidential real property) unless superseded by the mid-quarter convention (explained next). Under the half-year convention, property is treated as if you placed it in service in the middle of the year. You are allowed to deduct only one-half of the depreciation allowance for the first year. This is so even if you place the property in service on the first day of the year. Under this convention, property is treated as disposed of in the middle of the year, regardless of the actual date of disposition.

The half-year convention means that property held for its entire recovery period will have an additional year for claiming depreciation deductions. Only one-half of the first year's depreciation deduction is claimed in the first year; the balance of depreciation is claimed in the year following the last year of the recovery period.

Example

A desk (seven-year property) is placed in service on January 1, 2005. Without regard to expensing, one-half of the depreciation deduction that would otherwise be claimed in the first year is allowed. Normal depreciation is claimed in years two through seven. The remaining depreciation is claimed in the eighth year.

Mid-Quarter Convention

Under the *mid-quarter convention*, all property placed in service during the year (or disposed of during the year) is treated as placed in service (or disposed of) in the middle of the applicable quarter. The mid-quarter convention applies (and the half-year convention does not) if the total bases of all property placed in service during the last three months of the year (the final quarter) exceeds 40 percent of the total bases of property placed in service during the entire year. In making this determination, do not take into consideration

Example

You are on a calendar year. In January 2005, you place in service machine A, costing $3,000. In November 2005 you place in service another machine, machine B, costing $10,000. You must use the mid-quarter convention to calculate depreciation for both machines. This is because more than 40 percent of all property placed in service during the year ($13,000) was placed in service in the final quarter of the year ($10,000). (Actually, 77 percent of all property placed in service in the year was placed in service in the final quarter of the year.)

Example

Continuing with the same machine situation, except that machine B is placed in service in January and machine A is placed in service in November. In this instance, the mid-quarter convention does not apply because only 23 percent of all property placed in service in 2005 was placed in service in the final quarter of the year.

residential or nonresidential real property or property placed in service and then disposed of in the same year.

Mid-Month Convention

This convention applies only to real property. You must treat all real property as if it were placed in service or disposed of in the middle of the month. The mid-month convention is taken into account in the depreciation tables from which you can take your deduction. Simply look at the table for the type of realty (residential or nonresidential) you own, and then look in the table for the month in which the property is placed in service.

Depreciation Methods

There are five ways to depreciate property: the 200-percent declining balance rate, the 150-percent declining balance rate, the straight-line election, the 150-percent election, and the ADS method. Both 200-percent and 150-percent declining balance rates are referred to as accelerated rates.

You may use the 200-percent rate for three-year, five-year, seven-year, and 10-year property over the GDS recovery period. The half-year or mid-quarter convention must be applied. The 200-percent declining balance method is calculated by dividing 100 by the recovery period and then doubling it. However, as a practical matter you do not have to compute the rates. They are provided for you in Tables 14.2 and 14.3, which take into account the half-year or mid-quarter conventions.

If the 200-percent declining balance rate is used, you can switch to the straight line in the year when it provides a deduction of value equal to or greater than the accelerated rate. Of course, total depreciation can never be more than 100 percent of the property's basis. The switch to straight line merely accelerates the timing of depreciation (the total depreciation is, of

TABLE 14.2 MACRS Rates—Half-Year Convention

Year	Three-Year Property	Five-Year Property	Seven-Year Property
1	33.33%	20.00%	14.29%
2	44.45	32.00	24.49
3	14.81	19.20	17.49
4	7.81	11.52	12.49
5		11.52	8.93
6		5.76	8.92
7			8.93
8			4.46

TABLE 14.3 MACRS Rates—Mid-Quarter Convention (200% Rate)

Year	First Quarter	Second Quarter	Third Quarter	Fourth Quarter
	Three-Year Property			
1	58.33%	41.67%	25.00%	8.33%
2	27.78	38.89	50.00	61.11
3	12.35	14.14	16.677	20.37
4	1.54	5.30	8.33	10.19
	Five-Year Property			
1	35.00	25.00	15.00	5.00
2	26.00	30.00	34.00	38.00
3	15.60	18.00	20.40	22.80
4	11.01	11.37	12.24	13.68
5	11.01	11.37	11.30	10.94
6	1.38	4.26	7.06	9.58
	Seven-Year Property			
1	25.00	17.85	10.71	3.57
2	21.43	23.47	25.51	27.55
3	15.31	16.76	18.22	19.68
4	10.93	11.97	13.02	14.06
5	8.75	8.87	9.30	10.04
6	8.74	8.87	8.85	8.73
7	8.75	8.87	8.86	8.73
8	1.09	3.33	5.53	7.64

course, limited to the basis of the property). Table 14.4 shows you when it becomes advantageous to switch to the straight-line rate.

You use the 150-percent rate for 15- and 20-year property over the GDS recovery period. Again, you must also apply the half-year or mid-quarter convention. You change over to the straight-line method when it provides a greater deduction. Tables for this rate may be found in IRS Publication 946, *How to Depreciate Property.*

Residential and nonresidential realty must use the straight-line rate (see Tables 14.5 to 14.7). *Straight line* is simply the cost of the property divided by

TABLE 14.4 When to Change to Straight-Line Method

Class	Changeover Year
Three-year property	3rd
Five-year property	4th
Seven-year property	5th
10-year property	7th
15-year property	7th
20-year property	9th

TABLE 14.5 Rates for Residential Realty Years (27 Years), Straight-Line, Mid-Month Convention

Year	Month in the First Recovery Year the Property Is Placed in Service					
	1	2	3	4	5	6
1	3.485%	3.182%	2.879%	2.576%	2.273%	1.970%
2–9	3.636	3.636	3.636	3.636	3.636	3.636
Year	7	8	9	10	11	12
1	1.677%	1.364%	1.061%	0.758%	0.455%	0.152%
2–9	3.636	3.636	3.636	3.636	3.636	3.636

TABLE 14.6 Rates for Nonresidential Realty Years (31.5 Years), Straight-Line, Mid-Month Convention

Year	Month in the First Recovery Year the Property Is Placed in Service					
	1	2	3	4	5	6
1	3.042%	2.778%	2.513%	2.249%	1.984%	1.720%
2–7	3.175	3.175	3.175	3.175	3.175	3.175
8	3.175	3.174	3.175	3.174	3.175	3.174
9	3.174	3.175	3.174	3.175	3.174	3.175
Year	7	8	9	10	11	12
1	1.455%	1.190%	0.926%	0.661%	0.397%	0.132%
2–7	3.175	3.175	3.175	3.175	3.175	3.175
8	3.175	3.175	3.175	3.175	3.175	3.175
9	3.174	3.175	3.174	3.175	3.174	3.175

TABLE 14.7 Rates for Nonresidential Realty Years (39 Years), Straight-Line, Mid-Month Convention

Year	Month in the First Recovery Year the Property Is Placed in Service					
	1	2	3	4	5	6
1	2.461%	2.247%	2.033%	1.819%	1.605%	1.391%
2–39	2.564	2.564	2.564	2.564	2.564	2.564

Year	7	8	9	10	11	12
1	1.177%	0.963%	0.749%	0.535%	0.321%	0.107%
2–39	2.564	2.564	2.564	2.564	2.564	2.564

the life of the property. However, you begin depreciation with the month in which the property is placed in service. This makes the rate vary slightly over the years. The tables can be used to calculate depreciation for residential and nonresidential real property using basic depreciation (GDS). If you place nonresidential realty in service in 2004, be sure to use the 39-year table. For all tables, find your annual depreciation rate by looking in the column for the month in which the property was placed in service (for example, for calendar-year businesses, March is 3; August is 8). Then look at the year of ownership you are in (e.g., the year in which you place property in service, look at year number one).

Example

You are on a calendar year and placed in service a factory in April 2002. In 2005, your depreciation rate is 2.564 percent. You found this rate by looking at the table for 39-year nonresidential property under month 4, year 4.

Tables for depreciation of residential and nonresidential real property using ADS as well as years after year 9 for residential and pre-May 13, 1993, nonresidential realty may be found in Appendix A of IRS Publication 946, *How to Depreciate Property.*

You can elect to use the 150-percent rate for properties eligible for the 200-percent rate. If the election is made, the 150-percent rate is used over the ADS recovery period. Again, a half-year or mid-quarter convention is applied and there is a changeover to the straight-line method when it provides a greater deduction. The election may be advisable if you do not think you will have sufficient income to offset larger depreciation deductions. It may also be advisable to lessen or avoid the alternative minimum tax.

Note

Once you make the election to use the 150-percent rate over the ADS recovery period, you cannot change your mind.

Alternative Depreciation System

You must use the alternative system (ADS) (and not the basic system, GDS) for the following property (see Table 14.8):

- Listed property not used more than 50 percent for business. Listed property includes cars and other transportation vehicles, computers and peripherals (unless used only at a regular business establishment), and cellular telephones.
- Tangible property used predominantly outside the United States.
- Tax-exempt use property.
- Tax-exempt bond-financed property.
- Imported property covered by an executive order of the president of the United States.
- Property used predominantly in farming and placed in service during any year in which you elect not to apply the uniform capitalization rules to certain farming costs.

The ADS requires depreciation to be calculated using the straight-line method. This is done by dividing the cost of the property by the alternate recovery period. In some cases, the recovery period is the same as for the basic system; in others, it is longer.

You can elect to use ADS for other property in order to claim more gradual depreciation. The election applies to all property within the same class placed in service during the year (other than real estate). For residential rental and nonresidential real property, you can make the election to use ADS on a property-by-property basis.

TABLE 14.8 Recovery Periods under Alternative Depreciation System

Property	Years
Cars, computers, light-duty trucks	5
Furniture and fixtures	10
Personal property with no class life	12
Nonresidential/residential real estate	40

An election to use ADS may be helpful, for example, if you are first starting out and do not have sufficient income to offset large depreciation deductions. Use of ADS can help to avoid alternative minimum tax and the special depreciation computations required for alternative minimum tax.

For property placed in service after December 31, 1999, you can calculate depreciation for regular tax purposes using the same recovery periods as required for alternative minimum tax purposes. This eliminates the need to make any adjustments for alternative minimum tax and to keep separate records of depreciation taken for regular and alternative minimum tax purposes.

Bonus Depreciation

Prior to 2005, there was a special rule, called *bonus depreciation*, that allowed you to deduct 50 percent of the cost of property (other than realty) in the year in which it was placed in service. This rule applied in addition to any expensing election that was claimed. However, bonus depreciation expired on December 31, 2004, and Congress did not extend it.

Recapture of Depreciation

If you sell or otherwise dispose of depreciable or amortizable property at a gain, you may have to report all or some of your gain as ordinary income. The treatment of what would otherwise have been capital gain as ordinary income is called *recapture*. In effect, some of the tax benefit you enjoy from depreciation deductions may be offset later on by recapture.

Also, if you sell or otherwise dispose of real property (e.g., residence containing a home office) on which straight-line depreciation was claimed after May 6, 1997, all such depreciation is taxed as capital gain up to 25 percent. This taxable portion is referred to as *unrecaptured depreciation*. The treatment of income from depreciation recapture is explained in Chapter 6.

Recordkeeping for Depreciation

Since depreciation deductions go on for a number of years, it is important to keep good records of prior deductions. It is also necessary to maintain records since depreciation deductions may differ for regular income tax purposes and the alternative minimum tax. Recordkeeping is explained in Chapter 3.

Limitations on Listed Property

Certain property is called *listed property* and is subject to special depreciation limits. Listed property includes:

- Cars
- Other transportation vehicles (including boats)

- Computers and peripherals, unless used only at a regular business establishment owned or leased by the person operating the establishment. (A home office is treated as a business establishment.)
- Cellular telephones (or similar telecommunication equipment)

These are the only items considered listed property because they have been specified as such in the tax law. For example, fax machines and noncellular telephones are not treated as listed property.

It is advisable to keep a log or other record for the use of listed property. This will help you show that business use is more than 50 percent. However, if you use listed property, such as a computer, in a home office whose expenses are deductible, the Tax Court says you do not need records. The reason: Recordkeeping for business use does not apply to computers used at a place of business (which includes a home office that is the principal place of business and that is used regularly and exclusively for that business).

If business use of listed property is not more than 50 percent during the year, the basic depreciation system cannot be used. In this case, you must use the ADS. Under this system, depreciation can be calculated only with the straight-line method. Divide the cost of the property by the alternative recovery period. For cars, computers, and other listed property, the alternative recovery period happens to be the same as the basic recovery period—five years.

Use of the ADS means that instead of accelerating depreciation deductions to the earlier years of ownership, depreciation deductions will be spread evenly over the recovery period of the property.

Note

Weigh carefully an election to use ADS. If you make the election to use ADS, you cannot later change your mind.

Putting Personal Property to Business Use

You may already own some items that can be useful to your business, such as a home computer, office furniture, and a cell phone. You don't have to go out and buy new items for the business; you can convert what you already own from personal to business use.

For depreciation purposes, the basis of each item is the lower of its adjusted basis (usually its cost) or its value at the time of conversion. For most items that decline in value over time, this means that depreciation is usually based on value. But for other property, such as realty that typically increases in value, depreciation is usually based on adjusted basis.

Example

In 2003, you purchased a computer for home use at a cost of $3,000. In 2005, you start a business and begin to use the computer for business activities. Its value in 2005 is $1,000. For depreciation purposes, you are limited to $1,000; in this case the computer's value is lower than its adjusted basis.

Example

In 2003, you bought your home for $200,000. In 2005, you start a business from home and use 10 percent of the space exclusively for this purpose. The house is now worth $240,000. For depreciation purposes, you are limited to $20,000 (10 percent of $200,000); in this case the adjusted basis is lower than the home's current value.

You cannot use first-year expensing for property you convert from personal to business use in a year that is after the year you acquired the property. The law limits expensing to the year in which property is initially placed in service (and that is usually prior to the year it is first used in business).

Amortization

Certain capital expenditures can be deducted over a term of years. This is called *amortization*. This deduction is taken evenly over a prescribed period of time. Amortization applies only to the following expenditures:

- Intangibles acquired on the purchase of a business
- Business start-up costs and organizational expenses
- Construction period interest and taxes
- Research and experimentation costs
- Bond premiums
- Reforestation costs
- Pollution control facilities
- Costs of acquiring a lease

Intangibles Acquired on the Purchase of a Business

If you buy a business, a portion of your cost may be allocated to certain intangible items:

- Goodwill
- Going concern value

- Workforce in place
- Patents, copyrights, formulas, processes, designs, patterns, and know-how
- Customer-based intangibles
- Supplier-based intangibles
- Licenses, permits, and other rights granted by a governmental unit or agency
- Covenants not to compete
- Franchises (including sports franchises), trademarks, or trade names

These items are called *Section 197 intangibles,* named after a section in the Internal Revenue Code. You may deduct the portion of the cost allocated to these items ratably over a period of 15 years.

Example

You buy out the accounting practice of someone else. As part of the sale, the other accountant signs a covenant not to compete with you for two years within your same location. You may amortize the portion of the cost of the practice relating to the covenant over 15 years.

Section 197 intangibles do not include interests in a corporation, partnership, trust or estate, interests in land, certain computer software, and certain other excluded items. Also, you cannot amortize the cost of self-created items. Thus, if you generate your own customer list, you cannot claim an amortization deduction.

ANTICHURNING RULES. If you already own a business with goodwill and other intangibles, you cannot convert these into Section 197 intangibles, for which an amortization deduction would be allowed, by engaging in a transaction solely for this purpose. Special antichurning rules prevent amortization for intangibles acquired in transactions designed to create an acquisition date after August 10, 1993 (the date on which Section 197 intangibles came into being) for assets that were previously owned as of that date.

DISPOSITIONS. If a Section 197 intangible is sold at a loss but other such intangibles are still owned, no loss can be taken on the sale. Instead the bases of the remaining Section 197 intangibles are reduced by the unclaimed loss. The same rule applies if a Section 197 intangible becomes worthless or is abandoned. No loss is recognized on the worthlessness or abandonment. Instead, the bases of remaining Section 197 are increased by the unrecognized loss.

Self-Created Intangibles

If you create an intangible, such as a trademark, you cannot amortize the costs you incur (e.g., registration fees to the U.S. Patent and Trademark Office and attorney's fees). These costs are capitalized (carried on the company's books as an asset).

Business Start-Up Costs and Organizational Expenses

When you start up a business, you may incur a variety of expenses. Ordinarily these are capital expenditures that are not currently deductible. They are expenses incurred to acquire a capital asset, namely, your business. However, the tax law allows you to write off start-up costs. The timing of your deduction depends on when you started your business.

- For start-up costs paid or incurred before October 23, 2004—you can elect to amortize start-up costs over a period of not less than 60 months.
- For start-up costs paid or incurred after October 22, 2004—you can elect to deduct $5,000 in the first year, with the balance of start-up costs amortized over 180 months. However, if costs exceed $50,000, the $5,000 immediate deduction is reduced dollar-for-dollar, so that no immediate deduction can be claimed when start-up costs exceed $55,000. In this case, *all* start-up costs must be amortized over 180 months.

If you sell your business before the end of the amortization period or the business folds before that time, you can deduct the unamortized amount in your final year.

BUSINESS START-UP COSTS. Generally, you think of start-up costs as expenses you pay during the first few years of your business. But for tax purposes, the term "start-up costs" has a very specific meaning. These include amounts paid to investigate *whether* to start or purchase a business and *which* business to start or purchase (this is called the *whether and which* test for determining amortization of start-up costs). Expenses related to these activities are treated as start-up expenses. Examples of start-up costs include:

- A survey of potential markets
- An analysis of available facilities, labor, and supplies
- Advertisements for the opening of the business
- Travel and other expenses incurred to get prospective distributors, suppliers, or customers
- Salaries and fees for consultants and executives, and fees for professional services

Other similar expenses are amortizable if they would have been deductible if paid or incurred to operate a going business and were actually paid or incurred prior to the commencement of business operations. Otherwise such expenses must be treated as part of the cost of acquiring a capital asset—the business. For example, legal fees to prepare contracts for the purchase of a business are no longer start-up fees but, rather, are expenses that must be added to the cost of the business.

Once you have passed the start-up phase and identified a target business you want to acquire, you can no longer amortize related expenses under this rule.

Example

You are looking for a business to buy and have your accountant review the financial data from several prospects. You then zero in on one business and examine its financial data in detail. The accountant's fee related to the general search is amortizable, but the fee related to the detailed examination of the target business is not.

ORGANIZATIONAL COSTS FOR A CORPORATION.   If you set up a corporation (C or S), certain expenses unique to this form of business can be written off under the same rules that apply to business start-up costs. These expenses include the cost of:

- Temporary directors
- Organizational meetings
- State incorporation fees
- Accounting services for setting up the corporate books
- Legal services to draft the charter, bylaws, terms of the original stock certificates, and minutes of organizational meetings

You can deduct any other organizational costs if they are incident to the creation of a corporation, they are chargeable to the capital account, and the cost could have been amortized over the life of the corporation if the corporation had a fixed life.

You cannot amortize expenses related to selling stock, such as commissions, professional fees, and printing costs.

ORGANIZATIONAL COSTS OF A PARTNERSHIP.   If you set up a partnership, certain expenses unique to this form of business can be written off under the same rules that apply to business start-up costs. As in the case of corporate organizational costs, partnership organizational costs include those that are incident to the creation of a partnership, are chargeable to the capital account, and would have been amortizable over the life of the partnership if the partnership had a fixed life.

Syndication costs to sell partnership interests are not treated as amortizable organizational costs. These nonamortizable costs include commissions, professional fees, and printing costs related to the issuing and marketing of partnership interests.

Computer Software

There are several different rules for treating the cost of software:

- If it is purchased separately from the purchase of a computer (i.e., it is not bundled with the hardware), the cost can be expensed. Alternatively, if expensing is not elected, the cost can be amortized over 36 months. However, if the useful life of the software is less than 36 months, amortize it over its useful life. If it has a useful life of less than one year (e.g., an annual tax preparation program), deduct it in full in the year of purchase (in effect, the same write-off as expensing but there is no taxable income limitation in this instance as there is for expensing).

- If it is bundled with hardware, depreciate as part of the hardware (generally over five years as explained earlier in this chapter).

- If it is purchased as part of the acquisition of a business, it is amortized as a Section 197 asset over 15 years.

- If it is developed by you for use in your business, treat it as a research and development cost (explained later).

- If it is leased, deduct the lease payments over the term of the lease as you would any other rental expense.

Research and Experimentation Costs

If you have research and experimentation costs, you have a choice of ways to deduct them. You can claim a current deduction for amounts paid or incurred in the year.

Alternatively, you can elect to amortize them over a period of not less than 60 months. Where you do not have current income to offset the deduction, it may be advisable to elect amortization.

You may be able to claim a tax credit for increasing your research and experimentation program. For further information on this credit, see instructions for Form 6765, Credit for Increasing Research Activities. The research credit is further explained in Chapter 23.

Legislative Alert

The research credit expires on December 31, 2005, unless Congress extends it.

Bond Premiums

If you pay a premium to buy bonds (a cost above the face amount of the bonds), you may be required to—or can elect to—amortize the premium. For taxable bonds, there is an election. You can amortize the bond premium or instead treat the unamortized premium as part of the basis of the bond. The bond premium is calculated with the amount that the bond issuer will pay at maturity or the earlier call date if it results in a smaller amortizable bond premium attributable to the period ending on the call date. Do not take into account any premium paid for a conversion feature. (Dealers in taxable bonds cannot deduct the amortizable bond premium.)

For tax-exempt bonds you must amortize the premium. However, you do not deduct the amortizable premium in calculating taxable income.

If you are required or elect to amortize the bond premium, decrease the basis of the bond by the amortizable premium.

Reforestation Costs

If you spend money on forestation or reforestation—planting and seeding, site preparation, and the costs of seeds, tools, and labor—you can elect to deduct up to $10,000 ($5,000 for married persons filing separate returns) in the year paid or incurred.

Costs in excess of the amount deducted are amortized over 84 months. The 84-month period begins on the first day of the first month of the second half of the tax year in which the amortizable basis is acquired.

Example

On January 1, 2005, you incur reforestation expenses of $20,000. You can deduct $10,000 on your 2005 return and charge the remaining $10,000 to the capital account, amortizing the expenses over 84 months. The monthly amortization is $119.50 ($10,000 ÷ 84). The amortization deduction on your 2005 return is $714.30 ($119.50 × 6 months). In 2006, your amortization deduction is $1,434 ($119.50 × 12 months).

Pollution Control Facilities

If you set up a pollution control facility for a plant or other property in operation before 1976, you can elect to amortize your costs over a period of 60 months. A certified pollution control facility is depreciable property that is a new identifiable treatment facility used to abate or control water or atmospheric pollution or contamination by removing, altering, disposing of, storing, or preventing the creation or emission of pollutants, contaminants, wastes, or heat. It must be certified by state and federal certifying authorities. The amortizable cost cannot include amounts recovered through its operation, such as through sales of recovered wastes. The certifying authorities will note this fact and limit the amortizable costs accordingly.

Costs of Acquiring a Lease

If you pay a fee to obtain a lease, you can amortize the cost over the term of the lease. The lease term includes all renewal options if less than 75 percent of the cost is attributable to the term of the lease remaining on the acquisition date. The remaining term of the lease on the acquisition date does not include any period for which the lease may be subsequently renewed, extended, or continued under an option exercisable by the lessee.

Depletion

Depletion is a deduction allowed for certain mineral properties or timber to compensate the owner for the use of these resources. *Mineral properties* include oil and gas wells, mines, other natural deposits, and standing timber. In order to claim depletion, you must be an owner or operator with an economic interest in the mineral deposits or standing timber. This means that you are adversely affected economically when mineral properties or standing timber is mined or cut. Depletion is claimed separately for each mineral property, which is each mineral deposit in each separate tract or parcel of land. Timber property is each tract or block representing a separate timber account.

Note

Claiming depletion may result in alternative minimum tax (AMT) both for individuals and C corporations (not otherwise exempt from AMT).

Methods of Depletion

There are two ways to calculate depletion: *cost depletion* and *percentage depletion.*

COST DEPLETION. Cost depletion is determined by dividing the adjusted basis of the mineral property by the total number of recoverable units in the property's natural deposit (as determined by engineering reports). This figure is multiplied by the number of units sold if you use the accrual method of accounting, or the number of units sold and paid for if you use the cash method. Cost depletion is the only method allowed for timber. The depletion deduction is calculated when the quantity of cut timber is first accurately measured in the process of exploitation. Special rules are used to determine depletion for timber, and the deduction is taken when standing timber is cut.

PERCENTAGE DEPLETION. Percentage depletion is determined by applying a percentage, fixed by tax law according to each type of mineral, to your gross income from the property during the tax year (see Table 14.9).

The deduction for percentage depletion is limited to no more than 50 percent (100 percent for oil and gas properties allowed to use percentage depletion) of taxable income from the property calculated without the depletion deduction and certain other adjustments. However, for 2005, percentage depletion on the marginal production of oil or natural gas by independent producers and royalty owners is *not* limited to taxable income from the property (figured without the depletion deduction).

Only small producers are allowed to use percentage depletion for oil and gas properties. If you use percentage depletion for mineral properties but it is less than cost depletion for the year, you must use cost depletion.

Partnership Oil and Gas Properties

The depletion allowance, whether cost depletion or percentage depletion, must be calculated separately for each partner and not by the partnership. Each partner can decide on the depletion method. The partnership simply allocates to the partner his or her proportionate share of the adjusted basis of each oil and gas property. Each partner must keep this information separately. In separate records the partner must reduce the share of the adjusted basis of each property by the depletion taken on the property each year by that partner. The partner will use this reduced adjusted basis to figure gain or loss if the partnership later disposes of the property. (This partnership rule also applies to members in LLCs.)

S Corporation Oil and Gas Properties

The depletion allowance, whether by cost or by percentage, must be computed separately by each shareholder and not by the S corporation. The same rules apply to S corporations that apply to partnerships, with some modifications. To

TABLE 14.9 Percentage for Mineral Properties

Type of Property	Percentage
Oil and gas—small producers	15.0%
Sulfur, uranium, and U.S. asbestos, lead, zinc, nickel, mica, and certain other ores and minerals	22.0
Gold, silver, copper and iron ore, and certain U.S. oil shale	15.0
Coal, lignite, sodium chloride	10.0
Clay and shale used for sewer pipe	7.5
Clay used for flowerpots and so on, gravel, sand, stone	5.0
Most other minerals and metallic ores	14.0

enable a shareholder to calculate cost depletion, the S corporation must allocate to each shareholder his or her adjusted basis of each oil and gas property held by the S corporation. This allocation is made on the date the corporation acquires the property. The shareholder's share of the adjusted basis of each oil and gas property is adjusted by the S corporation for any capital expenditures made for each property. Again, each shareholder must separately keep records of his or her pro rata share of the adjusted basis of each property and must reduce that share by depletion taken on the property. The reduced adjusted basis is used by the shareholder to determine gain or loss on the disposition of the property by the S corporation.

Where to Claim Depreciation, Amortization, and Depletion

All Taxpayers

In general, depreciation, including any first-year expense deduction, is computed on Form 4562, Depreciation and Amortization, regardless of your form of business organization. However, special rules apply to different entities.

If an election is made to use the 150-percent rate for property that could have used the 200-percent rate, you make the election by entering "150DB" in column (f) of Part II of Form 4562.

An election to use ADS is made by completing line 15 of Part II of Form 4562.

If depletion is taken for timber, you must attach Form T to your return.

In general, recapture of the depreciation and the first-year expense deduction is computed on Form 4797, Sales of Business Property, regardless of your form of business organization (explained in Chapter 6).

See Figure 14.1 (pages 326–327) for a completed Form 4562 and an accompanying worksheet to show depreciation for a florist shop business that placed equipment in service in both the current year and in prior years.

Employees

You complete Form 4562 only if you place depreciable property in service in the current year or have amortization costs that begin in the current year. For example, if you buy a laptop computer this year for your work and you want to claim a first-year expense deduction, you must file Form 4562. You do not have to complete Form 4562 if you are deducting job-related car expenses using either the standard mileage rate or actual mileage rate; you need only complete Form 2106, Employee Business Expenses, or Form 2106-EZ, Unreimbursed Employee Business Expenses. Your deductions are then entered on Schedule A as miscellaneous itemized deductions subject to the 2-percent-of-adjusted-gross-income floor.

Self-Employed

You complete Form 4562 only if you place depreciable property in service in the current year, are claiming depreciation on a car (regardless of when it was placed in service), claim a deduction for any car reported on Schedule C or Schedule C-EZ (or Schedule F for farming operations), or have amortization costs that begin in

FIGURE 14.1 Depreciation Worksheet

Description of Property	Date Placed in Service	Cost or Other Basis	Business/Investment Use %	Section 179 Deduction	Depreciation Prior Years	Basis for Depreciation	Method/Convention	Recovery Period	Rate or Table %	Depreciation Deduction
Building	2-2-02	$65,000	100%		$4,793.75	$65,000	SL/MM	GDS 39	2.564%	$1,666.60
Desk and Chair	2-2-02	600	100%	$600	-0-	-0-				-0-
Refrigeration equipment	2-2-02	4,500	100%		3,204.00	4,500	200DB/HY	GDS/5	11.52%	518.40
Work tables	2-2-02	1,200	100%		854.40	1,200	200DB/HY	GDS/5	11.52%	138.24
Cash register	2-2-02	270	100%		192.24	270	200DB/HY	GDS/5	11.52%	31.10
Subtotal—2002 Property										2,354.34
Delivery truck	4-16-03	31,500	100%	31,500	-0-	-0-				-0-
Typewriter	7-3-03	300	100%		103.14	300	150DB/HY	ADS/6	16.41%	49.23
Subtotal—2003 Property										49.23
Computer	6-21-05	3,000	100%	3,000	-0-	-0-				-0-
File Cabinets	9-9-05	475	100%	475	-0-	-0-				-0-
Store counters	11-1-05	1,870	100%	1,870	-0-	-0-				-0-
Van	11-16-05	32,500	100%	32,500	-0-	-0-				-0-
Subtotal—2005 Property				37,845						
Grand Total—2005				$37,845						$2,354.34

Form **4562**	**Depreciation and Amortization**	OMB No. 1545-0172
Department of the Treasury Internal Revenue Service	**(Including Information on Listed Property)** ► See separate instructions. ► Attach to your tax return.	2**005** Attachment Sequence No. **67**
Name(s) shown on return	Business or activity to which this form relates	Identifying number

Part I **Election To Expense Certain Property Under Section 179**
Note: *If you have any listed property, complete Part V before you complete Part I.*

1	Maximum amount. See the instructions for a higher limit for certain businesses	1	$105,000
2	Total cost of section 179 property placed in service (see instructions)	2	
3	Threshold cost of section 179 property before reduction in limitation	3	$420,000
4	Reduction in limitation. Subtract line 3 from line 2. If zero or less, enter -0-	4	
5	Dollar limitation for tax year. Subtract line 4 from line 1. If zero or less, enter -0-. If married filing separately, see instructions	5	

	(a) Description of property	**(b)** Cost (business use only)	**(c)** Elected cost
6			

7	Listed property. Enter the amount from line 29	7	
8	Total elected cost of section 179 property. Add amounts in column (c), lines 6 and 7 . . .	8	
9	Tentative deduction. Enter the **smaller** of line 5 or line 8.	9	
10	Carryover of disallowed deduction from line 13 of your 2004 Form 4562	10	
11	Business income limitation. Enter the smaller of business income (not less than zero) or line 5 (see instructions)	11	
12	Section 179 expense deduction. Add lines 9 and 10, but do not enter more than line 11 . . .	12	
13	Carryover of disallowed deduction to 2006. Add lines 9 and 10, less line 12 ►	13	

Note: *Do not use Part II or Part III below for listed property. Instead, use Part V.*

Part II **Special Depreciation Allowance and Other Depreciation (Do not** include listed property.) (See instructions.)

14	Special allowance for certain aircraft, certain property with a long production period, and qualified New York Liberty Zone property (other than listed property) placed in service during the tax year	14	
15	Property subject to section 168(f)(1) election	15	
16	Other depreciation (including ACRS)	16	

Part III **MACRS Depreciation (Do not** include listed property.) (See instructions.)

Section A

17	MACRS deductions for assets placed in service in tax years beginning before 2005	17	
18	If you are electing to group any assets placed in service during the tax year into one or more general asset accounts, check here . . . . ► ☐		

Section B—Assets Placed in Service During 2005 Tax Year Using the General Depreciation System

(a) Classification of property	**(b)** Month and year placed in service	**(c)** Basis for depreciation (business/investment use only—see instructions)	**(d)** Recovery period	**(e)** Convention	**(f)** Method	**(g)** Depreciation deduction
19a 3-year property						
b 5-year property						
c 7-year property						
d 10-year property						
e 15-year property						
f 20-year property						
g 25-year property			25 yrs.		S/L	
h Residential rental property			27.5 yrs.	MM	S/L	
			27.5 yrs.	MM	S/L	
i Nonresidential real property			39 yrs.	MM	S/L	
				MM	S/L	

Section C—Assets Placed in Service During 2005 Tax Year Using the Alternative Depreciation System

20a Class life					S/L	
b 12-year			12 yrs.		S/L	
c 40-year			40 yrs.	MM	S/L	

Part IV **Summary** (see instructions)

21	Listed property. Enter amount from line 28	21	
22	**Total.** Add amounts from line 12, lines 14 through 17, lines 19 and 20 in column (g), and line 21. Enter here and on the appropriate lines of your return. Partnerships and S corporations—see instr.	22	
23	For assets shown above and placed in service during the current year, enter the portion of the basis attributable to section 263A costs . .	23	

For Paperwork Reduction Act Notice, see separate instructions.   Cat. No. 12906N   Form **4562** (2005)

FIGURE 14.1 *(Continued)*

the current year. Your deductions are then entered on Part II of Schedule C or Schedule C-EZ (or Schedule F). Depreciation and first-year expensing not included in Part II of Schedule C (for cost of goods sold) are entered on a specific line in Part I of Schedule C or as part of total expenses on Schedule C-EZ.

Partnerships and LLCs

You complete Form 4562 only if you place depreciable property in service in the current year, are claiming depreciation on a car (regardless of when it was placed in service), or have amortization costs that begin in the current year. The partnership or LLC decides on the depreciation method and whether to claim a first-year expense deduction. Ordinary depreciation is then entered on Form 1065 and is taken into account in calculating a partnership's or LLC's ordinary income or loss. Depreciation is reported on a specific line on Form 1065 and is reduced by depreciation included in the cost of goods sold. Similarly, depletion (other than on oil and gas properties) is part of a partnership's or LLC's ordinary income or loss and is reported on the specific line provided for depletion.

Amortization items, such as a deduction for organizational expenses, are part of other deductions. An explanation for these items is included in a separate statement attached to the return.

First-year expense deduction is a separately stated item reported on Schedule K, and the allocable portion is passed through separately to partners or members on Schedule K-1.

Depletion of oil and gas properties is also a separately stated item reported on Schedule K. The allocable portion is passed through separately to partners and/or members on Schedule K-1.

S Corporations

You complete Form 4562 only if the corporation placed depreciable property in service in the current year, is claiming depreciation on a car (regardless of when it was placed in service), or has amortization costs that begin in the current year. The S corporation decides on the depreciation method and whether to claim a first-year expense deduction. Ordinary depreciation is then entered on Form 1120S and is taken into account in calculating an S corporation's ordinary income or loss. Depreciation is reported on a specific line on Form 1120S and is reduced by depreciation included in the cost of goods sold. Similarly, depletion (other than of oil and gas properties) is part of an S corporation's ordinary income or loss and is reported on the specific line provided for depletion.

Amortization items, such as a deduction for organizational expenses, are part of other deductions. An explanation for these items is included in a separate statement attached to the return.

The first-year expense deduction is a separately stated item reported on Schedule K, and the allocable portion is passed through separately to shareholders on Schedule K-1.

Depletion of oil and gas properties is also a separately stated item reported on Schedule K. The allocable portion is passed through separately to shareholders on Schedule K-1.

C Corporations

Form 4562 must be completed if any depreciation is claimed (regardless of the year in which the property is placed in service) or if amortization of costs begins in the current year. The depreciation deduction is then entered on Form 1120 on the specific line provided for depreciation. This deduction must be reduced by depreciation claimed in the cost of goods sold or elsewhere on the return. Depletion is entered on the specific line provided for depletion. Amortization is part of other deductions, an explanation of which must be attached to the return.

CHAPTER 15

Advertising Expenses

You may run advertisements in newspapers, on the radio or television, or in magazines or trade journals to sell your products or services. You can deduct these costs, as well as the costs of other promotional activities. At the same time, you will discover that some costs cannot be deducted or that certain costs need to be deducted as another type of business expense.

In this chapter you will learn about:

- Ordinary advertising expenses
- Promotion of goodwill
- Prizes, contests, and other promotional activities
- Help-wanted ads
- Where to deduct advertising expenses

Ordinary Advertising Expenses

Like all other business expenses, advertising costs must be ordinary and necessary business expenses in order to be deductible. They must have a reasonable relationship to your business activities, and they must be reasonable in amount. However, there are no guidelines on what is "reasonable" in amount.

Deductible advertising expenses include the costs of:

- Business cards
- Ads in print or the media (such as newspaper or magazine advertisements, charitable organization publications, radio or television spots, or on-line messages)

- Ads in telephone directories (such as Yellow Page listings)
- Web site costs (e.g., monthly fees to America Online or a point-to-point protocol [PPP] account to provide access to the Internet as well as web-master fees)
- Package design costs that are part of an advertising campaign
- Billboards (rental fees are an advertising expense)
- Signs with a useful life of not more than one year. (Signs expected to last longer than a year can be depreciated, as explained in Chapter 14.)

In the case of signs placed on the sides of cars or trucks, only the cost of the sign is deductible as advertising. The cost of the driving is not an advertising expense (although business use of the car may be otherwise deductible as explained in Chapter 9).

Example

The cost of metal or plastic signs with a life of more than one year have to be capitalized. The cost of restaurant menu folders are currently deductible, since the folders have a life of not more than one year.

Some businesses treat the cost of maintaining their web sites as an advertising expense. The IRS has not yet ruled on whether this treatment is correct. However, if a business uses the site for advertising (e.g., a law firm that posts its areas of specialty and personnel) and not for selling (e.g, a bricks-and-mortar store that posts its online catalog and accepts purchases through the Internet), it seems reasonable to handle the cost in this manner.

Promotion of Goodwill

Expenses designed to create goodwill in the public's eye rather than to obtain immediate sales are also deductible. In fact, the advertising program can be of a long-term nature and still result in an immediate deduction. The IRS has ruled that the ordinary costs of advertising are currently deductible despite the fact that they produce a long-term benefit.

In some instances, design costs may be considered deductible advertising expenses. In one case, the Tax Court said that graphic design costs could be currently deductible as advertising expenses even though they may produce future patronage or goodwill. The IRS has announced its disagreement with this decision so if you claim a deduction for package design costs you may face an IRS challenge.

Example

The costs of installing window treatments in model homes as part of an advertising campaign are currently deductible. The costs are incurred to promote the name of the business.

The cost of distributing a company's samples can be deducted as an advertising expense where the distribution is designed to engender goodwill.

Creating and maintaining a web site is another key way to keep your company name before the public. While there have not yet been any cases or rulings on the extent to which web site-related expenses are deductible, it can certainly be argued that these expenses relate to creating goodwill for the company.

Another type of advertising involves sponsorships of teams. Your business may, for example, sponsor a bowling team or a Little League team. In return for the sponsorship, your company's name is displayed on the team uniform and may also be a part of the team's name. These costs of sponsorship are deductible as advertising expenses.

Free services provided to generate goodwill cannot be deducted as an advertising expense. For example, in one case a doctor provided free medical services and deducted the value of his uncompensated services as an advertising expense. The Tax Court disallowed the deduction because the doctor's labor was not an expense (it was not an amount paid or incurred).

Personal versus Business Expenses

Expenses that smack of a personal nature may still constitute deductible advertising costs when it can be shown that the expenses were incurred primarily for business purposes. The following examples demonstrate when expenses may be considered primarily for business and when they may not.

Example

A restaurant chain owner who maintained show horses for the purpose of advertising the company's name was allowed a current deduction. But an owner who bought a horse, named it after himself, and entered it in shows was not allowed a deduction when he failed to show there was any connection between the horse and his business.

Example

A business owner who invited customers to his child's wedding reception could not deduct the cost for these guests as advertising. The nature of the expense was just too personal and the business aspect of the expense just too attenuated to make the cost a deductible advertising expense.

Example

An attorney was not allowed to deduct the cost of new suits as an advertising expense. He claimed he needed to look good to attract new clients. Again, the expense was personal in nature and so was not deductible.

Example

Costs of car racing by an officer of a computer research and design corporation were not deductible. Again, the expenses were personal in nature. In comparison, a meat processor that sponsored a race car could deduct expenses. The sponsorship allowed the company to display its logo on the car, and track announcers mentioned the car's sponsor during the race.

Lobbying Expenses

In general, the costs of advertising to influence legislation at the federal, state, or even local level are not deductible. Nondeductible expenses include:

- The costs of participating or intervening in any political campaign for or against any candidate in public office.
- The costs of attempting to influence the general public or segments of the public about elections, legislative matters, or referendums.
- The costs of communicating directly with certain executive branch officials in any attempt to influence the official actions or positions of such officials. These executives include the president, vice president, any officer or employee of the Executive Office of the President and the two most senior officers of each of the other agencies in the Executive Office, and certain other individuals.
- The costs of research, preparation, planning, or coordinating any of the activities already mentioned.

Not all lobbying expenses are nondeductible. You can still claim a deduction for de minimis in-house lobbying expenses. These are expenses that do not exceed $2,000 per year to influence legislation or communicate directly with a specified executive branch official. There is also an exception for expenses to influence local legislation, such as decisions by a local council. And, of course, professional lobbyists are entitled to deduct their own business expenses even though payments to them are not deductible.

Some types of goodwill activities may constitute deductible entertainment expenses (see Chapter 8).

Prizes, Contests, and Other Promotional Activities

Amounts paid for prizes, contests, and other promotional activities may be deducted as advertising expenses if you can show that the expenses have a relationship to your business. The amounts expended must be reasonable; they must not be out of proportion to the amount of business expected to be obtained as a result of the prize, contest, or other promotional activity.

Example

A restaurant owner gives away a car to the holder of a lucky-number ticket. These tickets had been distributed to patrons. The cost of the car was a deductible business expense.

Sponsorships of teams and other events can be deducted as advertising expenses (e.g., sponsorship of a tennis match or golf tournament).

Prizes and other awards given to employees are not treated as advertising costs. They are part of compensation (see Chapter 7).

Help-Wanted Ads

Most advertising is designed to sell products or services. However, you may also advertise when trying to fill a position in your company. The cost of running help-wanted ads in newspapers and trade magazines is deductible as an ordinary and necessary business expense. It is not an advertising cost.

If you are out of work and take out an ad in a newspaper to seek a position, again, the cost may be deductible, but not as an advertising expense. Instead, it may be deducted as a cost of finding a job. For a further discussion on deducting job-hunting costs, see Chapter 22.

Where to Deduct Expenses

Employees

An employee generally will not have any advertising expenses. He or she is only in the business of being an employee and need not promote that activity. When an employee takes out an ad in a newspaper or trade journal expressing availability for a new position, this expense may be deductible as a job-hunting expense.

Self-Employed

Advertising costs are deductible on Schedule C. There is a specific line for this type of expense. If you are eligible to file Schedule C-EZ, you claim advertising costs along with other deductible expenses.

Partnerships and LLCs

Advertising costs are trade or business expenses that are taken into account in determining the profit or loss of the partnership or LLC on Form 1065. They are entered in the category of Other Deductions on Form 1065. A schedule is attached to the return explaining the deductions claimed in this category. They are not separately stated items passed through to partners and members. Therefore, partners and members in LLCs report their net income or loss from the business on Schedule E; they do not deduct advertising costs on their individual tax returns.

S Corporations

Advertising costs are trade or business expenses that are taken into account in determining the profit or loss of the S corporation. They are reported on the specific line provided for advertising on Form 1120S. They are not separately stated items passed through to shareholders. Therefore, shareholders report their net income or loss from the business on Schedule E; they do not deduct advertising costs on their individual tax returns.

C Corporations

Advertising costs are trade or business expenses that are taken into account in determining the profit or loss of the C corporation. They are reported on the specific line provided for advertising on Form 1120. The corporation then pays tax on its net profit or loss. Shareholders do not report any income (or loss) from the corporation.

CHAPTER 16

Retirement Plans

The Social Security benefits you may expect to receive will make up only a portion of your retirement income. In order to help you save for your own retirement and to encourage employers to provide retirement benefits to employees, the tax laws contain special incentives for retirement savings. Broadly speaking, if a retirement plan conforms to special requirements, then contributions are deductible while earnings are not currently taxable. What is more, employees covered by such plans are not immediately charged with income. If you have employees, setting up retirement plans to benefit them not only gives you a current deduction for contributions you make to the plan but also provides your staff with benefits. This helps to foster employee goodwill and may aid in recruiting new employees. Dramatic law changes in recent years permit greater retirement savings opportunities than ever before.

The type of plan you set up governs both the amount you can deduct and the time when you claim the deduction. Certain plans offer special tax incentives designed to encourage employers to help with employee retirement benefits. Even though you may be an employer, if you are self-employed (a sole proprietor, partner, or LLC member), you are treated as an employee for purposes of participating in these plans.

In this chapter you will learn about:

- Qualified retirement plans
- Added costs for retirement plans

- Retirement plans for self-employed individuals: self-employed qualified plans, SEPs, and SIMPLE plans
- Salary reduction arrangements
- Individual Retirement Accounts (IRAs), including Roth IRAs
- Comparison of qualified retirement plans
- Nonqualified retirement plans
- Glossary of terms for retirement plans
- Where to claim deductions for retirement plans

For further information about retirement plans, see IRS Publication 560, *Retirement Plans for Small Business,* and IRS Publication 590, *Individual Retirement Arrangements.*

Qualified Retirement Plans

Qualified retirement plans provide retirement benefits and meet stringent requirements under federal law. Some of these laws fall under the jurisdiction of the Treasury Department and the IRS; others fall under the Department of Labor. Qualified plans allow employees to defer reporting income from benefits until retirement while at the same time allowing employers to claim a current deduction for contributions to the plans.

Income earned by the plan is not currently taxed. Eventually it is taxed to employees when distributed to them as part of their benefits.

Types of Retirement Plans

There are two main categories of plans: *defined benefit plans* and *defined contribution plans.*

DEFINED BENEFIT PLANS.   Defined benefit plans predict what an employee will receive in benefits upon retirement. This prediction is based on the employee's compensation, age, and anticipated age of retirement. It is also based on an estimation of what the plan can earn over the years. Then an actuary determines the amount that an employer must contribute each year in order to be sure that funds will be there when the employee retires. The employer takes a deduction for the actuarially determined contribution.

There are, however, variations of defined benefit plans. For example, in a cash balance defined benefit plan, benefits payable upon retirement depend in part on plan performance.

DEFINED CONTRIBUTION PLANS.   Defined contribution plans are more like savings accounts. The employer contributes to an account for each employee. The contribution is based on a defined formula, such as a percentage of the employee's compensation. The account may not really be a separate account. In corporate plans it is a bookkeeping notation of the benefits that belong to each employee. The benefits that are ultimately paid to an employee are based on what the contributions actually earn over the years.

There are a variety of plans under the umbrella of defined contribution plans. The most common is the *profit-sharing plan*. Under this plan, the employer agrees to contribute a percentage of employee compensation to the plan. The allocation is usually based purely on an employee's relative compensation (other factors, such as age, can be taken into account).

Another common plan is a *money purchase plan*. Under this plan, the employer also agrees to contribute a fixed percentage of compensation each year. Perhaps the most popular type of defined contribution plan today is the 401(k) plan (also called a cash and deferred compensation arrangement). The reason for its popularity: Contributions are made by employees through salary reduction arrangements that let them fund their retirement plan with pretax dollars. These employee contributions are called *elective deferrals*. Employers often match to some extent employee elective deferrals as a way of encouraging participation, something desirable so that owners, executives, and other highly-paid employees can benefit.

Regardless of the plan selected, all plans have the same requirements designed to ensure that they do not benefit only owners and top executives but also ordinary workers. Many of these requirements are highly technical. They are explained here so that you will recognize how complicated the use of qualified plans can become. It may be helpful to discuss your retirement plans or anticipated plans with a retirement plan expert.

Businesses that do not want to become involved with the complexities of qualified plans can use simplified employee pensions (SEPs) or savings incentive match plans for employees (SIMPLEs), discussed later in this chapter in connection with plans for self-employed persons.

Covering Employees

A plan will be treated as qualified only if it allows employees who meet certain requirements to participate and receive benefits under it. In general, the plan must satisfy one of three tests. The first test stipulates that the plan must cover at least 70 percent of all **nonhighly compensated employees.** This is called the *percentage test.*

Nonhighly compensated employees All employees who are not treated as highly compensated employees and do not have an ownership interest in the business. These essentially are rank-and-file employees.

Highly compensated employees   These include owners and highly paid
employees earning specified amounts ($95,000 in 2005). These amounts
are adjusted annually for inflation. Thus, the coverage test needs to be
checked annually.

Alternatively, the plan must cover a percentage of nonhighly compensated
employees that is at least 70 percent of the percentage of **highly compensated
employees.** This second test is called the *ratio test.* The third alternative is
called the *average benefit percentage test* (ABP test). This test also looks at
the percentage of nonhighly compensated employees to be sure that there is
no discrimination against them.

Participation

Participation is the right of an employee to be covered by a plan after meeting
certain participation requirements. In order to be qualified, the plan must not
only meet a coverage test but also meet a participation test. The plan must benefit the lesser of 50 employees or 40 percent or more of all employees. If an employer maintains more than one plan, participation must be satisfied by each plan
individually. The plans cannot be grouped together (aggregated) for this purpose.

There are also age and service requirements. The plan can defer participation until the later of the employee attaining the age of 21 or completing one
year of service. A two-year service requirement can be used if there is immediate and full vesting (vesting is discussed later in the chapter).

To ensure that coverage and participation requirements are satisfied,
401(k) plans can rely on a safe harbor. There is a choice (but you must use the
same choice for all participants). You can either:

- Contribute three percent of compensation (whether or not employees
  contribute to the plan).

- Make a matching contribution of 100 percent of employee elective deferrals, up to three percent of compensation, plus 50 percent of the deferral
  in excess of three percent, up to five percent of compensation. This trans-
  lates into the following match contribution percentage:

Employee's Elective Deferral (%)	*Your Match*
0%	0%
1	1
2	2
3	3
4	3.5
5 or more	4

Example

You have a 401(k) plan in which you and your eight employees participate. Table 16.1 shows what you would have to contribute under the safe harbor to ensure coverage and participation based on employee compensation.

TABLE 16.1 Safe Harbor Contributions by Employer (You) for Employees in 401(k) Plan

Employee	Compensation	Elective Deferral	Alternative 1	Alternative 2
You	$90,000	$10,500	$2,700	$3,600
#1	75,000	10,500	2,250	3,000
#2	60,000	0	1,800	0
#3	50,000	1,000	1,500	2,000
#4	40,000	0	1,200	0
#5	30,000	3,000	900	1,200
#6	25,000	2,500	750	1,000
#7	20,000	1,000	600	1,000
#8	20,000	0	600	0
			$12,300	$11,800

To enable you to encourage participation by rank-and-file employees (something especially important to small employers who do not want to make matching contributions as the means of ensuring necessary participation), you are permitted to use automatic enrollment. This means eligible employees are automatically enrolled in your plan and salary reductions fixed by you are contributed to the plan. If they want to opt out or change their salary reduction amounts, they must notify you of their intention.

Vesting

While the plan must permit certain employees to participate and have contributions made on their behalf, employers can, if they choose, require a certain number of years in the plan before benefits will belong absolutely to the participants. This delay in absolute ownership of benefits is called *vesting*. In order for plans to be qualified, employers cannot defer vesting beyond set limits.

For employer contributions not tied to employee elective deferrals, a plan can provide for *cliff vesting.* Under this type of vesting, there is no ownership of benefits before the completion of five years in the plan. At the end of five years, all benefits are fully owned by the employee.

The other vesting schedule is called *seven-year graded vesting.* This permits vesting of 20 percent of benefits after three years of service, with an additional 20 percent vesting for each year thereafter. Under this vesting schedule, there is full vesting after seven years of participation in the plan.

If a plan is weighted toward owners and highly compensated employees, it may be treated as a top-heavy plan even though it satisfies the coverage and participation tests discussed earlier. A top-heavy plan requires more rapid vesting for participants. Cliff vesting must result after three years of participation. Alternatively, there is a six-year graded vesting schedule.

For employer matching of employee elective deferrals, you must choose either of these alternatives: (1) 100 percent vesting after three years or (2) 20 percent vesting after two years of service, 40 percent after three years, 60 percent after four years, 80 percent after five years, with full vesting after six years.

Permitted Disparity

An employer can reduce the cost of covering employees by integrating the plan with Social Security. This means that the employer can take into account the employer contribution to Social Security for each participant. In effect, the employer's contribution to Social Security is treated as the plan contribution so the employer saves the cost of having to make this contribution a second time to a qualified plan. The employer payment of Social Security tax for each participant is deducted as taxes, not as a pension plan contribution.

Ordinarily the disparity in contributions to employees is viewed as discriminatory. But integrating Social Security contributions with plan contributions is viewed as permitted disparity (i.e., is not discriminatory). The rules for permitted disparity are highly complex, and different rules apply to defined benefit plans and defined contribution plans.

Obtaining and Maintaining Plan Approval

Your plan must be qualified and only the IRS can tell you if your plan falls within this category. You can use a master or prototype plan for setting up your retirement plan. Plans following these prototypes generally meet IRS requirements, although they are not deemed to have automatic IRS approval. If you design your own plan (or have a professional design one for you), in order to be qualified, the plan must obtain IRS approval. This approval is granted on the basis of how the plan is written and how it will operate. There is no requirement that you obtain approval prior to operating a plan, but it is a good idea to get it. The process is complicated, and the use of a tax or pension professional is advisable.

After initial qualification, your plan may be amended from time to time. For example, you may wish to make changes in how the plan operates—for example, increasing the percentage of compensation upon which your contributions are based. You must amend your plan to reflect law changes that are continually being made.

Note

Frequently you have an extended period of time to amend your plan documents to reflect law changes. But you must operate your plan in accordance with these new laws as soon as they become effective.

Compensation Limit

Benefits and contributions are based on a participant's taxable compensation reported on an employee's W-2 form. It does not include tax-free fringe benefits or other excludable wages.

The law limits the amount of compensation that can be taken into account. For 2005 there is a $210,000 limit. If an employee earns $225,000, only the first $210,000 is used to compute benefits and contributions.

For the Future

The compensation limit may be adjusted for inflation annually in increments of $5,000.

When both spouses work for the same employer, each can receive a contribution based on his or her respective compensation (up to the compensation limit). In the past, spouses working for the same employer were treated as one unit.

Contribution Limit

The contribution limit depends on the type of plan involved. For defined contribution plans, the 2005 limit is the lesser of 25 percent of compensation or

$42,000. This percentage is the top limit. Plans can adopt lesser percentages for contributions.

For defined benefit plans, there is no specific limit on contributions. Rather, the limit is placed on the benefits that can be provided under the plan. Contributions are then actuarially determined to provide these benefits. For 2005, the plan cannot provide benefits exceeding $170,000 per year, adjusted annually for inflation.

For the Future

The benefits limit may be adjusted annually for inflation in increments of $5,000.

Making Contributions

Contributions to defined benefit plans must be made on a quarterly basis. In order to avoid a special interest charge, contributions made in quarterly installments must be at least 90 percent of contributions for the current year or 100 percent of contributions for the prior year. If contributions are based on the current year, the balance of the contributions may be made as late as the due date for the employer's return, including extensions.

Contributions for defined contribution plans can be made at any time up to the due date of the employer's return, including extensions. In fact, contributions can be made even after the employer's tax return is filed as long as they do not exceed the return's due date. In effect, contributions can be funded through a tax refund.

Example

An employer (C corporation), whose 2005 return is ordinarily due on March 15, 2006, obtains a filing extension to September 15, 2006. The return is filed on June 1, 2006, and a refund is received on August 15, 2005. The employer has until September 15, 2006, to complete contributions to its profit-sharing plan, a deduction for which was reported on the return. The employer can use the refund for this purpose.

Note

Contributions to defined benefit plans subject to minimum funding requirements must be made no later than September 15 (even if there is an extension of time to file the return until October 15).

The only way to extend the deadline for making contributions is to obtain a valid filing extension. For example, an owner of a professional corporation on a calendar year who wants to extend the time for making contributions must obtain an extension of time to file Form 1120, the return for that corporation. To do this, Form 7004, Application for Automatic Extension of Time to File Corporation Income Tax Return, must be filed no later than March 15, the due date for Form 1120 for calendar-year corporations.

Filing Form 7004 gives the corporation an automatic six-month filing extension, to September 15. The corporation then has until September 15 to make its contributions to the plan.

Contributions generally must be made in cash. When cash flow is insufficient to meet contribution requirements (and there are no refunds available for this purpose, as explained earlier), employers may be forced to borrow to make contributions on time. In some instances, contributions can be made by using employer stock.

Borrowing from the Plan

Owners may be able to borrow from the plan without adverse tax consequences. The plan must permit loans, limiting them to the lesser of:

a. $50,000, or

b. The greater of one-half your accrued benefit or $10,000.

The loan must be amortized over a period of no more than five years (except for loans that are used to buy personal residences) and charge a reasonable rate of interest. As an owner, you cannot deduct interest on the loan.

The plan must also allow rank-and-file employees the opportunity to borrow from the plan on the same basis as owners and top executives.

Added Costs for Retirement Plans

In addition to the contributions you make to the plan, there may be other costs to consider. The type of plan you have affects the nature and amount of these added costs.

Whether you have a defined contribution or a defined benefit plan, you may be required to maintain a bond for yourself or someone else who acts as a fiduciary in your plan. You also must update your plan documents so that they reflect the latest law changes.

If you are approaching retirement age and want to obtain the maximum retirement benefits for your contributions (the biggest bang for your buck), you may want to adopt a defined benefit plan. Before doing so, it is important to recognize that these types of plans entail two additional costs not associated with defined contribution plans.

Bonding Requirement

To ensure that you will not run off with the funds in your company retirement plan, leaving participants high and dry, you are required to be bonded if you have any control over the plan or its assets. This includes, for example, authority to transfer funds or make disbursements from the plan. The bond must be at least 10 percent of the amount over which you have control. The bond cannot be less than $1,000, but it need not exceed $500,000.

No bond is required if the plan covers only you as the owner (a self-employed person or a single shareholder-employee) or only partners and their spouses.

Plan Amendments

You are required to keep your plan up to date and operate it in accordance with law changes that are enacted from time to time. The deadline for document compliance for law changes made in 2001 in most cases is the last day of the plan year beginning in 2005.

You may incur professional fees for updating plan documents. If your plan is a prototype plan provided by a bank, brokerage firm, mutual fund, or insurance company, however, there may be no charge for required updates.

If you discover errors in your plan (either in how it is written or how it is being operated), you can correct the errors and avoid or minimize penalties. If you do not take the initiative and the IRS discovers the problems, you can be subject to greater penalties, interest, and even plan disqualification. To correct problems, you can use the IRS's Employee Plans Compliance Resolution System (see IRS Rev. Proc. 2003-44, as modified by Rev. Proc. 2003-72, for details).

Actuarial Costs for Defined Benefit Plans

If you have a defined benefit plan, you must use the services of an enrolled actuary to determine your annual contributions. You must expect to pay for this service year after year.

Pension Benefit Guaranty Corporation Premiums for Defined Benefit Plans

The Pension Benefit Guaranty Corporation (PBGC) is a quasi-federal agency designed to protect employee pension plans in the event that the employer goes under. In order to provide this protection, the PBGC charges annual premiums for each participant in the plan. First, there is a flat-rate premium, which is currently $19 per participant (a different rate applies to multiemployer plans). Then, for underfunded plans of a single employer, there is an additional variable-rate premium of $9 for every $1,000 of under-

funding. (*Underfunding* means that the employer has not contributed sufficient amounts to pay all anticipated pensions that have already vested.)

Legislative Alert

A proposal has been made to overhaul the premium structure for the PBGC,
which includes increasing the flat-rate premium to $30 per participant and
indexing it for inflation.

There is now an online system, call My Plan Administration Account
(PPA), for paying premiums and filing returns. For information, go to
<www.pbgc.gov>.

Plan Start-Up Costs

If you set up a plan, you may be eligible for a special tax credit designed to
encourage small business owners to start retirement plans. A small employer
eligible for the credit is one with no more than 100 employees who received at
least $5,000 of compensation from the company in the preceding year.
However, the plan must cover at least one employee who is not a highly
compensated employee. Thus, a self-employed individual with no employees
who sets up a profit-sharing plan cannot claim a tax credit for any of her start-
up costs.

In addition to the employee requirement, to qualify for the credit you must
not have had a qualified plan in any of the three preceding years.

The credit is 50 percent of eligible start-up costs, for a maximum credit of $500.
The credit can be claimed for three years starting with the year in which the plan
is effective. However, you can opt to first claim the credit in the year immediately
preceding the start-up year based on costs incurred in the preceding year.

Example

Your corporation sets up a 401(k) plan in 2005 and the business qualifies as a
small employer. The corporation can opt to take a credit for start-up expenses
incurred in 2004 on its 2004 return.

The credit applies only to qualified start-up costs. These include ordinary
and necessary expenses to set up the plan, run it, and educate employees about
the plan and participation in it. Qualified expenses in excess of the $1,000
taken into account in figuring the $500 maximum credit can be deducted as
ordinary and necessary business expenses.

The credit is part of the general business credit.

Retirement Plans for Self-Employed Individuals

Self-employed individuals have three main options in retirement plans. First, they can set up qualified retirement plans, which used to be called Keogh plans. These plans may also known by other names. They have been called H.R.10 plans, reflecting the number of the bill in Congress under which qualified plans for self-employed individuals were created. They may also be called Basic Plans or some other name created by a bank, brokerage firm, insurance company, or other financial institution offering plan investments. A second option in retirement plans for self-employed individuals is a simplified employee pension plan (SEP). A third option in retirement plans is savings incentive match plan for employees (SIMPLE).

Self-Employed Qualified Plans in General

Qualified plans for self-employed individuals are subject to the same requirements as qualified plans for corporations. (Banks, brokerage firms, mutual funds, and insurance companies offering plans for self-employed individuals generally may denominate them as Keoghs, basic plans, or simply by the type of plan established, such as a profit-sharing plan.) Like corporate qualified plans, self-employed qualified plans must cover employees of a self-employed person on a nondiscriminatory basis. Also like corporate plans, they are limited in the amount that can be contributed and deducted.

There is an important distinction between self-employed qualified plans and corporate qualified plans: the way in which contributions are calculated on behalf of owner-employees.

Contributions to Self-Employed Qualified Plans

Contributions to all retirement plans are based on compensation. For qualified plans covering employees of corporations, this is simply W-2 taxable wages. For self-employed individuals under self-employed qualified plans, the basis for contributions is a little more complicated. Essentially, the basis for contributions on behalf of owner-employees is net earnings from self-employment. But this is not merely the net profit from your business on which self-employment tax is paid. Net earnings from self-employment must be further reduced by the deduction for one-half of the self-employment tax.

To calculate compensation of the owner-employee, start with the profit from Schedule C or Schedule C-EZ (or Schedule F in the case of farming) or the net earnings from self-employment on Schedule K-1 of Form 1065. For partners, this is essentially your distributive share of partnership income plus any guaranteed payments. Net earnings from self-employment from various activities are totaled on Schedule SE, Self-Employment Tax. After you have your compensation amount, subtract from this amount one-half of the self-employment tax computed on Schedule SE. This net amount is the figure upon which contributions to qualified retirement plans are based.

In order to make contributions on your own behalf, you must have net earnings from self-employment derived from your personal services. If you merely invest capital in a partnership while your personal services are not a material income-producing factor, you cannot make a plan contribution. If you are a limited partner, you cannot base a plan contribution on your distributive share of partnership income. Similar rules apply to members in LLCs. Income received from property, such as rents, interest, or dividends, is not treated as net earnings from self-employment.

CALCULATING YOUR CONTRIBUTION RATE. For self-employed individuals, the contribution rate must be adjusted for the employer deduction on behalf of yourself. This is a roundabout way of saying that the base percentage rate you use to determine contributions on behalf of employees, if any, must be adjusted for determining contributions on your own behalf. To arrive at this reduced percentage rate, divide the contribution rate, expressed as a decimal number, by one plus the contribution rate.

Example

The contribution rate for your profit-sharing plan is 25 percent. You divide 0.25 by 1.25 to arrive at the contribution rate on your behalf: 20 percent.

Remember, the maximum deduction for 2005 contributions cannot exceed the lesser of $42,000 or, $210,000 times your contribution rate.

Example

You maintain a 25-percent profit-sharing plan for your sole proprietorship, of which you are the only worker. In 2005 your net profit reported on Schedule C is $225,000. Your net earnings from self-employment for purposes of calculating plan contributions are $217,612 ($225,000 − $7,388 [one-half of the self-employment tax]). Your contribution is limited to $42,000 (20 percent of $210,000). You cannot base your contribution on your full net earnings from self-employment because of the $210,000 compensation limit and $42,000 deduction limit.

Simplified Employee Pensions in General

Simplified employee pensions, or SEPs, are another type of retirement plan that self-employed individuals can use to save for retirement on a tax-advantaged basis. (Corporations can use SEPs as well.) As the name implies, they do not entail all the administrative costs and complications associated with other qualified retirement plans. There are no annual reporting requirements, as is the case for qualified plans and qualified corporate retirement plans.

Simplified employee pensions are individual retirement accounts set up by employees to which an employer makes contributions, then deducts them. The contributions are a fixed percentage of each employee's compensation. To set up a SEP, an employer need only sign a form establishing the percentage rate for making contributions and for setting eligibility requirements. This is a one-page form, Form 5305-SEP, Simplified Employee Pension-IRA Contribution Agreement (Figure 16.1).

The form is not filed with the IRS. Instead, it serves merely as an agreement under which the employer makes contributions. The employer then instructs employees where to set up SEP-IRAs to receive employer contributions. Banks, brokerage firms, and insurance companies generally have prototype plans designed for this purpose.

The maximum deduction for a contribution under a SEP is essentially the same as for a deferred contribution plan: 25 percent of compensation or $42,000, whichever is less. For contributions made on behalf of self-employed individuals (called owner-employees), this percentage works out to 20 percent. As with other qualified plans, no more than $210,000 of compensation in 2005 can be taken into account in computing contributions.

Covering Employees

You must cover all employees who meet an age and service test. The SEP must cover employees who are 21 or older, earn over $450 in 2005, and have worked for you at any time in at least three out of five years. You can provide for more favorable coverage (for example, you can cover employees at age 18). The compensation requirement of $450 is adjusted annually for inflation in $50 increments.

Employees over the age of $70^1/_2$ can continue to participate in a SEP and receive employer contributions. However, required minimum distributions must also be made to these employees.

Salary Reduction Arrangements

Before 1997, a SEP of a small business (with no more than 25 employees who were eligible to participate in the SEP at any time during the prior year) could be designed so that employees funded all or part of their own retirement plans. Employees agreed to reduce their compensation by a set amount.

Form **5305-SEP** (Rev. March 2002) Department of the Treasury Internal Revenue Service	Simplified Employee Pension—Individual Retirement Accounts Contribution Agreement (Under section 408(k) of the Internal Revenue Code)	OMB No. 1545-0499 Do **not** file with the Internal Revenue Service

_____ makes the following agreement under section 408(k) of the
(Name of employer) Internal Revenue Code and the instructions to this form.

Article I—Eligibility Requirements (check applicable boxes—see instructions)

The employer agrees to provide discretionary contributions in each calendar year to the individual retirement account or individual
retirement annuity (IRA) of all employees who are at least _____ years old (not to exceed 21 years old) and have performed
services for the employer in at least _____ years (not to exceed 3 years) of the immediately preceding 5 years. This simplified
employee pension (SEP) ☐ includes ☐ **does not** include employees covered under a collective bargaining agreement,
☐ includes ☐ **does not** include certain nonresident aliens, and ☐ includes ☐ **does not** include employees whose total
compensation during the year is less than $450*.

Article II—SEP Requirements (see instructions)

The employer agrees that contributions made on behalf of each eligible employee will be:
A. Based only on the first $200,000* of compensation.
B. The same percentage of compensation for every employee.
C. Limited annually to the smaller of $40,000* or 25% of compensation.
D. Paid to the employee's IRA trustee, custodian, or insurance company (for an annuity contract).

_____ _____
Employer's signature and date Name and title

Instructions

*Section references are to the Internal
Revenue Code unless otherwise noted.*

Purpose of Form

Form 5305-SEP (Model SEP) is used by an
employer to make an agreement to provide
benefits to all eligible employees under a
simplified employee pension (SEP) described
in section 408(k).

Do not file Form 5305-SEP with the IRS.
Instead, keep it with your records.

For more information on SEPs and IRAs,
see Pub. 560, Retirement Plans for Small
Business (SEP, SIMPLE, and Qualified Plans),
and Pub. 590, Individual Retirement
Arrangements (IRAs).

Instructions to the Employer

Simplified employee pension. A SEP is a
written arrangement (a plan) that provides you
with an easy way to make contributions
toward your employees' retirement income.
Under a SEP, you can contribute to an
employee's traditional individual retirement
account or annuity (traditional IRA). You make
contributions directly to an IRA set up by or
for each employee with a bank, insurance
company, or other qualified financial
institution. When using Form 5305-SEP to
establish a SEP, the IRA must be a Model
traditional IRA established on an IRS form or
a master or prototype traditional IRA for
which the IRS has issued a favorable opinion
letter. You may **not** make SEP contributions
to a Roth IRA or a SIMPLE IRA. Making the
agreement on Form 5305-SEP does not
establish an employer IRA described in
section 408(c).

When not to use Form 5305-SEP. Do not
use this form if you:

1. Currently maintain any other qualified
retirement plan. This does not prevent you
from maintaining another SEP.

2. Have any eligible employees for whom
IRAs have not been established.

3. Use the services of leased employees
(described in section 414(n)).

4. Are a member of an affiliated service
group (described in section 414(m)), a
controlled group of corporations (described in
section 414(b)), or trades or businesses under
common control (described in sections 414(c)
and 414(o)), unless all eligible employees of
all the members of such groups, trades, or
businesses participate in the SEP.

5. Will not pay the cost of the SEP
contributions. Do not use Form 5305-SEP for
a SEP that provides for elective employee
contributions even if the contributions are
made under a salary reduction agreement.
Use Form 5305A-SEP, or a nonmodel SEP.

Note: *SEPs permitting elective deferrals
cannot be established after 1996.*

Eligible employees. All eligible employees
must be allowed to participate in the SEP. An
eligible employee is any employee who: (1) is
at least 21 years old, and (2) has performed
"service" for you in at least 3 of the
immediately preceding 5 years. You can
establish less restrictive eligibility
requirements, but not more restrictive ones.

Service is any work performed for you for
any period of time, however short. If you are
a member of an affiliated service group, a
controlled group of corporations, or trades or
businesses under common control, service
includes any work performed for any period
of time for any other member of such group,
trades, or businesses.

Excludable employees. The following
employees do not have to be covered by the
SEP: (1) employees covered by a collective

bargaining agreement whose retirement
benefits were bargained for in good faith by
you and their union, (2) nonresident alien
employees who did not earn U.S. source
income from you, and (3) employees who
received less than $450* in compensation
during the year.

Contribution limits. You may make an
annual contribution of up to 25% of the
employee's compensation or $40,000*,
whichever is less. Compensation, for this
purpose, does not include employer
contributions to the SEP or the employee's
compensation in excess of $200,000*. If you
also maintain a salary reduction SEP,
contributions to the two SEPs together may
not exceed the smaller of $40,000* or 25% of
compensation for any employee.

You are not required to make contributions
every year, but when you do, you must
contribute to the SEP-IRAs of all eligible
employees who actually performed services
during the year of the contribution. This
includes eligible employees who die or quit
working before the contribution is made.

Contributions cannot discriminate in favor
of highly compensated employees. Also, you
may not integrate your SEP contributions
with, or offset them by, contributions made
under the Federal Insurance Contributions Act
(FICA).

If this SEP is intended to meet the
top-heavy minimum contribution rules of
section 416, but it does not cover all your
employees who participate in your salary
reduction SEP, then you must make minimum
contributions to IRAs established on behalf of
those employees.

Deducting contributions. You may deduct
contributions to a SEP subject to the limits of
section 404(h). This SEP is maintained on a
calendar year basis and contributions to the
SEP are deductible for your tax year with or

* For 2003 and later years, this amount is subject to annual cost-of-living adjustments. The IRS announces the increase, if any, in a news release, in the Internal Revenue
Bulletin, and on the IRS Web Site at www.irs.gov.

For Paperwork Reduction Act Notice, see page 2.   Cat. No. 11825J   Form **5305-SEP** (Rev. 3-2002)

FIGURE 16.1   Form 5305-SEP

That amount, called an *elective deferral*, was then contributed to the SEP. Employees were treated as not having received the amount by which their salary was reduced so that they did not pay income taxes on that amount. Salary reduction arrangements in SEPs (SARSEPs), were repealed for 1997 and later years. However, employers that had SARSEPs before 1997 can continue these plans, and employees hired after 1996 may participate in these plans. So, for example, if you had a SARSEP plan in 1996, you can continue to fund it with salary reduction amounts in 2005.

Savings Incentive Match Plans for Employees

Self-employed individuals have another retirement plan alternative: Savings Incentive Match Plans for Employees (SIMPLE). These plans are open to **small employers** who want to avoid complicated nondiscrimination rules and reporting requirements. These SIMPLE plans can be used by corporations as well as by self-employed business owners.

Small employers Those employers with 100 or fewer employees who received at least $5,000 in compensation in the preceding year.

Simple Incentive Match Plans for Employees plans may be set up as either IRAs or 401(k) plans. The rules for both types of SIMPLE plans are similar but not identical. Employees can contribute to the plans on a salary reduction basis up to $10,000 in 2005 (plus an additional $2,000 if age 50 or older by the end of the year). Self-employed individuals can make similar contributions based on earned income.

Employers satisfy nondiscrimination rules simply by making required contributions. Employers have a choice of contribution formulas:

- Matching contributions (dollar-for-dollar) up to three percent of employee's compensation for the year. For example, in 2005, if an employee under age 50 earning $35,000 makes the maximum salary reduction contribution of $10,000, the employer must contribute $1,050 (three percent

For the Future

The elective deferral of $10,000 will be adjusted annually for inflation in increments of $500. The catch-up contribution for those age 50 or older by year-end is set to increase to $2,500 in 2006 and be adjusted annually for inflation thereafter in increments of $500.

of $35,000). The maximum matching contribution per employee in 2005 to a SIMPLE 401(k) is $6,300 (100 percent of the matching employee contribution, which is up to three percent of $210,000). However, there is no limit on compensation taken into account for employer matching contributions to a SIMPLE-IRA.

Note

An employer can elect a lower matching rate under certain conditions.

- Nonelective contributions of two percent of compensation (regardless of whether the employee makes any contributions) for any employee earning at least $5,000. For example, in 2005, if an employee's compensation is $25,000, the employer's contribution is $500 (two percent of $25,000). The maximum contribution per employee in 2005 is $4,200 (two percent of $210,000, the maximum compensation that can be used to determine contributions).

Self-employed persons can make employer contributions to SIMPLE IRAs on their own behalf as well as make their own contributions. In effect, they are treated as both employer and employee.

Employee and employer contributions vest immediately. This means that employees can withdraw contributions at any time (although withdrawals prior to age 59½ are subject to a 25-percent penalty if taken within the first two years of beginning participation, and 10 percent if taken after that period).

Employers who want to let employees choose their own financial institutions can adopt SIMPLE plans merely by completing Form 5304-SIMPLE (Figure 16.2). Employers who want to choose the financial institutions for their employees use Form 5305-SIMPLE. Whichever option is chosen, the form is not filed with the IRS but is kept with the employer's records. This form has the necessary notification to eligible employees and a model salary reduction agreement that can be used by employees to specify their salary reduction contributions. Employers who use SIMPLE plans cannot maintain any other type of qualified retirement plan.

Individual Retirement Accounts as a Plan Alternative

If the cost of covering employees is prohibitive for a self-employed individual, neither a qualified plan, a SEP, nor a SIMPLE plan may be the answer. Instead, the self-employed individual may want to use an IRA. In this case, the maximum that can be deducted is $4,000 (plus $500 if the person is age 50 or older by year-end). However, if a self-employed's spouse is a participant in a qualified plan, the self-employed person may deduct $4,000 only if the couple's combined adjusted gross income does not exceed $150,000. The $4,000 deduction phases out as the couple's adjusted gross income (AGI) reaches $160,000. If a self-employed

Form **5304-SIMPLE** (Rev. March 2002) Department of the Treasury Internal Revenue Service	**Savings Incentive Match Plan for Employees of Small Employers (SIMPLE)—Not for Use With a Designated Financial Institution**	OMB No. 1545-1502 **Do not** file with the Internal Revenue Service

_____ establishes the following SIMPLE
Name of Employer

IRA plan under section 408(p) of the Internal Revenue Code and pursuant to the instructions contained in this form.

Article I—Employee Eligibility Requirements *(complete applicable box(es) and blanks—see instructions)*

1   **General Eligibility Requirements.** The Employer agrees to permit salary reduction contributions to be made in each calendar year to the SIMPLE IRA established by each employee who meets the following requirements (select either 1a or 1b):

a   ☐ **Full Eligibility.** All employees are eligible.

b   ☐ **Limited Eligibility.** Eligibility is limited to employees who are described in both (i) and (ii) below:

    (i)   **Current compensation.** Employees who are reasonably expected to receive at least $ _____ in compensation (not to exceed $5,000) for the calendar year.

    (ii)   **Prior compensation.** Employees who have received at least $ _____ in compensation (not to exceed $5,000) during any _____ calendar year(s) (insert 0, 1, or 2) preceding the calendar year.

2   **Excludable Employees.**

    ☐ The Employer elects to exclude employees covered under a collective bargaining agreement for which retirement benefits were the subject of good faith bargaining. **Note:** *This box is deemed checked if the Employer maintains a qualified plan covering only such employees.*

Article II—Salary Reduction Agreements *(complete the box and blank, if applicable—see instructions)*

1   **Salary Reduction Election.** An eligible employee may make an election to have his or her compensation for each pay period reduced. The total amount of the reduction in the employee's compensation for a calendar year cannot exceed the applicable amount for that year.

2   **Timing of Salary Reduction Elections**

a   For a calendar year, an eligible employee may make or modify a salary reduction election during the 60-day period immediately preceding January 1 of that year. However, for the year in which the employee becomes eligible to make salary reduction contributions, the period during which the employee may make or modify the election is a 60-day period that includes either the date the employee becomes eligible or the day before.

b   In addition to the election periods in 2a, eligible employees may make salary reduction elections or modify prior elections _____ _____. If the Employer chooses this option, insert a period or periods (e.g. semi-annually, quarterly, monthly, or daily) that will apply uniformly to all eligible employees.

c   No salary reduction election may apply to compensation that an employee received, or had a right to immediately receive, before execution of the salary reduction election.

d   An employee may terminate a salary reduction election at any time during the calendar year. ☐ If this box is checked, an employee who terminates a salary reduction election not in accordance with 2b may not resume salary reduction contributions during the calendar year.

Article III—Contributions *(complete the blank, if applicable—see instructions)*

1   **Salary Reduction Contributions.** The amount by which the employee agrees to reduce his or her compensation will be contributed by the Employer to the employee's SIMPLE IRA.

2a   **Matching Contributions**

    (i)   For each calendar year, the Employer will contribute a matching contribution to each eligible employee's SIMPLE IRA equal to the employee's salary reduction contributions up to a limit of 3% of the employee's compensation for the calendar year.

    (ii)   The Employer may reduce the 3% limit for the calendar year in (i) only if:

        (1) The limit is not reduced below 1%; **(2)** The limit is not reduced for more than 2 calendar years during the 5-year period ending with the calendar year the reduction is effective; and **(3)** Each employee is notified of the reduced limit within a reasonable period of time before the employees' 60-day election period for the calendar year (described in Article II, item 2a).

b   **Nonelective Contributions**

    (i)   For any calendar year, instead of making matching contributions, the Employer may make nonelective contributions equal to 2% of compensation for the calendar year to the SIMPLE IRA of each eligible employee who has at least $ _____ (not more than $5,000) in compensation for the calendar year. No more than $200,000* in compensation can be taken into account in determining the nonelective contribution for each eligible employee.

    (ii)   For any calendar year, the Employer may make 2% nonelective contributions instead of matching contributions only if:

        (1) Each eligible employee is notified that a 2% nonelective contribution will be made instead of a matching contribution; and

        (2) This notification is provided within a reasonable period of time before the employees' 60-day election period for the calendar year (described in Article II, item 2a).

3   **Time and Manner of Contributions**

a   The Employer will make the salary reduction contributions (described in 1 above) for each eligible employee to the SIMPLE IRA established at the financial institution selected by that employee no later than 30 days after the end of the month in which the money is withheld from the employee's pay. See instructions.

b   The Employer will make the matching or nonelective contributions (described in 2a and 2b above) for each eligible employee to the SIMPLE IRA established at the financial institution selected by that employee no later than the due date for filing the Employer's tax return, including extensions, for the taxable year that includes the last day of the calendar year for which the contributions are made.

* For 2003 and later years, this amount is subject to annual cost-of-living adjustments. The IRS announces the increase, if any, in a news release, in the Internal Revenue Bulletin, and on the IRS's internet web site at www.irs.gov.

For Paperwork Reduction Act Notice, see page 6.   Cat. No. 23377W   Form **5304-SIMPLE** (Rev. 3-2002)

FIGURE 16.2   Form 5304-SIMPLE

individual contributes $4,000 to a Roth IRA, he or she cannot make deductible contributions to an IRA. Individual retirement accounts are discussed later in this chapter.

Salary Reduction Arrangements

Salary reduction arrangements are not limited to SIMPLE plans. Perhaps the most common form of salary reduction arrangement is elective deferrals to regular 401(k) plans. In fact, these plans have become the most popular form of retirement plans in recent years.

These 401(k) plans allow employers to offer retirement benefits to employees that are largely funded by the employees themselves. To encourage employees to participate in the plans (employers cannot force employees to make contributions), employers may offer matching contributions. For example, an employer may match each dollar of employee deferral with a dollar of employer contributions or some other ratio. Employers who offer 401(k) plans must be careful that stringent nondiscrimination rules are satisfied.

Essentially, these rules require that a sufficient number of rank-and-file employees participate in the plan and make contributions. If the nondiscrimination rules are not satisfied, the plan will not be treated as a qualified plan and tax benefits are not available. Explaining the advantages of participating to rank-and-file employees and offering matching contributions are two ways to attract the necessary participation.

Employees who take advantage of elective deferral options cannot deduct their contributions to the 401(k) plan. They have already received a tax benefit by virtue of the fact that deferrals are excluded from taxable income for income tax purposes. They are still treated as part of compensation for purposes of FICA and FUTA.

From an employer perspective, using 401(k) plans can shift the investment responsibility to employees. Instead of making all of the investment decisions, the employer simply has to offer a menu of investment options to employees. Then the employees decide how they want their funds invested. Employees can be as conservative or as aggressive as they choose. Treasury and Department of Labor regulations detail the number and types of investment options that must be offered and what must be communicated to employees about these investment options.

There is a dollar limit on the elective deferral. In 2005 the elective deferral cannot exceed $14,000. The catch-up (additional) elective deferral limit for those who attain age 50 by December 31, 2005, is $4,000.

Those who work for certain tax-exempt organizations—schools, hospitals, and religious organizations—may be able to make elective deferrals used to buy tax-deferred annuities, called 403(b) annuities. The same elective deferral limit applies here.

For the Future

In 2006, the elective deferral limit increases to $15,000 and the additional elective deferral limit for those age 50 and older by year-end increases to $5,000. After 2006, both limits will be adjusted annually for inflation.

One-Person 401(k) Plans

If you work alone, with no employees, can you have a 401(k) plan? The answer is yes, even if you are self-employed. This type of plan may enable you to maximize contributions because you can make both employee salary reduction contributions (elective deferrals) and employer contributions.

Example

You are self-employed, age 45, and have net earnings from self-employment of $140,000. If you have a profit-sharing plan, your contribution is limited to $28,000 (20% of $140,000). But with a one-person 401(k) plan, the maximum contribution of $42,000 can be attained with these earnings (salary reduction contribution of $14,000, plus employer contribution of $28,000). For those with an incorporated business, the maximum contribution is attained with salary of $112,000.

Loans from 401(k) Plans

The rules governing loans from 401(k) plans are the same as those discussed earlier in connection with loans from corporate plans. However, it should be noted that all participants, not just owners, are prohibited from deducting interest on plan loans. But the interest is really being paid to the participant's own account, so the loss of a deduction is not so important.

For the Future

Starting in 2006, 401(k) plans can offer a Roth 401(k) option. Contribution limits are the same as for regular 401(k)s. In fact, you can split contributions among regular and Roth 401(k)s, as long as the total does not exceed the annual limit. Contributions can be made to separate Roth 401(k) accounts with after-tax dollars (rather than salary reduction amounts). Withdrawals are completely tax-free if not made until at least five years have elapsed and you are at least age $59\frac{1}{2}$, are disabled, or use the funds up to $10,000 to pay first-time home-buying costs, withdrawals are completely tax free. Existing 401(k) plans must be amended to allow for Roth 401(k) contributions.

Individual Retirement Accounts

Another retirement plan option to consider is an IRA. There are now three types of personal IRAs to consider for retirement savings: traditional deductible IRAs, traditional nondeductible IRAs, and Roth IRAs. The maximum amount that can be contributed in 2005 is $4,000 (or taxable earned income if less than $4,000). If you have a nonworking spouse, the contribution limit is $4,000 for each spouse (as long as you have earned income of at least $8,000). Therefore the limit is considerably lower than the limit for other retirement plans.

For the Future

The contribution limit for IRAs increases to $5,000 in 2008. The additional catch-up contribution increases to $1,000 in 2006. The $5,000 limit will be adjusted annually for inflation in increments of $500; the $1,000 catch-up contribution limit will not be adjusted for inflation.

In addition to the basic contribution limit, those who attain age 50 by year-end can make additional catch-up contributions. The limit on catch-up contributions to IRAs in 2005 is $500.

If you are self-employed and have more than one business, you must aggregate your business income to determine compensation for purposes of calculating contributions. You cannot base an IRA contribution on a pension or annuity income or income received from property, such as rents, interest, or dividends. (A special rule allows alimony to be treated as compensation for purposes of IRA contributions.)

However, if you are in business and set up an IRA for yourself, you need not cover your employees. For some, this factor alone may dictate in favor of an IRA.

If you are age $70\frac{1}{2}$ and have a business, you cannot make contributions to a deductible or traditional nondeductible IRA. In this instance, you may want to explore other retirement plans, such as the Roth IRAs.

Individual Retirement Accounts and Other Retirement Plans

Whether you can make deductible contributions to both an IRA and another retirement plan depends on your overall income. Individuals who are considered active participants in qualified retirement plans cannot deduct contributions to an IRA if adjusted gross income exceeds a certain amount. More specifically, in 2005 no deduction can be claimed by an active participant when adjusted gross income exceeds $60,000 in the case of single individuals, $80,000 for married persons filing jointly and surviving spouses, or $10,000 for married persons filing separate returns. The deduction is phased out for AGI of up to $10,000 less than the phase-out limit (phase-out starts at $50,000 for singles; $70,000 for married persons filing joint returns). The phase-out limit for married persons filing jointly will increase until it reaches $80,000 to $100,000 in 2007.

You are considered an *active participant* if, at any time during the year, either you or your spouse is covered by an employer retirement plan. An employer retirement plan includes all of the following plans:

- Qualified pension, profit-sharing, or stock bonus plan
- SEP plan
- SIMPLE plan
- Qualified annuity plan
- Tax-sheltered annuity
- A plan established by the federal, state, or political subdivision for its employees (other than a state Section 457 plan)

If you are an active participant (or your spouse is an active participant) and your AGI is over the limit for your filing status, you can make a traditional nondeductible IRA contribution. There is no AGI limit on making this type of IRA contribution.

Alternatively, you may want to make contributions to a Roth IRA. Contributions must be based on compensation (just as they are for traditional IRAs), but there are some important differences between the new Roth and a traditional IRA. First, contributions to a Roth can be made regardless of your age. So, for example, if you have a consulting business and you are 75 years old, you can still fund a Roth IRA. Second, there are no required lifetime minimum distributions, as there are from traditional IRAs commencing at age $70\frac{1}{2}$. Third, contributions can be made regardless of whether you (or your spouse) are an active participant in a qualified retirement plan. Fourth, and most significantly, if funds remain in the Roth IRA for at least five years, withdrawals after age $59\frac{1}{2}$, or because of disability, or to pay first-time home-buying expenses (up to $10,000 in a lifetime) are completely free from income tax.

The five-year period starts on the first day of the year in which contributions are made (or to which they relate). So, for example, if you make a 2005 contribution to a Roth IRA on April 17, 2006 (the due date of your 2005 return), the five-year holding period commences on January 1, 2005, the year to which the first contribution relates. However, you can make Roth IRA contributions only if your AGI is no more than $95,000, or $150,000 on a joint return. (The contribution limit is reduced if your AGI is between $95,000 and $110,000 if you are single, or $150,000 and $160,000 on a joint return.)

In planning to maximize your retirement funds, you may want to convert your traditional IRAs to a Roth IRA if you did not do so already. You can convert if your

AGI is no more than $100,000 (regardless of whether you are single or married as long as you do not file a separate return if married). This will allow you to build up a tax-free retirement nest egg (provided the funds remain in the Roth IRA at least five years and are not withdrawn unless you meet a withdrawal condition). The price of conversion is that you must report all the income that would have resulted had you simply taken a distribution from your IRAs.

In deciding to use a traditional IRA, be aware of certain restrictions designed to encourage savings and prevent dissipation of the account prior to retirement. First, you generally cannot withdraw IRA contributions, or earnings on those contributions, before age 59½. Doing so may result in a 10 percent early distribution penalty. There are a number of exceptions to the early distribution penalty:

- Disability
- Withdrawals taken ratably over your life expectancy
- Distributions to pay medical expenses in excess of 7.5 percent of AGI
- Distributions to pay health insurance premiums by those who are unemployed (self-employed can be treated as unemployed for this purpose)
- Distributions to pay qualified higher education costs
- Distributions for first-time home-buying expenses (up to $10,000 in a lifetime)
- Involuntary distributions resulting from IRS levies upon IRAs to satisfy back taxes

Second, you must begin withdrawals from traditional IRAs no later than April 1 of the year following the year of attaining age 70½. The failure to take certain minimum distributions designed to exhaust the account over your life expectancy results in a 50-percent penalty tax. The minimum distribution requirement applies as well to qualified retirement plans, SEP-IRAs, and SIMPLE plans.

Comparison of Qualified Retirement Plans

The different choices of qualified retirement plans have been discussed at length. But how do you know which plan is best for you? There are several factors to consider:

- How much money do you have to set aside in a retirement plan? If your business is continually profitable you may want to commit to a type of plan that requires contributions without regard to profits. If your business is good in some years but bad in others, you may want to use a profit-sharing-type plan that does not require contributions in poor years.

- How much will it cost to cover employees? When there are few or no employees, then the choice of plan is largely a question of what will be the most beneficial to you. When a great number of employees will have to be covered, the cost may be too prohibitive to provide substantial retirement benefits. However, if your competitors offer plans to their employees, you may be forced to offer similar benefits as a means of attracting or retaining employees.
- How soon do you expect to retire? The closer you are to retirement, the more inclined you may be to use a defined benefit plan to sock away as much as possible.
- Also consider the costs of administration, the amount of entanglement with the IRS, and your financial sophistication and comfort level with more exotic arrangements.

Table 16.2 offers a comparison of the retirement plans.

TABLE 16.2 Comparison of Retirement Plans in 2005

Type of Plan	Maximum Contribution	Last Date for Contribution
IRA	$4,000 or taxable compensation, whichever is smaller ($4,500 for those 50 or older)	Due date of your return (without extensions)
SIMPLE plan	$10,000 (not to exceed taxable compensation), plus catch-up contributions, plus employer contributions	Due date of employer's return (including extensions)
SEP-IRA	$42,000 or 20 percent of participant's taxable compensation, whichever is smaller	Due date of employer's return (including extensions)
Qualified plan	Defined contribution plan— smaller of $42,000 or 20 percent of compensation (20 percent of self-employed's income)	Due date of employer's return (including extensions) Note: Plan must be set up no later than the last day of the employer's tax year.
	Defined benefit plan—amount needed to provide retirement benefit no larger than the lesser of $170,000 or 100 percent of the participant's average taxable compensation for highest three consecutive years	Due date of employer's return (including extensions) but not later than the minimum funding deadline. Note: Plan must be set up no later than the last day of the employer's tax year.

Defined Benefit Plans versus Defined Contribution Plans

Defined benefit plans offer owners the opportunity to slant more contributions to their own benefit, especially if they are older than their employees. However, most small business employers are moving away from defined benefit plans because of the complexities and costs of administration. Defined benefit plans are by far more costly to administer than defined contribution plans. First, there are the costs of plan design. Defined benefit plans may be specially tailored to each employer, whereas defined contribution plans generally use prototypes readily available. Second, there is the cost of the actuary to determine contributions necessary to fund the promised benefits. Third, there are annual premiums paid to the Pension Benefit Guaranty Corporation (PBGC), a federal agency designed to provide some measure of protection for employees (somewhat akin to FDIC insurance for bank accounts). These premiums are calculated on a per-participant basis, with an additional premium for underfunded plans (as discussed earlier in this chapter).

Another factor to consider when deciding between defined benefit and defined contribution plans is the timing of making contributions. Contributions to defined contribution plans can be made at any time during the year to which they relate but can also be made as late as the due date for the employer's return, including extensions. In the case of defined benefit plans, contributions must be made more rapidly than those to defined contribution plans. Defined benefit plans have quarterly contribution requirements, and the failure to make sufficient contributions quarterly can result in penalties.

Qualified Plan versus Simplified Employee Pension

If you use a profit-sharing plan, the contribution limit is the same for both self-employed qualified plans and SEPs. However, there are some reasons for using one or the other type of retirement plan.

A SEP offers a couple of advantages over self-employed qualified plans. A qualified plan must be set up no later than the last day of your tax year, even though contributions can be made up to the due date of the return, including extensions. In contrast, a SEP can be set up as late as the date for making contributions, which is also the due date of your return, including extensions. There is less paperwork involved in a SEP than in a qualified plan. While qualified plans must file information returns with the IRS annually, SEPs have no similar annual reporting requirements.

In the past, qualified plans offered one advantage over SEPs—the ability to use five-year averaging to reduce the tax cost on distributions. This option no longer applies and all distributions are taxed the same as distributions from SEP (i.e., ordinary income).

> **Note**
>
> Those who were born before 1936 can continue to use 10-year averaging to report distributions from qualified plans, an option not open to distributions from SEPs, regardless of the participant's age.

SIMPLE-IRA versus Self-Employed Qualified Plan or SEP

Business owners with modest earnings may be able to put more into a SIMPLE-IRA than a qualified plan. The reason: The employee contribution (which a self-employed individual can also make) to a SIMPLE-IRA is not based on a percentage of income but rather a dollar amount up to $10,000 in 2005 ($12,000 for those age 50 or older). (The 25-percent annual compensation limit applies to employee contributions to SIMPLE-401(k)s.) For example, assume a 40-year-old self-employed individual's net earnings from self-employment are $25,000. The top contribution to a SIMPLE-IRA is $10,750 ($10,000 salary reduction contribution, plus $750 employer matching contribution). In contrast, the contribution limit to a profit-sharing plan or SEP is only $5,000, considerably less than that allowed for a SIMPLE-IRA.

The bottom line is that business owners who want to maximize their retirement plan contributions need to run the numbers to determine which plan is preferable.

Nonqualified Retirement Plans

If you have a business and want to provide retirement benefits without the limitations and requirements imposed on qualified plans, you can use nonqualified plans. Nonqualified plans are simply plans you design yourself to provide you and/or your employees with whatever benefits you desire. Benefits under the plan are not taxed to the employees until they receive them and include them in their income. But the plan must restrict distributions to fixed events (e.g., separation from service, a fixed date, a change in company ownership or an unfortunate emergency) or participants become subject to interest and penalties.

There are no nondiscrimination rules to comply with. You can cover only those employees you want to give additional retirement benefits, and this can be limited to owners or key executives. There are no minimum or maximum contributions to make to the plan. However, because nonqualified plans give you all the flexibility you need to tailor benefits as you see fit, the law prevents you, as the employer, from enjoying certain tax benefits. You cannot deduct amounts now that you will pay in the future to employees under the plan. Your deduction usually cannot be claimed until benefits are actually paid to employees. However, there is one circumstance under which you can deduct these amounts: If you segregate the amounts from the general assets of your business so that they are not available to meet the claims of your general creditors, the amounts become immediately taxable to the employees and thus deductible by you.

How a Nonqualified Plan Works

Suppose you want to allow your key employees the opportunity to defer bonuses or a portion of their compensation until retirement. To do this, you set up a nonqualified plan. These employees can defer specified amounts until termination, retirement, or some other time or event. The employees in the plan must agree to defer the compensation before it is earned. They generally have no guarantee that the funds they agree to defer will, in fact, be there for them upon retirement. If your business goes under, they must stand in line along with all your other creditors. Employees should be made to understand the risk of a deferred compensation arrangement.

Once you set up the terms of the plan, you simply set up a bookkeeping entry to record the amount of deferred compensation. You may also want to credit each employee's deferred compensation account with an amount representing interest. In the past, there had been some controversy on the tax treatment of this interest. One court allowed a current deduction for the interest. The IRS, on the other hand, had maintained that no deduction for the interest could be claimed until it, along with the compensation, was paid out to employees and included in their income. However, that court changed its view and now agrees with the IRS. As long as receipt of the interest is deferred, so, too, is your deduction for the interest.

Rabbi Trusts

This is a special kind of nonqualified deferred compensation that got its name from the original employees covered by the plan—rabbis. The plans provide a measure of security for employees without triggering current taxation on contributions under the plan. Employers are still prevented from claiming a current deduction. These plans have now been standardized, and the IRS even provides model rabbi trust forms to be used on setting them up.

Glossary of Terms for Retirement Plans

The following terms have been used throughout this chapter in connection with retirement plans.

Catch-up contributions Additional employee contributions that can be made only by those who attain age 50 by the end of the year.

Compensation   The amount upon which contributions and benefits are calculated. Compensation for employees is taxable wages reported on Form W-2. Compensation for self-employed individuals is net profit from a sole proprietorship or net self-employment income reported to a partner or limited liability member on Schedule K-1.

Coverage   Qualified plans must include a certain percentage of rank-and-file employees.

Defined benefit plans   Pension plans in which benefits are fixed according to the employee's compensation, years of participation in the plan, and age upon retirement. Contributions are actuarially determined to provide sufficient funds to cover promised pension amounts.

Defined contribution plans   Retirement plans in which benefits are determined by annual contributions on behalf of each participant, the amount these contributions can earn, and the length of time the participant is in the plan.

Elective deferrals   A portion of the employee's salary that is contributed to a retirement plan on a pretax basis. Elective deferrals apply in the case of 401(k) plans, 403(b) annuities, SARSEPs (established before 1997), and SIMPLE plans.

Excess contribution penalty   A six-percent cumulative penalty imposed on an employer for making contributions in excess of contribution limits.

Funding   In the case of defined benefit plans, the amount of assets required to be in the plan in order to meet plan liabilities (current and future pension obligations).

Highly compensated employees   Owners and employees earning compensation over certain limits that are adjusted annually for inflation.

Keogh plans   A term that had been used to designate qualified retirement plans for self-employed individuals (also called H.R.10 plans). This term is no longer in use.

Master and prototype plans   Plans typically designed by banks and other institutions to be used for qualified retirement plans.

Money purchase plans   Defined contribution plans in which the annual contribution percentage is fixed without regard to whether the business has profits.

Nondiscrimination   Requirements to provide benefits for rank-and-file employees and not simply to favor owners and highly paid employees.

Participation   The right of an employee to be a member of the retirement plan and have benefits and contributions made on his or her behalf.

Pension Benefit Guaranty Corporation (PBGC)   A federal agency that will pay a minimum pension to participants of defined benefit plans in companies that have not made sufficient contributions to fund their pension liabilities.

Premature distribution penalty   A 50-percent penalty imposed on a participant for receiving benefits before age 59 ½ or some other qualifying event.

Profit-sharing plan   A defined contribution plan with contributions based on a fixed percentage of compensation.

Prohibited transactions   Dealings between employers and the plan, such as certain loans, sales, and other transactions between these parties. Prohibited transactions result in penalties and can even result in plan disqualification.

Required distributions   Plans must begin to distribute benefits to employees at a certain time. Generally, benefits must begin to be paid out no later than April 1 following the year in which a participant attains age 70 ½. Failure to receive required minimum distributions results in a 50-percent penalty on the participant.

Roth 401(k)s   401(k) plans funded with after-tax dollars that permit tax-free withdrawals if certain holding period requirements are met.

Roth IRAs   Nondeductible IRAs that permit tax-free withdrawals if certain holding period requirements are met.

Salary reduction arrangements   Arrangements to make contributions to qualified plans from an employee's compensation on a pretax basis. In general, salary reduction arrangements relate to 401(k) plans, 403(b) annuities, SARSEPs in existence before 1997, and SIMPLE plans.

Savings incentive match plans of employees (SIMPLEs)   IRA- or 401(k)-type plans that permit modest employee contributions via salary reduction and require modest employer contributions. SIMPLE plans are easy to set up and administer.

Simplified employee pensions (SEPs)   IRAs set up by employees to which an employer makes contributions based on a percentage of income.

Stock bonus plans   Defined contribution plans that give participants shares of stock in the employer rather than cash.

Top-heavy plans   Qualified retirement plans that provide more than a certain amount of benefits or contributions to owners and/or highly paid employees. Top-heavy plans have special vesting schedules.

Vesting   The right of an employee to own his or her pension benefits. Vesting schedules are set by law, although employers can provide for faster vesting.

Where to Claim Deductions for Retirement Plans

Employees

If you contribute to an IRA and are entitled to a deduction, you claim it on page one of Form 1040 as an adjustment to gross income. If you contribute to a salary reduction plan (such as a SIMPLE or a 401(k) plan), you cannot deduct your contribution.

All Employers

To claim the credit for plan start-up costs of small employers, file Form 8881, Credit for Small Employer Pension Plan Startup Costs. The credit is part of the general business credit and so must be entered on Form 3800, General Business Credit, if you have another credit that is part of the general business credit.

Self-Employed

Contributions you make to self-employed qualified retirement plans, SEPs, or SIMPLEs on behalf of your employees are entered on Schedule C (or Schedule F for farming operations) on the specific line provided on the form called, pension and profit-sharing plans. Contributions you make on your own behalf are claimed on page one of Form 1040 as an adjustment to gross income. Contributions you make to an IRA are also claimed on page one of Form 1040 as an adjustment to gross income.

Partnerships and LLCs

Deductions for contributions to qualified plans on behalf of employees are part of the partnership's or LLC's ordinary trade or business income on Form 1065. The deductions are entered on the line provided for retirement plans.

The entity does not make contributions on behalf of partners or members. Partners and members can set up their own retirement plans based on their self-employment income. Thus, if partners and members set up qualified retirement plans, they claim deductions for their contributions on page one of Form 1040.

As a practical matter, small partnerships and LLCs generally do not establish qualified plans for employees, since the partners and members do not get any direct benefit.

S Corporations

Deductions for contributions to qualified plans on behalf of employees other than more-than-2-percent employees are taken by the corporation as part of its ordinary trade or business income on Form 1120S. Enter the deduction on the line provided for pension, profit-sharing, etc. plans. This line includes contributions to nonqualified plans if the corporation is entitled to claim a current deduction for such contributions.

More-than-2-percent owners can set up their own retirement plans. If they do, contributions are deducted on page one of Form 1040.

C Corporations

C corporations deduct contributions to retirement plans on Form 1120. The deduction is entered on the line provided for pension, profit-sharing, etc. plans. This line includes contributions to nonqualified plans if the corporation is entitled to claim a current deduction for such contributions.

Other Reporting Requirements for All Taxpayers

Qualified plans entail annual reporting requirements. If you maintain a qualified plan, you must file certain information returns each year to report on the amount of plan assets, contributions, number of employees, and such (unless you are exempt from reporting). Information returns in the 5500 series are *not* filed with the IRS. Instead, these rules are filed with the Department of Labor's Pension and Welfare Benefits

Form **5500-EZ**

Department of the Treasury
Internal Revenue Service

Annual Return of One-Participant
(Owners and Their Spouses) Retirement Plan

This form is required to be filed under
section 6058(a) of the Internal Revenue Code.

▶ **Complete all entries in accordance with**
the instructions to the Form 5500-EZ.

Official Use Only

OMB No. 1545-0956

2004

This Form is Open to
Public Inspection.

Part I Annual Return Identification Information

For the calendar plan year 2004
or fiscal plan year beginning MM / DD / YYYY and ending MM / DD / YYYY

A This return is: **(1)** ☐ the first return filed for the plan; **(3)** ☐ the final return filed for the plan;

(2) ☐ an amended return; **(4)** ☐ a short plan year return (less than 12 months).

B If filing under an extension of time, check box and attach required information. (see instructions) ....▶ ☐

Part II Basic Plan Information -- enter all requested information.

1a Name of plan

1b Three-digit plan number (PN) ▶ ☐☐☐

1c Date plan first became effective MM / DD / YYYY

Caution: *A penalty for the late or incomplete filing of this return will be assessed unless reasonable cause is established.*

Under penalties of perjury and other penalties set forth in the instructions, I declare that I have examined this return, including accompanying schedules, statements and attachments, as well as the electronic version of this return if it is being filed electronically, and to the best of my knowledge and belief, it is true, correct and complete.

Signature of employer or plan administrator

SIGN HERE ▶ Date MM / DD / YYYY

Type or print name of individual signing as employer or plan administrator

For Paperwork Reduction Act Notice, see the instructions for Form 5500-EZ. Cat. No. 63263R Form **5500-EZ** (2004)

0 3 0 4 0 0 0 1 0 8

v7.1

FIGURE 16.3 Form 5500-EZ

Administration (PWBA) <www.efast.dol.gov>. There are penalties for failure to file these returns on time and for overstating the pension plan deduction.

Plans other than one-person plans must file Form 5500, Annual Return/Report of Employee Benefit Plan, each year. The return is due by the last day of the seventh month following the close of the plan year (July 31 of a calendar-year plan).

Those with one-person plans (and their spouses) can use a simplified information return, Form 5500-EZ, Annual Return of One Participant (Owners and Their Spouses) Pension Benefit Plan. This form need not be filed if plan assets at the end of the year do not exceed $100,000. However, if the plan assets exceed $100,000 in any year beginning on or after January 1, 1994, Form 5500-EZ must be filed even though plan assets dipped below $100,000.

For businesses that have defined benefit plans for which premiums must be paid to the Pension Benefit Guaranty Corporation, the deadline for premium payments is October 15 of the year following the end of the year for calendar-year plans of small employers (fewer than 500 participants) (e.g., October 16, 2006, for the 2005 year of a defined benefit plan on a calendar-year basis). Payment is accompanied by PBGC Form 1 or PBGC Form 1-EZ; for details about which form to use, where to file, and more, see <www.pbgc.gov>.

Example

You maintain a profit-sharing plan on a calendar-year basis. In 2004 your plan had $105,000 in assets. In 2005, due to fluctuations in the stock market, your plan assets are only $95,000. You must still file Form 5500-EZ for 2005, because plan assets exceeded $100,000 in a year beginning on or after January 1, 1994.

The return is due by the last day of the seventh month following the close of the plan year. Thus, if the plan is on a calendar year, the return is due no later than July 31 of the following year. Obtaining an extension to file an income tax return generally does *not* extend the time for filing these returns. However, if you are self-employed and obtain a filing extension for your individual return to August 15, you have until the extended due date to file Form 5500-EZ (Figure 16.3). If you do not have a filing extension for your personal return, you can request an extension of time to file Form 5500-EZ by filing Form 5558, Application for Extension of Time to File Certain Employee Plan Returns, to obtain an automatic two-and-a-half month extension (to October 15).

Note

There are no special annual reporting requirements for IRA plans, SEPs, or SIMPLE-IRAs.

CHAPTER 17

Casualty and Theft Losses

Earthquakes in Montana, floods in North Dakota, droughts in New Jersey, hurricanes in the Gulf Coast, ice storms in the Northeast—these are just some examples of the types of weather-related events that can do severe damage to your business property. Terrorist attacks are another means of causing damage to business property. If you suffer casualty or theft losses to your business property, you can deduct the losses. You may also suffer a loss through condemnation or a sale under threat of condemnation. Again, the loss is deductible. Certain losses—those from events declared to be federal disasters—may even allow you to recover taxes you have already paid in an earlier year. And special breaks apply to those who suffered losses in the September 11, 2001, terrorist attacks. But if you receive insurance proceeds or other property in return, you may have a gain rather than a loss. The law allows you to postpone reporting of the gain if certain steps are taken.

In this chapter you will learn about:

- Casualty and theft
- Condemnation and threats of condemnation
- Disaster losses
- Postponing gain on casualties, thefts, and condemnations
- Deducting property insurance and other casualty/theft-related items
- Where to deduct casualty and theft losses and related items

For further information about deducting casualty and theft losses, see IRS

Publication 547, *Casualties, Disasters, and Thefts (Business and Nonbusiness)*; IRS Publication 2194B, *Disaster Losses Kit for Businesses;* and IRS Publication 3921, *Help from the IRS for Those Affected by the Terrorist Attacks on America*.

Casualty and Theft

If you suffer a casualty or theft loss to business property, you can deduct the loss. There are no dollar limitations on these losses, as there are on personal losses. Nor are there adjusted gross income (AGI) limitations on these losses, as there are on casualty and theft losses to personal property.

Definition of Casualty

If your business property is damaged, destroyed, or lost because of a storm, earthquake, flood, or some other "sudden, unexpected or unusual event," you have experienced a *casualty.* For losses to nonbusiness property (such as your personal residence), the loss must fall squarely within the definition of a casualty loss. Losses to business property need not necessarily satisfy the same definition.

The tax law details what is considered a "sudden, unexpected or unusual event." To be sudden, the event must be one that is swift, not one that is progressive or gradual. To be unexpected, the event must be unanticipated or unintentional on the part of the one who has suffered the loss. To be unusual, the event must be other than a day-to-day occurrence. It cannot be typical of the activity in which you are engaged.

EXAMPLES OF CASUALTIES. Certain events in nature automatically are considered a casualty: earthquake, hurricane, tornado, cyclone, flood, storm, and volcanic eruption. Other events have also come to be known as casualties: sonic booms, mine cave-ins, shipwrecks, and acts of vandalism. The IRS has also recognized as a casualty the destruction of crops due to a farmer's accidental poisoning of his fields. Fires are considered casualties if you are not the one who started them (or did not pay someone to start them). Car or truck accidents are casualties provided they were not caused by willful negligence or a willful act.

Note

Business losses are deductible without having to establish that the cause of the loss was a casualty. Thus, if your equipment rusts or corrodes over time, you can deduct your loss even though it does not fit into the definition of a casualty loss (assuming you can fix the time of the loss). The reason for understanding the definition of the term "casualty" is that it determines where the loss is reported. It also comes into play in connection with deferring tax on gains from casualties, as discussed later in this chapter.

Progressive or gradual deterioration, such as rust or corrosion of property, is not considered a casualty.

PROOF OF CASUALTIES.   You must show that a specific casualty occurred and the time it occurred. You must also show that the casualty was the direct cause of the damage or destruction to your property. Finally, you must show that you were the owner of the property. If you leased property, you must show that you were contractually liable for damage so that you suffered a loss as a result of the casualty.

Definition of Theft

The taking of property must constitute a theft under the law in your state. Generally, *theft* involves taking or removing property with the intent to deprive the owner of its use. Typically, this includes robbery, larceny, and embezzlement.

If you are forced to pay extortion money or blackmail in the course of your business, the loss may be treated as a theft loss if your state law makes this type of taking illegal.

If you lose or misplace property, you cannot claim a theft loss unless you can show that the disappearance of the property was due to an accidental loss that was sudden, unexpected, or unusual. In other words, if you misplace property and cannot prove a theft loss occurred, you may be able to deduct a loss if you can establish a casualty was responsible for the loss.

PROOF OF THEFT.   You must show when you discovered the property was missing. You must also show that a theft (as defined by your state's criminal law) took place. Finally, you must show that you were the owner of the property.

Determining a Casualty or Theft Loss

To calculate your loss, you must know your **adjusted basis** in the property.

Adjusted basis   This is generally your cost of the property, plus any improvements made to it, less any depreciation claimed. Basis is also reduced by any prior casualty losses claimed with respect to the property.

You also need to know the fair market value (FMV) of the property. If the property was not completely destroyed, you must know the extent of the damage. This is the difference between the FMV of the property before and after the casualty.

Example

Your business car is in an accident and you do not have collision insurance. The car's FMV before the accident was $9,000. After the accident, the car is worth only $6,000. The decrease in the FMV is $3,000 ($9,000 value before the loss, less $6,000 value after the loss).

How do you determine the decrease in FMV? This is not based simply on your subjective opinion. In most cases, the decrease in value is based on an appraisal by a competent appraiser. If your property is located near an area affected by a casualty that causes your property value to decline, you cannot take this general decline in value into account. Only a direct loss of value may be considered. Presumably, a competent appraiser will be able to distinguish between a general market decline and a direct decline as a result of a casualty. The IRS looks at a number of factors to determine whether an appraiser is competent and his or her appraisal can be relied upon to establish FMV. These factors include:

- Familiarity with your property both before and after the casualty
- Knowledge of sales of comparable property in your area
- Knowledge of conditions in the area of the casualty
- Method of appraisal

Remember that if the IRS questions the reliability of your appraiser, it may use its own appraiser to determine value. This may lead to legal wrangling and ultimately to litigation on the question of value. In order to avoid this problem and the costs entailed, it is advisable to use a reputable appraiser, even if this may seem costly to you.

Appraisals used to secure a loan or loan guarantee from the government under the Federal Emergency Management Agency (FEMA) are treated as proof of the amount of a disaster loss. Disaster losses are explained later in this chapter.

You may be able to establish value without the help of an appraiser in certain situations.

If your car is damaged, you can use "blue book" value (the car's retail value, which is printed in a book used by car dealers). You can ask your local car dealer for your car's retail value reported in the blue book (or look it up at <www.kbb.com>). You can modify this value to reflect such things as mileage, options, and the car's condition before the casualty. Book values are not official, but the IRS has come to recognize that they are useful in fixing value. Of course, if your car is not listed in the blue book, you must find other means of establishing value. Value before the casualty can be established by a showing of comparable sales of similar cars in your area. According to the IRS, a dealer's offer for your car as a trade-in on a new car generally does not establish value.

Repairs may be useful in showing the decrease in value. To use repairs as a measure of loss, you must show that the repairs are needed to restore the property to its precasualty condition and apply only to the damage that resulted from the casualty. You must also show that the cost of repairs is not excessive and that the repairs will not restore your property to a value greater than it had prior to the casualty. Making repairs to property damaged in a casualty can result in double deductions: one for the cost of repairs and the other for the casualty loss.

Example

Severe flooding destroys a business owner's property. He is not compensated by insurance. The IRS, in a memorandum to a district counsel, allows him to claim a casualty loss for the damage as well as deducting the cost of repairs to the property where such repairs merely restore it to its precasualty condition.

The last piece of information necessary for determining a casualty or theft loss is the amount of insurance proceeds or other reimbursements, if any, you received or expect to receive as a result of the casualty or theft. While insurance proceeds are the most common reimbursement in the event of a casualty or theft, there are other types of reimbursements that are taken into account in the same way as insurance proceeds. These include:

- Court awards for damages as a result of suits based on casualty or theft. Your reimbursement is the net amount of the award—the award less attorney's fees to obtain the award.
- Payment from a bonding company for a theft loss.
- Forgiveness of a federal disaster loan under the Disaster Relief and Emergency Assistance Act. Typically, these are given under the auspices of the Small Business Administration (SBA) or the Farmers Home Administration (FHA). The part that you do not have to repay is the amount of the reimbursement. Services provided by relief agencies for repairs, restoration, or cleanup are considered reimbursements that must be taken into account.
- Repairs made to your property by your lessee, or repayments in lieu of repairs.

What happens if you have not received an insurance settlement by the time you must file your return? If there is a reasonable expectation that you will receive a settlement, you treat the anticipated settlement as if you had already received it. In other words, you take the expected insurance proceeds into account in calculating your loss. Should it later turn out that you received more or less than you anticipated, adjustments are required in the year you actually receive the insurance proceeds, as explained later in this chapter.

If the amount of insurance proceeds or other reimbursements is greater than the adjusted basis of your property, you do not have a loss. Instead, you have a gain as a result of your casualty or theft loss. How can this be, you might ask? Why should a loss of property turn out to be a gain for tax purposes? Remember that your adjusted basis for business property in many instances reflects deductions for depreciation. This brings your basis down. But your insurance may be based on the value of the property, not its basis to you.

Therefore, if your basis has been adjusted downward for depreciation but the value of the property has remained constant or increased, your insurance proceeds may produce a gain for you. Gain and how to postpone it are discussed later in this chapter.

CALCULATING LOSS WHEN PROPERTY IS COMPLETELY DESTROYED OR STOLEN. Reduce your adjusted basis by any insurance proceeds received or expected to be received and any salvage value to the property. The result is your casualty loss deduction. The FMV of the property does not enter into the computation.

If the casualty or theft involves more than one piece of property, you must determine the loss (or gain) for each item separately. If your reimbursement is paid in a lump sum and there is no allocation among the items, you must make an allocation. The allocation is based on the items' FMV before the casualty.

> ### Example
>
> Your machine is completely destroyed by a flood. You have no flood insurance, and the destroyed machine has no salvage value. The adjusted basis of the machine is $6,000. Your casualty loss is $6,000 (adjusted basis of the property [$6,000], less insurance proceeds [zero]).

CALCULATING LOSS WHEN PROPERTY IS PARTIALLY DESTROYED. Calculate the difference between the FMV of the property before and after the casualty. Reduce this by any insurance proceeds. Compare this figure with your adjusted basis in the property, less any insurance proceeds. Your casualty loss is the smaller of these two figures.

> ### Example
>
> Your machine is damaged as a result of a flood. You do not have flood insurance. The machine is valued at $8,000 before the flood and $3,000 after it. Your adjusted basis in the machine is $6,000. Your loss is $5,000, the difference between the FMV of the machine before and after the flood, which is smaller than your adjusted basis.

If you lease property from someone else (e.g., if you lease a car used for business), your loss is limited to the difference between the insurance proceeds you receive, or expect to receive, and the amount you must pay to repair the property.

Inventory and Crops

You cannot deduct a loss with respect to inventory or crops damaged or destroyed by a casualty. Your inventory account is simply adjusted for the loss. In the case of crops, the cost of raising them has already been deducted, so no additional deduction is allowed if they are damaged or destroyed by a casualty.

Recovered Property

What happens if you deduct a loss for stolen property and the property is later recovered? Do you have to go back and amend the earlier return on which the theft loss was taken? The answer is no. Instead, you report the recovered property as income in the year of recovery.

But what if the property is not recovered in good shape or is only partially recovered? In this instance, you must recalculate your loss. You use the smaller of the property's adjusted basis or the decrease in the FMV from the time it was stolen until you recovered it. This smaller amount is your recalculated loss. If your recalculated loss is less than the loss you deducted, you report the difference as income in the year of recovery. The amount of income that you must report is limited to the amount of loss that reduced your tax in the earlier year.

Insurance Received (or Not Received) in a Later Year

If you had anticipated the receipt of insurance proceeds or other property and took that anticipated amount into account when calculating your loss but later receive more (or less) than you anticipated, you must account for this discrepancy. As with recovered stolen property, you do not go back to the year of loss and make an adjustment. Instead, you take the insurance proceeds into account in the year of actual receipt.

If you receive more than you had expected (by way of insurance or otherwise), you report the extra amount as income in the year of receipt. You do not have to recalculate your original loss deduction. The additional amount is reported as ordinary income to the extent that the deduction in the earlier year produced a tax reduction. If the additional insurance or other reimbursement, when combined with what has already been received, exceeds the adjusted basis of your property, you now have a gain as a result of the casualty or theft. The gain is reported in the year you receive the additional reimbursement. However, you may be able to postpone reporting the gain, as discussed later in this chapter.

If you receive less than you had anticipated, you have an additional loss. The additional loss is claimed in the year in which you receive the additional amount.

Example

In 2005, your business car was completely destroyed in an accident. Your adjusted basis in the car was $8,000. The car had a value of $10,000 before the accident and no value after the accident. You expected the driver responsible for the accident to pay for the damage. In fact, a jury awarded you the full extent of your loss. However, in 2006, you learn that the other driver will not pay the judgment and does not have any property against which you can enforce your judgment. In this instance, you have received less than you anticipated. You do not recalculate your 2005 taxes. Instead, you deduct your loss (limited to your adjusted basis of $8,000) in 2006.

Basis

If your property is partially destroyed in a casualty, you must adjust the basis of the property:

- Decrease basis by insurance proceeds or other reimbursements and loss deductions claimed.
- Increase basis by improvements or repairs made to the property to rebuild or restore it.

Year of the Loss

In general, the loss can be claimed only in the year in which the casualty or other event occurs. However, in the case of the theft, the loss is treated as having occurred in the year in which it is discovered.

Condemnations and Threats of Condemnation

The government can take your property for public use if it compensates you for your loss. The process by which the government exercises its right of eminent domain to take your property for public use is called *condemnation*. In a sense, you are being forced to sell your property at a price essentially fixed by the government. You can usually negotiate a price; sometimes you are forced to seek a court action and have the court fix the price paid to you. Typically, an owner is paid cash or receives other property upon condemnation of property.

Sometimes the probability of a condemnation becomes known through reports in a newspaper or other news medium or proposals at a town council meeting. For example, there may be talk of a new road or the widening of an existing road that will affect your property. If you do not voluntarily sell your property, the government will simply go through the process of condemnation.

Where there is a condemnation, you may also voluntarily sell other property. If the other property has an economic relationship to the condemned property, the voluntary sale can be treated as a condemnation.

Not every condemnation qualifies for special tax treatment. When property is condemned because it is unsafe, this is not a taking of property for public use. It is simply a limitation on the use of the property by you.

For tax purposes, a condemnation or threat of condemnation of your business property is treated as a sale or exchange. You may have a gain or you may have a loss, depending on the condemnation award or the proceeds you receive upon a forced sale. But there is something special in the tax law where condemnations are concerned. If you have a gain, you have an opportunity to avoid immediate tax on the gain. This postponement of reporting the gain is discussed in Chapter 6.

Condemnation Award

The amount of money you receive or the value of property you receive for your condemned property is your *condemnation award.* Similarly, the amount you accept in exchange for your property in a sale motivated by the threat of condemnation is also treated as your condemnation award. The amount of the condemnation award determines your gain or loss for the event.

If you are in a dispute with the city, state, or federal government over the amount that you should be paid and you go to court, the government may deposit an amount with the court. You are not considered to have received the award until you have an unrestricted right to it. This is usually after the court action is resolved and you are permitted to withdraw the funds for your own use.

Your award includes moneys withheld to pay your debts. For example, if the court withholds an amount to pay a lien holder or mortgagee, your condemnation award is the gross amount awarded to you, not the net amount paid to you.

The condemnation award does not include **severance damages** and **special assessments.**

Severance damages Compensation paid to you if part of your property is condemned and the part not condemned suffers a reduction in value as a result of the condemnation. Severance damages may cover the loss in value of your remaining property or compensate you for certain improvements you must make to your remaining property (such as replacing fences, digging new wells or ditches, or planting trees or shrubs to restore the remaining property to its condition prior to the condemnation of your other property).

Special assessments Charges against you for improvements that benefit the remaining property as a result of the condemnation of your other property (such as widening of the streets or installing sewers).

TREATMENT OF SEVERANCE DAMAGES. Severance damages are not reported as income. Instead, they are used to reduce the basis of your remaining property. However, only net severance damages reduce basis. This means that you must first subtract from severance damages any expenses you incurred to obtain them. You also reduce severance damages by any special assessments levied against your remaining property if the special assessments were withheld from the award by the condemning authority. If the severance damages relate only to a specific portion of your remaining property, then you reduce the basis of that portion of the property.

If the net severance damages are greater than your basis in the remaining property, you have a gain. However, you can postpone reporting the gain, as discussed in Chapter 6.

Generally, you and the condemning authority will contractually agree on which portion of an award is for condemnation and which part, if any, is for severance damages or other awards. This allocation should be put in writing. You cannot simply go back after the transaction is completed and try to make an allocation. You may, however, be able to convince the IRS that the parties intended to make a certain allocation if the facts and circumstances support this argument. If there is no written allocation and you cannot convince the IRS otherwise, all of the amounts received will be treated as a condemnation award (and no part will be treated as severance damages).

TREATMENT OF SPECIAL ASSESSMENTS. Special assessments serve to reduce the condemnation award. They must actually be withheld from the award itself; they cannot be levied after the award is made, even if it is in the same year.

If a condemnation award includes severance damages, then the special assessments are first used to reduce the severance damages. Any excess special assessments are then used to reduce the condemnation award.

Disaster Losses

In the past several years, our country has experienced a large number of major disasters, including hurricanes, floods, fires, blizzards, earthquakes, and terrorist attacks. When large areas suffer sizable losses, the president may declare the areas eligible for special federal disaster relief. This disaster assistance comes in the form of disaster relief loans, special grants (money that does not have to be repaid), special unemployment benefits, and other types of assistance. Still, despite all these efforts by the federal government, as well as state, local, and private agencies, you may experience serious disruption to your business and loss to your business property. The tax law provides a special rule for certain disaster losses that will give you up-front cash to help you get back on your feet.

Typically, you deduct your loss in the year in which the disaster occurred. However, you may elect to deduct your loss on a prior year's return, which can result in a tax refund that may provide you with needed cash flow.

Example

In January 2006, you suffer an uninsured disaster loss of $25,000. You may, of course, deduct the loss on your 2006 return, which is filed in 2007 (assuming you are on a calendar-year basis). Alternatively, you may elect to deduct your loss on your 2005 return.

If your loss occurs later in the year, after you have already filed your tax return for the prior year, you can still get a tax refund by filing an amended return for the prior year. For example, if in the Example your loss occurred in December 2006 (after you filed your 2005 return), you can file an amended return for 2005 to claim the disaster loss.

You must make the election to claim the loss on the prior year's return by the later of:

- The due date (including extensions) for filing your income tax return for the year in which the disaster occurred, or
- The due date (including extensions) for the preceding year's return.

Not all seeming disasters qualify for this special tax election. To be treated as a disaster, your loss must have resulted from a casualty in an area declared by the president to be eligible for federal disaster assistance.

If you suffer a loss in your inventory due to a disaster, you need not account for your loss simply by a reduction in the cost of goods sold. Instead, you can claim a deduction for your loss. The loss can be claimed on the return for the year of the disaster or on a return (or amended return) for the preceding year. If you choose to deduct your inventory loss, then you must also reduce your opening inventory for the year of the loss so that the loss is not also reflected in the inventory; you cannot get a double benefit for the loss.

If you suffer a net operating loss (NOL) and you are in a federally-declared disaster area, you can carry the NOL back for three years (rather than the usual two years) to obtain a tax refund (see Chapter 4). Being in a disaster area, such as one of the many counties in the Gulf region declared eligible for federal disaster relief following Hurricane Katrina, may also entitle you to more time to file tax returns and complete other tax obligations. For details on Hurricane Katrina tax relief, see the New Releases for September 2005 at the IRS web site <www.irs.gov/newsroom/article/0,,id=108500,00.html>.

Deducting Property Insurance and Other Casualty/Theft-Related Items

It is well and good that you can write off your casualty and theft losses. But as a practical matter, you should carry enough insurance to cover these situations so that you will not suffer any financial loss should these events befall your business. If you carry insurance to cover fire, theft, flood, or any other casualty related to your business, you can deduct your premiums (see Chapter 21).

If you maintain a home office, you must allocate the cost of your homeowner's policy and deduct only the portion allocated to the business use of your home as part of your home office deduction (as discussed in Chapter 18). Be sure to check your homeowner's policy to see that it covers your business use. You may have to obtain additional coverage if you use your home for certain types of business activities. For example, if clients or customers come to your home, it may be advisable to increase your liability coverage. The cost of additional coverage for business guests (which may be in the form of a rider to your policy) may be rather modest. Similarly, your homeowner's policy may not cover business equipment in your home office, (e.g., computer, fax, or copying machine). Again, a small rider may be necessary to protect you against equipment loss.

If you are a manufacturer who includes business insurance as part of the cost of goods sold, no separate deduction can be taken for these insurance premiums.

If you self-insure to cover casualty or theft by putting funds aside, you cannot deduct the amount of your reserves. In this case, only actual losses are deductible, as explained earlier in this chapter. Self-insurance may be advisable to cover certain casualties that may not be covered by your policy. For example, your policy may not cover damage from civil riots. Self-insurance is also a good idea where you have a high deductible (for example, a state-prescribed deductible for flood insurance in a coastal area). Be sure to review carefully your policy's exclusions (the types of events not covered by your insurance).

Use and Occupancy Insurance

If you carry insurance to cover profits that are lost during a time you are forced to close down due to fire or other cause, you may deduct the premiums. If you then do shut down and collect on the insurance, you report the proceeds as ordinary income.

Car Insurance

The same rule that applies to business property insurance also applies to insurance for your car or other vehicles used in your business. This insurance covers liability, damages, and other losses in accidents involving your business car. However, if you use your car only partly for business, you must allocate your insurance premiums. Only the portion related to business use of your car is deductible. The portion related to personal use of your car is not deductible.

If you use the standard mileage allowance to deduct expenses for business use of a car, you cannot deduct any car insurance premiums. The standard mileage rate already takes into account an allowance for car insurance. Deductions for various types of insurance are discussed in greater detail in Chapter 22.

Appraisals

If your property is damaged by a casualty and you pay a qualified appraiser to establish the FMV of the property in order to prove your damage and the extent of your loss, you claim a separate deduction for appraisal fees. You do not take the appraisal fees into account when calculating your casualty loss deduction.

Where to Deduct Casualty and Theft Losses and Related Items

Employees

Casualty and theft losses to business property are calculated in Section B of Form 4684, Casualty and Theft Worksheet for Individuals. Losses are then netted against gains and are entered on Form 4797, Sales of Business Property. Your losses are entered directly on page one of Form 1040. They are not taken on Schedule A, as are casualty and theft losses to personal property (such as your personal residence). Nor are they limited by the $100 per casualty or 10-percent-of-adjusted-gross-income limitation that applies to casualty and theft losses to nonbusiness property.

If the casualty or theft happened to property used for both business and personal purposes, you must make an allocation. Only the business portion of the loss is free from the $100/10-percent limitations. For example, if you use a car 75 percent for business and 25 percent for personal purposes and the car is totaled in an accident for which you do not have collision insurance, 75 percent of your loss (the business portion) is claimed without regard to the $100/10-percent limits; the other 25 percent of your loss (the personal portion) is subject to both the $100 and 10-percent limits.

Self-Employed

Casualty and theft losses to business property are calculated in Section B of Form 4684. Losses are then netted against gains and are entered on Form 4797. The net result is then entered on page one of Form 1040; you do not enter the amount on Schedule C.

Losses from involuntary conversions are netted against gains and losses from Section 1231 property. This is essentially depreciable property, used in a trade or business and held for more than one year, that is not held for inventory or for sale to customers in the ordinary course of business. (Certain livestock, crops, timber, coal, and domestic iron ore can also be Section 1231 property.) Thus, even if you have a casualty loss, you may not get the benefit of the loss if you have gains from the sale or exchange of Section 1231 property. However, losses to inventory are taken into account in the cost of goods sold.

Partnerships and LLCs

The partnership or LLC reports income or loss from an involuntary conversion (casualty, theft, or condemnation) on Form 4797. The net gain or loss is taken into account when arriving at the total trade or business income or loss on Form 1065 on the specific line provided for net gain or loss from Form 4797.

Even if you are a silent partner in an activity that is treated as a passive activity, casualty and theft losses are not subject to the passive loss limitations. You may claim these losses as long as they are not a recurrent part of the business.

S Corporations

If the S corporation has income or loss from an involuntary conversion (casualty, theft, or condemnation), it must file Form 4797. The net gain or loss is taken into account in arriving at the S corporation's total trade or business income or loss on Form 1120S. Net gain or loss from Form 4797 is reported on the specific line provided on Form 1120S for this purpose.

Even if you are a silent partner in an activity that is treated as a passive activity (a shareholder who does not materially participate in the business), casualty and theft losses are not subject to the passive loss limitations. You may claim these losses as long as they are not a recurrent part of the business.

C Corporations

C corporations report net gains or losses from involuntary conversions on Form 4797 and then use the net amount to arrive at taxable income on Form 1120. Net gains or losses from Form 4797 are reported on the specific line provided on Form 1120 for this purpose.

CHAPTER 18

Home Office Deductions

Today over 40 million Americans work at home at least some of the time, and the number is growing. Computers, faxes, modems, and the information highway make it easier and, in some cases, more profitable to operate a home office. As a general rule, the cost of owning or renting your home is a personal one and, except for certain specific expenses (such as mortgage interest, real estate taxes, and casualty losses), you cannot deduct personal expenses. However, if you use a portion of your home for business, you may be able to deduct a number of expenses, including rent or depreciation, mortgage and real estate taxes, maintenance, and utilities. These are collectively referred to as *home office deductions*. They are claimed as a single deduction item. The deduction is allowed for both self-employed individuals and employees who meet special requirements.

In this chapter you will learn about:

- Home office deductions in general
- Special requirements for employees
- Allocating the business part of home expenses
- Deduction limits
- Special business uses of a home
- Ancillary benefits of claiming home office deductions

- Implications of claiming home office deductions on home sales
- Where to deduct home office expenses

This chapter covers home *office* expenses; however, you need not use your home as an office to claim this deduction. Home office is simply a name assigned to a category of deductible business expenses. For example, you may use your garage to do mechanical repairs, or a greenhouse to grow plants for sale. The expenses related to these uses may be treated as home office expenses.

It has long been thought that claiming a home office deduction is an automatic red flag for an audit. However, there are no statistics to show that this is true. If you meet the tests for claiming a home office deduction as explained in this chapter and you have proof of your expenses, you should have nothing to fear, even if your return is questioned.

For more information about home office deductions see IRS Publication 587, *Business Use of Your Home.*

Home Office Deductions in General

Whether you own your home or rent it, you may be able to deduct a portion of the costs of your home if you use it for business. This is so for both employees and self-employed individuals. However, the law is very strict on what constitutes business use of a home. First, you must use the portion of your home exclusively and regularly for business. Then you must meet one of three tests. The home office must be:

- Your principal place of business,
- A place to meet or deal with patients, clients, or customers in the normal course of your business, or
- A separate structure (not attached to your house or residence) that is used in connection with your business.

Exclusively and Regularly

Exclusive use of a home office means that it is used solely for your business activities and not for personal purposes, including investment activities. If you have a spare bedroom or a den that you have equipped with a computer, telephone, and perhaps a fax/modem, you cannot meet the exclusive use test for a home office if you also use that room as a guest room or family den.

The exclusive use test does not require you to set aside an entire room for business purposes. You can meet this test if you clearly delineate a portion of a room for business. It must be a separately identifiable space. However, you need not mark off this separate area by a permanent partition to satisfy the separately identifiable space requirement.

There are two important exceptions to the exclusive use requirement:

day-care facilities and storage space. Each of these exceptions is discussed later in this chapter.

The home office must also be used on a regular basis for your business activity. This determination is based on all the facts and circumstances. Occasional or incidental use of a home office will not satisfy this requirement, even if such space is used exclusively for business purposes.

Principal Place of Business

Your home office is treated as your principal place of business if it is the place where you conduct your business. It may be your prime activity or a sideline business. As long as it is the main location for the particular activity, it is your principal place of business. Generally this means the location where you earn your money. However, one court has recognized that a musician who spends considerably more time using one room in a home for practice so that she can perform with symphonies and make recordings can treat that room as the principal place of business. It remains to be seen whether this reasoning will be extended to other types of professionals—for example, an attorney who prepares and rehearses his opening and closing arguments in a home office.

Your home office is considered to be your principal place of business if it is used for substantial managerial or administrative activities and there is no other fixed location for such activities.

Example

You run an interior design business, seeing clients in their homes and offices. You use your home office to schedule appointments, keep your books and records, and order supplies. You can treat your home office as your principal place of business because you use it for substantial managerial or administrative activities and you do not have a store front or other office for such work.

Examples of substantial administrative or management activities include:

- Billing customers, clients, and patients
- Forwarding orders
- Keeping books and records
- Ordering supplies
- Reading professional or trade journals and papers
- Scheduling appointments
- Writing reports

Even if you perform administrative or management activities at places other than your home office, you can still take the home office deduction if you fall into one of the following categories:

- You do not conduct substantial administrative or management activities at a fixed location other than your home office, even if such activities are performed by other people at other locations. For example, another company handles your billing from its own place of business.
- You carry out administrative or management activities at sites that are not fixed locations of the business in addition to performing the activities at home. For example, you do these tasks in your car or in a motel room while on the road.
- You conduct insubstantial amounts of administrative and management activities at a fixed location other than the home office. For example, you do minimal paperwork at an office—not your home office—once in a while.
- You conduct substantial nonadministrative and nonmanagement business activities at a fixed location other than a home office. For example, you meet with or provide services to customers, clients, or patients at a fixed location other than your home office.
- You have suitable space to conduct administrative or management activities outside your home but instead choose to use your home office for doing these activities.

Example

Same as the earlier example, but you schedule appointments for your interior design business from your car phone. Because your car is not considered a fixed location, you can still claim a home office deduction.

MORE THAN ONE BUSINESS.　If you are an employee and also conduct a sideline business from a home office, you may deduct your home office expenses for the sideline business. The business activity from the home office need not be your main activity; the home office simply must be the principal place of business for the sideline activity.

However, if you conduct more than one activity from a home office, be sure that each activity meets all home office requirements. Otherwise you may lose out on deductions. For example, if you are an employee and also have a business that you run from your home, if you use the home office for your employment-related activities (and not for the convenience of your employer), then you fail the exclusive use test for the home-based business. You will not be able to deduct any home office expenses even though the home office is the principal place of business for the home-based activity.

Place to Meet or Deal with Patients, Clients, or Customers

If you meet with patients, clients, or customers in a home office, you can deduct home office expenses. The home office need not be your principal place of business. You can conduct business at another location, and your home office can be a satellite office. However, if you use your home office only to make or receive phone calls with patients, clients, and customers, you do not meet this test. While making or receiving phone calls can arguably be viewed as dealing with patients, clients, or customers, the IRS will not view it as such.

This test generally allows professionals—attorneys, doctors, accountants, architects, and others—to deduct home office expenses. Even though they have another office, they can still use a home office and deduct related expenses. Of course, the meeting or dealing with clients and others must be more than occasional; it must be on a regular basis. However, the home office must be used exclusively for business. You cannot use it for personal activities during the time when it is not used for business.

Example

An attorney with an office in the city has a den in her home in the suburbs that she uses to meet with clients on weekends and in the evenings. If the den is also used by her family for recreation, then it cannot be treated as a home office because it fails the exclusive use test. However, if it is used only for regularly meeting with her clients, home office expenses are deductible.

Separate Structure

If you have a separate freestanding structure on your property, you can treat it as a home office if you use it exclusively and regularly for your home office activity. A separate structure may be a garage, a studio, a greenhouse, or even a barn. It need not be an office in order for expenses to be deducted as home office expenses. Nor does the separate structure need be the principal place of your business activity. Further, it need not be a place to meet or deal with patients, clients, or customers in the normal course of your business. It simply must be used in connection with your business.

Example

You own a flower shop in town. You have a greenhouse on your property in which you grow orchids. You can deduct the home office expenses of the greenhouse.

What constitutes a separate structure? The answer is not always clear. In one case, the Tax Court treated a separate structure in a taxpayer's backyard as part of the house itself because of the close relationship to it. If your local real estate law treats a separate structure as *appurtenant* to the house, then it is not a separate structure for purposes of the home office deduction rules.

Examples of separate structures that may qualify as home offices include an artist's studio, a florist's greenhouse, and a carpenter's workshop.

Special Requirements for Employees

Telecommuters take heart. If you use your home for business, you can deduct home office expenses provided your use is for the convenience of your employer. However, this is not an easy standard to satisfy. There is no hard-and-fast rule for proving that your use of a home office is for the convenience of your employer. Neither the tax law nor regulations provide any guidelines.

Your home office use is not treated as being for the convenience of your employer simply because it is appropriate or helpful to your job; there must be a real need on the part of your employer for you to use an office at home. In this age of computers, if your employer allows you to telecommute from a home office because it suits your schedule, this is not necessarily for your employer's convenience. As long as your employer provides you with an office, there must be some other compelling reason for you to use a home office for business. Simply getting a letter from your employer that the home office use is for the employer's convenience may not be enough to satisfy the IRS if your return is questioned. But if your employer has no office space for you to use so that telecommuting is the only arrangement feasible, then clearly such arrangement is for the convenience of the employer. Of course, there may be situations where it is not clear whether the arrangement if for the convenience of the employer. Then, factors such as office space, arrangements with other workers, and other factors must be considered.

If you employ your spouse, you may be able to deduct home office expenses by requiring your spouse to use the home office for your convenience. There have been no cases or rulings testing this arrangement, but if there is a real need on your part for it, the arrangement just might work.

You cannot claim a home office deduction if you rent a portion of your home to your employer and then perform services in it as an employee. If you do rent space to your employer, the rent is still taxable to you.

Allocating the Business Part of Home Expenses

Some expenses of the home office are directly related to business use. For example, if you paint your home office, the entire cost of the paint job is a business expense. Other expenses are indirectly related to business use of your home office; rather, they relate to your entire home. Indirect expenses include:

- Deductible mortgage interest
- Real estate taxes
- Depreciation
- Rent
- Utilities
- Insurance
- General repairs to the home (such as servicing the heating system)
- Security systems
- Snow removal
- Cleaning

Only the portion of indirect expenses related to the business use of your home is deductible. How do you make an allocation of expenses? If you have five rooms and use one for business, can you allocate one-fifth of expenses, or 20 percent, for business? The answer is yes if the rooms are more or less the same size. This is often not the case. If rooms are of unequal size, you allocate expenses based on the square footage of business use. Determine the size of your home; then determine the size of your home office. Divide the size of your home office by the size of your home to arrive at a percentage of business use.

Example

Your home is 1,800 square feet. Your home office is 12 feet × 15 feet, or 180 square feet. Therefore, your home office use is 10 percent (180 divided by 1,800).

Once you have determined your business percentage, you apply this percentage against each indirect expense.

Example

Your business percentage is 20 percent and your total real estate taxes for the year are $5,000. You may treat $1,000 ($5,000 × 20%) as part of your home office deduction. The balance of your real estate taxes continues to be deductible as an itemized deduction on Schedule A.

Example

Your business percentage is 20 percent, and instead of owning your home you rent it. If your annual rent is $12,000, you may treat $2,400 ($12,000 × 20%) as part of your home office deduction. The balance of your rent is not deductible, since it is a personal expense.

You apply the business percentage against deductible mortgage interest. You can include a second mortgage and deductible points in this figure. Again, the portion of your mortgage interest not treated as part of your home office deduction continues to be deductible as an itemized deduction on Schedule A.

Casualty losses may be either an indirect or direct expense, depending upon the property affected by the casualty. If, for example, your home office is damaged in a storm and you are not fully compensated by insurance, you claim your loss as a direct expense. If, however, the damage is to your entire home (such as a roof leak), you treat the loss as an indirect expense. Remember that the limits on deducting casualty losses to nonbusiness property ($100 per incident/10-percent-of-adjusted-gross-income floor) do not apply to business casualties. See Chapter 17 for more information on deducting casualty losses.

If you rent your home, you can deduct the business portion of rent as an indirect expense. If you own your home, you cannot deduct the fair rental value of your home office. However, you can claim depreciation on your home office. See Chapter 14 for more information on depreciation.

Generally, utility expenses—for electricity, gas, oil, trash removal, and cleaning services—are treated as indirect expenses. The business portion is part of your home office deduction; the nonbusiness portion is not deductible. However, in some instances you may be able to deduct a greater portion of a utility expense. For example, if you can show that electrical use for your home office is greater than the allocable percentage of the whole bill, you can claim that additional amount as a direct expense.

The business portion of a homeowner's insurance policy is part of your home office deduction. It is an indirect expense. If you also pay additional coverage directly related to your home office, treat the additional coverage as a direct expense. You may, for example, carry special coverage for your home office equipment (computer, library, etc.). In fact, if you do not now maintain special coverage for home office equipment, you should check your homeowner's policy to see if damage or loss to your business equipment would be covered. You may think your computer is covered, but some homeowner policies may exclude business equipment. Also check whether your homeowner's policy covers personal liability for on-premises injury to patients, clients, and customers who visit your home office. Again, you may have to carry additional insurance for this type of liability.

Repairs may be direct or indirect expenses, depending on their nature. A repair to a furnace is an indirect expense; a repair to a window in the home office itself is a direct expense.

A home security system for your entire home can give rise to two types of write-offs. First, the business portion of your monthly monitoring fees is an indirect expense. Second, the business portion of the cost of the system itself may be depreciated. This depreciation also becomes part of your indirect expenses.

Telephone Expenses

Telephone expenses are not part of your home office deduction. They are separately deductible. However, if you maintain a home office, there is a special rule that limits a deduction for a telephone line: You may not deduct the basic monthly service charge for the first telephone line to your home as a business expense. You can, however, deduct business-related charges, such as long-distance calls for business or call answering, call waiting, and call forwarding. You can also deduct the entire phone bill of a second phone line used exclusively for business. You can deduct any additional lines used for business, such as dedicated fax lines.

Nondeductible Expenses

Not every home-related expense can be treated as a home office deduction. For example, the cost of landscaping and lawn care cannot be treated as a home office expense.

Deduction Limits

Home office deductions cannot exceed your gross income from the home office activity. For those who conduct their primary business from home, this gross income limit poses no problem. Income from the home office activity will more than exceed home office expenses. Thus, for example, if a dentist conducts his or her practice from a home office, there should be no problem in deducting all home office expenses. For those who use a home office for a sideline activity, however, the gross income limit may pose a problem.

What Is Gross Income?

For purposes of limiting home office deductions, *gross income* is income from the business activity conducted in the home office.

Example

A teacher who teaches full-time at school conducts a retail business from a home office. For purposes of limiting home office deductions, gross income includes only the income from the retail business.

To calculate gross income, look to your profit reported on Schedule C if you are self-employed, or the portion of your salary earned in the home office if you are an employee. You can adjust your Schedule C profit for certain items. If you sold your home, the portion of the gain related to the home office increases your gross income for purposes of limiting home office deductions. If you suffer a loss on the home office portion, you reduce your gross income.

If your gross income from your home office business activity is less than your total business expenses, your home office deduction is limited. Your deduction for otherwise nondeductible expenses (such as utilities or depreciation) cannot exceed gross income from the business activity, reduced by the business portion of otherwise deductible expenses (such as home mortgage interest or real estate taxes) and business expenses not attributable to business use of the home (such as salaries or supplies). This sounds rather complicated, but Form 8829, Expenses for Business Use of Your Home, incorporates this limitation. This rule merely orders the categories of deductions.

If, after applying this ordering of deductions, you still have unused home office deduction, you can carry forward the unused portion. The carryforward can be deducted in a future year when there is gross income from the same home office activity to offset it. There is no time limit on the carryforward. You can claim it even though you no longer live in the home in which the deduction arose, as long as there is gross income from the same activity to offset the deduction. Be sure to keep adequate records to support your carryforward deduction.

Special Business Uses of a Home

There are two exceptions to the exclusive use requirement: day-care facilities and storage space. If either of these exceptions apply, you can deduct your home office expenses even though the space is also used for personal purposes.

Day-Care Facilities

If you use all or part of your home on a regular basis as a facility to provide day-care services, you may claim home office deductions if you meet certain tests.

- You must provide day care for children, elderly persons (age 65 and older), or persons who are physically or mentally unable to care for themselves.
- You must have a license, certificate, registration, or other approval as a day-care center or family or group day-care home under your state law.

You can claim home office expenses if you have applied for approval and are awaiting it. You cannot claim home office expenses if your application has been rejected or your approval revoked.

Note: Special rules for meal costs of day-care providers are covered in Chapter 21.

CALCULATING YOUR HOME OFFICE DEDUCTION. If you use a portion of your home exclusively for day-care services (e.g., a basement playroom), you can deduct your expenses for any other type of business use of a home. If, however, you use a portion of your home for day-care services but also use it for personal purposes (e.g., your living room), you must follow special allocation rules to determine your home office deduction. You must compare the business use of the space with the total use of the space. There are two methods for making this comparison:

1. Compare the number of hours of business use in a week with the number of hours in a week (168 hours).

2. Compare the number of hours of business use in the tax year with the number of hours in a tax year (8,760 in a 365-day year).

Then this percentage is applied to the business percentage of total space.

Example

An individual uses her basement to provide day-care services. The basement represents 50 percent of her house's total square footage. She uses her basement for 12 hours per day, five days per week, 50 weeks per year, for day-care services. Her family uses the basement during the times it is not being used for day-care services. She uses her home for a total of 3,000 hours per year for business, or 34.25 percent of the total hours in the year (3,000 ÷ 8,760). In calculating the amount of indirect expenses allocable to her business use, she can deduct 17.13 percent (34.25% × 50%).

If meals are provided as part of the day-care services, the cost of the meals is not included in a home office deduction. It is a separate expense. In calculating the deductible portion of the meal costs, 100 percent of the costs to day-care recipients is deductible. If you also provide meals to employees, only 50 percent of the cost of meals for them is deductible. No percentage of the cost of meals consumed by you or your family is deductible. If you receive reimbursements under the Child and Adult Food Care Program under the U.S. Department of Agriculture, you must include in income any reimbursements in excess of your expenses for eligible children.

Storage

If space is used on a regular basis for the storage of your inventory or sample products, you can deduct home office expenses even though you also use the space for personal purposes and thus fail the exclusive use test. The storage space that is deductible is only the actual space used. For example, if a portion of a basement is used for storage, only the expenses related to that portion are deductible even if the rest of the basement is not used for other purposes.

Expenses of storage space are deductible even though the exclusive use test is not satisfied if:

- The home is the fixed location of the business activity (you run the business from home).
- The business activity is selling goods wholesale or retail.
- The space is used as a separately identifiable space suitable for storage.

Example

An individual runs from home a gift basket business and uses her family room to store samples. She may deduct the portion of the family room used to store her samples even though the family room is also used for personal purposes.

Ancillary Benefits of Claiming Home Office Deductions

Claiming home office deductions means more, tax-wise, than simply deducting the expenses related to that office. It means additional tax benefits may be available.

Having a home office means that travel to and from the office for business is fully deductible (there is no such thing as commuting from a home office). So travel from your home to a customer's location and back again is a fully deductible business expense. Business use of your car is explained in Chapter 9.

Having a home office also means it is not necessary to keep a log of computer use. A computer used in a regular business establishment is not treated as listed property for which an owner must prove business use exceeds 50 percent in order to claim first-year expensing or accelerated depreciation. A home office for which a deduction is allowed is treated as a regular business establishment. First-year expensing and depreciation are explained in Chapter 14.

Impact of Home Office Deductions on Home Sales

Claiming a home office deduction does *not* impact your ability to claim the home sale exclusion (up to $250,000 of gain; $500,000 on a joint return) if you otherwise qualify for it. In the past it had been reasoned that gain on the portion of the home used as a home office would have to be reported. However, recent regulations make it clear that the exclusion can be applied to the home office portion as well, as long as the office is within the dwelling unit.

However, any depreciation taken on a home office after May 6, 1997, must be *recaptured* at the rate of 25 percent (for taxpayers in tax brackets over this amount). This means you must report your total depreciation deductions related to home office use after this date and must pay tax on the total amount at the rate of 25 percent. You cannot use the exclusion to offset this tax.

You cannot avoid this recapture by choosing not to report depreciation to which you are entitled. Recapture applies to depreciation both allowed (the amount you actually claimed) *and* allowable (what you were entitled to claim). If you want to avoid depreciation recapture, you must sidestep the home office deduction entirely by disqualifying your home office. You can do this easily by *not* using the space exclusively for business. By disqualifying your home office, you lose out on depreciation but can still claim many related costs, such as office maintenance and utility costs, as ordinary and necessary business expenses.

Where to Deduct Home Office Expenses

Employees

Employees do not compute their home office deduction on Form 8829, Expenses for Business Use of Your Home. Instead, use the special worksheet in IRS Publication 587, which largely follows Form 8829. You will find this worksheet (Figure 18.1) on page 396.

Your home office deduction is entered on Form 2106, Employee Business Expenses, or Form 2106-EZ, Unreimbursed Employee Business Expenses, if you are otherwise allowed to use this form. Then the deductions from Form 2106 or 2106-EZ are entered on Schedule A as miscellaneous itemized deductions subject to the two-percent-of-adjusted-gross-income floor discussed in Chapter 1.

Remember that if you lease your home to your corporation, you cannot take any home office deductions (other than the mortgage interest, real estate taxes, and casualty and theft losses allowed to all homeowners).

Self-Employed

Self-employed individuals compute home office deductions on Form 8829, Expenses for Business Use of Your Home (Figure 18.2). This form allows you to calculate the portion of your home used for business. This portion, or percentage, is then used to allocate your home-related expenses. You also use the form to calculate any carryover of unused home office expenses.

If you first begin to use your home office this year and you own your home, you must also complete Form 4562, Depreciation and Amortization, to calculate the depreciation deduction entered on Form 8829.

Depreciation is explained in full in Chapter 14. Note that when you begin to use part of your home for business, it is depreciated as nonresidential realty over 39 years

Worksheet To Figure the Deduction for Business Use of Your Home

PART 1—Part of Your Home Used for Business:

1) Area of home used for business . . . . 1) _____
2) Total area of home . . . . 2) _____
3) Percentage of home used for business (divide line 1 by line 2 and show result as percentage) . . . . 3) _____ %

PART 2—Figure Your Allowable Deduction

4) Gross income from business (see instructions) . . . . 4) _____

	(a) Direct Expenses	(b) Indirect Expenses
5) Casualty losses	5) _____	_____
6) Deductible mortgage interest	6) _____	_____
7) Real estate taxes	7) _____	_____
8) Total of lines 5 through 7	8) _____	_____

9) Multiply line 8, column (b), by line 3 . . . . 9) _____
10) Add line 8, column (a), and line 9 . . . . 10) _____
11) Business expenses not from business use of home (see instructions) . . . . . 11) _____
12) Add lines 10 and 11 . . . . 12) _____
13) Deduction limit. Subtract line 12 from line 4 . . . . 13) _____

14) Excess mortgage interest	14) _____	_____
15) Insurance	15) _____	_____
16) Repairs and maintenance	16) _____	_____
17) Utilities	17) _____	_____
18) Other expenses	18) _____	_____
19) Add lines 14 through 18	19) _____	_____

20) Multiply line 19, column (b) by line 3 . . . . 20) _____
21) Carryover of operating expenses from prior year (see instructions) . . . . . 21) _____
22) Add line 19, column (a), line 20, and line 21 . . . . 22) _____
23) Allowable operating expenses. Enter the **smaller** of line 13 or line 22 . . . . 23) _____
24) Limit on excess casualty losses and depreciation. Subtract line 23 from line 13 . . . 24) _____
25) Excess casualty losses (see instructions) . . . . 25) _____
26) Depreciation of your home from line 38 below . . . . 26) _____
27) Carryover of excess casualty losses and depreciation from prior year (see instructions) 27) _____
28) Add lines 25 through 27 . . . . 28) _____
29) Allowable excess casualty losses and depreciation. Enter the **smaller** of line 24 or line 28 . . . 29) _____
30) Add lines 10, 23, and 29 . . . . 30) _____
31) Casualty losses included on lines 10 and 29 (see instructions) . . . . . . 31) _____
32) Allowable expenses for business use of your home. (Subtract line 31 from line 30.) See instructions for where to enter on your return . . . . 32) _____

PART 3—Depreciation of Your Home

33) Smaller of adjusted basis or fair market value of home (see instructions) . . . . 33) _____
34) Basis of land . . . . 34) _____
35) Basis of building (subtract line 34 from line 33) . . . . 35) _____
36) Business basis of building (multiply line 35 by line 3) . . . . 36) _____
37) Depreciation percentage (from applicable table or method) . . . . 37) _____
38) Depreciation allowable (multiply line 36 by line 37) . . . . 38) _____

PART 4—Carryover of Unallowed Expenses to Next Year

39) Operating expenses. Subtract line 23 from line 22. If less than zero, enter -0- . . . . . 39) _____
40) Excess casualty losses and depreciation. Subtract line 29 from line 28. If less than zero, enter -0- . . 40) _____

FIGURE 18.1 Worksheet to Figure the Deduction for Business Use of Your Home

Form **8829**	**Expenses for Business Use of Your Home**	OMB No. 1545-1266
Department of the Treasury Internal Revenue Service (99)	▶ File only with Schedule C (Form 1040). Use a separate Form 8829 for each home you used for business during the year. ▶ See separate instructions.	**2005** Attachment Sequence No. **66**
Name(s) of proprietor(s)		Your social security number

Part I   Part of Your Home Used for Business

1	Area used regularly and exclusively for business, regularly for daycare, or for storage of inventory or product samples (see instructions)	**1**	
2	Total area of home	**2**	
3	Divide line 1 by line 2. Enter the result as a percentage	**3**	%

● For daycare facilities not used exclusively for business, also complete lines 4–6.
● All others, skip lines 4–6 and enter the amount from line 3 on line 7.

4	Multiply days used for daycare during year by hours used per day	**4**		h r .
5	Total hours available for use during the year (365 days × 24 hours) (see instructions)	**5**		8,760 h r .
6	Divide line 4 by line 5. Enter the result as a decimal amount . . .	**6**	.	
7	Business percentage. For daycare facilities not used exclusively for business, multiply line 6 by line 3 (enter the result as a percentage). All others, enter the amount from line 3. . . . . ▶	**7**		%

Part II   Figure Your Allowable Deduction

8	Enter the amount from Schedule C, line 29, **plus** any net gain or (loss) derived from the business use of your home and shown on Schedule D or Form 4797. If more than one place of business, see instructions	**8**	

		(a) Direct expenses	(b) Indirect expenses		
	See instructions for columns (a) and (b) before completing lines 9–20.				
9	Casualty losses (see instructions)	**9**			
10	Deductible mortgage interest (see instructions)	**10**			
11	Real estate taxes (see instructions)	**11**			
12	Add lines 9, 10, and 11.	**12**			
13	Multiply line 12, column (b) by line 7		**13**		
14	Add line 12, column (a) and line 13			**14**	
15	Subtract line 14 from line 8. If zero or less, enter -0-			**15**	
16	Excess mortgage interest (see instructions) . .	**16**			
17	Insurance	**17**			
18	Repairs and maintenance	**18**			
19	Utilities	**19**			
20	Other expenses (see instructions)	**20**			
21	Add lines 16 through 20	**21**			
22	Multiply line 21, column (b) by line 7	**22**			
23	Carryover of operating expenses from 2004 Form 8829, line 41 . .	**23**			
24	Add line 21 in column (a), line 22, and line 23			**24**	
25	Allowable operating expenses. Enter the **smaller** of line 15 or line 24			**25**	
26	Limit on excess casualty losses and depreciation. Subtract line 25 from line 15			**26**	
27	Excess casualty losses (see instructions)	**27**			
28	Depreciation of your home from Part III below	**28**			
29	Carryover of excess casualty losses and depreciation from 2004 Form 8829, line 42	**29**			
30	Add lines 27 through 29			**30**	
31	Allowable excess casualty losses and depreciation. Enter the **smaller** of line 26 or line 30 . .			**31**	
32	Add lines 14, 25, and 31			**32**	
33	Casualty loss portion, if any, from lines 14 and 31. Carry amount to **Form 4684**, Section B . .			**33**	
34	Allowable expenses for business use of your home. Subtract line 33 from line 32. Enter here and on Schedule C, line 30. If your home was used for more than one business, see instructions ▶			**34**	

Part III   Depreciation of Your Home

35	Enter the **smaller** of your home's adjusted basis or its fair market value (see instructions) . .	**35**	
36	Value of land included on line 35	**36**	
37	Basis of building. Subtract line 36 from line 35	**37**	
38	Business basis of building. Multiply line 37 by line 7	**38**	
39	Depreciation percentage (see instructions)	**39**	%
40	Depreciation allowable (see instructions). Multiply line 38 by line 39. Enter here and on line 28 above	**40**	

Part IV   Carryover of Unallowed Expenses to 2006

41	Operating expenses. Subtract line 25 from line 24. If less than zero, enter -0-	**41**	
42	Excess casualty losses and depreciation. Subtract line 31 from line 30. If less than zero, enter -0-	**42**	

For Paperwork Reduction Act Notice, see page 4 of separate instructions.   Cat. No. 13232M   Form **8829** (2005)

FIGURE 18.2   Form 8829 for Home Office Deduction

(31.5 years if you began home office use before May 13, 1993). You must determine the basis of your home office in order to calculate depreciation. Basis on the conversion of property from personal use to business use is the lesser of the FMV of the office on the date you begin business use or the adjusted basis of the property on that date. If you are not sure about the FMV of your home office, get an appraisal. Ask a local real estate agent to assist you in this task.

The home office deduction calculated on Form 8829 is entered on a specific line on Schedule C for expenses for business use of your home. You cannot use Schedule C-EZ, Net Profit From Business, if you claim a home office deduction.

Farmers

Self-employed farmers who file Schedule F instead of Schedule C do not compute home office deductions on Form 8829. Instead, they should calculate these deductions on the Worksheet (see Figure 18.1) on page 396 in the same way as employees. Then the home office deduction is entered on Schedule F.

Partners and LLC Members

If you use a home office for your business, you figure your deductions in the same way as an employee. Use the Worksheet (Figure 18.1) on page 396 (do not use Form 8829 to figure your home office deduction).

CHAPTER 19

Medical Coverage

Medical coverage is an expensive personal expense for most people. So, for many, a job that provides medical coverage offers an important benefit. For the small business owner there is often a need to obtain personal coverage. It may also be imperative to offer medical coverage as a benefit to attract and keep good employees. A deduction of all or a portion of the cost of medical coverage is a significant cost-saving feature of providing such coverage.

In this chapter you will learn about:

- Deducting medical insurance
- Deducting health insurance for self-employed persons and more-than-2-percent S corporation shareholders
- Using medical reimbursement plans
- Shifting the cost of coverage to employees
- Setting up Health Savings Accounts (HSAs)
- Using Archer Medical Savings Accounts (MSAs)
- Using health reimbursement arrangements
- COBRA coverage
- Where to deduct health insurance costs

For more information about deducting medical coverage, see IRS Publication 535, *Business Expenses*, and IRS Publication 969, *Health Savings Accounts and Other Tax-Favored Health Plans*.

Deducting Medical Insurance

With rare exceptions, you are not required to provide medical insurance for employees. However, according to the Kaiser Family Foundation, 60 percent of all small businesses (with 3 to 24 employees) now offer this benefit to their employees. If you choose to provide medical insurance, you can deduct the cost of their group hospitalization and medical insurance. Deductible medical coverage also includes premiums for **long-term care insurance**.

Long-term care insurance An insurance contract that provides coverage for long-term care services necessary for diagnostic, preventive, therapeutic, curing, treating, mitigating, and rehabilitative services, as well as maintenance or personal care services required by a chronically ill person and provided pursuant to a plan of care prescribed by a licensed health care practitioner.

To be deductible long-term care insurance must:

- Be guaranteed renewable.
- Not provide for a cash surrender value or other money that can be repaid, assigned, pledged, or borrowed.
- Provide that refunds of premiums, other than refunds on the death of the insured or complete surrender or cancellation of the contract, and dividends under the contract may be used to reduce future premiums or increase future benefits.
- Not pay or reimburse expenses incurred for services or items that would be reimbursed under Medicare, except where Medicare is a secondary payer or the contract makes per diem or other periodic payments without regard to expenses.

Medical coverage provided to employees is treated as a tax-free fringe benefit. According to the IRS, medical coverage provided to a domestic partner is taxable to the employee because a domestic partner is not a spouse under state law. However, an employer providing such medical coverage can still deduct it (since the employee is taxed on the cost of coverage for a domestic partner as additional compensation).

The value of long-term care insurance provided through a cafeteria plan or other flexible spending arrangement is not excludable from the employees' income.

You deduct medical premiums according to your method of accounting. If you use the cash method, you generally deduct premiums in the year you pay them. If you are on the accrual method, you generally deduct premiums in the year you incur the liability for them (whether or not you actually pay the bill at that time). The IRS maintains that premiums covering a period of more than one year cannot be deducted except for the portion of the premium that relates to the current year.

You cannot deduct amounts you set aside or put into reserve funds for self-insuring medical costs (see medical reimbursement plans). However, your actual losses (when you pay for uninsured medical costs) are deductible.

COVERAGE FOR RETIREES.   You are not required to continue providing medical coverage for employees who retire (beyond COBRA requirements discussed later in this chapter). If you choose to pay for such coverage, you may deduct it. You may terminate your obligation for this coverage as long as you retained the right to do so in any plan or agreement you made to provide the coverage (for example, in an employee's early retirement package).

Special Rules for Partnerships and S Corporations

The business may provide coverage not only for rank-and-file employees but for owners as well. Partnerships and S corporations follow special rules for health insurance coverage provided to owners because owners cannot receive this benefit on a tax-free basis.

First, partnerships deduct accident and health insurance for their partners as guaranteed payments made to partners. Alternatively, partnerships can choose to treat the payment of premiums on behalf of their partners as a reduction in distributions. In this alternative, the partnership cannot claim a deduction.

S corporations deduct accident and health insurance for its shareholder-employees in the same way that it does for other employees.

Payment of accident and health insurance for a shareholder means the premiums are not treated as wages for purposes of FICA (includes Social Security and Medicare taxes) if the insurance is provided under a plan or system for employees and their dependents. Of course, even where the payment is not treated as wages for FICA, it is still taxable to the shareholder for income tax purposes.

A partnership or S corporation must report the medical insurance that it provides to owners on the owners' Schedule K-1. This is picked up by the partners and S corporation shareholders as income (unless, in the case of the partnership, the partnership does not claim a deduction). Owners may be entitled to deduct a percentage of health insurance, as explained in the next section.

Deducting Health Coverage by Self-Employed Persons and More-Than-2-Percent S Corporation Shareholders

Self-employed persons (sole proprietors, partners, and LLC members), as well as more-than-2-percent S corporation shareholders, may deduct the cost of health insurance they buy directly or receive through their business, but not as a business expense. Health insurance for purposes of the deduction includes the cost of long-term care insurance.

The deduction is taken from gross income on page one of Form 1040. This means the deduction is allowed even if the self-employed person does not itemize deductions. The policy can be purchased individually (it need not be purchased by the business).

The deduction cannot exceed the net earnings from the business in which the medical insurance plan is established. You cannot aggregate profits from two or more businesses to establish the net earnings ceiling required for deducting health insurance premiums. For S corporation shareholders, the deduction cannot be more than wages from the corporation (if this was the business in which the insurance plan was established).

You cannot take the deduction for any month if you were eligible to participate in any employer (including your spouse's) subsidized health plan at any time during the month. For example, suppose you are a single, self-employed individual and pay for your own health coverage. On July 1, 2005, you begin a job in which your employer provides you with health insurance. You can deduct the applicable percentage of your health insurance from January 1 through June 30, 2005 (the time you did not receive any subsidized health coverage).

In calculating self-employment tax, do not reduce net earnings from self-employment by your allowable medical insurance deduction.

Legislative Alert

Small business groups are pressing Congress to make the health insurance deduction for self-employed individuals and more-than-2-percent S corporation shareholders a business deduction rather than a personal one. This would have the effect of reducing the amount of self-employment income subject to self-employment tax and place such business owners on a par with C corporation owners. Small business would also benefit from the creation of Association Health Plans (AHPs), organizations regulated by the Department of Labor, to offer lower-cost health coverage.

Using Medical Reimbursement Plans

Businesses can set up special plans, called *medical reimbursement plans*, to pay for medical expenses not otherwise covered by insurance. For example, medical reimbursement plans can pay for the cost of eye care or cover co-payments and other out-of-pocket costs. Medical reimbursement plans are self-insured plans; they are not funded by insurance.

Medical reimbursement plans can cover only employees. These include owners of C corporations (but not S corporations). The plans cannot discriminate in favor of highly compensated employees, such as owners and officers.

The IRS has endorsed a way around the ban on deducting medical costs of self-employed owners. If the business has a medical reimbursement plan for employees and your spouse is an employee (nonowner), the medical reimbursement plan can cover the medical expenses of your spouse-employee and your employee's spouse (you) and dependents. In this way, your medical costs are deductible by the business and are not taxable to you.

Disadvantages

While self-insured medical reimbursement plans provide advantages to employers, there is a significant risk of substantial economic exposure (that claims will run higher than anticipated and planned for). This problem can be addressed by setting a dollar limit (such as $2,500) on medical reimbursements for the year.

Another disadvantage to this type of plan is the administration involved (reviewing and processing reimbursement claims). For a very small employer, however, this may not be significant.

Shifting the Cost of Coverage to Employees

Health insurance is increasingly costly to employers. There are several ways in which business owners can reduce their costs without putting employees out in the cold.

Sharing the Cost of Premiums

Instead of employers paying the entire cost of insurance, employers can shift a portion of the cost to employees. For example, employers may provide free coverage for employees but shift the cost of spousal and dependent care coverage to employees.

Flexible Spending Arrangements

Businesses can set up flexible spending arrangements (FSAs) to allow employees to decide how much they want to pay for medical expenses. Employees pay for medical expenses on a pretax basis. At the beginning of the year, they agree to a salary reduction amount that funds their FSA. Contributions to an FSA are not treated as taxable compensation (and are not subject to FICA). Employees then use the amount in their FSA to pay for most types of medical-related costs, such as medical premiums, orthodontia, or other expenses during the year that are not covered by medical insurance (including over-the-counter medications, such as pain relievers and cold remedies, not prescribed by a doctor). This plan cannot be used to pay for cosmetic surgery unless it is required for medical purposes (such as to correct a birth defect).

Your employee agrees to a monthly salary reduction amount of $100. This means that the employee has $1,200 during the year to spend on medical costs.

The downside for employers is that employees can use all of their promised contributions for the year whenever they submit proof of medical expenses. This means that if employees leave employment after taking funds out of their FSA but before they have fully funded them, the employer winds up paying the difference. So, for example, if an employee who promises to contribute $100 per month submits a bill for dental expenses of $1,200 on January 15 and leaves employment shortly thereafter, the employee has contributed only $100; the employer must bear the cost of the additional $1,100 submission.

Of course, the flip side benefits the employer. If employees fail to use up their FSA contributions before the end of the year or the two-and-a-half month grace period (referred to as the "use it or lose it" rule), the employer keeps the difference. Nothing is refunded to the employees.

Cafeteria Plans

Employers can set up cafeteria plans to let employees choose from a menu of benefits. This makes sense for some employers, since cafeteria plans allow working couples to get the benefits they need without needless overlap. For example, if one spouse has health insurance coverage from his employer, the other spouse can select dependent care assistance or other benefits offered through a cafeteria plan. Cafeteria plans do not require employees to reduce salary or make contributions to pay for benefits. Benefits are paid by the employer.

Premium-Only Plans

In these plans, employees choose between health coverage or salary. If they select the coverage, it is paid by means of salary reduction. In effect, employees are paying for their own coverage, but with pretax dollars. The employer deducts the compensation (whether the employee chooses the coverage or takes the salary). The only cost to the employer under this type of plan is the cost of administering it. (Many payroll service companies will administer the plan for a modest charge.) Bonus: Both the employer and employee save on FICA if the medical coverage is chosen.

Note

Health Savings Accounts (HSAs) cannot be part of cafeteria plans.

Setting Up Health Savings Accounts (HSAs)

The high cost of health insurance is considered by many small-business own-ers to be their number-one concern. Now there's a way to cut costs by 40 per-cent or more by combining a high-deductible (lower-cost) health policy with a special savings account called a Health Savings Account (HSA). As of March 2005, more than one million people were covered by HSAs.

MSAs Alternative

The Congressional experiment of combining high-deductible health insurance with savings accounts continues in the form of Archer Medical Savings Ac-counts (MSAs). (In 2001, the last year for which statistics are available, there were only about 61,000 individuals who claimed deductions for MSA contribu-tions.) These accounts are available only to self-employed individuals and small-business owners. There are many restrictions on eligibility. If eligible, you can use an MSA instead of an HSA. If you set up an MSA before 2004, you can roll over amounts to an HSA. MSAs are discussed later in this chapter.

Eligibility

HSAs are open to anyone who, on the first day of the month, is covered by a high-deductible health insurance plan, is not covered by another type of health insurance plan (other than worker's compensation, long-term care, disability, and vision and eye care) and who is not eligible for Medicare. This means that self-employed individuals, small-business owners, and those who work for small businesses and are under age 65 can use HSAs to obtain necessary health cov-erage. Each spouse's eligibility is determined separately; the fact that one spouse cannot have an HSA does not taint the other spouse's eligibility.

HSAs are available in all states. By September 2005, there were 83 insurers offering HSAs nationwide (not all in every state).

HIGH-DEDUCTIBLE PLAN. This is defined as a plan with an annual deductible of at least $1,000 for self-only coverage or $2,000 for family coverage and the sum of the annual deductible and other annual out-of-pocket expenses in 2005 is no more than $5,100 for self-only or $10,200 for family coverage (these dollar lim-its will be adjusted annually for inflation).

Benefits of HSAs

HSAs give you an affordable way to offer health coverage for yourself and your employees. This example from the National Small Business Association shows you how.

Example

A company with 15 employees is currently paying $72,000 for a low-deductible health insurance. It changes to a high-deductible health plan with a $2,500 deductible for participants. The annual cost of the new plan is $40,000. The company also contributes $1,000 to each participant's HSA, so its total cost is $55,000 ($40,000 insurance premiums + $15,000 HSA contributions). This is $17,000 less than the company was paying for high-deductible health coverage.

Contributions to HSAs are *not* subject to payroll taxes, which makes HSAs a better option than paying additional compensation to employees as a way to cover unreimbursed medical expenses.

Contributions

For 2005, contributions are limited to $2,650 for those with self-only coverage or $5,250 for family coverage (any plan other than self-only); these limits will be adjusted annually for inflation.

For those age 55 or older by year-end, the contribution limit is increased by $600 in 2005 (increasing in $100 increments to $1,000 by 2009). Contributions are fully deductible.

You are not required by law to make contributions for your employees, but if you choose to do so, it must be on a nondiscriminatory basis (you can't simply contribute for owners and not for rank-and-file employees).

Like IRAs, contributions to HSAs can be made up to the due date of the return (e.g., April 17, 2006, for 2005).

Taxation of HSAs

There is no current tax on earnings in HSAs. Funds withdrawn from HSAs to pay medical costs are not subject to tax. Money can be taken out for any purpose, but nonmedical withdrawals are taxable and there is a 10 percent penalty (the penalty is waived for disability or attainment of age 65).

When taking withdrawals for medical purposes, you are not required to prove this to the financial institution acting as the account's trustee or custodian. If you maintain the accounts for your employees, they are not required to prove the purpose of their withdrawal to you (it is their responsibility). But you should save receipts and other proof to show that the withdrawals should not be subject to a 10 percent penalty if you are under age 65.

Note: Employees own their HSAs and can take them when they leave the company.

For more information on HSAs, including a list of insurers and financial institutions offering HSAs, go to <www.hsainsider.com>.

Archer Medical Savings Accounts (MSAs)

Small employers and self-employed individuals can use MSAs in lieu of Health Savings Accounts to combine low-cost high-deductible health coverage with a savings-type account.

Eligibility

Archer MSAs are open only to small employers (those with 50 or fewer employees) and self-employed individuals with high-deductible plans. In 2005, they are health insurance plans with an annual deductible between $3,500 and $5,250 for family coverage, or $1,750 and $2,650 for single (self-only) coverage. The health insurance must have an annual limit on out-of-pocket expenses of $6,450 or less for families, or $3,500 or less for singles.

Legislative Alert

Archer MSAs are set to expire at the end of 2005 unless Congress again extends the law.

Contributions

As in the case of HSAs, employer contributions to MSAs for employees are not taxable to employees. Contributions are limited to 75 percent of the annual deductible for family coverage or 65 percent of the annual deductible for self-only coverage.

If a high-deductible health plan is not in place for the entire year, the contribution is limited to the ratable portion of the annual deductible for the time the plan is in effect.

These same contribution limits apply to self-employed individuals and employees who make contributions on their own behalf. Personal contributions within these limits are deductible. Contributions must be made in cash (they cannot be made in the form of stock or other property). The contribution must be made no later than the due date of the return (without regard to extensions).

Contributions can only be made on behalf of individuals who are under age 65. However, those age 65 and older have the option of selecting Medicare-MSAs, which is a type of coverage alternative to traditional Medicare (called "fee for service"). Medicare-MSAs are not funded by employers, employees, or self-employed individuals; they are funded entirely by contributions from the federal government. Medicare-MSAs will not generate any tax deductions for small businesses nor for self-employed individuals.

MSAs versus HSAs

While the options are strikingly similar, MSAs have not achieved any significant success in the public eye. This is partly because the plans are temporary
(MSAs are due to expire at the end of 2005).

As discussed earlier, those with existing MSAs might want to continue funding them rather than changing plans. However, there is the option to roll over
funds in MSAs to HSAs (see above).

Health Reimbursement Arrangements

If you want to limit your outlays for employee medical costs, consider a
relatively new option called a health reimbursement arrangement (HRA). You
contribute a fixed amount to an account for each employee that can be tapped
to cover unreimbursed medical expenses. You complement the HRA by
switching medical insurance to a less extensive, less costly plan. Overall you
save on your medical costs. And the HRA does not entail any costly and
complex design requirements associated with other types of plans such as
flexible spending arrangements within cafeteria plans (for details on HRAs
see Rev. Rul. 2002-41).

The benefit to your employee is that neither contributions to nor qualified
reimbursements from the plan are taxable. Funds in the account can be
accessed by credit or debit cards that you set up for this purpose. Also, unused
amounts in an employee's account can be carried forward and used in future
years (there is no use-it-or-lose-it feature).

COBRA Coverage

Employers who normally employ 20 or more employees and who provide
coverage for employees must extend continuation coverage (referred to as
COBRA—the initials for the law that created continuation coverage). COBRA
entitles employees who are terminated (whether voluntarily or otherwise)
to pay for continued coverage of what they received while employed. It also
covers families of deceased employees and former spouses of divorced employees. COBRA coverage generally applies for 18 months (36 months in
some cases).

Employers can charge for COBRA coverage but only up to the cost of the
coverage to the employer plus an administrative fee. This limit on the total
cost to the individual for COBRA coverage is 102 percent of the cost of the insurance. Employers who fail to provide COBRA and/or to provide proper notice
of COBRA can be subject to a substantial penalty.

A number of states have their own COBRA rules, referred to as *mini-COBRA*.
Be sure to check any state law requirements on providing continuation health
coverage to terminated employees.

Note

Federal COBRA does not include the cost of long-term care insurance.

Where to Deduct Health Insurance Costs

Employees

If you pay for your own health insurance, you can deduct premiums only as an itemized deduction on Schedule A. Premiums, along with other unreimbursed medical expenses, are deductible only to the extent they exceed 7.5 percent of adjusted gross income.

Health Savings Account contributions are treated separately from other medical expenses. If you make contributions to HSAs or MSAs, they are deductible on page one of Form 1040 (regardless of whether you itemize your other deductibles). You must complete Form 8889 to claim a deduction for HSA contributions or Form 8853 to claim a deduction for MSA contributions.

Self-Employed

Coverage provided to employees is fully deductible on Schedule C (or Schedule F for farming operations). The cost coverage for the self-employed person is deducted on page one of Form 1040.

Contributions to a Health Savings Account or Archer MSA on your own behalf are also deductible on page one of Form 1040. You must complete Form 8889 to claim a deduction for HSA contributions or Form 8853 to claim a deduction for MSA contributions.

Partnerships and LLCs

Insurance paid by the partnership is deducted on Form 1065. Coverage for partners is included in guaranteed payments and reported to them on Schedule K-1. If the partnership chooses to treat the payment of insurance premiums for partners as a reduction in distributions, no deduction can be claimed.

The cost of coverage for partners is deducted on page one of their individual returns (Form 1040). You must complete Form 8889 to claim a deduction for HSA contributions or Form 8853 to claim a deduction for MSA contributions.

S Corporations

Insurance paid by the S corporation is deducted on Form 1120S. Coverage for more-than-2-percent S corporation shareholders is reported to them on Schedule K-1.

The cost of coverage for more-than-2-percent S corporation shareholders is deducted on page one of their individual returns (Form 1040). You must complete Form 8889 to claim a deduction for HSA contributions or Form 8853 to claim a deduction for MSA contributions.

C Corporations

Insurance paid by the corporation is deducted on Form 1120.

CHAPTER 20

Deductions for Farmers

Business owners engaged in farming activities may be entitled to special deductions not claimed by other businesses. These special deductions are in addition to the same types of deductions that other business owners enjoy. A *farm* includes stock, dairy, poultry, fish, fruit, and truck farms. Thus, it encompasses plantations, ranches, ranges, and orchards.

Farmers have been given these special rules in recognition of their unique business arrangements and to make their tax reporting easier. Some of these rules have been highlighted in other parts of this book. For example, farmers (other than farming syndicates) generally are allowed to use the cash method of accounting to report their income and expenses.

In this chapter you will learn about:

- Farm expenses
- Farm losses
- Farm-related tax credits
- Nondeductible farm-related expenses
- Where to deduct farm-related expenses

For further information about deducting farming expenses, see IRS Publication 225, *Farmer's Tax Guide*.

Farm Expenses

Ordinary and necessary business expenses related to farming generally are deductible. The timing of the deduction is determined by your method of accounting (cash or accrual). However, in addition to the types of expenses claimed by nonfarm businesses, farmers may be able to claim deductions for expenses unique to farming activities and in ways more favorable than general tax rules would allow.

Prepaid Farm Supplies

If you are on the cash method of accounting, expenses generally are deductible when paid. However, if you prepay farm supplies, they must be deducted ratably over the period during which they will be used unless you qualify for an exception to this prepayment rule.

Prepaid farm supplies include:

- Feed, seed, fertilizer, and similar farming supplies not consumed during the year (other than what is on hand at the end of the year but would have been consumed had it not been for fire, storm, flood, drought, disease, or other casualty).

- Poultry bought for use in your farm business that would be deductible in the following year if you had capitalized the cost and deducted it ratably over the lesser of 12 months or the useful life of the poultry.

- Poultry bought for resale and not resold during the year.

Prepaid farm expenses are deductible to the extent they do not exceed 50 percent of other deductible farm expenses in the year (including depreciation and amortization). Any prepaid expenses in excess of this limit are deductible in the following year.

Example

In 2005, you bought fertilizer ($4,500), feed ($1,500), and seed ($750) for use in the following year for a total of $6,750. Your other farm expenses in 2005 total $12,000. You can deduct prepaid expenses up to $6,000 (50% of $12,000). The excess $750 is deductible in 2006, the year in which such items will be consumed.

If you are a *farm-related taxpayer* (your main home is a farm, your principal business is farming, or a member of your family lives on the farm or has farming as his or her principal business), you are not subject to the 50 percent limit if:

- Your prepaid farm supplies expense is more than 50 percent of your other deductible farm expenses because of a change in business operations caused by unusual circumstances, or

- Your total prepaid farm supplies expense for the preceding three years is less than 50 percent of your total other deductible farm expenses for those three years.

Livestock Feed

Generally, even though you are on the cash basis, feed must be deducted in the year that your livestock consumes it. However, if you meet all of the following three tests for the advance payment of feed, you can deduct in the year of payment the cost of feed your livestock will consume in a later year (subject to the prepaid farm supplies limit):

1. The expense is a payment for the purchase of feed and not a deposit. A binding contract for delivery shows this is not a deposit.

2. The prepayment has a business purchase and is not merely a tax avoidance scheme. A business purpose would include securing more favorable payment terms and prices.

3. The deduction of these costs does not result in a material distortion of income. For example, if this is your customary practice, then the deduction will have roughly the same impact on your income each year and will not produce a material distortion.

This limit on deducting the advance payment of feed does not apply to the purchase of commodity futures contracts.

Labor and Related Costs

You can deduct reasonable wages that you pay for regular farm labor, piecework, contract labor, and other forms of labor hired to work your farm. This includes payments to your spouse or child as long as there is a true employer-employee relationship.

You can also deduct related costs including:

- The cost of maintaining houses and their furnishings for tenants or hired help (e.g., heat, light, insurance, depreciation, and repairs).

- Insurance related to the workers (e.g., health insurance and workers compensation).

- Employer's share of FICA on farm wages.

You must reduce your deduction for wages by any employment tax credits you may be entitled to claim on such wages. These credits are explained in Chapter 7.

Breeding Fees

Cash method farmers may deduct breeding fees as a farm business expense. Accrual method farmers must capitalize such fees and allocate them to the cost basis of the calf, foal, and so on to which they relate.

Fertilizer and Lime

You have a choice of when to deduct the cost of fertilizer and lime used to enrich, neutralize, or enhance farmland.

- You can deduct it in the year you paid or incurred the expense (subject to the prepaid farm supplies rule discussed earlier in this chapter), or
- If the benefit from the material lasts more than one year, you can capitalize the cost and deduct a part of it each year in which the benefit lasts.

After you make your choice, you cannot change your reporting method without IRS consent.

Depreciation

Property used in farming generally is subject to the same depreciation rules as property used in nonfarm businesses. The rules for depreciation are discussed in Chapter 14. However, certain farming property has special recovery periods. Table 20.1 shows the recovery periods for property used in farming.

Instead of depreciating certain farm-related property, you may claim a first-year expense deduction (see Chapter 14). The limit for 2005 is $105,000. In addition to equipment and machinery used in farming, this deduction can be taken with respect to single-purpose agricultural or horticultural structures, grain bins, and drainage facilities.

Soil and Water Conservation Expenses

Generally, soil and water conservation expenses must be capitalized. However, you can elect to deduct such expenses within limits. The deduction cannot be more than 25 percent of gross income from farming. Expenses must be consistent with a plan approved by the Natural Resources Conservation Service (NRCS) of the Department of Agriculture or a comparable state agency.

Expenses eligible for this special write-off include:

- Treating or moving earth (e.g., leveling, conditioning, grading, terracing, contour furrowing, and restoration of soil fertility)
- Constructing, controlling, and protecting diversion channels, drainage or irrigation ditches, earthen dams, watercourses, outlets, and ponds
- Eradicating brush
- Planting windbreaks

TABLE 20.1 Recovery Periods for Farm Property

Type of Property	General Depreciation System	Alternate Depreciation System
Agricultural structures (single purpose)	10	15
Airplanes and helicopters	5	6
Cattle (dairy or breeding)	5	7
Cotton-ginning assets	7	12
Drainage facilities	15	20
Farm building (other than single purpose)	20	25
Fences (agricultural)	7	10
Goats and sheep (breeding)	5	5
Grain bins	7	10
Hogs (breeding)	3	3
Horses (age when placed in service)		
Breeding and working (12 years or less)	7	10
Breeding and working (more than 12 years)	3	10
Race horses (more than two years)	3	12
Horticultural structures (single purpose)	10	15
Logging equipment and machinery	5	6
Machinery and equipment (nonlogging)	7	10
Tractor units (over-the-road)	3	4
Trees or vines bearing fruit or nuts	10	20
Truck		
Unloaded weight		
13,000 pounds or more	5	6
Weight less than 13,000 pounds	5	5
Waterwells	15	20

They also include assessments by conservation districts for any of these expenses (but not more than 10 percent of your deductible share plus $500 and subject to the total limitation).

Reforestation Expenses

You can deduct up to $5,000 annually ($10,000 if married filing jointly) in qualified reforestation expenses. Amounts in excess of this dollar limit can be amortized over 84 months. For further details, see Chapter 14.

Miscellaneous Expenses

Ordinary and necessary business expenses common to all businesses (e.g., advertising costs or attorney's fees) are deductible. Other expenses specific to farming activities that may be deductible as ordinary and necessary expenses include:

- Chemicals
- Fuels and oil
- Freight and trucking
- Ginning
- Insect sprays and dusts
- Litter and bedding
- Livestock fees
- Storage and warehousing
- Tying materials and containers
- Veterinary fees and medicine

Farm Losses

If your deductible farm expenses exceed your farm income, you have a loss from the operation of your farm. The amount you can deduct of your farm loss may be limited by a number of rules. However, consider how the following rules may especially impact on farming activities.

PASSIVE ACTIVITY RULES.   Losses from an activity in which you do not materially participate and any rental activity cannot exceed your income from passive activities. Thus, if you own the farm but do not work it yourself, you may not be able to deduct your losses.

AT-RISK RULES.   These rules, which limit your deduction for losses to your economic investment, apply to farming activities in the same way in which they apply to nonfarming activities.

HOBBY LOSS RULES.   If you are not engaged in the farming activity with a realistic profit motive, then your losses are not deductible. They do not carryover to another year; they are gone forever. There is considerable litigation each year involving *gentlemen farmers* and their success in deducting losses depends on demonstrating a profit motive.

Net Operating Losses

Farmers are subject to special rules for net operating loss (NOL) carrybacks. For losses incurred in 2005, instead of the two-year carryback applicable to most other businesses, farmers can use a five-year carryback for farming losses. However, there is a three-year carryback for the part of the NOL attributable to a presidentially-declared disaster.

You can choose to forgo the carryback and simply carry forward the loss for up to 20 years. There is no special carryforward period for farmers. For farms operated through a partnership or S corporation, the losses pass through to the owners who claim the NOLs on their individual returns.

Net operating losses—figuring them and claiming quick refunds—are discussed in greater detail in Chapter 4.

Farm-Related Tax Credits

Farmers may be entitled to claim the same tax credits available to other businesses (discussed in Chapters 7 and 23). For example, if they pay wages to certain types of workers, they may be eligible to claim employment credits. But, there are also credits unique to farmers.

Farm-Related Credits

In addition to credits available to nonfarm businesses, certain credits may be unique (or more relevant) to farmers. These include:

KEROSENE FOR HOUSEHOLD USE.   The credit is the amount of excise tax paid on kerosene used in your home for heating, lighting, and cooking.

FEDERAL TAX PAID ON FUELS.   The credit is the amount of excise tax paid on gasoline, special motor fuels, and compressed natural gas used on a farm for farming purposes. Through September 30, 2005, farmers may not claim a credit or refund for undyed diesel fuel or undyed kerosene (the credit is allowed only to the ultimate vendor, a seller registered with the IRS to sell such fuel to the user of the fuel). Starting October 1, 2005, the credit is claimed by the ultimate purchaser, rather than the ultimate vendor—the farmer who bought the fuel and did not resell it.

FUELS USED IN OFF-HIGHWAY BUSINESS USE.   The credit is for the amount of excise tax paid on fuels used in running stationery machines (such as generators), for cleaning purposes, or in other vehicles not registered for highway use. However, if undyed diesel fuel or undyed kerosene is used on a farm, the fuel is not considered as being used in an off-highway vehicle.

Claiming a Credit or Refund

You can claim the aforementioned credits for fuel-related excise taxes on your income tax return. The credits are claimed on Form 4136. Alternatively, you can claim a refund of the excise taxes you already paid. The claim for refund can be made for any quarter of your tax year for which you can claim $750 or more.

If for any quarter the excise tax paid on all fuels used for qualifying purposes is less than $750, you carry the amount over to the next quarter of your tax year to determine if you can claim at least $750 for that quarter. If you cannot claim at least $750 at the end of the fourth quarter of your tax year, you must claim a credit on your income tax return.

You can use Form 8849 to file a claim for refund. If you file Form 720, you can use the Schedule C portion of Form 720 for your claims, rather than Form 8849.

You must file a quarterly claim by the last day of the first quarter following the end of the last quarter included in the claim. If you do not file a timely refund claim for the fourth quarter of your tax year, you will have to claim a credit for that amount on your income tax return.

If you claimed taxes as an expense deduction that reduced your income, you must now include any credit or refund of excise taxes on fuels.

Example

A cash basis farmer filed his 2004 Form 1040 return on April 15, 2005, on which he deducted gasoline that included $110 of excise tax. He then claimed a credit of $110 for excise tax paid on fuel. The $110 is reported as additional income in 2005.

Waiver of the Right to Claim a Credit or Refund

If fertilizer or pesticides are applied to your farm aerially or otherwise, you can waive your right to claim a credit or refund. The waiver allows the applicator to claim the credit or refund. (You may even be required to make the waiver part of your contract with the applicator.)

To make a waiver, you must sign an irrevocable statement knowingly giving up your right to the credit or refund. The statement must clearly identify the period covered by the waiver. The waiver must be signed before the applicator files his or her return. A sample waiver (Table 20.2) is reproduced on page 419.

WAIVER OF RIGHT TO CREDIT OR REFUND

I hereby waive my right as owner, tenant, or operator of a farm located at:

_____

Address

to receive credit or refund for fuel used by:

_____

Name of Applicator

on the farm in connection with cultivating the soil, or the raising or harvesting of any agricultural or horticultural commodity. This waiver applies to fuel used during the period:

_____

Both Dates Inclusive

I understand that by signing this waiver, I give up my right to claim any credit or refund for fuel used by the aerial applicator or other applicator of fertilizer or other substances during the period indicated, and I acknowledge that I have not previously claimed any credit for that fuel.

_____

Signature

_____

Date

TABLE 20.2 Sample Waiver

Exemption from Excise Tax on Fuels

As a farmer, you can buy diesel fuel and kerosene excise tax free (and so are not eligible to claim any credit with respect to these fuels). To obtain tax exemption, you must provide the vendor with a signed certificate and keep a copy of it with your other business records. A sample Exemption Certificate (Table 20.3) is reproduced on page 420.

For more information about these special tax credits, see IRS Publication 378, *Fuel Tax Credits and Refunds*.

Nondeductible Farm-Related Expenses

Not every expense of the farm can be written off. Some expenses are personal in nature and are nondeductible. Other expenses may be subject to limitations. Nondeductible expenses include:

- Personal or living expenses that do not produce farm income (e.g., taxes, insurance, and repairs to the home). If you pay expenses (such as electricity) that is used for both personal and farm purposes, you must allocate the expenses accordingly (and deduct only the farm portion). While

---

EXEMPTION CERTIFICATE

(To support vendor's claim for credit or payment under section 6427 of the Internal Revenue Code)

Name, Address, and Employer Identification Number of Seller

The undersigned buyer ("Buyer") hereby certifies the following under penalties of perjury:

A. Buyer will use the diesel fuel to which this certificate relates either—(check one):

1. ❏ On a farm for farming purposes (as defined in §48.6420–4 of the Manufacturers and Retailers Excise Tax Regulations) (and Buyer is the owner, tenant, or operator of the farm on which the fuel will be used).

2. ❏ On a farm (as defined in §48.6420–4(c)) for any of the purposes described in ¶ (d) of that section (relating to cultivating, raising, or harvesting) (and Buyer is not the owner, tenant, or operator of the farm on which the fuel will be used).

B. This certificate applies to the following (complete as applicable):

   1. If this is a single purchase certificate, check here ❏ and enter:

      a. Invoice or delivery ticket number _____

      b. Number of gallons _____

   2. If this is a certificate covering all purchases under a specified account or order number, check here ❏ and enter:

      a. Effective date _____

      b. Expiration date_____
      (*period not to exceed 1 year after effective date*)

      c. Buyer account or order number _____

■ Buyer will provide a new certificate to the seller if any information in this certificate changes.

■ If buyer uses the diesel fuel to which this certificate relates for a purpose other than stated in the certificate Buyer will be liable for any tax.

■ Buyer understands that the fraudulent use of this certificate may subject Buyer and all parties making such fraudulent use of this certificate to a fine or imprisonment, or both, together with the costs of prosecution.

Signature and Date Signed

Printed or Typed Name and Title of Person Signing

Name, Address, and Employer Identification Number of Buyer

TABLE 20.3 Sample Exemption Certificate

personal expenses are not deductible, there is one exception. You may claim a tax credit for the excise tax on kerosene used in your home for heating, lighting, and cooking (discussed earlier in this chapter). Also, a portion of the home may qualify for a home office deduction as discussed in Chapter 18.

- Expenses of raising anything consumed by you and your family.
- The value of animals or crops you raised that died. The costs of raising the animals or crops were separately deductible (under the rules discussed throughout this chapter).
- Cost of raising unharvested crops sold with land owned more than one year if you sell both at the same time to the same person. Instead, add these costs to the basis of the land for purposes of determining your gain or loss on the sale. Similarly, the cost of unharvested crop you buy with land is added to the purchase price of the land. This cost is then taken into account to determine your profit (or loss) when you later sell the land.
- Fines and penalties. However, penalties you pay for exceeding marketing quotas are deductible. If such penalties are paid by the purchaser of your crop, you simply report the net amount you receive as income (you do not claim a separate deduction for the penalties).

Where to Claim Farming Expenses

Self-Employed

Farming expenses are deductible in Part II of Schedule F. There are specific lines for various types of farming expenses. There is also a catchall line for reporting other expenses. If there are more than six other expenses, attach a statement to the return listing these other deductions.

Partnerships and LLCs

Farming expenses are deductible in Part II of Schedule F. There are specific lines for various types of farming expenses. There is also a catchall line for reporting other expenses. Schedule F is attached to the partnership return, Form 1065.

Most expenses are not separately stated items passed through to partners and members. They are simply part of the entity's ordinary business income or loss. Therefore, partners and members in LLCs report their net income or loss from the farm on Schedule E.

S Corporations

Farms operating as S corporations claim deductions on the corporation's return, Form 1120s. Most expenses are not separately stated items passed through to shareholders. They are simply part of the corporation's ordinary business income or loss. Therefore, shareholders report their net income or loss from the farm on Schedule E.

C Corporations

Farms operating as C corporations report their expenses on the corporation's return, Form 1120. This form contains separate lines for deducting certain costs. Other costs must be reported on the catchall line for "other deductions" with an explanation attached. Shareholders do not report any income (or loss) from the corporation.

All Taxpayers

The credit for federal tax on fuels is figured on Form 4136, Credit for Federal Tax Paid on Fuels.

Instead of claiming the credit on the current return, taxpayers may be entitled to a refund. The refund is claimed on Form 8849, Claim for Refund of Excise Taxes.

CHAPTER 21

Domestic Production Activities Deduction

How often does Uncle Sam reward taxpayers for simply doing a good job? Now there is a new deduction that is designed to encourage domestic production activities and is expected to save businesses $76 billion in tax dollars over the next 10 years. Also referred to as the "manufacturer's deduction," this new write-off effectively slashes the tax rate applied to such activities and does not require any additional cash outlay to qualify.

In this chapter you will learn about:

- Background to the new deduction
- Qualified production activities
- Figuring the deduction
- Special rules for pass-through entities
- Where to claim the domestic production activities deduction

Background

In the past, there were two special tax regimes designed to assist U.S. companies doing business abroad: the domestic international sales corporation (DISC) and the Extraterritorial Income Exclusion Act. The World Trade Organization viewed these regimes as discriminatory in favor of U.S. companies, and the European Union was authorized to impose sanctions on U.S. goods. In response, these regimes have been replaced by a new deduction for domestic production activities. The new deduction does *not* require any foreign distribution of goods or services; it is based on producing things within the United States.

The new rules took effect on January 1, 2005. The old extraterritorial income (ETI) regime is repealed but continues to provide some benefits under a transition rule not discussed in this book.

Qualified Producers

Only "qualified producers" can claim the deduction. The term is not limited to traditional manufacturers in the United States. It applies to a business that engages in any of the following activities:

- Selling, leasing, or licensing items manufactured, produced, grown, or extracted in the United States in whole or significant part (see safe harbor discussed later).

- Selling, leasing, or licensing films produced in the United States.

- Construction in the United States Construction includes both erection and substantial renovation of residential and commercial buildings.

- Engineering and architectural services relating to a construction project performed in the United States.

- Software developed in the United States, regardless of whether it is purchased off-the-shelf or downloaded from the Internet. The term "software" includes video games. But, with some de minimis exceptions, the term does not include fees for online use of software, fees for customer support, and fees for playing computer games online.

While it could be argued that every business produces something, not every business is treated as a qualified producer. Businesses engaged in the following activities are specifically *not* qualified producers:

- Cosmetic activities related to construction, such as painting.

- Leasing or licensing to a related party.

- The sale of food or beverages prepared at a retail establishment. However, if a business both manufactures food and sells it at a restaurant or take-out store, income and expenses can be allocated so that those related to manufacture and wholesale distribution qualify for the deduction. Thus, in the so-called "Starbucks" situation, roasting and packaging coffee beans could qualify, but selling the beans or brewed coffee at stores would not.

Safe Harbor

The deduction is limited to activities that are in whole or "in significant part" in the United States. Under a safe harbor, labor and overhead costs incurred in the United States for the manufacture, production, growth, and extraction of the property are at least 20 percent of the total cost of goods sold of the property.

Even if you fail to meet this safe harbor, you can still demonstrate that the activity is "in significant part" a U.S. activity based on all the facts and circumstances.

Figuring the Deduction

The deduction is 3 percent of income from domestic production activities and is figured on Form 8903, Domestic Production Activities Deduction (Figure 21.1). "Income" means gross receipts reduced by certain expenses.

For the Future

In 2007, the deduction percentage increases to 6 percent. Starting in 2010, the deduction percentage will be 9 percent, which results in an effective top tax rate on corporations of 32 percent (instead of the maximum 35 percent rate).

Allocable Gross Receipts

Start with gross receipts from qualified domestic production activities. If your business is entirely domestic, then all gross receipts are taken into account. If you have both domestic and foreign activities, use any reasonable method to allocate gross receipts to qualified domestic activities.

Under a de minimis rule, if less than 5 percent of total gross receipts are derived from nonqualified domestic production activities, you do not have to make any allocation; all gross receipts are treated as attributable to qualified domestic production activities.

If there is a service element in the activity, allocate gross receipts between the qualified activity and the services. However, no allocation is required if the gross receipts relate to a qualified warranty and other gross receipts from these services are 5 percent or less of the gross receipts from the property.

Allocable Cost of Goods Sold and Related Expenses

Next, reduce these gross receipts by the cost of goods sold and related expenses. Related expenses include direct costs of production, plus a portion of indirect expenses. The allocation is based on your books and records if possible, or if not, on any reasonable method. Small businesses (those with average

Form **8903**	**Domestic Production Activities Deduction**	OMB No. 1545-xxxx
Department of the Treasury Internal Revenue Service	▶ Attach to your tax return. ▶ See separate instructions.	20**05** Attachment Sequence No. **143**

Name(s) as shown on return | Identifying number

1 Domestic production gross receipts **1**

2 Allocable cost of goods sold **2**

3 Directly allocable deductions, expenses, or losses **3**

4 Indirectly allocable deductions, expenses, or losses **4**

5 Add lines 2 through 4 . . . . **5**

6 Subtract line 5 from line 1 . . . . **6**

7 Qualified production activities income from pass-through entities:

If you are a—	Then enter the total qualified production activities income from—
a Shareholder	Schedule K-1 (Form 1120S), box 12, code P . . . . . .
b Partner	Schedule K-1 (Form 1065), box 13, code T . . . .
	Schedule K-1 (Form 1065-B), box 9, code S2 . . . . . .

7

8 **Qualified production activities income.** Add lines 6 and 7. If zero or less, enter -0- here, skip lines 9 through 15, and enter -0- on line 16 . . . . **8**

9 Income limitation (see instructions):
● Individuals, estates, and trusts. Enter your adjusted gross income figured without the domestic production activities deduction . . . .
● All others. Enter your taxable income figured without the domestic production activities deduction (tax-exempt organizations, see instructions) **9**

10 Enter the smaller of line 8 or line 9. If zero or less, enter -0- here, skip lines 11 through 15, and enter -0- on line 16 . . . . **10**

11 Enter 3% of line 10 . . . . **11**

12 Form W-2 wages (see instructions) **12**

13 Form W-2 wages from pass-through entities:

If you are a—	Then enter the total Form W-2 wages from—
a Shareholder	Schedule K-1 (Form 1120S), box 12, code Q . . . . . .
b Partner	Schedule K-1 (Form 1065), box 13, code U . . . .
	Schedule K-1 (Form 1065-B), box 9, code S3 . . . . . .

13

14 Add lines 12 and 13 . . . . **14**

15 Form W-2 wage limitation. Enter 50% of line 14 . . . . **15**

16 Enter the smaller of line 11 or line 15 . . . . **16**

17 Domestic production activities deduction from cooperatives. Enter deduction from Form 1099-PATR, box 6 . . . . **17**

18 Expanded affiliated group allocation (see instructions) **18**

19 **Domestic production activities deduction.** Combine lines 16 through 18 and enter the result here and on Form 1040, line 35; Form 1120, line 25; Form 1120-A, line 21; or the applicable line of your return **19**

For Paperwork Reduction Act Notice, see separate instructions.   Cat. No. 37712F   Form **8903** (2005)

Printed on recycled paper

FIGURE 21.1 Form 8903 for Domestic Production Activities Deduction

annual gross receipts of $25 million or less) can use a simplified method to allocate deductions on relative gross receipts.

Design and development costs, including packaging, labeling, and minor assembly operations, are *not* taken into account in determining manufacturing or production activities.

The deduction applies for both regular and alternative minimum tax purposes, so claiming it will not trigger or increase AMT liability.

Limitations on the Deduction

The deduction is subject to two limitations:

1. It cannot exceed taxable income (for C corporations) or adjusted gross income for sole proprietors and owners of partnerships, limited liability companies, or S corporations.

2. It cannot exceed 50 percent of W-2 wages. W-2 wages includes both taxable compensation and elective deferrals (e.g., employee contributions to 401(k) plans).

For purposes of the W-2 wage limitation, it appears that *all* wages of a business, not just those related to domestic production, are taken into account when applying this limitation. There are three methods provided for determining W-2 income. One method looks to the lesser of Box 1 or Box 5 of Form W-2, while the other alternatives are more complex.

Note: For exporters, there is another limitation related to the phase-out of the tax rate on extraterritorial income (ETI). But some businesses that are exporters may be able to qualify for both benefits.

Pass-through Entities

The deduction is applied at the owner (not entity) level. This means that the business must allocate gross receipts, cost of goods sold, and related expenses from qualified production activities to the owners so they can claim the deduction on their personal returns.

A special allocation rule applies for purposes of the limitation to 50 percent of W-2 wages. The allocation of this amount is the lower of the owner's allocable share of wages or two times 3 percent of production activities income for 2005.

Where to Claim the Deduction

Self-Employed

The domestic production activities deduction is figured on Form 8903, Domestic Production Activities Deduction.

The deduction is then entered in the "Adjusted Gross Income" section of Form 1040. It is *not* a business deduction reported on Schedule C.

Partnerships and LLCs

The domestic production activities deduction is figured on Form 8903, Domestic Production Activities Deduction. However, the partnership or LLC does not claim the deduction; it is a pass-through item.

The information necessary to enable owners to figure their share of this deduction is reported to them on line 13 Schedule K-1 (Code "S"). Owners then figure the deduction, applying their own adjusted gross income limitation, and enter the deduction in the "Adjusted Gross Income" section of Form 1040.

S Corporations

The domestic production activities deduction is figured on Form 8903, Domestic Production Activities Deduction. However, the corporation does not claim the deduction; it is a pass-through item.

The information necessary to enable owners to figure their share of this deduction is reported to them on line 12 of Schedule K-1 (Code "O"). Owners then figure the deduction, applying their own adjusted gross income limitation, and enter the deduction in the "Adjusted Gross Income" section of Form 1040.

C Corporations

The domestic production activities deduction is figured on Form 8903, Domestic Production Activities Deduction, and entered on Form 1120.

CHAPTER 22

Miscellaneous Business Deductions

Some miscellaneous business items defy classification. Still, you may be able to deduct them.

In this chapter you will learn about:

- Other business expenses in general
- Job-seeking expenses
- Moving expenses
- Educational expenses
- Charitable contributions made by your business
- Dues and subscriptions
- Legal and professional fees
- Supplies, materials, and uniforms
- Insurance
- Payments to directors and independent contractors
- Penalties, fines, and damages
- Meal costs for day-care providers
- Expenses of disabled persons
- The dividends-received deduction
- Where to deduct miscellaneous business expenses

Some of these deductions apply only to individuals; others apply only to corporations. Review all of the categories to see which deductions may apply to you. Checklists of deductible and nondeductible expenses are found in Table 21.1.

For more information on other business expenses, see IRS Publication 535, *Business Expenses.*

Other Business Expenses in General

You generally can deduct any business expense if it is considered ordinary and necessary. It need not fit neatly into a specific category as long as it meets three tests:

1. The expense must be related to the business you carry on (be it employment or a business you own).

2. The expense cannot be a capital expenditure. *Capital expenditures* are costs related to the acquisition of a capital asset. For example, you cannot deduct the cost of improvements to property. These costs are capital in nature. However, some capital expenditures can be recovered through deductions for depreciation or amortization (see Chapter 14).

3. The expense must be **ordinary** and **necessary.**

Ordinary   Common and accepted in your business.

Necessary   Helpful or appropriate to your business. To be necessary, an expense need not be indispensable. For example, if you send flowers to your employee in the hospital, you may deduct the cost of the flowers.

Another requirement that applies to all deductions is that the expenses must be reasonable in amount. What is reasonable is a question of fact based on the particular situation. Checklists of various miscellaneous deductions related to your business status can be found toward the end of this chapter.

Job-Seeking Expenses

Being an employee is treated like a trade or business. It is considered to be the business of being an employee. Therefore, certain expenses related to getting a job may be deductible as ordinary and necessary business expenses. These include:

- Cost of resumes
- Postage and telephone charges

- Travel costs for interviews
- Career counseling
- Advertising your availability in a newspaper or magazine

These costs are deductible if you are already in a job and are seeking a new one. If you lost your job because you quit, you were fired, or your company downsized, you can still deduct these expenses as long as you are still in the business of being an employee. You cannot deduct these expenses if you have been out of the job market for many years, because you are no longer considered to be in the business of being an employee. Thus, for example, women who return to the job market after a number of years of staying home to raise children cannot treat their job-hunting costs as deductible business expenses.

You cannot deduct the expenses of obtaining your first job. You are not yet in the business of being an employee.

If you are laid off and receive outplacement services from your former employer (such as office space and resume counseling), you need not include this benefit in income. It is treated as a tax-free fringe benefit. If you pay for these services yourself, they are deductible.

If you receive reimbursement from a prospective employer for the costs of traveling to an interview, you cannot deduct your costs. But the good news is that you are not taxed on the reimbursement.

Employer Reimbursements and Outplacement Services

If you are an employer and reimburse a prospective employee for the costs of traveling to an interview, you can deduct the allowance as a business expense. You do not have to treat the reimbursement as wages or as payments subject to employment taxes.

If you provide outplacement services for discharged employees to help them find new employment, you can deduct your costs as a business expense. Some of your costs may fall into specific deduction categories. For example, if you rent a separate office for use by discharged employees looking for new employment, you treat the cost of the office as a rental deduction. Utilities related to the office are deducted along with other utility costs.

Moving Expenses

If you move your business to another location (e.g., you relocate your offices to larger quarters) or you move equipment to another location (e.g., you move machinery from one plant to another), your moving costs are deductible. There is no requirement that your new location be any special distance from the old one.

In general, if you personally move from one home to another, you cannot deduct the cost of moving your furnishings and family because these are personal expenses. However, if you relocate because of a change in jobs or a new business, you may be able to deduct your moving expenses. The tax law allows a personal deduction for moving expenses for certain job-related moves.

To claim deductible moving expenses, you must show three things:

1. That your move was of a sufficient distance (distance test).
2. That you worked at your new location for the required length of time (or were prevented from doing so) (time test).
3. That, if you are an employee, your expenses are not paid or reimbursed by your employer.

Distance Test

The distance between your new job or business location and your former home must be at least 50 miles more than the distance between your old job or business location and your former home. If you move to another city or state, generally you have no difficulty in satisfying the distance test. Where you simply move across town, be sure that the move is of a sufficient distance to make your expenses deductible.

Example

You take a job in the same metropolitan area, but way across town. You move to an apartment in the part of town in which your new job is located. The distance between your new job location and your former home is 57 miles. The distance between your old job location and your former home is 5 miles. The distance test is met because the difference is at least 50 miles (57 miles − 5 miles = 52 miles).

In calculating the distance test, use the most commonly traveled routes between locations. You need not measure distance "as the crow flies."

What if you have been out of work a long time or you are changing from part-time to full-time employment? In this case, the new job location must be at least 50 miles from your former home.

Usually the distance between your new home and job locations is not considered. However, if the distance between your new home and new job location is more than the distance between your old home and new job location, you may not be able to deduct your moving expenses. The only way to deduct moving expenses in this situation is to show that you are required to live in your new home as a condition of employment or the move results in an actual decrease in commuting time or expense.

Work in Your New Location (Time Test)

If you are an employee, you must remain on the job at your new location for at least 39 weeks during the 12-month period that starts with your arrival at the new location. You need not stay with the same employer for all those weeks. You can get another job in the same location and deduct moving expenses as long as the total employment time is at least 39 weeks. In general, only full-time employment is used to satisfy the 39-week requirement, although there is a special rule for certain seasonal employment.

If you are laid off or fired from your employment without any willful misconduct on your part, the 39-week test is waived. The time test is also waived if you fail to meet the 39-week requirement because of circumstances beyond your control—strikes, temporary absences, illness, natural disasters, and such. The time is waived if you are transferred from your new job to another location for your employer's benefit. According to the IRS, this waiver does not apply if you request a transfer for your benefit. The waiver does not apply if you resign, are fired for willful misconduct, or reach the mandatory retirement age of your new employment where you anticipated this retirement.

If you are self-employed or a partner or an LLC member, there is a 78-week test. You must work full-time in your business for 78 weeks in a 24-month period beginning with the move to the new location. At least 39 weeks must occur within the first 12 months of arrival.

You need not wait out the time requirements before claiming the deduction for moving expenses. You can deduct your costs in the year of the move under the assumption that you will meet the time test. If you do not (e.g., if you move again before the end of the 39 or 78 weeks), then you must report your deduction as income in the subsequent year. Alternatively, you can amend the earlier return to delete the deduction for moving expenses.

If you are not sure whether you will meet the time test, you can file your return for the year of the move without the deduction and then amend it after the time test has been satisfied.

Change in Employment Status

If you change your employment status to that of an employee (e.g., if you shut down your business and find a job in your new location), you need only meet the 39-week test. If you change your employment status from employee to self-employed person before satisfying the 39-week test, you must meet the 78-week test to deduct moving expenses.

Deductible Moving Expenses

Only certain moving expenses are deductible. You may deduct the actual cost of moving your household goods and personal effects. What constitutes a *personal effect* has been rather liberally interpreted. For example, one taxpayer was able to deduct moving costs for a sailboat. The cost of packing, crating, and transporting furniture, the related insurance, and some storage costs are examples of deductible expenses.

You can also deduct the travel costs for you and members of your household. You need not all travel together. For example, you may relocate immediately and your family may follow when your old home is sold or when the school year ends. Keep track of all transportation expenses for you and members of your household.

Travel costs include transportation and lodging to get from your old home to your new one. If you travel by your car, you can use a standard mileage allowance of 15 cents per mile for driving from January 1, 2005, through August 31, 2005, and 22 cents per mile from September 1, 2005, through December 31 2005, plus tolls and parking (you cannot deduct your mileage at the business mileage rate even though the move is business-motivated). Alternatively, you can deduct your actual expenses for gas, oil, and repairs on the trip, plus tolls and parking. You cannot deduct the cost of meals on the trip from your old home to your new home.

If your employer pays your moving expenses or you receive reimbursement from your employer, you cannot deduct your costs. Your employer will not include the reimbursements in your income if the employer believes that you would have been entitled to a deduction had you not received reimbursement.

As an employer, if you pay employee moving expenses, you may deduct the costs even though they are not taxable to the employee.

Educational Expenses

If you take educational courses, you may be able deduct their cost as a business expense (or you may qualify for new tax credits, explained later under personal education incentives). The tax law clearly states what types of educational courses are deductible and what types are not.

You can deduct education courses that are primarily undertaken to:

- *Maintain or improve skills required in your employment or in your business.* If you have been away from the job market for some time, you may no longer be considered in a business (the business of being an employee). In this case, education costs are not deductible.

- *Meet the requirements of an employer or applicable law or regulations imposed as a condition of retaining your salary, status, or employment.* For example, continuing professional education courses are deductible as business expenses.

You cannot deduct education courses designed to:

- *Meet minimum educational requirements.* This precludes you from deducting the cost of obtaining any professional degree in law, accounting, medicine, or dentistry. The fact that you may already be performing service in an employment status within the profession does not necessarily mean that you have met the minimum education requirements. For example, if a second-year law student is hired to do research, the cost of the third year of law school is not a deductible education expense since the student has not yet met the minimum education requirements to practice law (three years of law school and admission to the bar). If new minimum requirements are imposed after you have met old minimum requirements, however, the cost of taking the additional courses is deductible.

- *Qualify you for a new business.* A mere change in duties is not treated as a new business if it involves the same general type of work. For example, all teaching and related duties are treated as the same general type of work. However, if the education qualifies you for a new business, you cannot deduct courses even though you intend to remain in your old line of work. For example, a certified public accountant (CPA) who attends law school at night cannot deduct the cost of courses, since this leads to a new line of work—law. This is so even if the CPA never plans to practice law. A bookkeeper who takes courses to get a B.A. in accounting cannot deduct education expenses because the courses lead to a new business of being an accountant. However, a practicing attorney who takes courses toward an LL.M. can deduct expenses because the courses do not lead to a new line of work.

- *Relate to something that does not pertain directly to your business.* For example, an attorney could not deduct the cost of an English course that he argued would help him write better briefs. The courses were not directly related to his business of law even though they were helpful to his work.

Deductible Expenses

If education costs are deductible, the following types of expenses may be deducted:

- Tuition and fees
- Books
- Travel costs to and from school

These travel costs include going to or from home to school, as well as travel between work and school. If you attend a seminar at a resort, see Chapter 8 to

Note

You cannot deduct your education costs if you claim an education credit for the same expenses, as explained later.

determine whether or to what extent you may deduct your education-related travel costs.

However, you may not deduct the cost of travel as a form of education. Thus, for example, an architect cannot deduct the cost of a trip to Rome to look at ancient Roman architecture as an educational expense. However, if the architect takes education courses in Rome on architecture, then the cost of the trip may become deductible.

Employer-Paid Education

If your employer pays for the cost of your courses, you cannot take a deduction. Employer-provided education may be a tax-free fringe benefit on which you are not taxed. Such benefits are discussed in Chapter 7. If you have a C corporation and the corporation pays your education costs, the corporation can deduct the costs whether or not you are taxed on the benefits.

Personal Education Incentives

There are a number of personal tax incentives designed to encourage higher education, whether or not it is job-related. Here are some to consider:

- *Hope credit.* There is a credit of up to $1,500 per student for the cost of tuition and fees for the first two years of college (100 percent of the first $1,000 of tuition, plus 50 percent of the next $1,000 of tuition). The full credit can be claimed for the taxpayer, spouse, or dependents, but only if adjusted gross income (AGI) is below threshold amounts ($43,000 for singles or $87,000 for married persons filing jointly in 2005). The credit phases out for AGI between $43,000 and $53,000 for singles ($87,000 and $107,000 on a joint return). No credit can be claimed if AGI is over $53,000 for singles (or $107,000 on a joint return). No credit can be claimed by a married person who files a separate return.

- *Lifetime learning credit.* There is a credit of up to $2,000 (20 percent of up to $10,000) per return for the cost of tuition and fees for any college, graduate school, or vocational training. Like the Hope scholarship, the lifetime learning credit can be claimed for the taxpayer, spouse, or dependents, but only if AGI is below those same threshold amounts. Unlike the Hope scholarship, there is no limit on the number of years you can claim this credit. This credit cannot be claimed if the Hope credit is elected for any student (but you can claim the credit for any other eligible student). For example, if your child begins college and you take a graduate course, you can elect the Hope credit for your child and the lifetime learning credit for yourself if your AGI is below the threshold amount.

- *Deduction for tuition and fees.* There is an above-the-line deduction of up to $4,000 ($2,000 for certain higher-income taxpayers) for tuition and related expenses for higher education. However, the deduction in 2005 can be claimed only if modified AGI is no more than $65,000 for singles and $130,000 on a joint return ($80,000 for singles and $160,000 on joint returns for the $2,000 deduction limit). Even one dollar of excess AGI means no deduction can be taken.

Legislative Alert

The above-the-line deduction for tuition and fees is set to expire at the end of 2005 unless Congress extends it.

- *Interest on student loans.* Interest of up to $2,500 on student loans is deductible as an adjustment to gross income on page one of Form 1040. Qualified interest is interest paid on the loan during the first 60 months in which interest payments are required. The full deduction can only be claimed if your AGI is below a threshold amount ($50,000 for singles or $105,000 on a joint return). The deduction phases out over the next $15,000 of adjusted gross income, so that no deduction can be claimed once adjusted gross income exceeds $65,000 for singles or $135,000 on a joint return.
- *Penalty-free IRA withdrawals.* Withdrawals used to pay qualified higher education costs by those under age 59$\frac{1}{2}$ are not subject to the 10 percent premature distribution penalty. However, using IRA funds for education is still costly since the distribution is subject to regular income tax and you lose the opportunity for tax-free compounding.

Charitable Contributions Made by Your Business

Your business may contribute cash or property to various charities. In general, the amount of your charitable contribution is deductible, but there are certain limits and requirements that must be followed. Donations of your time and effort are not deductible.

Example

An attorney performs services for a charitable organization. She cannot deduct the value of her uncompensated legal services as a charitable contribution.

If your employees donate their vacation, sick, or personal leave in exchange for your making cash payments to a charity for Hurricane Katrina victims, you can deduct the amount of your cash payments (the leave donations are *not* included in employee income).

Unincorporated Businesses

Individuals can deduct charitable contributions only as itemized deductions. For example, if you are a partner and the partnership makes a charitable contribution, the contribution is passed through to you as a separately stated item and you then deduct it on your Schedule A as an itemized deduction. The same is true for members of LLCs and shareholders in S corporations. Self-employed individuals who file Schedule C do not take business-related charitable contributions as a business expense. Charitable contributions are reported as an itemized deduction on Schedule A. Similarly, an employee who makes a charitable contribution at work (e.g., amounts are withheld from pay as contributions to the United Fund or another charity) deducts the contribution on Schedule A as a charitable contribution (not as an employee business expense). Charitable contributions by individuals are subject to certain AGI limits.

Donations of property by a partnership, limited liability company, or S corporation can affect the owner's basis in his or her business interest.

Example

Suppose a partnership owned equally by two individuals donates a painting worth $80,000 that the partnership bought for $50,000. Each partner can deduct $40,000 on his or her individual return (50% of $80,000). However, each partner must also reduce the basis in the partnership interest by $25,000 (50% of the property's basis).

Sometimes it is not clear whether an expense is a charitable contribution or some other business expense. For example, if you pay to run an ad in a journal of a tax-exempt organization, the expense may be an advertising expense rather than a charitable contribution.

Corporations

Corporations may make charitable contributions and deduct them on their returns. The contributions must be made to public charities. The corporation cannot take a deduction if the organization receiving the contribution benefits any private shareholder or individual.

The corporation's accounting method may affect the timing of the deduction for a contribution. Cash method corporations deduct the contribution only in the year it is actually made. Corporations on the accrual method can choose to deduct contributions made within two-and-a-half months after the close of its year as having been made in the prior year. To do this, the board of directors of the corporation must authorize the payment of the contribution within two-and-a-half months after the close of the year. This authorization should be reflected in the corporate minutes.

A corporation can deduct only charitable contributions that total no more than 10 percent of its taxable income. Taxable income for purposes of this limitation does not include the deduction for contributions, the deduction for dividends received and dividends paid, net operating loss (NOL) carrybacks, and capital loss carrybacks.

Contributions in excess of the 10-percent limit can be carried forward for up to five years. If the corporation makes contributions in the carryforward years, the current deductions are taken into account before the carryforwards. Carryovers of excess charitable contributions cannot be deducted in a subsequent year if they increase a net operating loss carryover.

Corporations cannot claim a charitable contribution deduction for amounts given to an organization that conducts lobbying activities on matters of direct financial interest to their business.

Inventory

If you donate items from your inventory, the deduction is limited to the fair market value (FMV) of the property on the date of the contribution, reduced by any gain that would have been realized if you had sold the property at its FMV instead of donating it. Be sure to remove from opening inventory any contributions you make (namely, the costs for the donated property included in prior years). These costs are not part of the cost of goods sold for the year in which the contribution is made.

If you have excess or dated inventory that you wish to dispose of but do not know the organization interested in it, consider working with an organization that can find a place for your inventory. Here are two examples:

- Gifts in Kind at <www.giftsinkind.org>
- National Association for the Exchange of Industrial Resources at <www.naeir.org>
- World Vision's Gifts-in-Kind Program at <www.worldvision.org>

Donations for the Ill, Needy, or Infants

If a C corporation donates items from inventory to a public charity or an operating foundation where the inventory will be used for the care of the ill, the needy, or infants, add to the deduction 50 percent of the difference between the basis and the FMV of the inventory (but not more than 200 percent of the basis of the property). This special inventory rule does not apply to S corporations.

Scientific Property Used for Research and Computers for Education

A C corporation can claim a larger deduction than ordinarily allowed if certain scientific property used for research is donated to an institution of higher education or computers are donated to schools or libraries. This special rule allows the corporation to increase its deduction by 50 percent of the difference between its basis and the FMV of the property (but not more than 200 percent of the basis of the property). This special deduction is not allowed for S corporations, personal holding companies, or service organizations.

Legislative Alert

The enhanced deduction for donations of computers and peripherals is set to expire on December 31, 2005, unless Congress again extends it.

Appraisal Rules for Corporate Donations

All corporations that donate property valued at more than $5,000 must obtain a qualified appraisal. However, certain property donations are exempt from this requirement: donations of inventory, publicly traded stock, intellectual property, and vehicles for which a written statement is obtained from the charity.

If the deduction for a donation is more than $500,000, the appraisal must be attached to the return.

Contributions for Relief to Tsunami Victims

All businesses that donated cash during January 2005 to organizations providing relief to tsunami victims had the option to deduct the contributions on 2004 returns; if such deduction was claimed, it cannot be taken on 2005 returns. If this election was not made, then the contributions are deductible on 2005 returns.

This special rule does not apply to contributions of property. Such contributions made in January 2005 are deductible only on 2005 returns.

Contributions of Intellectual Property

All types of businesses may make charitable contributions of their intellectual property. The deduction for such contributions is limited to the lesser of the basis of the property or its fair market value. Intellectual property includes:

- Patents
- Copyrights

- Trademarks
- Trade names
- Trade secrets
- Know-how
- Software
- Other similar property or applications

ADDITIONAL DEDUCTION BASED ON INCOME. You can also deduct an amount based on the income derived by the charity from the intellectual property. The amount of the additional deduction is the applicable percentage found in Table 22.1.

No additional deduction can be claimed after the legal life of the intellectual property ends or after the 10th anniversary of the donation, whichever happens first.

Note: The additional deduction cannot be claimed if intellectual property is donated to certain private foundations.

How will you know how much income the organization derived from your donated property? At the time you make the donation, inform the organization that you intend to claim the additional deduction. The organization is then required to file Form 8899, Notice of Income from Donated Intellectual Property, showing the income it derived from the property.

TABLE 22.1 Applicable Percentage for Additional Contribution

Tax Year	Deductible Percentage
1	100%
2	100%
3	90%
4	80%
5	70%
6	60%
7	50%
8	40%
9	30%
10	20%
11	10%
12	10%

Dues and Subscriptions

Dues

Certain dues are deductible; others are not. Dues paid to unions are deductible. If you pay dues to professional, business, or civic organizations, they, too, are deductible, as are dues to the following:

- American Bar Association, American Institute of CPA, American Medical Association, and other professional associations
- Chambers of commerce, business leagues, trade associations, boards of trade, real estate boards, and business lunch clubs
- Civitan, Rotary, Lions, and other civic organizations

However, no deduction is allowed for dues to other types of clubs, such as athletic, sporting, airline, hotel, or other recreational clubs, even though membership is for business.

Subscriptions

The cost of subscriptions to business or professional publications is deductible. However, if you are on the cash basis and prepay subscriptions—that is, your subscription covers a period of more than one year—your deduction may be limited to the cost related to one year. You can deduct an allocable portion of the subscription cost in each succeeding year.

Example

In January 2005, you pay for a three-year subscription to a trade magazine. Your total cost is $150. (Assume you are on a calendar year for reporting your income and deductions.) In 2005, you can deduct $50 (one-third of your total cost). In 2006 and again in 2007, you can deduct $50, the remaining portion of your subscription cost.

Legal and Professional Fees

Legal and professional fees related to your business are deductible. Professional fees may include, for example, not only legal fees but also accounting fees, actuarial fees, systems analyst fees, and appraisal fees.

Legal Fees

Legal fees for business matters generally are deductible. For example, when a company pays legal fees to defend against charges of mismanagement of their retirement plan, the fees are currently deductible as an ordinary and necessary business expense.

Fees related to wrongful discharge actions are also deductible, as are legal fees incurred by a corporate director to defend against stockholder allegations of misconduct. Other deductible legal fees are those for tax advice or to obtain an IRS ruling.

Limits on Deducting Legal Fees

If legal fees are incurred to acquire a capital asset, they are not separately deductible. Instead, they are added to the basis of the asset. For example, if you pay attorney's fees to handle the closing when you buy your office building, the fees cannot be currently deducted. They are part of the basis of your office building and are recovered through depreciation.

Legal fees that are personal in nature cannot be deducted at all. For example, legal fees to pursue a personal injury action are not deductible even if the injury occurred on a business trip. Also, legal fees to prepare your will are not deductible even if your will provides for the disposition of your business upon your death. Similarly, legal fees for divorce are not deductible even though they relate to preserving your interest in a business. However, if part of the fees deals with tax issues, you can deduct the allocable portion of the fees for tax advice.

Legal fees to incorporate your business are part of incorporation fees that may be amortized. Similarly, legal fees to set up partnership or LLCs may be amortized as organizational costs for a partnership. Amortization of incorporation fees and partnership organizational costs are discussed in Chapter 14.

Accounting and Tax Preparation Fees

If you pay an accountant to show you how to set up your books or to keep your books for you, the accounting fees are deductible. Also deductible are fees for accounting advice, such as advice on whether to change your method of accounting or your method of inventory.

Accounting fees incurred in investigating whether to buy a business are not currently deductible but may qualify as start-up expenses that can be amortized over a period of up to 60 months. Amortization of start-up costs is discussed in Chapter 14.

The same rule applies to tax assistance fees paid to contest a tax deficiency. The portion related to business income is deductible on Schedule C; the portion related to nonbusiness income is deductible on Schedule A.

If you pay an accountant or other tax professional (paid preparer) to complete your tax return for your business (Form 1065, Form 1120, or Form 1120S), the cost is fully deductible on the appropriate return. If you are self-employed, the allocable cost of preparing Schedule C is a deductible business expense that can be claimed on Schedule C. The balance of tax preparation fees is deductible as a miscellaneous itemized expense on Schedule A, subject to the two-percent-of-adjusted-gross-income floor.

Recovering Legal Fees and Other Costs from the Government

If you are involved in a tax dispute with the IRS and you win, you may be able to make the government pay any reasonable costs of your tax contest. You must have exhausted your administrative remedies and have substantially prevailed in your tax dispute. The IRS has the burden of proving that its position in going after you was substantially justified. If the IRS did not follow published regulations, revenue rulings, revenue procedures, information releases, notices or announcements, private letter rulings, determination letters, or technical advice memoranda issued to you, then there is a rebuttable presumption that the IRS's position was not substantially justified. Also, the fact that the IRS has lost in other appellate courts on substantially similar issues must be taken into account in determining whether the IRS's position was not substantially justified. If you succeed, you can recover attorney's fees at the rate of $150 per hour in 2005. In limited circumstances, a higher award may be possible.

If you are successful in your claim to recover costs from the government (e.g., if the IRS fails to prove that it was substantially justified in its position), you cannot also take a deduction for these costs. If you have already taken a deduction for your costs, you must include the government's award in your income.

The opportunity to recover legal fees from the government is limited to individuals with a net worth below $2 million per individual. In the case of businesses, the net worth requirement is below $7 million and fewer than 500 employees.

Lobbying Costs

Fees paid to professional lobbyists to influence legislation on the federal, state, or local level are not deductible. However, in-house lobbying costs up to $2,000 are deductible.

Supplies, Materials, and Uniforms

The cost of incidental supplies and materials used in your business are deductible as ordinary and necessary business expenses. However, if you are on the cash basis and order such large quantities that the supplies or materials will last you more than a year, you can deduct only the portion of the cost related to supplies or materials expected to be used within the year.

Postage

The costs of postage, overnight delivery charges, and other mailing and shipping costs are deductible.

Books, Software, and Equipment

Books, software, and professional equipment that normally have a life of less than a year can be deducted. For example, if you buy a business book that is updated annually, you can deduct its cost. By the same token, if you buy tax return preparation software that applies to one tax year, you can deduct its cost. However, if you buy a professional library or other equipment that can be expected to last for more than a year, its cost must be depreciated. See Chapter 14 for depreciation rules.

Uniforms and Clothing

The cost of uniforms required by the job generally is deductible. Thus, for example, the cost of nurse's uniforms is deductible. However, clothing that is adaptable to ordinary street use is not deductible even if used solely in business.

> **Example**
>
> An actor who buys a tuxedo for a role cannot deduct the cost because the tuxedo is adaptable to street use—in other words, it can be used in other ways than on-the-job uses.

Nondeductible clothing costs cannot be transformed into deductible costs by calling the clothing something else. For example, an attorney cannot deduct the cost of business suits by claiming they are an advertising expense, even though a prosperous look is a way of attracting new clients. If the cost of the clothes is deductible as a business expense, then the cost of cleaning and altering the clothes is also deductible.

Insurance

The cost of most types of business-related insurance is deductible. (Medical insurance is discussed in Chapter 19.) Examples of other deductible insurance include:

- *Casualty insurance* to cover flood, fire, storm, and other casualty destruction to property. Casualty insurance may include coverage for data recovery necessitated by destruction or damage to a computer system. This may be a separate policy or part of a comprehensive casualty insurance policy. Casualty insurance also covers loss of property by theft. Check to make sure your policy covers theft of laptop computers. If the policy does not provide this specific coverage, you can obtain a separate policy for this purpose. You may need separate coverage for certain casualties, such as floods, earthquakes, and wind damage.

- *Accident and health insurance* (including long-term care insurance). The business can deduct this coverage for its employees, spouses, and dependents. Employees can exclude this benefit from their income (with a limited exclusion for long-term care insurance). Self-employed individuals (partners, LLC members, and more-than-2-percent S corporation shareholders) cannot enjoy this tax-free fringe benefit. Instead, self-employed persons and more-than-2-percent S corporation shareholders can deduct a percentage of their health insurance costs on their individual returns. (Deducting medical coverage is explained more fully in Chapter 19.)

- *Errors and omissions insurance* to provide protection for doing or failing to do something in the line of work (similar to professional liability coverage but for nonprofessionals). Self-employed individuals can carry the coverage to protect themselves. Businesses can carry the coverage to protect themselves with respect to the acts of their employees.

- *Employer practices liability (EPL)*, a relatively new type of coverage that protects employers from claims by employees based on sexual harassment, age discrimination, wrongful termination, or other similar work-related claims.

- *Group-term life insurance* for employees. This type of coverage allows employees to name the beneficiaries who will receive the proceeds. What is more, up to $50,000 of coverage is not taxable to employees if the coverage is provided on a nondiscriminatory basis (coverage does not favor owners and top executives at the expense of rank-and-file employees). (This type of coverage is discussed in more detail in Chapter 7.)

- *Key-person life insurance* for employees. This type of coverage protects the business from the loss of a key employee. The proceeds are payable to the business, allowing it to look for replacement help and to cover losses in the interim.

- *Credit insurance* to cover nonpayment of debts owed to the business.

- *Overhead insurance* to cover the costs of rent, salaries, and other overhead expenses during periods of illness by the owner.

- *Business interruption coverage.* Like overhead insurance, this type of coverage provides payment during a period in which a business is forced to close, such as during a natural disaster or a civil riot.

- *Worker's compensation.* Businesses are required to provide coverage for employees.

- *Automobile insurance* on business cars. However, if you use the IRS's standard mileage rate to write-off car expenses in lieu of deducting actual costs, you may not separately deduct car insurance. This expense is built into the standard mileage rate.

- *Professional liability coverage* to provide protection from malpractice claims. However, premiums paid to physician-owned carriers may not be deductible unless most of the policyholders are not economically related to one another and none of them owns a controlling interest in the insuring company.

- *Cyber-liability coverage* to provide protection from copyright or trademark infringement or actions arising from misinformation on your web site. This coverage may supplement professional liability or other coverage or act as a stand-alone policy. Why supplement professional liability coverage with cyber coverage? If you do not charge for advice or other information provided on your web site, then your professional liability coverage will not protect you from claims because you do not have an attorney-client or doctor-patient relationship required as a condition of protection under your professional liability policy.

- *Product liability coverage* to provide protection from claims that products you manufacture or sell are defective and have caused injury to the public.

- *Performance bonds* to ensure the faithful performance of employees, and bonds to ensure a company's performance on a contract. These are also called surety bonds.

- *Fidelity bonds* to protect clients and customers against theft or embezzlement by company employees.

- *Pension Benefit Guaranty Corporation (PBGC)* premiums for defined benefit plans to provide a minimum retirement benefit to employees if the plan goes under. (This premium amount is discussed in Chapter 16.)

Disability insurance you pay for your employees is deductible. But if you buy insurance coverage for yourself, you cannot deduct your premiums even though the insurance relates to your work. Of course, if you receive benefits under a policy you took for yourself (in which premiums were nondeductible), you are not taxed on the benefits.

In most cases, insurance premiums are currently deductible in full. However, if you are on the cash basis and your premium covers a period of more than one year, you may deduct only the portion of the premium related to the current year. The balance of the premium is deductible over the period to which it relates.

If you are a business owner and enter into a cross-purchase buy-sell agreement with other owners to acquire the interests of an owner who dies, the agreement may be funded with life insurance. In this instance, the cost of the premiums is not deductible. The reason: No deduction is allowed for premiums paid on life insurance if you are, directly or indirectly, the policy beneficiary.

Example

A and B are partners in the AB Partnership. They have a buy-sell agreement that requires A to buy B's interest in the event of B's death, and vice versa. A takes out life insurance on B and will use the proceeds of the policy to buy out B's interest if B dies before A. Similarly, B takes out life insurance on A. Neither A nor B may deduct the premiums on this life insurance arrangement even though there is a business reason for the purchase.

Interest on Life Insurance Policies

If you take out a loan on a life insurance policy covering the life of anyone in whom you have an insurable interest, you may not deduct the interest on the loan. So, if you borrow on a policy maintained to fund a buy-sell agreement, you may not deduct the interest. Corporations (and other nonnatural persons) generally may not deduct a portion of interest on any of their outstanding loans to the extent of any *unborrowed policy cash value* (cash surrender value of the policy reduced by any loans). This interest deduction rule, however, does not apply if the business owns a policy covering only one individual who owns at least 20 percent of the business or is an employee, officer, or director of the company.

Payments to Directors and Independent Contractors

Payments to directors and independent contractors are not treated as compensation. Rather, they are miscellaneous payments that are deductible as a business expense. Since they are not compensation, they are not subject to employment taxes. However, you must report nonemployee compensation of $600 or more on Form 1099-MISC (see Appendix).

Individuals who work for their corporations and also serve as directors may receive both salary (as an employee) and self-employment income (as a director). Such individuals may be able to reduce the tax on directors' fees by setting up retirement plans based on this self-employment income. For a discussion of whether a worker is an employee or an independent contractor, see Business Organization, Chapter 1.

Penalties, Fines, and Damages

If you contract to perform work and are subject to penalty for noncompletion or lateness, you can deduct the penalty.

Example

You contract to remodel a kitchen. The contract calls for a penalty if the job is not completed within a month. You do not bring the job in on time and must pay a penalty for each day beyond the month. You can deduct this penalty.

You can also deduct compensatory damages paid to the government. However, you cannot deduct nonconformance penalties imposed by the Environmental Protection Agency for failing to meet certain emission standards.

If you lose a business lawsuit and must pay damages, you deduct your outlays. For example, if you lose a malpractice case and your insurance carrier pays 95 percent of the damages while you pay five percent, you can deduct your payment.

If you are subject to governmental fines or penalties because you violated the law, no deduction is allowed. Such penalties include:

- Amounts paid as penalties to plead no contest or to plead guilty to a criminal offense
- Penalties imposed by federal, state, or local law (e.g., additions to tax imposed by the Internal Revenue Code)
- Payments to settle actual or possible civil or criminal litigation
- Fines for violation of housing codes
- Fines by truckers for violating state highway maximum weight limits or air quality laws
- Civil penalties for violating federal laws on mine safety or discharge into navigable waters

Nongovernment fines or penalties are deductible. For example, one broker who was fined by the Chicago Mercantile Exchange for violating trading limitations was allowed by the Tax Court to deduct his payment.

Treble Damages for Antitrust Violations

One-third of the treble damages—three times the actual damages—for antitrust violations is deductible; the balance is treated as a nondeductible penalty.

Restitution Payments

These payments generally are regarded as fines and are deductible. However, if restitution payments are made in lieu of a prison sentence, they are viewed as a nondeductible governmental penalty even though the funds go to a private person rather than to the government.

Related Expenses

Certain expenses related to nondeductible fines or penalties may themselves be deductible. For example, legal fees to defend your business against prosecution or civil action for a violation of a law imposing a fine or civil penalty are deductible.

Meal Costs for Day-Care Providers

If you provide family day-care services and include meals to children you are caring for, you can deduct the cost of the meals. There are two ways to figure your deduction:

1. Your actual costs, for which you need records and receipts to support your deduction.
2. Reliance on an IRS per diem amount, for which you need only keep records of the number of children you care for and the meals they consume.

The per diem amounts are based on a per person rate. The rates for 2005 may be found in Table 21.1 Rates for 2006 are slightly higher.

To use the standard rates you must provide care in your home to minor children, other than children who are full-time or part-time residents in your home. If you opt to use the standard meal rates, you must do so for all food costs provided to eligible children during the year.

Expenses of Disabled Persons

Individuals with handicaps or disabilities may incur certain expenses to enable them to work. For example, a blind individual may hire a reader. In general, the cost of work-related expenses of disabled persons is deductible.

TABLE 22.2 Standard Meal and Snack Rates for 2005

Your Location	Breakfast	Lunch and Dinner	Snack
States other than Alaska and Hawaii	$1.04	$1.92	$0.57
Alaska	$1.64	$3.11	$0.92
Hawaii	$1.20	$2.25	$0.67

Sometimes it may be difficult to decide whether the expense is a personal medical expense that is subject to a 7.5-percent-of-adjusted-gross-income floor or a business expense. If the expense is required for the individual to perform his or her job and the goods or services are not used primarily for personal purposes, the expense can be treated as a business expense. For example, attendant care services at the office generally are treated as business expenses. You must show a physical or mental handicap that results in a functional limitation to employment, such as blindness or deafness.

Work-related business expenses of handicapped persons are itemized deductions that are not subject to the two-percent floor. If the handicapped person is self-employed, the expenses are deductible as any other business expense on Schedule C.

If you, as an employer, incur special costs because of compliance with the Americans with Disabilities Act, you may deduct these costs as ordinary and necessary business expenses. If they are capital in nature, you may be able to claim a special deduction or credit, as explained in Chapter 10.

The Dividends-Received Deduction

Corporations cannot deduct the dividends they pay out to shareholders. But C corporations may be able to claim a special deduction for a percentage of certain stock dividends they receive. This is called a dividends-received deduction. Other taxpayers—individuals, partnerships, LLCs, and S corporations—cannot claim this deduction.

Percentages of the Dividends-Received Deduction

The percentage of the dividend that can be deducted depends on the amount of stock your corporation owns and the type of company paying the dividends. Other factors may operate to further limit the percentage.

FORTY-TWO PERCENT DEDUCTION. If your corporation owns less than 20 percent of the preferred stock issued before October 1992 of a taxable public utility, your dividends-received deduction is limited to 42 percent of the dividends received from that public utility. If your corporation owns more than 20 percent of the utility, the dividends-received deduction increases to 48 percent.

SEVENTY PERCENT DEDUCTION. If your corporation owns less than 20 percent of the stock of the dividend-paying corporation, your dividends-received deduction is 70 percent of the dividends you receive from that corporation.

EIGHTY PERCENT DEDUCTION. If your corporation owns at least 20 percent of the stock of the dividend-paying corporation, your dividends-received deduction is 80 percent of the dividends you receive from that corporation.

EIGHTY-FIVE PERCENT DEDUCTION. For one year, from October 22, 2004, through October 21, 2005, a corporation that is a U.S. shareholder of a controlled foreign corporation (CFC) can claim an 85 percent dividends-received deduction (DRD) with respect to certain cash dividends it receives from its CFCs.

ONE HUNDRED PERCENT DEDUCTION. If your corporation and the dividend-paying corporation are members of an affiliated group, all of the dividends received are deductible. The full deduction also applies to small business investment companies that receive dividends from domestic corporations.

Other Limits on the Dividends-Received Deduction

In addition to the percentage limitation, other limits may apply to reduce or eliminate entirely the deduction.

LIMIT FOR DEBT-FINANCED PORTFOLIOS. If your corporation borrows to buy or carry a stock portfolio, the 70-percent and 80-percent dividends-received deductions must be reduced by the percentage related to the amount of debt.

OVERALL LIMIT. There is an overall limit on the deduction for dividends received. This limit is calculated on Schedule C of Form 1120.

NO DEDUCTION ALLOWED. Certain types of deductions do not qualify for the dividends-received deduction. These include dividends from:

- Foreign corporations (with limited exceptions).
- Real estate investment trusts.
- Corporations whose stock has been held for only 46 days or less during the 90-day period beginning on the date that is 45 days before the date on which the shares become ex-dividend.
- Corporations whose stock has been held for 91 days or less during the 180-day period beginning on the date that is 90 days before the date on which the shares became ex-dividend, if the stock has preference as to dividends and the dividends received on it are attributable to a period of more than 365 days.
- Tax-exempt corporations.
- Corporations to which your corporation is obligated (pursuant to a short sale or otherwise) to make related payments for positions in substantially similar or related property.

See Table 22.3 for a checklist of deductible and nondeductible expenses.

Where to Deduct Miscellaneous Business Expenses

Employees

In general, employee business expenses are deductible as itemized expenses on Schedule A, subject to the two-percent-of-adjusted-gross-income floor discussed in Chapter 1.

SPECIAL RULE FOR PERFORMING ARTISTS. Expenses are fully deductible from gross income if you meet certain tests:

- You must perform services as a performing artist as an employee for at least two employers.

TABLE 22.3 Checklists of Deductible and Nondeductible Expenses

Deductions for Self-Employed Individuals

Abandonment of assets, loss for

Accounting fees

Acquiring a lease, cost of

Actuary fees for defined benefit plans

Advertising

Agreement not to compete

Air transportation taxes

Allowances and returns

Amortization of acquired intangibles

Association dues

Attorney's fees

Automobiles (see Cars)

Bad debts

Bank fees

Black Lung benefit trust contributions

Bond premium

Bonus depreciation

Bonuses to employees

Breach of contract damages

Bribes

Buildings, demolition of

Business conventions

Business interruption insurance

Capital losses

Cars

Casualty insurance

Casualty losses

Cellular phones

Commissions paid to independent contractors

Computers

Conventions

Copyrights

Cruise ship, conventions on

(Continued)

TABLE 22.3 *(Continued)*

Deductions for Self-Employed Individuals
Dependent care
Depreciation
Dues for professionals
Education expenses
Employee compensation
Employment taxes
Entertainment expenses
Equipment
Excise taxes
Experimental costs
Fax machines
Fines
First-year expensing of equipment
Franchise fees
Franchise taxes
Freight
Fuel taxes
FUTA tax for employees
Gifts
Going concern value
Goodwill
Handicapped, improvements for
Health insurance for employees
Health savings account contributions
Home office expenses
Insurance
business interruption
car
casualty
cyber-liability
errors and omissions
health
liability

TABLE 22.3 *(Continued)*

Deductions for Self-Employed Individuals
long-term care
malpractice
overhead
workers' compensation for employees
Intangible drilling costs
Interest
Internet-related fees
Involuntary conversions
Journals
Kickbacks
Labor costs
Lease payments
Legal fees
Liability insurance
Libraries
License fees
Maintenance costs (repairs)
Malpractice insurance
Materials
Meals for business
Medical insurance
Medical reimbursement plans
Mortgages
Moving expenses
Net operating losses
Office in home
Oil and gas wells
Organizational expenses
Outplacement services for employees
Overhead insurance
Pagers
Patents

(Continued)

TABLE 22.3 *(Continued)*

Deductions for Self-Employed Individuals
Penalties
Pension plans
Pollution control facilities
Postage
Qualified retirement plan contributions
Real estate taxes
Reforestation expenses
Registration fees
Removal of architectural barriers
Rent
Research costs
Retirement plan contributions
Royalty payments
Sales tax
Section 197 intangibles
Self-employment tax
SEP-IRAs
sick pay to employees
SIMPLE plan contributions
Software
Start-up costs
Subscriptions
Supplemental unemployment benefits for employees
Supplies
Tax return preparation fees
Thefts
Timber
Tools
Trade names
Trademarks
Transportation expenses
Travel expenses
Trucks (see Cars)

TABLE 22.3 *(Continued)*

Deductions for Self-Employed Individuals

Unemployment payments to state compensation fund for employees

Uniforms

Use tax

Utilities

Vandalism

Wages for employees

Work clothes

Workers' compensation for employees

Deductions for Employees

Advances for travel and entertainment expenses

Association dues

Automobiles (see Cars)

Bad debts

Breach of contract damages

Breakage charges

Business conventions

Cars

Cellular phones

Cleaning costs for deductible uniforms

Computers

Conventions

Cruise ships, conventions on

Dependent care

Depreciation

Dues for professional associations/unions

Entertainment expenses

Equipment

Fax machines

First-year expensing of equipment

Gifts

Health savings account contributions

Home office expenses

(Continued)

TABLE 22.3 *(Continued)*

Deductions for Employees
Impairment-related job expenses
Insurance for business, car
Interview expenses
IRAs
Job-hunting expenses
Journals
Jury fees returned to employer
Lease payments for business property
Legal fees
License fees
Materials and supplies
Meals for business
Moving expenses
Nonbusiness bad debts
Office in home
Performing artist expenses
Resumes
Section 1244 losses
Small tools
Subscriptions
Supplies
Tax return preparation fees
Telephone
Tools
Transportation expenses
Travel expenses
Trucks (see Cars)
Uniforms
Union dues
Utilities in a home office
Work clothes

TABLE 22.3 *(Continued)*

Deductions for Small Corporations

Abandonment of assets, loss for

Accident and health plans, contributions to

Accounting fees

Acquiring a lease, cost of

Actuary fees for defined benefit plans

Advances for travel and entertainment expenses

Advertising agreement not to compete

Air transportation taxes

Allowances and returns

Amortization of acquired intangibles

Amortization of premium on bonds

Appraisal fees

Association dues

Attorney's fees

Automobiles (see Cars)

Awards and prizes to employees

Bad debts

Bank fees

Black Lung benefit trust contributions

Bond premiums

Bonus depreciation

Bonuses

Breach of contract damages

Bribes

Buildings, demolition of

Business conventions

Business interruption insurance

Capital losses

Cars

Casualty insurance

Casualty losses

Cellular phones

Charitable contributions

(Continued)

TABLE 22.3 *(Continued)*

Deductions for Small Corporations
Commissions paid to independent contractors
Computers
Conventions
Copyrights
Cruise ships, conventions on
Dependent care
Depreciation
Disability insurance
Dividends-received deduction
Education expenses
Employee benefit plans
Employee compensation
Employment taxes
Entertainment expenses
Equipment
Excise taxes
Experimental costs
Fax machines
FICA
Fines
First-year expensing of equipment
Foreign taxes
Franchise fees
Franchise taxes
Freight
Fringe benefits
Fuel taxes
FUTA tax for employees
Gifts
Going concern value
Goodwill
Group term life insurance
Handicapped, improvements for

TABLE 22.3 *(Continued)*

Deductions for Small Corporations
Health plans, contributions to
Health savings account contributions
Incorporation fees
Insurance
business interruption
car
casualty
cyber-liability
employer practices liability
errors and omissions
group term
health
key person life
liability
life
long-term care
malpractice
overhead
workers' compensation
Intangible drilling costs
Interest
Internet-related fees
Involuntary conversions
Journals
Kickbacks
Labor costs
Lease payments
Legal fees
Liability insurance
Libraries
License fees
Life insurance
Maintenance costs (repairs)

(Continued)

TABLE 22.3 *(Continued)*

Deductions for Small Corporations
Malpractice insurance
Materials
Meals for business
Medical insurance
Medical reimbursement plans
Medicare tax
Mortgages
Moving expenses
Net operating losses
Oil and gas wells
Organizational expenses
Outplacement services
Overhead insurance
Patents
Penalties
Pension plans
Pollution control facilities
Postage
Prizes to employees
Qualified retirement plan contributions
Real estate taxes
Reforestation expenses
Registration fees
Removal of architectural barriers
Rent
Research costs
Retirement plan contributions
Royalty payments
Salaries
Sales tax
Section 197 intangibles
SEP-IRAs, contributions to
Sick pay
SIMPLE plans, contributions to
Social Security tax
Software

TABLE 22.3 *(Continued)*

Deductions for Small Corporations

Start-up costs

State income tax

Subscriptions

Supplemental unemployment benefits

Supplies

Tax return preparation fees

Telephone

Thefts

Timber

Tools

Trademarks

Tradenames

Transportation expenses

Travel expenses

Trucks (see Cars)

Unemployment payments to state compensation fund

Unemployment tax (FUTA)

Use tax

Utilities

Vacation pay

Vandalism

Wages

Workers' compensation insurance

Workforce in place

Worthless securities

Deductions Not Allowed

Advances to one's corporation (they are loans or contributions to capital)

Anticipated liabilities

Architect's fees (generally capitalized)

At-risk, losses in excess of

Bad debt deduction for income not reported

Bar examination fees

Car used for commuting

(Continued)

TABLE 22.3 *(Continued)*

Deductions Not Allowed
Club dues for recreational, social, and athletic clubs
Commuting expenses
Containers treated as part of inventory
Corporation's expenses paid by shareholder under no obligation to pay them
Demolition of entire buildings
Disability insurance for yourself
Dividend payments
Educational costs to meet minimum job requirements
Embezzlement losses of income not yet reported
Estimated tax penalties
Extortion payments
Federal income tax
FICA by employees
Fines
401(k) contributions by employees
Gifts to business clients or customers over $25
Hobby losses
Interest on life insurance policy loans funding buy-sell agreements
Inventory
IRA contributions by participants in qualified plans with AGI over set limit
IRA rollovers
Job-hunting costs for a first job
Land costs
Lobbying expenses (other than de minimus in-house)
Not-for-profit activity losses
Passive activity losses in excess of passive activity limits
Payments to a minister for prayer-based solutions to business problems
Penalties paid to the government
Political contributions
Reimbursed expenses (payments received by employees under accountable plans)
Related parties, losses on sales to
Salary reduction contributions to retirement plans
Self-insurance reserve funds
Spousal travel costs

TABLE 22.3 *(Continued)*

Deductions Not Allowed
State and local income taxes on self-employment income
Tax penalties
Travel costs as a form of education
Treble damage awards—two-thirds

- Your business deductions must exceed 10 percent of your gross income from the performance of services.
- Your AGI without regard to these business deductions must not exceed $16,000.

If you meet these tests to fully deduct your expenses, they are not claimed as itemized deductions on Schedule A, but rather as an adjustment to gross income on page one of Form 1040. Be sure to write "QPA" next to your deduction.

HANDICAPPED PERSONS.   Business-related expenses of disabled or handicapped individuals are itemized deductions that are not subject to the two-percent floor.

MOVING EXPENSES.   Moving expenses that are not reimbursed by an employer are deductible from gross income on page one of Form 1040. They are deductible regardless of whether other deductions are itemized. The moving expense deduction is not subject to the two-percent floor. Complete Form 3903, Moving Expenses, to determine your deductible moving expenses.

EDUCATION CREDITS.   The Hope and lifetime learning credits are figured on Form 8863, Education Credits, the amount of which is then entered on page two of Form 1040.

Self-Employed

Certain items discussed in this chapter are itemized on Schedule C. These include commissions and fees, insurance, and legal and professional services. Other miscellaneous business expenses discussed in this chapter are grouped together and deducted as other expenses on Schedule C. Other expenses are separately listed and explained in Part V of Schedule C. You can use Schedule C-EZ only if total business expenses do not exceed $5,000.

For self-employed farmers, certain expenses discussed in this chapter, such as insurance, are itemized on Schedule F. Other miscellaneous business expenses, such as legal and accounting fees, are grouped together and deducted as other expenses on Schedule F. Farming expenses are explained in Chapter 20.

Moving expenses are a personal expense claimed directly on your Form 1040 rather than on Schedule C. You figure your deductible moving costs on Form 3903 and then enter the deduction on page one of Form 1040 as an adjustment to gross income.

Education credits (Hope and lifetime learning credits) are personal credits claimed directly on your Form 1040. You figure your credits on Form 8863, Education Credits, and then enter the credit amount on page two of Form 1040.

Partnerships and LLCs

All of the miscellaneous business expenses discussed in this chapter to which a partnership or limited liability company is entitled are entered on Form 1065 as other expenses. Attach a schedule to the return, itemizing these expenses.

Charitable contributions made by the partnership or LLC are subject to limitations and are treated differently. Contributions are reported on Schedule K and passed through to partners/members on Schedule K-1. These are separately stated because they are subject to limitation at the owner level. Partners/members report their net income or loss from the business on Schedule E. However, separately stated items are reported on the owner's personal return in the appropriate space. For example, charitable contribution deductions are reported on the owner's Schedule A.

Partners and LLC members who have deductible moving expenses claim them on page one of their Form 1040. Partners and LLC members who are eligible for education credits claim them on page two of their Form 1040. For details, see Employees.

S Corporations

All of the miscellaneous business expenses discussed in this chapter to which the S corporation is entitled are entered on Form 1120S as other deductions. Attach a statement to the return explaining these deductions.

However, deductions that are subject to special limitations at the shareholder level are separately treated items reported on Schedule K and passed through to shareholders on Schedule K-1. For example, charitable contributions by the S corporation are separately stated items because they are subject to limitation at the shareholder level. Shareholders report their net income or loss from the business on Schedule E. Separately stated items are reported on the shareholder's personal return in the appropriate space. For example, charitable contribution deductions are reported on the owner's Schedule A.

Shareholders who are also employees of their S corporations and who have unreimbursed moving expenses compute them on Form 3903 and then enter the deduction on page one of Form 1040 as an adjustment to gross income.

C Corporations

Miscellaneous business expenses are taken into account in determining the profit or loss of the C corporation on Form 1120. The corporation then pays tax on its net profit or loss. Shareholders do not report any income (or loss) from the corporation.

Charitable contributions by the corporation, as well as NOLs and special deductions for dividends received, are listed separately on Form 1120. All other miscellaneous deductions are grouped together and reported as other deductions. Attach a schedule to the return explaining these deductions.

If a corporation claims a dividends-received deduction, it must also complete Schedule C, "Dividends and Special Deductions," of Form 1120. The net amount of the dividends-received deduction is then entered on page one of Form 1120 after any NOL has been taken. The dividends-received deduction is not part of the other deductions reported on this form.

All Businesses

If your business makes payments of more than $600 to independent contractors for services during the year, you may be required to file an annual information return, Form 1099—Miscellaneous Income. Report the payments as nonemployee compensation in the appropriate box on the form. Also use this form to report payments to corporate directors.

Form 1099-MISC must be furnished to independent contractors and corporate directors no later than January 31 of the year following in which payments were made. Copies of Form 1099 must also be sent to the IRS, along with a transmittal form, Form 1096, Annual Summary and Transmittal of U.S. Information Returns. This must be done by February 28 of the year following the year in which payments were made. However, you have until March 31 (or the next business day if March 31 falls on a weekend or legal holiday) if you file Form 1099 electronically.

CHAPTER 23

Roundup of Tax Credits

Just as deductions offset business income, tax credits offset tax liability. In effect, tax credits are considerably more valuable than deductions since they offset taxes on a dollar-for-dollar basis.

Businesses may be entitled to a variety of credits that Congress created to encourage certain activities—hiring special workers, using alternative energy sources, pouring money into research, and so on. Not every business credit applies to small business owners (but are all listed within this chapter to alert you to their existence).

Many of these credits have been discussed throughout this book in the chapter to which they relate. However, here you will find a roundup of tax credits, a brief explanation of what they are all about, and where you can find more information on them within this book (see Table 23.1, page 478).

In this chapter you will learn about:

- Employment-related credits

- Capital construction-related credits

- Other tax credits

- Where to claim tax credits

Employment-Related Credits

The tax law encourages you to hire certain workers by permitting you to claim tax credits for certain wages you have paid.

WORK OPPORTUNITY CREDIT. A credit applies for hiring workers from certain economically-disadvantaged designated groups. The credit is 40 percent of first-year wages up to $6,000 for those who work at least 400 hours (25 percent for those who work a minimum of 120 hours but less than 400 hours). Wages taken into account for purposes of summer youth employees are limited to $3,000. Thus, the top credit is $2,400 per employee ($1,200 for summer youth).

Legislative Alert

The work opportunity credit is set to expire on December 31, 2005, unless Congress again extends it.

WELFARE-TO-WORK CREDIT. A credit applies for hiring certain long-term family assistance recipients as a means of encouraging their employment. The credit is 35 percent of first-year wages up to $10,000, plus 50 percent of second-year wages up to $10,000. Thus, the top credit per employee is $3,500 in the first year and $5,000 in the second year. *Wages* for purposes of this credit include not only salary but also health care benefits, educational assistance, and dependent care assistance.

Legislative Alert

The welfare-to-work credit is set to expire on December 31, 2005, unless Congress again extends it.

FICA ON TIPS. If you own a food or beverage business, you may claim a credit for the employer portion of Social Security and Medicare taxes (FICA) on tips in excess of those treated as wages for purposes of satisfying the minimum wage provisions of the Fair Labor Standards Act. The credit applies to tips both on premises as well as off premises (e.g., earned for pizza deliveries).

EMPOWERMENT ZONE EMPLOYMENT CREDIT. A credit of 20 percent of the first $15,000 of wages may be claimed for workers who perform services in designated empowerment zones. Wages taken into account for the welfare-to-work credit or the work opportunity credit may not also be used for the empowerment zone employment credit.

Note

Employment credits reduce both your deduction for wages as well as your tax liability. Employment taxes (other than the empowerment zone employment credit) are part of the general business credit.

INDIAN EMPLOYMENT CREDIT. A credit of 20 percent of the first $20,000 in wages and health care costs may be claimed for employing Indian tribe members who live and work on a reservation. The top credit is $4,000 per employee.

Legislative Alert

The Indian employment credit is set to expire on December 31, 2005, unless Congress again extends it.

COMMUNITY RENEWAL EMPLOYMENT CREDIT. A credit of 15 percent may be claimed for wages up to $10,000 paid to full-time or part-time workers within the renewal communities. Generally, the same rules for the empowerment zone employment credit apply to the renewal community employment credit.

WORK-RELATED PERSONAL CREDITS. If you work as an employee or as a self-employed person, you may be eligible for certain personal tax credits.

EARNED INCOME CREDIT. Workers whose income is below threshold amounts may be eligible to claim an earned income credit. This credit is a type of negative income tax—it may be paid even though it exceeds tax liability. The amount of the credit depends on the number of qualifying dependents, if any, and AGI. A portion of the credit may be advanced to workers as a payment in their salary check.

DEPENDENT CARE CREDIT. Whether you are an employee or a business owner, if you hire someone to look after your children under age 13 or a disabled spouse or child of any age so that you can go to work, you may claim a personal tax credit. The credit is a sliding percentage based on your AGI. The top percentage is 35 percent, but scales back to 20 percent for AGI over $43,000. The percentage applies to eligible expenses up to $3,000 for one dependent and $6,000 for two or more dependents.

Capital Construction-Related Credits

The tax law encourages certain types of construction.

DISABLED ACCESS CREDIT. If you make capital improvements to make your premises more accessible to the handicapped, you may qualify for a credit of 50 percent of expenditures over $250, but not over $10,250. Thus, the top credit is $5,000. If you claim this credit you cannot claim depreciation on these costs.

LOW-INCOME HOUSING CREDIT. If you invest in the construction or rehabilitation of housing for low-income individuals, you may be eligible for a tax credit of 70 percent of new construction or 30 percent of federally subsidized buildings. The credit is claimed over a 10-year period.

REHABILITATION CREDIT. If you rehabilitate or reconstruct certain buildings, you may claim a credit of 10 percent of your costs if the building was originally placed in service before 1936. If the building is a certified historic structure listed on the National Register of Historic Places, the credit is 20 percent of your expenditures. To qualify, your expenditures must be more than the greater of $5,000 or your adjusted basis in the building and its structural components.

NEW MARKETS CREDIT. To encourage investments in certain economically-disadvantaged areas, you may claim a credit for purchasing stock in a community development entity (CDE). A CDE is a domestic corporation or partnership that provides investment capital for low-income communities or persons, maintains accountability to the residents of the area, and has been certified as a CDE by the Community Development Financial Institutions (CDFI) Fund of the Department of the Treasury. The credit is claimed over a period of seven years. The amount of the credit is the equity investment multiplied by 5 percent in years one through three and 6 percent in years four through seven. The credit is subject to recapture if the CDE ceases to be qualified, the proceeds cease to be used to make qualified investments, or the investment is redeemed by the entity (there is no recapture if you merely sell your investment).

Other Tax Credits

Other tax credits in the law are intended to encourage specific things—research, alternative energy consumption, and so on.

CREDIT FOR EMPLOYER-PROVIDED CHILD CARE FACILITIES AND SERVICES. You can claim a credit for providing child care facilities and child care referral services. The credit is 25 percent of qualified facility expenses, plus 10 percent of referral service costs, for a maximum credit of $150,000. If a company builds a child care facility, the basis of the facility for purposes of depreciation must be reduced by the expenses taken into account in figuring the credit. If the facility ceases to be used for child care within 10 years, the credit is subject to recapture.

RESEARCH CREDIT. If you engage in research and experimentation, you may claim a credit of 20 percent of increased research activities (increased costs this year compared with a base period that is usually the three preceding years). Alternatively you may claim a flat percentage of gross receipts on average for a four-year period. The credit percentage (2.65%, 3.2%, or 3.75%) scales up with the percentage of gross receipts. There is no dollar limit on the credit, but the credit cannot exceed taxable income from the business that produced the credit.

Legislative Alert

The research credit is set to expire on December 31, 2005, unless Congress again extends it.

ALCOHOL FUELS CREDIT. The credit applies to alcohol (ethanol and methanol) you sold or used as fuel in your business.

ENHANCED OIL RECOVERY CREDIT. The credit applies to certain oil recovery costs if you are in the oil and gas business.

FEDERAL EXCISE TAX ON FUELS. The federal excise tax you pay on certain fuels used in your business (particularly farming activities) may be claimed *either* as a credit or a tax refund. The credit is the amount of this tax paid on fuel used in machinery and off-highway vehicles (such as tractors) and on kerosene used for heating, lighting, and cooking on a farm.

FOREIGN TAX CREDIT. If you pay tax to a foreign country—on business income or investments made abroad—you may be eligible for a tax credit. The purpose of the tax credit is to prevent you from paying tax twice on the same income (once to a foreign country and again on your federal income tax).

RENEWABLE ENERGY PRODUCTION CREDIT. The credit is the cost of selling electricity produced from alternative energy sources within 10 years of placing the production facility in service.

CREDIT FOR SMALL EMPLOYER PENSION PLAN START-UP COSTS. Small employers (those with no more than 100 employees who received at least $5,000 of compensation in the preceding year) may claim a tax credit for starting up a qualified retirement plan. The credit is 50 percent of administrative and employee-education expenses up to $1,000, for a top credit of $500. The credit may be claimed for three years, starting with the year in which the plan becomes effective or the prior year. (This credit is explained in Chapter 16.)

CREDIT FOR QUALIFIED ELECTRIC VEHICLES. If you buy an electric car, you may claim a credit in 2005 of 10 percent of costs up to $40,000, reduced by 25 percent (maximum credit of $3,000). (This credit is explained in Chapter 9.)

PUERTO RICO ECONOMIC ACTIVITY CREDIT. A credit, based on certain wages and depreciation, can be claimed against any federal tax attributable to income from active business activities in Puerto Rico. However, wages taken into account for this credit may not be used for purposes of the research credit—no double-dipping is permitted.

ORPHAN DRUG CREDIT. If your business engages in research on diseases and afflictions that are not widespread, you may claim a special credit for your related expenses.

BIODIESEL FUELS CREDIT. This credit is the sum of two tax credits: the biodiesel mixture credit and the biodiesel credit. There is a higher credit limit for agribiodiesel.

LOW-SULFUR DIESEL FUEL PRODUCTION CREDIT. Small business refiners can claim a credit for the production of low-sulfur diesel fuel that complies with the EPA's Highway Diesel Fuel Sulfur Control Requirements. A small refiner is one with an average daily domestic refinery run for a one-year period ending on December 31, 2002, that is 155,000 barrels or less.

MARGINAL OIL AND GAS WELL PRODUCTION CREDIT. The credit is $3 per barrel of qualified crude oil production and 50 cents per 1,000 cubic feet of qualified natural gas production.

MINIMUM TAX CREDIT. If you paid AMT in a prior year, you may be eligible for a tax credit this year. Different rules apply to individuals and C corporations. (This credit is explained in Chapter 26.)

For the Future

Starting in 2006, there are new energy-related tax credits. For instance, there is a credit of $2,000 per dwelling for the construction of energy-efficient homes. There are also credits for energy production and certain investment.

General Business Credit

Most tax credits discussed in this chapter are part of the general business credit. This means that after figuring each separate credit, there is an overall limit to credits under the general business credit. Total credits in excess of these limits can be carried back and/or forward within limits.

The general business credit is comprised of the following:

- Investment credit (rehabilitation credit, renewal energy credit, reforestation credit, and the credit from cooperatives)
- Work opportunity credit
- Welfare-to-work credit
- Credit for alcohol used as fuel
- Research credit
- Low-income housing credit
- Enhanced oil recovery credit
- Disabled access credit
- Renewable electricity production credit
- Indian employment credit
- Credit for FICA on tips
- Orphan drug credit
- Credit for contributions to selected community development corporations
- Renewal community employment credit
- Credit for employer-provided child care facilities and services
- Credit for small employer retirement plan start-up costs
- New markets credit
- Biodiesel fuels credit
- Low-sulfur diesel fuel production credit
- Marginal oil and gas well production credit

The empowerment zone employment credit is not part of the general business credit and is not subject to the general business credit limitations. Excess empowerment zone credits may be carried over in a manner similar to the general business credit.

Credit Limitations

First you figure each separate credit of the general business credit and then total them. The total is then subject to special limits, determined by your regular and alternative minimum tax liability and certain other tax credits. Your limit is your net tax liability (regular tax reduced by certain personal credits, including the foreign tax credit), reduced by the greater of:

- Your tentative AMT liability (figured before comparing it with regular tax).
- Twenty-five percent of regular tax liability (before personal tax credits) over $25,000.

Example

In 2005, your regular tax liability is $12,000. You are entitled to claim $1,000 in personal tax credits. You have no AMT liability. Your general business credit is limited to $11,000 (net tax liability of $11,000, reduced by zero since you do not have any AMT liability and 25 percent of your regular tax does not exceed $25,000).

SPECIAL LIMIT ON THE RESEARCH CREDIT.   The credit cannot exceed the taxable income from the business that produced the credit.

CARRYBACKS AND CARRYFORWARDS.   If the credit limitation prevents you from claiming the full general business credit that you are otherwise entitled to, you do not lose the benefit of this excess amount—you simply cannot claim it in the current year. You may be able to use the excess credit to offset your tax liability in prior and/or future years.

You may carry back the excess amount to 2004. If there continues to be an excess (it exceeds the credit limitation for 2004), you may then carry forward the excess up to 20 years.

OLD CREDITS.   If you had credits arising in tax years beginning before 1998 that could not be currently claimed because of the credit limitation, this excess was subject to a three-year carryback period and a 15-year carryforward period. Be sure to segregate your pre-1998 and post-1997 excess credits. All excess pre-1998 amounts are added together and treated as one credit carryforward.

EXPIRED CARRYFORWARDS.   If you still have unused amounts and the carryforward period expires or the business ceases (or you die), the unused amounts may be deducted in the year after the carryforward expiration or in the year of business cessation (or death). However, to the extent the credit relates to the research credit, it must be cut in half before deducting it.

Where to Claim Tax Credits

Self-Employed Individuals

Employment tax credits are reported on Schedule C as a reduction to wages paid to employees. (Schedule C-EZ cannot be used if you have employees so no credits are reported on this form.) All other credits—both business and personal—are claimed directly on Form 1040.

Farmers

The credit for federal excise tax on fuels is claimed directly on Form 1040 (it is not reported on Schedule F). All other credits are also claimed directly on Form 1040.

Partnerships and LLCs

All business credits pass through separately to owners and are claimed on their individual returns.

S Corporations

The credit for the federal tax on fuels is claimed by the S corporation on Form 1120S. All other business credits pass through separately to shareholders and are claimed on their individual returns.

C Corporations

All tax credits are claimed on Form 1120. Some credits are taken into account on Form 1120, Schedule J, "Tax Computation," in figuring tax liability while other credits are claimed directly on Form 1120 as an offset to tax liability.

All Taxpayers

All taxpayers use the same form, Form 3800, General Business Credit, for figuring the general business credit, limitations, and carrybacks/carryforwards. However, if you have only one credit that is part of the general business credit, you need not complete Form 3800. Instead, complete the form for the specific credit and then figure the general business credit limitation on a separate attachment.

When claiming any carrybacks or carryforwards, you must attach your own explanation that includes the following information:

- The year in which the credit originated
- The amount of the credit
- The amount allowed in the year of origination
- The amount allowed in each carryback year
- The amount allowed in each carryforward year

TABLE 23.1 Guide to Tax Credits

Business Credits	Tax Form	More Info
Alcohol fuels credit	Form 6478	
Credit for FICA tax on tips	Form 8846	Chapter 7
Credit for qualified electric vehicles	Form 8834	Chapter 9
Disabled access credit	Form 8826	Chapter 10
Employer-provided child care facilities and services credit	Form 8882	Chapter 23
Empowerment zone employment credit	Form 8844	Chapter 7
Enhanced oil recovery credit	Form 8830	
Federal excise tax on fuel	Form 4136	Chapter 13
Foreign tax credit		
corporations	Form 1118	Chapter 13
individuals	Form 1116	Chapter 13
General business credit	Form 3800	Chapters 7 and 23
Indian employment credit	Form 8845	Chapter 7
Investment credit (rehabilitation credit, renewal energy credit, reforestation credit, and the credit from cooperatives)	Form 3468	Chapter 10
Minimum tax credit		
corporations	Form 8827	Chapter 26
individuals	Form 8801	Chapter 26
New markets credit	Form 8874	Chapter 23
Orphan drug credit	Form 8820	
Renewal electricity production credit	Form 8835	
Research credit	Form 6765	Chapter 14
Small employer retirement plan start-up costs credit	Form 8881	Chapter 16
Welfare-to-work credit	Form 8861	Chapter 7
Work opportunity credit	Form 5884	Chapter 7
Personal Work-Related Credits	**Tax Form**	**More Info**
Earned income credit	Form EIC	Chapter 7
Education credits	Form 8863	Chapter 21
Dependent care credit	Form 2441	Chapter 7

Tax Planning for Your Small Business

CHAPTER 24

Income and Deduction Strategies

Understanding what income you must report and the various business deductions you may claim is only half the job. You must also know when to report income and when to postpone it, when to claim certain deductions and when not to claim them. You should also be aware of the common traps that business owners often fall into with their income and deductions.

In this chapter you will learn about:

- Tax-saving tips
- Common errors in claiming deductions, and how to avoid them

Finally, it is important to recognize that you should not always go at it alone. You may need to get the assistance of tax professionals or additional information from the IRS. You need to know how to obtain referrals to tax professionals. You also need to know some important IRS telephone numbers to call for assistance. This information is included throughout this chapter for your convenience.

Tax-Saving Tips

Tax-Planning Decisions

Some deductions are under your control because you can decide whether to incur the expenditure. Also, sometimes you are permitted to make tax elections on when to report income or when to claim write-offs. Here are some pointers that can help you minimize your income and maximize your deductions. Or, you can follow the reverse strategy if you already have losses for the year and want to accelerate income to offset those losses (and defer deductions).

- *Cash-basis businesses.* If you account for your expenses and income on a cash basis, you can influence when you receive income and claim deductions for year-end items. For example, you can delay billing out for services or merchandise so that payment will be received in the following year. In deferring income for services or goods sold, do not delay billing so that collection may be in jeopardy. This income deferral strategy is more important than ever in view of declining personal income tax rates.

  On the flip side, you can accelerate deductions by paying outstanding bills and stocking up on supplies. As the personal income tax rates decline over the next several years, this deduction acceleration strategy becomes more important—the higher the income tax rate, the more valuable the deduction.

  However, in accelerating deductions, do not prepay expenses that relate to items extending beyond one year. For example, if you pay a three-year subscription to a trade magazine, you can deduct only the portion of the subscription (one-third) that relates to the current year; the balance is deductible in future years as allocated.

- *Accrual method businesses.* The board of directors of an accrual-basis C corporation can authorize a charitable contribution and make note of it in the corporate minutes. A current deduction can be claimed even if the contribution is paid after the end of the year (as long as it is paid no later than two-and-a-half months after the close of the year). Charitable contributions are discussed in Chapter 22.

  Similarly, accrual method businesses can accrue bonuses and other payments to employees in the current year that are paid within two-and-a-half months of the close of the year. However, this rule does not extend to payments to S corporation owner-employees—payments are deductible only when received by the owner-employees.

- *Owner participation.* If you own a business, be sure that your level of participation is sufficient to allow you to deduct all your losses under the passive loss limitation rules. Increase your level of participation and keep records of how and when you participated in the business. Passive loss rules and the various participation tests under these rules are discussed in Chapter 4.

- *Increase basis to fully utilize losses.* If you are an owner in a pass-through entity, your share of losses generally is deductible only to the extent of your basis in the business. Explore ways in which to increase your basis so that the losses can be fully utilized. For example, if you are an

S corporation shareholder, you can increase basis by lending funds to your business. Basis rules and their impact on deducting losses are discussed in Chapter 4.

- *Minimize FICA.* Owners who work for their corporations may be able to extract distributions on a FICA-free basis by arranging loans or rentals to the business and taking payments in the form of interest or rents. Of course, these arrangements must be bona fide. However, S corporation shareholders who perform substantial services for their corporation should not erroneously characterize compensation as dividends.

- *Review qualified plan selection.* If you are self-employed and use an IRA, SEP, SIMPLE, or other qualified plan to save for retirement, review your choice of plan annually to see if it optimizes your benefits while keeping costs down.

  Similarly, corporations should review existing plans to see whether terminations or other courses of action are warranted as cost-cutting measures. If you want to terminate one plan and begin another, do not do so without consulting a pension expert. You must be sure that your old plan is in full compliance with the tax laws—including recent changes—before it is terminated.

- *Carry medical coverage for yourself and employees.* Buy the kind of coverage you can afford. The business picks up the expense for your personal insurance protection. Even if you cannot receive this benefit on a tax-free basis (if, for example, you are a partner or S corporation shareholder who must include business-paid insurance in your income), you can deduct a percentage of the coverage on your individual return.

  You can reduce the cost of coverage to the business by buying a high-deductible plan that allows employees to contribute to medical savings accounts on a tax-deductible basis. Alternatively, you can make deductible contributions to Health Savings Accounts (HSAs) on behalf of your employees. You can shift most of the cost of coverage to employees by adopting a premium-only cafeteria plan.

  If you have a C corporation and are a shareholder-employee, you can institute a medical reimbursement plan to cover out-of-pocket medical costs not otherwise covered by insurance (such as dental expenses, eye care, or prescription drugs). Medical coverage strategies are discussed in Chapter 19.

- *Institute other employee benefit plans.* If you have a C corporation that is profitable and you are a shareholder-employee, you may be able to turn your nondeductible personal expenses into deductible business expenses. For example, you can have the corporation institute a group term life insurance plan for employees and obtain tax-free coverage up to

$50,000. Of course, in weighing the advantages and disadvantages of employee benefit plans, be sure to consider the cost of covering rank-and-file employees, since most benefit plans have strict nondiscrimination rules. Also, take into account the fact that employer-paid educational assistance and adoption plans cannot give more than 5 percent of benefits to shareholders owning more than 5 percent of the stock, making such plans undesirable for such closely held corporations. Employee benefits are discussed in Chapter 7.

- *Reimbursement arrangements.* If your company reimburses you for travel and entertainment costs, be sure that the arrangement is treated as an *accountable plan.* This will ensure that not only does the company save on employment taxes but also that you are not taxed on reimbursements, since your offsetting deductions would be subject to the two-percent-of-adjusted-gross-income floor. With an accountable plan, the company deducts the expenses and no income is reported to you. Reimbursement arrangements are discussed in Chapter 8.

- *Take optimum write-offs for business equipment purchases.* When the business can benefit from a larger deduction, instead of depreciating the cost of equipment over the life of the property, consider electing first-year expensing (e.g., a deduction of up to $105,000 in 2005). Alternatively, when the business cannot benefit from a current depreciation deduction because it does not have sufficient income to offset the deduction, consider electing alternative depreciation to spread deductions over future years. Time business equipment purchases carefully in view of the mid-quarter convention. Depreciation and expensing are discussed in Chapter 14.

- *Abandonment versus selling of property.* If you have property that simply is of no value to the business, you may want to abandon it rather than sell it for a nominal amount. This will allow the business to take an ordinary loss deduction rather than a capital loss on a sale. A sale of Section 1231 property may result in a capital or ordinary loss, depending on other Section 1231 transactions for the current year and prior Section 1231 losses. Abandonment of property and Section 1231 property are discussed in Chapter 6.

- *Disaster losses.* If you suffer a disaster loss to business property in an area declared by the president to be eligible for federal disaster assistance, consider claiming the deduction on a return for the year preceding the year of the loss if this will give you needed cash flow or result in a greater benefit from the deduction. Disaster losses are discussed in Chapter 17.

- *Elect to forgo a net operating loss carryback.* If the business has an NOL in 2005, it can generally carry the loss back two years (three years for small business disaster losses; five years for farmers and ranchers; 10 years for product liability) and forward for 20 years. Alternatively, it can elect to forgo the carryback and simply carry the loss forward. Where a corporation was in a low tax bracket in prior years but is in a higher tax bracket now (and expects to remain in a high bracket in the future), it may be advisable to elect to forgo the carryback. If the business simply does not have any prior income to offset by an NOL, do not make an election; simply carry the loss forward. By not making the election, you preserve the right to carry back the NOL if the IRS subsequently audits an earlier return and income results. Net operating losses are discussed in Chapter 4.

- *Review the business structure.* Changes in the business climate, in business goals, tax laws, and state laws may warrant a change in the form of business organization. For example, your business may start as a sole proprietorship; later you may want to incorporate in order to take advantage of certain employee benefit plans. Review the options that will afford tax reduction and other benefits. Business organization is discussed in Chapter 1.
- *Do year-end planning.* Businesses have an opportunity to save on taxes with year-end planning. Well-timed deductions may prove advantageous. Begin year-end planning well before the end of the year in order to have time to implement your decisions.
- *Stay abreast of tax law changes.* New opportunities are continually being created—through Congressional action, court decisions, and IRS rulings. You need to know what these changes are in order to take advantage of them. Download a free Supplement to this book (available February 1, 2006) on tax developments affecting small businesses from <www.jklasser.com>.

Audit-Proofing Your Return

Perhaps the number one audit trigger for small business is improper classification of workers. Small business owners may treat workers as independent contractors when they should be treated as employees. If the IRS successfully reclassifies workers as employees, you could owe back employment taxes, interest, and penalties as well as risk loss of qualified status for your retirement plan. In other words, the monetary risks of misclassification are substantial.

You can rely on a safe harbor to avoid misclassification. You need to show that it is an industry practice to treat such workers as independent contractors. All company practices should be consistent.

- Contract terminology in any agreements with these workers should reflect independent contractor status.
- Form 1099-MISC should be issued each year to all your independent contractors.

- Treat all workers on a consistent basis every year (independent contractors should remain independent contractors).
- Treat all workers with similar responsibilities on a consistent basis (all workers who handle a particular job should be treated *either* as employees or independent contractors, depending on the circumstances).

Many audit problems arise in connection with deductions. Your goal should be to claim all the deductions to which you are entitled in order to minimize your business income. At the same time, you want to *audit-proof* your return to avoid confrontations with the IRS. The following are some tips you can use to ensure that your write-offs will be allowed.

- *Report business income.* While there is an underground economy operating strictly for cash, do not join these ranks. The failure to report income can result in criminal charges punishable by fines and jail time. The IRS is becoming increasingly sophisticated about discerning unreported income. It has developed audit guides for various industries to enable its auditors to detect unreported income. For example, by examining the amount of flour ordered by a pizzeria, the IRS can determine how many pizzas should have been sold—the failure to fall within reasonable parameters can lead to charges of failing to report income.
- *Keep good records.* You need proof to back up your deductions, such as when the expense was paid or incurred, the amount of the expense, and why you think it is deductible. If you develop good recordkeeping practices, you will automatically be assured of the necessary evidence to support your deductions. For example, if you want to claim deductions for travel and entertainment expenses, you must have certain proof of expenditures. Using a computer to keep your books and records can simplify both recordkeeping requirements and tax return preparation. Recordkeeping is explained in detail in Chapter 3.
- *Formalize agreements between corporations and shareholders.* If loans are made to or from shareholders, be sure that the interest rate, terms of repayment, and other particulars of the loans are written down. Have the note signed by all of the parties. Formal agreements should also be made if property is leased by a shareholder to the corporation. In addition to promissory notes, contracts, or other agreements between the parties, it is a good idea to put any agreements into the minutes of the corporation.
- *Be careful when claiming deductions and credits.* Make sure you meet eligibility requirements before taking write-offs. Be aware that the IRS may flag returns that claim excessive deductions. Some tax professionals advise that you keep deductible expenses under 52 percent of gross income on Schedule C (50 percent on Schedule F) and suggest that deduc-

tions over 67 percent of income on Schedule C (or 71 percent on Schedule F) are likely to attract IRS attention. These numbers are only guidelines; claim *all* deductions to which you are entitled. Even if the IRS examines your return, you can prove entitlement to your write-offs.

- *Supply all necessary information.* In completing business returns, be sure to fill out all forms and schedules required. Also include all required information for claiming certain deductions. For example, if you have a bad debt, you cannot simply deduct the loss. You must attach a statement to the return detailing the nature and extent of the bad debt.

- *Review the IRS audit guide for your industry* (if such a guide has been released). This guide is used by IRS personnel to review returns of businesses within an industry and thus provides key information about what the IRS is on the lookout for. Currently there are more than three dozen guides available free from the IRS at <www.irs.gov/businesses/page/ 0,,id=7045,00.html>.

- *Ask for the IRS's opinion.* If you are planning a novel transaction or want to take a deduction about which you are unsure, you may be able to get the IRS's view on the situation. You may want to request a private letter ruling. If the ruling is favorable, you can be confident of your position. If it is unfavorable, you may be able to modify the situation as the ruling suggests. The IRS charges a user fee for issuing letter rulings (the amounts vary). Before asking for a ruling, though, it may be better to discuss the situation with a tax professional who can research existing precedent and help you prepare a ruling request.

- *File on time.* If you delay filing, you face not only penalties and interest but also the loss of deductions. For example, you must claim a deduction for contributions to a qualified retirement plan no later than the due date of your return. If you cannot meet the filing deadline, be sure to ask for a filing extension in a timely manner. File the correct form for claiming a filing extension appropriate to your business return. (See Table 24.1.) Also, check state income tax rules for filing extensions that may require a separate form.

- *Get good advice.* If you are unsure of whether you need to report certain income or whether you are entitled to claim a particular deduction, ask a tax professional. You may have special questions concerning the new tax law.

  Be sure to understand the protection you receive from attorney-client privilege. This privilege also applies to accountants and other federally authorized tax practitioners with respect to federal civil tax matters. But it does not apply to mere tax return preparation, state tax matters (unless your state extends similar protection), or other federal nontax matters (such as securities matters).

TABLE 24.1 Forms for Filing Extensions

If You File:	Ask for an Extension On:
Schedule A, Form 1040, for employees	Form 4868
Schedule C, Form 1040, for sole proprietors	Form 4868
Schedule F, Form 1040, for farmers	Form 4868
Form 1065, for partnerships and LLCs	Form 8736
Form 1120, for C corporations	Form 7004
Form 1120S, for S corporations	Form 7004

Planning Ahead

The ever-changing tax laws make it challenging to devise long-term tax strategies for your business. Still, it is important to be able to plan ahead so you can decide in which year it may be more favorable to purchase capital equipment, hire new workers, or take other actions that can affect your after-tax profits.

Many of the tax changes that take place each year are the result of cost-of-living adjustments (COLA). Others are the product of phased-in law changes, while still others are IRS devised. In Table 24.2 you will find a listing of some common scheduled adjustments and law changes affecting small businesses over the next several years.

Common Errors in Claiming Deductions, and How to Avoid Them

The IRS has compiled a list of errors that arise with great frequency on business returns in connection with deductions. By being forewarned of these errors, you should be able to avoid them.

Salary of Corporate Officers

Some corporations have been claiming deductions for management or consulting fees paid to the corporation's owners. At the same time, these corporations have not claimed deductions for salary. This leads the IRS to conclude that the corporations are misclassifying payments to corporate officers as fees rather than compensation in order to avoid payroll taxes. Corporations may be liable for penalties for failing to withhold and deposit payroll taxes and for failing to file required payroll tax returns. Of course, sometimes payments to shareholders may very well be management or consulting fees for occasional outside assistance. But if these individuals conduct the actual business of the corporation—perform the services for which the corporation

TABLE 24.2 Tax Items and Their Changes

Item	COLA/Law Change/IRS	Other Information
Adjustment to tax brackets for individuals (sole proprietors and owners of pass-through entities)	COLA	All brackets above 10% annually; 10% bracket COLA in 2004 and after 2008
Zero percent capital gains rate for community renewal property	Law change	Applies only to property acquired before January 1, 2010
Wage base for Social Security portion of FICA/self-employment tax	COLA	
Adoption assistance—excludable amount	COLA	
Standard mileage rate for business mileage	IRS	IRS-adjusted figure reflecting cost of gas, etc.
Dollar limits on depreciating vehicles under 6,000 pounds	IRS	IRS-adjusted figure
Inclusion amount for leased vehicles	IRS	IRS-adjusted figure
Transportation fringe benefits	COLA	
Per diem travel rates	*	
Deductible meal costs for Department of Transportation employees	Law change	No changes after 2008
Health savings accounts—annual deductible range and limit on out-of-pocket expenses	COLA	
Elective deferrals to 401(k) and SIMPLE plans	Law change	Increases scheduled to sunset after 2010
Contributions and benefits limits for qualified retirement plans	COLA	
First-year expensing	COLA	Applies to property placed in service before January 1, 2008
New York Liberty Zone leasehold improvements—five-year recovery period	Law change	Applies only to improvements made before January 1, 2007
Expensing of remedial environmental cleanup costs	Law change	Expires after 2005 unless extended by Congress

(Continued)

TABLE 24.2 *(Continued)*

Item	COLA/Law Change/IRS	Other Information
Credit for electric vehicles—reduction in credit in 2006	Law change	Expires after 2006 unless extended by Congress
Domestic production activities deduction percentage	Law change	Increases in 2007 to 6% and in 2010 to 9%

*These rates are adjusted each October 1 (the start of the federal government's fiscal year) by the General Services Administration.

was organized or provide management services on a full-time or consistent basis—the payments look more like compensation.

S corporations especially may also fail to deduct compensation paid to owner-employees and instead call distributions to them *dividends.* The rationale for this strategy is to reduce the corporation's liability for payroll taxes. Again, the IRS has identified this strategy as a common error and has imposed penalties on S corporations that have followed it. If an owner-employee performs substantial services for the S corporation, some reasonable amount of payment for services must be treated as deductible compensation subject to payroll taxes.

Below-Market Loans

Loans from shareholders to their corporations that bear an interest rate lower than the applicable federal rate (a rate set monthly by the IRS, which varies with the term of the loan) result in phantom or *imputed* interest. Shareholders must report this interest; corporations can deduct the imputed interest. If the corporation fails to take an interest deduction, the IRS may conclude that the shareholder has not really made a loan but rather a contribution to the capital of the corporation, and no deduction for the corporation will be allowed.

Loans to shareholders from their corporations may also present tax deduction problems. Shareholders are entitled to deduct imputed interest in this case (as business or investment interest), with the corporation picking up the imputed interest as interest income. Unfortunately, some corporations are failing to report the income, but they are still showing the loan on their balance sheets. This is an unnecessary error for corporations to make. If the shareholders are also employees of the corporation, then the corporation can claim a deduction for compensation to the shareholder-employees to offset the imputed interest income. If, however, the shareholders are not employees of the corporation, the payments to them must be treated as dividends, which are not deductible by the corporation.

Travel and Entertainment Deductions

Some businesses claim a full deduction for business meals and entertainment. They do not correctly apply the 50-percent limit on these deductions. This problem commonly occurs for meals and entertainment away from home.

Bad Debt Deductions

Some individuals are claiming bad debt deductions as ordinary losses rather than short-term capital losses. In other words, they are classifying the bad debt as a business bad debt when, in fact, it may be a nonbusiness bad debt. For example, if a shareholder has a bad debt for a loan to the corporation, the loan should be treated as a nonbusiness bad debt because it is not incurred in a trade or business; rather, it is made to protect one's investment as a shareholder.

Casualty Losses

Some businesses fail to reduce deductions for casualty losses by any insurance reimbursements received. This results in an overstatement of casualty losses.

Claiming Losses in General

Some taxpayers claim losses in excess of amounts that are otherwise allowed. They fail to observe the passive loss limitation rules that limit loss deductions for activities in which there is no material participation. Just because someone owns stock in an S corporation, for example, does not mean that he or she is a material participant in the business. The shareholder must meet special material participation tests to deduct losses in excess of passive income.

Other taxpayers may be deducting hobby losses in excess of income from this type of activity. While income from a hobby-type activity is fully taxable, losses are deductible only to the extent of income from the activity.

Also, some shareholders in S corporations claim losses in excess of their basis in the corporation. Losses are deductible only to the extent of a shareholder's basis in stock and loans to the corporation. Basis is adjusted annually for various transactions—shareholder's distributive share of S corporation income that is taxable to the shareholder, distributions by the corporation, and losses claimed. Losses in excess of basis are not lost. They can be carried forward and used in a subsequent year when there is sufficient basis to offset them.

Tax Assistance

Your primary focus should be on running your business and making it profitable. This may leave you little or no time to attend to tax matters. It may be cost effective to use the services of a tax professional to maintain your books and records, file your returns, and provide needed tax advice.

There are many different types of tax professionals to choose from. The particular type of counsel you seek depends in part on your needs and what you can afford to pay for the services provided. The types of tax professionals you can consult include:

- Accountants
- Enrolled agents
- Certified public accountants (CPAs)
- Tax attorneys

Storefront tax return preparation services may provide assistance with filing your returns. They generally are not staffed to provide tax guidance.

Keep in mind that any information you disclose to an attorney is completely confidential under the attorney-client privilege. This privilege has been extended to other federally authorized tax practitioners (such as accountants) in civil tax matters. However, it does not apply to the following situations:

- Tax return preparation
- Criminal tax matters
- State tax matters (unless there is a special state-created accountant-client privilege)
- Matters involving other federal agencies (such as the Securities and Exchange Commission)

If there is anything you absolutely want to remain confidential, then you must use an attorney. The attorney may hire an accountant to perform accounting tasks and, as the attorney's agent, tax information disclosed to the accountant in this situation remains completely confidential.

If you do not know the name of a specific individual to help you, ask business acquaintances for referrals. Another source of references is the Yellow Pages of your phone book. Then, if you wish to check whether a particular CPA is licensed as claimed, you can call your state Society of CPAs. Similarly, if you want to check on a particular attorney, call your state Bar Association. Do not hesitate to ask the professional what he or she charges for the services to be provided.

Help from the IRS

The IRS now has a web site exclusively for small business and self-employed individuals <www.irs.gov/businesses/small/index.htm>. This site contains industry-specific information so, for example, if you are in construction you will find the hot issues relating to the construction industry. You will also find audit guides that tell IRS agents what to look for when examining returns of businesses within your industry. And you will find links to other tax sites that may be helpful to you. At present there are only a dozen industries, but the IRS plans to expand its coverage.

The IRS provides a number of publications, some of which have been mentioned throughout the book, that can give you important information on income and deductions. Table 24.3 lists some of these publications.

These publications are available directly from the IRS by calling (800) 829-3676 or by visiting your local IRS office, post office, or library. You can also download them from the IRS web site at <www.irs.gov>. Forms are also available by fax by dialing (703) 321-8020 (a toll call).

The IRS provides a number of resource tools on CD-ROM. These include the Small Business Resource Guide, the Virtual Small Business Workshop, and Introduction to Federal Taxes (all of which are free).

Another valuable source of assistance is the instructions for particular tax returns. For example, if your business is an S corporation, you can obtain guidance on claiming various tax deductions from the instructions for Form 1120S.

You may want to attend a free IRS seminar offered to new business owners. Topics covered in these seminars include recordkeeping, tax filing requirements, employment taxes, and federal tax deposit rules. There are also special seminars for different types of businesses (e.g., S corporations). To find out about a seminar in your area, call the IRS's Taxpayer Education Coordinator (listed in your local phone book and available through the IRS's general number, (800) 829-1040. Or your can learn with your computer using the Virtual Small Business Workshop (mentioned earlier).

If you have questions, you may direct them to the IRS. There is a special telephone number to call for questions about your business return: (800) 829-4933. However, do not simply rely on statements made to you by someone in your local IRS office or over the telephone. If you want to rely on IRS advice, be sure to get it in writing. The IRS is not bound by oral advice, but it is bound by any written advice it may give you.

If you have a thorny tax issue involving substantial dollars and are not sure how the IRS will rule on the subject, you may want to obtain a special ruling. You can ask for a private letter ruling without the assistance of a tax professional, but this may not be the best course of action. You need to frame your question appropriately. Also, you need to supply a great deal of information to the IRS before it will take any action. A tax professional can ensure that your request will receive the attention you desire. The procedure entails the payment of a user fee that must accompany your ruling request.

If you have a problem with the IRS and cannot seem to get a satisfactory

TABLE 24.3 IRS Publications of Interest

Publication Number	Title
15	Circular E, Employer's Tax Guide
15A	Employer's Supplemental Tax Guide
15B	Employer's Guide to Fringe Benefits
51	Circular A, Agricultural Employer's Tax Guide
225	Farmer's Tax Guide
334	Tax Guide for Small Business
378	Fuel Tax Credits and Refunds
463	Travel, Entertainment, Gift, and Car Expenses
510	Excise Taxes
521	Moving Expenses
526	Charitable Contributions
533	Self-Employment Tax
534	Depreciating Property Placed in Service before 1987
535	Business Expenses
536	Net Operating Losses
537	Installment Sales
538	Accounting Periods and Methods
541	Partnerships
542	Corporations
544	Sales and Other Dispositions of Assets
547	Casualties, Disasters, and Thefts (Business and Nonbusiness)
550	Investment Income and Expenses
551	Basis of Assets
552	Recordkeeping for Individuals
560	Retirement Plans for Small Business
583	Starting a Business and Keeping Records
584B	Business Casualty, Disaster, and Theft Loss Workbook
587	Business Use of Your Home (Including Use by Day-Care Providers)
590	Individual Retirement Arrangements (IRAs)
595	Tax Highlights for Commercial Fishermen

TABLE 24.3 *(Continued)*

Publication Number	Title
908	Bankruptcy Tax Guide
911	Direct Sellers
925	Passive Activity and At-Risk Rules
946	How to Depreciate Property
954	Tax Incentives for Distressed Communities
963	Federal–State Reference Guide
966	Electronic Federal Tax Payment System (Answers to Most Commonly Asked Questions)
969	Health Savings Accounts and Other Tax-Favored Health Plans
1066	Small Business Tax Workshop Student Workbook
1220	Specifications for Filing Forms 1098, 1099, 5498, and W-2G Electronically or Magnetically
1518	IRS Tax Calendar for Small Business and Self-Employed
1542	Per Diem Rates (available online only)
1544	Reporting Cash Payments of over $10,000
1635	Understanding Your EIN
1779	Employee Independent Contractor Brochure
1875	Employer/Tip Income Reporting
1932	How to Make Correct Federal Tax Deposits
1976	Independent Contractor or Employee?
2194B	Disaster Losses Kit for Businesses
3144	Tips on Tips (A Guide to TIP Income Reporting) for Employer
3402	Tax Issues for Limited Liability Companies
3151A	The ABC's of Federal Tax Deposits
3518	Beauty Industry Federal Tax Guidelines
3780	Tax Information for Small Construction Businesses
3909	IRS e-file for Business Fact Sheets and Q&As
3998	Choosing a Retirement Solution for Your Small Business
4035	Home-Based Business Tax Avoidance Schemes

answer, you may want to ask the IRS to direct your question to its Problem Resolution section.

Tax Help through the Small Business Administration

The Small Business Administration (SBA) has teamed up with the IRS to provide tax assistance to small business owners. You can obtain a free CD-ROM entitled *Small Business Resource Guide: What You Need to Know About Taxes and Other Products* available at <www.sba.gov> or (800) 827-5722.

Small business tax forms and publications are now available at all 73 of the SBA's Business Information Centers (BICs) and One-Stop Capital Shops. IRS technical specialists are also available at BICs in Atlanta, Boston, Chicago, and Los Angeles one day per week to provide seminars, workshops, and one-on-one assistance (but not with tax preparation).

CHAPTER 25

Tax Strategies for Opening or Closing a Business

Two of the most challenging times of running a business are, perhaps, the start-up and close-down phases. Taxwise, there are certain opportunities that should not be overlooked.

In this chapter you will learn about:

- Initial tax decisions to make
- Tax identification numbers
- Tax reporting in the first year
- How to write off start-up costs
- Aborted business ventures
- Steps to closing down a business
- Setting up a business bank account and credit card
- Tax reporting in the final year

For further information, see IRS Publication 583, *Starting a Business and Keeping Records*.

Initial Tax Decisions to Make

When you start a business of any kind, whether a full-time or part-time one, you need to make certain choices. Here is a checklist of the elections, choices, and decisions to make when commencing a business (the chapter in which the item is discussed is also noted):

- *Type of entity* (Chapter 1). Should you incorporate? Form an LLC?
- *Tax year* (Chapter 2). Should you use a calendar year? A fiscal year (and which fiscal year)?
- *Accounting method* (Chapter 3). Should you use the cash method? Accrual method? Some other method?
- *Equipment* (Chapter 14). Should you start with the things you already own? Buy new equipment? Lease new equipment?
- *Home office* (Chapter 18). Should you start from home? Rent space? Buy a facility?
- *Professional advisors* (Chapter 22). Who is going to be your company attorney? Accountant? Insurance agent?

None of the decisions you make initially are carved in stone. You can make changes, but often they come with tax consequences. For instance, if you start as a corporation and then want to become a limited liability company, you may incur taxes upon the corporation's liquidation. Similarly, when you change tax years or accounting methods, you may have additional income to report from the changeover.

It is always a good idea to work with knowledgeable professionals to get started on the right foot. The money you pay for this advice can be considerably less than the cost of mistakes for doing things incorrectly on your own.

Tax Identification Numbers

For personal returns, your Social Security number is your tax identification number. But for business you may have several different numbers.

Your tax identification number is a nine-digit number unique to you. You use this number when filing tax returns, making tax deposits, hiring employees, opening a business bank account, applying for a loan, and setting up a qualified retirement plan. Usually you use a federal employer identification number (EIN) obtained from the IRS as your tax identification number (even if you are not an employer because you do not have any employees).

If you are a sole proprietor (or the sole owner of a limited liability company), you can usually use your Social Security number as your tax identification number on your income tax return. But even this type of business must use an EIN for a business bank account, to report payroll taxes, and to start a Keogh, SEP, or SIMPLE plan. And, in this era of identity theft, you may want to use an EIN if you pay an independent contractor $600 or more for the year and are required to report this income to the IRS and the contractor on Form 1099-MISC, so that you do not have to give your Social Security number to the contractor.

Where to Get Your EIN

You can obtain your federal EIN by completing IRS Form SS-4, Application for Employer Identification Number, online at www.irs.gov/businesses/small/article/0,,id=102767,00.html and click on "apply online now" (see Chapter 1).

When you apply online, the IRS automatically enrolls you in the Electronic Federal Tax Payment System (EFTPS) (www.eftps.gov). This electronic system enables you to make tax payments, including estimated taxes, through your computer. After automatic enrollment you will receive an enrollment confirmation, along with a PIN and instructions within a few days. You do not have to use EFTPS (unless tax deposits exceeded $200,000 two years ago), but may choose to do so for the convenience. Millions of small businesses have voluntarily signed on to use EFTPS.

State EINs

States may assign their own tax identification numbers (also called business registration numbers) to your business for unemployment insurance reporting for employees and for other purposes, typically at the time you register to do business in your state. For more information about your state EIN, contact your state tax, revenue, or finance department.

If you do business in Georgia and New York, you can register with the IRS and state in one step (go to www.irs.gov/businesses/small/article/0,,id=111949,00.html and click on the applicable state).

Resale Number Distinguished

Business owners are responsible not only for income and employment taxes, but also for state and local sales taxes on the goods and services they sell. In order to properly remit sales tax that you collect to your state and to avoid paying sales tax on items you buy for resale, you need a resale number (states without sales tax—Alaska, Delaware, Montana, New Hampshire, and Oregon—do not issue resale numbers). Your state sales tax number (called a resale number, a seller's permit, or sales tax license) is *not* the same as your federal tax identification number.

Once you have your resale number, your state may permit you to continue to use it as long as you are in business; in other states you must renew the resale number periodically. For information on obtaining a resale number, contact your state tax, revenue, or finance department.

Tax Reporting for the First Year

Most businesses do not start on January 1, so the first year of business may be a "short year" (less than a full 12 months). From a tax-reporting standpoint, a return must be filed for the short year. For example, if a business that reports on a calendar-year basis starts to operate on August 10, 2005, it must file a return for 2005. It does *not* have to prorate deductions for the period in which it operates.

Indicate on the appropriate tax return that this is the first year of the business. This is done as follows:

- Schedule C—Line H.
- Form 1065—Line G(1)
- Form 1120S—Line F(1)
- Form 1120—Line E(1)

How to Write Off Start-Up Costs

Once you're in business, most expenses become deductible items (tax rules may affect when you can claim deductions or may place certain limits on the amount you can write off). Before you open your doors, you do not have a business in which to claim the deductions. Therefore, it is important to separate start-up costs from those incurred by an operating business.

Start-up costs may be deductible once you actually start your business, but they are not deductible during your preopening phase.

A complete discussion of items viewed as start-up costs and how to deduct them is to be found in Chapter 14.

Setting Up a Business Bank Account and Credit Card

Once you have set up your business and obtained your tax identification number, it is highly advisable to set up a separate business bank account. Use this account exclusively to deposit business receipts and to pay business expenses. Do not commingle the funds in your business bank account with your personal money.

If you are self-employed, it is also advisable to set up another account for your personal estimated taxes. Use this account to set aside the funds needed to pay your quarterly estimated taxes. Often small-business owners who were formerly employees of large corporations that had withheld income taxes on their behalf are unfamiliar with estimated tax requirements on their share of business income and can fall short of the money needed to meet this tax obligation.

It is also a good idea to use a separate credit card solely for business purchases. Having both a separate business bank account and credit card simplifies recordkeeping for your business. Further, it helps to show that you are running your company in a businesslike fashion in case the IRS questions whether losses should be disallowed under the hobby loss rules (see Chapter 4).

Aborted Business Ventures

What happens if you investigate the purchase of a business or the start of a venture but the deal never goes through? Or if you hire an architect to design a building but never get town approval for the construction? The costs of starting up and organizing a business are not immediately deductible in full (but may be amortized, as explained in Chapter 14). However, the costs of an aborted business venture are immediately deductible.

To deduct your costs, you must have proceeded beyond a general search. Once you focus on a particular business and the deal falls through, you can deduct your expenses. Mere investigatory expenses are not deductible; only those related to a specific business are. Thus, for example, if you travel to look at various business opportunities, you cannot deduct your travel costs. But once you select one particular business and begin drawing up contracts, your legal costs for the contracts are deductible even if they never get signed.

Expenses of Winding Up a Small Business

Unfortunately, the cold statistics show that many small businesses fail. Some last longer than others, but a large number of ventures will reach a point where they are so unprofitable that the owners must simply give up. Certain expenses relate to the closing up of a small business. They are deductible business expenses.

Unamortized Costs

If you have been amortizing certain items, such as organizational or incorporation fees, you can deduct the unamortized amounts on a final return for the business. For example, say the business was formed in 2002 and elected to amortize organizational costs over 60 months, but it goes under after only 36 months. You can deduct 24/60 of your organizational costs on the final return, in addition to any of the amortization allowed for the final year of the return.

Other Expenses

You may incur special costs for going out of business. For example, a corporation may have to pay a special fee to the state corporation or franchise department when terminating. There may also be additional legal and accounting fees for winding up a business. Again, these costs are deductible business expenses.

Professionals who wind up their practice but continue to carry professional liability coverage to protect themselves from claims arising from work already performed can deduct the insurance premiums in full as a current deduction in the final year of the practice.

Tax Reporting in the Final Year

As is the case in starting a business, most businesses do not shut their doors on December 31, so the final year of business may be a "short year" (less than a full 12 months). From a tax-reporting standpoint, a return must be filed even though the business did not operate for the entire year. For example, if a business that reports on a calendar year basis ceases operations on August 10, 2005, it must file a return for 2005. It does *not* have to prorate deductions for the period in which it operates.

Indicate on the appropriate tax return that this is the final year of the business. This is done as follows:

- Schedule C—no entry required
- Form 1065—Line G(2)
- Form 1120S—Line F(2)
- Form 1120—Line E(2)

Special Rules for Corporations

Corporations must notify the IRS of their termination. This is done by filing Form 966, Corporate Dissolution or Liquidation, with the IRS within 30 days after the plan or resolution of liquidation is adopted.

You must also follow state rules for dissolving your corporation. Even if you shut your doors for business, you have to formally terminate the corporation under state law in order to avoid continuing tax and fee obligations to the state. In order to dissolve the corporation, your state tax obligations must be up to date; you cannot dissolve the corporation if you owe the state any money.

CHAPTER 26

Alternative Minimum Tax

Reducing regular tax is only half the battle that a small business owner wages to increase after-tax returns. Minimizing or avoiding alternative minimum tax (AMT) where applicable is a second important front that must be addressed. Some business owners may find themselves subject to AMT if they have certain substantial deductions and/or credits.

In this chapter you will learn about:

- Alternative minimum tax basics
- Exemption for small corporations
- Deduction limits for AMT
- Credit offsets
- Minimum tax credit

Alternative Minimum Tax Basics

Alternative minimum tax is designed to ensure that all taxpayers pay at least some tax. Years ago, with tax shelters and other loopholes, wealthy individuals and corporations often paid little or no tax. In an effort to make all taxpayers share the tax burden, an AMT was imposed.

The AMT is a separate tax system, with its own deductions and tax rates. A taxpayer computes the regular income tax as well as a tentative AMT. The extent to which the tentative AMT exceeds regular tax liability is reported as AMT.

For the Future

As the individual income tax rates decline over the next several years, an increasing number of business owners may find themselves subject to the AMT on their share of business preferences and adjustments as well as on personal items.

Alternative minimum tax liability for individuals can be reduced by certain personal tax credits, including a limited foreign tax credit (corporations can reduce their AMT liability only by a limited foreign tax credit). There are two different AMT structures: one for C corporations and another for individuals.

C corporations pay AMT at the rate of 20 percent. This rate is applied to *alternative minimum taxable income* (AMTI) reduced by an exemption amount of $40,000 (reduced by 25 percent of the amount by which AMTI exceeds $150,000). Alternative minimum taxable income includes an *adjusted current earnings* (ACE) adjustment. This adjustment is designed to measure income tax on as broad a basis as it is for financial reporting purposes.

Individuals have a two-tier AMT rate structure of 26 percent on the first $175,000 of income subject to AMT, plus 28 percent on any excess amount. The amount subject to these tax rates is reduced by an exemption amount of $58,000 on a joint return, $40,250 for singles, and $27,000 for married filing separately. This exemption amount is phased out for high-income taxpayers (e.g., no exemption may be claimed on a joint return when AMT income exceeds $330,000).

For the Future

The current exemption amounts are set to drop in 2006 to $45,000 on a joint return and $33,750 for singles unless Congress again extends the higher exemption amounts.

Who is subject to AMT? Potentially all businesses are subject to AMT. However, small C corporations may be exempt, as explained later in this chapter. Owners of pass-through entities (partnerships, LLCs, and S corporations) figure AMT on their individual returns. They include business items passed through to them and identified as AMT items on their Schedule K-1.

Exemption for Small Corporations

Small corporations are entirely exempt from AMT.

Small corporation   A C corporation with average gross receipts of $7.5 million or less for the prior three tax years ($5 million for the first three years, or portion of time in business).

Example

X, Inc., a C corporation, had average gross receipts of $275,000 for the three-year period that included 2002, 2003 and 2004. For 2005, X is a small corporation and therefore is exempt from AMT.

New C corporations (those with the first tax year being 2005), other than those aggregated with other corporations, are exempt from AMT in 2005 without regard to gross receipts. The tax law simply assumes that start-ups are small corporations.

Once your business is established as a small corporation, it retains that status (and is exempt from AMT) as long as its average gross receipts for the prior three-year period do not exceed $7.5 million. The first year of small corporation status is ignored for purposes of this three-year period.

Note

While a C corporation generally can claim a tax credit with respect to AMT liability incurred in a prior year, a small corporation can claim only a limited AMT credit.

LOSS OF SMALL CORPORATION STATUS.   If your business succeeds to the extent that it loses its small corporation status, special AMT rules continue to apply to *formerly small corporations.* These rules simplify AMT for such corporations. In general, these corporations start fresh for certain AMT items and never have to make certain AMT adjustments.

Deduction Limits for Alternative Minimum Tax

Certain deductions that were allowed for regular tax purposes may be disallowed or modified for AMT. The following deductions that were claimed on individual returns may not be deducted for AMT purposes:

- Personal exemptions
- Any addition to the standard deduction

- Itemized deduction for taxes
- Itemized deduction for miscellaneous expenses

The following deductions that were claimed on individual returns must be modified for AMT purposes:

- Investment interest.
- Itemized deduction for medical expenses (only expenses in excess of 10 percent of adjusted gross income are deductible for AMT purposes, while those in excess of 7.5 percent of AGI are deductible for regular tax purposes).
- Itemized deduction for home mortgage interest (only interest to buy, build, or substantially improve a principal residence or second home is deductible for AMT purposes, while interest on home equity loans used for other purposes may be deductible for regular tax purposes).
- Depreciation.
- Net operating losses (NOLs).
- Mining exploration and development costs (the regular tax deduction must be amortized over 10 years).
- Research and experimentation expenditures (costs must be amortized over 10 years if you are not a material participant in the business).
- Passive activity losses from nonfarming activities (losses are adjusted for items not deductible for AMT purposes).

ADJUSTMENTS FOR DEPRECIATION.   The depreciation method that you use for regular tax purposes may require that an adjustment be made for AMT purposes. For AMT purposes you are allowed only a limited depreciation deduction. If you claimed more for regular tax purposes, you must adjust your AMT income accordingly.

For property (other than real property) acquired after 1986, your AMT depreciation is limited to the 150-percent declining balance method, switching to straight line when a larger depreciation deduction results. For real property acquired after 1986, your AMT depreciation is limited to straight line over 40 years.

Note

Different adjustments apply to property placed in service before 1987. Follow the instructions to Form 6251.

For real property placed in service after December 31, 1998, an AMT adjustment is no longer required. For personal property placed in service after this date, a depreciation election can be made to use the same depreciation method for regular and AMT purposes so that an AMT adjustment is avoided. By making this election, depreciation is figured using the 150-percent declining balance method over the regular tax recovery period (instead of the 200-percent declining balance method). For an explanation of these depreciation methods, see Chapter 14.

PREFERENCE ITEMS.   Certain items that may have escaped the regular tax is subject to AMT. These include:

- Tax-exempt interest on private activity bonds issued after August 7, 1986.
- Exclusion of 50 percent of the gain on the sale of small business stock (see Chapter 5).
- Oil and gas preferences.
- Accelerated depreciation on real property acquired before 1987.

NET OPERATING LOSSES.   The NOL deduction for regular tax purposes must be adjusted for AMT. This is because only a limited NOL deduction is allowed for AMT purposes. The NOL for AMT purposes is the regular tax NOL except that the nonbusiness deduction adjustment includes only AMT itemized deductions (i.e., state and local taxes and certain other deductions cannot be used to figure the NOL deduction).

You may be able to eliminate your AMT liability because of your NOL deduction. However, the NOL deduction cannot be more than 90 percent of AMT income (without regard to the NOL deduction). If you cannot use all of your NOL because of the 90-percent limit, you may carry it back and forward under the applicable carryback/carryforward periods (explained in Chapter 19). However, the carryback and carryforward NOLs are also subject to the 90-percent limit.

OTHER ADJUSTMENTS AND PREFERENCES.   In figuring AMT income on which AMT tax is imposed, certain income items are also given special treatment. These include incentive stock options, long-term contracts, tax-exempt interest on private activity bonds, and basis adjustments for AMT gain or loss.

For C corporations other than small C corporations, the key adjustment that can trigger AMT is the ACE adjustment. However, since small corporations are exempt from AMT, this adjustment is not explained further.

Credit Offsets

Only certain tax credits can be used to offset AMT liability. Components of the general business credit *cannot* be used to offset this tax. In 2005, the only credits that can offset AMT liability include:

- *Foreign tax credit. **Note:*** In the past there had been a 90 percent limit on the amount of the foreign tax credit that could be used as an offset, but this limit was repealed, effective after December 31, 2004.

- *Certain business credits.* Alcohol fuel credit and credit for electricity or refined coal (for tax years ending after October 22, 2004).
- *Certain personal tax credits.* Owners of pass-through entities who have AMT liability do not lose the benefit of personal tax credits, such as the child tax credit, education credits, and the adoption credit.

Legislative Alert

Using personal credits to offset the alternative minimum tax and regular tax liability expires at the end of 2005 unless Congress extends this break. If it is *not* extended, then the only personal credits offsets are the adoption credit, the nonrefundable portion of the child tax credit, and the retirement savers' credit.

Minimum Tax Credit

If you paid AMT last year, you may be eligible for a tax credit this year. Different minimum tax credits apply for individuals and corporations.

Individuals

You qualify for a minimum tax credit if you meet any of the following three conditions:

1. You paid any AMT in 2004.
2. You had an unused minimum tax credit that you carried forward from 2004 to 2005.
3. You had certain unallowed business-related credits in 2004.

The credit is the amount of AMT paid in 2004 reduced by the part of the tax related to exclusion items (standard deduction, medical expenses, taxes, miscellaneous itemized deductions, gains on small business stock, tax-exempt interest from private activity bonds, and depletion). The credit may be increased by minimum tax credit carryforwards and unallowed credits for nonconventional-source fuel, orphan drugs, and electric vehicles.

Compute the credit on Form 8801. If the credit exceeds your AMT liability for 2005, the excess amount may be carried forward and used to offset AMT liability in a future year. There is no limit on the carryforward period.

Corporations

Unlike an individual's minimum tax credit which is limited to exclusion items, corporations that paid AMT in a prior year may claim a tax credit in 2005 if they have no AMT liability this year. Compute the credit on Form 8827, Credit for Prior Year Minimum Tax—Corporations.

Where to Figure Alternative Minimum Tax

Self-Employed

If you have any adjustments or preference items, you must complete Form 6251, Alternative Minimum Tax—Individuals. You may or may not have any AMT liability.

Partnerships and LLCs

The business reports an owner's share of AMT items on Schedule K-1. As an owner, you must complete Form 6251 to see if you owe any AMT.

S Corporations

The business reports an owner's share of AMT items on Schedule K-1. As an owner, you must complete Form 6251 to see if you owe any AMT.

C Corporations

Small C corporations exempt from AMT are not required to complete any special forms. Other C corporations figure their AMT liability on Form 4626, Alternative Minimum Tax—Corporations.

CHAPTER 27

Other Taxes

Federal income taxes may be your primary concern and your greatest tax liability, but as a business owner you may have other tax obligations as well. You may owe state income and franchise taxes, employment taxes, sales and use taxes, and excise taxes.

In this chapter you will learn about:

- State income taxes
- Employment taxes
- Sales and use taxes
- Excise taxes

For more information about various other taxes, see IRS Publication 15, *Circular E, Employer's Tax Guide;* IRS Publication 15-A, *Employer's Supplemental Tax Guide;* IRS Publication 15-B, *Employer's Guide to Fringe Benefits;* and IRS Publication 510, *Excise Taxes.*

State Income Taxes

You may owe state income taxes on your business profits in each state in which you do business. Your obligation does *not* depend on where the business is set up. For example, if you incorporate your business in Nevada but operate in California, you owe income taxes to California, the state in which you do business. (And you may owe a tax or fee to Nevada as well.)

Generally, state income taxes depend on having a nexus (connection) to the state. This is based on having a physical presence there, which may be evidenced by maintaining an office or sending a sales force into the state; merely shipping goods into the state without some additional connection is not enough to establish a business presence within the state. You may have a nexus to more than one state, no matter how small your business is.

If there is a business connection to more than one state, the business income is apportioned among those states. Apportionment is based on a sales factor, a payroll factor, and a property factor (each state has different apportionment formulas). The apportionment rules are highly complex, but there is some flexibility that permits you to shift income into the state with the lower taxes within certain limits.

If you are a sole proprietor or an owner of a pass-through entity, you must file a state income tax return in every state in which your company does business (if such state has a personal income tax). For example, if an LLC does business in 12 states, all of which impose an income tax, each member of the LLC must file a personal income tax return in those 12 states.

Of course, even if you do business within a state, there may be no tax liability. For example, Wyoming does not have a personal or corporate income tax so there is no tax even if you do business in this state.

The filing deadlines for state business returns are not the same as the federal deadlines in all cases, so check with your state tax authority for the forms to file and when to file them. You may also need to obtain a state tax identification number for your business.

Corporations

Corporations may owe state corporate income tax. In some states this is called a **franchise tax.**

Franchise tax   State tax imposed on a state-chartered corporation for the right to do business under the corporate name within the state (it has nothing to do with whether the business is a franchise).

S corporations in most states are taxed in the same way as they are taxed for federal income tax purposes (i.e., income, losses, etc. pass through to shareholders to be reported on their personal income tax returns). However, if the S corporation has shareholders who are not residents of the state, special rules may apply (for example, the corporation may be required to make tax payments on behalf of these shareholders).

In most taxes, the S election for state tax purposes is automatic if a federal election is filed. However, in about half a dozen states you must file a separate state tax election for S corporation status (merely filing the federal election is not sufficient for state tax purposes).

Some states, such as New York and Rhode Island, allow S status but also impose an annual corporate-level tax for the privilege of being an S corporation. The corporate-level tax applies even though the income and deductions of the corporation pass through to shareholders and are taxed on their personal returns.

Some localities, such as the District of Columbia and Louisiana, do not recognize S corporation status. They tax the entity as a regular C corporation.

For more information about the state income taxes, contact the tax or revenue departments of each state in which you do business. You can find contact information in Table 27.1.

Employment Taxes

You may be liable for the payment of certain taxes with respect to the compensation you paid to your employees. If you own a corporation, these obligations apply even if you are its *only* employee. As a small business owner, you need to know what taxes you are responsible for, where and when to deposit the taxes, and what returns you must file for employment taxes. The returns you must file are discussed later in this chapter. In this section you will learn about employment taxes and where to deposit them. The deductibility of these taxes is discussed in Chapter 13.

You may find assistance on employment tax obligations for small businesses at <www.irs.gov/businesses/small>. You should also contact your state tax department to learn about your state employment tax obligations.

Employment Tax Obligations

The Federal Insurance Contribution Act (FICA) set up a (Social Security and Medicare) system to provide for old age, survivors, disability, and hospital insurance of workers. Both you, the employer, and your employees contribute to this system. The Federal Unemployment Tax Act (FUTA), together with state unemployment systems, provides payment to workers in the event of unemployment. Only employers pay this tax.

You must withhold from your employees' wages income tax and the employee portion of Social Security and Medicare tax. These taxes are referred to as *trust fund* amounts because you, as employer, are holding the funds in trust for your employees. You must pay over these amounts to the IRS. You must also pay the IRS the employer portion of Social Security and Medicare tax, which is the same amount that the employee paid, plus FUTA.

TABLE 27.1 State Tax Authorities

State/Agency	Telephone	Web Site
Alabama—Department of Revenue	(334)242-1170	www.ador.state.al.us
Alaska—Department of Revenue	(907)465-2300	www.tax.state.ak.us
Arizona—Department of Revenue	(602)255-3381	www.revenue.state.az.us
Arkansas—Department of Finance and Administration	(501)682-2242	www.arkansas.gov/dfa
California—State Board of Equalization—Franchise Tax Board	(800)400-7115 (800)852-5711	www.boe.ca.gov www.ftb.ca.gov
Colorado—Department of Revenue	(303)238-7378	www.revenue.state.co.us
Connecticut—Department of Revenue Services	(800)382-9463 (860)297-5962 (out of state)	www.drs.state.ct.us
Delaware—Department of Finance	(302)577-8200	www.state.de.us/revenue/default.shtml
District of Columbia—Department of Finance and Revenue	(202)727-4829	http://dc.gov/index.asp
Florida—Department of Revenue	(850)488-6800	http://sun6.dms.state.fl.us/dor/
Georgia—Department of Revenue	(404)417-4477	www2.state.ga.us/Departments/DOR
Hawaii—Department of Taxation	(808)587-4242	www.state.hi.us/tax/tax.html
Idaho—Department of Revenue and Taxation	(208)334-7660	http://tax.idaho.gov/index
Illinois—Department of Revenue	(217)782-3336	www.revenue.state.il.us/
Indiana—Department of Revenue	(317)232-2240	www.in.gov/dor/
Iowa—Department of Revenue and Finance	(515)281-3114	www.state.ia.us/tax
Kansas—Department of Revenue	(785)368-8222	www.ksrevenue.org
Kentucky—Revenue Cabinet	(502)564-4581	www.state.ky.us/agencies/revenue
Louisiana—Department of Revenue	(225)219-2448	www.rev.state.la.us/
Maine—Maine Revenue Services	(207)287-2076	www.maine.gov/revenue
Maryland—State Department of Assessments and Taxation	(410)260-7801	www.marylandtaxes.com
Massachusetts—Department of Revenue	(617)887-6367	www.dor.state.ma.us
Michigan—Department of Treasury	(517)373-3200	www.michigan.gov/treasury
Minnesota—Department of Revenue	(651)296-3781	www.taxes.state.mn.us
Mississippi—State Tax Commission	(601)923-7000	www.mstc.state.ms.us
Missouri—State Tax Commission	(573)751-4450	http://dor.state.mo.us

TABLE 27.1 *(Continued)*

State/Agency	Telephone	Web Site
Montana—Department of Revenue	(406)444-6900	www.discoveringmontana.com/revenue
Nebraska—Department of Revenue	(402)471-5729	www.revenue.state.ne.us/
Nevada—Department of Taxation	(775)687-4892	http://tax.state.nv.us/
New Hampshire—Department of Revenue Administration	(603)271-2186	www.state.nh.us/revenue
New Jersey—Department of the Treasury	(609)292-5185	www.state.nj.us/treasury/taxation
New Mexico—Taxation and Revenue Department	(505)827-0700	www.state.nm.us/tax
New York—Department of Taxation and Finance	(800)972-1233	www.tax.state.ny.us
North Carolina—Department of Revenue	(919)733-3991	www.dor.state.nc.us
North Dakota—Tax Commissioner	(701)328-2770	www.state.nd.taxdpt/
Ohio—Department of Taxation	(800)282-1780 (individuals) (888)405-4039 (businesses)	www.tax.ohio.gov
Oklahoma—Tax Commission	(405)521-3214	www.oktax.state.ok.us
Oregon—Department of Revenue	(503)378-4988	www.dor.state.or.us
Pennsylvania—Department of Revenue	(717)783-3682	www.revenue.state.pa.us
Rhode Island—Department of Administration	(401)222-3050	www.tax.state.ri.us
South Carolina—Department of Revenue	(803)898-5000	www.sctax.org
South Dakota—Department of Revenue	(605)773-3311	www.state.sd.us/drr2/revenue/revenue.html
Tennessee—Department of Revenue	(615)253-0600	www.state.tn.us/revenue
Texas—Comptroller of Public Accounts	(512)463-4444	www.window.state.tax.us/m23taxes.html
Utah—Tax Commission	(801)297-2200	http://txdtm01.tax.ex.state.ut.us/
Vermont—Administration Agency	(802)828-2505	www.state.vt.us/tax/index.htm
Virginia—Department of Taxation	(804)367-8005	www.tax.state.va.us/
Washington—Department of Revenue	(800)647-7706	http://dor.wa.gov
West Virginia—Department of Tax and Revenue	(304)558-3333	www.state.wv.us/taxdiv/
Wisconsin—Department of Revenue	(608)266-2772	www.dor.state.wi.us
Wyoming—Department of Revenue	(307)777-7961	http://revenue.state.wy.us

FICA. The tax rate for the Social Security portion of FICA is 6.2 percent of the first $90,000 of wages in 2005. This wage base is adjusted annually for inflation. This means that you must withhold from the employee's compensation this amount of tax. In addition, as an employer, you must also pay the same rate of tax. The tax rate for the Medicare portion of FICA is 1.45 percent on all compensation. There is no wage base ceiling for purposes of computing this tax. You must withhold this amount from the employee's compensation and pay a similar amount as the employer.

FUTA. The tax rate for FUTA is 6.2 percent of the first $7,000 of each employee's wages. However, you may claim a credit for payments to state unemployment funds of up to 5.4 percent of taxable wages if all state payments were made in a timely fashion. Thus, the effective FUTA rate in most cases is 0.8 percent of the first $7,000 of each employee's wages.

INCOME TAX WITHHOLDING. In addition to FICA and FUTA tax you may owe, you may also be required to withhold income taxes from employee compensation. Your withholding is based on each employee's withholding allowances and marital status as reported to you on Form W-4, Employee's Withholding Allowance Certificate. These forms should be completed when employment commences and need not be updated each year (unless the employee chooses to do so). If an employee fails to complete Form W-4, then withhold as if the employee were single with no withholding allowances.

In the past, employers were required to submit W-4 forms on which employees claimed exemption from withholding even though wages were $200 or more per week or more than 10 withholding allowances. This requirement was dropped as of April 14, 2005, because the IRS has stepped up enforcement efforts to identify employees who are seriously underwithheld; employers must still retain these forms and make them available to the IRS if requested.

It is important to note that the definition of compensation is, in some instances, different for purposes of income taxes and employment taxes. For example, a salary reduction that is contributed to an employee's 401(k) plan or Savings Incentive Match Plan for Employees (SIMPLE) plan is not treated as compensation subject to income tax. However, the salary reduction is still subject to employment tax.

Table 27.2 can be used to determine your employment tax obligations for various fringe benefits you may provide to employees in 2005.

EMPLOYING FAMILY MEMBERS. If you are self-employed and employ your child who is under age 18, his or her wages are not subject to FICA. If you employ your spouse in your business, his or her wages are fully subject to FICA. If you have a corporation that employs a child un-

> **CAUTION**
> The IRS looks closely at family hiring. Make sure that the wages are reasonable for the work performed. Keep timesheets as proof of work performed by your relatives.

TABLE 27.2 Your Employment Tax Obligation on Common Fringe Benefits

Fringe Benefit	Withhold Income Tax	Pay Social Security and Medicare Taxes	Pay Federal Unemployment Tax (FUTA)
Achievement awards (within limits)	No	No	No
Adoption assistance up to $10,630	No	No	No
Athletic facilities	No	No	No
Company car personal use	Yes	Yes	Yes
De minimis benefits	No	No	No
Dependent care assistance up to $5,000			
Rank-and-file employees	No	No	No
HCEs* (if plan discriminates)	Yes	Yes	Yes
Education assistance up to $5,250—not job related	No	No	No
Any job related	No	No	No
Elective deferrals to 401(k), SEP, or SIMPLE plans	No	Yes	Yes
Employee discounts			
Rank-and-file employees	No	No	No
HCEs* (if plan discriminates)	Yes	Yes	Yes
Flexible spending arrangement salary contribution	No	No	No
Group term life insurance	No	No up to cost of $50,000 of coverage	No
Health insurance			
Rank-and-file employees	No	No	No
More-than-2-percent S corporation shareholders	Yes	Yes	Yes
Health savings account contributions	No	No	No
Lodging on the premises	No	No	No
Meals on the premises	No	No	No
Medical care reimbursements under a self-insured plan	No	No	No
Moving expenses	No	No	No
No-additional-cost services	No	No	No
Stock options			
ISOs	No	No when granted; yes when exercised	No when granted; yes when exercised

*HCEs are highly-compensated employees—owners and employees earning over a set dollar limit that adjusts annually for inflation.

(Continued)

TABLE 27.2 *(Continued)*

Fringe Benefit	Withhold Income Tax	Pay Social Security and Medicare Taxes	Pay Federal Unemployment Tax (FUTA)
Employee stock purchase plans	No	No when granted; Yes when exercised	No when granted; Yes when exercised
Nonqualified stock options	Yes when exercised	Yes when exercised	Yes when exercised
Supplemental unemployment compensation plan benefits	Yes	No	No
Transportation benefits			
Rank-and-file employees	No	No	No
More-than-2-percent S corporation shareholders	Yes	Yes	Yes
Vacation pay	Yes	Yes	Yes
Working condition benefit	No	No	No

der age 18, his or her wages are still subject to FICA. Your child's wages are exempt from FUTA until he or she reaches age 21.

LEASED EMPLOYEES. If you lease employees from a corporation that supplies workers for your business, the employees may be treated as in the employ of the corporation that does the leasing rather than as your employees. The leasing corporation, and not you, is responsible for the payment of employment taxes.

Special Rules for Tips

Tips that employees receive are taxable wages for purposes of employment taxes. Employees are *supposed* to report their tips to employers so that employment taxes can be applied. However, as a practical matter, this is not always the case.

The U.S. Supreme Court has said that the IRS can use an estimated aggregation of unreported tips to assess FICA tax on employers; the IRS does not have to audit each employee to determine actual unreported tips for purposes of determining the employer share of FICA.

To avoid this forced rate upon employers, the IRS has developed voluntary compliance agreements for industries, such as the restaurant industry, where tipping is customary. These agreements are designed to enhance tax compliance among tipped employees through education and avoid employer examination during the period that the agreements are in place. They include:

- Tip reporting alternative commitment (TRAC)—avoids the establishment of a tip rate, requires employers to educate employees on tip reporting requirements, requires employees to report monthly to employers, and provides for audits of those employees who underreport.

- Tip rate determination agreement (TRDA)—sets a tip rate through employers cooperating with the IRS, requires employees to sign a Tipped Employee Participation Agreement with the employer (75 percent of whom must sign).

- Employer-designed tip reporting alternative commitment (EmTRAC)—solely for those in the food and beverage industry whose employees receive both cash and charged tips, this program generally follows the TRAC program.

Depositing Employment Taxes

When employment taxes must be paid to the IRS is determined in part by the size of the tax liability. More precisely, employment taxes are deposited with a federal depository (certain banks) along with a deposit coupon, Form 8109, Federal Tax Deposit Coupon. (Ask at your local bank to determine whether it is qualified to accept employment tax deposits on behalf of the IRS.) Deposit slips are furnished to you by the IRS. New employers can expect to receive a coupon book within five to six weeks after applying for an employer tax identification number (EIN). The federal depository then turns the funds over to the government. The reporting of these deposits is made quarterly for Social Security and Medicare tax and income tax withholding, and annually for FUTA tax.

Employers of very small businesses may be able to pay employment taxes directly to the IRS along with their quarterly tax returns. Employers of larger businesses (those with aggregate federal tax deposits over $200,000 two years ago) must pay employment taxes via electronic transfer under the Electronic Federal Tax Payment System (EFTPS).

Example

If your tax deposits first cross the $200,000 threshold in 2005, you are not required to use EFTPS before 2007.

Although you are not *required* to pay your employment taxes by electronic transfer (unless your aggregate federal tax deposits exceeded $200,000 two years ago), you are *permitted* to do so. Many small businesses find paying by electronic transfer convenient, which they activate with their computers or a telephone call to their bank. And studies have shown that businesses using EFTPS to pay their taxes have significantly fewer penalties assessed. About 2 million businesses, many of them small businesses, have already enrolled in

EFTPS (about 6,500 enroll each week). Small businesses that have been subject to penalties on late deposits can receive an automatic refund by enrolling in EFTPS and making timely deposits for four quarters; at the end of this one-year period the IRS will look back up to one year prior to EFTPS enrollment and refund any penalties. If you wish to voluntarily enroll, you can do so online at <www.eftps.gov> or call 1-800-945-8400 or 1-800-555-4477.

Unless you are permitted to remit employment taxes with the return as explained later, you must deposit income tax you withhold from your employee's compensation as well as both the employer and employee portion of Social Security and Medicare taxes. This is done by electronic transfer under EFTPS or by mailing or delivering the required amount to a Federal Reserve Bank or an authorized financial institution.

DEPOSIT DATES.   Depending on the size of your payroll, you are put on one of two deposit schedules, *monthly* or *semiweekly.* (See Table 27.3.) The IRS notifies all employers each November of their schedule for the coming calendar year. The determination of your deposit schedule is based on your employment taxes during a lookback period (two years prior to the upcoming year). If your employment taxes were $50,000 or less in the lookback period, you are on a monthly deposit schedule. If your employment taxes exceeded $50,000 in the lookback period, you are on a semiweekly deposit schedule. It is important to note that even if you are put on a monthly deposit schedule, you need not file the quarterly employment tax return monthly or more frequently unless the IRS instructs you to file Form 941-M, Employer's Monthly Federal Tax Return. Remember, the amount of your employment taxes, not the time you pay your employees (i.e., weekly, semimonthly, monthly), determines your depositor status.

If the bank is closed on the required deposit date, the deposit is made on the next banking day.

PAYMENT WITH RETURNS.   Instead of depositing employment taxes, you can pay them directly to the IRS along with your return if your net tax liability for the quarterly return is less than $2,500. Thus, for example, if you have one employee

TABLE 27.3 Deposit Schedule

Type of Deposit Schedule	Due
Monthly	15th day of the following month
Semiweekly Payment on Wednesday, Thursday, and/or Friday	Following Wednesday
Payment on Saturday, Sunday, Monday, and/or Tuesday	Following Friday

who earned only $10,000 for the quarter, employment taxes will be under $2,500, so you can pay them directly to the IRS when you file your return, Form 941. If you are not sure whether your quarterly employment taxes will cross the $2,500 threshold, it is advisable to deposit the taxes monthly in order to avoid a penalty.

For FUTA taxes, the deposit threshold is $500 (up from $100 in 2004). This means that companies with eight or fewer employees can pay this tax annually when the annual FUTA return is filed.

Penalty for Failure to Pay Employment Taxes

As an employer, you are required to deduct and withhold income taxes and FICA from your employee's compensation. If you fail to do so, or if you withhold an insufficient amount, you are still liable for the correct amount.

There is a 100-percent penalty imposed on persons who are responsible for paying employment taxes but fail to do so. This penalty, called the *trust fund recovery penalty* (because an employer pays income tax withholding and the employee's share of Social Security and Medicare taxes into a trust fund maintained by the government for the employee's benefit), is a personal one against an owner, officer, or other responsible person. Thus, for example, a shareholder in a corporation who serves as company president may be personally liable for this penalty even though a shareholder generally is not liable for corporate debts.

Even if there is more than one responsible person, the IRS can collect the entire tax and penalty from one person. It is up to that one person to try to recover a portion of the payment from other responsible persons. If you make a written request, the IRS must notify you of the name of the person that it has determined to be responsible and whether it has attempted to collect the penalty from other responsible persons. There is a *federal right of contribution* (to collect a share of the penalty by someone who has paid it from someone else who is also responsible) where there are multiple responsible persons.

Penalty for Delinquent Deposits

Unless you can show reasonable cause for failing to deposit required amounts or paying deposits directly to the IRS instead of depositing the employment taxes, you will be subject to a penalty. The penalty schedule is designed to encourage employers to comply with deposit requirements as quickly as possible. Thus, the penalty is 2 percent if deposits are made from one to five days late; it increases to 5 percent for deposits six to 15 days late. The penalty jumps to 10 percent for deposits more than 15 days late, deposits made at unauthorized financial institutions or directly to the IRS, and amounts paid to the IRS within 10 days of a first notice asking for tax due. A 15-percent penalty applies to amounts outstanding more than 10 days after a first notice from the IRS

CAUTION

In view of this substantial penalty, it is essential that employment taxes be paid. If you are experiencing a cash crunch, see that these taxes are paid before satisfying other creditors.

of amounts due or the day on which you receive a notice and demand for immediate payment, whichever is earlier. However, you can designate the period for which payment is made to avoid cascading penalties.

State Employment Tax Obligations

As mentioned earlier in this chapter, as an employer, you should check out your obligation, if any, for state employment taxes.

Special Rules for Self-Employed Individuals

Self-employed individuals—sole proprietors, general partners, and LLC members who are not treated as limited partners—are not employees of their businesses even though they may be compensated for their services. Thus, they are not subject to FICA. However, self-employed individuals bear the same tax burden as owners who work for their corporations. Self-employed individuals pay both the employee and employer portion of FICA, called self-employment tax (SECA). The rate for self-employment tax is 12.4 percent on net earnings from self-employment up to $90,000 in 2005 and 2.9 percent on all net earnings from self-employment tax. To more closely equate self-employed individuals with corporations, self-employed individuals may claim a deduction for one-half of self-employment tax (what amounts to the employer portion of FICA). However, they pay self-employment tax on more than just an amount that could be called a salary. Sole proprietors pay self-employment tax on the net income reported on Schedule C (or Schedule F for farming activities). This is so even if they do no work at all for their business and hire someone else to run it. General partners and LLC members who are not treated as limited partners pay self-employment income on their distributive share of income from the partnership or LLC and on guaranteed payments to them.

Limited partners (and LLC members treated as limited partners) are not subject to self-employment tax on their distributive share of partnership income. They are viewed as mere investors. At the present time, there is no guidance on how to treat LLC members for purposes of self-employment tax. The IRS was prevented, by law, from issuing regulations on this issue before July 1, 1998. The IRS has still not given any indication of forthcoming regulations on this issue.

Unlike FICA, self-employment tax is not deposited with a Federal Reserve Bank or other authorized financial institution. Instead, it is paid along with income taxes. This means that self-employed individuals must ensure that quarterly estimated taxes cover not only their income tax obligations but also their self-employment tax for the year. Self-employed individuals are not subject to FUTA. They cannot cover themselves for periods of no work because, by definition, self-employed persons are never employed.

State Income Tax Withholding

If your business is located in a state that imposes a personal income tax, you are required to withhold state income tax from your employees' compensation. You can obtain information about state withholding rates by contacting your state tax authority (see Table 27.1).

If you have employees who live in another state, you are only required to withhold tax for the state in which your business is located. (The employees may be entitled to a credit for taxes paid to another state.) However, you *may* withhold state income tax for the state in which the employees reside so that they do not have to grapple with state estimated taxes. If you make such an accommodation, you must still withhold state taxes for the state in which your business is located. If you do business in more than one state and have employees who work in more than one location, you must withhold state income tax in each state in which they work. In one case, for example, withholding was required for a professional baseball player for each state in which he played ball, not just in the home state. Withholding in this case was based on the number of days he played in each of these other states.

Employment Tax Filing for All Businesses

If you have employees (even if you are your corporation's only employee), you must report quarterly to the IRS. Use Form 941, Employer's Quarterly Federal Tax Return, to report any income tax withholding and FICA withholding and payments made during the quarter. More than three million small businesses are eligible to file their quarterly returns using the 941TeleFile system. Under this system, quarterly payroll returns are filed by telephone. This system automatically calculates the tax and tells you any balance that is owed. Potentially eligible small businesses were sent 941TeleFile packages. If you think you are eligible but did not receive one, contact the IRS.

For the Future

Starting in 2006, the IRS may implement a proposal to allow small employers that deposit less than $2,500 quarterly to file Form 941 annually (instead of quarterly), provided the business has an on-time payment record for at least two years.

You must also file an annual return to report the payment of federal unemployment insurance. Use Form 940, Employer's Annual Federal Unemployment (FUTA) Tax Return. Alternatively, you may be able to use a simplified form,

Form 940-EZ, Employer's Annual Federal Unemployment (FUTA) Tax Return, if you meet the following tests:

- You paid unemployment contributions to only one state.
- You paid all state unemployment contributions by January 31.
- All wages for FUTA tax were also taxable for state unemployment tax purposes.
- All wages were paid in a state other than a credit reduction state.

Employment tax forms can be signed by facsimile, including alternative signature methods such as computer software programs or mechanical devices.

Note that reporting for employment tax obligations is separate from income tax reporting.

SPECIAL REPORTING FOR EMPLOYING A WORKER IN YOUR HOME.   If you are a sole proprietor and have a nanny or other household employees, as well as regular business employees, you can report the FICA and FUTA taxes for your household employee on Schedule H and pay the taxes with your Form 1040. Alternatively, you can report and pay the FICA taxes for your household employee with the quarterly reports for your regular business employees on Form 941, and you can pay the FUTA taxes on Form 940 or Form 940-EZ.

Sales and Use Taxes

There is no federal sales or use tax. But there are over 7,500 states, counties, cities, and towns with their own sales taxes, in many cases generating the greatest revenue for these jurisdictions. Many also impose a **use tax.**

Use tax   Tax imposed on the purchaser of certain goods from out-of-state vendors.

The rules for these taxes vary considerably from one locality to another. For example, the sale of one type of product may be subject to sales tax in one state but exempt in another. Because these taxes produce significant revenue in some places, taxing authorities may be aggressive in their collection activities, so you should understand your responsibilities.

Sales Taxes

If you sell goods or provide certain services within a state that has a sales tax, as the vendor you are required to collect the tax from the purchaser and remit the tax to the state agency. Generally, the same test used for state income tax purposes to determine whether you do business within a state applies for sales tax purposes as well. If you do not do business within a state, you are not required to collect sales tax on goods shipped within that state. If you sell online, you may or may not have a presence in another state (for example, maintaining a server in another state may establish a nexus there).

Currently, it is not well established whether Internet sales to a customer in another state are subject to sales tax. The federal moratorium on state sales tax, titled the Internet Tax Nondiscrimination Act (which is set to apply only through November 3, 2007), applies only to the tax on Internet access, not to Internet sales. Revenue-hungry states may rush to impose new Internet-related taxes and clarify when online sales are subject to sales taxes.

Familiarize yourself with how the sales tax works. For example, if goods are returned and you refund the purchaser's money, you may be entitled to a deduction or credit for the sales tax you originally collected.

When you must remit sales tax to the state depends on how much you collect. You must also file certain returns reporting your collection activities.

Contact your state tax authority (see Table 27.1) to request a sales tax package. This will explain whether you must collect tax (and how much) and when to pay it to the state and file sales tax returns.

Use Taxes

If you buy goods out-of-state, you may be liable for a use tax on the purchase. (In effect, your state is collecting the sales tax you would have paid had you made the purchase in-state.) Generally, the tax is imposed on the purchaser (though some states may collect the tax from the seller).

Before you pay any use tax, check to see if the sale is exempt from the tax. Exemptions often exist for items that will be resold (including components of products for resale), used for capital improvements, or used in research and development.

Even if the vendor does not charge a use tax because it has no responsibility to pay the tax to your state, you may still be liable for it. In effect, you may be required to "self-assess" the tax.

Excise Taxes

An excise tax is a tax imposed on the manufacture and distribution of certain nonessential consumer goods, such as spirits and tobacco, although it now applies to many essential goods and services as well (such as gasoline and telephone service). Until the advent of the income tax in 1913, the federal government ran entirely on excise taxes. Today, excise taxes are only a small part of the government's revenue, but may still be an obligation for you. In 2003 (the last year for which statistics are available), more than half a million taxpayers filed returns for heavy highway vehicle use tax and nearly 200,000 for federal excise tax on certain fuels.

Excise taxes include:

- Environmental taxes on the sale or use of ozone-depleting chemicals
- Communications and air transportation taxes
- Fuel taxes
- Manufacturers' taxes on various items (including sport fishing equipment, bow and arrow components, etc.)
- Retail tax on the sale of heavy trucks, trailers, and tractors (imposed on the seller)

Many small companies have no liability for excise taxes because of the nature of their business. However, there are no specific exemptions from these taxes because a business is a small one (for example, small farmers are subject to certain fuel taxes, although they may be entitled to a credit or refund).

The deduction for excise taxes is discussed in Chapter 13. Tax credits for certain farm-related excise taxes are discussed in Chapter 20.

CHAPTER 28

Online Filing and Information

In 1998 Congress announced that its policy was to promote paperless filing of tax returns. It set a goal that 80 percent of all federal tax and information returns be filed online by 2007. In furtherance of this goal it instructed the IRS to promote the use of electronic filing through its *e-file* system and, to date, the IRS effort has been highly successful.

In this chapter you will learn about:

- Online filing of business income tax returns
- Paying taxes online
- Online filing of other business returns

For more information about the electronic federal tax payment system see IRS Publication 966, *Electronic Federal Tax Payment System (Answers to Most Commonly Asked Questions)*.

Online Filing of Business Income Tax Returns

In the case of electronic filing of tax returns, the future is now. About 66 percent of all individual income tax returns are now filed electronically, many of which include returns of sole proprietors, partners, limited liability company members, and S corporation shareholders. The number of C and

S corporations filing their returns electronically has not yet been reported (their option to file electronically did not take hold until July 2004 when all necessary corporate forms and schedules were available for electronic filing). There are several reasons for the increased interest in using electronic filing—even though it is not mandatory.

- *Faster refunds.* Those who are owed a refund can expect to receive it in about half the time that it would take had the return been filed the traditional way in paper form. With electronic filing of returns and direct deposit of refunds, you can receive a refund in as little as seven days.

- *Accuracy.* There is a less than one percent error rate with electronically filed returns (compared with a more-than-20 percent error rate for paper returns). This is because the IRS reviews the return before accepting it. The IRS acknowledges acceptance of a return within 48 hours of submission. This acknowledgment is your proof of filing and assurance that the IRS has your return information.

- *Convenience.* You can use your personal computer to file your return seven days a week, 24 hours a day. If you lack the software to *e-file,* you can use an authorized IRS *e-file* provider (for a modest fee). In 37 states you can file your federal and state returns simultaneously. If you owe taxes, you can file early and postpone payment until the return's due date. (Payment can be made by authorizing an automatic withdrawal [direct debit] from a savings or checking account, payment by credit card [American Express, Discover, or MasterCard], or by mailing a check payable to the United States Treasury along with Form 1040-V, Payment Voucher, to your service center.)

If you *e-file,* then you do not have to attach any information returns that would otherwise be required. For example, if you are a sole proprietor but your spouse is an employee with a W-2 form, that form need not be sent to the IRS if you file your return electronically.

ELECTRONIC SIGNATURES.   In the past, in order to file a return electronically you were required to follow up with another form to indicate your signature. Today, the signature of an electronically-filed return is handled through a *self-select personal identification number* (PIN). This is a self-created five-number code that is used in conjunction with your prior year's adjusted gross income, total tax, and date of birth to verify that the return being filed is your own. You do not have to register your PIN number, nor even notify the IRS. But if you are a sole proprietor filing a joint return, both you and your spouse need a PIN.

If you do not choose to use a PIN or need to attach either of the above forms, then you must send Form 8453-OL, U.S. Individual Income Tax Declaration for an *e-file* Online Return to your IRS service center when the return is accepted. This form indicates that you agree with the return information that has been submitted.

DEEMED FILING DATE. An electronically-filed return is deemed timely if it is transmitted on or before the due date *and* an acknowledgment of processing by the IRS is issued.

Sole Proprietorships

You can *e-file* your income tax return if you are a sole proprietor filing a Schedule C, C-EZ, or F. Virtually all the forms and schedules you need can be filed electronically.

Partnerships and LLCs

Form 1065 may be filed electronically. In 1999, only 143 returns were submitted in this manner. Other than large partnerships (those with 100 or more partners), there is no requirement to use *e-file*. But the same benefits of *e-filing* for individuals applies to partnership returns.

S Corporations

The 1120/1120S *e-file* program began in February 2004. S corporations with total assets over $50 million and 250 or more returns filed annually (including income tax, excise tax, information—W-2 and otherwise—and employment tax returns) *must* file Form 1120S electronically. Whether *e-file* is used, if the corporation owes any income tax it must deposit it electronically if it is otherwise required to use EFTPS as explained later in this chapter.

S corporation shareholders can, however, file their personal tax returns electronically, even if the corporation files by mail (and vice versa). Thus, they can obtain the benefit of *e-filing* on their share of business items.

For the Future

Starting in 2007 (for 2006 returns), the mandatory electronic filing requirement will apply to S corporations with total assets over $10 million. There are no current plans to further reduce the mandatory threshold, requiring small S corporations to file electronically, although the IRS encourages them to do so.

C Corporations

The return can be filed under the 1120/1120S *e-file* program. C corporations with total assets over $50 million and 250 or more returns filed annually (including income tax, excise tax, information—W-2 and otherwise—and employment tax returns) *must* file Form 1120 electronically. Whether *e-file* is used, you must still deposit corporate income taxes electronically if you are required to use EFTPS as explained later in this chapter.

For the Future

Starting in 2007 (for 2006 returns), the mandatory electronic filing requirement will apply to C corporations with total assets over $10 million. There are no current plans to further reduce the mandatory threshold, requiring small C corporations to file electronically, although the IRS encourages them to do so.

Paying Taxes Online

Some businesses *must* deposit their taxes through the Electronic Federal Tax Payment System (EFTPS) while others may choose to do so. Under this payment method you authorize the transfer of funds from your bank account by using your telephone or personal computer. This payment method can be used whether or not returns are filed electronically and enables you to designate the amount of payment to be made. You can also designate in advance the time you wish payment to be made. As long as the transfer is initiated at least one business day before the due date of the deposit, the electronic fund transfer is considered timely.

Required Use of EFTPS

You are required to use this method of payment in 2005 if you meet either of the following conditions:

- You used EFTPS in 2004.
- You had total tax deposits (employment tax, excise tax, and corporate income tax) in 2003 of more than $200,000.

If you are required to use EFTPS but fail to do so, you may be subject to a 10 percent penalty.

Voluntary Use of EFTPS

While most small businesses are *not* required to use EFTPS, they may wish to do so—for their own convenience. You initiate payment so you remain in control of your funds until you want them disbursed to the government. You receive an acknowledgment number as a record of your payment.

You may voluntarily participate in EFTPS. To obtain more information in EFTPS or to enroll in the system, call (800) 555-4477 or (800) 945-8400. If you enroll, you can use the Internet or receive free Windows-based software for use on your PC. You also receive a PIN to use when making payments.

Electronic Transfer Payment Methods

There are different ways you can make an electronic transfer of funds to the government:

- Through EFTPS-OnLine <www.eftps.gov>. This is a secured web site that individuals and businesses can use to pay taxes through the Internet. After enrolling online, you'll receive a confirmation kit by mail, including instructions for obtaining your password (a PIN number is mailed separately). Payments can be scheduled in advance and even canceled, with instant acknowledgments to confirm transactions.

- Directly to EFTPS through your PC or telephone. You choose the automated clearing house (ACH) debit method when you enroll. Then, when you want to make a payment, you instruct EFTPS to transfer funds from your account to the U.S. Treasury.

- Through your bank or other financial institution through its payment service. You choose the ACH credit method when you enroll and follow the bank's instructions on how to direct payment. Before designating a particular financial institution, check whether they can accommodate this payment method. Also ask about any fees or other charges for using this payment method.

If you use a payroll company to process your payroll, you may also authorize them to pay your employment taxes. Special enrollment rules for EFTPS apply in this case. You can also enroll separately so you keep the flexibility of making your own electronic payments.

Online Filing of Other Business Returns

At present, employment tax returns and employee benefit returns are not required to be filed online. Certain information returns *must* be filed online by certain taxpayers—others who are not required to do so may choose to file online.

Employment Tax Returns

Employment tax returns may be filed electronically. These include:

- Form 940, Employer's Annual Federal Unemployment (FUTA) Tax Return
- Form 941, Employer's Quarterly Federal Tax Return

You must request IRS authorization to participate in the *e-file* program for employment returns. You do so by submitting a letter of application (LOA)—on paper or electronically—to the IRS requesting authorization to participate. Letter of application and other *e-file* information about employment forms can be found in IRS Publication 3715, *Technical Specifications Guide for Electronic Filing of Form 940, Employer's Annual Federal Unemployment (FUTA) Tax Return* (which contains a sample LOA) when filing Form 940, and IRS Revenue Procedure 2001-9 (see Internal Revenue Bulletin 2001-3 at page 328, for Form 941).

If you need any technical help with *e-filing* these returns, contact the Electronic Filing Help Desk in Austin, Texas, at (512) 460-8900, or Memphis, Tennessee, (901) 546-2690 ext. 7519.

Information Returns

You may choose to submit certain information returns to the IRS electronically even though you must provide paper returns to your employees or others. You *must* file electronically if you file 250 or more information returns (Form 1042-S, 1098, 1099, 5498, 8027, or W-G).

You do not have to be concerned about the security of the information you submit in this manner. The IRS has set up FIRE (Filing Information Returns Electronically) to protect the confidentiality of the data you submit. To learn more about FIRE, see <www.irs.gov/taxpros/article/0,,id=98045,00.html> or call the Martinsburg Computer Center at (304) 263-8700.

You can provide information returns to payment recipients electronically *if* they consent to receive them in this manner. So, for example, if you paid an independent contractor $1,200 in 2005 and want to send the Form 1099-MISC to her electronically, you must obtain her consent to do so.

EMPLOYEE BENEFIT RETURNS.   Forms in the 5500 series may be filed electronically with the Department of Labor (not with the IRS). For information about EFAST (ERISA Filing Acceptance System) and EFAST *e-filing* employee benefit returns, see <www.efast.dol.gov/qaabout_efast.html>.

DUE DATE OF ELECTRONICALLY FILED INFORMATION RETURNS.   Filing electronically extends the due date of Forms 1098, 1099, and W-2G from February 28 to March 31. For example, for 2005 information returns, you have until March 31, 2006, to *e-file* the returns with the IRS. For Form 1042-S, the due date remains

March 15, the same date for paper returns. Similarly, the due date for furnishing information returns to payment recipients (January 31) remains the same (use of electronic filing does not extend this date). Of course, if the due date falls on Saturday, Sunday, or legal holiday, the due date of an electronically filed return is extended to the next business day.

Excise Tax Returns

Under the ExSTARS (Excise Summary Terminal Activity Reporting System), terminal operators and bulk fuel carriers can file their monthly information returns (Fuel Transaction Reports) electronically instead of using paper returns.

Information Returns

Businesses are in a unique position to monitor certain activities with which they are involved, and the federal government has harnessed this power by requiring certain reporting for tax and financial purposes. Reporting enables the government, where possible, to make sure that income is reported as it should be and to keep tabs on certain monetary activities.

Reporting requirements vary from return to return. However, filing deadlines are completely independent of your tax year (when you file your income tax return). If a filing deadline falls on a Saturday, Sunday, or legal holiday, then the deadline becomes the next business day that is not a Saturday, Sunday, or legal holiday.

The IRS has completely revised its electronic reporting system, called Filing Information Returns Electronically (FIRE). The former dial-up connection can be replaced by an Internet system at http://fire.irs.gov. When using the FIRE system, you are informed of the status of submissions ("good," "bad" or "not yet processed"). Usually it takes about 20 days for processing.

The following is a review of the most common business-reporting requirements, some or all of which may apply to you. (Some of these responsibilities are explained in greater detail within the book as indicated.)

Dividends

WHO MUST REPORT.   If your corporation pays out dividends or distributions to shareholders (including yourself), payments of $10 or more ($600 or more for liquidations) must be reported to the IRS and to the recipient.

File Form 1099-DIV, Dividends and Distributions. Request a copy other form from the IRS at (800) 829-FORM or purchase it from an office supply company (the form is a triplicate form that cannot be downloaded from the IRS web site). The IRS copy of Form 1099-DIV must be accompanied by Form 1096, Annual Summary and Transmittal of U.S. Information Returns.

WHEN TO REPORT.   Furnish the recipient with a copy of the form no later than January 31 of the year following the year in which dividends or distributions were paid.

File the form with the IRS no later than February 28 of the year following the year in which the dividends or distributions were paid. But if you file the form electronically, you have an additional month (to March 31) to file with the IRS.

WHERE TO REPORT.   The filing location you use depends on where your corporation is located—there are four IRS service centers in which this information return is filed.

PENALTIES FOR NONFILING.   The amount of the penalty for late filing depends on how late you are—the quicker you correct the nonfiling, the smaller your penalty will be. For example, the penalty is $15 per information return if you miss the due date but then file correctly within 30 days (up to a maximum penalty of $25,000 for small businesses). You are a small business if your average annual gross receipts for the three most recent tax years (or the period for which you are in existence, if shorter) are $5 million or less.

Large Cash Transactions

WHO MUST REPORT.   If you receive more than $10,000 in cash in one or more related transactions in the course of your business, you must report the transaction to the IRS. You must also report your reporting to the party that paid you. "Cash" for reporting purposes does not mean only currency; it includes cashier's checks, money orders, bank drafts, and traveler's checks having a face amount of $10,000 or less received in a transaction used to avoid this reporting requirement.

File Form 8300, Report of Cash Payments Over $10,000 Received in a Trade or Business.

WHEN TO REPORT. The form must be filed with the IRS by the 15th day after the date the cash was received. For example, if you receive a payment of $12,000 on February 1, 2006, you must report it by February 15, 2006. If the deadline falls on a Saturday, Sunday, or legal holiday, file by the next business day.

You must give a written statement to the party who paid you, but you have until January 31 of the year following the year in which the cash was received to do so. For example, on that February 1, 2006, cash payment, your written statement must be furnished by January 31, 2007.

WHERE TO REPORT. File Form 8300 with the IRS, Detroit Computing Center, P.O. Box 32621, Detroit, MI 48232 (regardless of where you file your business return).

PENALTIES FOR NONFILING. Unless you can show your failure to timely report the transaction to the IRS and to the payer was due to reasonable cause, you may be subject to penalties. A minimum penalty is imposed if you intentionally or willfully fail to report the transaction. Criminal penalties (fines and imprisonment) can result if you cause or attempt to cause a business to fail to file a required report or file a report containing a material omission or misstatement of fact or for structuring a transaction to avoid reporting requirements.

Payments to Independent Contractors

WHO MUST REPORT. If you use independent contractors, freelancers, or subcontractors in your business and pay them $600 or more within the year, you must report these payments to the IRS as well as the contractors. In most cases, payments to corporations are not subject to this reporting requirement.

File Form 1099-MISC, Miscellaneous Income. Request a copy of the form from the IRS at (800) 829-FORM or purchase it from an office supply company (the form is a triplicate form that cannot be downloaded from the IRS web site). The IRS copy of Form 1099-MISC must be accompanied by Form 1096, Annual Summary and Transmittal of U.S. Information Returns.

WHEN TO REPORT. You must furnish a copy of the form to the independent contractor no later than January 31 of the year following the year in which the payments were made.

You must provide the IRS with its copy no later than February 28 of the year following the year of payment. But if you file the form electronically, you have an additional month (to March 31) to file with the IRS.

If you need additional time to file, request a filing extension on Form 8809, Request for Extension of Time to File Information Returns.

WHERE TO REPORT.   The filing location you use depends on where your business is located—there are four IRS service centers in which this information return is filed.

PENALTIES FOR NONFILING.   The amount of the penalty for late filing depends on how late you are—the quicker you correct the nonfiling, the smaller your penalty will be. For example, the penalty is $15 per information return if you miss the due date but then file correctly within 30 days (up to a maximum penalty of $25,000 for small businesses). You are a small business if your average annual gross receipts for the three most recent tax years (or the period for which you are in existence, if shorter) are $5 million or less.

Pension and Retirement Plan Distributions

WHO MUST REPORT.   You must report any distributions from qualified retirement plans to the recipient of the distributions as well as to the IRS.

Furnish Form 1099-R, Distributions from Pensions, Annuities, Retirement or Profit-Sharing Plans, IRAs, Insurance Contracts, Etc. and file Copy A of this form with the IRS. Submit the copy with Form 1096, Annual Summary and Transmittal of U.S. Information Returns.

WHEN TO REPORT.   You must furnish a copy of the form to the distribution recipient no later than January 31 of the year following the year in which the payments were made.

You must provide the IRS with its copy no later than February 28 of the year following the year of payment. But if you file the form electronically, you have an additional month (to March 31) to file with the IRS.

If you need additional time to file, request a filing extension on Form 8809, Request for Extension of Time to File Information Returns.

WHERE TO REPORT.   The filing location you use depends on where your business is located—there are four IRS service centers in which this information return is filed.

PENALTIES FOR NONFILING.   The penalty is $25 per day for late filing, up to a maximum of $15,000.

Retirement and Employee Benefit Plans

WHO MUST REPORT.   If you have a qualified retirement plan, such as a profit-sharing plan, or an employee benefit plan, such as a funded deferred compensation plan, you must report annually on the plan's activities. Reporting includes information on annual contributions, distributions, and the number of participants.

File Form 5500, Annual Return/Report of Employee Benefit Plan. If you are self-employed and the only participant is you (or you and your spouse, or you and your partners and spouses), you can file Form 5500-EZ, Annual Return of One Participant (Owners and Their Spouses), a simplified form. You do not have to file *any* form if you qualify to file Form 5500-EZ and plan assets did not exceed $100,000 in any year after 1993.

WHEN TO REPORT. The form is due on the last day of the seventh month following the close of the plan year (for example, for the 2005 plan year that is on a calendar year, July 31, 2006).

If you need additional time to file, request a filing extension on Form 5558, Application for Extension of Time to File Certain Employee Plan Returns. If you obtained an automatic six-month filing extension for your personal income tax return, you automatically have until October 16, 2006, to file Form 5500 or 5500-EZ for 2005 (attach a copy of your personal extension when you file the form).

WHERE TO REPORT. File the form with the Pension and Welfare Benefits Administration (not with the IRS), which is now called the Employee Benefits Security Administration (the addresses for paper filing, filing by disc, CD-ROM, or tape; or by private delivery service are listed in the instructions to the form).

The form can be *e-filed* through a filing professional. For more information, click on <www.efast.dol.gov>.

PENALTIES FOR NONFILING. The late filing penalty is $25 per day (up to $15,000). Various other penalties may also be imposed.

Small Cash Transactions

WHO MUST REPORT. If you are in a business that sells or redeems money orders or traveler's checks in excess of $1,000 per customer per day or issues your own value cards, you are asked by the government to report suspicious transactions that exceed $2,000. Such businesses include convenience stores, groceries, liquor stores, travel agencies, courier services, and gas stations (the government estimates that there are about 158,000 business within these categories and that they provide financial services of $200 billion each year).

Suspicious activities include a customer who:

- Attempts to bribe or threaten you or your employee
- Buys multiple money orders in even hundred-dollar denominations or in unusual quantities

- Provides false or expired identification
- Refuses to proceed with a transaction once you notify him/her that a form will be completed
- Tries to keep the transaction from being reported or asks you how to avoid reporting requirements
- Works with one or more other individuals who split up to conduct separate transactions that combine for more than $3,000

File Form TD F 90-22.56, Suspicious Activity Report by Money Services Businesses. Filing the form does not give you any financial exposure; you have complete protection from civil liability (the person you report cannot sue you for damages).

WHEN TO REPORT.   File the form within 30 days of the suspicious activity.

WHERE TO REPORT.   File the form with the U.S. Treasury Department's Money Services Businesses Division, Detroit Computing Center, Attn: SAR-MSB, Box 33117, Detroit, MI 48232-5980.

PENALTIES FOR NONFILING.   None since filing is voluntary.

Wages

WHO MUST REPORT.   If you have any employee (including yourself if your business is incorporated), you must report annual compensation and benefits to the employee and to the Social Security Administration.

File Form W-2, Wage and Tax Statement, with the Social Security Administration and furnish a copy to the employee. Also file Form W-3, Transmittal of Income and Tax Statement, with the Social Security Administration.

For the Future

Starting in 2007, large employers (those filing 250 or more W-2 forms) must file electronically. Smaller employers can continue to file paper forms, but are encouraged to file electronically through an extended filing deadline.

WHEN TO REPORT.   Different deadlines apply to different parties:

- *Employees.* Furnish the form to them by January 31 of the year following the year in which the wages were paid (whether you furnish the Form W-2 by paper or electronically).

- *Social Security Administration.* File the forms by February 28 (March 31 if filing electronically).

You can request additional time to file with the Social Security Administration by sending Form 8809, Request for Extension of Time to File Information Returns, to gain an additional 30 days to file. But you must still furnish the form to employees by the regular deadline; there is no extension in this case.

WHERE TO REPORT. File the forms (copy A of W-2 and the entire page of W-3) with the Social Security Administration, Data Operations Center, Wilkes-Barre, PA 18769-0001. If you use certified mail, change the zip code to 18769-0002. If you use an IRS-approved private delivery service, add "Attn.: W-2 Process, 1150 E. Mountain Drive" to the address and change the zip code to 18702-7997.

PENALTIES FOR NONFILING. The amount of the penalty for late filing depends on how late you are—the quicker you correct the nonfiling, the smaller your penalty will be. For example, the penalty is $15 per information return if you miss the due date but then file correctly within 30 days (up to a maximum penalty of $25,000 for small businesses). You are a small business if your average annual gross receipts for the three most recent tax years (or the period for which you are in existence, if shorter) are $5 million or less.

For more information about wage reporting, see Chapter 7.

Index